In loving memory of Charles (1902–1987) and Florrie (1906–1993) who had so little,
yet who gave so much…and to whom, like so many of their generation,
motor racing meant 'BRM'…

*"The British, the British, the British are Best,
So Up with the British and Down with the Rest."*

after Flanders & Swann

_B.R.M._

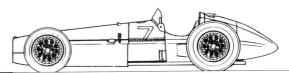

THE SAGA OF BRITISH RACING MOTORS

VOLUME I - FRONT ENGINED CARS 1945–1960

DOUG NYE WITH TONY RUDD

MRP

FOUR VOLUMES

This volume – as Doug Nye indicates in his Introduction – was originally planned as the first of a two-part complete history of BRM, but subsequently the project has been expanded into a projected four-volume set. Revealed here is the story of the front-engined cars from 1945 to 1960, whilst Volume 2 is devoted to the spaceframe-chassised cars produced from 1959 to 1965. Volume 3 will continue the story through the monocoque V8 Formula 1 and Tasman cars campaigned from 1964 to 1969, leaving Volume 4 to cover the history of the H16 and V12-cylinder cars run from 1966 onwards, and the conclusion of the BRM saga.

MRP PUBLISHING LTD
PO Box 1318, Croydon CR9 5YP, England

First published 1994 by Motor Racing Publications Ltd
Reprinted 2003

A catalogue record for this book is available from the British Library

ISBN 0 947981 37 3

Printed in Great Britain by
The Amadeus Press, Cleckheaton, West Yorkshire

Bound by MPG Books Ltd, Bodmin, Cornwall

Contents

Introduction

The three initials 'BRM' – derived jointly from 'the British Racing Motor' and 'British Racing Motors' – are known throughout the motor racing world. From the marque's inception in 1945, until the end of its significant life as a satellite of The Owen Organisation in 1974, BRM's existence was high-profile, action-packed, often sensationally controversial...

This is the first of a projected two-volume complete history of BRM – Volume 1 offered here telling the story of the team and its cars and career during the front-engined era, 1945–1960, while Volume 2 will cover the rear-engined story from 1960 to the final demise of the serious Formula 1 team at the end of 1974, followed by the shadowy half-life which it endured for a few years more...

In its early years BRM became a byword for disappointment, frustration, the dashing of public hopes which had been raised sky-high upon a flimsy balloon of rash publicity.

BRM had been conceived during the final stages of the Second World War and was launched amidst the elation of victory and the eager expectation of an early return to what had once passed for normality. Its promoters had spent the six long years of war incurably starstruck by the charismatic glamour of Grand Prix racing's Age of Titans through the 1930s. They and their early supporters were fired by dreams of a place at the Grand Prix winner's table, not for themselves you understand, but "for reasons of national prestige...". Does one scent a charlatan there? For sure, some were, but for each charlatan involved there were a dozen more perfectly sincere and genuine patriots on board. For King and Country was a potent motive around those war years. For many the dream soon soured. For many more – the majority of average motor sporting enthusiasts – the twilight of old-style good-hearted British patriotism, proud yet blind, warming yet self-destructive, natural, laudable, sometimes laughable – became perhaps the BRM project's most potent motivation.

For years before the war, top-class motor racing had been ruled by Nazi Germany – now humbled – and as international racing resumed it was another former enemy state – Italy – which reigned supreme. Many British enthusiasts genuinely perceived production of a Grand Prix car capable of toppling Johnny Foreigner to be indeed a pressing matter of national prestige.

Barely aware of what would prove to be a postwar world of grim recession, depression, deprivation and gloom, the BRM project plunged ahead...

In parallel with the costly Bristol Brabazon transatlantic airliner programme and the catastrophic British African ground-nut scheme – seeking to make peanuts grow where they could not – for long years when motor racing would never hit the headlines short of some awful accident, 'the BRM' became another national *cause celebre*.

For an entire generation the fortunes of the project and of the team built around it brought unprecedented prominence to Grand Prix racing. Whatever else was achieved by BRM, it certainly made both the British motor industry and the general public more motor racing-minded than ever before. In many ways BRM laid the foundation upon which British manufacturers – BRM included – could establish an unprecedented dominance over almost every significant class of motor sport worldwide.

Yet I know of no other motor racing subject which is more daunting to any would-be historian.

More than any other motor racing marque, BRM has attracted both the staunchest and most partisan of supporters, and the most entrenched and damning of critics...

Many times during my researches, rabid BRM supporters have urged me "Don't jump on the bandwagon and go poking fun at BRM", or have simply demanded that I should "...not write anything which will destroy the reputation of those great men who put British motor racing on the map. BRM was the British answer to Mercedes-Benz, don't you destroy that impression...".

Yet just as often I have been earnestly advised "not to waste your time on the history of BRM, bunch of over-publicized incompetents – at best BRM was staffed by glorified garage mechanics and managed by a bunch of conmen...".

The tragedy of both these extremes is the inflexibility of mind which they express. Nothing in life is so comfortably black or white. Truth and reality are all about shades of grey – collate five eyewitness testaments to any one man's character and while the drift may be common, the detail and degree will always differ.

Against this background, I began my serious work on the marque's history as far back as 1978, well aware of the fact that if I put together the kind of book I wanted to write – which was to present the most detailed and comprehensive history that anyone has ever attempted of any Formula 1 racing team – I would simultaneously antagonize both BRM's most rabid supporters and its most implacable detractors.

As a researcher and writer I have only ever been interested in presenting – upon the evidence available – objective truth. If my presentation of the BRM story in the following pages causes irritation, or dismay, or derision, then I can only invite those I have upset to weigh the available evidence as carefully, and I hope as impartially as I have done, and to reach their own conclusions... I would hope that on balance they may judge that I have, at least, been fair.

I decided early on that fully to understand and appreciate BRM demands a basis of understanding of the project's famous forerunner, English Racing Automobiles – 'ERA'.

Consequently, the early chapters which follow relate an inside story of ERA – and of its own background and formative influences – which has hitherto remained largely hidden, or forgotten, and certainly very largely unpublished.

Most significantly, many of the personal relationships – the lifelong friendships and in some cases the most bitter of antipathies – which shaped and dictated the course of BRM history were established during the days of ERA, or even earlier, and as far as I have been able to unravel them they are all addressed and described in what follows.

Motor racing is a complex exercise, particularly at its topmost levels. It is the nearest that industrial endeavour may approach to wartime demands and pressures short of war itself. To attack motor racing successfully demands total dedication and devotion, and invariably submergence of self to the common aim.

In many ways the story of BRM is one of dedication and devotion by a loyal band whose efforts were constantly betrayed by those most

likely to claim these qualities as their own. Above all it is a story of unswerving faith and commitment by one whose entire active life was one of Faith – in Christ and in people, and in particular in British engineering and the working man, a faith which was not always repaid as one might have hoped it should have been...

In what follows I have attempted to present the life and times of British Racing Motors against the life and times, and changing fortunes – and attitudes – of Great Britain itself. I have also tried very hard to demonstrate how motor racing success and failure is a technical exercise dependent totally upon the talent, dedication and commitment not merely of well-publicized racing drivers and high-profile team principals, but more so of the entire and so-often unsung team working with them, without whom not one racing car would ever make its way to the starting grid.

Any attempt to aim so high would have been impossible without the patient support and encouragement of many 'BRM people' – including, I am happy to relate – the project's founding father, the late Raymond Mays, who could not have been more supportive, nor more helpful, during the final years of his long life. My main collaborator has been Tony Rudd – whose own splendidly readable autobiography is greatly recommended and who has been an outstandingly reliable witness whose long-suffering patience, constant readiness to assist, and valued criticism and encouragement have been absolutely invaluable.

And perhaps above all, the depth of detail which I have been privileged to present here would never have emerged had it not been for the generosity and enthusiasm of David and John and Jim Owen, of The Owen Organisation, who over a period of too many years – for which I apologize! – made available for my examination their late father Sir Alfred's staggeringly extensive industrial archive.

Acknowledgements

'The BRM book' has been an ever-present part of my professional life – fettling part of it here, some of it there – for almost 16 years. In that time the remarkable thing to me has been the number of people who have kept faith with my word that it would be finished "one day" – headed by those thanked above.

Although it simply is not 'done' for an author to thank his publisher, I have never respected convention, and for his enduring faith, patience and forebearance, John Blunsden of MRP certainly deserves some kind of medal. He has been sorely pressed for many years by my "propensity for procrastination..." – to quote an early report upon goings-on at Bourne – yet has (almost) always remained entirely supportive, understanding and mysteriously confident of the manuscript's eventual delivery...

In any case it was he – as Associate Editor of *Motor Racing* magazine – who caused the trouble in the first place, in December 1963. He took the 18-year-old office boy to visit BRM at Bourne. That boy was me – bemused to be greeted there with cries of "Hello Chris..." because I was at that time (apart from size) Chris Amon's double. That first experience of a Formula 1 car factory was entirely overwhelming – and I have spent much time around them ever since.

Two men we met that day were Alec Stokes and Aubrey Woods, and both for many years have given unstintingly of their time and knowledge in helping me to understand BRM and BRM people. Raymond Mays himself gave me much time to explain his view of the story in the final years of his long life, as also did the late, great Harry Mundy, Stan Hope and Dave Turner. Paul Berthon helped paint in background details of his late brother, Peter, while special thanks go to PB's daughter, Jacquie, for putting up with my intrusions and for loaning family photographs. I hope despite some inevitable censure she feels I have dealt justly with her late father...

A.F. Rivers Fletcher – of Brooklands, ERA, 'Rembrandt get-togethers' and Rubery Owen PRO fame – and his wife Penny deserve another medal for enduring what I am certain must many times have been my unwelcome objectivity, but Rivers has been faultlessly helpful.

Amongst the many former BRM employees who have helped with reminiscences of goings on there I must single out Phil Ayliff, Colin Atkin, Maurice Dove, Dick Salmon and John Sismey for special mention. Maurice and Dick have been particularly helpful in providing photographs. John provided access to a wealth of reference material. Ken Richardson and his son Paul have both been of considerable help in painting in the former Chief Mechanic's view of times at both ERA and BRM. My old friends and colleagues Geoff Goddard and Denis Jenkinson have provided help, photographs, reference and reminiscence in no particular order throughout all the long years...

Charles Picton – a great BRM enthusiast – provided unstinted access to the magnificent collection of BRM works drawings which he bought at the 1981 Christie's auction.

Others who have helped with photographs, information, recollection and opinion over the long years are as follows:

Kathy Agar at LAT Photographic – the *Motor Sport* magazine photo files – Cyril Atkins, the former BRM Chief Mechanic, but who during the period covered by this Volume served with 'The Enemy' – Vandervell's *ThinWall Special* and Vanwall team – the staffs of *Autosport* magazine and Haymarket Publications photo library, Tony Brooks, Robert Brooks, Fred Burt, Pat Carvath, Colin Crabbe, Neil Corner, Dick Crosthwaite, Dave Curry's ScanCam photographic library in Auckland, New Zealand, Bernard Cahier, Bill and Rob Clark in New Zealand, Jabby Crombac, Yves Debraine, Juan Manuel Fangio, Rob Fowler, Bob Fox, late of Rubery Owen, Howden Ganley, John Gardiner, Graham Gauld, John Godfrey, who painted in so much of the local Lincolnshire attitude towards BRM goings on during the period in question, Jose Froilan Gonzalez, Ken Gregory, Guy Griffiths, Dan Gurney, Rick Hall, Bruce Halford, John Harper, David Hayward, Sid Latter, Robs Lamplough, Karl E. Ludvigsen, whose technical motor sporting writings over such a long period have set a standard all who follow strive to match, The Royal Air Force Museum at Hendon, Kathy at Quadrant Picture Library, Jonathan Day at the National Motor Museum Photographic Library, Beaulieu, Barry Lake in Australia, the late Hon. Patrick Lindsay, Nick Mason, Tony Matthews, for his supreme cutaway artistry, Danny Margulies, the late Anthony Mayman, Mandy McKenna at the Hulton-Deutsch Collection, Tony Merrick, Stirling Moss, Lord Edward Montagu, of the National Motor Museum, John Olliver, Tim Parnell, for recollections of his late father Reg's dealings with BRM, John Pearson, David Phipps, Anthony Pritchard,

Peter Putterill, of the Bourne Society, Duncan Rabagliati, of the Formula 1 Register, John Ross, for his long years of patience after loaning me some of the fine BRM photographs reproduced within these pages, Tony Sadler, Dr Paul and Mrs Betty Sheldon, of the Formula 1 Register, the late Peter Spear, Mike Stowe, the Hon. Amschel Rothschild, Gordon Wilkins, Mick Walsh, of *Classic & Sportscar* magazine, Tom and Kevin Wheatcroft, of the Donington Collection of Single-Seater Racing Cars, for so many years of ready access to their BRM V16 and Type 25 cars, spares and above all the surviving V16 drawings, David Weguelin, whose tremendous ERA book pre-empted much of my work in this area and for being an all-round good egg, Geoffrey Wilde, of Rolls-Royce, who answered so many daft questions with abiding patience and enthusiasm, and Mrs Nan Tresilian – his widow – for sharing fond memories of the late, great Stewart S. Tresilian.

But in any work of this kind there will always be those involved with the team who pass unmentioned, but who deserve enduring credit for the roles they played in the reality. RM's long-faithful secretary, the late Miss Sybil Ingoldby, was one of two life-long spinster sisters, a Sunday School teacher and relief church organist who tolerated RM "and his little ways" for many long years, often with wry humour.

PB's – and later Tony Rudd's – secretary, Mrs Marjorie Walker, was an absolute pillar of strength, peerlessly discrete, capable and completely trustworthy. She supported her husband, war-disabled with shell shock and, as Tony recalls, "neither PB nor I could have operated without her holding the fort and guarding our backs..."

James Sandercombe – sometime Comptroller, long-time BRM Company Secretary – quite properly felt when approached that it would be inappropriate for him to assist in my researches. 'Sandy', a wartime Captain in the Royal Corps of Signals, was seconded to the BRM project from Rubery Owen and is widely recalled for his absolute incorruptibility, for the way he "carefully concealed great enthusiasm for motor racing and performed many thoughtful acts of kindness and consideration for the staff – yet would always appear embarrassed when thanked..."

His secretary was Mrs Joan Bryden, wife of race mechanic Cyril, and Dick Salmon's sister-in-law.

The Maltings machine shop was run long-term by Cyril's taciturn elder brother Les, an absolutely brilliant machinist and fine planner, who aspired to the post of Works Manager, whereupon Wally Wakefield assumed responsibilities for the machine shop.

Purchase manager and storekeeper Clarence W. 'Clarrie' Brinkley – sometimes known as 'Brink' – was an ex-ERA racing mechanic, famous for having once rolled a double-deck Thorneycroft canvas tilt truck carrying two cars *en route* from Bourne to Donington. Les Bryden christened him 'The Lalograph' for "letting his lal out..." – waffling on (BRM was a great place for nicknames).

In any such organization there will have been those who made friends and some who made enemies amongst their colleagues, yet regardless of minor personality clashes all of BRM's people commonly united against external criticism. Many from both sides of various divides have been of enormous assistance to me in presenting what we hope is a true and objective view of what went on out there in the Lincolnshire wilds for so many years – and which had such a profound effect in so many ways upon the development of British motor racing...

Here I fear I will inevitably have omitted some who have helped over the past 16 years, to whom I can only apologise, as I must for the occasional error of fact which may – perhaps inevitably – have escaped our eye. The responsibility for that is entirely mine – the credit for what BRM ultimately achieved belongs to those who cared, and who worked so desperately hard, for all those long years of the marque's turbulent life. I promise not to take so long – God willing – to complete Volume 2... which is a deliverance my long-suffering wife Valerie, and children Kirsten and Peter, keenly await; 'BRM' having played such an ever-present role in our family life.

Doug Nye

Farnham, Surrey,   Doug Nye
March 1994

STYLE NOTE

Before embarking upon the following text it is important to understand that much of it comprises direct quotation from contemporary letters, memoranda, notes and internal company reports.

Since nearly all the originals are unsuitable for adequate photographic reproduction it has been necessary to typeset them for inclusion within the following text. To keep faith with contemporary written standards and customs as applied by the characters in our long story, we have typeset all this material absolutely as faithfully as possible, without – except where stated – making any conscious alteration or correction whatsoever to their original structure, spelling, style and punctuation...

Thus, if the initials 'BRM' are rendered 'B.R.M.' in one letter, but not in another,

or a date is rendered 'July 10' in one place, '10 July' in another or 'July 10th' in a third, this is merely a matter of faithful reproduction as originally written. Neither, where in some of Harry Schell's memorable broadsides 'Behra' is spelled 'Berha' or he describes himself as 'iIii", or if a bleat from Jo Bonnier spells Peter Berthon's surname 'Burthon', is this due to any failure of our proof-readers – we are simply reflecting the original material as accurately as possible...and thereby, we hope, retaining the original's maximum inference, tone and character short of direct – and in terms of legibility practically impossible – photographic reproduction.

We hope our readers will appreciate the time-consuming care expended to this end.

PART ONE

Raymond Mays...

Eastgate House, Bourne – Raymond Mays' lifelong home. The year of his birth, 1899, was the last of Queen Victoria's long reign, it saw the Boer War begin, the death of Johann Strauss, the development of aspirin and magnetic sound recording. All RM's racing cars would be developed, designed, built and prepared behind the imposing House..

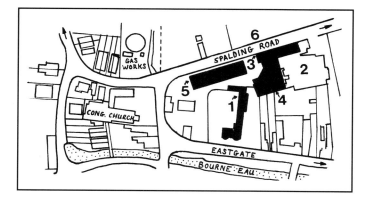

Bourne Local Plan
*South-eastern corner of Bourne, town centre arrowed to the top left, Spalding to the right:
1 – Eastgate House; 2 – What became the Delaine coach company garage, incorporating
the original ERA works; 3 – The Old Maltings; 4 – The built-on BRM works of the
'50s–'70s; 5 – The 1960-built BRM engine/panel/race shop which replaced the
Folkingham Compound; 6 – Site of Raymond Mays & Partners post-Maltings garage.*

BOURNE

Bourne in Lincolnshire might be described as a typical, small, rural English market town; compact, quiet and largely unremarkable despite its lengthy history.

It stands on the edge of the East Anglian Fens – the flat drained marshlands which plain away north-eastwards, flat as a billiard table, eventually to submerge beneath the grey North Sea in the great bite of The Wash. Due north of Bourne, rising ground fringes the Fens, while to the west the town is backed by the hummocky hills of what further north become the Lincolnshire Wolds.

In antiquity the Romans came to Bourne, excavating the Car Dyke nearby – Britain's earliest canal – originally to transport stone or in an attempt to drain the Fens. In the 11th Century, Hereward the Wake, legendarily the last Saxon noble to resist the invading Normans, was based there, and in 1605 the Gunpowder Plot was hatched in Bourne's Old Red House.

More peaceably, the town also became established as a centre of the wool trade. A 1920s' census quoted its population as 4,343, mostly dependent upon agriculture, tanning and wool. But then, for a heady period around the Second World War, one of its sons gave Bourne a unique and glamorous new claim to fame.

His name was Raymond Mays – and he made Bourne the focus of British motor racing ambition, and home to his creations: 'The English Racing Automobile' and 'The British Racing Motor'…

For many years, the Mays family had been prominent within Bourne's wool, tannery and fertilizer trade. Both Ray's father and grandfather were christened Thomas William Mays, after whom the company was named T.W. Mays & Son. These three generations all lived in Eastgate House – a tall, rambling, mainly Victorian pile which, with its outbuildings and grounds, plays a major role in the story to follow.

As its name suggests, it stands in Bourne's eastern outskirts, its grounds once backing onto the main A15 Spalding Road nearby to the north. To the south, the House overlooked the quiet side-road – Eastgate – from which it took its name. Eastgate was narrow, and quiet, edged opposite the House by the Bourne Eau, a sluggish, almost stagnant stream linked to the nearby Car Dyke. The Bourne Eau was so often clogged with floating rubbish, the locals sometimes pronounced its Norman name 'Bourne Eeugh'! It combined

with the adjoining Mays businesses – a tannery, a slaughter-house and other pungent premises further along Eastgate to the right (when facing it) of the House itself – to make this by no means the most fashionable end of town…

The property there had been acquired in 1794 by a local miller named Thomas Chamberlain, Eastgate House being built to replace some cottages destroyed by fire. A scroll bearing the initials 'JC' and dated '1796' above one door is thought to commemorate the birth of John Chamberlain, who in 1827 built an adjoining brewhouse, bakehouse, barns and stables. The Mays family eventually acquired the property in 1856. Thomas William the younger married a girl some 20 years his junior, and on August 1, 1899, Anne Mays gave birth there to their only child – Thomas Raymond Mays.

As a boy he quickly discarded his first name, and subsequently became famous to the motor racing world at large as Raymond Mays, to his intimates as Ray, and within his own team and businesses simply as 'RM'…

His father, Tom, was an enthusiastic motorist before the First World War. Tom Mays took his son on motoring business trips around the countryside – which near Bourne is an open-air motoring dream; flat and fast across Fenland, or winding, climbing and swooping through the inland hills towards Stamford and Grantham.

Motoring magazines were always to be found at Eastgate House. Ray avidly read them all. He was fired by pictures of the works racing Vauxhall KN at Brooklands, and soon painted the initials on his bicycle to relive in his imagination the exploits of factory driver A.J. Hancock.

From 1908–12 Tom Mays entered his own Vauxhall and Napier road cars in local speed events and often hired factory mechanics to tune them in the outbuildings behind Eastgate House. Ray rode with these "fearless men" on their test runs along the flat Fenland roads, later recalling vividly how "…these speed bursts were to me the supreme thrill, bringing the realization that to race was the great ambition of my life…"

He would never display much mechanical aptitude or interest, but was riveted absolutely by the glamour and adulation he attached to fast cars and to those who drove them… In 1912 he entered Berystead House at Oundle School, west of Stamford. During five years there, he played tennis passably and rugby well, and won a reputation as something of a dandy – always snappily-dressed, impeccably well-groomed. He also assumed a certain stature as the son of a 'motoring' father. He was wildly enthusiastic about Vauxhall cars – so well-engineered by Laurence Pomeroy Sr – and even conducted a lengthy schoolboy correspondence with the great man himself. In later years 'Pom' Sr's technical-journalist son would play a significant role in the evolution of Ray's great creation – BRM.

During school holidays Tom Mays took his son to local sprint and hill-climb meetings, and eventually south to the great Brooklands Motor Course where at last Ray actually saw the Vauxhall KN and A.J. Hancock in action.

In 1917, as the First World War climaxed, the Guards Brigade circulated the public schools seeking limited numbers of "boys who were tall enough" – according to Ray – to volunteer for service. In December 1917 he reported for training at Bushey Hall, in Hertfordshire, and was commissioned as a Grenadier Guards officer in May 1918. He reported for duty to Chelsea Barracks, but was allowed by Pa to take a private room in the nearby Grosvenor Hotel. He later recalled: "…life at Chelsea was strenuous, but I had a wonderful time in London during those final few weeks' training…"

There he became totally stage-struck. He was smitten by London's theatre, and became a devoted 'stage-door Johnny', idolizing musical stars like Jose Collins and Winifred Barnes. Into his 'teens he had already realized he was more attracted to male than female company, but above all he simply courted star quality, glamour and fame.

His unit left for France in October 1918, bound for the front line at Cambrai, which would prove to be the decisive battle of the war. Perhaps the Hun heard he was on his way; the Hindenburg Line was breached, the Allies broke through, and the broken Hun retreated. The Armistice followed before Ray saw action, leaving his Guardsmen to march triumphantly through France and Belgium to occupy Cologne by Christmas.

He returned home soon after, surrendering his commission to enter Christ's College, Cambridge. There he renewed acquaintance with old friends from Oundle like D'Arcy Hann and Lewis Motley, and a fellow car-enthusiast named Charles Amherst Villiers. Amherst was a budding and ambitious engineer fresh from wartime work on aero engines at the Royal Aircraft Factory, Farnborough.

At Cambridge, Ray ostensibly read engineering. But nearly 60 years later he would confess to ERA researcher David Weguelin who wrote, "…in the three years he was at Cambridge he had attended only four lectures, and it was only when his name became associated with…motor sport that his lecturers knew who he was…"

Tom Mays intended his son to join the wool firm after graduation, but Ray's own ambitions lay first in motor racing, and failing that – on the stage…

During 1920, in Cambridge, he saw a 1½-litre Speed Model Hillman in Herbert Robinson's showroom, and what followed set the tone for virtually his entire adult life. Undeterred by being unable to afford the asking price, he first focused all his considerable charm on the hapless Robinson, suggesting special terms in return for which he would run the car in speed events to promote the Hillman name. The startled agent agreed to think it over. Meantime, Ray pestered Pa to buy him the car, more or less as his 21st birthday present. Tom Mays surrendered, Robinson agreed a special price, and RM's entrepreneurial charm had scored its first motor racing success…

1921

Amherst Villiers honed his skills in tuning the Hillman after Ray had entered it in his first event – a Cambridge University Automobile Club hill-climb – which he won. Confidence and ambition swelled as the two undergraduates stripped the car, rebuilt its engine and had a slender pointed-tail body made. Hillman's contemporary works car, driven by George Bedford, was named *Mercury*, so Ray now had the name *Quicksilver* signwritten on his new car in his favourite colour – blue.

The remodelled Mays Hillman then made its debut in the Inter-Varsity hill-climb at Aston Clinton, near Tring, where Ray set fastest time of the day (FTD) again to give Cambridge victory over Oxford. The motoring press published his photograph and

RM – the gay young blade in 1922, cutting a dash for the camera behind the wheel of Cordon Rouge – the first of his sprint Brescia Bugattis. While Ray established himself as a driver, both the USSR and Fascist Italy were founded, in Paris James Joyce published Ulysses, and the first FA Cup Final at Wembley was won by Bolton Wanderers…

he used the cutting as his introduction to write to Zenith Carburettors, describing his ambitions and tuning plans and suggesting some assistance might be of mutual benefit.

H. Kensington 'Bertie' Moir duly arrived in Cambridge on Zenith's behalf, laden with a range of alternative carburettors to experiment on *Quicksilver*. He was accompanied on some of his visits by Miles Thomas, editor of *The Light Car*, and when he wrote "Mays is a real amateur enthusiast and shows promise of becoming a good driver", the young man from Bourne gained new stature.

Ray's next sporting target was to race at Brooklands, and in search of 'bits' he visited Hillman in Coventry, collecting some useful spares and meeting both Captain John Black and S.B. Wilks, who in later years would feature in the ERA and BRM saga.

Ray won his first Brooklands race and finished second in another that day. Minor speed events and hill-climbs yielded further awards as the year progressed, but his debut at Shelsley Walsh hill-climb – an event of major national importance at the time – was disappointing. He had also met Lionel Martin at Brooklands, and at the Spread Eagle 'climb near Salisbury he drove the Hillman to second place and Martin's 1½-litre Aston Martin to third in its class.

Meanwhile, T.W. Mays & Son was hit hard by the postwar recession. Tom Mays sold his beloved 30/98 Vauxhall to a Mr Cobb – whose son John would eventually set the perpetual Brooklands Outer Circuit lap record and later become the Fastest Man on Earth…

Ray's Cambridge days ended and he returned to join the family business in Bourne, where Pa spelled out the grim economic facts of life. Ray's racing days looked over before they had really begun. The Hillman reverted to road tune and Ray was despatched to Clark, Son & Morland – a related company – in Glastonbury to learn the rudiments of the wool trade. They processed rug skins selected personally by Tom Mays and freighted south on specially chartered trains.

1922

While in Glastonbury that chill winter of 1921–22, Ray heard that a limited number of Brescia Bugattis were to be sold in Britain. He contacted Major Lefrere – Bugatti's London representative – to suggest a part-exchange, his old Hillman for a new Brescia. Lefrere had heard of this persuasive young man from Lincolnshire and arranged for dealer B.S. Marshall of Hanover Square to handle the deal. Early in 1922 the first three new Brescias arrived in England – one for works driver Leon Cushman, one for Eddie Hall, and the third for Raymond Mays…

He was £300 short of the balance price yet talked Marshall into accepting the Hillman plus what cash he could spare as deposit, the rest to follow in instalments – *sans* security!

Brainsby's of Peterborough sprayed the car in Ray's own mixture of battleship-grey and blue, and first time out at the Laindon hill-climb in Essex, RM and the Brescia Bugatti set second FTD in class. At Dean Hill they set FTD, and on his return to Bourne Tom Mays allowed a young company apprentice named Harold Ayliffe to work essentially on Ray's

Bugatti. Many years later his son, Phil Ayliffe, would become BRM's chief mechanic…

Many excellent results followed in that period's more or less *ad hoc* public-road sprints and hill-climbs. All were technically illegal, run with only tacit blessing from local magistrates while the constabulary looked the other way. But these events were well-publicized, and the motor trade certainly applied the American dictum of "Win on Sunday, Sell on Monday" by advertising their successes.

These events are important in our BRM story, as the 1920s saw Raymond Mays making many of the contacts and friends who later contributed what he never could to his great projects…money and technical support. For example, it was at Chatcombe Pitch that he first met the very wealthy owner-driver of a Vauxhall 30/98 – Humphrey Cook.

A rather solemn, introspective man, tubby Humphrey Cook had inherited a fortune and the family wholesale drapery business, Cook Son & Co of St Paul's, London, at the age of 12 when his father died. He went to Oxford, developed a taste for neither education nor business, and embarked instead upon a leisurely life centred around spending his considerable private income on fine cars and foreign travel.

Meanwhile, as the important South Harting and Shelsley Walsh hill-climbs loomed near, RM sorely needed new tyres while owing all his savings to Marshall for the next instalment on the Brescia. So he wrote to Englebert Tyres, Speedwell Oil and Lodge Plugs, relating his achievements, ambitions and current requirements, and inviting their support. He promptly won free supplies from them all!

Ray later described this letter-writing as "…the most distasteful day's work I had ever set myself", but any such sentiment I frankly doubt. He had in fact discovered his own rare talent to persuade others to finance his racing; support which he was able to repay with public promotion of a degree almost unprecedented in any British sport. He would maintain a prodigious and often importunate correspondence with big business and component suppliers alike for over half a century to follow…

1923

During the winter of 1922–23, Amherst Villiers stayed at Eastgate House to develop the little Bugatti. Tom Mays took him and Ray down to London for the annual Olympia Motor Show, where they met the heads of Englebert, Speedwell and Lodge and negotiated a retainer for the new season, plus free supply of product. In return Ray virtually promised to break the prestigious Shelsley Walsh hill-climb record. Then Lefrere of Bugatti offered free spares, and the Marshall debt was also settled.

Villiers greatly modified the Bugatti, Ray first set FTD at Angel Bank and later shattered the Shelsley record with a climb in 51.9 seconds, beating the 30/98 and TT Vauxhalls which he still admired so much. It was his first great win on the stage he would love best.

After that season Ray met Lefrere again at Olympia to receive a letter from Ettore Bugatti, inviting him to visit the factory at Molsheim, in Alsace.

Humphrey Cook suggested that Ray and Villiers should accompany him and his mechanic, Jennings, and take in Molsheim during a Continental tour in the 30/98. But when they arrived at the famous Bugatti plant *Le Patron* was rather cool, surprised that Ray had not brought with him the highly-tuned Brescia he had heard so much about. Still he agreed to rebuild the car at Molsheim and also to supply an additional new 1½-litre Brescia on very favourable terms.

Tom Mays desperately wanted his son to settle properly into the family business, but even he could not resist offering some support to Ray's 'wild ambitions' so he now paid expenses for him and Villiers for a maximum five days to take the Brescia back to Molsheim. There Ettore Bugatti drove the highly-tuned car and professed himself "delighted". Villiers was to stay in Molsheim to help rebuild the old car and prepare the new one, so Ray went home by train, leaving his engineer friend there to help in the work…

1924

Ray was remarkably successful in attracting trade backing for 1924, donations totalling no less than £1,000[1]…

Before the two Brescias arrived at Bourne, Ray had been dining one night in a London restaurant when the attractive red-and-gold label on a bottle of G.H. Mumm & Co's *Cordon Rouge* Champagne caught his eye. He wrote to Mumm in Reims, seeking permission to use their insignia and name on one of his Brescias to advertise their product. They readily agreed, despatching three dozen bottles to confirm the deal. Ray then arranged similar support for his new sister car from the distillers of *Cordon Bleu* Brandy.

Now *Cordon Rouge* – the older car – was to be his 'racer', while the new *Cordon Bleu* would run as a 'standard production' sports.

Brainsby's of Peterborough sprayed both Brescias in his special RM shade of grey-blue, and their new red and blue promotional motifs were then signwritten into place.

The Mays Brescia Bugattis subsequently came to typify this great age of British sprint racing through the early 1920s. *Cordon Bleu* was converted to four-wheel braking by British Wire Products Ltd, makers of Whitehead front-wheel brakes. They also supplied free parts plus £500 – over £14,500 by 1993 values – as Ray's retainer. Come BRM days they would be asked for more…

Meanwhile, *Cordon Rouge* was beaten into an unaccustomed second place at Aston Clinton (despite breaking the old 'climb record) by Grand Prix driver Dario Resta in a new supercharged 2-litre GP Sunbeam. Returning home, Ray and Villiers animatedly discussed supercharging, but the Brescia engine was unsuitable.

Ending 1924, Ray could reflect upon three seasons' competition which had yielded over 100 first-class awards and 11 course records. He had profited greatly by continuously developing his cars, never relying upon his undoubted driving skill alone. But continuous development had drained available

1. **Using the Central Statistical Office's price deflator tables, £1,000 in 1924 represents just over £29,000 by 1993 values.**

finance. During a lurid incident at Holme Moss *Cordon Bleu*'s now highly-tuned engine had 'run away' and broken. Consequently Ray approached Selwyn Francis Edge of AC Cars, who loaned a sprint car in which Ray set FTD and clipped *nine seconds* off the Saltersford 'climb record.

1925

Coincidentally, Humphrey Cook commissioned Amherst Villiers to produce and fit a Roots-type supercharger for his TT Vauxhall. Ray then arranged with AC for Villiers to supercharge their sprint car for 1925. To cover costs and settle outstanding debts the two Brescias were sold; *Cordon Rouge* to F.B. Taylor, the Birmingham Bugatti agent, and *Cordon Bleu* to a young, "fair-haired and rather dreamy" Oxford undergraduate named Francis Giveen… Raymond Mays was always attracted to fair-haired, good-looking young men.

By this time, his ability to 'do a deal' seemed all pervasive. Villiers used Italian Memini carburettors on the AC in return for which Ray persuaded the company to provide the instruments, plus a sizeable fee, plus workshop space to build the car in their London depot (to be nearer AC's plant at Thames Ditton). As Ray, from his army days, knew the manager of the Grosvenor Hotel he arranged a room there "on special terms" for himself and Villiers and another friend named Arthur Selby-Bigg. Edge provided a new six-cylinder 2-litre AC as a road car "in return for good publicity", and by the spring of 1925 the blown AC sprint car was ready, along with the sister blower for Cook which was to be fitted at Vauxhall's Luton factory. Sadly, the AC engine soon gave trouble, while the mercurial Villiers' attention was further diverted by a commission to design a Napier Lion-engined Land Speed Record car for Malcolm Campbell.

Tom Mays was being driven to distraction. He threatened to stop Ray's salary unless he worked consistently in the family business. But Ray was committed to Edge and the AC agreement. The new sprint season opened on March 28 at the famous Kop hill-climb. There, the fearless Giveen – who had already rolled *Cordon Bleu* when practising under Ray's tuition through the tight ess-bend and up the brief hill at Toft, between Bourne and Stamford – lost control of *Cordon Bleu* and charged the crowd. Several spectators were hurt and the meeting was abandoned. Government instantly clamped down on these mad-cap meetings, and a total ban on public-road speed events soon followed. The last fixtures of this rip-roaring era were held on April 4, 1925, along the Whitecross Road out of Hereford towards Hay-on-Wye, and on the Brentnor Straight near Tavistock.

J.A. Joyce's works AC won at Brentnor, but F.B. Taylor was fastest at Whitecross in *Cordon Rouge* – a fitting finale to an era in which Raymond Mays and his Bugattis had so excelled.

In contrast, the supercharged AC proved a costly failure. Villiers set up his own engineering works at Colnbrook, Middlesex, and as Tom Mays' health failed, Ray faced the winter of 1925–26 with no racing car, no money, many unpaid bills and the prospect of unglamorous work in the wool trade as an unglamorous substitute for competition motoring.

RM about to break the Shelsley Walsh hill-climb record in H.F. Clay's modified TT Vauxhall, sans front brakes, in 1926. His passenger on the 49.4sec climb would be Amherst Villiers. The mechanic is Harold Ayliff – Tom Mays' chauffeur, later a haulier in Bourne, then landlord of The Anchor pub in Eastgate. His son Phil would become BRM's Chief Mechanic...

1926

He consoled himself in amateur dramatics and considered a professional stage career until Harold Clay loaned his TT Vauxhall for Shelsley Walsh, the steep little hill-climb surviving the Government's ban since it was wholly on private land.

Villiers helped prepare the car and rode as passenger while Ray lowered the record to 49.4 seconds. Later that day Basil Davenport's GN climbed faster still, and for the rest of 1926 Ray "...did no other racing and had very little fun generally...being committed to saving every possible penny to complete payment of my AC debts..."

Meanwhile, however, Ray had developed a close friendship with a teenage Flying Cadet from the nearby Royal Air Force College at Cranwell. His name was David Gam Harcourt Wood. He came from Caer-Beris, in Breconshire, was an outstanding athlete and Rugby back, and his brother Beris would subsequently become a minor 'Bentley Boy' racing driver. David Harcourt Wood had entered Cranwell on January 15, 1925, by which time another new Flying Cadet set to assume vital importance in our story had already completed four months of his Cranwell course...

Peter Loraine Ashton Berthon – destined to serve as Chief Engineer of both ERA and BRM – was one of seven children of Colonel Charles Peter Berthon of the East Yorkshire Regiment, an old soldier who had fought in the Boer War and who lost a leg in the First World War. Peter – subsequently known in BRM-ese as 'PB' – had been born at Maymyo, Burma, on September 20, 1906, and educated at Christ's Hospital, the famous Bluecoat School at Horsham in Sussex.

Even as a very small boy he had displayed innate mechanical talent, dismantling clocks, bicycles, even the kitchen mincer "to improve them". His brother Paul recalled PB actually making a clock from scratch while still very young, and building radio sets of his own design in his early 'teens. He loved tinkering with the family's Model T Ford and Darracq cars, and on September 4, 1924, he entered the RAF College Cranwell to become an able – if often lazy and undisciplined – Flying Cadet. He was held back one term after failing his exams, which presumably left him in the same course as Harcourt Wood, through whom he met "the racing motorist from Bourne" – Raymond Mays.

David Harcourt Wood's relationship with Ray ended tragically on November 12, 1926, when he was killed in a flying accident at Caistor, Lincolnshire, aged only 19. Cranwell's CO broke the news to Ray by telephone and soon after, Peter Berthon arrived at Eastgate House to return an inscribed keepsake which Ray had given to Harcourt Wood. They began discussing motor cars and motor racing and Ray discovered that this dazzlingly handsome young man seemed only too willing and apparently able to help develop whatever competition car he, RM, might obtain.

Today the Cranwell staff describe the College's 1920s' engineering course as "rudimentary at best", but it provided the only formal engineering training which Peter Berthon ever received. He would never attain any formal engineering qualifications, but his intuitive 'feel' for things mechanical founded a considerable if controversial career which would be closely interwoven with that of Raymond Mays.

But first he was committed to a flying career in the RAF.

On December 10, 1926, within a month of Harcourt Wood's fatal accident, he passed out from Cranwell. Next day he was granted his permanent commission as an RAF Pilot Officer, and on January 10, 1927, he was posted to No. 19 (Fighter) Squadron based at Duxford near Cambridge.

They were operating the Gloster Grebe biplane, and so 20-year-old P/O Peter Berthon became a professional fighter pilot...

1927

At Olympia for the 1926 Motor Show, Raymond Mays had met Frank Seddon, British manager of Mercedes-Benz, who some weeks later offered him the supercharged 2-litre four-cylinder Targa Florio model which had been handled by Mayner in 1926, plus a retainer, all expenses, free maintenance and transport and a factory mechanic for the forthcoming season. Ray was also free to accept any retainer fees or bonuses from accessory suppliers. Once again, he had landed squarely on his feet. T.W. Mays & Son's fortunes had also recovered, and with his bonus and salary savings Ray managed to settle the AC debts.

But barely six months into his RAF career, Peter Berthon apparently crash-landed his Gloster Grebe, up-ending it in a field and emerging quite badly knocked about. He spent part of his convalescence that summer accompanying Ray and the 2-litre Mercedes-Benz to Aston Clinton for their debut, and subsequently – following advice from Amherst Villiers – he helped prepare the car in the garages behind Eastgate House.

PB was an extraordinary man. He was always prone to changeable, but when in favour, all-absorbing enthusiasms. When gripped by a craze for motor racing, or astronomy, or sailing, or radio, or later hi-fi and television, he would immerse himself totally for weeks on end in whatever interest had bubbled to the surface. While recovering from his accident during that summer, his energetic enthusiasm was fired by Ray and the racing Mercedes.

He moved into Eastgate House, and on November 2 resigned his RAF commission "on account of ill-health", to join the Mays wool business. The object was largely to help prepare Ray's racing cars, but there were other attractions at Bourne too.

Motor race engineering was to become PB's full-time business, but passing enthusiasms and female distractions would divide his attentions at many crucial times in the years to come. He was a dazzlingly handsome, amoral young man, and with Tom Mays ailing and infirm, for a very brief period Anne Mays became involved in a relationship with her son's newfound friend.

Many familiar with the Eastgate House *menage* as the 1920s ran into the 1930s recall both mother and son being equally infatuated with PB – who despite his close and long-lived friendship with RM was very much a lady's man...

Even so, Ray adored him, and subsequently wouldn't make a move without consulting him. Unlike PB, Ray was a decidedly gay young man in both contemporary and modern connotations of that word, but he always ensured that his private life was very private, and discreet. Homosexuality in 'tween-wars upper-middle-class Britain was a closed world, new friends introduced by old, a secret, enclosed freemasonry of its own. Few of Ray's close menfriends came from inside racing...most of his racing associates got to know and like and respect him firstly as the dashing driver, then remained loyal

if detached when they knew him better. He was always a good friend to have, and both could and would move mountains to help those loyal to him. But certainly prewar he also had a towering ego. He relished being the central attraction of an admiring coterie and was demonstrably convinced the world owed him a living. Yet in return he could, and often did, deliver the goods... His was becoming a household name.

His Mercedes season of 1926 was very successful. Late that year Frank Seddon brought over one of the works' notoriously tricky, short-wheelbase 2-litre straight-eight GP cars. At Brooklands, Ray and PB shared a terrifying ride in it, after which De Hane Segrave told them "you're damned lucky to be alive, and if you take my advice you'll never drive that car again!"

Ray had lapped at 116.91mph, reaching 130mph along the Railway Straight. There was very little effeminate about his driving, but his polished skill, highly attuned to unleashing maximum effort over a brief period of time, always shone most brightly in explosive-effort sprint events.

1928

Tom Mays' deepening frailty forced Ray to play an increasing role in the wool business, together with his company managers and PB, who helped him select and buy rug skins around the country. Early in 1928 Ray was holidaying with his father at Canford Cliffs in Bournemouth while considering a replacement for the Mercedes deal. Amherst Villiers had been irritated by Humphrey Cook selling his Villiers-supercharged TT Vauxhall to Jack Barclay, the dealer, with its full potential still untapped. Now he and Ray bought it between them, plus related spares, for £275.

Villiers had it rebuilt in his Colnbrook works and late in July 1928 it was completed, rebodied and sprayed 'Mays blue'. Ray drove down in his 2-litre Lagonda – which of course had been acquired on part-payment with promise of "good publicity".

On July 28 the revamped *Vauxhall-Villiers* made its debut at Shelsley Walsh and Ray set second FTD in it behind Davenport's GN. He then raced and sprinted the car successfully until its engine failed on Southport Sands.

1929

Through the winter of 1928–29 considerable modifications were made to the *Vauxhall-Villiers* and in the second Shelsley meeting Ray smashed Davenport's record, using twin rear wheels to improve traction. Shell Oil and KLG Plugs backed him that year, and they made great play of his success. At Olympia, Lagonda displayed a blue 3-litre saloon behind a notice declaring its sale to "Mr. Raymond Mays", whose star status – by the standards of that time – was firmly established upon the small English motoring stage.

However, he was certainly no enormous superstar at that time...such accolade then being reserved for the likes of Segrave, Campbell, Birkin and Barnato. Neither is it true the entire establishment had fallen prey to his dazzling charm. After all, didn't he have to tap the trade to sponsor his racing – and worse yet, wasn't his father – the tanner and fertilizer manufacturer – only 'the bone man' from Bourne?

Ray liked to portray himself as being decidedly upper-middle-class – certainly ex-public school and Guards Brigade – but Oundle was not Eton and in a highly class-conscious society, even disregarding his personal orientation, some believed breeding mattered, and occasionally when he "got above himself" they told him so. Subsequently, when patrician Dick Seaman felt himself sold short by ERA, the upstart bone man's son would hear all about it…

1930

For the new season, the *Vauxhall-Villiers* was again rebuilt. With 20lbs boost its 3-litre four-cylinder engine reached an astronomical 6,000rpm and Villiers fitted an intercooler between blower and inlet ports to reduce charge temperature. Contributions to the renamed *Villiers Supercharge* were made by Clayton-Dewandre servo brakes, India tyres, Zenith carburettors, Andre dampers, Shell oil, BTH magnetos, Ferodo brake linings, Jaeger instruments and Kayser Ellison steels. The car was intended partly to promote Villiers' new series of superchargers which he had designed in conjunction with a brilliant young engineer named Tom Murray Jamieson. They were intended to match a range of production car engine sizes, but unfortunately the new car misbehaved, preventing Ray from competing in the first Shelsley 'climb – the first

meeting he had missed there since 1921.

In his absence, Austrian visitor Hans Stuck promptly set a sensational 42.8-seconds 'climb record, driving his special Austro-Daimler. Ray subsequently set FTD in the later Shelsley meeting that season, but rain prevented him attacking 'The Stuck Record'.

1931

For 1931, Melville of India Tyres contracted Ray for a series of promotional events using the *Villiers Supercharge* and later a 4½-litre sports Invicta, which naturally was purchased "at a special price" from Captain Noel Macklin of Invicta Cars. Amherst Villiers had become involved with 'Tim' Birkin in producing the Blower Bentleys and soon redirected his attention towards aero-engines, whereupon Humphrey Cook financed Ray's purchase of Villiers' share in the *Supercharge*. Murray Jamieson had left Villiers to become a consultant to Austin's experimental and racing department. But early in 1931 he, Mays and Peter Berthon combined at Eastgate House to modify the Invicta's Meadows engine, helped by mechanic Alf Buckle, on loan from Henry Meadows and destined to become a full-time ERA mechanic.

Tom Mays, meanwhile, was bedridden. Ray's devotion to racing did little to bolster the family business, but Tom accepted that his son was driven to follow his own path…and

Tom Mays' company transport was press-ganged into service to haul RM's competition cars…becoming a familiar sight on the roads around Bourne, which became his testing ground.

Amherst Villiers – polymathic genius – shows off what is better known today as the Vauxhall-Villiers. Initially he supercharged this basically 1922 3-litre TT Vauxhall for Humphrey Cook in 1926. Cook sold it, unproven, to Jack Barclay, who raced it unblown in 1927, Amherst and RM then buying it jointly for 1929 and continuing development until 1933.

when Ray eventually drove the Invicta away into India's agreed six-week tour of agents it was Peter Berthon who stayed in Bourne to handle company business…

1932

Despite a costly season with little real success, India renewed its support for 1932, Ray using the Invicta and the ageing *Villiers Supercharge*. But when he could not approach the Stuck record at Shelsley Walsh he regretfully concluded that the old TT Vauxhall-based special had reached the limit of its development. In the September Shelsley meeting, the white Invicta with its blue upholstery set a new sports record, but the lovingly prepared *Villiers* snapped its very expensive crankshaft.

However, Ray's old acquaintance Humphrey Cook had been very impressed by the speed and reliability which Jamieson – assisted by Berthon, to whom Ray was far more inclined to give the credit – had engineered into the Invicta. Cook now suggested that if Noel Macklin would co-operate financially and in kind, he would underwrite a new Invicta to uphold British racing prestige internationally. Bentley's racing days had ended the previous year, and the patriotic Cook was anxious to perpetuate their British success in international sports car racing.

Plans centred upon a new 5-litre supercharged engine to assume Bentley's mantle at Le Mans, but agreement could not be reached so this Invicta scheme collapsed. It remains a mere hint of what would follow.

Meanwhile, on June 2 that year, Peter Berthon married a rather exotic, certainly an extrovert and often quite outra-geous (and very glamorous) lady – Lorna Mary Wiltshire.

Even to their daughter, Jacqueline, this spectacular lady tended to tell differing stories about her background. Jacquie told me: "I think her father worked in the Polish Embassy in Istanbul, and her mother was a famous temple-dancer, known as 'The Rose of Turkey'. She was adopted into a huge Greek family and eventually came to England at the age of 16 with a Scottish diplomatic attache named Wiltshire. She sometimes told me she sang at The Cabaret Club in London, and she was certainly a solo dancer…and a really extraordinary character…"

Annie Mays still reputedly carried a torch for PB, and she was appalled at his marriage. One story of her revenge which became a favourite of many ERA veterans involves her tossing the entire contents of his room at Eastgate House out of its window, down into the yard – his gramophone was smashed to pieces, while before tossing out his suits and shirts she cut off all the sleeves and trouser-legs with a pair of scissors. Ever after she referred to Lorna Berthon darkly as 'The Terrible Turk'…

1933

During the winter, work began yet again to repair and prepare the old *Villiers Supercharge*, but while on a wool trade trip to the Midlands, Ray and PB visited Victor Riley at his Coventry factory. They suggested to him that tremendous publicity could be generated if Ray could break the Hans Stuck record at Shelsley in a 1½-litre Riley sports car. 'VR' was fascinated by these magnetically persuasive visitors. PB was despatched to examine the six-cylinder engine parts in the factory and he declared that a redesigned cylinder head and supercharger

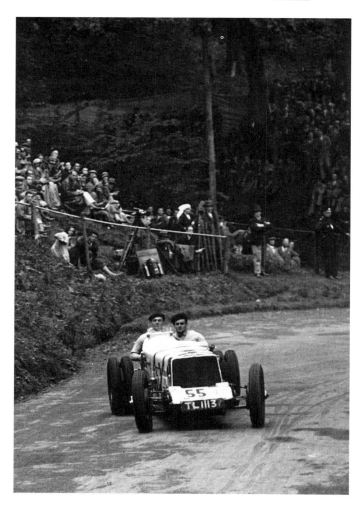

Twin rear wheels on the Villiers Supercharge helped RM dominate his favourite hill-climb at Shelsley Walsh. Here in the Esses in 1931 passenger PB understandably tenses while Ray holds TL 1113's full-blooded powerslide. Neither man was faint-hearted...and those were hard times – the height of the Great Depression sparked riots in London and Glasgow, proposed pay cuts saw the Invergordon Mutiny rock the Royal Navy and HM Government abandoned the Gold Standard, devaluing the Pound.

Shelsley 'climb of 1933. There, despite being damaged *en route*, the old lady achieved the fastest-yet wet climb in 44.8 seconds.

The new Berthon/Barratt/Jamieson-modified Riley engine with its balanced Jamieson crankshaft first ran unsupercharged, but when the new blower was fitted it developed 147bhp at 6,500rpm in its first power-run at Coventry. Humphrey Cook was somehow interested financially at this time, as the possibility was discussed of running a team of similar 1½-litre Rileys in the Mannin Beg race at Douglas, Isle of Man.

That was not possible, but after further development the

1933 – Kay Petre, the darling of the Brooklands set, strikes a pose in The White Riley for the press photographers.

could be accepted by a slightly modified existing bottom end. With more power the light and limber Riley would have a power-to-weight ratio matching Stuck's Austro-Daimler. After completing their wool commitments the duo returned that evening to see VR, who accepted their proposal, provided a 12/16 model chassis and immediately drew a £300 cheque – nearly £10,900 by 1993 values – to float the project.

Berthon pored over Riley's works drawings in a room on the third floor of Eastgate House, and in May a young professional draughtsman named Aubrey Barratt was engaged – fresh from a Daimler apprenticeship – and set to work drawing the engine modifications in the attic there. Ray also commissioned Murray Jamieson to design a suitable 100mm supercharger. Later colleagues of PB's swear he could never read a technical drawing. Be that as it may, he took credit in conjunction with Jamieson for what became Raymond Mays' famous *White Riley*.

Meanwhile, the equipe was provided with two Riley saloons which accompanied the *Villiers Supercharge* to the first new engine was installed in its special chassis with off-white bodywork and blue-upholstered cockpit and Ray drove it to Brooklands for its race debut – road-registered KV 5929.

There it proved extremely smooth and powerful, the engine revving to 8,000rpm, until its blower-drive sheared. Then at Shelsley Walsh Ray smashed Stuck's famous record – at 42.2 seconds – only for Whitney Straight twice to lower that mark later in the day with his 3-litre GP Maserati. Ray then broke the Stuck record again in the *Villiers*, but could not better Straight's best of 41.4sec.

Even so, a 1½-litre British sports car had shattered Stuck's famous record and Mays and Berthon had fulfilled their promises to Victor Riley and their other backers. By the end of that season the *White Riley* had only existed for less than six months yet had proven itself indisputably Britain's fastest 1500.

ENGLISH RACING AUTOMOBILES

While Raymond Mays was pondering future proposals to Victor Riley looking forward to 1934, a letter arrived at Eastgate House from Humphrey Cook. He had followed the *White Riley*'s career with great interest, and considered its engine good enough to form the basis of a new 1½-litre *Voiturette* single-seater racing car. He suggested that if Mays and Berthon were interested they should meet him to discuss foundation of a company to build and race this British car internationally.

At this range one can imagine how much Cook's proposal must have excited RM and PB. The trio met and agreed to set up a company as suggested, defraying some of the cost of a works team by also building a few cars for customer sale. On the question of factory premises, it seems certain that Ray was not about to entertain the inconvenience of uprooting himself from Bourne, and Cook agreed that in any case both his and Peter Berthon's commitments to T.W. Mays & Son meant they should stay put. Ray suggested that Cook should finance establishment of a factory behind Eastgate House and a gentleman's agreement followed, without written contract, to proceed as discussed.

Accordingly, 'English Racing Automobiles Ltd' was registered on November 6, 1933, with a nominal capital of £10,000 comprising 9,990 £1 Preference Shares and 200 Ordinary Shares of one shilling each. This nominal £10,000 capital represents over £360,000 at 1993 values…

According to A.F. Rivers Fletcher – who came to know the trio exceptionally well as perhaps their leading fan and most loyal supporter – the alternative title 'British Racing Motors' was considered even at this very early stage. It was rejected in favour of 'English Racing Automobiles' on the basis that FIAT's initials had quickly been rendered 'Fiat' in popular speech, so 'ERA' could handily become 'Era', whereas there's not a lot one can do with the admittedly onomatopoeic 'Brm'…

But, as it happened, the initials ERA would become and remain famous in their own right…

Initially, each of ERA's founders drew a salary of £250 a year (about £9,000, 1993). Mays (number one driver and Director) and Berthon (Designer and Director) each held just £2 10s-worth of shares while Cook (as Managing Director)

held the balance and financed the entire operation. Any prize money plus all accessory retainers and bonuses were the company's, to offset expenditure. Ray was to handle all contracts with accessory firms and attract as much additional capital as possible.

Subject to Victor Riley's agreement, Ray gave ERA all rights to the *White Riley*-developed engine, while Riley would help manufacture and machine mechanical parts, at least until the new Bourne plant was running.

Ray asked his invalid father to allow erection of a small factory in the orchard behind Eastgate House, in addition to use of their small adjoining Maltings, flanking the Spalding Road. Tom Mays agreed and the Maltings were quickly converted, while the orchard plot was sold to Humphrey Cook for a nominal £50 and a small new corrugated-clad factory was built there.

Freddie Gordon Crosby, *The Autocar* artist, designed a badge suggesting 'The dawn of a new Era', with a circular insignia bearing the ERA initials from which radiated the rays of the rising sun. This appeared only on the first prototype car, being quickly replaced by an interlinked three-circle badge giving more prominence to the ERA letters. This badge was jointly designed by PB and an RAF friend of his – the diminutive station commander at Duxford – Hugh Lewis Pingo Lester. He would later become an avid supporter of both ERA and BRM and as an inventive engineer in his own right would play a small role in BRM's wartime foundation.

The Bourne duo approached Reid Railton – of Thomson & Taylor, the Brooklands car preparation specialists – to design and build a suitable single-seat racing car chassis. According to Ray's account it was to incorporate "some of Peter Berthon's ideas", though their extent is now impossible to determine. Murray Jamieson was also enlisted to design and produce the supercharger, and one of his closest friends recalled asking him one day: "How much of the ERA did Peter Berthon design?" After much thought, Murray quizzically replied: "An oil-pipe…?"

The *White Riley*-type cylinder block was further modified, but Berthon and Barratt's proven cylinder head with its numerous holding-down studs and Jamieson's counter-balanced crankshaft were to continue unaltered. A specially-built Wilson pre-selector gearbox made by Armstrong Siddeley was chosen because its clutchless changes were considered to give the driver an advantage since he could keep both hands on the steering wheel when he hit the 'clutch pedal' to engage the pre-selected gear. Jamieson's blower was to be updated to deliver some 15lbs boost against the *White Riley*'s 12lbs. Improved valves and cooling followed. The target was 170bhp from the 1½-litre engine, while a 1,100cc version was also planned.

Into 1934, ERA Ltd became established at Bourne in the former Eastgate House orchard beside the Spalding Road. A Heenan & Froude dynamometer was installed to brake-test engines, and an engine assembly shop under Alf Buckle was set up on the first floor of the old Maltings. The new building's ground floor comprised machine shop and engine assembly area, engine test-bay and tool and fuel stores, while the parts stores and offices were upstairs where the design staff (Aubrey Barratt, and later his assistant) resided.

Several new employees were engaged, one of them a tall, lean, penetratingly blue-eyed local mechanic named Ken Richardson. His father was a publican and butcher in Bourne, and as a boy Ken had watched RM's Bugattis and Vauxhall "whizzing about…I'd hang over the gate at Eastgate House to see what was going on in the yard and garages there. I was running a garage for a chap down Wisbech way when Peter Berthon rang me out of the blue to ask if I'd join ERA. I asked 'When d'you want me to start?'. 'Tomorrow' he said, so I accepted and gave my chap only about two to three hours notice. It was as sudden as that. I just wanted to go racing. It was a fantastic chance, and I grabbed it…".

Thomson & Taylor were finishing Reid Railton's first two chassis frames at Brooklands, and Humphrey Cook frequently visited from London to study progress. Two self-employed 'panel bashers' – the brothers George and Jack Gray, all the way from Emsworth on the Hampshire coast – built the new single-seater bodyshells (and postwar some of the BRM V16

body panels) on visits to Bourne, and everything developed with astonishing speed; celerity which would be sadly lacking, due to all manner of circumstances, with BRM postwar…

Unfortunately, before the prototype ERA could be completed, Tom Mays died, aged 78.

The wool business' future now fell on RM's shoulders at a time when he was fully-extended in the ERA venture; but he was fortunate in that T.W. Mays & Son had good professional managers. For him there was no going back.

1934

Not since 1924, 10 years previously, had a British car and driver won a European race of Grand Prix status, nor had Britain been represented at all in European events for 'proper' racing cars. Now, in 1934, a brand-new Grand Prix Formula was being introduced as racing emerged from the austere

Right: April 1934 – RM and PB with the bare bones of ERA prototype 'R1', fresh from Thomson & Taylor at Brooklands. Note Ray's shorter left arm, legacy of a boyhood accident in the Eastgate House yard beyond the wall when he fell on ice and smashed his elbow. Also launched in 1934 were mandatory UK driving tests, the Cunarder RMS Queen Mary and F. Scott Fitzgerald's Tender is the Night. Hitler established himself as German Fuhrer while Oswald Mosley – whose son Max would become President of the modern FISA motor sporting authority – held a mass meeting of his British Fascists at Olympia. But Henry Cotton ended US golfing dominance by winning the Open Championship at Sandwich.

Below: May 1934 – the prototype ERA chassis 'R1' shows off its brand new unpainted body panelling, by brothers George and Jack Gray, outside the just completed ERA workshop behind Eastgate House. Its radiator cowl bears the original, short-lived, rising sun badge designed for the project by The Autocar's artist, Freddie Gordon-Crosby.

Depression years. A supplementary 1½-litre class for racing *Voiturettes* continued internationally, while an 1,100cc small car division also assumed special significance in Britain. Thus the stage was set for ERA...

The new Bourne-based marque's original target was to field two cars in the races at Douglas, Isle of Man, on May 30, 1934. Cook was to drive an 1100 in the small-capacity Mannin Beg race, and Mays a 1500 in the large-capacity Mannin Moar. When this proved impossible, ERA's small staff concentrated upon Ray's 1500. This first ever British-built central-seat road racing car – ERA 'R1A' – was wheeled into the yard of Eastgate House in mid-May. Problems were revealed in preliminary Brooklands testing, and during practice around Douglas' bumpy streets the new car proved itself a terrifying handful. There was no option but to withdraw from the race.

New rear springs, and suspension and steering modifications were then made in time for the Empire Trophy race at Brooklands, where Ray was to share 'R1A' with Cook. After a series of minor problems at least they finished, unclassified.

ERA then made its foreign debut, Ray retiring from the first heat of the Dieppe GP when a rocker broke. The second car – 'R2A' – was hastily completed with the prototype 1,100cc engine for Cook to accompany Ray's 'R1A' in the August Bank Holiday meeting at Brooklands. Both cars, fitted with plywood mudguards, trade plates and silencers, were tested by RM and PB around a public road circuit which they had often used, leading from Bourne out to the Great North Road at Colsterworth, south to Stamford, then back to Bourne along the country roads. Drive this tortuous and hilly loop enthusiastically today in a modern road car and one soon gets sweaty and breathless... In an ERA it must have been sensational!

At Brooklands, Cook won a handicap race and set a new 1,100cc lap record on the Mountain Circuit at 72.37mph. The more severely handicapped 1500 finished second in one race and set a new class record at 76.5mph...

The two ERAs then broke 1,100cc and 1,500cc standing-start records for the kilometre and mile, by which time 'R3A' was approaching completion with a 2-litre sprint engine, aimed at the Shelsley record. Ray drove this new car on the road from Bourne to Malvern and duly set Shelsley FTD in pouring rain.

The new marque's first serious road race – and in fact the first long-distance road race ever to be run on the English

August 28, 1934 – Brooklands: Ray in 1,500cc 'R1' and Humphrey Cook in 1,100cc 'R2' both broke International standing-start kilometre and mile speed records on this day. Beyond RM stand the talented, tragically ill-fated, Tom Murray Jamieson, PB and Madge Cook (left); the white(ish) overalled mechanics are (left to right) John Lea – with Jaguar postwar – Alf Buckle and ERA truck driver Lawrence.

mainland – followed at Donington Park near Derby. There Ray won the Nuffield Trophy at 61.51mph, and Cook's 1,100cc sister car finished fifth. To close this maiden ERA season, Ray then took the 2-litre to Brooklands for the Mountain Championship and finished second behind Straight's 2.9-litre Maserati. Hans Ruesch's similar car held the world standing-start kilometre record at that time, at 88.87mph. Ray attacked this record with 'R3A', which became the smallest-capacity car to break it – at 89.73mph.

The ERA was a success, and having overcome its teething troubles, Humphrey Cook forwarded more capital to provide extra staff, to extend the premises at Bourne and to produce customer cars for sale to approved drivers.

The South African amateur, Pat Fairfield, placed the first order, wisely opting for an 1100 since his previous experience had been restricted to a Riley sports. Richard John Beattie Seaman followed, his immense skills having just been honed on an MG K3 under the Whitney Straight team banner.

Ending their very first season, on Monday, "the 26th day of November 1934, at 5 o'clock in the afternoon..." ERA's Board met in the offices of W. Lewis Shepherd – Cook's and the company's solicitor – at 46 Queen Anne's Gate, Westminster, London SW1.

At that time, Cook had received certificates for £9,490-worth of £1 ERA Preference Shares to cover monies already advanced. ERA's current account was £37 4s 8d in credit, but an additional £1,000 had been received in deposits for the two cars ordered – £500 each from Fairfield and Seaman. Ray anticipated at least two further orders. He, PB and Cook then discussed provision of the cash required to manufacture the cars and to meet current liabilities, which their minutes listed as follows:

Outstanding trading accounts	–	£608 7s 1d
Due to Cook for loans by him	–	£1,150 0s 0d
Estimated cost of building new factory wing at Bourne	–	£300 0s 0d
Total	–	£2,058 7s 0d

Cook agreed to advance a further £2,000 (over £72,000, 1993 value!) that December. They then reviewed salaries, and upon Cook's proposal, seconded by Mays, PB's salary was doubled as from New Year's Day, 1935, to £500 (about £18,000, 1993). But in return Cook wanted him to work full-time for ERA and to relinquish his duties for T.W. Mays & Son. This would throw extra family-business load upon RM's shoulders – Ray argued – so upon Cook's proposal, seconded by Berthon, RM's £250 *pa* was raised to £400.

Bourne's racing car business had been well and truly launched...

1935

The ERA story has been well told by David Weguelin's *The History of English Racing Automobiles Limited* (White Mouse Editions/New Cavendish Books, London, 1980) but David had no access to some forgotten source material within RM's own files which throws new light on some aspects of ERA's development and thus adds shape to the background of BRM.

Briefly, ERA's career unfolded into 1935 as Fairfield's 1,100cc 'R4A' was completed alongside Seaman's black-painted 'R1B' – first of a new B-Type series of production models with softer rear springs, extra chassis cross-bracing beneath the seat and other modifications (though in truth every ERA was an individual). Fairfield's 'R4A' was to be campaigned as an occasional works entry.

The English-domiciled Siamese, Prince Chula Chakrabongse, then bought 'R2B' for his cousin Prince Birabongse Bhanubandh as a 21st birthday present. Their new car would run in blue – later heightened with yellow – as the Princes' idea of Siamese racing colours. They christened it *Romulus*, and in the hands of young 'B. Bira' it would become the most successful of all customer ERAs.

Meanwhile, the 1934 prototype car 'R1A' was sold to the Hon. Brian Lewis (later Lord Essendon), while 'R2A' went to the hard-driving Greek, Nicky Embiricos, who subsequently had it converted to Tecnauto independent front suspension. Car 'R3A' was acquired by the immensely fast young Anglo-Brazilian owner/driver Luis Fontes.

F.R.W. 'Lofty' England joined ERA that season as a mechanic. He recalled: "I first went to ERA after Whitney Straight packed up at the end of 1934. Charlie Newcombe had been my boss for Straight in Milan [where that team's Maseratis had been prepared] ...and before that at Birkin's. He had come home ahead of me and was already at ERA so I joined up with him there.

"I wasn't impressed with what was going on, which was mainly preparing the ex-1934 cars for the 1935 season and trying to get more power – nor for the lack of respect shown behind his back by Mays and Berthon for that charming man Humphrey Cook. After attending one Brooklands meeting I decided to have another spell in London, my home town, so I then worked there for Alvis until about November '35, when I went back to ERA.

"They had made their third customer car for 'Bira' in a big hurry when Chula decided to give him one for his 21st birthday. When they made its engine they were short of some parts so fitted two same-side camshafts (I don't remember whether inlet or exhaust side) and a smaller supercharger, the size used on the 1,100cc engine but with higher speed gears as used in the normal 1,500cc size. The result was that the car went well, started on the handle and did 6mpg instead of the usual 4mpg! I had many times told Berthon that in my opinion for a supercharged engine the valve overlap was excessive and what they did with the 'Bira' engine brought it down to a more reasonable amount. They never seem to have asked themselves *why* the 'Bira' car went so well – later when I worked for 'Bira' we changed the camshafts that way on all his three ERAs."

Early that season, Ray set the first-ever sub-40 second records at Shelsley Walsh in both his 1,500cc and 2-litre cars, and Fairfield then won both the 1,100cc Mannin Beg at Douglas and the Nuffield Trophy at Donington Park.

But even then, with ERA barely 18 months old, the always easily discouraged Humphrey Cook was depressed. On June 6 – as the works team prepared for its second Continental foray, to the 1,500cc Eifelrennen at Nurburgring, Germany – he wrote the following letter in his uneven, tight and angular hand, from Upper Brook Street (Tel: Mayfair 4170) to RM at Bourne:

My dear Ray,

Am enclosing cheque for £500 to cover expenses until we get back. I am very worried indeed as, unless we can sell a car or two, *I am afraid that there will be no alternative but to 'pack up'.* [my italics, DCN] The £2,000 balance, which I am still holding with Shepherd, is already earmarked, what with Burt's & Mathieson's deposit & our other liabilities; in fact, if we stopped everything now, a considerable amount more would still have to be found to settle all our debts. I think every nerve ought to be strained to get orders & to cut down expenses as much possible, so as to keep the business going as long as possible on its present capital. After we get back from Nurburg, I think all our efforts should be concentrated on the Empire Trophy, so as to get the cars properly prepared & not have the everlasting rush at the last moment, as now. With this end in view, I suggest that we do not try & do too much racing, with our limited staff & number of cars & that we definitely cut out Kesselberg & Donington.

If we give plenty of time for good preparation for the Empire Trophy & Dieppe, I am sure it is better than trying to sandwich in other events in between. I hope you & Peter will agree to this, as there are only 2½ weeks between returning from Nurburg & the Empire T., which is not too long to get a lot of cars ready, properly, without undue haste... Also, get the original correspondence about Nurburg, so that we know what is really due to us.

Yrs. ever
Humphrey

P.S. Don't forget to bring your A1 Licence.

Their Eifelrennen trip was in fact triumphant. Dick Seaman battled with RM until his new car faltered, leaving Ray to win at 68.99mph, with Tim Rose-Richards third, Seaman fourth and Cook fifth, all in ERAs. Paul Berthon accompanied brother Peter there, and in the 1980s could vividly recall the thrill as "...the Mercedes-Benz and Auto Union mechanics from the main race crawled all over our cars and just couldn't believe the company hadn't existed only 18 months before..."

This was generally a successful season for ERA though marred by PB and RM foolishly attempting to palm-off Seaman with a used engine represented as new, and some very slipshod preparation of his customer car.

This ambitious and wealthy young man, determined to race in the most professional manner, simply *blasted* RM, PB and ERA when he discovered their mindless fraud. Cook was not amused.

Seaman set up his own racing 'shop in garages behind his mother's house in fashionable Ennismore Gardens, Knightsbridge, London. Thereafter, he shone in his well-prepared black ERA. He set second FTD at the Grossglockner mountain climb, won the 1500 Coppa Acerbo and Prix de Berne and was second-quickest behind Stuck's GP Auto Union at Freiburg, beating Ray's best time there by fully 11

seconds... Seaman then completed this great half-season by winning the Masarykring 1500 race at Brno, Czechoslovakia. Meanwhile, the novice, 'Bira', scored a string of second places in 'R2B', *Romulus*.

By that September, *Motor Sport* could enthuse:

Continental organisers are ordering new gramophone records of the British National Anthem to play at the end of their races, for the E.R.A. is regarded as unbeatable. Maserati and Bugatti – names to conjure with – have been subdued...

Cook's philanthropy and the combined efforts behind ERA had achieved both their patriotic and sporting aims. Both the popular and specialist British press took up the story, ERA had made its mark, RM's public stature towered while PB was lauded as 'a brilliant racing car designer'. But behind the public facade, things were not so rosy.

Beyond Seaman's condemnation, money remained short. Late that same season, Ray was beating the bushes in his inimitably importunate style, clearly pressured by Cook to secure extra or alternative sponsorship. He had tried Lord Wakefield – of Castrol – and had failed, when Victor Riley encouraged him to approach Lady Houston – famously patriotic backer of the Schneider Trophy-winning Supermarine seaplanes.

Consequently, on December 2, 1935, Ray wrote to her, his letter clearly presaging the arguments he later evolved to launch the BRM:

Dear Lady Houston,

Knowing your public spirit and keen desire for the eminence of British prestige, I feel I may permit myself to approach you on behalf of an endeavour which I, and others with me, are making.

In the past it has been said, and truly said, that British endeavour had been sadly lacking in the design and development of the advanced automobile design expressed in racing cars. In consequence valuable national prestige has been lost to this country and has been gained by Italy and France, and now Germany.

I set out some two years ago to endeavour to produce an example of British Automobile Engineering which would be equal, if not superior to the best examples emanating from Europe...

No attempt has been made, and no attempt is contemplated to exploit commercially the results obtained. In other words, no endeavour has been made to produce cars for sale, and beyond the sale of 12 cars to certain approved drivers no revenue from this source has been forthcoming nor is expected...

We desire, if possible, to continue our efforts because greater success is in sight... Mr. Humphrey Cook, who has so generously provided the financial support up to the present time, feels that having done so much the financial burden should not be born in the future solely by him.

Because I feel that a great opportunity to place British supremacy pre-eminent in advanced automobile engi-

A distant relationship – ERA Chief Engineer Peter Berthon with financial backer Humphrey Cook, who competed 14 times in the early works cars through 1934–35 then twice more, winning the Albi GP with RM in 1937. Quick to despair and easily depressed, Cook rapidly became darkly suspicious of PB's probity and dedication to the cause. After the final split in 1939, Cook remained upon surprisingly cordial terms with RM, but never regarded Berthon as warmly.

neering may be hindered and perhaps lost, I now approach you in the hope that you will see in our efforts something which may justifiably enlist your valuable encouragement… I sincerely hope we may secure your interest to further our work.

He – and Cook – must have been sadly disappointed by the clipped response from Lady Houston's home at Hampstead Heath, London NW3, dated December 18, 1935. It even misspelled RM's surname: Raymond Mayes. Esq.,

Dear Sir,
I very much regret that it is impossible for me to approach Lady Houston with the matter you mention. She is far from well and has already too many existing claims on her time and energy to permit her to take on any fresh interests.
Please accept my sincere regrets,

Yours Faithfully,
B.D.R.
Secretary.

1936

During 1936, ERA scored more success, thanks largely to the applied skills of the Siamese Princes, Chula and 'Bira', with *Romulus*. More customers had appeared and extra staff were engaged at Bourne, including a young engineer named Harry Mundy who joined Aubrey Barratt's design team. Harry had served an Alvis apprenticeship in Coventry when he "…heard of this works in the little orchard at Bourne and saw an ERA job advertised – I wrote in, and got it…".

He was later to play a leading role in designing the V16 BRM before joining Coventry Climax with another (briefly) ex-ERA man – Walter Hassan.

The Chula/'Bira' White Mouse Stable team achieved ERA's major international successes that season, winning at Picardie and Albi in France and also in the 1½-litre *Coupe Rainier* at Monte Carlo where Marcel Lehoux's works-entered 'R3B' finished second and Embiricos third in 'R2A'. 'Bira' won on his adopted home soil in the JCC International Trophy at Brooklands, beating Mays, although Ray won the Mountain Championship race there and of course became Shelsley Champion yet again – his name by this time synonymous with the picturesque Midlands venue. During this season his new works car 'R4B' was using an experimental Zoller vane-type supercharger mounted behind the engine, projecting into the cockpit, in place of the original Jamieson compressor.

Lofty England: "That year Marcel Lehoux – who I knew since he had driven for Straight in the Spanish and Algerian GPs of 1934 – drove for ERA. He drove to win and was second at Monaco first time out for ERA, after a first-lap shunt which left him pushing his car across the Casino Square to restart it. In later races he was dogged by various troubles but after the race at Albi he personally got an entry in the Deauville GP by telling the organizers he would run a 2-litre ERA, but he actually ran a 1.5. A hard course on brakes suited the ERA, but sadly he was killed running second behind a 3.8 Alfa when hit up the back by Farina, whose car by that time was short of brakes. Only Percy Pugh – Cook's personal mechanic who he sent to Bourne to help out and keep an eye on things – was there with me. After Bremgarten in August we rushed home to get the cars ready for the JCC 200 at Donington the following Saturday, for which the Mays car was fitted with an extra fuel tank to go through non-stop, while the other cars were not!

"Mays wasn't fast in practice and asked me what was wrong with his car? I suggested he should let Fairfield try it. To my surprise he agreed. Fairfield broke the lap record on his first flying lap…

"After a few laps in the race, Mays came in to complain of oil on his vizor, and he then repeated this stopping act on which I expressed my views… After that race I went to the Isle of Man to ride in the Manx GP, and while there heard from ERA that my services were no longer required. I finished second in the Lightweight Manx GP, and then joined Dick Seaman…and when he went to Mercedes-Benz for 1937, I went to 'Bira' as Chief Mechanic…"

Lofty ended up with William Lyons at SS Cars, renamed Jaguar postwar. He became Service Manager there, ran Jaguar's multiple Le Mans-winning racing operation through the 1950s and after Sir William Lyons' retirement in the 1960s ultimately replaced him as Chief Executive. A man whose opinions one respects…

Poor Lehoux's Deauville crash destroyed 'R3B' – the only one of the 17 'Old English Upright' ERAs to be written-off. 'R5B', christened *Remus*, went to Chula as the second car for 'Bira', and other customers included former Bentley Boy Dr J.D. Benjafield for 'R6B', Cyril Paul for 'R7B', Frances, the Earl Howe 'R8B', Dennis Scribbans 'R9B', Peter Whitehead 'R10B' and Reggie Tongue 'R11B'. A new works car, 'R12B', was also produced for Ray's own use at the end of that season.

Right: July 20, 1935 – ERAs dominate the Dieppe GP starting grid; Dick Seaman's troublesome 'R1B' (number 10), RM in 'R1A' (2), Pat Fairfield in 'R4A' (12), 'B.Bira' behind in 'R2B' (8), Humphrey Cook in 'R2A' (6) on row three. That year saw 'Swing' music born and Penguin Books triggering the paperback revolution…times were changing, economic activity accelerating. Earl Howe – in the low-slung Delage on row two – would order an ERA for 1936.

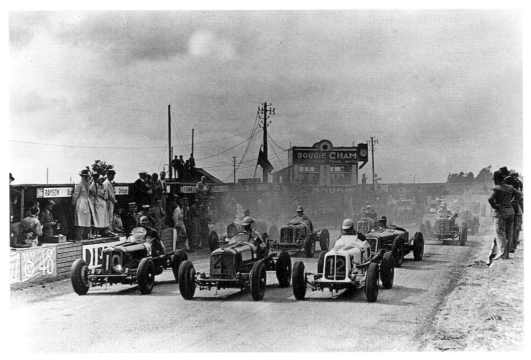

Below: April 10, 1936 – Coupe Rainier, Monte Carlo. The glamour of international motor racing utterly mesmerized RM, seen here with his team of ERAs on Monte Carlo's Quai Albert 1er. In the wider world, German troops entered the Rhineland, the Spanish Civil War began and King Edward VIII abdicated to marry Wallis Simpson.

More significantly, ERA thoughts now turned seriously towards capitalizing upon their name through a road-going 'Pleasure Car' project, but their relationship with Riley (Coventry) Ltd – who were of course major engine component suppliers – was troubled.

In May 1936, Riley instructed B.S. Gorton, a Coventry solicitor, to institute proceedings against Raymond Mays for non-payment of debt. But Ray could *always* charm Victor Riley in particular, although his brother Rupert was a distinctly harder nut to crack…

Irrespective, six days after the first ranging shots by solicitor Gorton, Ray could still receive the following from VR:

> One thing…which I have not failed to notice, is the splendid manner ERA cars have been doing [*sic*] recently and there is no doubt that you have more than achieved the purpose for which you set out originally. Once again, let me say that all concerned deserve the greatest credit. With kind regards and every good wish, believe me to remain,
>
> Yours sincerely,
>
> *Victor Riley.*

But by May 1937, Riley's Company Secretary was far less cuddly. Then he would write:

> We have received an enquiry for an E.R.A. type cylinder block.
>
> In the ordinary course we should refer the customer to your goodselves but seeing that your account is in such an unsatisfactory condition and you refuse to deal with same, we are not in a position to grant you any more credit in order to supply this order.
>
> This letter is also to advise you that failing a cheque by the end of this week, our solicitors will be instructed to proceed…we have (previously) stopped proceedings in order that you might send us forward a cheque but it is several months ago and you take no further notice so that we are left with no other procedure than that which we now tell you we shall definitely take…

ERA had managed to survive to the end of 1936, but could they see out the New Year?

1937

During the winter of 1936–37, 'R4B' and 'R12B' were reconstructed as C-Type ERAs, their channel-section chassis being cut in half and the front ends replaced with new boxed-in fabrications carrying Porsche-type independent front suspension and hydraulic brakes. Maserati's new 6CM *vetturetti* with IFS had finished 1–2 in the 1936 Eifelrennen at Nurburgring, drivers Trossi and Tenni beating five live-axled ERAs. The Porsche-type torsion-bar and trailing-arm IFS system – though costly – now appealed greatly to PB who

would retain it in his postwar BRM.

Pat Fairfield became Ray's factory team-mate, until in June he was fatally injured while driving a Frazer Nash-BMW at Le Mans. Arthur Dobson, who had bought 'R7B' from Cyril Paul and proved himself a fast and smooth driver, joined the team for the rest of that season, winning the JCC '200' at Brooklands.

ERA fortunes peaked, with 17 major victories in Britain, Europe and South Africa. Amongst other successes, Fairfield won the South African GP and Crystal Palace Coronation Trophy, Ray the British Empire and International Trophy races, Eugen Bjornstad – 'R1A' 's new Norwegian 'owner' (he didn't pay up) – the Turin 1500 race, Charlie Martin – new owner of 'R3A' – the 1500 AVUSRennen in Berlin, 'Bira' the 200-Miles at Douglas and so on.

Through the following winter into January 1938, Ray, the Earl Howe and Norman Wilson raced their cars in South Africa, Ken Richardson accompanying RM there as mechanic on 'R4C'.

During 1937 the Bourne-built *Voiturettes* had raised British stature to almost unprecedented heights in international open-wheeled motor racing, but all this in a class supplementary to proper Grand Prix racing which the German state-backed teams totally dominated.

Yet despite this success, the writing remained very much on the wall. ERA's finances had always been stretched taut, and even adoption of high-pressure Zoller supercharging was really just an expedient to keep the ageing design competitive.

A new 3-litres supercharged/4.5-litres unsupercharged Grand Prix Formula was on its way for 1938–40, with an accompanying sliding scale of alternative capacities-cum-minimum weights. RM and PB ambitiously authorized initial design studies for an ERA GP project as early as September 1936. But there was no money to build anything very exotic, although a 3-litre V12 was at least discussed. It would have mated two 1500 blocks on a common crankcase, rather like Riley's Autovia V8 concept, but it seems doubtful if Cook – who might have been expected to fund it – was included in the discussion!

Failing that, an alternative stretch of the existing six-cylinder seemed most likely, achieving something around 2.4 litres and powering a very much more modern and lighter chassis clothed in more aerodynamic bodywork with much-reduced frontal area.

During 1936, the intractable prototype Zoller engine had proved its mettle on high-speed circuits, but elsewhere suffered badly from poor low-speed torque away from slow corners. The Zoller blower boosted the six-cylinder engines at 26–28psi (giving *c.*230bhp) compared with the Jamieson blower's 19psi, which offered some 40 horsepower less. But a string of Zoller engine failures centred around weak con-rods, so for 1937 PB had them redesigned with more beefy little ends and larger diameter gudgeon pins. While Mays and Berthon progressed this work, Cook was kept largely in the dark.

He had despaired of the Zoller-blown engines being anything other than "…chronically and incurably unreliable". He wanted the idea shelved, and only when PB could demonstrate a Zoller-blown engine surviving prolonged full-throttle running on the test-bed would Cook authorize the 1937 C-Type cars.

Transmission then became their Achilles heel, but they still achieved some genuine success.

At Bourne, meanwhile, Annie Mays – who had always been quite an extrovert and eccentric lady – shook the mechanics one day when she appeared in the ERA workshop brandishing a Derringer...

Ken Richardson: "She had a bee in her bonnet about us possibly forgetting something while we were preparing Ray's car. That day she was waving this pistol about, we didn't know whether it was loaded or not, so we were all dodging about in case it pointed at us! She said 'You take care building that car. If anything ever happens to my Raymond I'll shoot you all dead!'

"We believed her too – she adored him, he absolutely worshipped her, and we thought she was just bats enough to pull the trigger..."

ERA chronically needed commercial income. To provide it they re-employed – in May 1937 – the consultant engineer Tom Murray Jamieson BSc (Eng), AMIAE, MSAE, fresh from his excellent work with Austin's experimental department for which he had produced a superb series of 750cc racing cars culminating in the legendary 'OHC Racer'.

Handsome, bespectacled, a brilliant design engineer, 'Jamie' returned to work at Bourne, setting up home with his soon-pregnant young wife at 10 Rutland Terrace in nearby Stamford, not far from the modern home there of Peter and Lorna Berthon. He was to create a 4-litre road-going high-performance ERA 'Pleasure Car' and also to help PB, Aubrey Barratt and Harry Mundy in design of the potential Grand Prix ERA for 1938–40.

The 4-litre road car was to use an all-aluminium six-cylinder single-overhead-camshaft engine to challenge Lagonda in that expensive market sector.

Harry Mundy: "This was my primary job at Bourne with Jamieson, and a prototype engine was built and tested, briefly. It had a wedge-type combustion chamber which I carried on postwar in the first Climax fire pump engine...but unfortunately the concept of the car was a big mistake, because they insisted on competing with Lagonda. Money was always short...I think parts of the gearbox were detailed, but the all-independent chassis never emerged. If ERA had just done a 1½-litre sports car and put a big ERA label on it, it would have sold like hot cakes..."

The truth is that 'they' tried to do that *as well*...

In parallel with his commitments to Humphrey Cook and ERA, Ray had founded a garage business named 'Raymond Mays & Partners Ltd', which he based in part of the Maltings complex behind Eastgate House, flanking the corrugated-clad ERA works. It was nothing very grand, but it held a Bentley agency which kept Ray in a new luxury road car each year. One of his major partners in this business was Lancelot Prideaux Brune. He and his wife, Constance, were a deeply-religious couple, two of RM's most loyal friends and supporters. Their house at Limpsfield, in Surrey, was unpromisingly titled *Thrift Wood*, but Prideaux Brune's main business was The Winter Garden Garages Ltd, which he ran from 17 Macklin Street, London WC2.

Ray was also very friendly with a businessman and financier named Philip Merton, who was one of five directors of British Brands Ltd, a company with interests in confectionery and food. It was chaired by G.W. Cadbury, and its head office was in Drayton House, Euston Road, London WC1. We will hear more of Philip Merton...

It was also during this season that Tony Rudd – later PB's assistant and subsequent successor as Chief Engineer of BRM – first became 'hooked' on motor racing, thanks to Prince Chula, the White Mouse Stable, and their ERAs. The Rudd family lived at Stony Stratford, in Buckinghamshire.

Anthony Cyril Rudd, BSc (Eng), FSAE, had been born on March 8, 1923, was educated at Ratcliffe School, Wolverton, "...and in 1936–37, at the age of 14, my ambition was to become an RAF pilot. My aunt had a friend, one of whose four daughters was Lisba Hunter who became Chula's fiancée. In 1937, *en route* to Donington Park for the Nuffield Trophy, Chula and Lisba Hunter, plus 'Bira' and his fiancée Ceril Heycock called to see my aunt, and arranged for their White Mouse Stable transporter to stop by on the way back to their Garage in Dalling Road, Hammersmith, for me to see the legendary *Romulus*.

"I was hooked for ever more, and in 1938 Chula and Lisba took me to races and in my holidays I spent time at the White Mouse Garage where they maintained the cars..."

Their generosity was to have enormous ramifications.

1938

For 1938, Chula bought 'R12B' ex-works in C-Type form despite its B-Type chassis suffix. It was the first Zoller-blown ERA in private hands and once Lofty England had rebuilt it, the cousins christened it *Hanuman* after the Siamese Monkey God. In 1939 'Bira' lapped Reims in it at 100mph before an almighty accident which wrote-off its frame, leaving the White Mouse mechanics to rebuild the car around a new chassis as *Hanuman II*. The original frame parts were preserved in store, and in the late 1970s were resurrected to give us simultaneously two *Hanumen*...

During the winter of 1937–38, much design effort (and money) was expended on 'the Grand Prix car' at Bourne, but one new D-Type version of the existing model was also produced.

The converted C-Type chassis frames, with their welded-on IFS front ends, had tended to crack amidships at the welded joint. ERA frame material was 3 per cent nickel-steel. Bourne's welding wasn't quite up to that, and their welds were brittle. Now PB had a new frame assembled from boxed, lighter-gauge side members supplied by an outside specialist sub-contractor, and made distinctive by several large lightening holes along their length.

That outside supplier was a large concern based at Darlaston, near Wednesbury, in Staffordshire's 'Black Country'. Its name was Rubery Owen & Co Ltd, and it would play the decisive role in BRM postwar...

Ray's number one works car 'R4B/C' was rebuilt around this unique, 70lbs-lighter chassis frame as 'R4D', while the car's original frame then seems to have been used to rebuild Howe's 'R8B/C' for the new 1938 season.

Alongside at Bourne, the year-old 4-litre pleasure car project progressed quite well, and RM had approached the manic-depressive Captain John P. Black, then Managing

Most consistently successful of all ERA owner/drivers, the Siamese Prince 'B. Bira' notched 10 significant wins 1935–39 in ERA 'R2B' Romulus, his 21st birthday present from his cousin Prince Chula – right background, eyes raised. All their cars were impeccably prepared under the direction of Stan Holgate and Shura Rahm (right). Note the White Mouse Stable emblem upon Shura's overalls. Chula and 'Bira' would introduce future BRM Chief Engineer Tony Rudd to motor racing.

Director of The Standard Motor Company Ltd in Coventry, to produce it in volume...

However, Standard already supplied William Lyons' SS Cars company with engines and other components. When Black told Lyons of ERA's possible rival 4-litre, SS's guv'nor threatened to find another supplier.

It was high-level poker. Few would have been as accommodating to Lyons as Black had been. But Bill Lyons was a master player, and Black was susceptible to stone-faced argument... On April 28, 1938, he wrote to Ray, explaining that Standard could *not* after all manufacture the proposed 4-litre ERA.

Philip Merton had been interested in marketing it, and on May 5 he responded:

> Ray has sent me your letter of the 28th April the contents of which we all naturally very much regret to note.

He asked if Black would be willing to introduce them to Wilks of Rover, to see if Rover instead might be interested in building the ERA.

Black responded:

> ...quite frankly, I am practically certain that they would not be the slightest bit interested, as their present production facilities are fully occupied. Nevertheless, I am quite prepared to put you in touch with my brother-in-law if you think it is worthwhile in view of the above mentioned circumstances...

On May 24, Merton wrote to Humphrey Cook:

> You will undoubtedly be delighted to hear that the whole distribution programme now looks like being settled on the best terms. Charles Follett will be sole Distributor for London and the Home Counties, and Mr Prideaux-Brune [sic] will form a company E.R.A. Sales to work the wholesale distribution throughout Great Britain.

> Charles Follett and Mr. Prideaux-Brune were able to agree terms which I think are also acceptable to us.

> Privately Charles Follett informed me that he was most pleased to learn that we were dealing with a man [of] whom he had heard and knew had unlimited means at his disposal...

With the prospect of ERA Sales Ltd Handling along these lines, Merton seemed to believe that only manufacturing capacity and the international situation – imminent war with Germany – now threatened the ERA road car's future.

Cook was not so optimistic.

Previously, on April 25, 1938, Murray Jamieson had written to his good friend – and great fan – Bert Hadley, the young works Austin racing mechanic and driver, telling him in part about progress at Bourne on the 4-litre. He wrote cheerfully:

> My dear Bert,
> As you will gather, I have been busy – now being a fully-fledged FATHER...The SON and his MOTHER are both doing 100% well...The touring car goes on a (slightly) pace. Two first engines just finishing assembly. Clutches finished. Gearboxes partly machined. Axles and so on partly in hand. I built the first two engines for £1,000, over half being in tools, patterns, dies and so on. All work done out, so includes overheads and all.
> Racing cars are progressing with much telephoning, telegraphing, tremendous efforts, night shift, boloney, at exclusive and enormous expense. Cars appear in 1959" [sic – he surely meant 1939 or, come to think of it, maybe he didn't?].
> Let's have your news from time to time. And MUCH better luck next time. International Trophy? Or nothing?

> Yours ever,

Within two weeks of writing this letter, 'Jamie' kissed his wife, and new baby son, goodbye in Stamford and drove away down the A1 Great North Road to Brooklands to watch the May 7 JCC International Trophy race. Handicap channels were arranged at the Fork there to equalize the lap times of small and large-capacity cars, and Ray's 'R4D' was beaten into second place by Percy Maclure's fleet Riley and the narrow margin of 1.2 seconds.

Before the start Ken Richardson saw Murray Jamieson: "I'd walked up to the end of the pits and saw him there. He said 'Ken, I'm not feeling very well' and he certainly looked bad, I think he'd eaten something which didn't agree with him. I said 'Come down to the pit and I'll have a cup of tea ready for you.' He said 'Thanks, I'll see you later, I'm just going to watch the start now'...

"I went back to the pits, and during the start Joseph Paul's Delage caught fire, there was a collision and it veered off through some railings into where Jamieson was watching..."

Two hapless spectators were killed – a Miss Peggy Williams dying instantly, while 'Jamie' was fatally injured by the Delage and the collapsing railings, and succumbed soon after in Weybridge hospital.

Ken Richardson had the job of driving his abandoned Austin back home to that neat terraced house overlooking the water meadows in Stamford...

"He was brilliant, a great designer, but you know he couldn't even fix his own road car; used to ask me to fix his Austin or whatever. His new 4-litre aluminium engine flexed under power, but otherwise looked ever so good on the test bed."

Immediately after this sad event, Humphrey Cook told friends the 4-litre project could not possibly survive. He had regarded it as something of a renaissance for the stillborn 5-litre supercharged Invicta proposal of 1932, but now its cessation reflected ERA Ltd's declining fortunes, and the lack of custom for their now ageing *Voiturette* design. The truth was that Jamieson's death had left ERA doomed.

The staff at Bourne was thinned down, but in the drawing office Aubrey Barratt, Harry Mundy and design-engineer Frank May – who before coming to Bourne had served his apprenticeship at Daimler, followed by spells at Lea-Francis, Riley (on the Autovia) and then Daimler again – were now fully engaged in finalizing design and organizing manufacture of the new GP car. Had expense been no object, ERA's directors would dearly have liked to produce a full 3-litre supercharged Grand Prix car 'for Britain'. But Cook had already spent more than enough. Therefore a mongrelized project had been launched to produce instead a low-slung and aerodynamically efficient new car, powered by a derivative of the 2-litre engine used in Ray's 'R4B/C/D' works car. ERA laid pilot plans to build four of these new cars for 1939, intending to field two in each major race, with two in reserve. But even this would prove over-ambitious.

Still the dauntless RM, PB and Merton devised alternative road car schemes to generate some revenue; one for a Standard-based road car to carry the charismatic Raymond Mays name, the other for a whole range of small-engined ERA-Standard sports cars, a project presaging the Mini-Cooper 20 years before its time.

And in July 1938, RM and PB, in partnership with L.G.O.

Prideaux Brune and Philip Merton, founded 'Shelsley Motors Ltd' to build a hastily cobbled-up high-performance 'Raymond Mays Special' car, based upon Standard Flying 14 V8 parts. The cars were to be assembled at Bourne in Raymond Mays & Partners' workshop in the Maltings on Spalding Road.

Ken Richardson recalled that Shelsley Motors simply took delivery of four complete new Standard V8s purchased by Prideaux Brune and whose bodies were removed at Bourne. Their chassis were then stiffened and revamped with new IFS front ends designed by Frankie May, and after the specialist Gray Brothers (visiting coachbuilders) had dragged their feet, the cars were ultimately rebodied by REAL Coachworks in Ealing, West London. Only these four Raymond Mays cars were completed, the original programme having apparently envisaged a three or four-month time-scale.

Prideaux Brune had put up £1,000 for the conversion work and by January 19, 1939, expressed his dissatisfaction to PB, writing:

...I must sound again the oft-repeated warning that unless things can be speeded up very considerably we shall fail with this car. We are already too late to catch

Peter Berthon, who was a dazzlingly handsome young man between the wars, looks matched by his exotic – and daring – wife to be, Lorna...dubbed 'The Terrible Turk' by Ray's mum, Anne Mays.

Highlife: The responsibilities of team direction and business management were never allowed to interrupt RM's social calendar. An inveterate musical theatre buff, he also loved the buzz of nightclub life, but here he's mixing business with pleasure, sharing a table next to his youthful 'Mam', with Rudi Caracciola , Louis Chiron and – extreme right – Rene Dreyfus; Ray rubbing shoulders with Grand Prix drivers he would never match, yet whose home fame he could equal in Britain.

much of the trade this year, and the Shelsley money is being spent very fast. Actually about £600 of the £1,000 is now spent...What is to be done when all the money is gone? I do not know, but my experience so far will not make me feel eager or even willing to find any more....We have paid Gray £45.10.0 so far, and...we have one cowl and one wing to show for it...At the pace we are going we shall miss this year's sales altogether which will damage the future of the car very badly, and our money will be exhausted...I know [Philip] feels the same as I do, and in fact he seems to me to have lost interest to some extent...

Ten years hence lack of progress at Bourne would become a familiar war cry for BRM's backers.

On September 5, 1938, RM and PB visited Standard in Coventry to outline their new plans to John Black for a less expensive, higher-volume co-production sporting car. He received them enthusiastically and production and marketing plans promptly forged ahead...but ERA's time was running out fast...

That same month, Humphrey Cook and his accountants regretfully concluded that any Grand Prix aspirations for the new E-Type should be abandoned, and instead a modified 1½-litre six-cylinder engine be installed in the new rolling chassis for *Voiturette* racing.

Efforts were redoubled to find backing, and The ERA Supporters' Club had been formed under the wildly enthusiastic leadership of A.F. Rivers Fletcher, but although it succeeded in subscribing some funds they could only amount to a mere drop in the ocean...

Frankie May left for a third spell at Daimler, leaving Barratt and Mundy to complete detail design of Berthon's E-Type scheme. The new car was to use a twin-tube chassis, slung low on Porsche IFS and initially a swing-axle rear end, while the engine used a bigger bore and shorter stroke, plus a longer but slimmer Zoller supercharger slung alongside the crankcase and delivering 28psi boost, aiming at "around 250bhp" at 8,000rpm.

Pre-selector gearboxes made way for a lighter and simpler five-speed manual, but Harry Mundy told me: "This unit hadn't been designed very well, in that it wouldn't go together in assembly. I sorted that out and redesigned a few of the gears and bearing arrangements. Then they decided to seat the driver lower, so I designed some drop gears to go behind the engine and drop the prop-shaft lower beneath the seat, then to step-up the drive again into the rear-mounted gearbox. The original swing axle of course proved as Auto Union had previously shown that it had severe limitations for a racing car of that performance..."

The E-Type gearbox was not to be the last mechanism incapable of assembly to be designed at Bourne but – with the arguable exception of the supercharged AC – the car itself was the first notable racing failure to be associated, in part, with Raymond Mays.

Imagine now the excited anticipation at Bourne as Captain

THE ERA-STANDARD –
PB's CONCEPT LETTER

On September 6, 1938, the day after his meeting with Captain Black of Standard, Peter Berthon wrote to him, in part as follows, confirming ERA's road car proposals:

...we would like to confirm the various points we discussed in connection with your 10 H.P. E.R.A. Sports Car, and also to put forward our further views which you may think worth considering.

We are both terribly enthusiastic with the whole scheme and are convinced that the car is the ideal type to sell under the E.R.A name, which has built up its racing prestige in the small car class. We feel that it is essential that the car, besides bearing the frontal appearance of an E.R.A. Racing car, is assembled here at Bourne and should carry some feature about the engine that is essentially E.R.A. the suggestion being a new cylinder head which will enable us to get the increased perfor-mance, i.e. an output of 50B.H.P. and which in production would hardly raise the cost to any appreciable extent.

The idea of assembling and servicing the car from the Bourne Works would definitely give it a home in a racing establishment, which would strongly appeal to the type of people who would purchase, and furthermore, the racing successes and achievements could be directly applied and advertised with the information that the car is built by the same skilled staff and mechanics who do the racing work.

We also feel that the owner of this type of Sports Car is the young man who likes to go to the Works and talk about it. Besides considerably enhancing the chances of success of the car, the scheme would fit in with the present activities of E.R.A. and fill the breach on the lines we spoke about yesterday.

As regards ways and means, we would summarise the suggestions to date as follows:

That the Car is produced and marketed through the Standard distributing organisation if possible, and by E.R.A. Motors Ltd, of which company the Directors would be yourself, Philip Merton, Raymond Mays and myself.[2]

The Standard Motor Company would supply components in assembled sets, leaving only the final assembling to be done at Bourne. Bodies would of course be also delivered to Bourne.

As regards finance, if the Standard Motor Company could arrange to extend to E.R.A. (Motors) Limited a floating credit, it would fit in admirably with the present scheme and enable us to put the whole thing over with a very minimum of capital.

As regards the car itself, we are absolutely confident that to guarantee a performance of 90 miles an hour with an open 2-seater would ensure the scheme going over in a big way, and furthermore, is consistent with all that the name E.R.A. represents, which is primary [sic] perfor-mance. To enable this performance to be satisfactorily achieved, the engine must be capable of producing 50B.H.P. which in itself presents absolutely no difficulty.

The question of bodies is equally important, and we feel it essential that both in the open 2-seater sports and coupe types, really modern streamline shape with a flat under-shield must be fitted.

I am sending catalogues of the present Alfa Romeo. Unfortunately they do not include the open 2-seater to which I refer. However, the frontal appearance as presented by the 8C2990B[3] [sic] is the type of front treatment we have in mind. The front and rear wing treatment of both the Alfa types can be carried out on both the open and coupe type bodies, and the fared rear appearance of the 'Mille Miglia' saloon would give the rakish lines we want to achieve.

I have been into the question of tyre sizes and axle ratios and find that a 4.7 axle with a 16.00" x 5.50" tyre would give 95m.p.h. at 5400r.p.m.; which is exactly what is wanted with the improved engine output. Average driving speed 70–80m.p.h. would lie between 4200 and 4800 revs.

We should both like to impress upon you how pleased we are that we have at last come to some arrangement which connects with the Standard Motor Company, if only for the reason that we have always recognised your concern as the most go ahead of present day Motor Car Manufacturers...

2. Note – no place for Humphrey Cook? RM and PB seem clearly to have been planning for the future...

3. The correct model name is of course '8C-2900B'.

Black and his Chief Engineer Ted Grinham studied PB's proposals for the small-car ERA-Standard project, and conducted an enthusiastic six-week correspondence concerning its development. To handle the project as suggested by PB the Bourne premises must surely have been greatly extended, and many extra staff employed. But on 'Guy Fawkes morning', November 5, 1938, this devastating bombshell dropped onto RM's doormat:

STRICTLY PRIVATE & CONFIDENTIAL.
My dear Mays,

It is with personal regret that I am compelled to write this letter.

From the beginning of our negotiations concerning the proposed small E.R.A. car I have informed you on many occasions of my understanding with Mr. Lyons, the Chairman and Managing Director of S.S. Cars Limited, and I now confirm what that arrangement is, viz: that if for any reason either Mr. Lyons or myself consider the action of the other to be a breach of our obligations, which are only moral, then either of should [sic] be free to go our own way.

At the time of my negotiations with you, I, personally, did not consider my action as a breach, but, on further consultation with Mr. Lyons, he has left no doubt in my mind as to his views.

I am, therefore, compelled to give you formal notice that I cannot proceed any further in this matter.

You will appreciate, I am sure, the large volume of business that Mr. Lyons and myself have built up

August 2, 1937 – JCC International Trophy, Brooklands: Ken Richardson and Marshall Dorr savour another success with RM and the famous works ERA which began life as 'R4B' and went through C-Type and D-Type development in its 15 years at Bourne. Beyond stand Humphrey Cook (right) – who had just retired 'R12C' – and Peter Berthon. From 1935–39, Ray accumulated 13 race wins and seven hill-climb FTDs in 'R4B/C/D'. His 37 postwar outings in it from 1946–50, mainly hill-climbs, included only nine race entries, but yielded 17 FTDs and two third places, both in Jersey, in 1947 and – his last ERA race – 1949. An intended International Trophy entry then fizzled in a practice breakage. His farewell in 'R4D' came on September 23, 1950 – fourth at his beloved Shelsley Walsh...

together in S.S. Cars, which is now an important factor in our total volume, and to allow that turn-over to go to a possible competitor would be sheer madness.

So Bill Lyons had killed the ERA-Standard idea, but ERA's principals would continue to consider alternative road car programmes while Ray's trader friends modified their marketing schemes to match...

1939

Into the New Year, ERA maintained two possible avenues of approach towards a production road car. Philip Merton offered the remains of the Murray Jamieson 4-litre project to Alan Good, owner of Lagonda. And despite Captain Black's gloomy predictions that his brother-in-law's company was "...fully committed" (in part – after the Munich Crisis of October '38 – to panic rearmament), Ray succeeded in interesting Wilks of Rover in possible ERA road car production... although I cannot say to what extent. Additionally, RM and PB were putting together a new deal with Major Antoine Lago's Talbot company in Suresnes, Paris, to collaborate over a new sports car project as a 'homer' – without necessarily involving either Cook or ERA...

But having funded ERA for five costly years, Humphrey

Cook was by this time a terminally reluctant backer, clearly taken for granted by his co-director duo at Bourne. His relationship with Raymond Mays and more so with Peter Berthon was by this time frosty. To heighten internal tensions, design-draughtsman Aubrey Barratt was unhappy with PB taking total credit for much that he regarded as his work, and he unburdened himself to Cook.

Against this background, and with RM's active encouragement, Philip Merton and Charles Follett made Cook an offer they felt he could not refuse...involving whatever kind of pleasure car project ERA might eventually launch.

On January 19, 1939, from his home at 1 Avenue Lodge, Avenue Road, London NW8, Merton composed a four-page foolscap letter to Cook at his home in Upper Brook Street.

He detailed the plans he had laid with Follett, "...with the principal idea that the suggestions contained herewith will be helpful and an asset to both you and your Co-Directors [ie RM and PB] in continuing to keep the E.R.A. team racing...". He proposed a take-over of the finance and, therefore, the control of ERA Motors Ltd, whereupon the company would immediately undertake to produce a pleasure car bearing the name 'ERA'. ERA Motors Ltd would then guarantee to ERA Ltd a minimum income of £5,000 *per annum* as long as ERA continued to race successfully:

The definition of what successful racing means might

be defined as gaining success in two major English International events, and participating, when possible, in the premier 1500cc foreign events with 50% success.

This guaranteed minimum income would be made up of Royalties from a sliding scale of, say, £5 for each of the first 1,000 E.R.A. Pleasure cars sold, £3 for the second 1,000, and £1 for each car sold after this figure has been reached.

Ambitious plans indeed, particularly with war looming, unless the partners had trusted Neville Chamberlain's paper agreement with Hitler in Munich. Merton's promised "guaranteed income" was to commence on January 1, 1940, "…and payments will be made as each car is sold. Adjustment, however, to be made at the end of each 12 months".

He continued:

It being thought that immediate cash will be necessary, an immediate payment of £1,000 will be made for, say, the Good Will of the name of E.R.A. It must be remembered that this is not assessing the value of the name at £1,000, but that the continuous Royalty is doing this on a basis that has already been agreed elsewhere…

He requested a 10-week option on this offer, after which:

If we have not signed to take up these obligations within that period, then E.R.A. Limited may call the deal off.

On the other hand, we are not prepared to consider or take up this proposition unless we are given a definite answer within 7 days from the date of this letter…

Humphrey Cook, perhaps understandably incensed by Merton's unnecessarily brutal "seven-day ultimatum", flatly rejected the idea.

On March 3, Ray wrote to Prideaux Brune:

Yesterday I went to Coventry to have further talks with Wilks – In view of the co-operation and interest he has shown in the original proposition I brought before him, I thought it only fair to tell him all about the Lago scheme – particularly so because I do not like the idea of losing Wilks' possible co-operation in the future…I told him quite a lot about the present position and I still think he is interested enough to be helpful to us in the future…

There is no surviving evidence available to me of just what these discussions and proposals involved…

But amidst all this manoeuvring, in mid-March, Humphrey Cook had a letter published in *The Motor*, harshly distancing himself from Shelsley Motors at Bourne and putting RM into a rare old flap at Eastgate House. Cook's letter then sparked a response from Prideaux Brune who on the 21st wrote to Ray of an impending meeting with Cook the following Thursday evening, which RM, PB and Merton should also attend.

He also wrote to Cook:

It seems to me that things have now reached a stage where we must get a better understanding between E.R.A. Ltd., and Shelsley Motors. Your letter of the 29th of February and your letter in last week's *Motor* made it clear to me that you were not entirely happy about the arrangements made last summer between us, and I have now heard from Peter Berthon of the action you took last Friday after his departure.

You will remember that after some considerable negotiations you and your co-directors came to an agreement with me to the effect that I was appointed sole Distributor for the proposed E.R.A. car.

This agreement was arrived at in May 1938. Shortly after that it was decided by Messrs E.R.A. Ltd., not to continue with the production, although I have never been notified of this fact officially.

In July of last year, Philip Merton saw me and placed before me the Raymond Mays – Standard proposition, and two of the main reasons for this scheme given to me then and adhered to throughout were
1. That it would be some recompense to me for the failure to carry out the agreement in connection with the E.R.A. car.
2. That it would afford some income to E.R.A. Ltd., as a certain sum per car would be paid by Shelsley Motors Ltd., to E.R.A. in return for certain facilities at Bourne.

I asked how you stood, and I was told that you did not wish to enter into any commercial obligations but that you were fully acquainted and in agreement with all that was suggested. I was satisfied with that information and entered into the scheme.

After some months of experimental development work, which, as it was bound to do, has proved rather costly, we are about to go into production, and it does seem unfair on me (in fact on all of us) that at this stage you should suddenly start to take unfriendly action both at Bourne and in the Press. I have never had any wish to interfere in any way with your activities at Bourne; I have always taken a keen interest in the development of the E.R.A. car and have always wished to do all I can to help things along. The Shelsley business has gone too far for it to be stopped or at this stage moved, so it would seem to me that we must get together, talk the thing out frankly and openly, and arrive at a mutual understanding…

Undoubtedly they had their meeting but its fall-out ultimately ended the RM/PB/ERA partnership…

Before that could happen, long-rumoured moves by enthusiasts finally materialized to organize an ERA support fund.

At the end of March the British Motor Racing Fund was announced by Desmond Scannell, Secretary of the British Racing Drivers' Club. His statement reported that:

Mr. Humphrey Cook, having spent approximately £75,000 on these cars during the past five years, has announced that he will be compelled to curtail his support of E.R.A. There are now four racing cars built or in the process of building valued at approximately £25,000 which Mr. Cook is confident will be capable of performances equal to or better than those of any continental challenger, but a sum of approximately £12,000 *per annum* will be required to race and maintain them. Of this sum Mr. Cook is prepared to contribute approximately one-third in 1939 and 1940, subject to this Fund providing the remaining two-thirds, approximately £12,000...

Thirty-two assorted dignitaries publicly patronized the Fund, requesting public contributions of £1 for 1939–40. Scannell's statement included a paragraph whereby Cook guarded against perceived abuse involving Shelsley Motors' Raymond Mays Special plans – a necessary precaution considering the deep suspicion with which a large body of British motor sporting opinion regarded anything to do with Mays and Berthon:

> No part of the Fund will be expended in the promotion or fostering of any form of commercial undertaking. In the event of the E.R.A. Company engaging in any activity other than motorcar racing, the disposal of the Fund will be in the hands of the Trustees...

The first new car – E-Type ERA 'GP1' – was tested by Ray during the spring at Donington Park and Brooklands, revealing many problems. He told me: "I felt at that time when money was so tight, that we should have concentrated on 'R4D'. The old car was clearly at the peak of its development. It was clearly capable of lapping any British circuit faster than anything else, short of the German or Italian factory teams..."

An entry was made for 'GP1' in the JCC International Trophy at Brooklands on May 6, but practice problems sidelined it so Ray raced 'R4D' instead, only to retire from what was to be his last race in a works-entered ERA.

On the following Monday he took out the repaired E-Type, lapped fully 11 seconds faster than his best race lap in the D-Type, and topped 156mph at the end of the finishing straight...

But now both he and Humphrey Cook had become convinced – for opposing reasons – that their best course was to dissolve the partnership. On May 9, 1939, Desmond Scannell issued the following statement:

> Mr Humphrey Cook, founder and sponsor of E.R.A. Ltd. (English Racing Automobiles), has today announced that his works at Bourne, Lincolnshire, will close down on 26 May next, after which date E.R.A. Ltd. will be defunct...It is understood that Mr. Cook has intimated to the Trustees of the Racing Fund that after 26 May he is prepared to transfer to them all the assets of E.R.A. Ltd., together with the new cars, of course, to be administered by them as a national organisation.
>
> Thus it appears that the future of the E.R.A. cars depends entirely on the response to the appeal for the British Motor Racing Fund.

It flopped, raising little more than £1,000...whereas Cook regretfully estimated that ERA had finally cost him around £90,000 over five years. [4]

RM officially resigned his position as Director of ERA Ltd

on May 24, 1939, and PB followed on June 1. On May 31 Cook had moved the company's Registered Office from Eastgate House to Donington Park, where Fred Craner of the Derby & District Motor Club provided premises beside the circuit in the outbuildings at Coppice Farm. Cook had decided to persevere until season's end, taking those staff members who wanted to go with him – including Aubrey Barratt and Alf Buckle – together with the new E-Type and all related material. Arthur Dobson was works driver, but poor technical preparation then delayed 'GP1''s race debut until Albi in mid-summer where he crashed mildly after leading off the line.

Cook sold the old No. 1 works car – 'R4D' – effectively to Ray complete with many spares and alternative 1,500cc and 2-litre engines, and mechanics Ken Richardson and Marshall Dorr stayed on in Ray's otherwise deserted former ERA works to maintain it. They resprayed the car black and silver, and Ray then made his independent debut in it at Shelsley Walsh in June, setting his sixth record there – and his twelfth Shelsley FTD – in 37.37 seconds, a record destined to survive for a decade.

Now whether Cook fully appreciated to whom he was selling 'R4D' actually seems a moot point...

Ray for years would declare that its purchase was made possible for him "by old and dear friends"; in fact the publicity-shy Lancelot and Constance Prideaux Brune. But did Cook know for whom the car was intended when he agreed to its sale? Ray was certainly cock-a-hoop in a letter to Philip Merton dated May 15, 1939:

> I am sure you will be pleased to hear that after a really *terrific* wangle, I have managed to purchase the 1938 ex Works 1½ litre E.R.A. car. I will tell you all about this when we meet.
>
> No doubt you will have read all the news in the papers concerning E.R.A. and on the strength of this I do feel that I should like to publish a letter in the motor papers, saying that I, on behalf of somebody else, approached Humphrey Cook concerning the sale of this Company. I suggest something on the[se] lines....
>
> Concerning the unfortunate and sudden closing down of E.R.A. Limited, I think it only fair to state that I, on behalf of a large financial organisation, approached Humphrey Cook concerning the sale of E.R.A. Limited. This organisation would have been prepared to buy the Company to complete the new racing cars and to race them and continue in an endeavour to uphold British prestige in the motor racing world, which Humphrey Cook has been doing for the last five years.
>
> This organisation fully appreciated the enormous amount of money spent and the large part played by Mr.

4. **A rough guide of comparative monetary value between 1938–39 and 1993 may be deduced from the London Central Statistical Office's long-term price index. Judging £1 Sterling as a value of 100 for January 1974, its relative value in 1938 was 17.4, which by 1993 had inflated to approximately 550! Thus Cook's estimated personal expenditure of £90,000 on ERA represents a 1990s value of some £2.84 million – all from his personal account... Using another measure of relative value, Tony Rudd's 'Ford Cortina Formula', the basic mid-range Ford of 1939 cost £150, against some £9,000 in the early 1990s – equating Cook's £90,000 to over £5.4 million in automotive terms!**

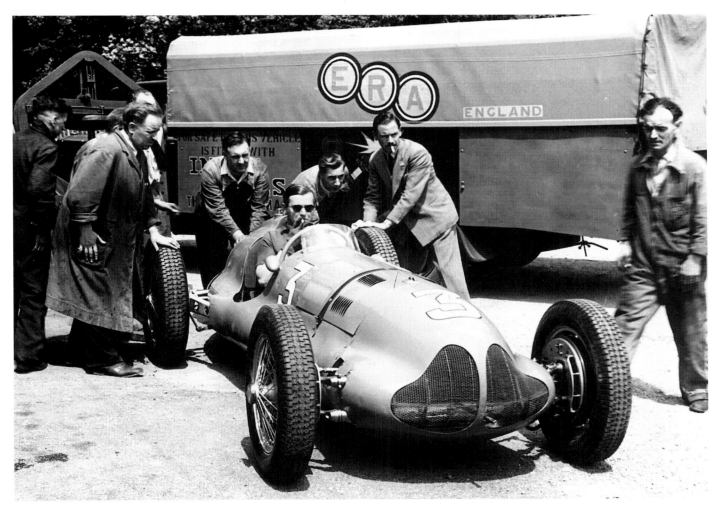

June 10, 1939 – Nuffield Trophy meeting, Donington Park – Percy Pugh (work coat) and Humphrey Cook's new Team Manager Philip Mayne (by the left-rear wheel, 'gasper' between lips) supervise as the revamped ERA team's works driver Arthur Dobson prepares to practice in the definitive new E-Type. The car non-started, its new engine not yet run in.

Humphrey Cook, in this endeavour and to relieve him of this financial burden were prepared to carry on…

As it was, Humphrey Cook had had more than enough of RM and PB's carryings-on at Bourne and although the trio would remain on surprisingly good personal terms well into the 1960s all business relations between them were emphatically over…

Meanwhile, during that 1939 season, 'Bira' had won the Nuffield Trophy from Ray and Peter Whitehead, then Ray held off 'Bira' to win the Crystal Palace Cup. He drove Antoine Lago's prototype Talbot *Monoplace Centrale* in the French GP until its fuel tank split, and survived 'R4D' throwing a wheel at Albi where Dobson's new works-entered E-Type led before spinning off in a minor incident. At the new Prescott hill-climb Ray set FTD, and he won yet again in the Brooklands Campbell Trophy the following week. On Tuesday, August 8, 1939, he took 'R4D' out again onto Brooklands' artificial Campbell road circuit, and raised the lap record there from 75.94 to 77.79mph.

On August 26, the Imperial Trophy race at South London's

Crystal Palace circuit saw Ray in 'R4D' chase Bert Hadley's baby Austin OHC Racer in company with Dobson's 'R9B' until a tyre rolled off its rim, the Mays crew having reduced pressures too much in an attempt to improve grip on a rain-damped surface.

Ray was then due to sail to Thailand for a Christmas invitational race organized by Chula, but nine days after the Crystal Palace meeting, Great Britain declared war on Germany, and motor sport became a memory.

The British Motor Racing Fund was liquidated, and Cook's ERA Ltd at Donington Park closed down…

ERA – THE DYING EMBERS – 1939–45

In his well detailed autobiography, *Split Seconds*, written in 1950, Ray quite properly projected the prewar split between Cook and himself as "perfectly amicable, almost affect-ionate…" because indeed, despite all their differences, they remained remarkably friendly, but in 1944 the old embers certainly flared when Laurence Pomeroy, FRSA, MSAE, tried

Tantalizing target – October 2, 1937 – the Donington Grand Prix, Donington Park, set entirely new standards of motor racing performance before the British public, to shattering effect. "It was like the arrival of the men from Mars…" Upon first sight, one enthusiast simply gasped: "Strewth! So that's what they're like." Here three of the 600-horsepower straight-eight Mercedes-Benz W125s lead Rosemeyer's ultimately victorious rear-engined V16-cylinder Auto Union through the first corner, Redgate. RM and PB could only drool…and dream…

to buy the ERA name from Humphrey Cook to found a postwar mass-production car project.

'Pom' was the rotund and erudite Technical Editor of *The Motor* magazine, and son of the great Laurence E.Pomeroy of Vauxhall fame with whom the schoolboy Raymond Mays had once so eagerly corresponded.

'Pom' was a cheerful soul. He mentioned his negotiations simply by chance to Peter Berthon, and triggered a furore…

On June 22, 1944, Ray wrote testily to Cook, complaining that:

> I have heard through Peter Berthon, who has heard through Pomeroy, that he is negotiating with you for the use of the name E.R.A. I must say I am surprised that you have never mentioned this to me. As you will know, my last wish is to attempt to stand in the way of any such deal, because naturally if you can cash in on any of the assets it is right and natural that you should wish to do so. Nevertheless, I do strongly feel that certain other facts should be taken into consideration, because the value of the name E.R.A. was jointly made by you, Peter and me.
>
> You put your money into E.R.A., for which I was most grateful; however, the fact must not be over-looked that it is useless for any one to put their money into anything unless there is a good article to be backed. The 'White Riley' was the car that made E.R.A. possible, and as you know this was entirely financed by me personally, by other accessory people who backed me, and also by Victor Riley personally. The knowledge put into this car

was partly the culmination of the many years which I had spent in connection with development work, experimenting and supercharging, with Peter, Amherst Villiers, and Murray Jamieson…This experience enabled all of us to gain most valuable knowledge…

> When E.R.A. was formed it was merely a gentleman's agreement between the three directors, and in my enthusiasm, being only too keen to get a real British Racing car going, I did not ask for any of the goodwill for our past work, which I should have been justified in doing.
>
> The whole point is that E.R.A. was made possible by all three of us and not by any of us alone…therefore whatever may be the value of this name to-day, I am sure you would be the first to agree that we are entitled to our fair share of the value of the name of E.R.A.…
>
> I hope you and Anne are well. My mother joins me in all good wishes.
>
> Yours ever,

Humphrey Cook responded on June 24 – the Royal Mail was quicker then, even in wartime!:

> Referring to the proposed sale of the name E.R.A. to Pomeroy & his associates.
>
> I cannot agree with you that I *ought* to have mentioned this to you or to anybody, as, if you remember,

the original agreement was that, until all my original outlay of capital & interest had been paid, no shareholders were entitled to anything. As the proposed price is considerably below what has been put into E.R.A., I do not see that it concerns anyone but myself legally.

Anyway, you seem to be jumping to conclusions rather rapidly. I have never said that you should not have some consideration, should the sale materialize &, in any case, it will be some years before any money appears, so there is no hurry & no need for alarm.

I am only concerned with selling the name: Pomeroy & his associates are the buyers & it is for them to come to terms with any other parties interested on 'compensation' grounds…

He then tossed this stun grenade into his parting sentence:

…Just one point. You say that E.R.A. was made possible by all three of us. I quite agree, but it came to grief not through all three of us, but through two of us &, in my own defence, I have to say that I was *not* one of the two.

Hoping you are all well at Bourne

Yrs. Humphrey

This argument raged for some time, poor 'Pom' adopting the shaken and bemused air of one who has blundered, all unsuspecting, into a minefield. He repeatedly emphasized he had "no wish to be involved in any personal controversies in this matter", nor should he "take sides".

Ray and PB seem to have realized that the 1939 Merton-Follett-inspired entity, ERA Motors Ltd, could share the magic name, and by August 23 with 'Pom' 's input they had concocted a detailed scheme for postwar ERA production cars.

On August 23, K. Vickery[5] of Mortimer Engineering Co Ltd, 2 & 3 Station Parade, Upper Clapton Road, London E5 (which – as we shall hear – was the company then owned and run by PB in conjunction with co-directors R.J. Millidge, Chris Shorrock and Wing Commander H.L.P. [Pingo] Lester), wrote to Ray, enclosing "copy of Agreement as arranged with Mr. Berthon".

This quite remarkably detailed and ambitious document runs to four jam-packed pages, proposing in essentials that a resuscitated ERA Motors Ltd should purchase from 'Pom' all drawings, calculations, sales data and other information relative to four and six-cylinder 1,100cc cars which he proposed, offering £3,000 payable £500 in cash within three years and £2,500 in £1 Ordinary Shares immediately.

ERA Motors would give 'Pom' an option of becoming within six months Technical Director of the company at a salary of not less than £1,000 *pa* for two years, and for five years subsequent thereto at not less than £2,500 *pa*.

In return 'Pom' would set up the requisite organization for the production of prototype cars and introduce the necessary finance. Humphrey Cook was invited to grant ERA Motors an option to purchase the exclusive use of the name 'E.R.A.' and all associated goodwill.

Peter Berthon's draft proposal included this paragraph: "(1) Reconstructing the Board of Directors by the appointment of a new Chairman acceptable to H.W.C. [Cook] in addition to P. Berthon *who shall remain a director*" [my italics, DCN] – PB was obviously defending himself against Cook's by this

time loudly (and often) declared mistrust.

Under the subsequent nine clauses, Cook was supposedly to receive £10,000 in cash and £2,000 Ordinary Shares in the company on signature of the purchase agreement, plus £28,000 in cash by quarterly instalments of £1,250 "…or 35/- per car sold whichever be the greater sum…".[6] By 1946 failure to meet the option or sale conditions would revert all rights to the name etc to Cook without prejudice to any claims he might have against the company for unpaid balances. But in return Cook should agree not to dispose of ERA Ltd without consent of ERA Motors or alternatively without a proviso that ERA Ltd "…shall not enter into the business of designing, testing or manufacturing self propelled vehicles or aircraft…" – areas in which PB and his associates clearly at that time had other ambitions. Cook was also to give ERA Motors Ltd first refusal "…of any sale of the 1939 Racing Cars or any agreement to lease or loan them for racing purposes".

The 10th clause then read:

In consideration of securing the exclusive benefits of the technical and racing experience gained in 1934–9 with E.R.A. Ltd., E.R.A. Motors Ltd. agrees to pay Messrs. P. Berthon & R. Mays the sum of £4,000[7] of which £1,000 shall be satisfied by 1000 ordinary £1 shares in the Company and the balance at the rate of £600 p.a. or 5/– per car sold whichever is the greater.

The Company shall not be liable to make this payment unless and until the option agreement with H.W.C. is taken up.

The floating of shares in ERA Motors Ltd was proposed to raise some £25,000 to finance manufacture of a four-cylinder and two six-cylinder prototype cars, with spares and testing. The company should then be expanded:

…into an organisation capable of designing, assembling and selling automobiles at the rate of at least £1,000,000 p.a. and that for this purpose the capital would have to be enlarged to at least £250,000; preferably £400,000…

PB also suggested:

…that the arrangement first mentioned can be implemented within the next 2–3 months. On this assumption it is believed that the E type [*sic*] 6 cyl. can be ready for production by *Jan. 1946* or at latest *May 1946*.

5. **This is believed to be one name adopted by Mrs Krivickas, later better known at Bourne as 'Katie Vickers' – PB's long-time secretary and sometime travelling partner…**

6. **Relating 1946 £1 Sterling purchasing power to that of 1993, these figures represent respectively approximately £195,000 in cash; £39,000-worth of ordinary shares; £546,000 in cash by instalments of over £24,000 "or just over £33 per car sold…". This would have been a better deal than John Cooper accepted for the Mini-Cooper, but one cannot escape the conclusion from figures such as these, in view of immediately postwar commercial conditions, that RM, PB and their associates were dreaming utter pie in the sky…**

7. **Over £78,000!**

He continued:

> Assuming that production of civilian cars restarts during the next 12 months it is of great importance that the new car should be released to the public as soon as possible and that agencies etc. be fixed up. In this connection there are good reasons for opening with the E type [not to be confused with the 1939 racing model].

He listed these as:

> (1) *Prestige*: This car with high efficiency engine and 90 m.p.h. maximum establishes the production car as a direct descendant of the racing models…(2) Commercial experience shows that it is far easier to sell a popular version of an expensive article than a de luxe edition of a cheap one i.e. sales of 4 cyl. F type will be helped by prior existence of E type but the reverse does not hold good…(3) *Saving Time*: E type production on a small scale can start with more simple jigs and tools than F type which is planned for larger quantities and lower machining costs…

It is interesting to note how Berthon ignored the Cook 1939 racing car known as the E-Type ERA in describing his/'Pom''s proposed production six-cylinder as the E type, and that a converted Fiat engine should have powered the economy F type.

His paper further considered rectification of initial faults which would be eased and expense minimized:

> …if the output in the first 6 months is say 500 cars and not say 2,500 cars…to step straight into the sale of 100 cars per week would involve a fully fledged sales and production organisation starting ab ovo…gradual growth over the first 12 months is greatly to be preferred.

Accurately foreseeing postwar supply shortages – although grossly under-estimating their severity – he continued:

> With an initial output of say 15–20 cars per week it is relatively easy to build and hold supplies for some weeks.

For this reason he felt:

> …that the F type should be introduced when the E type has been in production about 12 months; but that if the first Motor Show is in October-November 1946, then both models should be presented.

Longer term the company should develop:

> …a 'b' type using a simplified all-ferrous F type engine; orthodox clutch driving direct to 4 speed clash type box; all metal pressed body; simple fittings and equipment price £225 1939 value. This should have wide appeal in the export field…

Then came the glamour:

> To support the type of sale envisaged a small (but of necessity successful) racing programme will be desirable. For the first 3 years after the War (say 18 months of E.R.A. Motors public activity) the existing B & C type E.R.A. racing cars should suffice for adequate advertising.
>
> Thereafter support of sports car racing, say Le Mans; T.T.; Italian 1000 Miles and Belgian 24 Hrs. would be advisable. This requires a special organisation within but apart from the production and engineering departments. This dept. could start in a small way by preparing standard cars for special demonstrations e.g. 80 miles in 1 hr on 2 galls on an *autobahn*; 60 m.p.h. average for 24 hrs at Donington and so on…

He further proposed that ERA Motors should – like MG, Riley and SS – be responsible for design & development, sales, service and assembly of finished components but expounded a plan for a separate works and one-off specialist job plant, plus an: "Experimental station in Europe handling long-term test of current and proposed models…"

Judged by ERA's prewar standards, the financial figures as much as the ambition revealed in this grandiose scheme are simply mind-boggling. No doubt much was window-dressing to camouflage a device aimed primarily at up-staging Pomeroy's proposals to Cook, and so to prevent him obtaining the ERA name to the exclusion of RM and PB.

If this was in fact the proposal's only aim, it apparently succeeded. But on the day that Ray received the draft proposals from PB, 'Pom' wrote:

> Cook tells me that he thinks the conditions under which racing will be resumed after the war are so uncertain, both in respect of the time that will elapse and the type of race that will be run, that it is not possible for him to make any definite plans for the latest type 1½-litre cars. He is unwilling to sell them as he thinks this uncertainty makes it impossible to fairly assess their worth. The future of these cars and E.R.A. Limited must remain undecided for some time…

Summarizing Cook's attitude to ERA's name and goodwill, he also reported:

> …he will be unwilling to sell the name for a smallish sum (e.g. £5,000 to £10,000) to any new or existing company manufacturing cars on a very limited scale… comparable with Invicta, H.R.G. and so on…companies of this kind are not really in a position to compete in the post-war market and the net gain to Cook is really insufficient to make the transaction worth while…he is greatly concerned that if he sold the name to a large concern or to some financial group who might re-sell it, it would be 'vulgarised' by being attached to the wrong type of car… Rather than follow either of the above courses he would prefer to let the whole thing die out and become an honoured and historic name but one without any current life and existence. Alternatively, he is agreeable to accepting a reasonable sum from some concern in whom he has confidence, who plans to build

a type of car which he thinks could be reputable. He believes that a fair value for the name, bearing in mind the cost to him of building it up, and the terms under which he would be prepared to go ahead, would be £40,000 and he is agreed that a car which would be really up to date, a cross between as it were, the Riley 9 and Lancia Aprilia…capable of being run at sports car races…would be appropriate to the name…

'Pom' added significantly that one of Cook's conditions:

…and I speak here frankly, is that the said organisation will not be *controlled* or dominated by Peter although Humphrey has not the slightest objection to his being connected with it as a member of the board or in a consultative capacity…

By October 12, 1944, 'Pom' sounded desperate as he wrote to Ray:

…it seems to me that the only person or persons who are justified in making a cash payment to secure E.R.A. Motors Limited are the people who will be making further investments for the production of prototype cars, and the position here is complicated by the fact that really nothing can be done until there is an agreement between E.R.A. Motors and Cook and he, in turn, will not make a move until the board of the company and its control is reconstituted.

As things stand the matter is in danger of being held up indefinitely and as you know, a great deal of time has already passed since the discussion was initiated. However, I do not despair that something can be made of it…

But nothing was. Humphrey Cook rebuffed both Pomeroy's original approach and the combined and grandiose 'Pom'/PB/RM proposals, and he did indeed keep ERA himself. It was not until 1946, with RM and PB deeply embroiled in the birth of their BRM project – that Cook re-activated ERA Ltd, his long-faithful personal mechanic Percy Pugh finding suitable new premises in Dunstable, his home town. Aubrey Barratt was re-enlisted as Chief Engineer, and on May 13, 1946, ERA Ltd's new office was officially registered at Half Moon Hill, London Road, Dunstable, Bedfordshire.

Cook planned to complete two E-Types – 'GP1' and 'GP2' – for sale, and to find customers for a follow-up batch of six more, plus all spares and service. In March 1947 Barratt became a director of ERA Ltd, and on August 23 Leslie Johnson – who had ordered E-Type 'GP3' at the turn of the year – joined the Board. By mid-November 1947, Johnson had bought out Cook's failing interest. Towards the end of 1948 Barratt and Pugh left, and early in 1949 Pomeroy introduced his friend Prof. Dr. Robert Eberan von Eberhorst – prewar Auto Union chief development engineer – to both ERA and Jowett's of Idle, Yorkshire.

Eberhorst joined ERA Ltd to design what became the 'big-tube chassis' Jowett Jupiter, with newcomer David Hodkin, ex-aeronautical engineering, as his assistant. Into 1950 Dunstable also began work on an F-Type 500cc Formula 3 car

project, and by 1951 finally abandoned all further development work on the misbegotten and legendarily unsuccessful E-Types. Hodkin began design of a big-tube-chassied G-Type 2-litre Formula 2 car for 1952 to use Bristol power and many sophisticated ideas, which in practice flopped, despite the services of one S.C. Moss as driver.

Leslie Johnson eventually sold the entire G-Type project, before Hodkin could completely debug it, to Bristol's as basis for their Le Mans sports cars, but his already suspect health broke, and as a sick man he sold the company to Zenith Carburettors. In 1958 ERA's name was carefully changed to 'Engineering Research Application Ltd', retaining both those famous initials and Pingo Lester's old prewar logo, and it is fighting for survival in Dunstable as I write – over 30 years later.

Meantime, just as ERA Ltd had begun to struggle arthritically into its postwar period, Raymond Mays and Peter Berthon had launched BRM around their prewar achievements, charisma, fame…and in some important sectors, their notoriety…

THE BRITISH UNION

In 1939, after the collapse of their hopes for a Grand Prix ERA, and the split from Humphrey Cook and ERA Ltd, RM and PB had endlessly discussed alternative fund-raising schemes to finance what would in effect become a British national Grand Prix car…

At that time there were very few full-blooded single-seat racing cars in Britain, and most of them had been built by ERA. Add a few Altas and assorted specials, several imported Maseratis and obsolescent Alfa Romeos and that was Britain's armoury. The only road racing venues were the artificial Campbell Circuit crossing the infield at Brooklands, plus the genuine roadways at Donington Park (very good but rather narrow) and Crystal Palace (very tight, short and sinuous).

Laurence Pomeroy calculated that, up to 1939, Italian marques had won 58 major GP-status races, Germany – not in contention for as long – had won 57, and France 53. German cars had secured 52 of their 57 major victories within the 1930s, against 39 for the Italians. So how many had British cars won? Four – and three of them with cars palpably copied from original French and Italian designs.

Despite this unpromising background, by 1939, ERA's successes in Europe had broadened Britain's status which had been hard-won in sports car racing by the likes of Bentley, Lagonda and MG.

Late in 1938, *The Motor* published some percipient articles by 'Pom' envisaging "British Racing Cars to beat the World". The magazine's November 22 issue then published reaction to the original story, from 'Pom''s illustrious father, from Cecil Kimber of MG and from Brooklands tuning specialist Robin Jackson.

'Kim' was interested in the technical potential of Britain building a Grand Prix team to compete successfully with Germany, but having just visited Mercedes-Benz and Auto Union he emphasized the reputed £250,000[8] state subsidies which supported their racing programmes.

Robin Jackson – urging Government support – considered: "…The cars should be built by a company independent of any car manufacturer or other existing organisation" and emphasized the folly of entering the existing Formula, when it must surely be better to await a new one when everybody could start level.

Then 'Pom Sr', worldly-wise in both British and American industry, wrote:

> Business, social activities and entertainment, sport and politics are no longer separate entities but form a compound so definitely related to national prestige that even the result of a prize fight may be regarded as an important national issue. There is, therefore, every reason to utilize the engineering skill and technical resource of British automobile engineering to produce a racing car of spectacular performance, not only for the respect that may be inspired in other countries but for its effect on raising the morale of our own country.
>
> The first essential is for those concerned to realize that a million pounds is indeed an insignificant amount of money regarded from the viewpoint of a percentage of the national turnover, or, for that matter, the turnover of the motor industry as an appropriation for advertising.
>
> …Given the money, and thus the enterprise, there would seem little doubt as to the result. This country has for a good many years produced the fastest cars in the world [the Parry Thomas, Malcolm Campbell and Henry Segrave Land Speed Record contenders] incidentally by private enterprise. The knowledge and experience thus gained are available. Further, when it comes to a showdown, the British engineer by temperament, experience and training is a combination of the scientific and the empiric, a happy medium between the oft-time delusive logical tenacity of the German and the antlike methods of American research and development. In brief, more brains per dollar.
>
> I think it was S.F. Edge who, years ago, coined the phrase that all cars which engaged in competitions are better than those which don't, and in those days it was true…In the last 15 years the production expert has dominated motor car design, reduced costs of production and made the motor industry the mighty thing it is. But, in the interests of the industry itself, a healthy injection of new engineering technique is required to maintain demand and meet competition. Design in terms of thin tin and thick cast iron will not last for ever. The concentration of the best skill available on the problems of design and production of a world-beating racing car cannot but have important repercussions on the type of cars best suited for normal use.
>
> Your efforts to this end command the most serious consideration of the country and the motor trade…

Of course, kind words from father to son, but compelling

8. **Both Mercedes-Benz and Auto Union claimed their Nazi subsidies were only a drop in the ocean relative to their actual expenditure on racing. This 1938–39 subsidy figure represents a 1993 value of over £8.1 million… The World Championship Williams-Renault team's budget (without engine costs) in 1992 was around £22 million, which strongly supports these prewar claims from D-B and AU that they were in fact State 'under-funded'.**

stuff, indeed.

At Bourne, Ray was a compulsive reader of the motoring press and I feel certain he and PB must have seen these articles and sympathized with the sentiments expressed, particularly by 'Pom Sr', whom Ray still deeply admired. In 1979, when I last talked with him, he disclaimed any memory at all of these articles, but in reality he simply must have seen them and they surely gave him another nudge towards what became BRM.

Meanwhile, 'Pom Jr' had outlined an imaginary national racing car which he called 'The British Union'. He proposed a 135-degree V16-cylinder engine with high-pressure supercharging, carried in a stressed-skin monocoque chassis, and enclosed within wheel-enveloping streamlined bodywork. His engine's crankshaft was divided amidships by a central timing gear and supercharger drive, while the broad vee angle kept the engine mass low and compact to minimize frontal area and lower the car's centre of gravity.

His engine's 135-degree vee angle gave even firing intervals and decent balance, and its multiplicity of small cylinders allowed high rotational speeds without unduly high piston velocities and inertia loads. It also provided massive piston area. Pom suggested that experience with such a 3-litre V16 could provide data for either a 1½-litre straight-eight or a 750cc in-line 'four', where, in the latter class "…we have obtained in England higher outputs per litre than on any other power unit in the world", this reference being to Hubert Charles' MGs and to the Austin OHC Racer, as developed by the late Tom Murray Jamieson.

This all, surely, struck a chord in the hearts of the Bourne duo, for they knew 'Pom' well and I have no doubt their shared thinking must have prompted some of what he wrote. All three admired Daimler-Benz's way of racing to the point of pure idolatry, and both Mays and Berthon were desperately keen to go GP racing. It was evident that the 1½-litre supercharged *Voiturette* class would effectively provide the Grand Prix Formula for 1941–43. Around the time of the split from Cook in May 1939, the Bourne duo took a first step towards establishing their own 'British Union', by setting-up a company named 'Automobile Developments Ltd'.

But they didn't get very far as it became obvious war was imminent, and all their other activities meant ADL made little progress before September 1, when Hitler's forces invaded Poland. Two days later Neville Chamberlain declared the failure of his appeasement policies, and for the second time in a quarter-century war broke out with Germany.

RM, PB AND THE WAR YEARS, 1939–45

During the war, Automobile Developments Ltd (ADL) lay fallow while Ray – forlorn without racing – had to concentrate upon T.W. Mays & Son's wool brokerage and fertilizer businesses, or at least do his bit to contribute while his full-time managers bore the load… Ray also told me he did unspecified work "…for the Admiralty".

He was 39 when the war began, 45 when it finished; Peter Berthon respectively 33 and 39…difficult years for a chap.

The war years saw Ray taking 'R4D' around a lengthy series

of fund-raising events; Red Cross garden parties, fetes and Warship Weeks, delivering lectures and collecting donations for charity, War Bonds etc. Many a lay audience who had never even seen a motor race were thrilled by his glamorous image, the sight (and feel) of 'R4D', and the exciting picture he painted of his sport. His evangelism paid off handsomely postwar, when the British public were hungry for any spectacle and flocked to see motor racing in unprecedented numbers. For many, the first racing car they had ever seen at close quarters would have been 'R4D'.

For the motor racing enthusiast there were wartime functions, first run in Chessington, Surrey, and later in the Rembrandt Hotel, South Kensington, arranged by the energetic Rivers Fletcher – late of the ERA Supporters' Club.

Meanwhile, Peter Berthon had been in Paris when the war broke out, working in Tony Lago's Talbot factory at Suresnes. Major Lago was an acquaintance of RM's and PB's and had invited Mays to drive his brand-new Talbot-Lago *Monoplace Centrale* 4½-litre GP car on its debut in that year's *Grand Prix de l'ACF* at Reims-Gueux. After that outing PB had been collaborating with Lago on design and development work and it is not without significance that the Major had a 3-litre twin-supercharged V16-cylinder GP engine drawn and ready for production there whose blueprints Berthon must have seen. It was to have been a 45-degree vee unit, designed by ex-Fiat engineer Walter Becchia, to replace the marque's production-based in-line six-cylinder unblown 4½-litre GP unit. But the money never became available to build this supercharged V16. Of more interest, perhaps, to PB would have been discussion of Lago's new plans to scale down this design into a supercharged 1½-litre V16 for 1940–41, known as the 'Talbot-Lago 1500–1940' project.

Little progress had been made, however, when the new war with Germany broke out. PB was promptly seconded onto aircraft work at Suresnes until the 'Phoney War' ended and the Nazis' *Blitzkrieg* suddenly swept through the Low Countries to engulf France itself.

Safely home, PB then began running his own light engineering company, Mortimer Engineering Ltd, in premises at 38–40 Upper Clapton Road, London E5, in the capital's run-down East End, and according to his brother Paul, he had "…quite a profitable war manufacturing precision tank gunsights and similar equipment…"

Naturally, PB moved his family – wife Lorna and daughter Jacqueline – from Stamford down to London. Jacquie had gone to boarding school aged only four-and-a-half, but in 1988 she offered this romantic, little-girl picture of family life: "We lived in a wonderful Spanish-style studio house at 102A Drayton Gardens, Kensington, and later moved next door into number 102. My father's work on tanks also took us up to Lancashire for a while.

"He rented a wonderful rambling old bungalow for us somewhere near Clitheroe. The owner had gone to Africa and everything inside was painted ghastly red and green. Daddy immediately repainted it all white. It was fun there. We grew our own vegetables. Mother had never ever seen a hedgehog, and one day there was a terrific panic when one appeared and she tried to stone it to death! Daddy revived it, he was marvellous with animals.

"I'd bought an Alsatian puppy called Max, he bought an Alsatian bitch named Sheila of Friega, but she was pregnant so suddenly we had 10 Alsatians in all and he sat up all night playing vet. I also had two Belgian hares who'd sit on my lap and eat with us, and the Alsatian puppies would play with the hares, which really amused him…

"At Mortimer Engineering in the school holidays I was given a job sticking stamps on envelopes, for which I was paid 10s a week – jolly good money then… They were always terribly busy. Pingo Lester was one of Daddy's partners there, I adored him – he was wonderful to me…"

Once the Normandy landings had succeeded in June 1944 it was clear victory was near, and ADL's objective to build something like 'The British Union' was taken off the back burner where it had simmered so long.

During this period the great controversy erupted over Pomeroy's approach to purchase the name and goodwill of ERA from Humphrey Cook. As already related, PB became deeply involved in planning a competitive production car programme for the return of peace. He was also deeply committed to Mortimer Engineering, so when Ray began to expound seriously upon imminent foundation of a British Union-type GP project, PB was unable immediately to commit himself to it.

Ray, of course, totally relied upon Peter's technical advice, but PB's engineering background was certainly inadequate to create a world-beating Grand Prix car from scratch. The likes of Reid Railton, Murray Jamieson, Aubrey Barratt, Frank May and Harry Mundy had done the technical donkey work at ERA. Certainly PB made the ultimate technical decisions, but he was never 'The Great Designer' as Ray projected him, and as PB himself was regrettably slow to refute.

His enemies are harsher. They simply say Peter Berthon was a con-man.

Harry Mundy's view was better balanced: "Peter was a truly *charming* man. I liked him immensely, he had a good engineering 'feel', but his limited technical training left him severely restricted. And he would seldom make his appearance at Bourne until mid-morning; Ray spent half-days working for the wool business or gallivanting off to the London theatre, and Jamieson – well, I don't know what he was like at Austin's, but at ERA he never came in before 11am…

"This general lack of discipline came from the top, and it was always Peter Berthon's greatest failing…"

PB's reluctance, or more charitably his simple oversight, in not publicly sharing technical credit at ERA had ultimately contributed to the schism there. In April 1939 Humphrey Cook had written to Sammy Davis – 'Casque' of *The Autocar* – to correct a previously published error describing Aubrey Barratt as "a draughtsman". Cook emphasized that Barratt was "a designer" and that ERAs were the joint efforts of Peter Berthon and Aubrey Barratt.

The man in question felt his contribution had been ignored too long and had threatened to sue unless a correction was printed. He had done most of the E-Type work and felt that unless he made this clear PB would again steal all the thunder. Ironically, with benefit of hindsight, he might have been happy for PB alone to carry the E-Type can…

So, come the winter of 1944–45, if Berthon was not

equipped to design a world-beating new Grand Prix car, then such a man was sorely needed. To plug the gap, in December 1944 Ray enlisted help from an extremely capable design engineer who – according to Harry Mundy – had qualified originally as a surveyor. He then became an engineer at Douglas motorcycles in Bristol where he worked with Frank Stark – who subsequently joined Rolls-Royce and much later played a further role in BRM experiments. He had moved on to Amherst Villiers' establishment in Sackville Street, London, working under Murray Jamieson on supercharger design for the Dorothy Paget team 'Blower' Bentleys. On Jamieson's behalf he then did some ERA work, before spending the later war years on Rolls-Royce aero engines, via the Rover/Whittle gas turbine drawing office at Barnoldswick. When Rolls-Royce began to put the Welland turbine into production they moved the entire 'Barlick' operation to Derby.

Enter Eric George Richter...

When Ray approached him, Eric Richter was still working for Rolls-Royce in Derby. Tall, dark, heavily bespectacled and hawkish, he was a highly intelligent, dogmatic, impatient and somewhat eccentric man. His workmates found him explosively unpredictable. His friendship was hard to win, his respect harder still. He never suffered fools gladly and could be brutally outspoken, but for those who bridged the gap his friendship was highly rewarding. His fertile mind bubbled with design ideas, he especially liked motorcycles and racing cars and he could be great fun. He was very independent, a streak manifested in a rather Bohemian dress style – loud check shirts and jackets, bright-coloured socks (if any at all) and sandals. Crucially, skilled men in those days had to work where they were told to. At Rolls-Royce, by 1944, he was bored.

When Ray contacted him to invite design help on a potential GP car, Eric Richter's enthusiasm ignited...

Fortunately for posterity, fragments of their winter correspondence have survived.

On December 5, 1944, Richter wrote from 62 Ashbourne Road, Derby, to RM in Bourne – using the respectful introduction "Dear Mr. Mays" – to confirm a forthcoming visit "...about the subject of new urge producers...".

Then breathlessly on December 13, again to:

Dear Mr. Mays,

You say that you are dead keen to do something on the lines we talked about. To say that I am dead keen is a typical British under-statement! I simply cannot wait! I have already devoted much thought to one of the more important problems and have arrived at a satisfactory solution pending the arrival of daylight.

I was much impressed by your insistence on a pre-selector gearbox and your implied dislike of the Wilson type owing to maintenance troubles and the like. In consequence of this, I have designed a Hydraulic-mechanical pre-selector mechanism to be used in conjunction with a synchromesh gearbox. It is exceedingly simple and I wonder it has not been thought of before. Its operation is exactly the same as a Wilson, so there would be nothing to get used to or experiment with in driving technique...

I would like to take this opportunity of saying how

very much I enjoyed the week-end and how exhilarating it was to breathe some of the old atmosphere again; also to thank you for your welcome and the import of the matters we discussed.

With kind regards to your mother and yourself...

Yours Sincerely,

Eric G. Richter.

P.S. Standing on Bourne station, I noticed the name Britannia on a cable drum. It struck me as not altogether inappropriate to the project in which we are interested.

We cannot know today just how close 'the BRM' came to being 'the Britannia'...

On December 28, a hand-written letter to Ray from Eric read in part as follows:

...I have not written before as I have nothing definite to say – as a matter of fact I was very much afraid that I had said too much in the first place, and have been in rather a wild mental skid trying to justify what I said about a self-changing gearbox.

However, I have just this minute solved the control problem, with the aid of paper models of hydraulic cylinders and am now quite confident that it will work. I will now set about making a reasonable drawing for your, or the patent agent's, edification.

Regarding the engine: I have done a good deal of work with a slide rule, plus one or two head layouts and can see no reason at all why we should not at least approach 400bhp with 1½-litres. I had toyed with the idea of a rear engined device – but have come to the conclusion it is a bad thing (except that it might be more comfortable in a vertical direction ONLY). For various reasons I favour a V12 – it has much to recommend it, unless you particularly don't like it. High r.p.m. are obtainable with very low rubbing speeds and inertia loadings, and as the cylinders will be small, the valve gear will be small and light, too.

He confirmed a meeting between them for January 6, 1945, and added:

...I must say that I am selfish enough – and interested enough – to hope that this will be a purely technical meeting with no extraneous matters to sidetrack the proceedings – except, of course, the inevitable 'ways and means' sub-committee!

Please excuse pen – it is too late to start typing at this hour of the night.

With all good wishes for the New Year to you all...

On January 3 to Ray:

> I have had several long spells at the board every night for this last week with some material progress…Tonight I have been having a look at the engine, which is not as easy as I thought. (I didn't think it would be.) As you know quite well, almost every point is a matter of opinion and what would suit one engine, will not suit another – and certainly will not suit other conditions. To eliminate as much opinion as possible I would like yours on various aspects of the design, particularly as to the limitations which must be observed.
>
> To make this unit an overhead camshaft V12 will necessitate a bonnet about two feet wide unless it is to have local bulges. This strikes me as being prohibitive. In fact it would be very little wider to make it a flat 12 which is rather surprising. To reduce the width it could be made a straight eight, but then it will be so long – and unpleasant things can happen to long crankshafts which it might take considerable development work (and expense) to eradicate. Strangely enough, the chief cause of the great width is the tentative use of an aluminium head. A bronze head with the valves running direct on the seats seems to be indicated – as on the *Villiers Supercharge*. What do you think about that? Personally I favour the idea, but if it does NOT work at our intended MEP[9] it would mean a completely new head to alter it, and there goes the expense again.
>
> Quite obviously, it all boils down to a question of money, to put it bluntly, and/or time, which is virtually the same thing. With the E.R.A. you had a good start and did wonders with it, but if we are going to do MUCH better, as we must, I am afraid it means a bit of groping – starting with a brand new engine and limited facilities. It is considered reasonable here to take five years to produce such a thing – and that would not be markedly different from the previous standard production. So you see what we are up against. Certainly we have a free hand and IT CAN BE DONE, but I think it only reasonable that I should not optimistically minimise the difficulties.
>
> I need hardly repeat that I am as enthusiastic as you are and if you say it is possible, in the directions which I have mentioned, then I can do it. I have a very good idea of the money which has been spent in the production of an engine with which I am familiar and it is a *very* terrifying figure! This may sound very pessimistic but it may only be one of the penalties of knowing too much… As Wing Commander Lester said at the Birmingham bother, we have got to be absolutely superior to all competition which I think can best be achieved by anticipating difficulties rather than by overcoming them after they have arisen…

This remarkable far-sighted, analytical and indeed prophetic letter was typical of Eric Richter, a now little-known and shadowy figure, but a fine detail designer of the kind invaluable to great conceptual thinkers. He has never been given public credit for his considerable fine work on motor racing projects. He not only played a critical role in creating the reliable mechanicals of the V16 BRM, but subsequently did similarly uncredited work on the World Championship-winning Vanwall GP engine, and later still on the Rover gas turbine power units which eventually took BRM into battle at Le Mans!

But by March 8, 1945, it sounds as if his not always realistic conceptual thinking was beginning to run riot. Perhaps this alarmed RM – it must certainly have steadied PB. By this time Richter was addressing RM as "My dear Ray", and he asked:

> What do you think about the shape of this car? Do you want it low and wide *a la* Merc., or as nearly like the E.R.A. as can reasonably be obtained? The point is of considerable importance as it has a bearing on the type of engine fitted. I am quite sure that I am going to fit the engine across the frame with the final drive as I have already described in order to avoid the slightest trace of torque reaction, so that the car will be completely inert laterally. In this case it will be desirable to keep the engine as short as possible, which a V12 will do.
>
> As a further technical perfection, the drive will be taken from the centre of the crankshaft, so that we shall have an engine which is virtually two V6's, – which will be quite satisfactory as a whole, but equally quite useless in two halves; or rather, in ONE half. Now, if we make the engine two straight fours (a total of eight cylinders) we have a perfectly usable four cylinder 750cc if we wish to use one half in anything else. Moreover, and this is the great point, I have a perfectly good sectional drawing of TMJ's masterpiece[10] which could be adapted to our use and would save us a lot of costly experimental work.
>
> BUT, this arrangement would make an engine something like 50% longer than a twelve and, under exactly the same internal conditions, about 87% as powerful. Also it would have larger and less reliable pistons and valves and would almost certainly weigh a little more.
>
> I could quite easily design the twelve to be short enough to go across the width of the present car, but that could not be done with an eight. Do we want to be able to use half of it on the one hand, or do we want the car so narrow on the other?

He went on, revealingly, to mention use of aeronautical Lockheed air strut suspension and to infer that his transverse-engined GP car concept would also be rear-engined after all:

> If we are going to use the Lockheed suspension it would be lighter and simpler to place the cylinders close to the wheels, in which case it would be necessary to bring the body right out to enclose the whole of the back of the car (excluding the wheels of course) when there would be sufficient room inside to enclose the longer engine. It is all very problematical. As designer, I quite realise that all this is my worry and am only too pleased to undertake it and provide a satisfactory solution – but

9. **Mean Effective Pressure – the measure of work done by pressure created within the cylinder during combustion.**

10. **Tom Murray Jamieson's 750cc Austin OHC Racer.**

at this stage it is more a question of policy on which I should like your pronouncement…

He then extolled the virtues of gold bearings, enabling use of more oily and therefore more acid lubricants than hitherto, recommending Johnson Matthey & Co of Hatton Garden as suppliers of precious metals for industrial use and asking Ray to approach C.A.Vandervell – meaning G.A.Vandervell, not his father CAV:

> …who make admirable strip bearings…As the actual bearing metal is only a few thous., thick the question of cost on even cheap cars hardly arises…

He also requested PB's address "as I should like to exchange a few written ideas with Peter". Perhaps it was then that RM and PB became alarmed at the blossoming theoretical jungle into which their chosen 'designer' seemed to be leading them.

Richter was progressively made aware that PB was Ray's only 'designer', but the duo had drawn him in and he became captive to both their charm and to his own enthusiasm for the new GP car project. PB's thinking finally dominated the general BRM concept, but Richter probably did most to make it work as well as it did in early form. As Harry Mundy told me: "…he was a *very* clever man", and all who knew the often acid

Mundy will appreciate this is praise indeed.

In addition to his East End factory at Mortimer Engineering, PB also ran a drawing office in his home at 102 Drayton Gardens and wangled an old ERA associate to work for him there. Rivers Fletcher: "Before the start of the war I had joined the Auxiliary Fire Service as a driver, and we were subsequently made full-time firemen until the end of the Blitz. I was on night duty two weeks out of three and if there were no alerts I would work for Peter who was screaming for draughtsmen. But he quickly got fed up with me just doing two weeks out of three and said: 'This is too bloody silly, you ought to be here full-time.' Anyone with a certain technical background was put on technical reserve for the services – he was RAF and I was Royal Naval Reserve, RNR. Through Mortimer Engineering, Peter had contracts with the Ministry of Aircraft Production and the Admiralty so he applied to the proper authorities and had me transferred. So I became a jig and tool designer for him – though to be truthful I wasn't very good at it…"

Early in 1945, Jacquie Berthon returned to Drayton Gardens from boarding school: "I knew Harry Mundy was working there part-time, but another drawing board had been set up and this tall, dark, rather forbidding man – who actually turned out to be quite nice – was working at it. He was Eric Richter…" In effect Automotive Developments Ltd had been activated. 'The Mays Project' was about to begin.

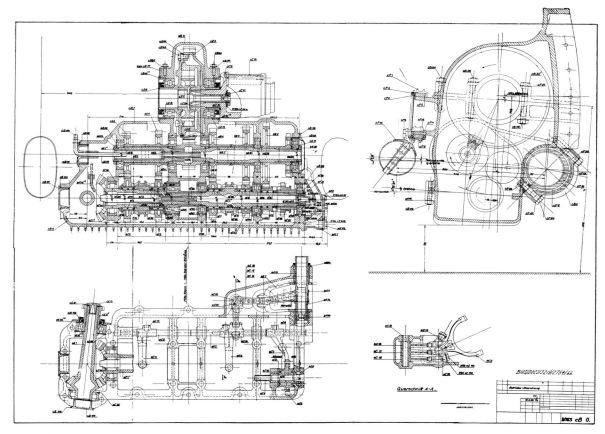

Bridging the war years and linking the postwar Mays Project to the prewar Mercedes-Benz racing programme which RM and PB so admired, this drawing of the 1939 W165 transaxle was one of those which would find its way to Bourne via Cameron Earl, spoils from his BIOS trip No 3219 – an investigation of Daimler-Benz and Auto Union racing developments – in 1947. It would provide the basis of the BRM V16 gearbox.

PART TWO

The V16 BRM

The Mays Project takes shape, 1948. In the panelled study at Eastgate House, the balding RM and the older, heavier, lined PB (right) and administrator, later BRM Company Secretary, James Sandercombe (seated) show off the styling model of the V16 BRM, styled by Walter Belgrove of Standard, to three principals of the newly-formed British Motor Racing Research Trust; Alfred Owen (left), Denis Flather and Bernard Scott of Lucas. Behind the model are Bob Henderson Tate of the all-powerful Ministry of Supply and publicist Walter Hill.

THE MAYS PROJECT

Through that winter of 1944–45 British industry was completing wartime contracts and vigorously planning its return to peacetime production. RM and PB listed companies they believed might be interested in backing a British Grand Prix car project to boost national prestige abroad. Recalling their prewar problems with the ERA 'Pleasure Car' they avoided initial contact with established motor manufacturers, and concentrated instead upon component and accessory companies – those unlikely to be interested in building complete rival cars of their own.

On March 2, 1945, Raymond Mays launched his appeal by writing to a number of such companies.

Now PB and Eric Richter between them argued out the basis of a racing car design to improve upon all known super-charged 1½-litre standards. 'Pom' 's prewar 'British Union'-style arguments on the merits of piston area and a multiplicity of small cylinders prevailed over Richter's preference for a V12. Since it was now going to be a V16, 'Pom' 's preferred 135-degree vee angle was also confirmed. Thoughts of anything so outlandish as a transverse rear-engined layout were dumped in favour of a conventional front-engined configuration, with the engine and driveline raked across the chassis to enable the driver to sit low. The bodylines matched.

Most notably, Richter's wartime experience of Rolls-Royce aero engines confirmed PB's opinion of the vast strides they had made – in common with all major combatants – in high-pressure centrifugal supercharging. Consequently E.W. Hives, CH, MBE, Managing Director of Rolls-Royce at Derby, figured high on RM's mailing list.

Replies to 'The White Paper' were slow, and tense days passed at Eastgate House until one morning Ray received simultaneous invitations to visit A.G.B. Owen – head of the vast Rubery Owen Group of companies at Darlaston – and Oliver Lucas of the Joseph Lucas electrical concern in Birmingham. Lucas' office was closer to Bourne, so Ray arranged to see him first, before driving on in the latest of his long series of Bentley saloons to meet Owen.

Lucas met him in company with Bernard Scott, his personal assistant – later to become Sir Bernard Scott, Chairman of both Lucas and the SMMT – and they listened rapt as the 46-year-old star driver told his story, emphasized his past success and glowingly described Peter Berthon's capabilities, his plans, hopes and needs. Lucas listened intently, invited Ray to lunch with his fellow directors, and after a brief private meeting told his visitor: "You've won the day…how much do you want from us?"

No idea of a detailed budget had yet occurred to RM or PB – still just enthusiastic amateurs looking for whatever they could get. Ray knew he dare not hesitate, yet neither should he ask too much, nor too little. So he asked crisply for £1,000 in cash plus free manufacture of parts. Equally crisply, Oliver Lucas accepted, and RM left Birmingham for Darlaston with a £1,000 cheque[11] in his pocket and a firm promise for £4,000-

---

11. **A roughly equivalent 1993 value for such a cheque would be over £19,500 – on the Rudd 'Cortina Formula' over £20,300 – the parts value no less than £78,000…**

worth of equipment for the new GP car.

While he drove towards Darlaston, Oliver Lucas telephoned Owen to tell him he was backing the project. Ray later wrote:

> Mr. Owen was prepared for me…I had never met him before and I was at once taken by him. He has magnetic eyes that look through you. He looks you directly in the face and I think he sums you up straight away. He has a very gentle manner and a gentle voice and is obviously a man of the highest possible integrity… He let me talk. He listened, saying remarkably little, pencilled a few notes on his pad, and as with Oliver Lucas, it was his patriotism which was kindled…

Alfred Owen matched the Lucas offer, and this devoutly religious, immensely determined and amazingly energetic businessman was to carry BRM fortunes on his broad shoulders for decades to follow…

Naturally, many rebuffed Ray's 'White Paper', but at least with men of such stature as Owen and Lucas behind him, his toe was in many doors. Their support attracted more as he travelled, met and talked his head off in the months which followed. Although some 'surefire' companies refused support, surprise offers were made by smaller fry. More offered assistance should the project prove successful.

This understandably irritated Ray, as what he needed was support to launch the project – he could not offer "…an investment in a sure return. I needed people who had faith, faith in me and faith in British skill and engineering knowledge. We would have had the car in three dimensions far more quickly and more professionally if some of those short-sighted men had shown that faith…"

He spent hours on his telephone at 'Bourne 17' talking to would-be supporters. Slowly 'The Mays Project' was taking shape, and already with the £2,000 donated by Owen and Lucas, serious design had begun…

THE DESIGN TAKES SHAPE

Harry Mundy had spent the war in the Royal Air Force. He had been a reservist prewar during his time at ERA, and as he became convinced war was inevitable he returned to his native Coventry, and worked briefly at Morris Engines before being activated as an RAF officer in August 1939. He rose to the rank of Wing-Commander and spent the last year of hostilities on the technical development staff of Air-Commodore F.R. 'Rod' Banks, Director of Engine Research and Development at the Air Ministry, whose brilliant career had included formulation of the Schneider Trophy-winning high-performance aviation fuels. As an Air-Commodore, Banks was only entitled to a Flight-Lieutenant as his PA, and in order to enhance Harry's rank and have him paid what Banks thought he was worth, Harry was listed as a Development Engineer. Banks was a most important figure in the aircraft world and very rank conscious. Harry Mundy thus came highly recommended…

He had maintained contacts with his old associates from ERA, and in 1945, as Peter Berthon and Eric Richter began to

RM's 'WHITE PAPER' – MARCH 2, 1945

The initial circular letter which launched 'The Mays Project' was richly worded to suit the atmosphere of the time, and leaned heavily upon Raymond Mays' image as Britain's leading motor racing personality. It also leaned heavily upon his favoured ploy of presenting himself as spokesman for an upsurge of popular sentiment. Addressed to the principals of a broad cross-section of the British accessory and component industry, it read as follows:

I have given a good deal of thought to the future of motor sport in this country, particularly motor racing.

This has been inspired largely by the import of the innumerable letters which I am constantly receiving from servicemen all over the world. It would appear that the mechanization which nowadays forms so large a part of their lives, has made a deep impression which manifests itself in a greatly increasing interest in motor racing. In these letters their constant query is – 'What is being done about the future of motor racing in England?'

You will appreciate, as my correspondents do, that I have given the best part of my life to motor racing, and the valuable research and development that goes with it, and would ordinarily be keen to continue to do so.

I am all the more keen in view of the general interest I have mentioned which, I think you will agree, augurs well for the future popularity of the sport in this country. In fact as I see it, it might well become our premier sport if suitably promoted.

I feel very strongly that the ultimate in any activity is of direct value to the country achieving it. There is no doubt that the motor and associated industries have achieved it in the mechanization of our forces. It is only fitting that this superiority should be perpetuated as a gesture to the technicians and servicemen who have made our victory possible – no less than to the masses who have patiently endured so much. It becomes therefore, incumbent on those of us who have the ability to try to produce a car which will securely hold our place in the very forefront of international competition.

I have been approached by numerous people about this matter, many of whom have suggested the inauguration of a public subscription to enable such a car to be built. However, past experience has shown me that this is not altogether the most satisfactory procedure. In any case it would be preferable to produce and prove the vehicle before it was offered to the public, as it were, but more particularly such a scheme would give the sponsors quite the wrong sort of publicity at the wrong time. After such a car had been run to the satisfaction of those responsible for it, then some consideration might well be given to a public fund.

My position is that I am able to get the preliminary design work on a suitable car started immediately, and can find much of the necessary cash towards the materialization of the design. I should be very interested to know if you are sufficiently interested to make a material contribution towards this end. Not only would the idea generally benefit our engineering industries, but the sport side of the venture would be well worth while, as much valuable publicity would rightly accrue to those who participated.

It would, moreover, remove England from the back seat in which she languished all too long in pre-war competitive motoring.

So far, all the surviving engineers who previously assisted me in my racing ventures have prepared the broad designs of a suitable vehicle embodying the features dictated by successful participation in every type of event. I have every confidence that the result would transcend anything which has previously been associated with my name.

It is difficult to explain, within the confines of a reasonable letter, the scheme as I have developed it so far, but I very sincerely hope that you will be interested. I now look forward to hearing from you and then I trust we shall be able to arrange a mutually convenient time for me to pay you a personal visit, when we could discuss the project in greater detail.

Yours Truly,

scheme their projected V16, PB re-enlisted Harry's help, ostensibly for Automobile Developments Ltd. Richter was then still effectively trapped in his reserved occupation at Rolls-Royce and could only contribute in his spare time. Banks' command was based in Hackney, London, and Harry spent his evenings working for PB at Drayton Gardens on initial layout drawings.

After VJ day in August 1945 Banks allowed Harry afternoons off to spend more time at Drayton Gardens working on 'the car'. Once ADL had the capital provided by Owen and Lucas, Richter was engaged full-time, and when Mundy left the RAF in January 1946 he followed suit, ruefully surrendering his Wing-Commander's pay – which including allowances for special duty, marriage, separation and batman totalled some £1,800 a year – to accept instead £12 10s[12] a week plus £2 10s expense allowance as Chief Designer, superior to the increasingly marginalized Richter... "Enthusiasm was the thing...we were laying down a world-beater."

Not that he agreed with the glamorous concept chosen by PB. While Richter preferred a V12, Mundy believed a V8 would have been ideal.

In 1939 two 1½-litre supercharged Mercedes-Benz *Voiturettes* had been designed and built in secret to make surprise entries in the Tripoli GP, in which they shocked Alfa Romeo and Maserati by blowing Italy's best hopes into the sand dunes. They had finished first and second, and were powered by supercharged V8 engines. Now, postwar, the Italian cars were sure to reappear, but the Mercedes-Benz W165s would not.

Mundy: "When I first joined I said we should be doing a V8, but they said no, that would be like the Tripoli Mercedes. I couldn't see why that was bad! Berthon was fixated with

12. This £12 10s per week wage in 1946 had approximately the same purchasing power as £244 per week in 1993. Hardly over-generous for a 'Chief Designer'...

16 cylinders. He had been quite friendly with old 'Pom' who had propounded this theory of piston area." With hindsight Harry insisted: "…piston area didn't matter so much in those days when you were running a supercharged Formula. We should have been working on a V8 – and of course that, combined with quite the wrong choice of centrifugal supercharger, ultimately killed our chances…"

Others differed on both number of cylinders and choice of supercharger, and above all on "the set-up" itself…

But ADL was aiming to produce a car which would set out probably in 1948 with more power than any foreseeable competitor and possessing sufficient development potential to go on defeating all comers into 1950–51.

RM followed up his first contact with Rolls-Royce in the autumn of 1945, and asked Hives and his Joint Managing-Director-cum-Chief Engineer, A.G. Elliott, CBE, to design and build for ADL's 'Mays Project' a very special supercharger whose power band should also be wide enough for road racing. This last requirement should be remembered, for many BRM detractors have since concluded that ADL either ignored or was ignorant of the known limitations of centrifugal supercharging. Where initial design is concerned, neither charge stands up although ADL's original concept submitted to Rolls-Royce specified 150-grade aviation fuel, which would have required a space-consuming intercooler. When this was made clear to them they changed to alcohol fuel to save space – Tony Rudd: showing they weren't that bright – it's first year stuff.

'E', as Elliott was known within Rolls-Royce, then sent for Geoffrey L. 'Oscar' Wilde, of the Compressor Section of RR's Experimental Department. 'Oscar' recalled: "He gave me the job of making proposals to supercharge a 1½-litre engine to produce 400 brake horsepower. At the time of that meeting between RM and E, Rolls-Royce had not committed itself to fund the building and testing of a supercharger. E wanted to consider the proposals before he was prepared to commit the company to what would be a considerable investment of resources."

One of Wilde's colleagues was Frank J. Allen, a brilliant man, older than 'Oscar' and known as 'Prof' from his habitually rather distracted, absent-minded manner. Despite his seniority in years Allen happily deferred to Geoffrey Wilde's command of their department, and by November 17, 1945, they had produced initial estimates of engine performance for E and had suggested to him design of a small two-stage centrifugal supercharger – report and drawing No. ALN 1108.

'Oscar': "This initial proposal embodied an intercooler between the supercharger and the engine to reduce the charge temperature entering the cylinders, but ADL resisted this to simplify engine installation. The aesthetic lines of the car and frontal area reduction were always treated as key factors. But it was essential to cool the charge flow to produce the power required and to avoid the destructive effects of detonation. So the alternative course was adopted, of using methyl-alcohol fuel with a very high latent heat of evaporation to reduce the charge temperature…

"E accepted these proposals. In December 1945 and January '46 there were further meetings in Derby between E

ALFRED OWEN – A MAN COMMITTED

Alfred George Beech Owen was one of Britain's leading industrialists, running an extraordinary family business, Britain's largest privately-owned industrial group.

His empire traced its foundation back to the brothers John T. and Tom W. Rubery, who in 1884 had opened their own light steel fabrications shop in Booth Street, Darlaston, Staffordshire. Four years later Tom Rubery withdrew so 'Rubery Bros' became 'Rubery & Co'.

On July 4, 1893, John Rubery wrote to his business associates and neighbours:

> Dear Sir, I beg to inform you that Mr. Alfred Ernest Owen of Wrexham, Denbighshire, has become my partner. The partnership business will be carried on under the style of 'Rubery & Co.' and the respective partners will sign as below… (signed) John T. Rubery with a sample signature A.E. Owen.

Rubery's new Welsh partner was the only son of Alfred Owen, JP, born on May 10, 1869. After schooling at Arnold House, Chester and Cambridge House, Waterloo, he had become one of three premium apprentices in Taylor's Engineering Works at Sandycroft, Chester. After five hard years there he took a Marine Engineering course in Liverpool, before moving to Darlaston – aged 24. When he went into partnership there with John Rubery, their works consisted of a smith's shop and a template shop, housing 24 employees.

A.E. Owen was both a fine engineer and a dynamic businessman. His company was 'in' at the foundation of the motor industry, and grew with it, and in July 1900 he married Florence Lucy Beech. By 1905 the company name changed to 'Rubery, Owen & Co.' and in 1910 the elderly John Rubery, without an heir, sold his interest to his partner.

The company expanded rapidly through the First World War, and survived the depression of 1920. Thereafter, the Darlaston premises mushroomed to include "…a number of contiguous but separate factories" devoted broadly to motor frames;

structural steelwork for buildings, bridges and piers; sheet metal and turned components and vast quantities of nuts and bolts for the aircraft industry; and disc and wire-spoked motor wheels.

A.E. Owen was a paternalistic employer and a pioneer in industrial welfare. As early as 1912 he had provided a company recreation ground including bowling greens and tennis courts – "decidedly a novelty in the grim setting of Black Country manufacture" – and an Institute with canteen, staff dining room, billiards hall and reading room. Into the late 1920s Rubery Owen employed around 1,600 workers; they all knew the boss at least by sight – and he knew hundreds of them by name. He was described as "a man of moderate tastes and regular habits, with strong artistic inclinations", until late in 1929, after attending an ex-Servicemen's supper at the works, he collapsed. Five years earlier he had undergone apparently successful surgery for a duodenal ulcer. But this recurrence proved fatal. He died on December 30 that year, aged 60.

He left three children, Alfred George Beech Owen – born April 8, 1908 – Ernest William Beech Owen and Helen Jean Beech Owen. Shares in the family business were divided equally between them, and would subsequently be divided again to provide equal shares in turn for their children. Rubery Owen was most unusual in paying its shareholders no dividend. Instead it paid them only a salary.

A.E. Owen had always flown the company ensign from his Darlaston buildings and on his death-bed he urged young Alfred, "keep the flag flying…"

Alfred was only 21. He had been educated at Lickey Hill School, then Oundle – Raymond Mays' old school – before going up to Cambridge to read engineering at Emmanuel College. There he heard and responded to the call of Christ and committed his life to Him. Soon after this conversion he met *La Marechale*, General Booth's daughter, who asked him: "What are you doing for the Lord?" From that moment on he regarded his whole life as an act of service to God.

Upon his father's death he abandoned his unfinished degree course, and on January 6, 1930, assumed control of Rubery Owen. On October 8, 1932 he married Eileen Kathleen Genevieve 'Viva' McMullan. They would have five children, widely spaced – Helen Grace, Alfred David, John Ernest, Jean and Robert James. Alfred Owen delighted in the company of young people. One of his favourite sayings was: "Do not break a child's spirit."

As a young man he ran a children's service, he became an incredibly active and much-in-demand lay preacher and was a Crusader leader throughout his active life. He became a tireless Council Chairman for Dr Barnardo's orphanages, President of the West Midlands Boys' Brigade, Chairman of the National Sunday School movement, a Trustee of the Grubb Institute, Treasurer of Birmingham Youth for Christ and into the 1950s a leading organizer of Dr Billy Graham's first evangelical Crusade in Britain.

He also served on numerous hospital committees and as early as 1934 had begun a lifetime of civic service by being elected to the Darlaston Urban District Council. He was its Chairman from 1942–46 and 1952–54, while in his hometown of Sutton Coldfield he became a Council member in 1937 and Mayor in 1951. For 17 years from 1949 he was a member of Staffordshire County Council and from 1955–62 served as its Chairman.

Add other duties as sometime Pro-Chancellor of Keele University, Vice-Chairman of the National Savings Movement, Deputy Chairman of the Welsh Development Corporation, Chairman of Governors for Bishop Vesey's Grammar School, President of St John's Ambulance for Staffordshire *and* a Director of Walsall Football Club and the list is still not exhausted!

Yet in parallel with all these time-consuming responsibilities he still presided day-to-day – with the able support of his qualified engineer brother Ernest – over Rubery Owen & Co's continued rapid expansion. They steered it successfully through the Great Depression, it became an armaments giant through the Second World War and was then quite literally converted back from armour plate to ploughshares, and motor industry parts, and nuts and bolts, all the minutiae of manufacturing, postwar.

His personal mixture of hands-on and delegated manage-ment, his business flair and level-eyed, softly-spoken magnetism developed Rubery Owen into an international business empire with worldwide interests. His father had once told him that real business success was measured not by how much money you could make, but by how many people you could employ. To the despair, on occasion, of his accountants, Alfred Owen's interest was always more in people than in profits.

Under his direction the Group thrived and grew. He had an unusual management style, monitoring a constant incoming flood of management letters, memos and reports from the dozens of subsidiary companies – including BRM in years to follow – before scribbling the barest bones authorizations or instructions which were then transcribed for him in a style he approved by his personal secretary – for many years the redoubtable Miss Edith 'Polly' Ramsden – supported by a handful of assistant secretaries. His wishes would then be typed *en clair*, ready for signature. Once approved, he would append his rounded initials 'AGBO' or, to those he knew well, normally an 'A' alone.

Tall, imposing, fiercely bushy-eyebrowed, he struck an aldermanic figure in his grey, sober suits – but his manner startled many who were meeting him for the first time; softly-spoken, quiet, gentle mannered, almost diffident. He was a good listener, a sympathetic man…yet some who read him simply as a bible-thumping soft touch were riding for a fall. He was an immensely determined man once he had decided a course to follow. Once that course was set, little could deflect him. This trait alone would sustain BRM for two decades and more.

His sober suit was more often crumpled, sometimes stained, than sharply pressed. With the abstracted air of an absent-minded professor, it was not unknown for Alfred Owen to have buttoned his jacket crookedly, or to leave one shirt collar turned up, or to be wearing odd socks. Such niceties as sartorial display were always unimportant to his devout and brimming mind. His favoured wear for inclement outdoor events would be a similarly well-creased and shabby macintosh.

He was a man of the simplest tastes except in his motor cars. He favoured Rolls-Royce built Bentleys, which he drove himself, with great enthusiasm and at immense speed. And if a lengthy journey involved a stop for lunch or dinner it was never Alfred Owen's style to find a five-star hotel or lavish restaurant. The greasiest of 'greasy-spoons' or the most jam-packed of '40s/'50s transport cafes would find his Bentley, inevitably gasping-hot and ticking, abandoned outside while its owner/ driver – this leading British industrialist, with his staff worldwide numbered in tens of thousands – would be happily enjoying a fry-up inside, his nose buried in the daily paper, or in company reports; never happier than when he was amongst 'real people'.

Alfred Owen was, altogether, a most unusual and extraordinary industrialist. And a man of towering, unswerving faith…

Home of the Project: BRM's buildings alongside Spalding Road at Bourne photographed shortly before their demolition in the early 1980s. Left: The long and ancient Maltings in which Raymond Mays & Partners built their road car in the 1930s, and which later became home to Automobile Developments Ltd's – later BRM's – drawing office and machine shop. The far entrance leads into the Delaine coach company garage, ERA's prewar works. Below: Yard view of the Maltings with BRM's 1960s build-cum-race shop intruding at the left – 30 years later it was an auction hall…

and RM which I also attended. I don't remember Peter Berthon attending any of these early meetings…

"Frank Allen and I continued to work on the project off and on through 1946, mostly in the evenings. We were fully committed to aero engine work during the day, the years 1945 to 1948 being particularly exacting with the launching of two new Rolls-Royce aero engines – the Avon axial jet and Dart turbo-prop."

According to Rolls-Royce, when the war had begun, methods of estimating piston-engine power output were poor, particularly for supercharged aero engines. Between 1939 and 1941 a better method was evolved by a Rolls-Royce team under Dr S.G. Hooker, CBE [13], then Assistant Chief Experimental Engineer, Aero Division. Wilde and Allen were two of his team.

By the time they began research, serious car design had begun with Richter working at Drayton Gardens and Mortimer Engineering, while Harry Mundy was despatched to Bourne to re-activate some of the old facilities behind Eastgate House.

There, Ray had sold the abandoned ERA factory to Smith's – the local bus company. His old mechanics Jack Wylde and Charlie Davey were preparing 'R4D' in the private garages behind Eastgate House, while Raymond Mays & Partners Ltd still operated as an everyday garage on the ground floor of the Spalding Road Maltings. Ken Richardson had spent time during the war on the Rolls-Royce test flight at Hucknall Aerodrome, and was given a good job at Rover, trouble-shooting on their RR-licenced Meteor V12 tank engines. Now Ray asked him to return to the fold at Bourne, where he initially took over the running of RM & Partners, but would also work on 'R4D'.

The ancient Maltings building was decidedly dilapidated,

13. **Tony Rudd: This is pure Hooker propaganda. It was always possible to predict the potential maximum power very accurately, based upon air ingestion. It was when the predicted power failed to appear that the fun would begin, measuring air consumed, heat rejected to oil and water, exhaust gas analysis, so many variables along the way…**

but space was available on its first floor which RM and PB now had converted into offices for ADL Ltd and their 'Mays Project'.

Harry Mundy: "I helped Percy Larkin, the local umm – man – to put in new floors and then the following winter was terribly hard, typical of the conditions in which the V16 was designed, and it was bitterly cold in what became our drawing office. Late snow hung around for weeks and we just had a couple of tiny electric fires to take off the chill. Pingo Lester brought us in some silk flying gloves which we wore while working at our drawing boards – it really was *that* cold!"

Harry was in charge of this embryo drawing office, and the first draughtsman he hired was John A. Cooper, a former colleague at Alvis prewar, who was later to become Sports Editor of *The Autocar* and a great pal of young Stirling Moss', but would die in a Frazer Nash in a road accident in 1955. Frankie May returned after his wartime spell at Daimler and when RM interested Girling in the scheme they seconded to Bourne a draughtsman named Tony Sadler. Having set out much of the original scheme, Eric Richter was employed on other projects for Mortimer Engineering, and he would only move late to Bourne.

There his strange personal mix of excellent design engineer and 'mad genius' typified the whole incredible project. He was certainly brought to Bourne as an original thinker to temper the workmanlike experience of Frank May and the crisp practicality of Harry Mundy, and as a pure design team they would prove a strong combination, peculiarly managed.

Harry recalled Richter as being, "…an odd character. For example he would take endless trouble in the way he would pose questions to you, so you could only answer him the way he wanted. He seemed to regard this as some form of intellectual victory, manipulating your mind to say what he wanted you to say. But this was just his way… And he was *bloody* good."

ADL's drawing office at Bourne was not, however, devoted to work on the racing car. PB arranged several outside contracts on behalf of both Mortimer Engineering and ADL, and John Cooper – for example – spent hardly any time at all on the V16 during his spell there. PB had a deal going with Lucien Wagner's Imperia company in Belgium which had built cars prewar around German Adler front-drive units. With Adler now in the Russian Zone, Wagner contracted PB to produce a replacement front-drive system plus transmission and suspension for Imperia. But Wagner eventually negotiated an alternative scheme direct with Standard so Cooper's efforts were wasted.

Maurice Taylor, a Daimler apprentice during Frank May's time there, passed through ADL briefly, followed by a Rover man named Norman Bryden, who soon returned to head Rover's engine design office. But two young local draughts-men arrived who were to stay with BRM for many, many years. They were Aubrey Woods and Alec Stokes.

Aubrey Woods: "I started at Bourne in August 1946. I came from Stamford originally but had got a job on jig and tool design for Percival Aircraft at Weybridge in Surrey. I didn't like that at all, and when I saw an advert for work on an exciting Grand Prix project I applied and went to Kendrick Mews, Kensington [Aubrey recalls this as PB's London office of the time, prior to Drayton Gardens as others recollect] and met PB and Harry Mundy, and discovered to my astonishment the job was going to be in Bourne, barely 10 miles from home!

"I worked for a while there in Kendrick Mews, with Richter and also Rivers Fletcher. I remember meeting Lorna for the first time there – I'll never forget it – she was wearing only the flimsiest dressing gown and flaunting everything. She was a very exotic lady…at one stage I had to design monograms for her to sew onto her gowns and underwear.

"When I arrived at the Maltings, Harry Mundy, Frank May, Tony Sadler and Maurice Taylor were there. Eric Richter was on holiday. Then one morning this OEM motorcycle came charging into the yard, ridden by a wild-eyed bearded bloke wearing canvas trousers, a cheque shirt, sandals and no socks. That was Richter – a complete nut-case, but brilliant. He did the engine layouts complete. PB never drew, he didn't even sketch, but he could explain what he had in his mind's eye – and you drew everything for him just from his description. Harry was a great character, easy to get along with, and a right piss-artist.

Top: ADL's drawing office on the Maltings' first floor, Frankie May (left) at the board with Alec Stokes, Aubrey Woods third-left. PB's white miniature poodle took a liking to Aubrey's board, and shoes. Alec recalls many a cry of "My foot feels warm again! Aaah – that baloody dog!!!!…". Centre: The original engine build shop overlooking the yard, a prototype de Dion tube upon the floor. An assembled engine could be lowered by the hoist (top) through a trapdoor into a waiting chassis in the build 'shop below. Above: Meanwhile, on the Maltings' ground floor, the embryo machine shop was taking shape…

"The drawing office was on the Maltings' first floor and there were only floorboards between us and the Raymond Mays & Partners paint shop down below, which you could see through the gaps where the draught came whistling in. In November Alec Stokes joined us, and it was *freezing*…"

Alec was from Bourne. His father was a policeman, "…a 6ft 6in big-hitting batsman for the local cricket club". He'd been in the force for 30 years being posted all around Lincolnshire before finally settling in Bourne. It was hard to be accepted as Alec recalled of his home town: "Here for the first five years you're a foreigner. For the second five years you're a stranger, only after 10 years or more you're accepted, and that depends on you passing your probation OK. Playin' for the cricket and soccer clubs made it easier for me…"

Like Aubrey Woods, Alec had strong wartime industrial training and experience behind him: "I'd been a seven-year general engineering apprentice at Scunthorpe Steel Works, right from an initial two years at College to the final 18 months in the drawing office. We were taught to do just *everythin'* in between.

"I'd been on jig and tool design at Mirlees Blackstone [the Stamford diesel engine manufacturer] for nine months when I got my job at BRM as a detail draughtsman in November '46. I was 21½… We whinged an awful lot but never left…"

"BRM was like a big family. We'd all fight somethin' terrible between ourselves but any attack from outside would immediately push us all together, united, to repel boarders. There was a lot of 'Bourne against the outside world' in that, and we did finally get it right in the early '60s…

"When I joined they'd started to design about everything for the car – engine and chassis – but they hadn't started to build anything yet. We'd probably see PB one day a week and come summertime he'd disappear for a month or more. It was all run on the 'Gentlemen of Sport' principle. Nobody could get at PB to change his ways. He was the supremo, but it was hard when you couldn't proceed because you needed his say-so and he was away.

"I started detailing the gearbox, then went onto assembly drawings and finally got drafted into general gearbox design. The V16 gearbox was virtually an exact copy of the prewar 1½-litre Mercedes. Harry had got drawings of it [via Cameron

Earl, who compiled the immediate postwar BIOS[14] intelligence report on German GP car technology]. We were searching for something in his absence and found these drawings he'd been cribbing from. Of course PB and RM knew, but I don't think us lower orders were meant to!"

Aubrey: "That bitter winter was incredible. Snow drifts blocked the road outside and filled the yard, there were icicles

Above: On the Maltings' first floor, senior designer Frankie May and Bob Marshall at one of the ADL drawing-boards. The Raymond Mays & Partners garage stores and spray shop were visible through gaps in the floorboards beneath them, which passed icy draughts in winter, paint mist when the sprayer was at work… Left: Picture Post photographed the ADL design team examining this V16 scuttle tank drawing – PB presides, with the great Harry Mundy (left), the unsung Eric Richter (standing), RM and Frankie May (right).

inside from the Maltings' gutters and there we were trying to draw in our overcoats, thoroughly chilled and demoralized, and Percy Larkin would yank open the door at regular intervals and bawl: 'Buckets and shovels are outside!'

"PB always liked us to prepare four or five alternative schemes for any one job, after which you just had to wait until he put in an appearance when he'd pick the one he liked. He couldn't stress a thing to save his life, but he had a good eye – he was an instinctive engineer, and I thought a good one…"

Harry was quite settling in to Bourne. He would marry a local girl whose brother 'Taffy' Harris was headmaster of the local school. Harry had bought a plot of land in what would become known as Mill Drove on which he built himself a modernistic house there "with tiny windows", as Aubrey Woods recalled, which "looked like a cinema, so we christened it 'The Odeon'…". Meanwhile, at the Maltings site behind Eastgate House a new engine test house and a large stores building were being erected for ADL. The Standard Motor Company was footing most of the bill for the former, and both were erected by an outside contractor named Smith, introduced by PB, who subsequently turned out to be his employer, so drawing the profit!

Aubrey: "The Test House was actually three buildings, one within another, a box, within a box, within a box, to kill the noise. Ray's friend Pingo Lester had a house and a little development 'shop at Osterby, where Tony Rudd later lived in a flat. The Test House doors were wooden with metal sheet cladding which Pingo made up, forming them like a metal box, then having the doors delivered to his workshop where they just slid them into these fabricated steel boxes and then welded them up…setting fire to the wooden door inside!"

Anne – or 'Maisie' Mays as the locals sometimes referred to her – was still very much in evidence at Eastgate House and around the Maltings. Rivers Fletcher has described her as 'The Dowager Duchess of Eastgate House' – "…she was placed on a pedestal by her son, she was spoiled, waited upon and respected like the royalty she obviously believed she was…". She certainly had some – ahem – unusual ways, one of ADL's raw recruits, only a few days into his new job, being accosted by her behind the Maltings: "She said: 'Hello, I don't recognize you, do you like working for my Raymond?' What startled me wasn't so much the way she asked the question – expecting an enthusiastic 'Yes' – as what she was wearing; just a pair of knickers, wellington boots and gardening gloves…"

A local legend also gained currency amongst the mechanics which would have done credit to scriptwriters Ray Galton and Alan Simpson if true; 'Maisie' parading nude in the window at Eastgate House, for the benefit of the Bourne Gasworks staff opposite. This really was not the most attractive side of town…

At one stage Aubrey Woods was recruited by RM and 'Mam'

14. **British Intelligence Occupation Survey of German industry, prepared by HM Government's Technical Information and Document Unit, 40 Cadogan Square, London, SW1 and reported by Cameron C. Earl following "BIOS Trip No. 3219; April 22nd – May 20th, 1947". The unfortunate Mr Earl was subsequently killed while driving one of Bob Gerard's ERAs on the new Motor Industry Research Association test-track near Nuneaton, triggering a ban on the running of racing cars there.**

to redesign their kitchen in Eastgate House: "…and I had to go down to Harrods with RM to buy the bits." Everyone at ADL was roped-in to assist in some way, at some time. Ray could act very much as the local Squire…ADL's staff very much his retainers…

When new factory space was needed, the House's old conservatory was demolished, and its enormous and ancient vine cut down. Percy Larkin was given the job, Ray ordering: "Chop it down, Percy." He'd just started when a horrified Mrs Mays appeared, screaming: "Larkin! Stop that at once!" She then toddled off only for Ray to reappear, demanding: "Percy! Why haven't you cut down that vine?" Larkin explained, Ray ordered him to proceed, and left. Re-enter Mrs Mays: "Larkin! I told you to stop that!" Ray reappeared: "Percy! Cut it down!" The indignant Larkin stood, glared from mum to son, then hurled his axe to the ground and bawled: "Boogah yer bloody vine – do it yer bloody selves" and stamped off home, not returning until RM had visited him to make peace.

On one occasion RM invited new boy Aubrey to visit the house that evening, to see his collection of trophies and paintings. Percy Larkin overheard and took the young draughtsman to one side: "Young man, d'you mind if I tell you something?" Aubrey: "I said 'No' to Ray and there was never, ever, another approach like that, and from that day on we got on *absolutely* like a house on fire. I always called him 'Mr Mays' until one day he just said: 'Listen, call me Ray' so 'Ray' it was ever after except in others' presence, when it was 'Mr Ray'. He enjoyed that. He had his faults, of course, but he was marvellous; unlike some, if he couldn't do you a good turn, he would *never* do you a bad one…"

PB meanwhile would eventually become "Peter" to Aubrey, who became his closest collaborator, but it was always "Mr Berthon" in company.

Today, as then, Bourne looks and feels like an isolated country town, but actually it made a good enough base for such a sophisticated engineering project. It was only 90 minutes by road or train from such centres as Coventry, Derby and London. A large pool of highly-skilled local labour was available, well trained in the diesel engine works at nearby Peterborough and Stamford, and in the high-precision armaments works in Grantham. Men of that calibre would be employed as time went by, particularly in the machine shop, but in these pioneering days as ADL developed, good garage hands were good enough – and some became BRM stalwarts. ADL's first shopfloor employee was one such – Dave Turner.

"In wartime I'd worked for Dennis Kendall, the Grantham MP. His armaments works made Oerlikon cannon. Eighteen months before the war ended he began to develop a cut-price people's car. It was all-aluminium, in sections, firstly a three-cylinder radial two-stroke designed by Beaumont. That was hopeless, so Musnick, a Pole, designed a four-stroke radial, which had so much power loss it was hopeless too. Then Kendall bought two-cylinder air-cooled Gregoire engines and I helped build three of these Kendall cars and a tractor, and got sent out to Bombay for nine months to demonstrate the cars for Rajah Jemnigah. Laurence Pomeroy had a lot to do with Kendall, and after it packed up I went to work in Woolf's Garage here in Bourne until one evening Peter Berthon came round and offered me a job, and I took it.

Majoring upon the charismatic Mays connection, Union flag pre-eminent, an early – rejected – draft design for the BRM badge.

"I really got on well with Berthon, told me I was his right-hand man, he did. The first machine tools arrived, and I helped put them in on the Maltings' ground floor with a machinist from Stamford, Bert Alliss, a little feller…"

Two capable brothers from Grantham named Cyril and Les Bryden started work in the new machine shop in the spring of 1947, as the last snows finally thawed and the V16's major component drawings were completed. PB had remained London-based throughout this period and played little part in detailing the design. Mundy: "I cannot stress too highly that as a man I liked Berthon immensely, but Alec's right, he did lack discipline and application. He just didn't give enough time and dedication to the project and in that crucial early period he was terribly remote, living in London. Once he had chosen the basic things like 16 cylinders, 135-degree vee, Rolls-Royce centrifugal supercharger…we were left to do the schemes and detail them as we saw fit…

"Richter of course set down some basic things on the engine and with Frank May tied the whole thing together. Frank drew all the valvegear and sorted out the initial problems there. I did the original chassis layout, placing the engine at an angle, and then went on to detail the transmission while Tony Sadler drew the frame and suspensions.

"Berthon had decided – quite wrongly – that we should stay with the Porsche trailing arm front suspension as used in the later ERAs and he pushed Lockheed air struts to replace conventional springs and dampers – but that was virtually the extent of what real designing he did…"

Lacking any formal engineering training beyond his RAF Cranwell course, PB is recalled as being unable either to produce a technical drawing or to read one properly. His 'feel'

was the thing. His forte was in handling the parts once made and being able to 'read' whether they were right or wrong or could be improved. Mundy also discovered – as would many after him – that once the engine was running and breaking Peter Berthon had a remarkable intuitive ability to identify what had failed first amongst a shambles of twisted and heat-blued wreckage.

While towards the end of 1947 the Daimler-Benz gearbox blueprints had filtered through, by some astonishing means as early as 1946 one of the surviving 1939 Mercedes-Benz factory GP cars had been brought to England from Czechoslovakia. It had been acquired, despite the stifling bureaucracy of new-Socialist Britain and new-Communist Czechoslovakia combined, by a fly Walton-on-Thames car dealer named John Lawrence. There is a story that the car went to Bourne for ADL's inspection – again untrue – and it was in fact sold quickly to Don Lee in the USA who entered it for the 1947 Indianapolis 500-Miles speedway classic…without success.

This car, however, was one of a pair secreted away in Prague, and when Ray enlisted moral assistance for his project from the Ministry of Supply they offered to clear a Board of Trade permit to import a foreign racing car for experimental research. In February 1948, Everard Taylor of the Ministry of Supply arranged a BoT licence – No. M/66960 – to import a 1939 3-litre Mercedes-Benz racing car from Czechoslovakia. This would have given PB something tactile which he could fully have appreciated, but officialdom and diplomacy foundered and the car remained in Czechoslovakia – eventually in the National Technical Museum of Prague – until 1974 when it came to Britain for a spell on loan to the Donington Collection of Single-Seater Racing Cars.

While ADL's drawing office at Bourne wrestled with their side of the project, Wilde and Allen at Rolls-Royce continued their spare-time work on the supercharger. Geoffrey Wilde: "I first visited Bourne in September 1946. By then we had worked out the performance of the 1½-litre engine with methyl-alcohol fuel. We had also investigated increasing supercharge at lower crank speeds by incorporating two and three-speed supercharger driving gear ratios, and by the simpler alternative of applying variable inlet swirl to the supercharger, to be known as vortex throttling…

"By October 1946, we were visiting RM and PB in Bourne and also meeting and corresponding with Harry Mundy whom we thought of as chief designer. A number of supercharger design features were resolved in a meeting at Bourne on December 4, 1946, including the principle of vortex throttling which was a vital part of the proposed supercharger specification. These proposals had been approved by E, and by February 1947 he had agreed to sanction additional design effort on the supercharger under my direction. It was clear by then that Rolls-Royce had agreed to fund the supercharger's design and development, which meant that Lord Hives – 'Hs' to us – had given his approval."

By the end of April they had completed design of the supercharger with automatically-operated vortex throttle, and design of its gear drive which incorporated a flexible torque driveshaft from the engine crankshaft, and a slipper clutch. These drawings were despatched to RM on May 2, 1947 with separate notes to Mundy and Richter. By the end of

V16 – THE DESIGN CONCEPT

It has not been possible to unravel, satisfactorily, the various strands involved in the original design concept for the V16 BRM engine. However, Laurence Pomeroy essentially set down PB's thought processes, no doubt coloured by his own ideals and tempered by Eric Richter's input, as follows:

Engine power is determined by piston speed, piston area and mean gas pressures acting upon the piston – and piston speed was for practical purposes limited to below 4,000ft/min. Assuming that mechanical and volumetric efficiencies be maintained, mean gas pressure would be proportional to the manifold pressure applied. This left the proposition that for a given design, power output became proportionate to piston area and manifold pressure.

Since piston stroke was limited by the restriction on piston speed, it followed that maximum piston area within a proscribed cylinder volume could only be achieved either by adopting a very large bore and very short stroke, or by multiplying the number of cylinders. The search for piston area and power within a capacity ceiling so confined as 1,500cc then led inevitably to multiple cylinders and high rotational speeds offered by a short-stroke crankshaft. Several V16-cylinder engines had been produced and had run successfully before the war, most notably the Porsche *Buro*-designed Auto Union of 1934–37. For the 3-litre Formula of 1938–40, Wifredo Ricart had produced a 135-degree V16 for Alfa Romeo, with the typically Alfa Romeo feature of having its crankshaft divided centrally by a spur gear inserted between Nos. 4 and 5 crank webs. This provided a power take-off to drive the camshafts and also engaged with a separate spur beneath it which then drove a long torsion shaft at half crankshaft speed which was coupled to the clutch, and thence through the driveline to the rear wheels.

This system avoided problems of torsional vibration over a wide range of engine speeds, and although never properly developed this Italian V16 allegedly produced as much as 500bhp at a heady 9,000rpm, on only 22lbs' boost. ADL's V16 would now mirror this basic layout.

To supply the volume of air demanded by a 1,500cc V16 running perhaps to 12,000rpm (or more) would require two Roots-type superchargers in series, the first perhaps 10 inches long, and even this formidable installation problem would produce no more than 25lbs – or 2.7ata – boost.

Vane-type blowers, it was reasoned, could efficiently supply boost at up to 35lbs – or 3.3ata – but with a limit of around 5,000rpm they would have to be geared down to 0.4-times crankshaft speed. This would then demand two such blowers, each measuring perhaps 10in by 10in and so creating another formidable installation problem.

By comparison, a centrifugal blower of the type used in Rolls-Royce aero engines could provide very high pressure boost from an extremely compact and lightweight package. Prewar experience had shown that this type of supercharging, in which delivery pressure falls off very rapidly with reduced speed, was perfectly suited to flat-out constant-speed racing as on the American speedways, but was hopeless for road racing, in which engine revs rose and fell constantly over a very broad band, and where mid-range punch away from slow corners could be a decisive factor. In fact those really in the know about compressors knew that the way ahead was with the axial type. Rolls-Royce could have provided one for BRM – at vast expense – but they would never be asked, and so the 'cheaper' solution would be offered and accepted.

'Pom' quoted a typical boost curve for a centrifugal supercharger showing, say, 27lbs boost at 8,000rpm, which then fell abruptly to only 13lbs at 5,000rpm and absolute zero at 4,000rpm. Conversely then, its output was rising from one atmosphere at 4,000rpm, through 1.85ata at 5,000rpm and then soaring to 2.8ata at 8,000rpm.

'Pom' wrote, and PB would have agreed:

The statement that a V16 engine offers the highest practicable power output from 1½-litres of engine capacity and that the use of centrifugal blowers is a considerable convenience from the viewpoint of maximum air delivery with minimum size and weight, may be taken as incontrovertible. The ability beneficially to use the power output available will depend upon the resistance represented by weight and frontal area, and the roadworthiness of the car...

Indeed – there's the rub.

July 1947, all detail drawings of the supercharger's main components and of its drive had been completed and despatched to ADL.

Five superchargers were ordered, to be made and built at Rolls-Royce. The first, with special drive parts for testing on R-R's No.1 300hp Test Plant, was ready by October 1948, and testing began there on December 15...which, as it happened, would prove to be a year to the day before the completed prototype BRM's public unveiling.

Long before that time, drawings for the major items, like the divided crankcase halves and cylinder heads, had been issued to sub-contract suppliers, the bulk of this draughting work having been completed by March 1947.

It was at this point that the fragmented project began to hiccup for Bourne's drawings had first to be approved by PB at Drayton Gardens, and he put them out for manufacture from there. Bourne maintained direct contact with the foundries on complex items like the crankcases and heads, but equally-vital components suffered early delays when the drawings went to London and stayed there – because Berthon was away...

Mortimer Engineering was losing money, and more of his time was committed to an attempt to save it. Then developed one of his all-conquering passions as his brother Paul – a wartime MTB skipper – took him sailing and PB was hooked by it.

He bought himself a 40ft Robert Clark cutter named *Ortac* after the channel between France and Alderney. It had been built in 1936 for Colonel C.F. King, father of Charles Spencer King of postwar Rover fame, and Berthon would sail her away for days and often weeks on end. In his absence, ADL project work was stalled, and although Mays understood his

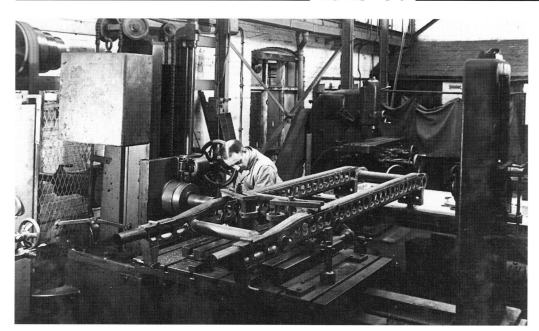

Rubery Owen's frame section at Darlaston fabricated the chassis-frames for the new V16 BRM Project 15. Here the prototype frame lies locked into its flatbed jig, upper and lower mainframe longerons already united by welded-on fletch plates, lightened and stiffened by those nicely formed swaged-edge holes.

independent-spirited friend's ways, their increasingly impatient backers did not…

Certainly the Rolls-Royce engineers had grave doubts. Geoffrey Wilde: "We knew little of PB's engineering background. When initially estimating performance of the 1½-litre engine we had appealed to him through RM for test data on racing engines. We received a power curve in October 1946 for a six-cylinder ERA engine [actually No.5018 from RM's 'R4D'] Zoller-supercharged to a maximum boost of 31lbs gauge at 7,500 crank rpm and 263bhp power. We wanted further information on such factors as blower hp, volumetric efficiency of the cylinders, mechanical losses etc – but nothing appeared that helped us in analyzing and predicting engine performance.

"We were rather surprised, because we had understood from RM that PB had been responsible for ERA's considerable successes prewar. Neither ever mentioned the late Murray Jamieson, and we only heard from another source that he had largely been responsible for developing the ERA engine…"

During their visits to Bourne, PB was "…often elusive, and it was virtually impossible to sit down with him to go methodically through our work". The Rolls-Royce men came to insist upon dealing with Harry in order to bring some order and proper date-targeting into the programme. Chief Draughtsman Frank May struck them as competent, but they had hardly any contact with Eric Richter who by this time had been shunted sideways into ADL contract design work.

They were surprised that PB "…never encouraged Harry Mundy to participate. In fact we discovered that none of the technical information which we gave to RM and/or PB ever reached HM, who by August 1948 was signing his letters 'Project and Development Engineer'. Consequently, we thought the engineering management of the project was unsatisfactory. It was not methodical. It was lacking in foresight, often in crisis and suffered poor team leadership. There is no doubt in my mind that this contributed significantly to unnecessary delays in the engine testing and development programme, particularly during 1949–1950…

"It did not help that this development work came increasingly under the spotlight of publicity. I fear that decisions made were sometimes the consequences of publicity-pressures, and were not in the best interests of engineering requirements…"

Clearly, there were yawning cracks in the BRM edifice.

THE WAYS OF INDUSTRY

Throughout this lengthy design period, Raymond Mays had been talking his head off in industry to drum-up support in money and kind.

Back in 1945 his original mailing list had purposely excluded established motor manufacturers, but once he had established a firm base he approached the man who had been so co-operative prewar – Sir John Black, head of the Standard Motor Company.

Black was an extrovert and extravagant character, but as a manic depressive was entirely victim to mood. He was a snappy dresser who operated in considerable style. When Ray visited his Coventry office, tea was served in cups monogrammed 'JB' in gold. RM was organizing a luncheon for his new backers in the Angel Hotel at Bourne and invited Black to attend. The day before the function Black telephoned to say he could not attend after all, but he was sending his deputy Alick Dick "…and he is going to hand you a cheque for £5,000…". He also offered to cast and machine many of the V16's major mechanical components without charge.

Many smaller cash donations flooded in, demonstrating widespread faith in RM as cheques were made payable to his personal account. Even before the end of 1946 he recalled being "quite alarmed by the dimensions the fund was reaching, and by the management the project began to demand."

Clockwise from right: Top end of the V16 engine showing the pairs of tandem heads for each bank, the rearward pair here united; note the hemispherical combustion chambers. Crankcase bottom half showing the output shaft spur-gear driven from the centre of the crankshaft, centrifugal water pump on the right-side flank. Prototype engine part-assembled, upper half comprising the 135-degree vee block. Almost complete V16 showing central camdrive gears. Fine engineering – not much was wrong mechanically with the BRM V16's bottom-end. Four V16 heads assembled in pairs with camshafts, magnetos and the cam-drive gear packs which would be re-used in the V8 programme. Gearbox assembly with casing cover to come. Two-piece crankshaft with its central power take-off gears, robust crankcase, tiny rods and Vandervell plain bearings.

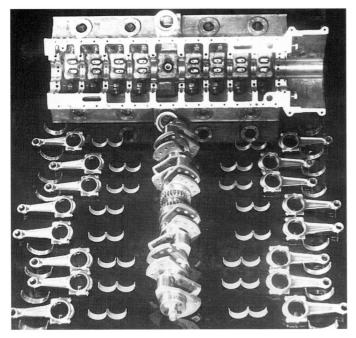

Assembly progressing in the Bourne build shop. Prototype No. I stands upon its road wheels, engine and gearbox installed, de Dion rear axle tube in its centre slide channel on rear of transaxle casing, prop-shaft to come – almost ready for George and Jack Gray's body panelling. The No. 2 frame is on trestles beyond the photographer's background board…

First public news of the project had broken at the start of March 1946, when a statement was released listing 22 industrial backers, ranging from the Aero Piston Ring Company to Tecalemit Ltd and including David Brown & Sons, Delaney-Gallay, Dunlop, ENV, Ferodo, Girling, High Duty Alloys, Lodge Plugs and Specialloid Ltd, all leading names in their respective fields.

The Autocar – clearly conscious of many prewar racers' somewhat 'arm's length' view of the Bourne duo – observed:

> The names of the firms are a guarantee that this is a serious enterprise, not merely the construction of a team to satisfy the sporting instincts of the few…

The Motor emphasized:

> No delivery date is promised, to quote a popular trade theme song, but…No single manufacturer in this country excepting Napiers and Sunbeams has ever made a GP winner; it will be exciting to see what the new syndicate can achieve.

Its piece ended with the far-sighted warning – perhaps since the author was well acquainted with PB's scheme:

> A possible danger, which must be guarded against, is over-elaboration, but Peter Berthon, who did the ERAs, will be on his guard against that…

So a complex consortium formed ranks behind RM's vision. Some formal structure became necessary, and on April 25, 1947, rules were adopted to form the 'British Motor Racing Research Trust'.

Rule Two declared loftily:

> The primary object of the Trust will be to promote, support and finance the development, production and

exploitation of new British racing cars by Raymond Mays, the racing motorist, with a view to obtaining information upon designs and materials from tests under racing conditions and to re-establishing and enhancing the prestige of Great Britain in the sphere of automobile engineering throughout the world (which said project is hereinafter called 'the Mays project').

Rule Seven stated:

> Ordinary members shall be persons, firms and bodies corporate who have a) subscribed or promised to subscribe to the funds of the Trust an amount of not less than £100 and b) indicated in writing their desire to be members, and in addition Raymond Mays and Peter Berthon. Ordinary members other than Raymond Mays and Peter Berthon shall be elected and may be removed by the Committee.

The Trust was to collect money and supervise its distribution to the separate manufacturing company of Automobile Developments Ltd, and to outside suppliers. By November 1947, Ray had collected a total of £20,297 in cash and had expended £15,025 on the project. On December 1 the balance of £5,316 was transferred to the Trust's account[15].

It is difficult for a modern readership (or authorship) to visualize the suffocating austerity of immediate postwar Britain. The country had effectively been bankrupted by six years of all-out war.

On July 26, 1945, Churchill's Conservative Party had been routed when a landslide General Election gave Clement Attlee's Labour Party an outright majority of 187 Parliamentary seats. They set out to build a brave new Britain. But in many ways, the rationing then applied was harsher than anything imposed during the war. Shortages of power and raw materials were exacerbated by that Arctic winter in 1947. An almost impenetrable bureaucracy controlled nearly everything as the Ministry of Supply wielded blanket control…and a very wet blanket at that.

Through its many influential sponsors, The Mays Project recruited help from Bob Henderson Tate, the MoS' National Controller for the North Midlands. He proved a good friend, and gained permission in his private capacity to join RM and PB on the board of ADL.

Through him, the ascetic Chancellor of the Exchequer, Sir Stafford Cripps[16], authorized the MoS to give priority material supply to the Project.

The Trust had begun operations officially on July 15, 1947, under the independent Chairmanship of public relations man Donald McCullough, well known at that time as question-master of the radio 'Brains Trust', while his brother Derek

15. **Again as a rough comparative guide, this total represents a 1993 value of about £370,000 collected, of which over £274,000 had been expended.**

16. **Cripps had been one of the first politicians to appear 'live' on BBC Television, when the tense dinner-jacketed announcer, awed by his stuffy reputation, solemnly introduced him as "The Right Honourable Sir Stifford Crapps…".**

No. 1 frame under assembly, on its wheels at last, transaxle and rear prop-shaft section in situ, de Dion tube in its central slide channel – the ill-fated pot-joint output shafts are within the cylindrical covers each side of the transaxle output. Note simple linkage picking-up bottom end of the tiny Lockheed air strut (foreground), short gearchange with the Mollart joints recalled by Ken Richardson, Porsche-type trailing-arm front suspension and steering arms.

Above: The No. 1 prototype under assembly on the ground floor of the Maltings extension, beneath the engine shop. Below: Hefty radiator and woefully flexible steering during installation with the first riveted heavy-gauge scuttle tank already saddled-up amidships. On the left of the picture, the three-leading-shoe Girling drum brake mechanism has already been fitted.

performed less formally as 'Uncle Mac' on the BBC's Children's Hour radio programmes. Donald McCullough was a motor racing enthusiast whom RM had met at a series of wartime functions. His after-dinner speeches were always lively and "…he knew all about publicity". He was dedicatedly, unquestioningly, patriotic – King, Country and Empire meant the world to him; he was perfect for the role as conceived and promoted by Mays.

Other Committee members were far more hard-headed, though faith and patriotism similarly figured high for differing objectives from man to man. Alfred Owen was there, alongside Bernard Scott, David Brown, Denis Flather of the Sheffield steel company – ensuring supplies of metal stock – Percy Bilton of Vigzol Oil, Captain J.C. Hopcraft of British Wire, R. Salter-Bache of Geo. Salter & Co, A.C. Burdon of Automotive Products and last (but formidably not least), G.A. 'Tony' Vandervell, Chairman of Vandervell Products, manufacturer of *ThinWall* plain shell bearings.

Early in December, details of the British Motor Racing Research Trust were released to the public in a London press reception. It was announced for the first time that their car was to be called the 'British Racing Motor', or 'BRM' for short.

The Autocar devoted three pages to this sensational story, describing the BRM as a national racing car despite emphasizing that:

> …the necessary finance has not been supplied by the Government but by various firms interested either in

the manufacture of cars or in components for cars…but whether or not the cars technically form a national team or not is of small importance as they will inevitably be regarded as the British racing team and a fair sample of what we can do from the engineering point of view…

They added this warning:

It is important to remember that…the organisation behind the team must be the best we can obtain. Many moments will come when the temptation to skip one or two phases in order to show the world that the work is proceeding will be exceedingly difficult to resist, just as when the cars are completed they should not race until they have been thoroughly tested, despite any opposition which might arise to this idea. A worse debut than that of the Arsenal[17] cannot be imagined…

Even the writer of that prophetic sentence could not have imagined what would, three years later, become gruesome reality.

A MATTER OF TRUST

By the end of 1947, it was already nine months since the first BRM drawings had been put out for manufacture, yet precious few parts had been delivered.

Free BRM work demanded valuable time in industrial toolrooms heavily committed to money-making production. Government was urging British industry to "export or die", despite crippling shortages of raw material, plant and skilled labour. ADL could hardly make a move without painstaking clearance through red tape – *nothing* was easy, and as weeks turned into months inflation meant every pound which had been donated bought less…

RM and the Trust's Finance Committee were continually scraping the barrel for more money. Ray was beginning to realize: "…I had a tiger by the tail…"

Not even their best friends would describe either Ray or Peter Berthon as a good industrial manager. Neither was suited to industrial disciplines by either training or temperament. When they conceived the project, they had given hardly any serious thought to costing it properly, nor of calculating how long design and development might realistically take. Neither, of course, for one single moment had there been any thought of trimming the design to match available finance. And, of course, there was no question of either of them trimming his own life-style to accommodate ever-intensifying demands upon his time.

In their defence, it was difficult to plan anything properly in the austerity of postwar Britain.

By the nature of the supporting Trust, few of their hugely more experienced backers could take a decisive role without estranging his peers. Each of these industrialists was used to

snapping his fingers within his own organization to make things happen. But here they had to trim opinions and ideas to suit the general consensus, and long periods between Trust meetings left the project adrift. Any sensible individual might just have admitted it was impossible and called the whole thing off. But at this stage nobody suggested they should.

So Ray maintained his prewar life-style, setting off from Bourne nearly every Friday either for a race or hill-climb with 'R4D' or for some assignation in London, dinner, a West End show…back Monday lunchtime, or evening. And PB, of course, was completely a law unto himself.

Ray's backers would certainly have brooked no such behaviour within their own empires. But here they all seemed mesmerized by his glamour and by the picture he continually painted of dedicated motor racing specialists working all hours towards their mystical and patriotic goal. Alfred Owen in particular maintained an almost unswerving faith in RM and PB and he provided a constant – though often constructively critical – bastion on which the entire project leaned.

Tony Vandervell, however, was a far tougher nut. He had first had dealings with RM in 1939 before his *ThinWall* bearings had been tested seriously in a racing engine. Ray had asked PB to make new rods for 'R4D''s 1½ and 2-litre engines to accept *ThinWall* bearings, while GAV – as Mr Vandervell was known within his own empire – donated £500 towards expenses on condition that Ray's Dodge van carried large 'ThinWall bearings' advertisements.

The experiment succeeded, so when approached postwar to join the Mays Project, GAV could hardly refuse, for he loved exciting engines and few promised more excitement than a centrifugally-supercharged 400-horsepower V16!

But he rapidly lost patience. The Trust had set up several committees to co-ordinate affairs with ADL. Owen and his material controller, W.J. Oldham, formed the Production Committee. Vandervell chaired the Finance and Planning Committee with RM and PB, while Cyril Mann of Power Flexible Tubing chaired the extraordinary Publicity Committee which included 24 member PROs from supporting firms. This hefty bias towards publicity rather than production became most evident…

As early as January 1948 – as the British railway network was nationalized – GAV was suspicious about Bourne's lack of visible progress. His financial man, Bill Robins, met P. Derek Warren of Goodman, Brown & Warren, Solicitors, of 30 John Street, Bedford Row, London WC1 – the Trust's legal advisors. Robins complained that the position had altered since the original agreement in three major respects.

Firstly, work was well behind schedule – BRM should have begun racing in the 1948 season but no chance survived of doing so. Costs had greatly inflated, and the demands upon free machining and gifts in kind had been greater than expected. GAV was particularly upset by the expense incurred in building Bourne's lavish new engine Test House even though it was being underwritten by Standard and Heenan & Froude.

He wanted the agreement with ADL tightened so that exploitation of the car should be controlled entirely by the Trust and in the event of a premature termination, the car should become the Trust's property and not ADL's, as agreed.

Otherwise GAV foresaw ADL breaking the agreement just

17. **The French Government-sponsored CTA-Arsenal broke its transmission on the startline when driver Raymond Sommer popped the clutch in that year's French GP at Lyons-Parilly.**

THE BMRRT SUBSCRIBERS

Into 1949 the list of subscribers supporting the British Motor Racing Research Trust's BRM project numbered no fewer than 124 including many of the best-known names amongst the British motor component and manufacturing industry plus many far more obscure concerns, the occasional motor club and a few enthusiastic individuals. The full list is as follows:

Abwood Tool & Engineering Co Ltd, Accles & Pollock Ltd, Aeroplane & Motor Aluminium Castings Ltd, Geo. H. Alexander Machinery Ltd, Alford & Alder (Engineers) Ltd, Edgar Allen and Co Ltd, Amal Limited, Andre Rubber Co Ltd, Messrs G. Angus & Co Ltd, James Archdale & Co Ltd, Austin Motors Ltd, Automotive Products Ltd.

Jack Barclay Ltd, T.M. Birkett & Sons Ltd, Birmingham Aluminium Casting (1903) Co Ltd, Thos. Bolton & Sons Ltd, Messrs James Booth & Co Ltd, James Briggs & Sons, British Belting & Asbestos Ltd, The British Piston Ring Co Ltd, The British Thermostat Co Ltd, British Wire Products Ltd, J. Brockhouse & Co Ltd, Brooke Tool Manufacturing Co Ltd, Brown Bros (Aircraft) Ltd, David Brown & Sons Ltd, Brown & Co Ltd (Colombo), Burgess Products Ltd, Burman & Sons Ltd.

Cambridge Instrument Co Ltd, Camelinat & Co Ltd, Capper Pass & Son Ltd, Carrier Engineering Co Ltd, Chloride Electrical Storage Co Ltd, Chas. Churchill & Co Ltd, Clifford Towers Temple & Co Ltd, Connolly Bros (Curriers) Ltd, Cooper & Co (Birmingham) Ltd, Cooper's Mechanical Joints Ltd, Coventry Gauge & Tool Co Ltd, Coventry Precision Engineering Co Ltd, Crypton Equipment Ltd, Messrs W.B. Cull & Sons Ltd.

Daley Bros, Delaney Gallay Ltd, Messrs Daniel Doncaster & Sons Ltd, Dowty Equipment Ltd, Ductile Steels Ltd, Dunlop Rubber Co Ltd.

Effingham Steel Works Ltd, Electro-Hydraulics Ltd, English Steel Corporation Ltd, ENV Engineering Co Ltd, Equipment & Engineering Co Ltd.

Fairman Precision Ltd, Ferodo Ltd, Messrs Thos. & John Brown Firth & Co Ltd, Fischer Bearings Ltd, Messrs W.T. Flather & Co Ltd, Ford Motor Co Ltd.

Messrs John Garrington & Sons Ltd, Girlings Ltd, Guest Keen & Nettlefolds Ltd.

Messrs J.J. Habershon & Sons Ltd, Hall & Pickles Ltd, Hampton & Beebee Ltd, Hardy-Spicer & Co Ltd, Messrs T.S. Harrison & Sons, Mrs M.A. Hassid, Heenan & Froude Ltd, High Duty Alloys Ltd, Holt & Mosedale Ltd.

Jenks Bros.

Messrs Richard Klinger Ltd.

The Lace Web Spring Co, Messrs Arthur Lee & Sons Ltd, Messrs F.H. Lloyd & Co Ltd, Lodge Plugs Ltd, Messrs Jos. Lucas Ltd, Messrs John Lund Ltd.

W.J. Mariner & Co Ltd, Marples & Beasley Ltd, Measham Car Sales Organisation, Mettoy Co Ltd, Mining & Chemical Products Ltd, Mollart Engineering Co Ltd, John Morgan Esq, Motor Components (Birmingham) Ltd, Motor Panels (Coventry) Ltd, Moy, Davis, Smith, Vandervell & Co Ltd.

D. Napier & Sons Ltd, Natal Motor Cycle & Car Club, National Standard Co Ltd.

Pinchin, Johnson & Associates Ltd, Poplars Manufacturing Co, Power Flexible Tubing Co Ltd, Pyrene Ltd.

Remax Ltd, Rubery Owen & Co Ltd.

Messrs Geo. Salter & Co Ltd, Messrs Jos. Sankey & Sons Ltd, Sheffield Forge & Rolling Mills Co, R.T. Shelley Ltd, Silentbloc Ltd, Slack & Parr Ltd, Frederick Smith & Co, Smiths Motor Accessories Ltd, Specialloid Ltd, Standard Motor Co Ltd, Standard Valves Ltd, Super Oils & Gaskets Ltd.

Tecalemit Ltd, Tube Investments Ltd, Tufnol Ltd.

United Wire Works Ltd.

Vandervell Products Ltd, Vigzol Oil Refining Co Ltd, Vokes Ltd.

Ward & Gladstone Ltd, Welding Technical Services Ltd, Messrs H. Wiggin & Co Ltd, Wilson Kyle Ltd, Messrs Jonas Woodhead & Sons Ltd.

Yorkshire Copper Works Ltd.

Each published listing of such supporters concluded with the following paragraph:

"In addition to the above Rolls-Royce Ltd are giving their invaluable co-operation regarding engine technique and the application of aero engine development that has taken place during the last world war."

---

to end it; and providing all subscriptions were then repaid, it would own the cars.

He could not accept that PB was working only part-time on the BRM project. Yet perversely this did not prevent him then demanding some of Berthon's time by awarding ADL another racing engine contract, this time for a motorcycle.

GAV was a director of Norton, whose famously pig-headed Chief Engineer, the Ulsterman Joe Craig, had achieved enormous success with his single-cylinder engine and saw no need to replace it. His Managing Director, Gilbert Smith, was more imaginative and he adopted GAV's suggestion to approach Berthon and ADL.

Typically, PB vacillated through much of 1948 before an agreement was finally reached between Norton Motors Ltd and ADL for design of a water-cooled four-cylinder racing motorcycle engine based upon V16 experience "...to be capable of winning international road races". In part-return, Norton's subsidiary R.T. Shelley Ltd was to pay £750 annually to the Trust for three years to aid BRM research.

Into 1949, Gilbert Smith would complain that no drawings had yet emerged from Bourne, even though – according to

ADL's time-sheets – Eric Richter during January that year spent 160 hours on the Norton engine scheme and his colleague John Botterill "20hrs on BRM and 148hrs scheming frame and rear suspension for motorcycle".

That same month, Draughtsman Astley (boy) spent: "...143hrs on BRM prints and office routine work; Marshall 122½hrs on tool and jig design for BRM; Stokes 116hrs on details of gearbox and engine test house, 52hrs on design of side-shift for Electro-Hydraulics Ltd; Woods 60hrs on engine test house and 108hrs on design of side-shift and rotating head mechanism for E-H Ltd..."

While its industrial backers were slow to deliver BRM components, ADL Ltd was earning its keep in the real world.

Electro-Hydraulics Ltd of Warrington was making suspensions for the BRM, and on November 15, 1948, a letter graphically illustrating problems all too prevalent amongst supporting companies was written by C.W. Sharp, E-H Ltd's Managing Director, to Alfred Owen as Chairman of the Production Committee:

Machining components for the car is interfering

The BRM five-speed transaxle was lifted from the Mercedes-Benz W165 V8 Voiturette design of 1939. This is a front-on view of the prototype unit ready for closure, power input from the prop-shaft at right, gearchange input at left.

with our aircraft work and after investigation today in regard to delays on Hermes, Prince and Sealand equipment I find we cannot tackle any more of this BRM work for some months... Incidentally we have already spent more than the £1,500 budgeted as our contribution to this venture...

On February 1, 1949 – the day that clothes rationing ended in Britain – Sharp reported that his company's expenditure on BRM had reached £2,942. He proposed to write-off the £1,442 overspent, but his situation was typical of The Mays Project through the late 1940s, and this was largely due to monetary inflation.

Another inherent feature created further delay.

While Aeroplane & Motor Aluminium Castings cast major components, and Standard Motors machined them, some items proved to be porous due to inexperienced designers and the problems of a small production run which would be sorted out by a second batch. Porous items like crankcase lower halves then had to go to Industrial Impregnations Ltd for processing, which then moved on to Bourne for testing, then away again to David Brown for surface grinding, and then back to Standard for machining! This included line-boring the main bearings, skimming top joint and water jacket facings, skirt cleaning, machining all oil gallery orifices, and extensive drilling and tapping of necessary bolt and stud holes.

This process alone occupied as much as three weeks of Standard's time against one week anticipated. Even then the crankcase had to go to Vandervell's in Acton for further operations before ultimately returning to Bourne for final assembly. In fact Bourne's own machine shop could machine

and line-bore accurately enough, and did so in later years.

In an unpublished memoir on the V16's birth, Peter Berthon cited seven types of machine forgings, each ordered with drawing between July and December 1947. The completed parts did not appear at Bourne until April 1948-January 1949, order to delivery thus taking from seven to 16 months. On non-ferrous components, citing three parts all ordered with drawing in September 1947, deliveries were not made until October 1948 at the earliest, May 1949 at the latest, delaying assembly from 13 to 20 months.

Some 350 companies throughout Britain were working on BRM components, and once Rolls-Royce finalized their supercharger design, it alone comprised 124 parts, many of which were sub-contracted through ADL at Bourne to 24 outside contractors. Once completed, they all had to be delivered to Derby for testing and assembly before the finished blowers could be delivered to Bourne to be mounted on the engines.

Not all these moves were justified on pure engineering grounds. Several contributing firms merely needed to be able to say: "We did that for the BRM."

A major industrial concern such as Rolls-Royce could have made much more of the car in-house. As it was, PB had some justification in observing querulously: "Some castings and forgings of the highest importance did not come into our hands until April or May of 1949. In these circumstances the fact that we were able to put an engine on the test-bed in June 1949 and show the motor car running to the world's press in December of the same year may not appear entirely without credit..."

Meanwhile, Alfred Owen soon twigged that ADL needed management and accountancy help. He seconded a Rubery Owen production engineer named J.K. Mason to manage the Bourne workshops, supported by weekly visits from the formidable W.J. Oldham, his Materials Controller, and also an equally rugged progress chaser, T.R.S. Lloyd. In the spring of 1948 he had already put in James Sandercombe to oversee production and keep the books in some semblance of order. 'Sandy', ex-Army, was a devout Christian who would serve as BRM's administrator, and later Company Secretary, far into the 1970s.

New offers of support still arrived, and when offers clashed, PB was cajoled into finding some way of using them. One example was a steel manufacturer, Oldham pressing PB to use their strip steel "for small brackets or straps etc..." just so they could advertise an association with "the BRM".

Despite all the problems and strife beneath the surface, and some entrenched cynicism from motor racing's hard-core RM/PB 'antis', the public at large believed in The Great Work. Many small firms wanted to ride on the bandwagon. The publicity machine was rolling well, to great – and increasingly dangerous – effect...

TROUBLE AT T'MILL 1948–49

Initially, the Trust had budgeted £50,000 expenditure over five years, including final tests and racing. As delays stretched and costs increased, that money was spread thin. Harry Mundy: "...sometimes we'd get a pay cheque from Raymond

Rolls-Royce's supercharger for the BRM was a work of art and fine science, which proved to be one of the project's successes. Above: Drive side with the input quill shaft at bottom. Above right: Intake side showing the inlet swirl vanes within and centrifugal whorl casing beyond. The 'dreadlock beads' are R&D pressure taps for testing only.

The prototoype two-stage centrifugal supercharger on Rolls-Royce's test rig, pressure taps and measuring devices festooned everywhere...

Mays' No. 2 account, then one from Peter Berthon's No. 3 account, then the next one from Ray again, only this time he'd say: 'Harry, my dear fellow, don't cash that for a while…'"

As parts deliveries accelerated, so alarming assembly problems emerged. On February 7, 1949, Jim Sandercombe reported to Alfred Owen:

> It is now apparent that the engine output shaft between the duplex gear and the clutch cannot be finally assembled until the clutch assembly is received from Borg & Beck, because the flange of the output shaft must be line-reamed to accommodate the bolt holes from the clutch back-plate…

He observed: "…I am afraid cases like this, unforeseen snags in the sequence of assembly, will frequently be encountered by us because we have not been 'in' since the beginning of the project. Those who have seem reluctant to divulge their knowledge in some instances…" That same day Ken Richardson was put in temporary charge of the engine shop "…and he seems to display that drive and technical ability which is so desirable here now", reported Sandy. He added that poor Mason was still troubled by boils which "naturally impair his efficiency" and (revealingly): "…the liquid air delivered last week for the inserting of the valve seats has now boiled away, unused. Mr Berthon has expressed a desire to be present when the first seats are put in their heads…" and of course he had been absent.

Another minor panic, creating much paperwork, occurred soon after when the time came to assemble the prototype engine's valvegear. *Nobody at ADL Bourne had a valve-spring compressor!*

The uncompromising Tony Vandervell was by this time beside himself. More than two years had passed since he'd joined the project, and still no car to see, nothing to race, not even an engine running in that expensive new Test House.

He decided it was time to run the project himself. If his fellow Trustees refused to make changes he threatened to resign and to withdraw his company's support.

Typically, when I pressed Ray on the subject the most he would gentlemanly admit to was "Vandervell always seemed to rub me up the wrong way…". GAV's opinion of RM and PB was fast declining, but not yet rock bottom. He simply felt they needed proper management, but he was increasingly suspicious about "…where's all the money going?"

Alfred Owen felt Vandervell's fears were exaggerated, and personally supported Mays. Following one notably stormy Committee meeting he expressed his startlingly bitter feelings to Don McCullough on February 14, 1949:

> Frankly, I was disappointed that our friend Vandervell did not stick to his guns and resign from the Finance Committee as he had promised, being so much out of sympathy with the efforts we have been making. It is not right or fair for a man holding position on the Finance Committee causing destruction to our efforts. He is one of the worst Fifth Columnists I have come across and frankly I never seem to know where I stand and neither do the committee…

By this time, the Trust had tried to discipline PB's determinedly free spirit. He responded bluntly that since their GP project contributed only a small proportion of his income, he owed it only a small proportion of his valuable time.

His BRM salary was only £500, though he and Ray both received £1,000 *pa* in expenses. The Trust admitted these arrangements were inadequate, but considered that since the cars should become RM's and PB's property upon the project's completion the deal balanced-out.

But Alfred Owen was harder than Vandervell suspected, and he insisted that both gentlemen should be tied down to ADL affairs. In February '49, he proposed that the agreement between the Trust and ADL should run for 10 years at the Trust's discretion and *only* should the Trust opt out would the cars, jigs and tools revert to RM and PB. Writing to Warren, the solicitor, he complained:

> Berthon never put in an appearance at all last week at Bourne and his absence caused considerable delays, contrary to the spirit of the arrangements that exist at the moment…I never expected to have to put a production man in fulltime at Bourne with weekly visits from Lloyd and Oldham and now to provide a financial advisor to get their books in order. I think that this has had to be done has caused the Trust to take a stronger line and that the agreement should only be broken at the discretion of the Trust…

That March, the new Test House bill was finalized at £7,000 against £6,000[18] quoted. Owen was furious: "No effort seems to have been made whatever to control the costs at all…Mr Berthon must take a considerable share of the responsibility for the expenditure exceeding so much the figure allowed for in the budget, without any sanction whatsoever." There was also that story that 'Mr Smith', the builder of the Test House whose bills the Trust paid, had actually been working for PB…

Oldham's regular 'spy' reports to Owen at this time often ended with such sarcastic – but illuminating – observations as "…I thought it as well that the matter should be brought to your notice knowing the propensity for over-optimism at Bourne".

Meanwhile, the hyper-active PR Committee's regular progress reports were being published widely in the press. Thousands of ordinary enthusiast readers followed them with eager anticipation – but of course they gave no clue to the turmoil behind the scenes.

There was, however, a growing tide of criticism for BRM's delays as 'the Continentals' like Alfa Romeo, Ferrari, Maserati and even Talbot-Lago were out there actually racing and winning while Britain's obsolete ERAs and inadequate Altas stood no chance.

March 1949 also saw the first V16 crankcase halves delayed at Vandervell's because they "…have run into unforeseen snags including the necessity to remove material from the inside walls of the crankcase to enable the crankshaft to

---

18. **These prices for the Test House correspond to 1993 values of over £115,000 charged, against only just over £98,500 quoted… Yet it was actually quite primitive by contemporary standards. We fear 'Mr Smith' made an excessive profit.**

Right: The famous BRM Test House at Bourne – financed by the Standard Motor Company – where the prototype V16 engine screamed its first and many subsequent builds coughed their last... The engine's front end, with supercharger, is to the right, output end on the Heenan & Froude brake amidships, the Ford donkey engine to motor the unit over is at the far left. The sound-proof window, right, is composed of transparent 'torpedo-glass' bricks.

Below: PB – an often charming man and an intuitive engineer whose capabilities many so-called 'experts' dismiss too readily; PB with the first V16 engine to be assembled. The four Lucas distributors were often troublesome. Pipes protruding beside the spark plugs are coolant intakes awaiting a water manifold when installed.

rotate...". Plainly, ADL's draughtsmen had not specified necessary dimensions to clear the crank, evidence of the DO's lack of experience, or ability...

In April the exasperated and often acid Oldham asked his boss "...to bring pressure to bear in the appropriate quarters allowing administrative and executive duties to be laid down at Bourne. I also had a chat on this matter with Berthon some weeks ago. His absence abroad and the propensity for procrastination which prevails means the matter is still in abeyance...in the absence from Bourne of Mays and Berthon there is no one individual in a position of real authority..."

When PB was there he found real problems, as he reported in detail on April 21:

> The crankshaft position is controlling the whole of our programme at the present time. The position is that through inaccuracies in the manufacture of the centre crankshaft gears (both David Brown and Coventry Gauge & Tool) together with the distortion of the half crankshafts during nitriding, plus a certain amount of bad lapping on the journals by English Steel, is preventing us from assembling a crankshaft with a runout on the main bearing journals of less .005/.006. This runout controls the cold clearance in the bearings and owing to the narrow width of the main bearing shells, we cannot hope to assemble and secure satisfactory lubrication results with more than .002 total cold clearance. Even this is excessive. English Steel are frightened of regrinding an assembled Crank as a whole, this being a difficult operation after nitriding and usually causing surface cracks. We have, in the past with E.R.A. crankshafts, always ground after nitriding without any

trouble [19] This work was carried out by Laystall...

...My feeling is that if we can secure one crankshaft that is reasonable and permits assembly and initial tests of the first engine, we then have time to take up the matter of re-grinding as a complete assembly for a second shaft with Laystall and English Steel...

Yours Sincerely,

At this time Ken Richardson, Jack Wylde, Charlie Davey and Dave Turner were completing a chain-driven ERA-engined ultra-lightweight sprint car for Ray, which he was intending to use as a competitive test-bed for such BRM items as the Lockheed suspension air struts. It should certainly have provided a great advance over the much larger and heavier 'R4D'. Ray had assured Oldham he would advise him of any components borrowed for this personal project, but Oldham exploded when he found the BRM's first special Borg & Beck clutch being fitted into it. A second set for the first BRM itself would be delayed for another four or five weeks.

Mundy in any case recalled how "...AP gave us an original clutch design the likes of which you have never seen – massive, huuuge, *tremendous*, like a bloody lorry clutch! We redesigned it as a small multi-plate thing and then sent the redesign back to AP. The Formula 1 clutches they use today [this conversation took place in 1979] aren't that far removed from our redesign for the V16..."

Vandervell now challenged ADL's accounts but as Alfred Owen wrote to McCullough "...we managed to find a way round". He ended that letter by confiding: "Whilst being fined in court for speeding I do not think this is as bad as it might have been..." The Rubery Owen chief might in many ways have been an austere man, but his remarkable energies were concealed behind a quietly spoken, gentle exterior, and they included a very real enthusiasm for motoring in earnest.

By this time the evident cracks in the whole facade were affecting morale at Bourne at precisely the time when the prototype was being slowly assembled and the entire works should have been electrified with excitement.

ADL's men largely regarded the Rubery Owen people with suspicion; Oldham and Lloyd in particular were "Owen's spies". In May 1949, Sandercombe was made Company Secretary, sharing financial responsibilities with RM to free Mason to run the workshops, but that unfortunate man was now under fire.

On May 2, Lloyd pulled no punches in reporting a whole litany of problems to Owen. In capital letters his communique listed:

(1) NOTHING CONCRETE HAS BEEN DONE REGARDING REORGANISATION AND CLARIFICATION

19. Rolls-Royce were absolutely right to refuse to grind a nitrided crankshaft. Rolls-Royce never did. It killed aircrew. The only way ERA had ever got away with it was because the piece cannot have been properly nitrided. PB's comment shows a regrettably limited knowledge and experience in metallurgy.

OF FUNCTIONS AGREED AT THE LAST TRUST MEETING...I am convinced that Mr. Mason is nowhere near up to the same standard as either Mundy or May; both these men know far more about the B.R.M., what is necessary and what has to be done, than Mr. Mason is capable of knowing.

(2) PROGRESS OF B.R.M. OVER THE LAST FEW WEEKS HAS BEEN VERY POOR....I feel there is a 'go slow' policy somewhere [the time] has been used to the advantage of the Sprint Car, the whole of the rear end for which has been completely assembled in the Fitting Shops and to the chassis frame over the last 2/3 weeks.

(3) THE FIRST CLUTCH I KNOW UNOFFICIALLY IS ALREADY AT BOURNE FOR THE SPRINT CAR...I feel we should insist that a clutch is now made available for the B.R.M. without further loss of time.

(4) THE PROMISE FROM DELANEY GALLEY FOR THE SUPPLY OF RADIATORS FOR THE CAR, i.e. TWO MONTHS, IS FAR FROM SATISFACTORY...

and more, much more...

A new man had joined ADL to become, briefly, chief mechanic. Phil Wilson was a tough, outspoken character experienced in wartime inspection. "I'd been posted to Enfield motorcycles in 1946, producing diesel gears etc for the Ministry of Supply. I got fed up, wrote to BRM and moved to Bourne. The first job I was given there was to fettle-up a propshaft UJ and by the time I'd finished it was sparkling and Peter Berthon said he'd never seen anything so good. I was eventually put in charge of building the first V16 with Dave Turner, but generally I wasn't impressed with the quality of the Bourne staff. They were just garage mechanics brought in to work on racing cars, and they didn't stand a chance..."

While the pugnacious GAV so exasperated and bewildered Owen, the tough bearings magnate merely wanted to start racing *NOW*. He argued that BRM personnel should gain experience despite the continuing delays to their own car, by racing another.

He was supplying *ThinWall* bearings to Ferrari in Italy, whose V12 cars were already out racing and winning with them. In January, Berthon's Ministry friend Everard Taylor persuaded the Board of Trade to re-issue an import licence on the unused old Mercedes-Benz permit.

Licence M/100397 was duly provided for Vandervell Products Ltd to acquire a Ferrari *Tipo 125* for "research into high-speed bearings for racing engines".

Ferrari's price was £4,360 until GAV admitted his intention to race the car, whereupon UK duty and purchase tax became payable because the original permit specified only testing and research. He was furious, but paid up regardless "to avoid any more messing about with Ministries...".

He then entered the Ferrari for the RAC British Grand Prix at Silverstone on May 14, 1949, paying the entry fee of £20. He christened the car the *ThinWall Special* to publicize his bearings, and named himself as reserve driver to Mays as number one. All British drivers were to receive £30 start money and the RAC organizers accepted this entry, despite objecting to the Special name. But they rejected Vandervell as reserve driver. Ray rated Ken Richardson's driving ability, so pressed his name as substitute, and the RAC accepted it instead.

The Ferrari was flown in from Italy, late of course, and once GAV settled the final bill of £5,430[20] with HM Customs the car was taken to Bourne for preparation and a coat of green paint.

Giulio Ramponi – a former Alfa Romeo and Scuderia Ferrari engineer who had become UK-based Racing Manager of Lodge Plugs – had helped Vandervell to arrange the Ferrari deal, and he was present at Bourne with detailed instructions to run the car.

Ray tested the Ferrari first on the wartime aerodrome at Folkingham, nine miles or so north of Bourne. He found its short wheelbase, V12 power and swing-axle rear suspension made it a vicious, twitchy beast. Phil Wilson recalls they found a problem in its oil system which was corrected – "…but after that they weren't going to change the oil filters, which…you do as a matter of course after a lubrication problem. Some of their people had no idea at all…"

May 14, 1949 – RAC British Grand Prix, Silverstone – 100 laps, approx 300 miles

The green Ferrari lapped Silverstone very slowly in official practice, Ray noticeably "flailing his arms less than usual". The car frankly frightened him and, already in his 50th year, he showed little relish for racing it. But he was under immense if tacit pressure from his Trust backers. He started way back on the fifth row of the grid and hardly featured on race day, though significantly now – with an estimated 120,000 crowd looking on – "fighting the wheel in corners far more than most". Eventually he handed over to Richardson who recalled that RM "…was pink round the gills, just scared stiff of that car", but within moments Ken himself had lost control and spun into the unprotected crowd at Abbey Curve – mildly injuring five spectators, including some of Napier's design staff. It was an inauspicious debut for – all bar the car – the BRM team, and particularly for Ken Richardson, would-be racing driver…

The battered Ferrari was subsequently stripped and inspected at Bourne, and its V12 engine run on the dyno. PB prepared a blunt technical report, which GAV sent on to bombard Mr Ferrari. PB described the car's performance as very disappointing, its power as totally inadequate, and he complained that its short wheelbase and weight distribution made it difficult to handle and its weight of 13cwt 40lbs – 1,496lbs – was too high. PB and GAV proposed extensive modifications before they would risk further bad publicity by running the car again. A longer-wheelbase chassis was proposed plus engine modifications.

The V12 engine was stripped at Acton, revealing that although it had run only 250 miles its gudgeon pins showed signs of seizing, galling and fretting due to running direct in the con-rods. GAV was irritated to find it was not fully equipped with his bearings, and he disliked both its lubrication system and the poor workmanship displayed by Ferrari's fitters. Its main bearing shells had been allowed too

20. This 1949 price relates to nearly £90,000 by 1993 values…

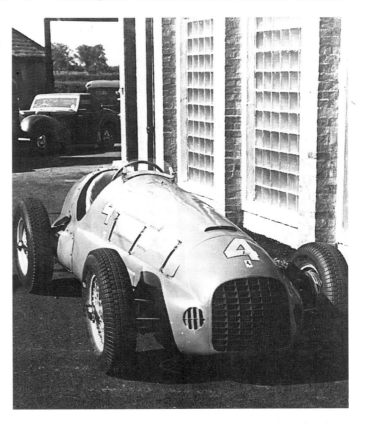

Vandervell's folly – the short-chassis Ferrari 125 which Tony Vandervell brought to Britain – and to the BRM equipe – for the 1949 British Grand Prix at Silverstone. Here it is at Bourne, ready to race, beside the new Test House. At Silverstone, officials would object to the jazzy number style, demanding white on black discs instead.

much clearance and its big-end bolts had been over-tightened 50 per cent.

He knew Ferrari was building a replacement four-cam two-stage supercharged V12 engine, and asked if he could have one. Ferrari eventually responded, saying how delighted he was with *ThinWall* bearings, listing his cars' many recent successes with them, and suggesting either that GAV return the unacceptable *Tipo 125* to Maranello for modification as requested or alternatively accept a replacement chassis. Eventually, at the end of the year, the unloved car was reassembled and returned to Modena by rail while GAV awaited its replacement.

On May 23, 1949, RM regretfully informed Owen: "The financial position of the Trust is now causing considerable anxiety. At date some £55,000 has been received and promises to the extent of £26,000 are outstanding. Present outgoings of ADL are some £400 per week…", its account was overdrawn by £700 or so. In response to an urgent telephone call the always-available Alfred Owen immediately provided £2,000 to satisfy ADL's hard-tried bank manager, Mr Appleyard, of the National Provincial Bank in Bourne.

At that time Phil Wilson and Dave Turner had just, at long last, finished assembly of the prototype V16 engine, Phil recalling: "The SU fuel injection planned for it wasn't ready so we cobbled it up instead with four small SU carburettors just to get it running."

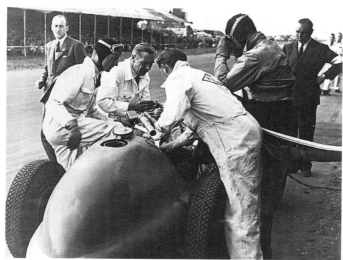

Dave Turner: "We had no assembly drawings for that first engine. The only drawings were machine drawings and nobody in the drawing office could help. But I'd built that many engines – been building 'em for years – it was more or less just common sense. Phil Wilson was pretty good but to me he seemed very slow. Peter Berthon used to call me his right-hand man for doing things quick…and the way it happened at BRM, that was most of the time…"

Eventually, Dave would build BRM's race-winning V16s, but Phil Wilson lapped-in each cylinder sealing ring "to two-tenths of a thou" by hand before assembly of these earliest prototypes, matching each one individually to its seating. Used rings were junked and never used twice. Through this early stage BRM had no problems of water leakage into the cylinders.

In fairness to both men it's probably true to say that Phil Wilson was used to toolmaker standards, Dave Turner was a garage mechanic. Both were good at their respective levels. Dave was malleable, Phil more abrasively self-confident. One fitted the BRM way of doing things – the other did not… One would survive some years there, the other would walk out in exasperation – and join Vandervell! Both were true to their own standards.

If there had been some development engineers with experience of high performance engines as well as designers, who came upon this dispute, they would have immediately recognized Wilson was right and many of the disastrous engine failures of 1950 and the first half of '51 would have been averted. They were due to the high cylinder pressures in the supercharged engine causing the joint rings to leak so that either all the coolant was blown out of the system or, worse, incompressible coolant leaked into the cylinder, the rod buckled, then broke and smashed the engine. Here, if the engineers had but known at the time, was the reason for many engine failures to follow.

When the first engine was at last ready to enter ADL's purpose-built Test House, The Mays Project was at long last approaching fruition – but Ray could hardly enjoy it. Though on the brink of fulfilment, The Mays Project actually faced disaster…

In the words of a report by Walter L. Hill of the Trust dated July 29, 1949:

> …Tuesday and Wednesday turned out to be very hectic and there is little doubt that the whole financial set-up is in the most parlous state.

The Trustees held an emergency meeting, agreeing to raise sufficient money to pay present accounts and overheads until the end of August, while the Finance Committee would chase promised but unpaid subscriptions. Alfred Owen promised another £1,500, Tony Vandervell, Denis Flather and Percy Bilton £500 each. The general consensus was that sufficient funds could be assembled to clear £15,000 outstanding debts and obtain subscriptions totalling at least £2,000 per month to complete the three years. The minutes added:

> It was emphasised that when racing commenced further additional commitments to the tune of £1,000 per car per race would be incurred but it was thought that racing successes would make it much easier to collect money and obtain influential subscribers.

> It was rumoured that a prominent oil company [Shell] was waiting for the Trust to go bust so that they could buy the pieces and finish and operate the cars as a Shell team.

On August 17 another meeting resolved to set up a Reorganization Committee including Owen, Flather, Vandervell, Bilton, Scott and Burdon, with full powers to act on behalf of the Trust. In Owen's absence on holiday, Vandervell was appointed Chairman with his man Robins as Secretary.

He went straight for the jugular, insisting Robins first prepare a Statement of Accounts up to July 31, 1949.

This revealed that ADL's creditors – including the emergency money advanced by Rubery Owen – totalled £15,141 18s 3d while creditors of the Trust itself amounted to £934 10s 4d. These ADL figures far exceeded those presented

to the Trust Committee, leaving around £10,000 to be found instead of £8,000[21] as previously reported. Since the Trust had very little guide as to how ADL was spending its money, Clifford Towers, Temple & Co, of 45/6 Bucklersbury, London, EC4 were instructed to make an immediate and thorough investigation, GAV undertaking to pay their fees.

The new Committee – dominated by Vandervell's forceful personality – then resolved to apply to the BoT to change ADL's name to 'BRM Limited'. Resignation of the existing board was to be demanded *en bloc*, to be replaced by the Trustees – Owen (absent, remember), Scott and Vandervell. A special Sub-Committee consisting of Scott, Vandervell and Robins was then appointed "to take immediate control of all expenditure and take such steps as they deem necessary to reduce expenses to an absolute minimum. In this respect Mr. Vandervell and Mr. Robins agreed to go to Bourne on Thursday night to review the position and they would stay there until joined by Mr. Scott on Saturday morning. Pending the appointment of a full time Manager of A.D.Ltd. Mr. Vandervell be appointed Managing Director…". He promptly drove to Bourne, where he grabbed effective control in what BRM old-hands recall today as "the Vandervell invasion".

Scott confronted Harry Mundy over his extra weekly expense payment, and stopped it. Even 30 years later Harry could still splutter at the memory: "That bastard Scott – I swore I'd get even with him!"

Ray telephoned Alfred Owen – the one man from whom he could always expect at least a fair hearing. Owen immediately interceded with Vandervell and insisted that while the Reorganization Committee was empowered to act drastically if necessary, he – Vandervell – on his own was *not* the Committee. Nothing should be done before further discussion by the full Trust board.

On September 5, Oldham warned Owen that: "You will be aware of certain jealous feelings against the unbiased efforts of yourself and your Company, if only insofar that we would be one of the biggest Creditors should there be a disaster, and I think this point annoys certain people who deliberately overlook the manner and spirit by which this has been brought about…I consider further procrastination by this latest Committee will intensify the seriousness in respect of outstanding Creditors, who may decide to take some drastic action which would have the result which I fear some people would welcome.

"As I see it, rightly or wrongly, you are likely to be placed in the position of calling for all the cards to be placed on the table and leading these stray members back to the Fold if the B.R.M. is to ever see the success for which we have all worked so hard…"

The auditors' investigation at Bourne reported – predictably – to GAV that ADL's book-keeping left much to be desired. Even a plumber's bill had gone unpaid for four

---

21. These figures correspond to 1993 values (£1 in 1949 = approx. £16.44 in 1993) as follows: ADL's creditors totalled £241,876; the Trust's £14,923; while what needed to be found amounted to some £159,700…not too horrific by modern standards but attitudes to credit and debt in the late 1940s were very different from those of the early 1990s. And after our experiences of the 1980s were the Trustees wrong in being so alarmed?

months while the sum involved passed through Raymond Mays & Partners, the garage business, before it had reached the plumber. PB was attacked for drawing £168 expenses "…in no way authorised…" for a trip to Italy:

> We think Mr. Berthon should be asked for a statement as to how this money was expended, more particularly as you [GAV] accompanied him on this trip, and inform us that you paid his fares and hotel expenses throughout…!

They also took exception to RM using a Dodge van which he had originally purchased with BRM sponsorship funds before transferring them, plus the van, to ADL. Since then he had continued to use the van in his racing activities with 'R4D' without paying ADL a penny for its running costs and 'hire'. This damaging report ended:

> We have been happy to assist you in your efforts with regard to this project as it interests us very much and, from the National point of view, has much to commend it. We will be equally happy to do anything further in our power to see this whole matter brought to a successful conclusion. We say this in spite of the opposition encountered by us in carrying out our original instructions, opposition, we feel, brought about by personal interests being placed far above those of the project.
>
> As a Trustee of this concern, receiving as it does large sums of money from a very wide 'public' you have a very clear duty to perform and this duty you must perform even if you are criticised for being pernicious.

PB's private company, Mortimer Engineering Ltd, closed down on August 26, 1949.

ADL's name was changed to BRM Limited, James Sandercombe becoming full-time Secretary at Bourne, saving the Trust professional fees. PB's position was reviewed "and it was considered that one of the weaknesses of the project administration up to date had been that Mr Berthon's services were only available on a part time basis." PB thereupon became a full-time "officer of the company" on a salary of £2,000 pa.

GAV's weekly expenditure limit on Bourne of only £50 was extended, while Bilton of Vigzol and Scott of Lucas promised £2,500 each supplemented by £2,000 from Burdon of Automotive Products. Owen paid off ADL debts of £2,500. Vandervell offered a similar sum "provided he was satisfied with the reconstruction proposals and provided the auditors' criticisms were dealt with to his satisfaction…".

By October 29, when ADL's board met at 15 Westbourne Road, Edgbaston, in Birmingham, they could at last begin to discuss motor racing…

RM, PB, Henderson Tate, Sutcliffe, Warren and Sandercombe were present, electing Burdon, Flather, Owen and Scott to the board of ADL/BRML. Ray resigned the Chairmanship to be replaced by Flather. Duties were assigned to each Director; PB taking charge of design and development, Mays of racing and PR, Henderson Tate Government liaison, Owen production, Burdon development, Flather finance and administration and Scott racing and PR with Ray. They voted to direct full effort to produce the first car with all possible speed.

To Mays' and Berthon's alarm by disregarding their advice, the meeting further resolved that the optimum date for the car's first test should be at Folkingham Aerodrome – which the Air Ministry had agreed to let them rent – no later than December 1, just five weeks hence.

Racing objectives were to be "First Car at Pau, on April 10th, 1950… As an alternative, Paris, on April 30th, 1950…and if possible, Silverstone, on May 13th, 1950".

Henderson Tate was applying to the Government for financial help. He was to take a Government official around the works at Bourne. PB suggested Folkingham be prepared for running tests, that the windows of the 'bungalows' there be repaired and the runways and perimeter track swept, also to carry out fencing required near the bungalows and to submit a cost estimate of the aerodrome buildings to be rented. At last Bourne's expenditure limit of £50 a week was released. While the Gray brothers had been building the body for the prototype car, Alfred Owen stated that he would ask Motor Panels (Coventry) Ltd to take on body-building for the second, free of charge.

After all the trouble and turmoil, a real V16-cylinder supercharged Grand Prix car was taking shape in the workshops at Bourne, and since early June the prototype engine had been running there in the Test House…

At last, at long, long last – 'The BRM' was almost a reality.

THE TESTING TIME

On June 9, 1949 the prototype BRM Type 15[22] engine had been motored-over and fired into life in the new, and costly, Test House at Bourne. Harry Mundy: "The first time the V16 fired the press were there even though it was well before the major press unveiling. Kay Petre was present in the Test House with Berthon and me and she wrote for the *Daily Graphic* at that time. We had the Ford V8 as a slave engine to motor it over and start it, and a freewheel arrangement in between which had to be disengaged as soon as the V16 fired. We had been motoring it over to check all the oil and water flows when Berthon decided to switch on the ignition and fire it up and we squirted it, just a *biiit*, and I know next morning – all euphoric – we went over and found the bloody ignition leads were all crossed over. That was the first time the BRM V16 ever fired. Perhaps it was an omen…"

On June 13 PB reported to Owen:

> The engine test is proceeding and I am endeavouring to press ahead with this work as fast as possible consistent with extreme care in order to avoid any unnecessary failure. Tests are being held up by many small preliminary details and minor troubles which constantly come to light. This is to be expected. As you know the engine is at the moment running in an unsupercharged condition and we are having a certain amount of difficulty with the distribution since the engine is of course designed for supercharged conditions. This being the first engine in the Test House

22. **Derived simply from "one-five", ie: 1.5 litres capacity.**

many small details in the fitting-up of the Test House are not quite right…

Aubrey Woods: "One of the first times the V16 ran it shattered the joints on the drive-shaft joining it to the Ford V8 slave motor and the shaft itself flew clean through one layer of glass bricks in the inner Test House wall, and lodged there in the cavity! If it had hit anyone on the way it would have taken his head off…In any case we'd had to tune-up that Ford engine quite a bit to make it man enough to motor the V16…"

PB's unpublished memoir recalled:

> The engine was first run on the bench unsuper-charged, with four downdraught carburettors, with a view to finding how it would behave mechanically. At this stage performance was irrelevant; the object was to raise the rpm progressively in easy stages, and watch the behaviour of valve gear, bearings, ignition, oil pumps etc… The supercharger was then added, and serious investigations were begun of valve and ignition timing and power output…

Mundy: "During bench tests one of the first things we found was that the valve rockers were just wearing out in 30 minutes or so! Richter was very clever here. By virtue of the geometry of the cams, when the rockers were closing the relative velocity between the rocker and the cam shot right up, although it was OK when it was opening. We had to redesign it and just put a finger rocker under the camshaft rather than the original which was on the side. That held us up again, as we had to have new camshafts made with revised lift. We found we had a cylinder liner problem due to differential expansion between steel liner and alloy block, but never any trouble at all with the bearings etc. Mechanically, it was pretty good from day one…"

On the Monday morning following the September board meeting at which the foundation of BRM Limited had been decided, Ray addressed the whole staff at Bourne to explain what was happening.

'Sandy' reported to Owen that in his view management control at Bourne was still insufficient, a proper chain of command had not been established but that "the drawing office however is virtually self-supporting and very efficiently run". Four days later Lloyd reported: "Everything has changed at Bourne, everybody is geed-up to get the first car completed." On October 11, Owen received a typically terse but incisive note from Vandervell:

> Dear Mr Owen, re British Motor Racing Research Trust…it is very encouraging to see that we now nearly share the same views.

By the end of that month, George Gray was finishing off the prototype car's body in the garages behind Eastgate House, shaping panels round the telegraph pole there. Three Rolls-Royce technicians were working until 11 at night to install the prototype engine's supercharger and finally decided that SU technicians would have to be brought in to balance the fuel pumps and carburettors to it. PB was still running his first

engine, gently, afraid it would break, but even so he was down to his last set of oil and water pump gears.

Phil Wilson: "On the four small SU carburettors and an unchanged 6:1 compression ready for supercharging I think it gave about 47 horsepower. When, later, the SU injection arrived I ended up fabricating about 17 alternative induction systems for various ideas. One day Scott of Lucas brought in some new distributors, saying: 'They're the best we've ever built' – and when we tested them they fell apart after 25 minutes…"

PB (in the winter of 1950–51): "Initially with the super-charger added there was no carburettor, and fuel was fed into the eye of the supercharger rotor by a metering pump of the type used on aircraft engines, responsive to rpm, boost and charge temperature. The fuel atomizing device in the supercharger inlet showed signs of requiring considerable investigation, so further running was done with two normal SU carburettors. These have been retained ever since as we have not had a test-bed engine available on which to complete this investigation…

"A lot of oil was thrown out of the crankcase breathers…There were two clues here, one that there was a lot of piston-ring blow-by, and the other that too much oil was being circulated. Wear and black marks on the cylinder bores further confirmed the former…and the original standard type of rings were changed for an improved design, with immediate improvement. The rate of oil circulation, and the oil pressure, were both reduced to much less than the original figures with no harmful effect at all, but with improved scavenging performance."

Dave Turner: "On carburettors we couldn't even-out its distribution at all, but once we got it running properly with its supercharger it was a wonderfully balanced engine. You could balance a sixpence on edge on it…"

Phil Wilson kept notes of the prototype BRM car's assembly in a soft-covered Challenge triplicate book. This flimsy record has survived.

It commences in July 1949 when Phil first drew components from the Bourne stores to build the second engine. On August 7 he wrote:

> Items required to complete assembly of 2nd Engine – Supercharger, S.U. Injection Pump, Clutch Housing, c/w withdrawal mechanism, Injection Units, Distributors & Coils, Induction System Type?, Rocker Covers to be fettled.
>
> [signed] P.H. Wilson

On September 9 parts were drawn to assemble "Engine No. 3. VE 3.". By the 19th Wilson was writing a memo to Mason listing outstanding items "…necessary to complete assembly of No.3 Engine for trial installation".

He recalled that when the car was *first* completed, its assembly had been so hurried that nobody could fit behind the steering wheel, apart from his own daughter who apparently became the first person actually to sit in the completed BRM V16's cockpit. It then had to be hastily rejigged to accommodate an adult male.

On November 16 and 21 Phil Wilson's notes describe "No.1 engine as fitted to chassis", and then on the night of November 28, 1949 the prototype car was finally assembled and ready to run...

Wilson couldn't stand Ken Richardson and Richardson couldn't stand Phil Wilson. Both were hard men; a pure case of diamond cut diamond. But when that first car was completed, it was apparently Ken Richardson who first drove it. It was late at night, a photographer had been cooling his heels all day and he finally rigged his floodlights outside the glass-brick windows of the Test House to 'shoot' this first BRM "...fresh from the oven".

It was around 11pm; Ken Richardson claims: "I was then pushed out through the gates onto the Spalding Road and we towed the car for a way, and fired it up. I drove it round the block, back down Eastgate and nipped into the yard again before the police arrived. That brought the lights on throughout the town. Funny thing was that amongst all the faces at the windows I recognized one in a bedroom he shouldn't have been in. Perhaps that was why he didn't complain!"

On November 29, 1949, Phil's notebook recorded as follows the BRM Type 15 car's first runs at Folkingham Aerodrome:

Fuel RR2. Oil SAE 30. Soft Water In Rad. Rear Struts 450lbs u. O/S Front Strut 420lbs u. N/S Front Strut 400lbs u.
   9 Laps Short Circuit.
   4 Laps Long Circuit.
1½ Gallons Oil after 3 Short Laps.
1 Gallon after 9 Laps.
Plugs mixed after 1st Change 47s removed & 51s fitted before Main Circuit used.
Tyre Pressures corrected to 25lbs Front 25lbs Rear Original Readings N.S. Front 28 OS 25.
N.S. Rear 25 OS 29.
Battery changed before car would run satisfactorily.

[signed] P.H. Wilson

'The BRM' was at last alive and running.

On December 3 the car was again taken up to Folkingham, started and ran briefly with Raymond Mays in its driving seat and Alfred Owen this time amongst the onlookers, thrilling to its V16 engine's shattering exhaust noise. On the 5th Owen wrote to Ray:

I should like to offer you my sincere congratulations on having thus far achieved the object on which you had set your heart...

After all they had been through, it was an emotional moment. That same day in London, Henderson Tate met Parliamentary Secretaries John Freeman and Jack Jones at the Ministry of Supply, reporting: "...both very interested in request for official assistance and being of the opinion that some should be granted. These were personal views..." followed the inevitable *caveat* of career politicians.

The following week Henderson Tate, accompanied by Sir

Bone of contention – PB's love of sailing became almost obsessional after he had purchased his Robert Clark cutter Ortac. While PB was absent afloat, BRM's design staff was too often left rudderless.

Archibald Brown and the Secretary to the Ministry, met Sir Stafford Cripps. No help was forthcoming...the BRM would never be Government-backed.

Meanwhile, once it had run, a Trust meeting decreed that it should be unveiled to the public at Folkingham on December 15. As Ray recalled: "Because we needed the public's support and backing and were financed by a large number of concerns all anxious to see the results of our work, we were forced to seek premature publicity. Manufacturers and the Trust were pressing us to show the car.

"Both Peter Berthon and I were dead against this public demonstration. We knew the car was not ready for showing, but it was understandable that other members of the Trust, who had after all put their own money into the project, wanted some tangible result for their efforts. There were fierce arguments; Peter and I lost them. We were overwhelmed and outnumbered by the less informed majority.

"Curiously enough, Alfred Owen was the only other member to see our point, although he was reluctant to put his weight too heavily on our side in case he should be thought, as a major contributor, to be forcing the issue...Donald McCullough, with a lifetime's experience of publicity and publicity methods, saw to it that we got a 'good press'. The

Hello, sailor – sorry, couldn't resist it: PB's younger brother Paul – a wartime MTB skipper – was blamed by BRM's men for having introduced their Chief Engineer to the nautical life. Here's Paul afloat with a particularly dapper RM.

16-cylinder BRM was hailed as a world-beater almost before the wheels had turned…"

PB was alarmed, writing to Bernard Scott on the 6th:

> On…the decision taken last week on publicising the BRM immediately I am rather upset that no consideration was given to the technical side. 1 – the bodywork is incomplete and unfinished and it will take us all our time working day and night to have this completed and painted and roughly finished for press photographs on Friday next. The paint is not promised until the end of next week so some interim colour may have to be used. 2 – arrangements we had made for brakes, suspension and steering tests will now have to be put off until after Friday, 15th December. 3 – the car will not be shown to specification as it is temporarily fitted with carburettors pending decisions on final mani-folding, type of fuel and calibration of injection pumps. I feel it would be the greatest mistake to forecast a programme for public issue or to make any intimation to the press as to when a car might appear…

His caution was wise and his recommendations justified,

but some involved at that time believe his and RM's fears were mainly "of being found out…".

Certainly some blame for the long delays attaches to them, but even so PB and RM were right to oppose premature public demonstration. As far back as 1947 Ray had warned of premature display, and had his backers referred to *The Autocar*'s original Trust story they would have seen how it warned against the temptation to skip stages in order to show the world that the work was proceeding.

The BRM's gestation had plainly taken far too long – yet its birth would still prove disastrously premature…

ENTER THE BRM

The BRM was unveiled to an invited audience at Folkingham Aerodrome on Thursday, December 15, 1949.

It was, by modern standards, a distinctly amateurish function, but these were austere times. It was held in a large, cold and draughty Maycrete hut beside Folkingham's control tower. Chairs had been arranged on three sides of a roped-off area around the prototype car, shrouded beneath a large parachute. The Trustees faced their guests from behind a top table, backed by a large Union Jack crudely pinned with engaging naivete to the hut's end wall…

For Raymond Mays and Peter Berthon this was a grotesque occasion. Ray had a raging temperature. Just for once his characteristic dowager-like protestation of being "not at all well" was perfectly genuine. And he was still mortified to see his creation's premature launch.

PB was acutely aware of the car's unreadiness, confiding as much to guests he knew. Yet for the general consumption of press, project subscribers and public at large, Donald McCullough introduced 'Britain's World-Beater' with a typical flourish, and to polite applause the mechanics pulled back the parachute to reveal the car's startling lines.

It was then wheeled out onto the airfield. RM squeezed into its confined cockpit, and the car was push-started, Ray blipping and whooping it away for a few demonstration laps. Of course the pale-green car with its skin-tight unlouvred bodyshell looked and sounded sensational…

Awe-struck newsmen excitedly telephoned their copy to Fleet Street, convinced that this magnificent new product of British genius would soon topple Alfa Romeo from Grand Prix dominance.

Richard Williams-Thompson was there for the BBC. His clipped, stilted wireless report on the Home Service the following week included… "Raymond Mays explained to me that Britain cannot afford to be left behind in the car racing world, and that through the medium of the BRM it will be possible for Britain to take her place in that world… In view of the initial success and outstanding promise of the scheme, I cannot see the Government refusing to support the Trust financially.

"Raymond Mays then had to leave me to go and demonstrate his car. The perimeter track of an aerodrome is not the best place to show off the capabilities of a racing car. Although Mays was not able to get out of second gear, he was able to drive it several times around the aerodrome at about

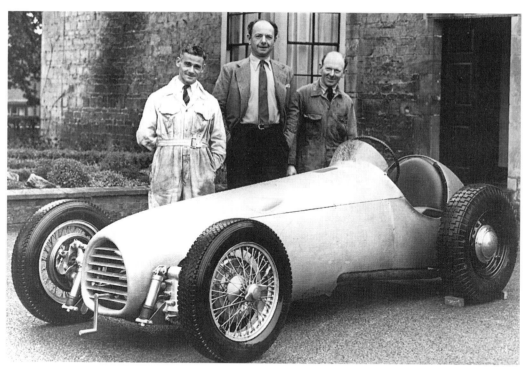

Left: RM outside Eastgate House with his two long faithful mechanics Jack Wylde and Charlie Davey, and the abortive ERA Special whose neat Gray brothers body had been part-shaped – like some of their early BRM panels – around a telegraph pole behind the House.

Below: The Eastgate House garages housed the ERA Special; assembly, the car featuring Lockheed air strut spring/damper units from the BRM programme with expensively cast chain-drive casings acting as rear suspension swinging arms. Note the massive Zoller vane-type supercharger between the driver's shins (bottom), spare casing on the workbench (below). BMRRT Trustees questioned how the car had been paid for, and by whom, but its uncontrollability on test was what killed it.

140 miles an hour. Everybody was most favourably impressed with the car as it flashed by. Though it is obviously too early to say finally what success the team of BRMs will have, I left the aerodrome feeling that at last Britain had got a British racing car which would sweep the board at future Grands Prix…"

The Autocar for December 16, 1949, observed judiciously:

> It is no secret that progress has been slower than originally hoped, but no one familiar with the frustrations and difficulties which accompany engineering work of the highest quality and precision in post-war Britain will be surprised at that. So far about £150,000 has been spent on the project in cash and kind, but during the whole period the purchasing power of the pound sterling has steadily declined[23] and it is clear that the contributions of existing members of the Trust need to be supplemented by new support if the cars are to be developed and operated on a scale necessary to make a full contribution to British prestige in international competition. The Government has shown a friendly interest in the project, but the money and effort have come from the voluntary contributions of companies and individuals…The real development work is just beginning…

23. In fact according to Whitehall figures, monetary inflation during the years 1946–49 diminished the value of £1 from the purchasing equivalent by 1993 values of £18.95 in '46 down to just £15.97 in '49 – a loss of nearly 16 per cent.

THE BRM TYPE 15 V16

When unveiled at Folkingham the BRM V16 possessed greater valve and piston area than any previous 1½-litre racing engine. Potentially, it could also reach higher rpm than anything previously attempted – the target as high as 14,500rpm. The declared intention was to race continuously between 7,000 and 10,000rpm, the engine peaking at around 12,000, at which it should have produced 400bhp.

Despite first running unsupercharged – only on carburettors – the plan was to supply the engine's huge appetite for air at such speeds via Rolls-Royce's centrifugal supercharger whose rotors would attain 40,000rpm.

The 135-degree V16 comprised effectively two 750cc V8s, mounted in tandem and separated amidships by an ancillary-drive train of spur gears. The upper crankcase half carried four individual four-cylinder blocks, each cast in RR50 aluminium alloy. Bore was only 49.53mm and stroke 48.26mm, providing a swept volume of 1,487.76cc. At 12,000rpm piston speed would be only 3,800ft/min. Since it was intended to maintain crankshaft speed above 6,000rpm a separate output shaft was located beneath the crankshaft and geared from it at half engine speed.

This shaft, with its duplex driving gears, was carried in a cast-magnesium lower crankcase half. These duplex gears also powered the front-mounted supercharger, a centrifugal water pump, and pressure and scavenge oil pumps on each side. The oil pumps could circulate up to 20 galls/min at 50psi.

The crankshaft itself ran in 10 main bearings. It was formed in two eight-cylinder halves, pulled together centrally by a differential-threaded bolt.

Once English Steel had begun to make the first crankshaft, some of their experts queried its balance. An outside consultant was then commissioned to calculate its torsional vibration characteristics. His name was Sydney Bailey. Like Harry Mundy he had been in the RAFVR, and during the war became a Squadron-Leader (Engineer) with Bomber Command, inevitably being nicknamed 'Bomber' Bailey by their aero engine suppliers.

Whenever the Command had identified engine problems, he had apparently forged the bullets which Air Chief-Marshal Harris then pumped mercilessly into Rolls-Royce, Napier and Bristol. So when the war ended there was a warm reception awaiting him in industry...

His wife, however, was a wonderful mathematician and they set up a crankshaft balance and stress consultancy for which he found the business while she did the calculations.

Where the BRM crankshaft was concerned, this problem was the first indication of Bourne's inadequacy in calculating dynamic crankshaft balance, but not the last, for such trials dogged them until 1962. At the time in question, the Bailey report triggered a Mark 2 design during 1949, which introduced two little flywheels each side of the central power take-off gear which drove the output shaft and all ancillaries. English Steel quoted several months delivery, so meantime a bolted-up Mark 1A hybrid shaft was made to get the V16 running. Bailey had reasoned that without the flywheel system, the two halves of the crank would oscillate and destroy that central gear train. Now, in practice, that gear train proved extremely reliable.

ThinWall main bearings were used, in bearing caps bolted laterally into the main bearing casting in addition to the usual vertical securing studs. Longitudinally, they were locked by round dowels.

Cylinder liners were in high-tensile cast iron. Each had a flange near its top end which bedded down onto the block as the four detachable cylinder heads were torqued down. The foot of each liner then compressed a Neoprene sealing ring to provide a water-tight lower joint.

The tiny aluminium pistons – about the size of a coffee cup – were machined from 'Y-alloy' forgings, while the tiny short-stroke con-rods were machined by Coventry Gauge & Tool from nickel-chrome steel. They again used *ThinWall* big-end bearings.

Each individual four-cylinder head was an RR53 aluminium-alloy casting, employing bridge clamps between the holding-down studs to distribute load between internally-cast struts bearing on the combustion chamber sections to minimize risk of head distortion. The chambers themselves were hemispherical with valves set at an included angle of 87½ degrees and seated on NMC inserts. On the exhaust side the valves were sodium-filled and the guides were in direct contact with cooling water.

Each cylinder bank was topped by twin overhead camshafts, which actuated the valves through steel rocking fingers, their clearances corrected by grinding half balls located between the rocker and valve stem during assembly. Double hairpin valve springs were used, and into late 1951 there was to be no recorded breakage despite valve gear tests running them up to 18,000rpm. Each camshaft ran in roller bearings, each pair being driven by a spur-gear train sub-assembled into an elegant light-alloy pack. Each pack could be withdrawn as a unit from the centre of the cylinder block.

Each front-half camshaft nose drove a specially-made three-contact Lucas distributor. The first contact broke the primary circuit, the second closed it again and the third – which could be switched-in manually – retarded the ignition for starting. Coil ignition had been chosen in view of the extreme engine speeds expected, ruling out magnetos since they allowed no time for magnetic flux to accumulate within the windings. There were four coils and current was provided by a small capacity – but physically heavy – Exide battery. One spark plug was centrally-placed in each combustion chamber – the V16 demanding 96,000 sparks per minute at peak revs...

Up front, Rolls-Royce's centrifugal supercharger was driven by a torsionally flexible shaft and a step-up spur gear train. The flexible shaft ran at 1.285 times crankshaft speed (a ratio of 27/21) which with the step-up gears provided an overall drive ratio of 3.25:1.

Geoff Wilde and Frank Allen subsequently compiled a detailed IME paper on their supercharger, presented in November 1964,[24] which describes in full their complex background researches, calculations and considerations.

While analyzing variation of power with engine speed, they calculated that if the centrifugal blower was geared to provide 34.5psi boost at 10,000rpm, the engine should develop 400bhp.

At 7,000rpm both boost pressure and power would fall to 22psi and only 220bhp respectively. Above 10,000rpm however, boost would soar to 65.5psi at 14,000rpm which would generate impossibly high cylinder pressures.

Such characteristics were typical of centrifugal supercharging – peak power at peak revs – which of course made such compressors eminently suitable for constant-speed use as in aircraft or American-style oval-track racing. Conversely, they were most unsuitable characteristics for road racing where acceleration and deceleration constantly alternate and a very broad rev range may be required.

To match the specified requirements of 400bhp at 10,000rpm, Wilde and Allen had decided upon full-throttle conditions of 41psi

24. Institution of Mechanical Engineers Paper Number AD P1/65.

boost from a supercharger pressure ratio of 2.8:1 and a rotational speed of 32,500rpm.

After years of intensive research into centrifugal supercharging for the wartime Merlin aero engine programme, the R-R men knew they could meet PB's conditions with a single-stage supercharger running at 70,000rpm. However, its impeller would have been only 4½ inches in diameter, which they considered too small for peak efficiency, while such high speeds would create mechanical problems with bearings, shaft seals and drive system. Neither would such a single-stage compressor offer much scope for future development.

So they chose instead a two-stage supercharger running at up to 45,500rpm (or 14,000 engine rpm) on that drive ratio of 3.25:1. The overall package would fit virtually into a 10-inch cube.

Its drive had to be flexible to withstand the sudden and rapid gear changes of a racing car being driven hard. The flexible drive torsion shaft provided a degree of cushioning, while a centrifugal clutch protected the supercharger gear and impellers from damage due to sudden changes in engine speed as in gear changes, backfires and mechanical failure.

To match the inherent characteristics of centrifugal supercharging to a road-racing engine, Wilde and Allen then proposed a system of 'vortex throttling'. This introduced an array of nine vanes into the supercharger intake, each of which could swivel about its individual vertical axis to vary swirl as air-fuel mixture passed by into the impeller stage. The swirl vanes were to be actuated by a servo piston controlled by boost pressure or engine speed. Below 9,000rpm these vanes would be set edge-on to the intake airflow to cause negligible pressure loss, but above 10,000rpm they would swivel progressively to swirl the incoming mixture in the same direction of rotation as the adjoining, fast-rotating impeller blades.

This would reduce the mixture's change of angular momentum through the impellers, and hence lower the temperature rise and pressure ratio achieved.

Ahead of these vanes was a normal throttle butterfly controlled by the driver, while further to enhance efficiency and response, fuel injection was specified into the eye of the supercharger, but PB felt he had enough development problems with the basic two-stage blower system and although an SU fuel injection and vortex throttle system was made it would never be raced. SU would instead design a special double-choke carburettor for the V16, which mounted on the supercharger nose. It created an intake pressure drop of around 1psi, consequently diminishing boost by 2½–3psi at 10,000rpm.

At the other end of the engine, the clutch, produced by Borg & Beck to ADL's redesign, was only 7½ inches in diameter despite having to transmit torque exceeding 400lbs.ft and running at 6,000rpm – both astronomical figures for the time.

It was a four-plate assembly with spring pressure augmented by centrifugal force on bob-weights attached to the operating fingers. Alternating with the steel driving plates were driven plates splined to the central output shaft and faced with Ferodo VG95 friction material secured by Redux cement and rivets. Both the head of the output shaft and the exterior casing had holes through which air was drawn over the interior. Interestingly this clutch was composed largely of standard parts. It weighed 29½lbs complete.

The engine and propeller shaft matched 1939 Mercedes-Benz practice in being set at a slight angle to the chassis centreline so that the prop-shaft passed between the driver's feet and then to the left of his seat to power a pair of bevel gears at the end of a five-speed gearbox-cum-final-drive unit set with its shafts

transverse across the rear frame. All its gears ran in constant mesh, and drive was taken off a pinion at the centre of the 'box to a large spur gear housing a ZF differential. The final-drive casing was cast in light-alloy. All gears were in case-hardened nickel-chrome steel and various ratios were available for the input bevels and final-drive gears to provide from 13mph to 17mph per 1,000rpm in top gear. With the highest available ratios top speeds through the gears were quoted as 95mph in 1st, 115mph in 2nd, 130mph in 3rd and 165mph in 4th. In suitable conditions top speed in 5th should have just topped 200mph...a magic mark for the Fleet Street pressmen.

A sliding-block or pot-type universal joint appeared on each side of the final-drive unit, carrying short half-shafts ending in Hooke-type universal joints inboard of the rear hub-carriers. The rear suspension was a de Dion type with these carriers linked by a tube passing behind the light-alloy final-drive casing and located laterally in its centre by a ball-pivoted block which slid vertically in a channel cast into that casing.

Fore-and-aft location (and brake reaction) was handled by a folded channel-section radius arm on each side, pivoted to the chassis at its forward end. A rotating joint in the centre of the de Dion tube permitted relative movement of each end as the wheels reacted on bump.

The chassis, built by Rubery Owen at Darlaston, comprised twin-tube side-members formed by two 2½in-diameter round-section chrome-molybdenum tubes – one above the other, united by webbing plate welded onto both sides of the assembly, the plates being lightened and made more rigid by a series of large swaged-edge holes. A similar crossmember braced the frame inboard of the radius arm pick-ups and normal tubular crossmembers appeared at front and rear. Despite its light weight and the wide spacing of these crossmembers the frame proved quite rigid...they said.

Its Porsche-type trailing-arm independent front suspension pivoted on light-alloy housings bolted to the frame at the front cross-tube junctions. Ball-joints on the links replaced conventional kingpins, as was usual with this system.

The suspension medium, front and rear, was by Lockheed compressed-air struts, which had been developed for aviation use. These units also incorporated hydraulic damping, were remarkably small and weighed only 4lbs each, far less than a conventional coil or leaf-spring and separate damper.

Those at the front were actuated by levers on the inner end of the pivot pins from the top trailing links, while at the rear the necessary leverage was provided by transverse arms linked by short rods to the hub-carriers. Total available suspension movement was as much as 6 inches front and 7 inches rear, though more restricted in practice.

A worm-and-nut steering box was mounted forward on the left side with a horizontal, rearward-facing drop-arm. A similar arm pivoted in a matching position on the right to provide a three-piece track rod. The steering column then had three UJs, passing down the centre of the engine vee.

The steering wheel in the very confined and thoroughly prewar cockpit had a wooden rim with domed aluminium studs projecting on its underside to provide the driver with a positive grip. There were 2¼ turns lock-to-lock.

Brakes were by Girling with three leading shoes operating within chromium-iron drums and magnesium-alloy back plates. The shoes were machined from light alloy and lined with Ferodo VG95 material. A Pesco servo pump was driven off an engine camshaft to circulate fluid through a circuit to the front brakes. Applying the brake pedal closed a valve, and pressurized this system to apply the front brakes directly. The fluid pressure also supplemented pedal pressure on the rear brake-circuit master cylinder. Both individual brake circuits shared a common fluid header tank on the central chassis crossmember.

Centre-lock wire wheels carried light-alloy rims, the rears being unusually wide for the time. They carried Dunlop tyres and were mounted on Rudge-Whitworth splined hubs.

To preserve a peerlessly lowline bodyshell, the radiator header tank was mounted remotely, behind the engine, leaving only the copper-film radiator matrix in the nose. Two modest body-top intakes fed cooling air over the header tank.

Separate water off-takes from each cylinder merged into two large pipes leading into this tank, a single pipe then connecting with the radiator, separate leads falling both sides to the water pumps.

A shallow oil cooler was mounted just below and behind the water radiator, while the dry-sump oil tank itself was mounted on the right of the frame alongside the angled engine. There were two fuel tanks, one intended to be of 50 gallons – but more like 48 in practice – mounted in the scuttle over the driver's legs and the other of 18 gallons occupying the forward part of that gracefully pointed tail. Behind it was a small gearbox oil tank, mounted on a tubular frame above the battery. Fuel delivery was by a Pesco engine-driven pump, and this tank arrangement was intended to minimize handling variations as fuel was consumed.

George Gray's body panelling was in aluminium, the car standing just 30 inches high at the scuttle. Although very reminiscent of Mercedes-Benz 1939 styling, its handsome proportions belied its large size – over 13ft long.

The cockpit was wide although the steering wheel projected too far into the driver's chest. The pedals were widely spaced with a right-side throttle as opposed to the Continentally-conventional centre-throttle. A stubby gear-lever projected on the right side in an exposed gate, and the handbrake lever had an almost vertical movement over on the left. The dash carried a bewildering array of development instruments, soon to be thinned drastically to just a quaint horizontal strip rev counter with insignificant lower numerals on the left side of the strip, leaping into bold and easily read prominence from '6' to '12' on the right. Over on the left side of the panel was a multiple dial, showing engine oil pressure and temperature and water temperature.

Main dimensions were: wheelbase, 8ft 2in; front track, 4ft 4in; rear track, 4ft 3½in; overall length, 13ft 2in. Weight was claimed to be around 1,700lbs (dry).

The BRM Type 15 had, at last, arrived...but when would it do battle?

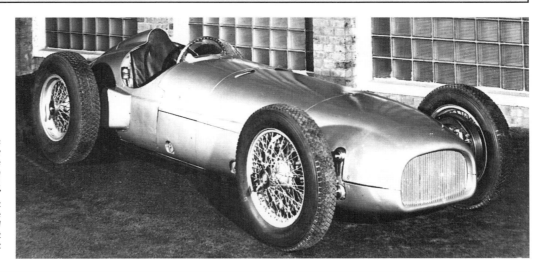

Opposing stories explain these striking press release shots of the prototype BRM – newly completed – outside the Bourne Test House – such as "the photographer had been cooling his heels all day until we finished it". In fact Louis Klemantaski – the great 'Klem' – had been retained by Lucas as Trust official photographer, and he recalled: "The car had been ready for several days and I planned the entire set-up – after dark, spotlit – for maximum dramatic effect…". It succeeded.

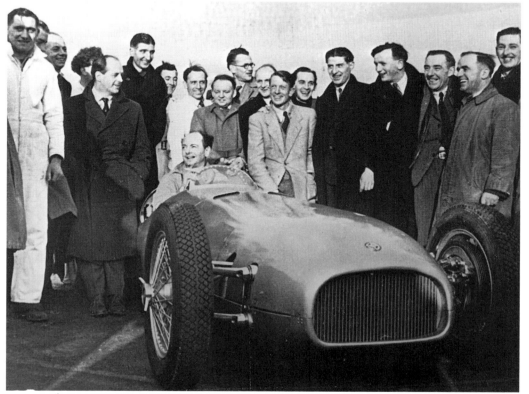

Above: Thursday, December 15, 1949 – press launch of the V16 BRM in building 355, Folkingham Aerodrome's former Crew Briefing Room, where USAAF Dakota crews had once been shown the Arnhem plan. What should have been The Great Day proved a trial for RM, standing here addressing the assembly despite 'flu, flanked by the Trustees. PB sits huddled in his overcoat (third from right) beneath that crumpled Union Jack. It was so cold even the rope encircling the car could not relax...

This relieved group poses for the press, including (left) Cyril Bryden, PB (on rear wheel), Frank May (behind RM in coat), tall Eric Richter, Harry Mundy, Ken Richardson, Aubrey Woods and (dark overcoat) the brawny figure of a happy Alec Stokes.

Right: Ray winding-up the prototype through the gears as he demonstrates the devastating noise of the V16 BRM for the first time to the press, high on the desolate aerodrome plateau at Folkingham. Still feeling – and looking – distinctly unwell, RM extols the BRM's virtues and promise to the gathered journalists, radio reporters, press and newsreel cameramen.

Below: RM had approached experienced ERA conductor Peter Walker – nicknamed 'Skid' Walker by the popular press prewar – to become one of BRM's first works drivers. Here he poses at Folkingham for Picture Post in the prototype car. Note how a starter-shaft hole has been crudely cut into its nose since the press launch, it wears three Dunlop five-stud tyres and one diamond-pattern R1, and still has its original cast badge – soon superceded by water-slide transfers.

IGNOMINY

As Mays and Berthon had feared, the BRM's public announcement triggered an immediate clamour for it to race. Of course, five years had already passed since the project's launch. Its existence and something of its progress had been public knowledge almost as long. By popular standards, it had already cost a fortune. Now Bourne's backers wanted some return on their investment. They demanded to see their BRM prove itself the world-beater they expected. After so many months and years of delay and prevarication any idea that it could still be unraceworthy was unacceptable.

In the Bourne Test House, engine runs continued, while at Folkingham Ken Richardson did the lion's share of test-driving. Geoffrey Wilde and 'Prof' Allen of Rolls-Royce became increasingly involved with ADL's Test House running: "At Bourne we were quite amazed by what we found and heard. Bench testing there was an undisciplined affair – ill-planned, poorly instrumented, with much 'driver-like' pumping of the throttle to give impressive bursts of sound and little idea of producing data for performance analysis. The general level of technical competence was not as high as the project required.

AFTER THE PARTY...

There were some strange goings-on after the Folkingham launch of the new BRM Type 15 that chilly December day. That year's motorcycle sidecar racing World Champions, rider Eric Oliver and passenger Denis Jenkinson ('Jenks' of *Motor Sport* magazine) were present. Neither had much regard for Mays and Berthon, and one look at the unlouvred body of the new BRM had them glancing at one another and muttering: "It's going to overheat". Both were impressed by its stunningly low build – "Nothing more than the headrest higher than the tops of its tyres" – but they knew Eric Richter vaguely through his Norton ties and he painted in much of the background, and voiced some of his own misgivings.

They were driving back via Bourne so they gave Richter a lift in their Ford van with the Norton motorcycle combination in the back. Partway there, the van ran out of petrol. They were beside a garage, with a windswept petrol pump, but the place was shuttered and looked deserted. Richter strolled across to the workshop door and peeped through, coming back chuckling to announce that all he could see was a bloke sitting on a chair, having his hair cut...

Nobody would sell them any petrol, so Oliver and 'Jenks' decided to syphon some out of their Norton instead. The problem was, they had nothing to syphon it into. 'Jenks' eventually found the solution, by using his wellington boot, and then pouring the fuel from it direct into the van's filler neck. Richter thought this was hysterical, roaring with laughter, and crying: "I've seen it all now!"

He had had quite a lot to drink, and was in a happy state. They deposited him back at the works and, soon afterwards, Mundy, Woods, Stokes and the others veered into the yard in one of the first canvas tilt Land-Rovers, parking it just beside the pocked, red-brick wall of the Maltings.

Aubrey Woods: "We were all high as kites and there was Richter in there, chain-smoking as usual and tossing his dog-ends out the window. One landed on the tilt of the Land Rover. After a while we became conscious of the smoke, and somebody yelled that it was on fire!"

It really had been a day to remember...

Peter Berthon used to disappear for long periods, and eventually we took command of the engine tests. Harry Mundy was pretty good, he was a real designer, but one day early on he was asking us how the engine was progressing and we said: 'Why do you ask?' and he astonished us by explaining: 'We're not allowed in, PB won't let us see it run.'

"This was incredible to us.

"At Rolls-Royce the leading designers naturally shared a major role in development. Certainly the scale of BRM's problems demanded all the co-operation they could get from all concerned. Really Peter Berthon was hopeless – you can't run the job if you want to take all the credit..."

The supercharger specialists desperately needed to assess the BRM cylinder and valve designs' volumetric efficiency. For this they needed air and fuel-flow measurements which ADL could not provide. Geoff Wilde again: "In desperation, Frank and I took measuring equipment and instrumentation from Derby to Bourne on Saturdays, often at considerable personal inconvenience. We could not spare any time during the week because of our aero engine commitments.

"We would make an early start, arriving at ADL at around 10am, but with the poor preparations and irritating delays, engine tests rarely began until mid-afternoon. In any case, PB rarely appeared before midday and he was the only person allowed to touch the throttle on the test bench. Frank and I dubbed him 'The Brain in the Bath' thinking that he would be lying there seeking inspiration. This stuck for years and fitted the image of the detached thinker which we believed he liked to project.

"However, when RM was there we were always very graciously received at Eastgate House and generously entertained to lunch. Seeing all his trophies and his fine collection of Gordon Crosby paintings was always a pleasure. It compensated for the disappointments and frustrations experienced during the day, followed by a late return to Derby. 'Hs' [R-R MD Lord Hives] was aware of my commitment on the BRM project, but I was not expected to give it any time that might reduce my development effort on the axial compressor of the new Avon jet engine. So as far as I was concerned the BRM supercharger became mainly an evening and weekend 'hobby', and to a lesser extent also to Frank Allen. Consequently, during 1947 to 1951 I was often working over 70 hours a week..."

In February 1950 a V16 power curve reached 395bhp at 10,000rpm with a 3.25:1 supercharger gear, but subsequent figures then disappointed. The Rolls-Royce men found that engine friction and pumping hp loss was higher than expected – by around 50 per cent...

PB seemed obsessed with peak power, and certainly with Test House security. This was ostensibly to prevent the opposition discovering what the BRM could do...but was it in part to prevent the Trustees from discovering what it could *not*?

Wilde and Allen were exceptions. Otherwise, only the fitters, less qualified than PB himself, were allowed in when the engine was running. And he also removed and hid the dynamometer data plate...

This, vitally, provided its calibration factor – a figure which, when divided into the load shown on the dyno, then multiplied by the dyno rpm, indicated engine output in horsepower. This explains subsequent violently conflicting accounts of the V16's actual output.

If Lucas or SU representatives – often quite senior within their own companies – should arrive to make tests, PB would allow them to monitor the engine while it was running light, yet politely show them the door when a power run began. The story was that BRM's insurance did not cover outside personnel.

About this time another ex-Rolls-Royce engineer, S.S. (Stewart Stewart, strangely enough) Tresilian, BA, AFRAeS, AMIME, MSAE, joined the team as a consultant. He was a genial giant of a man, a confirmed car enthusiast – a Grand Prix Bugatti owner – and an engineer of exceptional stature. He had joined Rolls-Royce direct from Cambridge in the late 1920s as one of their first graduate intake. He had been a member of their famous Schneider Trophy aero engine team and ultimately "left in a huff over two V12s", his largely forming the prewar V12 Lagonda engine for which W.O. Bentley took the credit. He had a spell with Bristol early in the war and was then seconded to the US 8th AAF dealing with problems in their European theatre. Postwar he returned to

Rolls-Royce at Hucknall, before falling out again with 'Hs'.

The Trust had also appointed, as team manager, J.B. 'Jack' Emmott, Chairman of Lockheed. On January 19, 1950, he minuted his thoughts for BRM's initial racing programme, suggesting two alternatives – the first short-term, racing one car with a second in reserve; the second a long-term policy for three race cars plus two in reserve at all times.

Emmott was a no-nonsense businessman, widely experienced in both engineering and motor racing. His wonderful prewar Multi-Union II Brooklands car had come within a whisker of smashing Cobb's 143.44mph Outer Circuit lap record there when driven by Chris Staniland. He wrote:

> As no English driver has had any experience of handling a racing car in a road race at the speeds predicted, it is seriously recommended that one of the leading Continental drivers be asked to try the car. Whether a Continental driver is employed or not, it is necessary to have an English driver in the car in order to develop the skills necessary to beat the Continental opposition. After serious consideration I recommend P.D.C. Walker to be engaged immediately for this purpose...
>
> Four drivers will be required, three plus a reserve... the activities and progress of other leading British drivers should be kept constantly in view...

For team equipment he recommended:

> ...for three cars, three 30cwt lorries with canvas roofs supported by detachable stays, six sets quick-life jacks, three sets refuelling equipment...mobile workshop, one dozen copper wheel hammers, six special plug boxes, four starter motors complete with certain special tools, overalls for 3 drivers plus a reserve driver plus three mechanics per car, 26 sets of overalls (two per man). Mechanics' overalls should be the same shade of green as the cars with the BRM badge on the pocket, drivers' overalls should be cream with the badge on the pocket, less likely to show slight dirtiness than pure white. Assuming three lorries and mobile workshop obtained free of charge, plus other items, total expenditure on pit equipment should not exceed £300.

The Rootes Group supplied and fitted-out a large Commer mobile workshop – registered KVP 362 – while Austin donated three Lodestar trucks as transporters – ETL 615, ETL 483 and KOM 257. Unfortunately, the Trust elected to have them all smartly painted in black with silver pin-lines; in Italy the livery of a hearse... Perhaps it was an omen?

Meanwhile, Vandervell had decided to withdraw from the project in all save an advisory capacity. He kept a foot in the camp because he still hoped ADL would provide Norton with a water-cooled four-cylinder racing engine running *ThinWall* bearings rather than Joe Craig's beloved ball and rollers in his wretched 'one-lunger'. Vandervell would eventually take Phil Wilson with him as Chief Mechanic for his own racing department, then being set-up at Acton to develop the series of *Thin Wall Special* Ferraris. (Although the first car had been called a *ThinWall Special*, from 1950 onwards the Ferrari's name was split into three separate words.) The racing department's activities would lead ultimately to the Vanwall which finally showed "that lot at Bourne" – just as much as "that lot in Maranello and Modena" – the proper way to go motor racing.

Once the second V16 engine was running at Bourne and the third was being assembled, Ken Richardson bore the brunt of the test driving on Folkingham aerodrome. Without ever admitting it, Ray was now feeling his age. He would seldom drive the car. Still both had 'moments' as Ray called them, one in his case when the suspension collapsed at around 140mph and in Ken's when the bayonet fastening of the steering wheel had failed to latch and it came adrift as he hurtled into a fast curve.

Ken had to be recovered several times from amongst the tall sunflower crop bordering the Folkingham test track. Several times PB infuriated him by remarking: "Going too fast again I suppose?" when in fact something else had come adrift. Ray Wood of Lucas proved an eye-witness ally, often watching the tests and one time riding pick-a-back on Ken's car to listen to some elusive ignition effect. He turned down Ken's offer of a second ride...

The car would approach 190mph on Folkingham's 2,000-yard runway. It could spin its wheels even in fifth gear – an impressive experience to relate in the bar, but hardly unexpected on the grit-strewn, crumbling aerodrome surface and of little practical use – indeed quite the reverse – in real racing.

PB and RM won Owen's support in resisting pressure to enter for the British and European GP at Silverstone in May 1950. They planned to debut the car instead in the *Daily Express*-sponsored BRDC International Trophy there that August. But King George VI, Queen Elizabeth and the Royal Family were to attend the British GP. On hearing this news the Trust immediately ordered Ray to demonstrate the BRM there, before their Majesties and the predicted 120,000 crowd.

PB was bitterly opposed. He was over-ruled again. The demonstration run went ahead. Peter Walker – who had driven his old ERA very well in the previous season's British GP – had been signed-on for a 350-guinea retainer and he stood by should Ray become 'unavailable'. RM had also contacted the great French gentleman driver Raymond Sommer about testing and possibly racing the BRM, and Sommer had responded with great enthusiasm.

Ray was available – of course – to show off the new prototype BRM No.1 to King George and his family at Silverstone, and to drive it on two medium-quick laps. The packed crowds were thrilled to see British racing's great hope, nemesis of all-conquering Alfa Romeo, yowling round the course. But after this brief glory serious testing continued at Folkingham, and suddenly BRM found themselves in deep trouble. Richardson had an engine wreck itself. So little remained intact that even PB's excellent 'feel' could not deduce the root cause. The third engine, untested, went straight into the brand-new second chassis.

Quite what could be learned from the constant running at Folkingham is a mystery. There, BRM had no competitive target lap times by which they could judge their own car. All they had was a measure of their own progress unrelated to any rival. Ken Richardson's racing experience was minimal. He

Left: May 13, 1950 – British and European Grand Prix meeting – 'Royal Silverstone', with RM explaining some of the finer points of the immaculately polished BRM prototype to Queen Elizabeth, while Princess Margaret asks Denis Flather if the man really sits in there? Her father, King George VI, in bowler hat seems impressed by the entire affair... But all enthusiasts were disappointed that the car would not be facing Alfa Romeo on the track.

Below: The car is wheeled from its transporter, at Royal Silverstone, Ken Richardson steering, engine builder Dave Turner (left), Ray Woods of Lucas and Clarrie Brinkley. The new nose cowl features a neatly-cut starter orifice, but that same original metal badge.

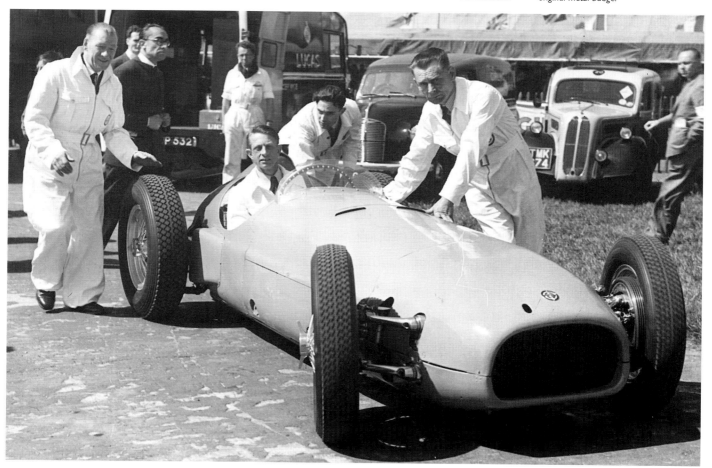

Just after 12 noon, on May 13, 1950 – British and European Grand Prix meeting, Silverstone: RM, demonstrating the deafening prototype car 'No 1', passes the pit line before a claimed 120,000 crowd and the Royal party. The BRM ran briefly between the second 500cc Formula 3 Heat and Final.

was undeniably a competent driver, and he knew every inch of the old ERAs, but apart from his brief and disastrous experience of the original *ThinWall Special* he had never driven another contemporary GP car and had no standard by which to analyze what he found in the BRM.

But when the car would run he drove lap after lap at Folkingham, happily revving the V16 high, spinning its wheels spectacularly in all gears, while objectively learning very little before its engine would break again…

Through the spring into the summer of 1950, work stumbled on, far into the nights at Bourne and in the racing shop at Folkingham. This was very much a dedicated team, working itself to extremes of fatigue but all its immense effort was unfocused and poorly organized. The aim was simply to run the car hard and hope reliability would emerge. PB and RM drove from the top, their men responded nobly, but few had the real ability – or authority – to step back and think. Tresilian was one, but he was not always listened to.

When Ken began to run hard, the engine first backfired, then misfired. Then con-rods would buckle, a piston shatter, the cylinder liner burst and the engine would break up. PB, Tresilian, Richardson, RM and the design team met consultant specialists in endless conferences, but no cause could be established so no immediate cure could be prescribed.

Raymond Sommer arrived and tried the car at Folkingham, paying his own way "for the fun of it" – a gesture typical of this engaging, friendly Frenchman. Ray recalled Sommer saying: "I have always been longing to find a car which is too much for me…this may be the car I am looking for – one that can master me…".

Such a remark certainly delighted and impressed the theatrical RM, but it makes precious little racing sense.

On July 5, RM informed the Trust that 39-year-old Reg Parnell had been invited for a trial drive "with a view to being available to drive at Silverstone if required and signing for 1951". The bluff, burly, Derby-based wheeler-dealer and pig farmer was happy for Sommer to drive in the Trophy race, and agreed to being reserve to Ray for '51. Ray reported:

He considered the car quite good from short acquaintance but was most unused to the necessity for keeping engine revs so high to obtain the best from the engine…

Reg signed on July 25, 1950 – for 50 guineas plus equal shares in 80 per cent of the prize money. The mechanics were to share 20 per cent, while Reg would also be paid all expenses while taking part in "training and racing".

That same month saw the Trust issue this cautious statement:

The BRM cars will be racing at Silverstone on 26 August as an essential part of their development, as only by racing can there be a proper assessment of performance and reliability, and the public are urged not to be too expectant at this juncture. The first full season of racing BRM cars will be in 1951.

'Development testing' continued apace, PB fiddling details but making little real progress towards curing the major failures. The promised flat had been prepared for him and Lorna on the upper storey of the Folkingham control tower. Until that time they had camped out in a caravan there. She provided tea and snacks for the exhausted mechanics as they and PB slaved away in the race 'shop nearby. Tres coined the phrase: "What? Here's a night and nobody working?" It summed-up BRM perfectly.

Nobody seemed to realize that a good night's rest could clear minds and talents, and a refreshed workforce would do more worthwhile work, and make fewer avoidable errors.

On August 19, a week before Silverstone, the Trust board meeting at Bourne heard Flather as Chairman stress the importance "…of smartness and precision at all times by BRM staff when racing". He wanted the racing committee to ensure if at all possible that Monsieur Sommer did not drive a Cooper (as invited) in one of the supporting races at Silverstone. But the French sportsman loved those little cars and stood a far

Left: August 26, 1950 – BRDC International Trophy, Silverstone – Ken Richardson warming-up the newly-completed race car 'No. 1' under Raymond Sommer's gaze (left). The white-overalled drinker is 500cc constructor/driver Wing Cdr Frank Aitken. Above: Haste – Sommer prepares for his brief race morning 'practice' – anxiety and fatigue are plain on many team faces. Note, no nose badge.

Below: BRDC International Trophy – only the early birds amongst the Silverstone crowd that day would have had any glimpse of the handsome BRM in action, like this – Sommer in the un-numbered car on one of his three practice laps.

better chance of winning a supporting race in one of them than of winning the Trophy race in the BRM…

PB himself described the run up to Silverstone like this: "We had a number of broken connecting rods, and even on several occasions the depressing sight of water pouring out of the exhaust pipes and out of the plug holes when the plugs were removed for inspection. This was accompanied by persistent misfiring and popping back at high rpm. All this was at its worst during the rush to get the cars ready for Silverstone during the first three weeks of August."

By the Monday evening, two days before the start of Silverstone practice, two BRMs were prepared and ready, the prototype and a new car. PB: "The problems were due to burst cylinder liners. We were working at absolute breakneck speed non-stop day and night to try and solve this problem, having been experimenting with carburation, induction pipes, ignition systems, supercharger drainage schemes, etc, for several weeks, in the frantic effort to cope with failed engines.

"To our horror, we were presented with a fountaining plug hole on the 24th [raceday being Saturday, August 26] which turned out to be another burst cylinder and badly bent connecting rod. There was obviously no hope of rebuilding this engine in time for the race, as we knew from experience our quickest possible time for getting an engine out, replacing a rod, and getting it back in the car. So one car was definitely out of the Silverstone race. We then concentrated everybody on getting the other car to the last day of practice."

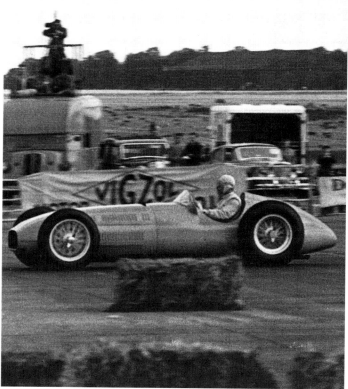

Ray went to Silverstone that Thursday to tell the Trust, press and race organizers that one car would be along shortly. *Motor Sport* described how:

> On the Thursday evening Raymond Mays made excuses on behalf of the B.R.M. Trust at a Press conference, during which Donald McCullough, Trust Chairman, made some tactless references to how embarrassed an individual firm would be if *their* contribution should cause the B.R.M. to retire from the race and how speedily they would seek to correct things…!

Recalling this clearly bungled conference, Ray merely admitted: "I did not enjoy that much."

He had been following Folkingham progress by telephone. It still looked as if one car could run in final, Friday, practice.

Ray and Sommer were staying at the Welcombe Hotel, Stratford-upon-Avon. Next morning RM awoke to a call from Folkingham. Ken Richardson had tested the surviving car at first light and, like its sister, it had cracked No. 8 cylinder liner…

Ray dropped Sommer at Silverstone to practise his sports Aston Martin and factory-loaned Cooper for the supporting races. The French star had ignored Flather's objections. RM then drove to Folkingham.

PB: "Only those who have been through a sustained pre-race effort of this sort will appreciate the disappointment to us all when, after a final check run, our second car presented us with the same symptom at 8.30am on the Friday morning, the last day of practice.

"Ray was sent for and after a very brief discussion it was agreed this was no way to go motor racing and we could not think of appearing the following day. On the engineering facts, we did not know how to make the engine work, and could not even get it to run on all cylinders. So we sent our men home, already nearly dropping with fatigue, and we ourselves departed to Silverstone to acquaint the BRM Trust Committee with the situation and as we thought to watch the motor racing in peace…"

RM drove PB, Ken and Tres back to Silverstone in his Bentley to announce BRM's withdrawal.

"On the way I said: 'I am sure it is better not to appear at all than to run and do badly. If we flop it could end the whole BRM project. We must not mar out efforts with a failure…'" He explained his decision to the BRDC officials and the *Daily Express* promotional people.

They gave him a dusty reception… PB: "On arrival at Silverstone we learned from our Trust and from the representatives of the *Daily Express* that there was a lot more to this racing than the cold engineering facts…"

All the organizers' and promoters' pre-race publicity had centred upon the BRM's racing debut. Non-appearance would cheat the vast crowd expected. Both organizers and sponsors pleaded for at least one car to start. The Trustees present over-ruled all Ray's arguments. Regardless of the risk of performing badly, the car must run. The RAC stewards agreed to allow BRM to start without formal practice, if the car could complete three 'quick laps' before 10am the following –

raceday – morning. 'Quick', ostensibly, meant an average speed of at least 80mph.

It was late afternoon. At Folkingham, after the order from RM and PB to abandon work, the weary mechanics had dispersed to home and bed. Ray, furious and tense – terrified of the public humiliation which he felt was looming large – telephoned Henry Coy, his Bourne garage manager, asking him to "…knock-up the boys". Then with PB beside him he drove the Bentley flat-out back into Lincolnshire.

Meanwhile, having built his engines ready for Silverstone, Dave Turner was on holiday with his wife in a caravan at Skegness. "They telephoned through to the caravan site and called me over the tannoy: 'Come on Dave you're needed here at Folkingham.' I was always at their beck and call. Now I had to build one engine overnight from two busted ones. I just abandoned the wife, got in the car and left – quick!"

By the time that RM and PB flurried up the winding lane onto the Folkingham plateau, 18 of their men were already hard at work in the race 'shop. Henry had toured the local villages to roust out the team. Both damaged engines were being stripped. Through a fifth consecutive 'all-nighter' the mechanics cobbled together one runner from the two.

PB: "The burst liner was replaced and the cylinder head refitted and timed, largely with the aid of bacon and eggs, black coffee and brandy, and the engine was run up successfully at 4.30am on Saturday, the day of the race."

Ray settled himself into the car's pale green cramped cockpit. The drawn, rocking mechanics inserted the electric starter shaft in its nose and pressed the button. Those 16 tiny pistons shuttled to and fro. The engine fired. She ran…

The *Daily Express* – relishing all this drama – had chartered a Silver City Airways Bristol Freighter. It flew in to RAF Cranwell – some 10 miles from Folkingham – to collect the car. The BRM was loaded aboard, accompanied by several mechanics, Dave Turner excepted. "RM later said: 'You're not on that plane David?' and I said 'No – don't bloody want to be.' He said: 'Are you scared of flying?' and I said: 'No, but I did see that film the other week, *One of Our 'Planes is Missing…*'"

The Bristol took off for RAF Bicester, close to Silverstone. Ray was already long gone, tearing back cross-country in the Bentley. One of BRM's three Austin Lodestar trucks met the Freighter at Bicester. The BRM was trans-shipped and Ken Richardson then hurried the Lodestar to Silverstone, flanked by police outriders. RM was waiting there, with Turner: "He was pacing up and down saying, 'Where have they got to?' I told him I didn't know, but I wasn't going to look for 'em. You had to give him what he give you otherwise the buggers'd treat you like dirt. Ray would, if you let him…"

The convoy arrived in the paddock at 9.40am.

The car was unloaded. Ray clambered aboard. Its engine was started and he drove a gentle warm-up lap in which the V16 ran clean, its shattering bark thrilling the vast majority of early-bird spectators present. Their anticipation was immense. So *this* was what the pre-race publicity had promised!

Sommer, wearing blue overalls with his 'SR' initials, a tiny French flash embroidered on the pocket, and blue linen helmet, then took over for his required three qualifying laps… The engine fired cleanly on all cylinders and those three laps averaged, respectively, 78.78, 81.24 and 79.99mph. He reported:

Above: BRDC International Trophy – Ray Woods of Lucas, Ken Richardson, Cyril Bryden, Dave Turner and Co push-start Sommer for his practice run. By this time someone had remembered to apply a badge transfer.

Left: RM returning the car to the paddock from the pits before those empty early-morning grandstands.

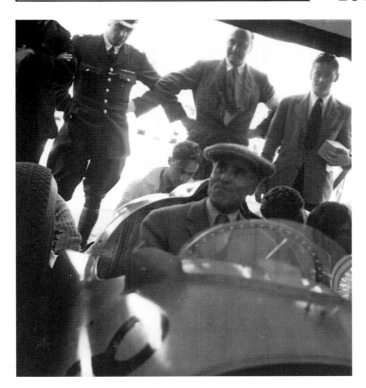

Honoured visitor, but a tragically ailing man – the legendary Tazio Nuvolari trying Sommer's BRM for size before the Trophy race. By this time race numbers have been applied. Note the heavy studding to provide finger grips on the woodrim steering wheel.

"The car is sliding about but the circuit is damp." The Stewards accepted the car as a starter, and a faulty rear hub race was quickly changed.

Before an estimated 150,000 crowd, the day's programme commenced with a 10-lap 500cc race in which Sommer finished second to young Stirling Moss, both driving Coopers. After a one-hour 2-litre Production Car race dominated by Ascari's Ferrari, the 15-lap Heat One of the International Trophy then fell to Farina's magnificent *Alfetta*. Then Sommer re-emerged in the BRM to start Heat Two from the back of the grid.

As Kenneth Evans dropped the Union flag the field blared away towards Woodcote Corner[25]...

Amidst the smoke of their departure the pale green BRM merely shuddered. It hardly moved at all.

Sommer, frozen-faced, was impotently whooping its engine, holding it in first gear, jabbing at the clutch pedal. He tried second gear, re-engaged the clutch, tried again – tried *everything*. To no avail. All connection had been lost between engine and rear wheels.

The BRM's debut race had ended at the instant it began. Both of its final-drive output shafts seemed to have sheared under load as Sommer popped the clutch.

The exhausted BRM crew simply stood and stared – utterly thunder-struck.

25. **The start and pit area at Silverstone in those days was situated close to Luffield Abbey Farm, on the gentle climbing straight between Abbey Curve and Woodcote Corner. It was not moved to its present, familiar situation, between Woodcote and Copse Corners, until 1952.**

As the last of its rival cars blared away out of sight round the distant Copse Corner, the BRM sat alone on the grid, Cyril Bryden, new recruit Willie Southcott, Ken Richardson, Dave Turner and the other mechanics running to assist. There was nothing they could do. They wheeled the car off onto the right-side verge. Sommer spread his hands to RM and PB, levered himself from behind their car's steering wheel and stood grim-faced beside it. This was the second time he had experienced such failure upon the debut of an important new car – the same thing had happened to him in the French national CTA-Arsenal Grand Prix car at Lyons in 1947.

Above the distant roar of the pack, by this time stringing out along Hangar Straight towards Stowe Corner, the packed crowds all round the course rumbled with disappointment – the PA system breaking the news. Near the start area some who could see the stricken BRM and the suddenly lonely group of figures examining it began to boo and jeer and some tossed coins into its cockpit...

Thousands anticipating the predicted sensational BRM debut had arrived too late to see its four brief exploratory laps. Now most of them – away from the immediate start area – had merely seen it growl by on its warm-up lap *en route* to the starting grid. Latecomers that day just missed it entirely.

Into the following winter, the *Daily Express* would cavil over paying BRM its promised starting money. On November 14 Ray would write to Donald McCullough: "As regards starting money – quite honestly I cannot remember if the car moved a few inches or if it did not..." Some very fine hairs were being split. Silverstone had provided more grotesque and enduring humiliation than even he had ever feared...

THE INQUEST

BRM's people had been braced to expect an early engine failure. Most expected another ruptured liner. But none had dreamed of such a body blow as this abject failure on the start-line.

Despite its many notes of caution, the Trust's PR output had persuaded the British press and public to expect great things. Certainly, as RM and PB had both insisted, none should have expected too much too soon. But how could a first race five-and-a-half-years after the project's inception justifiably be described as having been "too soon"?

This disaster was greeted with general derision and scorn.

Fleet Street journalists always react viciously when their own sensational predictions – founded in ignorance – are exposed as ill-informed and naive. The *Sunday Pictorial*'s piece, justifiably headlined "*FLOP*", was typical of the Street's output, simplistic and inaccurate – but certainly reflecting the British public's gut reaction as it proceeded: "*Four Years – 18 Men and £160,000, Much of it in Half-Crown Subscriptions – Went to Build the Racing Car that Would Not Start*".

The *Pictorial*'s journalists had confused membership of the BRM Association supporters club with that of the Trust funding the car's construction. The Trust had in fact helped launch the embryo Association with a donation of £1,000. As Publicity Director Percy Bilton of Vigzol later circularized BRMA members, he had asked the *Pictorial* for similar space

BRDC International Trophy – official photographer Louis Klemantaski's sequence of Sommer's start includes these frames: Left – the windswept Ken Richardson, Cyril Bryden and Dave Turner wheel Sommer onto his starting mark at the back of the grid. Arthur Ambrose clutches the spark plug box beyond. Future BRM driver Jack Fairman (moustache and tie – left of centre) is amongst the onlookers. Clockwise from below left: Sheer tension – Ken, Sommer, RM, Arthur and Dave await the start-up signal. Jack North offers up the trolley starter, PB (right), hands in pockets against the blustering wind. The flag is raised, Ray (left) wills success, Sommer hunches in anticipation, V16 whooping, reaching for first gear...

BRDC International Trophy – Top: Disaster! The flag has fallen, Sommer has dropped the clutch, surged mere feet abreast 'Klem' and the BRM has died, its transmission broken. Sommer is trying each gear in turn but finds no drive. Ambrose stands transfixed, others expressionless, some begin to smile… Above: "Clear my track!" – Desmond Scannell of the BRDC directs Richardson, Turner and Cyril Bryden to push the stricken BRM away. Right: Behind the timekeepers' control bus amused constabulary guard Britain's discredited worldbeater…

to respond, but they had replied: *"Would prefer await next B.R.M. demonstration but would give any contribution careful consideration..."* – Fleet Streetese for "get lost".

Even before the shocked team had packed their transporter amidst the rain showers at Silverstone, and while Sommer was racing a DB2 Aston Martin in the over 2-litre Production Car 'hour' before the Trophy race Final, the Trust Committee had convened an emergency meeting in the airfield's former Parachute Drying Shed. Some members declared this should be the end. The ignominy was unbearable. The supporting firms should cut their losses and run.

RM and PB emphasized instead that what had happened was an inescapable part of motor racing's risk. They had warned the Committee what might happen. The meeting resolved to investigate the car's failure in depth and to examine future plans in that light.

Clandestinely, Flather buttonholed Eric Richter and suggested to him that with Bernard Scott's support the entire project could shortly be removed from Bourne to a new site in the Midlands. Should that happen, RM and PB could well resign. Would he, Richter, accept the post of Chief Engineer? It appears that Richter could have been interested, he had certainly suffered the car's first-time failure very badly and was appalled by the lack of system – of discipline – all around him, but when whispers of this move reached Bourne there was Hell to pay. After a period freelancing, Eric Richter accepted a generous offer to follow Phil Wilson's lead and go to work for Tony Vandervell... [26]

Flather's flirtation with Richter, or vice versa, had far-reaching results. Flather was the only Trustee with any

---

26. On December 5, 1950, Eric Richter wrote as follows to Denis Jenkinson of *Motor Sport*:
    "You have probably heard that I have left the B.R.M. gang and am now free-lancing... *The* car goes well, but is a little unpredictable. *I* think, that in spite of its mathematical advantages, it has the wrong type of blower for a racing car: it is far too tricky over such a wide speed range. It is essentially a one-speed device – as an aircraft engine is for all practical purposes – and we should have known where we were much better with a multi-stage Rootes [*sic*]. The machinery part of the engine is reliable and the car is fast, but again, I think, suffers from insufficiently rigorous testing on an unsuitable course...I had a few words with them about the subject (and kindred matters) just after Silverstone – hence my monastic seclusion!"
    [In this same letter Richter explained that he had been waiting all morning with a stopwatch in hand before starting to write it, at precisely "12 noon, Dec 5th 1950, i.e. 4½ x 12 = 50"...] He continued:
    "I could not reply before, owing to there being no other reasonable factors of 50 – and when I first thought of [this one] I was in daily terror of its slipping past unnoticed..."
    Such cerebral juggling was absolutely typical of this very bright, rather eccentric and most unusual character.
    And where BRM were concerned he would return, but never to retrieve such prominence. Bourne was harsh upon those who abandoned ship and subsequently returned. Richter would find this in the mid-1950s, and Dave Turner too. Both were given a hard time there second time around.
    Tony Rudd: Richter should have known better – a Roots blower develops indigestion above 16/18psi, the internal compression between the rotors increases the work done and temperature rise so the thing falls right off the efficiency curve. To get the BRM boost he would have needed four blower stages with intercoolers *between* each one – bigger than the rest of the engine. He was on safer ground in his remarks on testing.

---

metallurgical connections. He would have been the most appropriate member to conduct any inquest – instead he effectively disqualified himself.

And Alfred Owen had missed it all...

He had been on holiday at *Cadwgan* in Dyffryn, Merionethshire, North Wales, and had planned to return home on the Friday before the race, then to go to Silverstone on the Saturday. But he had developed a septic throat and under doctor's orders could not travel. His sons David and John attended instead, under the wing of H.S. Holden, MD of one of the Owen Organisation's companies, Brooke Tool, who – ironically – had been responsible for machining the pot-joints which had fractured... But was their failure in any way Brooke's fault?

On the following Monday, August 28, Ray wrote to Owen's secretary at Darlaston, the formidable Miss Edith 'Polly' Ramsden:

> I am most distressed to hear about Mr Owen, do please convey messages to him from my mother and me and tell him that he is to be sure and take care of himself and get really fit before he comes back to work.
>
> Last Saturday was about the most cruel blow that could possibly happen. After all the terrific efforts of all of us here, and particularly those of Peter Berthon, Tressillian [*sic*] and the mechanics, who had literally hardly laid their heads on a pillow for weeks, you can imagine how we feel.
>
> After desperate efforts we got the car to Silverstone, it did its three official laps and was running well. The most extraordinary part is that the transmission of the B.R.M. had never given any trouble from the first day it was built, and to think that it has given trouble on the starting line is almost beyond comprehension.
>
> Naturally, I am heart-broken, but I am equally determined to succeed, which I know we shall do, particularly if Mr Owen fights with us.
>
> My mother sends her love to you and please give our kindest regards and all the best to Mr Owen.
>
> All good wishes,
> Yours very sincerely
>
> Ray.

Tom Blackburn of the *Daily Express* wrote generously to Donald McCullough:

> With regard to the B.R.M., I would not let it get anybody down. The way of the pioneer has always been very hard indeed and all the great wonders of the world and great developments have had their great disappointments and, in many cases, tragedies before the ultimate success.
>
> I believe the Trust made the right decision in coming to Silverstone. Naturally, I felt some responsibility for it. But the effort that was made was really grand and I am sure that such a spirit, backed by the experience of the

Trust, will finally produce the world-beater we are all waiting for…

The Trust issued an official statement reading:

> It was known by the Trust since May that the power available from the B.R.M. engine was insufficient in the lower and middle speed ranges. Effective steps were taken to remedy this, but the new parts were not available until early August…

This public assertion outraged the Owen Organisation's BRM progress chaser, W.J. Oldham, as we shall see shortly. The Trust statement continued:

> …Possibly as a result of the higher output obtained, a number of smaller troubles occurred such as oil pump failure, as late as Tuesday, August 22nd. The time taken to remedy these faults prevented full-scale track tests being made if the obligation to race one or two cars at Silverstone was to be met.
>
> After the failure of the car to start, an emergency meeting of the Trust was held at Silverstone, and Mr. Walter Hill was appointed to investigate the cause of the failure of the car, and to report in detail. The report is as follows:
>
> '(1) Transmission failure was due to the shearing of the inboard universal joint body at the roots of the spline; both sides had failed.
>
> '(2) From investigation it was apparent that the [inferring one] joint drive [sic] must have sheared either before or during practice laps. However, during the racing start, the whole of the power load was on one side only; hence the second failure.
>
> 'The Trust is alive to the necessity of issuing a more comprehensive statement as soon as possible.

[signature: Walter Hill]

It was left to Oldham to offer Owen – but certainly not the public media – more detailed information, at Dyffryn, on the Wednesday following the fiasco:

> You will have seen remarks…that the transmission failed, this being the axle shaft pot joint body part No. 20056, forgings ex-Firth Brown, machined by Brooke Tool, serrations at Coventry Gauge & Tool, this being the component which collapsed at the starting line. Yesterday Mr. Berthon said, after testing this item at Bourne, the test revealed they were low on Rockwell hardness figures. By the way, one set was delivered on the 14th December 1948 and the remaining sets on 29th April, 1949 and I reminded Mr. Berthon that these tests were somewhat tardy, in view of the delivery dates, *but he did not consider that the quality of work from Brooke Tool should require checking. Personally I do not agree with this attitude* [my italics – DCN. Modern teaching on Quality Assurance is that your supplier meets the

standard. The customer does NOT, and in fact cannot, 'inspect' quality into a piece. Point to PB]…

Oldham added that:

> …there can be little doubt, if any at all, that Brooke Tool have made the job in accordance with the drawings…

He then reacted to the Trust's press statement:

> You will probably already have seen the various Press comments and formed your own conclusions, especially in respect of today's remarks about waiting for new parts until early August. This statement by the Trust prevents me from registering an official protest, and [I] therefore request you to pursue the matter on my behalf, or, alternatively, consider relieving me of any responsibility in connection with any further work on behalf of the B.R.M. – my reading of these comments and the inference therein being that the Project was delayed due to parts not being available…

The incensed Oldham then listed the sub-contracted parts which had been unavailable during his earlier Bourne investigation of Whit-Monday/Tuesday, plus dates when his chasing had achieved their delivery. The final items required for Car 1 had in fact been delivered to Bourne on July 18 and, for Car 2, on July 31. Were they vital parts? Hardly.

Car 1's final delivery involved a handbrake cable from British Wire Products – Car 2's a rather more vital handed pair of Mollart gearchange universal joints…

PB evidently tackled Brooke Tool regarding heat treatment of the broken parts, Mr Holden retorting on August 31 that ADL's blueprint called for Firth Brown Nitralloy NCM 5 material to British Standard 970 Specification EN40U. Quoting the BS requirements, Holden pointed out that EN40U "must be delivered in Heat Treated Condition…The mechanical properties then give a minimum of 60 tons tensile with…a Rockwell C [hardness] equivalent of 28/34. See BS 970 page 100 (Mechanical properties). The Rockwell C Readings on Part No. 20056 (after events) was 32/34. No mention of any Heat Treatment other than that of Nitriding was called for on the Blue Print." He summed up tartly:

> You will observe therefore that not only were we not responsible for any Heat Treatment of this part other than Nitriding, but no Heat Treatment is necessary or called for on the Blue Print.
>
> It would seem that the selection of the material itself for the purpose in mind was the reason for the failure of the Joint…

Having made his point, Holden estimated three weeks' machining time for delivery of replacement parts.

In fact EN40 was and still is a crankshaft steel suitable for nitriding, but neither Holden nor anyone else involved in this investigation seems to have mentioned the Izod number which measures impact resistance, an important factor in any part subject to violent load fluctuations. The Izod number of EN40 was 35. There were plenty of steels around with an Izod of 50. Even a layman knows that as the steel gets harder it becomes more brittle which means a lower Izod number, suggesting EN40 was not at all the best material for such a tortured component.

Last word – internally – on the Silverstone failure came in a pot-joint body hardness investigation carried out by Rubery Owen on September 1. Chief Inspector G.R. Barnes concluded:

> …we are definitely of the opinion that the Hardness figures and Tensile Strength, together with the treatment of the material used in the production of the above component, are all within the limits laid down in Drawing No. 20056.

Supporting companies were circularized with a report finding that the faulty pot-joints used:

> …material although heat-treated within the broad limits of EN40U are within this specification but are on the low limit. Investigation has shown that these pot-joints are the originals which were fitted to the number one car and which have been running from the end of November last throughout the whole test period of getaways, development testing, etc… The failure can be attributed in the main to fatigue. With the material heat-treated to the higher limit of the EN40U specification these parts have a safety limit above the torque which can be applied, assuming the whole weight of the rear of the car to be on one wheel…new pot-joints have been put in hand with English Steel which will be treated to 100 tons tensile.

The report concluded:

> It is imperative that suppliers be made to realise the gravity of this national project. They must adhere to specifications and to delivery targets…

Whatever the truth of all this, a legend gained currency within BRM which some still believe is the real background to that Silverstone disgrace. Some claim that those first pot joints had been machined from simple bar stock drawn from the Maltings stores since the proper forgings had not yet arrived. The problem was that in any well-run stores the various types of material are colour-coded on one end for immediate identification. Any material drawn from stores should then be cut from the un-coded end of a bar. It's claimed that in ADL/BRM's case the storeman regularly cut off the coded bar ends, and then went around later when he had time, re-coding the bars from memory! In this case the code had been wrong, an entirely unsuitable grade material had been used to make those prototype joints, and Sommer's failure had been the result.

Tony Rudd: I had some sense during conversations with Denis Flather in later years that he had some inkling of this… But whatever really happened nobody seemed to have appreciated that the prewar Mercedes, from which the design

had been lifted, gave around 325bhp at 7,500rpm while the 1950 BRM engine could perhaps – not for long – deliver 400 at 10,500. Driveshafts think in terms of torque – twisting moment – and while the Mercedes engineers would have stressed for 228lbs/ft the non-existent BRM stress men should have aimed at 314lbs/ft, particularly since the V16 output shaft ran at half engine speed. Therefore, at best, the failure was due to design inadequacy – the components were just too small and made from unsuitable material. At worst the cause was undetected use of completely the wrong material with an inadequate design. In a normal organization the 'wrong' material would have been identified by checks during manufacture. If it was wildly wrong, the machinist should have picked it up, as 60-ton 30-Rockwell material is quite tough to machine, and there was never much wrong with the machine shop skills…

On balance of contemporary evidence, the colour-coding tale seems no more than legend, sadly believable only *because* this was BRM.

To sum up, the new marque's Silverstone humiliation had been caused by ADL's original design – and by the team's rash continued use of uninspected components which had already completed some 4,000 miles testing. It really was a case of 'no way to run a railway'…

Alfred Owen expressed his attitude to fellow Trustee Percy Bilton on September 8:

> I [am] still as 'sold' on the B.R.M. as always but am not at all happy with the existing set-up…I am sure if Peter and Ray are to be controlled (a suggested) Managing Director will have to be associated with one of the existing Directors if he is going to make any progress, having thereby a Court of Appeal.
>
> I am glad you took the initiative of sending Mr Hill up to investigate. I have appealed to Ray and Peter on many occasions re lack of any concrete information, in fact have had sit-down rows with Peter with Donald McCullough seeking as Chairman of the Trust Committee to try and make Peter realise what was wanted, but unless one continually sends people down to Bourne one gets no information whatever.
>
> I could tell you a sorry story of what I could only think has been intrigue and jealousy for I am certain that if I were to have continued in maintaining the contacts I had in July 1949 the present position would never have arisen but the whole of the show-down took place when I was away on holiday as you no doubt remember. If only we could get over this clash of personalities I should be very much happier to do what I have done in the past as I have got no ulterior motive whatever but simply to get racing cars produced without any publicity to myself whatever…

Hill's report on the situation at Bourne ran to five closely-typed foolscap sheets and was circulated to members that same day. He considered:

> A feeling of insecurity regarding the council's future thinking is found in the highest and the lowest at

THE FIRST TEAM MANAGER'S VIEW – JACK EMMOTT

In 1989, living in retirement in Switzerland, Jack Emmott looked back on BRM with little relish, recalling of the original launch at Folkingham: "The atmosphere there was one of anticipation that at last there was a British car which could match the foreign competition. I had the impression that this was the feeling of those whose knowledge of motor racing was fairly limited. For those who had a deeper knowledge of the art, there was a feeling of hope but not too much faith...

"Raymond Mays had invited me to become Team Manager in 1949, to be responsible for the team both during the run-up to the races and at the events themselves. My ability to do this..." – in addition to his industrial experience of running Lockheed and his racing activities with the prewar Multi Union Brooklands car – "...was based on the fact that I had had a long-standing relationship with Dick Seaman, who gave me a very clear picture of the way in which the Mercedes-Benz team was organized.

"However, after a fairly short time it became very clear to me that I was never going to have the authority and the co-operation which would enable me to bring the team to the point where it could mount a positive challenge to its contemporary competitors."

Even as BRM made its race debut in the International Trophy at Silverstone in August 1950, Jack made his exit:

"I had been at the circuit on the practice days and then arrived there at about 7.45am on race morning hoping we should have a car on the grid. It arrived at about 9.40am, and Mays did a lap to warm it up and then Sommer did the three laps necessary to qualify, but still at the back of the grid.

"Prior to that race, I had never met Sommer, nor was I ever introduced to him. As he was to drive the car in this event I thought the time had come to introduce myself. After he had done the qualifying laps, I saw him walking down behind the pit area towards the BRM pit together with Mays. As he came behind the pit, I moved forward to introduce myself, but to my total astonishment was brushed aside as if I did not exist...

"After the car failed on the starting line I was not present at the emergency meeting of the Trust. I could see very clearly there was no hope of real success unless I was left to operate with authority, and to stand or fall by results achieved. As this was not forthcoming, and as the cars were far from competitive, I quietly folded my tent..."

Bourne, and this harmfully affects the project... If the council still has confidence in Mays and Berthon it should say so. They are the professionals in the team, relying on the BRM for the principal part of their income...

He suggested that one car be maintained for the rest of the season for continuous track testing, while the second should be prepared for racing. The part-built third engine should be assembled and used for brake-testing.

Meanwhile, testing had resumed at Folkingham. PB recalled this period, later that winter, like this: "We failed a number more engines 'til we found that the trouble was somewhere in the ignition system, and we cured it completely by changing the position of the coils. They had been some way from the distributors, connected to them by a lengthy bundle of four leads, and owing to inductance it was possible for spark energy to be transferred to the wrong lead, causing misfiring and pre-ignition" (this subsequently proved to be untrue).

He continued: "In over 300 hours of bench testing and about 4,000 miles of track testing there were only two genuine mechanical weaknesses in the engine which were due to defective design. A big-end nut came off during track testing, due to a defective type of lock washer, and caused considerable damage. There were several failures of some hard steel spiral gears in the sump, driving oil and water pumps. This was cured by changing the material and design of the driven gear..."

In mid-September one car ran reliably and showed sufficient speed for Owen to telex an entry on September 19 for two races at the *Daily Graphic*-sponsored BARC Goodwood meeting on Saturday, September 30.

Dave Turner: "Between Silverstone and Goodwood I worked a week with no sleep at all and by mistake I over-torqued an engine by 100lbs too much. I used to log everything and I'd just written down the torque without a second thought. Then I had a couple of days off and when I came back PB said: 'I can't understand it, this car's going like a bomb, no trouble at all.' I thought about it, read my log, realized what I'd done and owned up. The casting material wasn't man enough to hold that torque and it was a hell of a job to put more meat into it, but it kept the engine water-tight all right. Like a lot of BRM development, we found that out by accident..."

By September 26 a BRM inventory check revealed that four chassis frames had been built, one "which may or may not be serviceable" being held at Motor Panels whose 'bashers' required "extra cover to bring the body panel position up to five car sets...".

Both complete cars were prepared for the Goodwood trip, and a successful test was completed there in the week preceding the race, using the ex-Sommer Silverstone car, based on frame 2. As the original prototype – ex-December press launch/ex-British GP demonstration car – was now ear-marked for use purely as a test vehicle and was subsequently cannibalized, the Sommer 'No. 2' car would eventually become logged as their 'No. 1' race car – the prototype or 'Test Car' being relegated to dismantled obscurity.

Reg Parnell – Goodwood lap record holder in his Maserati 4CLT – was to drive the 'Sommer car' at the Sussex circuit, and there he completed 13 laps in it on Friday, September 29, his fastest being timed at 1min 40.8sec, 89.1mph; only 0.8sec outside his record. In official practice he then got down to 1:37.6, fully 3.2sec quicker than his nearest rival in a thin field – Brian Shawe-Taylor in an ERA.

Raceday then dawned overcast and steady rain began to fall, first a drizzle, then a downpour. BRM's team was housed in seclusion at the scrutineering bay, away from the regular paddock stalls in another public relations blunder. But as Ken Richardson whooped Parnell's chosen 'No. 2' car out through the packed crowd into the collecting area ready for Reg to take over he could bask in – by the restrained British standards of the time – a wildly enthusiastic reception...

Above: September 30, 1950 – Goodwood: Ken Richardson is the envy of all present as he blips 'The BRM' out towards the circuit ready for Reg Parnell to take it out onto the streaming course (below) to start the Woodcote Cup and Goodwood Trophy.

September 30, 1950 – The Woodcote Cup *Formule Libre* race, Goodwood – 5 laps, 12 miles.

Ray stood on the grid, drawn and damp, wrapped in his heavy navy overcoat beneath a pale blue umbrella. Grid positions had been drawn by ballot, Parnell lining up the BRM in second place on the front row alongside Peter Whitehead's ERA to his right and his own Maserati – driven by Fred Ashmore – to the left. Belgian bandleader Johnny Claes sat in his chrome-yellow Talbot-Lago on the outside of the front row.

As the rain tippled down, Reg sat warming the V16 engine, its rippling exhaust blast clearing puddles behind the car and spitting atomized spray and rich black fumes at the Swiss Baron 'Toulo' de Graffenried on the row behind in his Maserati. Even the *Motor Sport* reporter – regarded as 'anti' by BRM people – recorded: "The note was really inspiring…"

As Ebblewhite of the BARC dropped the Union flag, Parnell – mindful of Sommer's mortifying experience – eased the BRM gently off the line, allowing both Whitehead and de Graffenried to charge ahead. But out in the country the pale green BRM hurtled into the lead, and 'Uncle Reg' simply splashed round in complete command exploiting as much of the new car's power advantage as he dared down Lavant Straight and back through the flat-out left-hand curve past the pits[27]. Whitehead retired, de Graffenried dropped back and

27. The famous Goodwood chicane was not introduced until the BARC Members' Meeting of March 22 opened the 1952 season there.

Above: On the wet Goodwood roadway Reg Parnell's race starts proved infinitely more successful than the unfortunate Sommer's. This is his second, from row two of the Daily Graphic Goodwood Trophy grid. Beyond, Brian Shawe-Taylor's endangered mechanics help to get ERA 'R9B' away.

Right: Pluming round the rain-soaked Sussex circuit, Parnell never pushed the BRM too hard, but always had sufficient performance – and courage – in hand to win both his races.

Right: "Blimey – it's a winner..." Dave Turner at Goodwood seems dumbstruck. Note the BRM's coolant header tank behind the engine and detached plug leads hanging over the cowling at right...

THE GREAT DAY AT GOODWOOD – FROM THE BBC HOME SERVICE

This was the climax of the live commentary broadcast by BBC Radio during the *Daily Graphic* meeting:

Raymond Baxter: "And here comes the BRM now, coming round going into one of its last laps [*noise of car*] the engine sounding as crisp and lovely as ever, and there's a long gap now before 'Bira' comes up – trying to get by Johnny Claes [*phonetic*]. He's lapping Johnny Claes, taking the wide line. In the meantime the BRM must be [*noise of car*] approaching to St Mary's very fast, so over to Robin Richards..."

Robin Richards: "And I can't see the BRM at the moment – there's no sign at the moment, but I'm peering out through this haze – yes, he's just in sight and he's got quite a comfortable lead. He's streaming down the straight now towards me and I can't even see 'Bira'; there's a tremendous lead – he's pulled nicely away in these last three laps. Just listen to him come by. He's approaching me now. Listen...[*noise of car*].

"And now 'Bira' is coming up – there must be a nice two hundred, three hundred, yards lead, and the BRM streaking away up to Lavant Corner – yes, he's just going into Lavant now. And now 'Bira's coming up behind, he's entering Lavant. Just braking and going in and he is into the corner now, and the BRM by this time is just streaking away up Lavant Straight and should come into your sight any time now, Raymond Baxter!

Raymond Baxter: "And I don't know how many thousands of eyes there are looking across into this bad visibility to see the BRM win this event, and it almost certainly shall [*noise of car*] but the excitement here is enormous and there's a terrific atmosphere of triumph in the air! I'm looking down the road now. Just at this moment the visibility has gone and got considerably worse again, but the BRM is just coming down Lavant Straight now – he's safely round Woodcote – he's coming down the left-hand curve – here he comes – chequered flag out for him – THE BRM WINS! [*Noise of car*]. And – relatively unusual thing at a motor race meeting – there's pronounced *cheering* as Reg Parnell wins the Goodwood Trophy of 1950 on the BRM..."

Postscript: When a recording of this live commentary was played on the BBC Overseas Service on October 1, 1950, it was introduced like this: "A good deal of publicity has been given in the Press over here, at any rate, to the teething troubles of Great Britain's new racing car, the BRM as it's called. But now 25,000 people at Goodwood have just seen the BRM overcome all difficulties, and some extremely bad weather into the bargain, to win its first two races under the noses of some of the best European machines and drivers..."

Some cautious voices (see text) ventured to point out that, perhaps, it hadn't been *quite* like that...

September 30, 1950 – Goodwood Trophy: BRM's second-ever race win, and the major success of this dank day as Reg Parnell wails home 12.4sec clear of 'B.Bira''s Maserati – yet to emerge from the gloom beyond. Earlier that afternoon Reg had won the Woodcote Cup by just 1.6sec from 'Bira'.

it was left to prewar ERA exponent Prince 'Bira' to close rapidly onto Parnell's tail in his latest Enrico Plate-prepared Maserati. The immaculate Siamese rushed up close to the BRM's tail under braking, only to fall away astern under acceleration. On the pit apron Ray looked worried to death, craning each time the car spumed by to keep it in sight as long as possible.

Then abruptly it was fifth time past the pits. With just 1.6sec separating Parnell and 'Bira', 'Ebby Jr' swung down his chequered flag. The BRM had won the first race it had actually started, averaging 78.5mph in foul conditions. And Reg Parnell had also set fastest lap, at a brave 82.01mph.

September 30, 1950 – *The Daily Graphic* Goodwood Trophy Formula 1 race – 12 laps, 28.8 miles

BRM drew a second-row start position for Parnell in this, the day's main race. Reg brought the car onto the grid, then clambered out to chat to Ray beneath that blue umbrella while the mechanics bundled a tarpaulin into their car's cockpit. "Then the B.R.M. was push-started, its grand exhaust note broke out, and Parnell again held its r.p.m. high..."

After another cautious start, this time Parnell took the lead from 'Bira' under acceleration away from the first corner, at Madgwick, the BRM snaking as its rear wheels spun under power. Parnell was struggling as the V16's front end also lacked bite and its front wheels visibly leaned outwards under lateral load. At times under braking, 'Bira''s Maserati closed right up onto the BRM's tail, but Parnell always had sufficient power to draw away along the straights. He never got into top gear, but as the rain fell more heavily he had time to crane round and peer behind him through the murk as he passed the pits on lap three.

The BBC radio commentary told the tale, as Parnell brought the BRM home to its second victory that day, this time beating 'Bira' by 12.4sec at an average of 82.48mph. Again the Derby farmer had set fastest lap, this time at 84.95. When presented with the Goodwood Trophy, filled with champagne, Parnell insisted upon RM enjoying the first sip...

With 'Bira''s little team at Goodwood was Tony Rudd: And 'Bira' complained that Reg had baulked him and nearly had him off the road several times. He said it was not an important enough race to risk his car in a senseless collision, and of all people Reg was the last one to tangle with in such a fashion… we have all heard this story repeated by many drivers…

Fleet Street went quite overboard in heralding the new British world-beater's brilliant victories. Amongst the responsible press even the *Daily Telegraph's* headline read: 'B.R.M. TRIUMPH RENEWS HOPES' and its report described how Parnell "…streaked past Bira after the first bend like a jet-fighter passing a bomber."

Amongst the specialist press, *Autosport* enthused:

> Goodwood, 30th September, 1950, was a red letter day for British motor racing…Reg Parnell gave positive proof of the raceworthy possibilities of the BRM…Parnell was the ideal demonstrator. On a circuit made treacherous by heavy rain, he went fast enough to keep in front, obviously driving the car well within its capabilities. After the Silverstone debacle, the satisfactory showing of the B.R.M. was heartening to its sponsors, and delighted the spectators…

Motor Sport – usually detested by rabid BRM supporters as a persistent 'knocker', but reacting to the mass media's treatment of the double-headed Goodwood success – was perfectly even-handed and objective:

> It was gratifying that the B.R.M. driven by Reg Parnell won both its races…what, then, did it all add up to? …Everyone, ourselves included, was delighted that the B.R.M. won, but it is nonsense to say that the car was proved a world-beater in full-length Grands Prix on its Goodwood showing or that it subdued 'strong opposition'. It raced, in fact, for just over 30 minutes, or 40.8 miles… In the light of the foregoing, enormous credit goes to Raymond Mays for immediately pressing for a B.R.M. entry in the 200-mile race at Barcelona, even at the risk of the cars 'blowing up'. That is a far more sensible test, one from which valuable lessons, victory or not, cannot fail to result, and it is high time the B.R.M. was tested in this manner… The thoughts and good wishes of every British enthusiast [are] with Mays and the Trust…

Yet again Alfred Owen had missed the races, Ray writing to him on the following Monday:

> You of all people have made this possible…The whole day was most satisfactory. The organisers were most helpful in every way, and the B.R.M. appearance was staged in a most dignified manner…

The next Trust meeting was scheduled for Tuesday, October 10, at the Royal Empire Society in North Avenue, London WC2. There it was decided to enter two BRMs in the Pena Rhin GP at Barcelona, Spain, on October 29. PB had previously flown out to Barcelona to inspect the city's very fast Pedralbes boulevard circuit. The Pena Rhin itself was effectively a Catalan businessmen's club, which had organized its own Grand Prix

race around the Pedralbes suburb since 1946. The 1950 race was a front-line event, but that year *neither* 'the Spanish Grand Prix' *nor* a World Championship round.

PB reported to the Trust meeting that the Pena Rhin had agreed to pay "the expenses of British Racing Motors Limited in Spain" plus starting money for two cars. Captain Hopcraft proposed the entry, Denis Flather seconded the motion and it was duly passed, drivers being nominated as Mr Reg Parnell and Mr Peter Walker with – as reserve – Mr Ken Richardson.

Also at that Trust meeting, general production was approved of sufficient components to provide four chassis, three with Mark 1 engines, the other with Mark 1A, complete, plus two Mark 1A engines and two sets of consumable engine and chassis spares.

The use of foreign drivers to ensure the best possible results had been discussed by the Trust. Tony Vandervell – now largely reconciled after his earlier eruptions – was keen. As early as September 22 he had sent, as he wrote to Owen:

> …a 'feeler' telegram to Ascari…to see whether he was interested. The reply I received was very encouraging, and I had to send a delaying telegram in order to obtain the Trust Council's permission to carry the matter to the concluding stages, if possible…it would appear that Ascari is willing but Commandant [*sic*] Ferrari has already made arrangements for him to drive. This seems to close the matter for Barcelona, but the door is still open for the future…

GAV continued:

> I would like to give my views on foreign drivers. To my mind there are only three top flight European drivers left, namely, Fangio, Farina and Ascari. Farina is in hospital, leaving only two. So it would appear we must fall back on English drivers. I would not recommend Bira to be employed. I do not think his sportsmanship at Goodwood [where he had reportedly brushed wheels with the BRM at one stage] was very encouraging, and there is bad feeling between Parnell and Bira. Furthermore, *a situation could very easily arise between any coloured and white person…* [My italics – DCN. One can imagine the Siamese Prince and even more so his patrician cousin and former racing manager Prince Chula having apoplexy had they heard GAV referring to them like this!] All these facts would not help to win races, and I would vote against it…

[signature]

Having now tasted some success, there was a movement within the Trust at this time for the Production Committee to resign, enabling RM and PB to run Bourne as of old with the "magic touch" which only pure-bred racing specialists could legendarily (mythically?) provide. Bernard Scott of Lucas was bitterly opposed, insisting that no such move should be made until a professional Controller had been assigned to Bourne. He warned: "Unless this is done there can be no end to present unsatisfactory position where clearly personal situations are being placed above best interests of project. Lucas Organisation will not accept decisions of present executive committee..."

This vexed question of a Controller at Bourne failing BRM's complete removal to a new base closer to the industrial Midlands became a *cause celebre*, which infuriated RM and PB and gave Owen – their main supporter – terrific problems as he became a cushion between them and their main critics, Scott and Flather – who had suggested the appointment of W.O. Bentley to run the project in place of them.

Meanwhile, the decision to enter the Pena Rhin GP had galvanized the works at Bourne and Folkingham. PB generally considered that the cars "had reached a stage of reasonable overall reliability and performance without vices. The road holding was considered to be good, and the steering improved after trackrod modification and by varying tyre pressures..." [28]

Modifications considered necessary but impracticable in the time available involved the drum brakes which PB knew might not last if used hard throughout a 200-mile race; too-heavy steering, particularly under acceleration in slow corners due – he suspected – to the ZF differential's limited-slip action; and performance clearly limited by the carburettor restriction, "...but it was impracticable to fit either larger or more carburettors immediately...".

"On brakes...", PB would recall "...we had made the usual multitudinous tests of front-to-rear ratio, pedal leverage ratio, materials for linings, drums, etc, and we had found ways of reconciling the usual incompatible demands of not enough available pedal travel, too heavy a pedal, too light a pedal, insufficient wearable depth of lining, drivers whose legs were too long, etc. We got the brakes so that they pulled the car up squarely without too much or too little pedal effort, and we could use up a fair amount of lining without adjustment. We tried to get better cooling to the brakes. They would get very hot indeed on occasions in the future and we had laboratory tests in hand on different materials, and to clear up the large number of unknowns and contradictory opinions on drum proportions. We thought some of the complication in our brake mechanism, put in to guard against troubles not found to be so serious after all, was not earning its keep. Our brakes juddered on occasion, but one or two cures were available for this and were to be tried shortly...

"The pneumatic suspension struts gave very little trouble and were thoroughly successful. Their advantages included a variable rate, variable with displacement, and weight no more than that of the usual shock absorber alone. As first tried they had only internal pneumatic damping which proved insufficient, but external hydraulic dampers were added temporarily, which were replaced by internal hydraulic damping built into the strut. Many combinations of strut damper settings were tried, and we found to our surprise that road holding and steering improved when we raised the tyre pressures..." (for Barcelona).

"Steering was at first much too heavy, owing to an incorrect guess at the box ratio required, and was soon improved, though we needed to get the steering effort lighter still if possible. When the car starts to go really fast we may have to revise our ideas again..." (They would indeed.)

Meanwhile, one of the most notable differences between

the cars built at that time involved the vast scuttle fuel tank and the long oil tank sited along the right side of the engine bay, as PB explained: "Fuel tanks were of a construction method successful on touring cars but not used before on racing cars, and suffered a good deal from leaks when first fitted. They had to be as light as possible, and were difficult to design correctly because of their awkward shape, the road shocks to which they were subjected, and the swilling about of fuel when part full under braking, cornering and accelerating loads. By plentiful reinforcing and stiffening they became better, but at the expense of much added weight.

"The cooling system at first lost water via the vent pipe, but a later header tank and slight pressurising avoided this... The long oil tank caused us some anxiety about oil surges leaving the pump dry, but we achieved control over the oil inside it by means of baffles and flaps. Pomeroy maintained that our exhaust pipes should be larger. We agreed, but we had to maintain *some* ground clearance." [29]

Jack Emmott's team-management role had been adopted by Peter Haynes, the Lucas competitions manager, but for most of the mechanics the Pena Rhin race would provide their first-ever trip abroad.

Ken Richardson was by far the most experienced Continental traveller amongst them, and when the two cars, race equipment and necessary spares were loaded aboard two of the Lodestars and the Commer workshop, PB took command of the convoy, led by Ken Richardson – at the wheel of the Commer – and at last, BRM went off to war in Europe...

SO THIS IS GRAND PRIX RACING?

BRM's transporter convoy sailed from Dover to disembark in Dunkirk at 4am on the Monday preceding the Spanish race. They faced a 900-mile drive, their speed set by the heavily-laden Commer. It would run out of puff on any appreciable hill but could cruise at 60-70mph on a level straight. Of the Austins, ETL 485 was the quickest – good for 68mph thanks to its rear axle ratio being 'longer' than its sisters. They reached Avalon on the first night, and Montpellier on the second, where the trucks were parked in the main square under an overnight guard of local *Gendarmes*. Barcelona was reached on the Wednesday, where PB, Ken and the nine mechanics met Parnell and Peter Walker, who had been learning the circuit in the latter's Jaguar XK120.

Back home, in London's Berkeley Hotel, Ray paced the carpet, chain-smoking and worried. PB had urged him to drive one of the cars at Barcelona, saying: "It's just your kind of circuit...", but Ray had demurred. He was in fact close to breakdown; his nerves worn to screaming pitch by that long, trying summer. He looked, and felt, ill. He told Alfred Owen

---

28. From PB's internal *'Technical Report to October 31st, 1950'*.

29. Tony Rudd: Exhaust pipes should be larger? I am very surprised at this. There is only one correct area of exhaust pipe for a given engine performance. The Massachusetts Institute of Technology published a paper on this around 1948 which was every engine designer's and tuner's Bible, including PB's. He certainly had a well-thumbed copy when I arrived.

FOLKINGHAM AERODROME

The tiny, straggly village of Folkingham lies across the main A15 road running north from Bourne towards Sleaford. Away to the west the ground rises, folded into abrupt humps and dips before opening out unexpectedly onto a high, bleak, plateau. Here stood Folkingham Aerodrome, today a barren wasteland, most of its concrete wartime runways long gone to provide motorway hardcore. Its remains are part cluttered beneath an enormous scrap-yard, although a small cluster of ex-BRM test house buildings are home to historic car restoration specialists Hall & Fowler.

The land here was first selected by the Air Ministry as a decoy airfield 'KQ Site' in 1940, intended to attract enemy aircraft away from nearby RAF Grantham. 'K Sites' were intended as look-alike daytime decoys, equipped with dummy hangars, aircraft and vehicles. 'Q Sites' on the same land were rigged with dummy flare-paths, or badly-masked lights to represent factories or railway marshalling yards. Folkingham KQ lay in Air Ministry area K2 and would have been crewed like its sisters by about 20 men who erected, maintained and operated its 'deceptions'.

By the end of 1941, night-time Q Sites had been credited with attracting 359 attacks, while the airfields they were defending had sustained 358 attacks. So the ploy was quite successful. As the German air offensive diminished into 1942, the number of operational decoy sites was rapidly reduced, but into 1943 contractors moved onto the plateau above Folkingham to develop it into a standard-pattern Heavy Bomber Station for No. 5 Group, RAF Bomber Command.

Before construction ended, several South Lincolnshire airfields were transferred to the USAAF for their Troop Carrier Groups. The new Folkingham Airfield was one of them, becoming US IXth Air Force 'Air Station 484'. It opened for business on February 5, 1944, under the 52nd Troop Carrier Wing. On February 24, Colonel James J. Roberts Jr led in the 313th TC Group's 29th, 47th, 48th and 49th Squadrons' combined total of 70 Douglas C47 Dakota transports.

From Folkingham – shortly before midnight on June 5, 1944 – the 508th Parachute Infantry and 82nd US Airborne took off for the Normandy Landings. Around 02.00 on June 6, the 313th TCG's C47s dropped 1,181 paratroopers intended for Dropping Zone 'N', some 5km south of Ste Mere Eglise. Three Folkingham aircraft were lost on this mission, and 24 damaged.

On June 7 a re-supply mission was flown by 52 Folkingham C47s, many sustaining further damage. Re-supply and advanced-area transport duties then kept the aerodrome busy until September 17, 1944, when the 313th TCG's C47s embarked the British 1st Parachute Brigade – bound for Arnhem.

Next day, 42 assault gliders were tugged from Folkingham to the Dutch battle zone.

After the 'Bridge Too Far' Battle of Arnhem had been fought, the station's C47 Squadrons were committed to Continental re-supply and casualty evacuation until, on February 23, 1945, the 313th TCG began to move to advanced airbases in France.

After barely 13 months' active service, on March 20, 1945, Folkingham closed to operational flying. The USAAF formally vacated the station on April 15 and on June 4 it joined 40 Group, RAF Maintenance Command, intended as a sub-site for 16 Maintenance Unit, Stafford. Then officialdom changed its mind, and on August 10, 1945, Folkingham Aerodrome was handed on to 22 Group, Technical Training Command, becoming home to No. 3 RAF Regiment Sub-Depot, preparing the Air Force's own soldier corps for posting overseas.

After this unit left in mid-1946, the site reverted to Maintenance Command in 1947, its runways, perimeter track, hard-standings and very many buildings distributed in five sites, surviving in generally good order. Through Henderson-Tate, of the Ministry of Supply, strings were pulled enabling BRM to use the aerodrome's runways and perimeter track as a test facility, and subsequently to rent premises there for their race-preparation and engine test 'shops. This BRM pound centred around the wartime control tower – subsequently converted to provide a flat for the Berthon family on the first floor while caretaker/go-for Jock Milne occupied the ground floor with his colony of cats sleeping in a chest of drawers.

When the RAF presence at Folkingham was ended, the Maintenance Command officers there threw a farewell party, to which Harry Mundy and his staff from Bourne were invited. It developed into "a gigantic booze-up in the Officers' Mess…", as Aubrey Woods recalled, "reminiscent of the BRM unveiling when we were all paralytic; Alfred Owen really didn't approve. This time I rode back to Bourne with Tony Sadler in his car, while Harry drove the rest down in his old fabric-bodied Alvis. He was going well until he reached the bend just beyond Rippingale crossroads, where he spun, rolled the car, it caught fire and burned out! Charlie Davey had been sitting in the back and he was clouted on the head by a spare diff which had been lying there. They all survived, but Harry went AWOL and wouldn't go to the police station until he'd sobered up!"

The lease arrangement between the Air Ministry and BRM specified that none of their installations could be permanent – everything had to be removable within 28 days' notice. This even

---

he could better serve the cause by staying in London to "…talk BRM to the important visitors I will meet at the Motor Show…".

In Barcelona, the team took residence at the Automobiles Fernandez Mercedes-Benz agency. In London's Steering Wheel Club odds of 10-to-1 were offered against a BRM win. In first practice both cars performed rather poorly. Ken Richardson was allowed to drive a considerable mileage in Peter Walker's car – chassis 'No. 2' – and when Walker finally had a go he spun while exploring how late he could brake. His tentative demeanour needled Vandervell, present with David Brown – and both became increasingly irritated by the inanity of another visiting Trustee, the garrulous Donald McCullough.

The V16s' carburation gave PB headaches and the mechanics late-night work, while a broken low-pressure oil pipe had to be repaired on Walker's car. The Ferraris of Ascari and Taruffi lapped in 2min 23.8sec, Serafini's third-quickest at 2:26.4[30], then Parnell's BRM 'No. 1' on 2:30.4. Walker managed 2:31.8, 0.4sec quicker than de Graffenried's Maserati and 1.8sec inside Louis Rosier's best with the Talbot-Lago. Final preparation began for the Sunday race…and the team's new-fangled, motorcycle-engined high-pressure refuelling system was started, and gingerly tested by the apprehensive mechanics.

30. All these times are quoted from BRM's *Orden de Salida* list provided to them by the Pena Rhin organizers. Some contemporary press accounts quote slightly different times.

entailed the Bourne drawing office designing a semi-mobile dyno test-bed.

The site remained home to BRM's racing team until 1959, during which period the surfaces of its runways and perimeter track had deteriorated so badly the 'test circuit' there was hazardous if not, quite useless.

Meanwhile, in March 1957, American President Eisenhower and British Prime Minister Macmillan had met in Bermuda, where they agreed that the RAF should develop a UK-based Strategic Missile Wing to bring potential Soviet targets within nuclear range. It would deploy new Intermediate Range Ballistic Missiles – the Douglas Thor IRBMs. They were to carry US nuclear warheads under dual-key Anglo-American control.

Four squadrons were to be formed, each with 15 missiles deployed on 20 dispersed sites. Folkingham was selected to house No. 223 (SM) Squadron, RAF, so BRM was given notice, ending its 10-year tenancy of most of the aerodrome.

Contractors moved in to build the standard Thor site, with three revetted concrete launch pads, on part of the plateau. Douglas Company technicians then followed to install the hardware. However, BRM was allowed to re-install its engine test equipment in another ex-USAAF building, further from the missile site, where it remained throughout the team's active life.

The fixed-site Thor system provided an arguable degree of nuclear deterrence but was, inevitably, vulnerable to pre-emptive attack. This was recognized even before it became fully operational (by May 1960) a month after the Tory Government had abandoned Britain's own intended replacement silo-launched Blue Streak ICBM system.

In May 1962, the US Secretary of 'Defense' – those colonials never could spell – announced that support for the RAF Thor force would end on October 31, 1964. In August, the Whitehall Ministry of Defence confirmed that Thor would be phased-out by the end of 1963, with no British replacement.

Only two of 12 RAF Thor test firings at Vandenburg AFB in California had been regarded as successful. The last Thor missile was returned to America on September 27, 1963, ending the RAF's brief dabble with strategic missiles...

They finally abandoned the Folkingham site, its runway concrete being salvaged after virtually all its many buildings had been demolished. Today, this bare, exposed corner of Lincolnshire lies abandoned to the elements, although into the mid-1990s Willie Southcott's old domain at the BRM dyno house survives amongst the small cluster of buildings in which former team mechanics Rick Hall, Rob Fowler and their men still make old racing cars – many of them BRMs – run so well...

October 26, 1950 – Pena Rhin Grand Prix, Pedralbes circuit, Barcelona, Spain – 50 laps, 195 miles

On race morning the BRMs were the last cars to arrive at the tarpaulin-draped scaffolding pits, behind which the Commer was parked. Parnell's blue-nosed 'No. 1' took position on the front row alongside the three big V12 Ferraris, 4.5-litre cars for Ascari and Serafini, a 4.1 for Taruffi. Walker's red-nosed 'No. 2' had created a minor panic with just an hour to go when a fuel tank was found to be leaking, and was hurriedly fixed.

After some confusion resulting in an initial false start, the flag fell and Parnell eased gently away.

Perhaps BRM's Pena Rhin race story is told best in PB's *Technical Report to October 31st 1950*, which he compiled for the Trust on November 15, while recuperating with his secretary, Mrs Vickers, at the sunny Hotel Miramar, Puerto Pollensa, Mallorca. His original is virtually unparagraphed and, therefore, difficult to read. I have merely paragraphed this version for clarity's sake; otherwise it is as Katie Vickers typed it, upon PB's dictation:

The Barcelona event was disappointing in results, but proved extremely valuable from the development point of view, particularly as three 4½ litre[31] unsupercharged Ferraris were competing which represent the most serious opposition at the present time.

The Course, although extremely fast, showed to have a bumpy road surface at racing speeds, and from observers opinions, it was considered that the cars looked steadier than the Ferraris and that the B.R.M.s were taking all bends at slower speeds than the Italian drivers, and on the two slow corners at each end of the straight, they appeared to lack acceleration and lost time initially on the "open out". It was confirmed also that the Italians had better brakes and were using them harder than our drivers. There were 3 practices of 3 hours each, but we practised on the Thursday and Friday only.

Parnell and Walker secured 4th and 5th fastest times (after the 3 Ferraris) but were 7 seconds per lap slower than Ascari's best time. This time was being lost mainly on the 2 slow corners due to poor initial "open out" when using 2nd gear, and generally through all bends due to our drivers using the brakes less and not driving with the same verve. The mid-range acceleration and up to about 150mph. was superior to that of the Ferraris, and our cars could catch up a certain amount every time pure acceleration was needed.

Parnell's car (blue) had a slightly higher maximum on the straight than Taruffi's Ferrari, possibly by 5m.p.h., although he could not pull more than 10,300r.p.m. Walker's car (red) appeared fastest and was able to pull 10,700r.p.m. This car was definitely faster than any Ferrari in maximum. Parnell seemed quite happy in the car, and was able to put up good lap times fairly consistently, but has not the flair to keep up with the best of the Italian drivers on the twisty section of the course.

Walker, to start with, was completely at sea, and was, on the average, 10 seconds a lap slower than Parnell, but managed towards the end of the second practice to make a supreme effort and do one lap equal to Parnell's best.

The total running in practice amounted to about half the race distance, i.e. 100 miles per car, the red car doing rather more than the blue, and throughout the cars behaved well with no signs of trouble apart from minor oil leaks and one broken supercharger oil feed pipe and low pressure feeds on both cars. Prior to the race it was found that the water blow-off valve was seized

31. Not strictly true, Taruffi's was a 4.1.

October 27, 1950 – the BRM team's Barcelona garage before Pena Rhin GP practice. BRM new recruit William George 'Willie' Southcott fastens the bonnet strap on Reg Parnell's assigned 'No. 1'. Willie was an absolute BRM stalwart until he succumbed to cancer in 1972. Ex-merchant navy, torpedoed twice, mined off the Normandy beaches, he had swallowed the anchor to become filing clerk in Rolls-Royce's photo-negative library in Slack Lane, Derby, before joining BRM. Arthur 'Hammy' Ambrose looks on as Chief Mechanic-cum test driver Ken Richardson prepares for some exploratory laps.

solid on the blue car, and that the front fuel tank on the red car had split on the right hand side on a seam near the frame. Generally, the bumpy circuit showed that the tank mountings and bodywork fastenings are not nearly good enough. Body panels were tearing at the joints and fastenings between tanks, and panels continually came adrift.

Parnell started in the 4th position on the front line, i.e. left hand side of the course, and Walker on the right hand position in the second line, the start being 4-3-4. Parnell made a poor getaway and nearly stalled his engine, but at the end of the straight caught up and was right on the heels of the three Ferrari's [sic]. Walker stalled his engine at the start and was 'push-started' after the field had left. Parnell maintained his position but came into the pits on the 3rd lap saying that the engine had no power and felt like an unsupercharged engine. Superficial inspection showed something seriously wrong with the supercharger and/or drive. This car was withdrawn.

Walker ran steadily at lap speeds varying from 2.38 to 2.46, which was not good enough to catch the two Gordini-blown 1500 Simcas. His car appeared to be running well and we brought him in for a fuel refill at 26 laps (50 lap race). Everything appeared O.K. at pit stops, tyres looked as though they had not done any work. [PB does not mention here that the refuelling system could not at first be started, costing much time – DCN]

Some laps after this car developed "missing" and waffle in the exhaust under full load. Walker came into the pits and complained the engine was missing but there was nothing that could be done. He was sent out again and the car appeared perfectly O.K. for some laps. He came in of his own accord a few laps later with gear box trouble, and said that he no longer had 4th and 5th gears. As there were not many more laps to go, he was sent out again to try and finish but came out again after 2 laps and gave up.

Impression was that Walker was not happy and was anxious to abandon the race. At the time of the pit stop he was in 5th place due to retirements, and would have got into 4th place as the Gordini Simca blew up a few laps later. Subsequent inspection showed that the plugs looked perfectly O.K. in this engine. Prior to Walker's pit stop, we noticed that oil was burning on the nearside exhaust tail pipe and it was obvious that oil was being lost from the gearbox, so that gearbox trouble was expected to follow.

The Ferrari's [sic] ran through without a pit stop. Ascari's rear tyres were through the tread and would not have lasted for more than a further 3 laps. The other 2 Ferrari's [sic] were in similar condition but the tyres were not quite so worn. Tarrufi's [sic] car finished with 25 litres (measured) in the tank, and it was noticeable that these engines were extremely clean after the race with clean cockpits and no oil leaks.

October 28, 1950 – Pena Rhin GP practice, Pedralbes, Barcelona: Jack North and Southcott (working on the Walker car) spare the photographers a wry glance as PB, Donald McCullough, Peter Walker, Ken Richardson, Trustee David Brown and Walter Hill of the BRM Association star.

Summarising the information learned from this event:

(1) A serious and immediate effort must be made to overcome the present restriction of carburettors by either using bigger carburettors, or changing over to fuel injection. The maximum time speed given for Parnell's car was 300km per hour (180m.p.h.) timed over a ⅛km stretch towards the end of the straight. This speed was unlikely and according to the r.p.m. reported by Parnell, our maximum speed did not exceed 165/170m.p.h. In any case Walker's car was the fastest on the straight.

(2) The present choice of gear ratios is not suitable and 3rd and 4th gears require to be raised in order to narrow the gap on the high range.

(3) The poor low speed "pick up" is causing loss of time when accelerating from slow corners (i.e. 30/35m.p.h.). This condition will be improved considerably by Rolls-Royce, but in any case drivers must master the technique of keeping the r.p.m. up and using all the ratios. Walker was particularly bad at this and has difficulty in appreciating that the engine must not be allowed to pull below 7,000r.p.m. Using bottom gears for the two slow corners makes more work for the Drivers and adds 4 additional gear changes per lap. It would be psychologically better if we calibrated our tachometers from 2,000 to 6,000r.p.m., instead of 4,000 to 12,000 as at present.[32]

(4) The weight of the car has been increased by approximately 2½cwt.[33] since the prototype was built, due to larger and heavier batteries, double weight of brakes due to additional and heavier components, larger and heavier water and oil radiators, heavier tanks due to reinforcing etc., which has made a serious difference to acceleration at low r.p.m. A serious attempt must be made to reduce the weight at least to the original designed figure of 1600lbs. dry.

(5) The brakes are still not satisfactory, although reasonably consistent, but they were not used hard by either driver during the practice or race. There may be some front wheel judder when the brakes are put on hard causing drivers to use them gently. Experience shows that "judder" is more prevalent when using Ferodo VG.95 linings, than when using Mintex M15.

(6) The fuel filling apparatus is unsatisfactory and should be scrapped. It is difficult to handle, erratic in performance, and the mechanics seem frightened of it. Although the conception is sound, the application of the 500c.c. single cylinder engine is unsatisfactory. Unfortunately, no accurate information could be collected concerning fuel consumption, as during practice it was found necessary to continually richen up the carburation in order to avoid "popping back" on the straights. (This circuit lies on the edge of the sea.)

(7) Although Walker's driving technique improved considerably during practice, it is obvious that drivers must have considerable experience and training in the handling of these cars prior to racing. Walker's ex-E.R.A. technique is a waste of time. Our drivers simply do not have the ability to maintain their speeds in the corners

---

32. **This is the beginning of the thinking which led to the BRM V16's horizontal strip tachometers merely presenting colours to the driver, his instructions then being to keep engine revs within the 'green' sector.**

33. **"2½cwt' – 'two and a half hundredweight', one hundredweight being the old English weight measure which equalled 112lbs, 50.8kg.**

as the best of the Italian and French appear to do.

(8) There is a good deal of cleaning up to do. There are far too many oil leaks and our pipework and general installation of accessories is not nearly good enough. A serious attempt should be made to reduce pipework to a minimum and use flexibles where-ever possible. The tanks showed a considerable amount of movement on such a rough circuit. The mountings must be redesigned and bodywork as far as possible isolated from tanks. Front tank particularly requires attention as excessive movement may be influencing the steering. The oil temperatures were running too high, 120°C on both cars, water 90–95°C on both cars, oil pressure 40/50lbs. according to oil temperatures, which are unsatisfactory. Cockpits still too hot under these conditions of fine weather, brilliant sunshine, ambient temperature off road probably 25–28°C.

(9) Tank capacities want reconsidering as these cars must be able to run 200 miles without refuelling. Ferrari claim 320 b.h.p. which figures cannot be far wrong. It can be assumed that they will push this up to 350–360 next year. The Alfa Romeo with their 12-cylinder [sic][34] 1½ litre can be expected to be nearer the 380 mark.

(10) General turnout was not good enough, and can be much improved. Arrangements for the race went awry due to the discovery of a fuel leak mentioned earlier in these notes, until a few hours before the race, and a very quick repair had to be made.

The mechanics overalls are particularly bad, they being of the wrong style for motor racing, together with an unsatisfactory fluffy material which picks up the dirt too readily.

Mrs. Parnell[35] kept a lap chart and our 2 drivers' practice lap times. This was well and efficiently done.

(11) The transporters are satisfactory, but better provision must be made for holding the Racing Cars in position, and prevent spare wheels etc. chafing on long journeys. The workshop lorry was found to be extremely useful and apart from a few minor points, the general installation seems practicable and works well. The speed of this vehicle is too slow as it limits the speed of the convoy, the ready maximum on the level not being more than 45m.p.h.[36] Peter Haynes of Lucas did an excellent job with the final installation and packing, and lists of spares. As a result of the experience gained on this trip,

34. PB was referring to the phantom flat-12-engined *Alfetta* replacement which was much-rumoured at that time, the dominant *Tipo* 158 *Alfetta* itself, of course, using a straight-eight supercharged engine.

35. 'Mrs Parnell' is sympathetic and tactful, but Reg was separated from his wife, and the lady in question, Reg's long-time companion, was Betty Offiler of the Derby brewing family, not son Tim's mother.

36. Tony Rudd takes considerable exception to this since he recalls personal experience of the maligned Commer being good for 70mph on the level: I suspect PB was grinding an axe against someone in the Midland AC who donated the vehicle. Moss had a similar one (later) for his cars which carried a lighter load. His mechanic 'Alf Francis' claimed 80mph. Our's was 6 inches lower and 3 feet longer, which should have given better aerodynamics...

THE BARCELONA FAILURES
PENA RHIN 1950

When stripped, the faults which had sidelined the cars of Parnell and Walker at Pedralbes were revealed as follows:

1. PARNELL's Car

A supercharger rotor bearing failed. This caused the quill shaft that drives the rotor to twist off and the supercharger stopped turning. The purpose of the quill shaft is to fail if anything goes wrong with the supercharger and avoid excessive damage, which it did in this case. The rotors had rubbed the casing very slightly, and the whole blower can be put back into condition by merely replacing the bearing.

The bearing is a special one for the high rotational speed of 45,000rpm, designed and made by Fischer[37].

Rolls-Royce have examined the bearing, and report that an incorrect design of cage was fitted...and that the cage failed first. The cage was of a type more suited to a roller bearing, having slots for the balls closed off by a plain bronze ring riveted on. It should have had hemispherical or circular recesses and been split through the plane of the balls.

The races showed signs that bronze powder was rolled into the surface by the balls, indicating that the case disintegrated first... Rolls-Royce are ascertaining from Fischers how such an unsuitable cage came to be fitted...

2. WALKER's Car

A stud came out of the gearbox and allowed all the oil to fall out in the road.

The entire box, casings, gears, shafts, bearings and differential are in the overheated condition that would be expected, and are scrap.

This stud was definitely a design defect. It was screwed into insufficient depth of aluminium in the casing and had only about three threads in the aluminium to hold in. Its tapped hole broke into the scavenge oil pump outlet so that when it fell out nothing stopped the oil from running out.

The stud was one holding the gearbox oil pump in position, and in this case the oil pump was assembled separately from the box and fitted at a late hour one night before leaving for Barcelona. The stud pulled out when the pump was being fitted and was replaced by the fitter with an Allen screw, which itself fell out during the race.

Though the fitter should have reported this, and either fitted an oversize Allen screw or positively locked it in position with wire, the initial mistake was defective design.

Other boxes will have stepped studs fitted to give larger diameter threads and will be wire-locked all together. The defect is being avoided on the new gearbox now being made.

37. In fact an unsuitable bearing had been fitted because BRM was tied to Hoffman, whereas Rolls-Royce *recommended* Fischer.

better provision for carrying spares have to be made in the future to prevent chafing of panels etc.

(12) The team behaved extremely well on this, their first Continental race, and with training through the winter, the mechanics we took will form a basis for a first class team next year.

Only one man can be in charge of such a team. It is quite impracticable to have discussions or hold meetings on the hour to hour decisions that have to be taken immediately. A proposed change of drivers was rendered impossible through a meeting called by the Chairman after second practice. It is quite useless to have any controlling personality who has not had vast experience of motor racing.

(13) The B.R.M. has shown in this, its first event, that it is sound proposition, and has the performance under present conditions effectively equal to that of the 4½ litre Ferrari. There is no question that the improvements that will be effected this winter by the fitting of the new type supercharger, better breathing and carburation arrangements, reduction in weight, slightly improved steering and better brakes, will give us a potential performance a good deal ahead of the opposition with reliability.

(14) The question of drivers is of paramount importance. If we must overcome the present handicap in time for next Season, which means that a serious programme of finding and training drivers through this winter must be tackled without delay.

(15) A Team Secretary who is responsible for financial and general arrangements is essential. It is too much to leave the whole of the organisation, finance, technical and race control to one person.

PB/KK   P.B.
15.11.50

Hotel Miramar,
Puerto Pollensa,
Mallorca,
Baleares.

PB fell ill during his post-race holiday, and stayed on Mallorca – and subsequently in Barcelona – longer than planned. Perhaps uncharitably, some team members recall that he often fell ill after a Continental race, particularly when he had drawn the start money as well… During this particular 'illness' he considered not only the race itself but also Bernard Scott's threatened reorganization of the BRM project. He wrote to Alfred Owen from Barcelona, saying in part:

…The results of the Barcelona event were disappointing but extremely valuable from the viewpoint of meeting the opposition and securing information about the cars and drivers under full Grand Prix racing conditions. The event has been very well worth while, and in fact without it, we may not have found some of the more important troubles until our first event next year.

My views for the immediate future of the project and control of the actual work in the main, line up with Ray's, and I think that one thing we have learned beyond any question is that the less people directly involved the better, and the more those who have to do the work are left alone to get on with it, the quicker we shall get results.

Briefly summarising my views on some of the points that have been under discussion:

(1) There have been only two important aspects of this project, (a) finances, (b) engineering. The Trust should control finances through their Trustees. Engineering should be left to the Engineers, and if the Trust have faith in their ability, they should give them maximum support and freedom of action. If the Trust lack confidence, they should say so and make immediate changes.

(2) The financial problem is all important. I do not believe the staff can settle to real hard work enthusiastically unless the finances are under-written by a number of firms over a definite period of at least 4 years which is now the life of the present Grand Prix Formula.

(3) The administration of the actual work and works is extremely simple and the important features are better, and closer liaison to secure speedier delivery of urgent requirements for development and production of the few cars laid down.

(4) The publicity and attempts at public finances have done us considerable harm. Our mission should be to proceed quietly with single aim of getting results.

(5) Any move to the Midlands or under the wing of any one concern would jeopardise the project at the present time. Should at a future date, the Trust find itself financially able to acquire and maintain a works on completely neutral territory with improved general facilities for the project, then is the time for consideration, but this should be a Trust undertaking through its own financial assets as a whole.

(6) It is quite impracticable to split the building of a few racing cars as suggested by Hill's report and discussed in Scott's letter. Races cannot be won by inspectors.

(7) I would not be willing to work under any Controller unless he was a man who knew a good deal more about the subject than I, and was of a calibre that one expects of a true Managing Director. I would vigorously oppose the installation of any opportunist.

(8) If the Trust members have thoughts on the position of Ray and myself and consider any changes necessary, they should make their motives clear. I believe our position is only thrown into relief through the difficulties that might arise in giving some form of Controller sufficient authority…

Kind regards,
Yours sincerely,

Ray had already aired similar sentiments about the threatened changes, having been particularly incensed by

October 29, 1950 – Pena Rhin GP: Peter Walker tippy-toeing his careful way around the Pedralbes circuit while, unknown to him, 'No. 2''s transaxle is leaking away its lubricant. The unusually-styled black race numbers replaced the white used in practice, confounding the Trust's film editors whose final 'race' footage includes many practice shots…

BARCELONA – A TRUSTEE'S VIEW

Tony Vandervell was unimpressed by BRM's display at Pedralbes, and he wrote the following – including his emphatic ideas for the way ahead – to Alfred Owen on November 3, 1950:

Dear Mr. Owen,

The Trustees

I have just returned from Barcelona. The results you already know. I bought some British newspapers on the way home and I see that the B.R.M. hits front page news again.

I feel it would be unwise at this stage to make comment on the performance at Barcelona, but one or two things were very obvious, and I had conversations with friends of mine, such as Ascari, who also made comments on the way we ran the race. It was generally accepted that Reg Parnell was the only driver worth worrying about, but unfortunately he did not last very long. If he could have kept going for two more laps I feel the blow would not have been so bad, because after a dismal start he had run through the field and was about to enter into competition with the Ferraris, which were by no means slow cars.

The performance made by Walker was, in my opinion, poor. At a 'briefing' meeting prior to the race, Walker said that the car was a difficult one to drive – that he had not driven it very much – that he thought he would do better as time went on – and that really we should not expect too much from him but he would do his best. This frank admission gave me some concern and I discussed the matter with Peter Berthon and Walter Hill after we had seen him perform during practice. It was quite obvious he was not at home in the car and he did not look part of it. Peter Berthon, Walter Hill and I decided at a meeting that we would do much better with Ken Richardson. We realized the complications that would arise out of such a decision at that late stage, and we might have been jumping out of the frying pan into the fire. However, we interviewed Walker and told him that he gave us some concern by the remarks he had passed, but he explained that he had probably expressed himself badly. It was then getting very late and I am afraid we were not all in agreement that a change should be made, although I thought that any change would have been better as it was quite obvious to everyone that Walker was not at home in the car.

This drives one to the conclusion that there is lacking an executive who would be prepared to make these unbiased decisions – where the Committee fails.

Parnell reported to me that the ultimate speed of the car was not up to his expectations, and its slow performance out of corners was disappointing. The brakes were also criticised. It was plain to see that the 4½-litre Ferraris were all round better cars, and their drivers and teamwork were to be admired. The Manager of the team asked me afterwards that when Parnell dropped out why didn't we replace Walker with Parnell. If Ascari's car had broken down he would have immediately taken over Serafini's car and there would have been no unpleasant feeling between anybody. They could not understand why this decision was not made as they said they race to win and not for personal feelings. I am only conveying to you what they conveyed to me and I hope you will not feel there are any thoughts of my own in this.

Since my return I have read the correspondence which has passed between members of the Reconstruction Committee also Denis Flather. Although there is something to be said on both sides, it is obvious that a reorganisation is very necessary so as to avoid this sort of thing happening. I think the question of expenses has always been unbusinesslike, and especially where there are public funds it should not be allowed to continue in this way. We had the same situation in Barcelona with Donald McCullough who really contributed nothing and was only ridiculed by those who were serious in the game of racing. Personally I contributed nothing to the project except that I was able to see at first sight how the setup was taking shape. Here again, most of it was decided in London by all and sundry, and in my opinion it did not produce a very attractive organisation.

I am sending you herewith some Press cuttings which you may not have seen, showing the unnecessary information imparted to the Press by Raymond Mays. I find it very difficult to understand this attitude, and I have tried for some time to think it was not deliberate but just through a course of circumstances. This kind of publicity stunt contributes little to the project and I think it is time the Trustees took strong action on the future running of the B.R.M.

There is a lot of development to be done on the car and many modifications will be necessary. This is going to cost a lot of money and we do not know at this moment what alterations are necessary. The cars are obviously too heavy. Starting from the line and acceleration low down is inadequate to meet the competition, and the front end does not appear to be as stable as others. The brakes we all know about. At this stage I do not know how this job is going to be tackled, and if we are to produce more cars I am wondering what modifications should be made. I am forced to the conclusion, although I hate to say it, that we have insufficient money to make more cars and carry out these modifications, and unless a large group get together and settle some of these engineering problems and eliminate all the other nonsense, our performance next year will be even more dismal. If we cannot be assured of adequate finances, then it would be far better to close the project down owing to lack of funds. If we should decide to take any other course there are one or two things that must be done. There will have to be rearrangement of the contract between Raymond Mays and Peter Berthon. That no paid servant can sit on the Executive Council, for obvious reasons, and the finance will have to be gone into in accordance with the programme as laid down by that Council, and there must be no interference from other people. The Council should be strengthened by more people in a position to advise and to pay, and we should have a financial brain to advise us in these complicated matters which arise from time to time.

Every expenditure should be examined, and people's expenses should not be paid unless they are authorised to go by the Council on some specific job. If the followers wish to accompany the cars they should undoubtedly pay their own expenses. Voluntary women helpers should not be part of the organisation, because if it is properly run their presence is not needed, and besides that it does not create a good impression on the basis of 'an ambassador for Britain'.

In conclusion, I think the Trustees should meet as soon as possible and decide a definite programme to clean up the mess, ruthlessly if necessary. When this is done they will be able to invite to the Council those people who can help strengthen the Board financially, technically and commercially. Until this is done I feel we shall just continue in the future like we have done in the past.

I am sending you an extra copy in case you would like to send it to Mr. Scott.

Yours sincerely,

discovering: "…incidents such as Bernard Scott and Flather, without the knowledge of anyone at Bourne, partly arranging that W.O. Bentley should be employed…neither Peter nor I were consulted. I do know the racing game and everybody connected with it well enough to advise accurately about outside help, should it be required (hence my suggestion, which was adopted, re Tresilian). I was actually told from an outside source about the W.O. Bentley suggestion, and you can imagine the reaction on the mind of an outsider when I said I knew nothing about this…".

Concerning the post of Controller, RM reminded the Trust that:

> The BRM project is essentially an engineering one. To my mind all that is required is a first class works manager, who has expert knowledge and a strong personality, and in addition an employee *permanently* in charge of progress… Quite frankly, if a controller at the salary suggested [£2,500 *pa*] were appointed, neither Peter Berthon nor myself would be agreeable to such an amount being paid to someone who has neither done anything towards the project, nor to someone whom it would be difficult to keep usefully employed…

He concluded:

> I know there is a tendency to wish to 'soft-pedal' my name and for me not to play so prominent a part in the project. Further, I consider that the suggested removal from Bourne partly comes under this heading. Unless there is a really sound reason for the works to be removed, I am strongly opposed to it and it would be against my wishes…

Referring to Barcelona he remarked:

> The new unsupercharged Ferrari's [*sic*]…are undoubtedly the fastest racing cars to date. In view of this, and as Barcelona was our first real test, the actual performance of the B.R.M.s is by no means unsatisfactory. Undoubtedly the B.R.M. power unit has more scope for development than the unsupercharged Ferrari.
>
> There will be further criticisms, as always in such a project as this one. However, the country as a whole is 100% behind us. I can speak with authority on this point…owing to the numerous letters I am always receiving, from the talks I give in all parts of the

country, and through the many people with whom I come into contact...

At the start of November, Alfred Owen went with RM to Derby to meet Lord Hives, newly appointed Chairman of Rolls-Royce. Mays and Owen were becoming increasingly united in thought and attitude towards the entire project. Ray certainly felt he could count on Owen's backing at least nine times out of ten, and after all that Owen had endured he was by this time implacably determined to see BRM achieve success – with or without the Trust...

Hs expressed continuing support for the project as it stood[38], retaining PB, RM and the plant at Bourne and Folkingham. He simply offered to do all he could to help attract more support from major motor manufacturers. Owen felt that "if only we could get a dozen firms putting up a regular amount each year the financial problems of the past would be at an end..."

Hs recommended an approach through the powerful Society of Motor Manufacturers & Traders (SMMT). He also arranged to meet William Lyons of Jaguar, Sir John Black of Standard and Waring of Lucas in a campaign to persuade seven companies each to contribute £10,000 a year for five years to the BRM project.

But he found 'Bill' Lyons implacably opposed to supporting anything which still involved RM and PB – that old prewar pigeon coming home to roost once more. In addition Lyons was deeply prejudiced against anything he regarded as 'queer', and where he was concerned Ray fell squarely into that category... In modern terms Bill Lyons had the reddest of red necks, RM was 'a queer', and therefore utterly detestable...

Unfortunately at that time Lyons was President of the SMMT and despite Owen taking him to visit Bourne he effectively vetoed any recommendation for that body's support of BRM unless sweeping changes were made – including the immediate dismissal of both Mays and Berthon. At one stage Owen wrote about Lyons to Hs:

> ...even whilst he feels as he does credit must go to Raymond Mays in that he was the first one to set about the problem as he did...From all my past dealings with Lyons I have always found him very obstinate...when once he

38. Geoffrey Wilde recalls: "I am sure that Hs had little faith in the ability of such an organization to manage the operation and get things done. He was very shrewd and had a lifetime's experience in 'driving' projects. He knew what was required, and did not see it in ADL-cum-BRM. He went along with R-R support with little comment for the first three years, but after the Silverstone failure had created great embarrassment and loss of confidence to all concerned, he began to discourage any deeper involvement by us. I have seen a memo from him dated July 1949 in which he expressed the view that: 'It would be the finest thing if the project were taken over by one of the oil companies' ...surely at the time when Vandervell and Scott were floating the idea of 'somebody like Shell' doing just that?"

Tony Rudd: Hs had become R-R Chairman in October 1950 and was in the thick of the Avon turbojet/Canberra sub-contract project and would not have had time for any messing about with BRM even had he been so inclined, which I'm sure he was not. He still referred to Jaguar as the "Wardour Street Bentley" and to RM as "that gilded Popinjay"...

BARCELONA – A DRIVER'S VIEW

On November 15, 1950, while on Mallorca PB was dictating his Pena Rhin technical report to Mrs Vickers, the much criticized Peter Walker wrote to Donald McCullough as Chairman of the Trust. He thanked him for his "help and encouragement" given in Barcelona and enclosed his considered report upon the BRM, dated two days previously. It provides a vivid insight into how the BRM V16 felt to an experienced driver. It read precisely like this:

Report on B.R.M. car driven by P.C.D.W. at Barcelona

First day's practice.
The car was driven slowly generally and an effort was made to learn the new technique of getting round slow corners fast without sufficient power, as this car was developing less power than usual low down in the range. An attempt to enter such corners faster in order to keep up the revs in 2nd. resulted in me turning the car round, which I think could have been avoided if the car had a greater lock. (for correction.)

The car behaved quite normally although it seemed to have less power low down (ie: 6000–9000R.P.M.) than when I drove it at Folkingham the previous week.

Second day's practice.
The first time the car reached 10,500R.P.M. down the straight practically resulted in a broken neck because the wind got under the peak of my crash hat! This was rectified by raising the screen 1½". During one of the first laps the car reached 10,700 on the straight apparently quite easily, but subsequently 10,500R.P.M. was it's [sic] limit. The straight was 1.6 miles long by car speedometer. The lack of power under 8000R.P.M. was very noticeable and made the car difficult to drive on the slower parts of the course. It was immediately apparent that the handling on fast corners (of which there was only one, approximately 130M.P.H.) and on the straight when going fast, was very very good.

My own impressions of the performance of my car during this day's practice were as follows: The car was some 8 seconds slower than Ascari's. I had thought that the difference would have been greater than that as it *felt* very slow on all corners (except the fast one) on the back leg of the course. The 8 seconds can be accounted for in various ways, in my opinion. Firstly that 3 seconds per lap were being lost through the *abnormal* lack of power low down, coupled with the fact that unluckily 2nd gear was just too high for five of the slow corners, and bottom was too low for all but two of them, ie: the ones at the start and the end of the straight. Secondly I am certain that I could have knocked 2 or 3 seconds off my time if it had not been such a momentous decision which precluded even the least risk being taken! Thirdly I am convinced that with a car like this a certain amount of practice under various track conditions is essential before a driver can really say he is giving of his best. The technique is so entirely different from any other racing car that I am sure that time will show big dividends, and the difference between driving the car and driving it with precision and confidence must be seconds per lap. This was most noticeable in the race when literally every lap seemed easier than the last. In my opinion this could account for as much as 3 seconds per lap, remembering how on past occasions even the most skilled drivers have knocked large lumps off lap times with practice when driving really fast cars for the first few times, for example Nuvolari in the Auto Union.

The race.
The engine was stalled on the line, partly due to my own clumsiness in not having the revs high enough (owing to the false start before the flag was even raised). The clutch was let in at about 6,500 but the engine spat back through the blow-off valves at the psychological moment and stalled. The oil pressure had been practically at 0 when the car arrived at the pit, but was normal on the line and stayed at 50 during the race.

The engine spat back about once or twice per lap during the race and the power was not there right from the start. It was inconsistent, and at certain times came right in. There was very little below 8000R.P.M. and the only place in the range where it was normal was over 10,000R.P.M. the difficulty being to get it up to that speed. The top speed reached on the straight was 10,000 on some laps, but more usually 9000R.P.M. At certain times I could pass Talbots easily and at others they could pass me. During the latter part of the race the car gave the impression of 'hanging back' rather like an E.R.A. just before piston trouble. (gearbox seizing?)
The gear changes were as follows:
2 corners: bottom
4 " 2nd.
1 " 4th.
and this entailed about 10 changes or more per lap, dependent upon how many of the intermediate gears were used.
The newly lined brakes were troublesome at first and

caused the front of the car to judder and bounce. This shaking at the front under the brakes was noticeable right through the race and could possibly be improved with lower front tyre pressures. The back end of the car was very steady under all conditions.

The steering on slow corners was heavy, and particularly noticeable when changing gear and steering in twisty parts of the course with one hand.

The brakes were very good when used hard on smooth parts of the course, but the stopping power was upset by front end instability on rough roads.

Control of the car was improved by fitting a foot rest, but for tall drivers I think the steering wheel should be 3" further away, but this is obviously a matter of personal preference.

No difference in stability was noticed between a full and a half empty tank.

Road holding on slow rough corners was not particularly good and the car was inclined to bounce across as if the tyre pressures were too high.

Front wheel flap (ie: side to side) which was so noticeable (from a spectator's point of view) at Goodwood seemed to have quite disappeared.

Oil temperature was normal but the water temperature gauge broke in practice.

These criticisms it is hoped will be taken in the spirit in which they are written, my only wish being to be of assistance in furthering the development of the B.R.M.

[signed] P.C.D. Walker

Such were the sensibilities within BRM that Walker's helpfulness finally counted against him. In contrast, Reg Parnell – never a man to commit himself to paper – merely called a spade a spade face-to-face. None could brood over his opinions and perceive hidden inferences between the written lines... He would survive as a BRM driver much longer than Peter Walker.

has got something into his mind with all the persuasion in the world one cannot make any impression…but I did hope you would be able to convince him…and so make him change his mind somewhat.

I know he has personal likes and dislikes which cause him to say many things and I sometimes wonder whether Hassett [actually Walter Hassan of Bentley, ERA, Jaguar XK and V12 and Coventry Climax fame] who was at one time Works Manager in the E.R.A. days and who was with Lyons at the time…did not perhaps put in a word to convince Lyons that the B.R.M. was similar to the E.R.A. set-up and as such there was not very much right with the project…

While Owen and Hives, he believed, were beating the bushes for funding, by November 7 Ray could report a long conversation with Ken Richardson upon his return from Barcelona. A new supercharger was being installed in Parnell's car, the gearbox problem was to be rectified on Walker's. Both BRMs were then examined and further tested to analyze their "exact condition".

He called Elliott at Rolls-Royce requesting Geoffrey Wilde and 'Prof' Allen's presence while Parnell's supercharger was

being stripped.

On Monday, November 13, Parnell's Barcelona car was tested at Folkingham with the spare supercharger installed but otherwise it had been untouched since its retirement at Pedralbes.

A compression test before running revealed 69–75lbs per cylinder, except No. 9 "which showed practically nil".

Ken warmed-up the car on Lodge 47 plugs, then had the 51s "which are used for racing" fitted straight from Walker's Barcelona race engine.

Despite a high wind and a wet 'normal' Folkingham circuit, he lapped in 1min 11sec against the V16 record of 1:06. He then ran the car on the outer circuit "for several miles, including three runs down the 2,000-yard runway" using 10,700rpm through the gears. The car pulled exactly 10,000rpm in fifth at the end-of-runway cut-off point.

Bad front brake judder was experienced – particularly on the right-side – but it seemed to improve as the barely-used Barcelona linings bedded in "…as they were fitted on the eve of the Barcelona race". (Interesting, then, that both Parnell and Walker had been sent to the start there on unbedded linings…)

Post-test compression checks confirmed the nil reading on

Pena Rhin pit stop – 'Klem' captured this refuelling stop for Peter Walker with Willie Southcott handling the hose, Ken Richardson half-hidden behind the pit-roof stanchion, Reg Parnell – long-since retired – reaching round PB, Dave Turner looking on, far right.

No. 9 cylinder: "most likely...damaged valve seats or a bent valve, possibly owing to small bits and pieces going through the engine when the rotors touched the casing owing to the ball race trouble at Barcelona...".

Next day Ray expressed his and PB's feelings and some contemporary rumours to Hives:

> We consider the Lyons attitude very dangerous at the present time. The success of the unsupercharged 4½-litre Ferraris at Barcelona have given rise to a general criticism of our more complicated 16cy. supercharged 1½-litre design. We understand that Lyons is being persuaded to make a 12cy. engine, using 2 banks of his 6cy. 3½-litre with reduced stroke, to total 4½-litres, and in view of his success with his 3½-litre engine, such a project might receive the support of the 'uncertains' at present connected with the B.R.M. Project...

He assured Hs that a V16 dyno run had just achieved:

> ...sufficient power on the mid and upper engine ranges to make us absolutely confident that the unsupercharged 4½-litre engines will have the utmost difficulty in obtaining higher figures...

He concluded:

You will remember...that Peter Berthon estimated the h.p. available at Barcelona was not more than 320. The Test Bed has shown this to be the case, but we have since located the very definite reasons for this poor output, the power now being over 400 at the same revolutions, i.e. 10,000. The power is still rising rapidly...we expect even higher figures at the 12,000r.p.m. maximum...

One suspects Ray was rather taken aback by Hives' reaction, which was to ask that his former employee Tresilian should prepare a further report for him on the technical situation – rather cutting down the RM/PB claims to size.

However, by mid-December 1950 Hs' efforts had achieved agreement from Leonard Lord of Austin, and from Lucas, to match his own pledge on behalf of Rolls-Royce, each company to contribute £10,000 *pa* for five years to BRM. Sir John Black of Standard would follow suit, despite Lyons' loudly conflicting advice. The Owen Organisation became a fifth contributing partner, and Bilton's Vigzol Oil the sixth.

Alfred Owen's diplomacy succeeded in dissuading the Bernard Scott and Denis Flather faction from pressing their Controller ideas upon Bourne, and a Rubery Owen appointee named Cliff Mander was made Production Manager there instead.

Thus prepared, both Trust and team could get ready for 1951.

A NEW NAME EMERGES

Tony Rudd made his first direct contact with motor racing in the school holidays of 1938. Basking in the glory of a successful School Certificate examination, he was taken to see the racing cars prepared for 'B. Bira' at Prince Chula's White Mouse Garage in Dalling Road, Hammersmith.

He was captivated, eager to see the cars actually race. On September 17 that year, Chula and 'Bira' took him to the 192-mile BRDC Road Race meeting on the Campbell Circuit at Brooklands. 'Bira' was driving *Romulus* with a 165hp Roots-blown engine installed, in preference to his 220hp Zoller-supercharged *Hanuman*, whose reliability was suspect, but against considerable odds, and Raymond Mays in 'R4D', he won.

Tony was ecstatic and hooked. He later said he learned several lessons that day: a mechanic's life was 99 per cent hard work and 1 per cent glamour – you had to finish to win – a race was not lost until it was over – you could win races by tactics even though you did not have the fastest car.

He attended another race on October 8 at Crystal Palace and soon decided he was going to design and build racing cars and not be a driver. From that point forward his school notebooks were covered with doodled designs for racing cars. His reading was *The Autocar, Speed* and *Motor Sport*, and after leaving school in the spring of 1939 he became an engineering apprentice at Rolls-Royce, Derby, where he found plenty of beer-mat race car engineering. ERA oil pumps appeared in the 'Tomb', the R-R rig shop, since ERA were using an early recticular-tin bearing alloy developed by R-R known as 'AC 9A' or 'Hall's metal' after their chief metallurgist. The engineering apprentice from the lab was much sought after for information. Then came the war.

In 1941, desperate for space, R-R's glamour cars – such as E.R. Hall's TT Bentley 'B35AE', and the Paulin-bodied Embiricos Bentley had been stored in a local garage. Some of the apprentices, Tony amongst them, were appalled by the cars' condition and volunteered to care for them in their precious spare time.

After the statutory two years in the workshops, Tony was then delighted to be attached to the staff of the company's prewar Chief Engineer – Motor Cars, the legendary 'By' in R-R-speak, R.W. Harvey Bailey. He had become Chief Technical and Development Engineer with responsibility for all the production R-R engines and for fixing any faults which arose in them. After a spell in the drawing office, Tony was required to record all service problems, make a statistical analysis of them and of how they were being cured. This information was then used by the equally legendary 'Hs'. Here Tony began to learn the ways of the mighty. Commanded by Hives upon a Thursday afternoon to investigate a statement that repaired engines were more reliable than new ones, he was asked: "How long?" "About a fortnight" was his reply. As Hs swept out he flung back "on my desk, Monday noon".

Another time Hs became embroiled in a dispute with Air Chief Marshal Sir Arthur Harris, Commander-in-Chief, Bomber Command, who claimed the unreliability of Rolls-Royce engines was delaying his plans to win the war by bombing. Hs said that Harris "never hears about all the engines that never go wrong". Tony's report, however, leaned

to Harris' side, much to Hs' disgust. This may have led to his description of Tony as "that clever bugger upstairs who makes figures stand on end".

Just postwar, Tony was being assisted in work on his own Aston Martin – which had all-independent suspension and an ex-Jock Horsfall[39] 2-litre engine – by a fellow enthusiast, an ex-ship's engineer, and a survivor of several wartime torpedoings. His name was Willie Southcott, and in 1950 he took a job as an engine specialist race mechanic with BRM.

Throughout this early postwar period Tony had precious little time to follow GP racing. But in 1948, when he heard 'Bira' was running the latest Maserati 4CLT in the first British GP at Silverstone and would welcome any help, his aunt – with whom he was staying – fell mysteriously ill and Tony's attendance became *vital* – and he subsequently served as one of 'Bira's team whenever he could, during his UK appearances.

Tony quickly came to believe that racing cars in general were designed and operated by persons far less gifted and well-trained than himself.

He also appreciated that motor racing was not all roses.

By 1950, it was obvious that the bolt-on power unit for aircraft was dead and that the gas turbine – buried in the wing as on the new DH Comet – was the way ahead. Therefore, Tony's department at Rolls-Royce could only contract, not grow, so he had to look to his future. He watched Alfa Romeo with interest in GP racing and was also intrigued by stories of the new V16-cylinder BRM for which Rolls-Royce was building the supercharger. Reduced pressure of work then gave him more time to accompany 'Bira' to the races, such as the Royal Silverstone meeting where Raymond Mays first demonstrated the BRM in public.

After accompanying 'Bira' and the Plate team Maseratis on a Continental trip – to Bari, Jersey and Albi – all in eight days, the cars were stressed beyond all reasonable limits and at the least provocation would hole their pistons. It felt like a week of piston changing.

'Bira' then decided to go fully independent for 1951, and asked if Tony would manage his 'team'. He was going to fit a new 4½-litre unsupercharged OSCA V12 engine into his existing Maserati 4CLT chassis.

Tony: I was very non-committal. Somehow 'Bira''s haphazard set-up did not seem to be the way to go motor racing, certainly not the way I had learned from Prince Chula and R-R. However, I agreed to go to Goodwood during my Easter holiday for the OSCA's debut. After practice, 'Bira' called from Dover where Customs were disputing his carnets for the car. It finally arrived late Sunday in the care of Reg Williams – an ex-White Mouse Stable mechanic – who spoke little Italian, and an OSCA mechanic who spoke no English.

Once we persuaded its engine to start, its oil pressure gradually subsided. Wilkie Wilkinson stopped by and diagnosed the trouble as oil in the tail tank taking too long to warm up. We therefore hung an oil can from the tree at the entrance to the Goodwood paddock tunnel and heated the oil over a petrol fire. Wilkie was right. It did the trick.

39. St John Horsfall, successful racing driver of ERA and Aston Martin cars, and single-handed winner of the 1948 Spa 24-Hours race in the first postwar 2-litre Aston Martin DB1 'LMA/48/1'.

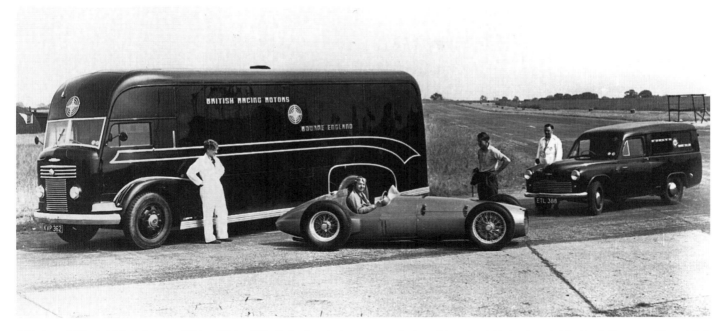

Folkingham, 1951 – publicity shot showing RM in a '51-spec V16 with its opened-out nose cone and unlouvred bonnet and side panels against the team's Commer mobile workshop, funded by the Midland Automobile Club, and the Rootes Group's presentation van at right. In the background can be seen the aerodrome's '2,000-yard runway' – main straight of the BRM test circuit.

After a few laps, 'Bira' coasted-in to report transmission failure, "because the V12's tremendous power had broken the Maserati gearbox". On the contrary, I found it had merely jumped out of gear.

Reg Parnell beat us in a five-lap race as the car was cutting-out due to lack of fuel pressure and the car was not set-up to run properly in the wet on Dunlops. I talked Dunlop into refitting the worn Pirellis on which it had arrived, and the Italian mechanic removed most of a newspaper from the fuel pressure relief valve...

'Bira' then went out and *won* the main event which triggered a tremendous party with Wilkie and David Murray.

It was by this time apparent that Tony's department at R-R had a limited future, he made unhappy noises and lobbied some of his friends to get back into the main stream of things at Derby, but all he heard were vague promises of a senior position in the Dart propeller turbine team some time in the future.

He missed the OSCA's outing at Bordeaux where 'Bira' finished third, and his final acquaintance with the car was then at the washed-out International Trophy meeting at Silverstone where he spent most of practice investigating why its scavenge system would not work.

Then he was on his way to Bourne. 'Bira', who was talking to RM about driving for BRM, had put in a word, and R-R, who had been asked for technical help and wanted to find out what was happening to their supercharger, saw a way of solving several problems in one go. He did not know then that he had been painted a vaguer but rosier picture.

He had learned much of what was right from Prince Chula. Tony: The ERA-patterned curtains from his study hang today in mine as a reminder of him. He had learned from the Maserati and the OSCA some mistakes not to make.

1951 – THE MOST TROUBLED YEAR

While young Tony Rudd was choosing between the security of a working lifetime with Rolls-Royce or the uncertain future offered by BRM, the Trust was studying possibilities for 1951.

By that time some £106,000 had been received in cash, and around £85,000-worth in kind. Expenditure totalled £97,000. As of August 26, 1950, assets had comprised the two complete cars plus one additional V16 engine under assembly, plus spares, tools, buildings, the Test House equipment etc – all valued at a total £24,000. The Trust had carefully hedged its bets, with a close check upon its assets should the entire project collapse.

It was anticipated, however, that supporters in kind would continue. The cash requirement to complete the cars and spares ready for a sensible racing season was estimated at £66,000. The cost of racing through a full European season was assessed as £13,000. Cash promised for the year had been £30,000 which left some £49,000 – a very considerable sum indeed[40] – to be found.

Further clouds were gathering as the Trust document concluded with this warning:

> If it is felt the BRM should continue beyond the 1951 season it is possible the Formula may be altered for 1952, which means a complete new racing car will have to be built from scratch, and if a similar programme of five racing cars is contemplated it is estimated that the following sum will be necessary to manufacture the cars: £140,000 – annual racing: £85,000...

40. At 1993 values these four sums of money represent approximately £1,012,000, £200,000, £460,000 and £614,000 respectively.

By this time all appreciated that the project's management was top-heavy, overloaded with important businessmen, each successful in his own right and each with his own emphatic ideas on the way ahead. Lord Hives told RM: "You can't run a racing car with a committee. One must choose men to run a project and then let them get on with it without interference..." Ray, of course, agreed.

At a meeting of the Executive Council on February 28, 1951, it was formally agreed that BRM Ltd was to be managed at Bourne by PB and RM, with a works manager and secretary. Ray was to be responsible for racing public relations, henceforth directed from Bourne, while PB remained responsible for R&D but relinquished direct responsibility for production. Mason, the beleaguered Works Manager, to be replaced by Pete Brothers, who in effect ran the Bourne machine shop. His writ did not extend to Folkingham, he had very little control and would last barely six months. Meanwhile Owen made Cliff Mander Production Manager, on equal status to RM and PB. Stewart Tresilian was also appointed to a full-time position.

The winter months really saw what Tony Rudd later termed "BRM's annual hibernation". Through the winter of 1950–51, engine testing had to stop at 5.30 every evening since BRM could not afford to pay overtime.

At Bourne a new fitter had just joined BRM, Colin Atkin, who would keep faith through thick and thin until 1976: "I was an ex-Army Engineer. I'd served my apprenticeship with Woolf's Garage in Bourne – where Dave Turner had been – and then BRM offered me the job and I started in the Old Maltings engine shop in January '51. Nice atmosphere there, generally. It was like somebody paying you to do your hobby. As a fitter, of course, you provided your own hand tools, but woe betide if Peter Berthon found you had an adjustable spanner – he wouldn't tolerate them at all.

"We all know Berthon's faults, but he was a genius. It's just that his brain would sometimes turn off! He was always a christian names man; he'd only use your surname if you'd done something wrong, and he was very quietly spoken. He only ever raised his voice if you'd done something really wrong. And he could be very sympathetic if you'd got a problem – I suppose he'd been through most things... He certainly had a reputation as a lady's man. Ken Richardson was the foreman, and wanted everyone to know it; and old Jack Wylde – RM's mechanic from prewar – was one of the finest fitters I ever saw. Charlie Davey was difficult. He seemed to resent most of us just breathing. Tresilian came across as a really good bloke, a fine engineer, and Willie Southcott – ex-Rolls-Royce and ex-Navy – was just fantastic. For years he virtually carried BRM on his shoulders engine-wise..."

When the generosity of such staunch supporters as David Brown and Percy Bilton topped-up funds, a sudden rush of rearmament orders – the Korean War had erupted – demanded time in industrial toolrooms which might otherwise have been devoted to BRM. This was the same old story...second time around.

Meanwhile, Ray had negotiated with M. Peyerimhoff, Secretary of the *AC Suisse* and organizer of the annual Swiss GP at Berne's fabulous Bremgarten forest circuit. The race date was May 27 and Peyerimhoff offered attractive terms for BRM to enter.

At an Executive Council meeting on April 19, it was agreed that the Swiss GP should be BRM's primary target, but the cars must first prove raceworthy. The Council was determined "...not to be stampeded into racing against its better judgement...".

PB had also decided that Rolls-Royce's magnificent vortex throttling system and SU's fuel injection were both beyond BRM's development capabilities. He had adopted instead the

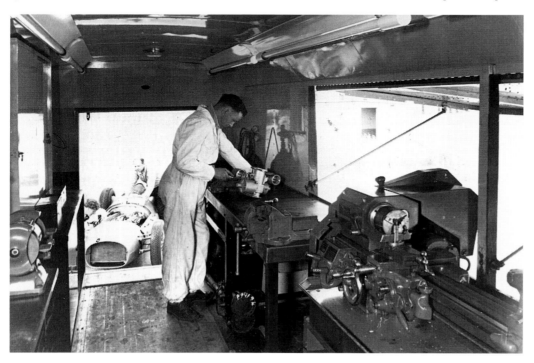

Interior of the team's well-equipped mobile workshop during the publicity photography session at Folkingham, early in 1951. Cyril Bryden was the racing team's machinist and 'drove' the mobile workshop lathe through the early '50s. He made most of BRM's carburettor needles and loved his weekend cricket – "Bin bashin' the willer a bit", he'd explain.

specially-made SU twin-choke carburettor which had not only a horizontal air intake but also horizontal dashpot pistons. This in effect combined all the problems of a downdraught carburettor with the disadvantages of a horizontal carburettor.

This hefty assembly was then mounted on an overhanging magnesium extremity of the engine. Magnesium offers low weight but with rigidity to match, so the carburettor vibrated violently, rendering its float chambers prone to flooding. The carburettor needles could also come clean out of their jets although nobody suspected it in 1950–51.

The engines' chronic plug-fouling was attributed instead to lubricating oil being blown past ineffective supercharger oil seals. Geoffrey Wilde and 'Prof' Allen therefore designed a fantastically elaborate safety-pinned and locking-wired seal system, and lived in blissful ignorance of PB's distrust of it as he insisted instead upon fitting a motorcycle-type oil feed restrictor to minimize oil flow into the blower. The Derby engineers were convinced their seal and drain system was effective since such features worked on aero engines and on the Rolls-Royce rigs. Tony: I was not quite sure as aero engines do not have to brake for corners. I would find PB's restrictor on the Sunday before the 1951 British GP, and when we ran with the valve wide open, after that race, the seals did not leak, although the engine still pulled oil past the piston rings, for which PB still tried to blame the blower.

The Council's technical report of the period preceding the Swiss race recorded:

Engine tests and development mainly consisted of work with the large rotor supercharger and the new twin-choke SU carburettor. Blower performance was found to be generally in line with the theoretical boost curve but matching showed that the supercharger was slightly too big and capacity had to be reduced by modification to diffuser vanes. The carburettor, while giving better performance, was difficult to tune as the two suction chambers were controlled by one throttle.

Due to inadequate location of the suction chamber pistons, seizing on the walls of the chambers occurred and special pistons and suction chambers were made from the solid at Bourne, and results with these were more satisfactory.

The original number one car in last year's form was used in road tests at Silverstone and Folkingham. Trouble occurred with flooding of float chambers and mounting these on rubber was of some help. It was found later that the flooding could be prevented by making both carburettors operate over the whole range (previously one carburettor had come in after the other).

Road performance was considerably improved and engine power was in excess of that which the drivers could easily handle. The modified steering which had been fitted reduced the tendency for wheel flap.

Tony: My recollection is that the float chambers were not actually rubber-mounted until Monza in September. However, the need for this may have been identified before then.

A test run was made at Silverstone on Monday May

14. Both 'Bira' and Parnell were at Goodwood ['Bira' having signed the same agreement with the company as had Parnell, but soon to ask to be released from it] …but Ken Richardson was able to put in one lap in one minute forty-nine seconds. These tests were cut short by a broken supercharger quill-shaft, which on examination was found to be down on the 90/95 tons called for on the drawing. A new quill shaft was rushed through at Bourne and all quill shafts were subsequently replaced. A second test was made at Silverstone on 17th May and 'Bira' lapped in one minute fifty seconds [Tony, who was uniquely close to 'Bira', is adamant that the Prince only ever drove a V16 at Folkingham and this report came as complete news to him. He doesn't believe 'Bira' ever drove a V16 at Silverstone, but both this report and Ken Richardson are adamant that he did]. While Walker was driving, two very heavy blow backs were heard and immediately afterwards he stopped. The car was returned to Bourne and the engine stripped for examination.

During this period car No. 2 was waiting an engine, and this was controlled by supercharger deliveries[41], and trouble was being experienced with bearings and seals. Both these difficulties were a question of oil supply and adequate drainage.

The third chassis was following close behind the second, all components being available except brakes, but here again the controlling factor will be the engine which was controlled by the supercharger…

BRM's Swiss GP entries were scrubbed.

One can imagine, reading the above, the hard-bitten Tony Vandervell's reaction to PB's continuing tale of mechanical woe.

During this period, Tony Rudd had joined the team, arriving at Bourne as a tousled, rather crumpled young man, his studiously scruffy appearance compensating for a natural shyness.

His always corrugated and dirty shirt collar quickly convinced the likes of Aubrey Woods and Alec Stokes in the drawing office, and Ken 'Tinker' Richardson and Dave Turner in the build and race shops, that he had only one shirt "…while his velvet cord jacket could stand up on its own…".

BRM's old hands quickly nicknamed their new boy 'Moleskin 'Arry', who recalls…

While I kept my Aston Martin in immaculate condition, nearly all of Rolls-Royce's bright young men had Austin Sevens for everyday use – the more disreputable the better – and mine was a 1926 fabric saloon with about seven spokes per 21-inch wheel, and magneto ignition. Travelling in it for my first morning with BRM the magneto expired, and I arrived at Bourne in the undertaker's best car.

I sought an interview with PB, when he arrived after lunch, to find out what my duties were. He had very important matters to attend to but would send for me and give me a

41. **Tony: The most crippling shortage was always crankcases, not blowers, since most engine failures damaged the crankcases beyond repair. PB is playing politics here, minimizing the failures and blaming the supercharger situation. Since nobody dare approach Rolls-Royce with a complaint, he was on safe ground!**

proper job list as soon as he could. In the meantime I was put in the care of Pete Brothers, who showed me round and introduced me. It appeared I was to be a mixture of Peter Haynes' representative at Bourne and PB's Personal Assistant.

I was surprised to find only a bare chassis frame in the car build shop and one engine in the engine shop. I was told there was more to see at Folkingham, in terms implying that the people up there were not very nice.

The next day I found my way to Folkingham where Ken Richardson presided. There were no racing cars there either. I was given a long list of parts and equipment required, and then went to look at the three Austin 5-tonners and the large Commer mobile workshop which were to be my responsibility. I was provided with a 44-item job list from Peter Haynes, the Team Manager. It ranged from making the Norton motorcycle-engined refuelling equipment [which had failed in Barcelona] work, to fitting the Commer workshop with better mirrors. I then recruited a fitter to care for the transport.

Back in Bourne I presented the Folkingham lists to 'Clarrie' Brinkley – the material controller. He was an ex-ERA mechanic who had been with RM since *White Riley* days. I later discovered he was known as 'The Lalograph' from his habit of adjuring people not to let their 'Lal' out, when he thought they were talking nonsense.

He promptly rang Ken Richardson to tell him he didn't need half the stuff on the list, another quarter he had no chance of getting anyway, while the remaining quarter had to be made by the machine shop. I retired to it, and presented the remains of my shopping lists to Les Bryden, the machine shop foreman. He had obviously had plenty of dealings with Ken Richardson's people up at Folkingham and said: "Tell Tinker he can have them next week."

PB then summoned me and tore me off a formidable strip because Folkingham hadn't yet received everything on Ken's list. My disillusion had been immediate, and very nearly complete.

I soon fell into the routine of chasing everything which Folkingham or the engine shop needed, from outside suppliers or the Bourne machine shop, first thing each morning. Then I'd check that Folkingham's needs hadn't changed overnight – which they often did – and then, armed with my collection of bits, I'd set off for Folkingham in the Austin Seven, looking like an itinerant tinker – no relation to the one resident at Folkingham.

Having sparred with Ken Richardson over short supplies, and tending to the racing equipment, I would return to Bourne. It was the same routine after lunch. And after tea...

BRM's normal working week was Monday to Friday, 8am to 10pm; Saturday and Sunday, 8am to 6pm, with the occasional all-nighter thrown in for good measure. But I could not see a racing car or engine growing as a result...

I asked build shop chargehand Jack North why he did not work two shifts as it was obvious that people were getting in each other's way. Only about six people can work effectively on a racing car, one at each corner and one each side, but he had about 10. His answer was that he himself had suggested it but PB had rejected the idea on the grounds there was not enough competent supervision.

It just seemed traditional to work that way at BRM. The general fatigue was obvious. Several fitters were on loan from the motor industry, so normal industrial pay rates had to be applied, including double time for working Sundays. This meant that while the normal BRM working week was stiff enough at 85 hours, scaling-up for overtime meant BRM paid for 115 hours. Since everyone was so tired and stale with this continuous overtime, only around 50 hours of their work was useful.

They were by no means slack or inefficient – *very* far from it – but they were simply worn out by this ludicrous working pattern. I never discussed why more men were not employed to reduce individual hours and so improve efficiency per man. One answer was that men of sufficient ability and drive could not be found.

Despite all this, the spirit certainly never flagged. Right to the end of my time at BRM this seemed a particular quality of the team's mechanics which other teams never achieved to the same degree.

And at that time we *fervently* believed that we were building a British car to beat the foreigners.

This problem of long hours was exacerbated by PB, justifiably in my opinion, insisting upon approving each modification and design. Since he had not mastered the art of being in two places at once, staff at Bourne were kept waiting for his arrival from Folkingham and *vice versa*, and whenever he was away in London or elsewhere, everything simply ground to a halt.

RM was always disinclined to take any major policy decisions without PB on hand to advise him, and they were often away together at various meetings and discussions.

It was obvious we would never make the Swiss race when, at the end of May, 'Bira' tested one car at Folkingham and it developed a gearbox oil leak due to the aluminium castings which served as a front gearbox mounting breaking. The escaping oil dripped onto the hot exhaust and burst into flames. 'Bira' did not approve of such behaviour and became an early member of the illustrious band of ex-BRM drivers...

Into June the pace hotted up with one car based at Folkingham on test, but more often than not minus an engine, while another was being built at Bourne. Towards the end of June I put 126 hours into one working week, and that was beaten by several of the mechanics...

Having missed the Swiss GP, BRM's target became the *Grand Prix d'Europe* at Reims-Gueux on July 1. PB's Technical Report for this period describes how:

> After the blow-up of No. 1 test car at Silverstone on 17th May, it was found that a broken connecting rod had seriously damaged the crankcase. At first over-speeding was considered a possible reason, but a check on the rod stresses confirmed that inertia loads of over 20,000rpm could be withstood...

Tony: If he really said 20,000rpm this had to be a guess. Stress goes up with the square of the speed, so it would be three times as great and the rods would be ridiculous.

> This failure resembled that which occurred last year due to ignition problems [*sic*]. No. 8 liner had burst

apart from mechanical damage to the skirt. Three other rods were deformed and the centres had been reduced by up to .015". The general evidence pointed to spurious sparks on wrong cylinders as other damaged rods were removed from cylinders having the longest ignition leads.

He paid tribute to Lucas' efforts in rearranging the plug leads to minimize induction effect between the longer ones:

> This was the second occasion that an engine had been damaged by a bent connecting rod and as a safety precaution, the rod was stiffened on some of its sections.
>
> No delivery of new machined engine castings had at this time been received and, due to damage, only two engines were available. Repairs to the damaged crankcase appeared impossible…

In fact Tres did not accept the spark jumping to adjacent plug leads causing massive destruction story. He had all the pieces of one failure laid out on the two-foot thick window sill of PB's office in the old Maltings. Tony: Citing my R-R defect investigation experience he invited me to look at them. I noted the connecting rod had broken after it had been twisted, so that the gudgeon pin axis was at some 30° to the crankpin instead of parallel. This indicated that the piston had encountered something incompressible such as coolant and was known as a hydraulicing failure. The next clue was the cylinder head joint ring, the subject of the Turner/Wilson dispute. It had the typical brown marks and stains of combustion gases blowing past it and was deformed, indicating it had partly collapsed as if it was made in too soft a material. We rang R-R for the material specification of the Battle of Britain Merlin single-piece block joint ring, which was a very similar application except that these Merlins had what is called free-standing liners, whereas the BRM had a top seating liner, like the later two-piece block Merlins, which however, did not have a joint ring at all. I sometimes suspect that Tres had already reached the same conclusions and was using me as an ally.

The machine shop was put to work making sealing rings in the new R-R material together with equipment to hand lap them against plate glass, after the required thickness had been determined by special gauges, liner lengths were adjusted and tolerances generally tightened up.

Ted Grinham of Standard agreed to carry out non-stop machining to deliver a complete engine set before the end of June. Rolls-Royce's men continued their supercharger seal work and a two-hour rig test was passed with flying colours. "This is the first blower which is considered to be raceworthy and the other two new type superchargers delivered recently had to be returned for the latest modifications before they could be raced…but…the delay in getting material for new engine and car components was seriously limiting our activities. No substantial deliveries had been made of the parts for additional engine sets ordered last season, and it appeared that the cycle was from nine to twelve months…" – No way indeed to run a racing team.

Neither Ferrari nor Alfa Romeo would have brooked such delays, but then both were tight-knit concerns with their own foundries, while the relatively tiny set-up in Lincolnshire was totally dependent upon industry at large. It had no choice.

BRM missed the race at Reims…

So the British GP became their target, at Silverstone on July 14, but in the immediate run-up the disturbing saga of engine failures continued. The Council reported:

> Although new type stiffened up cylinder liners were fitted to both engines it now seems fairly clear that the troubles recently met with were caused by carburettor flooding. Although carburation conditions were much improved prior to the (British GP) the optimum tuning could not be arrived at, due to the lack of time…

In fact while the machine shop at Bourne was producing new head sealing rings and equipment to hand-lap them in sets of four to suit the engine's four individual cylinder heads,

Testing was incessant whenever a car was available to run at Folkingham throughout the early months of 1951, normally with Ken Richardson driving, but occasionally – as here – with RM himself in charge. While an engine adjustment is made to this tail-less V16, PB seems lost in thought (right). In cold, wind or rain Folkingham could be dreadful, in the summer it could bake.

Left: July 14, 1951 – British Grand Prix, Silverstone. The two troublesomely-prepared V16s, 'No. 1' (race number 6) for Parnell and 'No. 2' for Walker, receive the final touches possible before the race beside one of the Austin Lodestar team transporters. Note how the nose cowls split horizontally, only the top half of Parnell's car's having been removed. Peter Knight of SU in jacket on right.

1951 British Grand Prix. Below: Ferrari newboy Jose Froilan Gonzalez – who will win this British Grand Prix for Ferrari to overturn Alfa Romeo's long postwar domination – tries Parnell's BRM for size; fellow Argentine driver Onofre Marimon (left) obscures RM, and Parnell and Walker stand beyond.

everyone was given the day off to gather strength for the team's first great race of 1951.

On the way home, the spokes in one of the rear wheels in Tony's Austin, which had now reached a critically low number, collapsed and the unfortunate car rolled over:

Damage was minor, I obtained a fresh wheel from the local breaker's yard, and that accounted for my day off.

We were all fired with determination to do well at Silverstone. RM stood on a bench in the racing shop at Folkingham and made an impassioned speech telling us all that we had to show some progress or the money would finally dry up.

None even dreamed that this would be the V16 BRM's *only* World Championship-qualifying race…

Then, in the words of the Council's report:

> …in the week prior to the actual race, one engine was seriously damaged about the valve gear due to lack of lubrication.

This unit had been hastily rebuilt after the previous failure and in the confusion it had been installed with the feed valve to its low pressure oil system shut off. The camshaft duly seized on the Sunday afternoon before Silverstone while Ken Richardson was driving and during a rare visit from A.G. Elliott of R-R. The supercharger, which was fed from the same system, had to be changed in case of damage.

Again, BRM was running out of time – there were plenty of problems to solve. At high rpm the engine threw oil from its crankcase breathers. Its enormous twin-horizontal-dashpot, SU carburettor still flooded its float chambers under vibration, filling the engine with raw fuel. Conversely, it would refuse to pick up under cornering loads because the fuel level in the chambers was too low. Setting float levels became a black art involving an array of special equipment, and no two people could agree how it should best be done.

Tony: We were thoroughly locked into the usual vicious circle of development, where as the engine became more reliable so it could be run longer and harder, and that brought more problems to light – and one just had to keep slogging away until they could be eliminated.

Naturally, the supporting companies had been told all this back in 1949, and throughout 1950, so by 1951 they were becoming very bored with hearing The Same Old Story.

In the midst of all this I had my own problems. Peter Haynes was unable to attend at Silverstone, and the

Everybody who was anybody wanted to try the BRM for size. After Gonzalez came Ferrari numero uno Alberto Ascari, attracting a quizzical look from RM (right) while Nino Farina of Alfa Corse (below) possibly felt – like Peter Walker – that the protruberant studding behind the steering wheel rim had been overdone. Note the extensive cockpit upholstery. BRM drivers were not entirely denied comfort...

motorcycle engine-powered refuelling equipment became my responsibility. At Barcelona it had refused to start at the crucial moment when Peter Walker came in. That problem had been sorted out, but now something else reared its head. As we filled the enlarged front tank via pipes from the rear tank, sometimes the U-shaped vent pipes would fill with fuel. This created an air-lock in the forward tank, which then refused to fill above one-third full, i.e. only some 20 gallons...

Driver-operated dump valves were made and fitted, but we had no chance to test them. The race was over 260 miles. The

cars held about 75 usable gallons and did about 2½mpg on the 1951 fuel which was a 70 per cent alcohol mix. If we got it right, we might – just about – get away with only one refuelling stop. The refuelling gear itself was an aircraft system feeding at 5 gallons (40lbs) per second. We would have to be very careful not to blow the bottom out of the tank with such a rush of fuel, and although the nozzle had a balanced reaction, there was quite a jerk when flow was started or shut off, demanding real muscle to control it.

We finally managed to try it all at dusk on the Friday before the race, after one car had been test-driven by both Parnell and Walker. At that time, with less than 24 hours to go, the second car was still unfinished. Around midnight, the overloaded racing shop electrical supply failed and all the lights went out. We drove the transporters up against the windows and worked on in their headlights. We finally left for Silverstone at 4am and arrived before the 7 o'clock deadline. The suspension had been modified and I didn't find time to check whether the quick-lift jacks would still fit and lift a complete car until midday. Nobody had a clue whether we would need a tyre change.

July 14, 1951 – RAC British Grand Prix, Silverstone – 90 laps, 262.8 miles

Without having practised, the cars started from the back of the grid, driven by Parnell and Walker. Earl Howe to RM, PB and the drivers: "Everybody is behind you, no matter what happens..."

Tony: We all stood in a trance watching the cars go out to the start. Most of the mechanics promptly nodded off...I had a job to keep the pit crew awake. There was soon a blistering Alfa Romeo-versus-Ferrari battle raging up front but our two cars were still running, seventh and ninth, when we made our first pit-stop.

It was obvious something was wrong from the way the drivers' heads had been nodding and lolling as they went by. I signalled Parnell in first with our green and white flag. They were supposed to operate their dump valves as they came in.

He got out of the car, which he was not supposed to do, saying: "It's burning me."

Nobody took any notice. He had stopped on my flag. Ken Richardson put the fuel in. 'Dunlop Mac' rushed forward to stop the tyre-changing crew as there was plenty of tread left. As I saw Ken finish refuelling I thought he was quick, and dived for the dump valves inside the cockpit. They had not been operated. I burned my hands on the cockpit sides. Reg was still grumbling about it burning him but PB said: "Never mind – get back in the car!" I began to sympathize.

He rejoined, and then Peter Walker came in. He seemed dazed, he hadn't operated his dump valves either and his car's cockpit was hotter still. When we checked we found we had put less than 50 gallons total into the two cars, instead of 60 gallons each. They would need a second stop! I hoped the motorcycle engine would start a second time and prepared

1951 British Grand Prix. Above: Only 11 months after the debutante BRM had sheared its transmission on this same stretch of track, and two years after Ken Richardson (left foreground) had spun the ThinWall Special Ferrari into the crowd here, Reg Parnell's 'No. 1' stands ready for the start, attended by Ray Woods (left), Ken Richardson, Cyril Bryden and (second right) Geoff Aldridge.

Left and centre: The under-achieving V16s of Parnell (6) and Peter Walker (7) during the Grand Prix. The Porsche-type front suspension's front wheel flap was plainly visible in corners, while cockpit heat and fumes severely affected both drivers. It speaks volumes for their appreciation of the race's significance to Trust and team alike that both endured...

Right: 1951 British Grand Prix – Geoff Aldridge, Willie Southcott, Tony Rudd and PB in pit counter conference.

Below: Race pit-stop – Parnell in, plainly disorientated and groggy, Tony Rudd (with flag) operating the fuel tank dump valves, while Ken Richardson, Jack North and Cyril Bryden attend to refuelling at the tail. PB – just beyond Tony – has spun around, perhaps to confirm that the Norton motorcycle-powered pressure refuelling apparatus is on song.

wads of cotton wool soaked in Aquaflavine burn dressing.

The two cars came round together as I pointed the fuel flag at Reg Parnell. While Ken refuelled his car, I opened the dump valves and wrapped Reg's legs in the cotton wool. I told him Ascari was out and Sanesi had been delayed so he was lying fifth, "…just keep going".

Peter Walker had also seen my signal, and thought I had meant him to stop as well, so he started to come in only to find us fully occupied with Reg. He was waved on. When he did come in he was given the same treatment and told he was lying seventh. He seemed barely able to take it in, but carried on, very bravely because he was obviously extremely groggy.

They still managed to bring both cars to the finish, one in the money, and the pressure from the sponsors was eased.

Parnell finished fifth, five laps behind Froilan Gonzalez's winning 4½-litre unsupercharged Ferrari, having averaged 90.50mph compared with the Argentine's victorious 96.11. Peter Walker finished seventh, another lap and 36.4sec behind his teammate, having averaged 89.11mph.

The well-wishers at Silverstone were incredible. Stirling Moss gave me a fiver to buy the mechanics a drink. The owner of the paddock ice-cream stall gave me his remaining stock. You would have thought we had won. We all slept like logs that night…

Right: Aftermath – Ronald Startup of Picture Post captured Peter Walker's poignant collapse immediately after the race, in the cool of this empty transporter. He had tottered from his BRM, painfully removed his shoes and socks, had burn cream applied to his blistered shins and feet, then asked simply to be left alone… Poor Walker – the once wealthy farmer/driver – would end his days as an alcoholic derelict in London streets and hostels…

1951 BRITISH GP – A DRIVER'S VIEW

On July 30, 1951, Peter Walker wrote from his home at Shobdon Court, Kingsland, Herefordshire, to Alfred Owen at Darlaston, enclosing this report to the Trust on his experience of the BRM at Silverstone:

British Grand Prix Silverstone, July 14th 1951
Report on performance of No. 7 B.R.M.

I drove the car for an hour on a damp road the evening before the race and, running in and using 8,500RPM towards the end of the period. Under these conditions the car seemed very controllable [sic] and the brakes were light and very good. Several attempts were made at a racing getaway at various revs and it was found essential to slip the clutch and do slow roll away starts owing to the fact that as the clutch took up the power dropped away too much to spin the wheels unless the clutch was let in at around 9,000RPM, when the power became too high to control the wheelspin properly.

I realise that much of what I say in this report is already known and steps have been taken to deal with the various points, such as the clutch.

At the start of the race the clutch was let in at 7,500 RPM and the motor nearly stalled. The clutch had to be released several times in order to get the car away. As it stands it is virtually impossible to get the car off the line at all fast. I realise that the remainder of my remarks are extremely critical and I would repeat my request at Barcelona which I made to Mr Vandervell that the opinion of several other drivers be asked without delay and that the car should be driven to the maximum against the watch on a circuit with a known lap speed, such as Lindley[43], Goodwood or Silverstone.

It is difficult to be constructively critical without a real knowledge of the design and the technicalities of construction, but I have driven enough fast cars to form the following conclusions.

A. The roadholding on corners which are taken at under 130 is very poor and the slower the corner the worse it is. The front and rear suspension seem to work in anything but sympathy. The front wheels, particularly the one with the weight off, flaps badly and this is transmitted up to the steering wheel. The steering is still too heavy when really being used and the car seems to understeer at the front and oversteer at the back if that is possible!

The car gives the impression of being too low and the back gives no warning at all before breaking away.

The rear suspension was very solid, especially towards the end of the race and in my opinion wants softening very considerably.

Power comes in according to the revs at which the engine is turning over at the time and not according to throttle opening. The fact that power continues to come in for an appreciable fraction of time after the throttle is closed makes cornering extremely difficult. Conversely the power is not there at the moment of opening the throttle and takes a fraction of a second to come in.[44]

The brakes were good, although still too heavy when used hard which makes the point at which they lock difficult to find. The brakes could not be used hard owing to the fact that my left foot could not be used to brace myself into the seat owing to the heat and I was being thrown all over the cockpit.

There was a fine spray of fuel coming up throughout the race which the heat was vaporising under my visor and this made it hard to see the track. This caused more discomfort and made driving more difficult than the overheating.

Cockpit and engine ventilation needs attention and I suggest that the continental practice of using a small

The Council reported:

Both drivers wanted to give up through heat and physical discomfort at their first pit stop but were persuaded to continue. Neither driver responded to the 'go faster' signal. [Tony: We NEVER gave them any such signal.]

The following facts were observed as a result of the race:

Tyre wear was remarkably small and much less than was found during the Silverstone tests.

Brakes were in excellent condition.

Oils – coolant, pressures and temperatures, were all normal. Consumption was about one gallon per car.

Fuel consumption was better than expected.

In Parnell's car, grit had caused the sticking of the carburettor pistons causing rich mixture and probably accounting for the fluffiness at high rpm.[42] All rotor arms in the distributors were loose.

In Walker's car, the gearbox was covered with grass and leaked badly through an opened cover plate. Carburettor pistons were sticking due to grit. Rotor arms were all loose, one contact breaker had closed by .006".

One plug lead was badly positioned and partly chafed.

The drivers complained bitterly of the heat and this is probably due to the side fairings of the body work which had not been continued far enough forward properly to insulate the exhaust system from the nearside of the cockpit. The drivers may have been partially doped, as to prevent possible hydraulicing due to flooding carburettors, a vent was taken from the back of the induction pipe. Unfortunately this vent was so placed that a stream of air was continually carrying fuel vapour into the cockpit.

Although both cars finished, the performance was disappointing, perhaps due to lack of practice on the part of the drivers and their being unable to give of their best due to heat and fumes. The drivers avoided changing gear whenever possible since the heat on the left leg was worsened when the clutch pedal was depressed.

42. Tony: 'Sticking due to grit' was surmise. Alcohol corrodes untreated magnesium, so immediately the cars stopped after the race I insisted fuel was drained from carburettors and fuel pumps and parts wiped with an oily cloth, earning a monumental bollocking from PB for this. Dave and Willie who did it swore there was no grit nor sticking before they cleaned them.

screen with a slot or gap underneath it be tried.

Seating position, driver's comfort, and such things as a foot-rest, heel and toe change and seat fitting will have to be dealt with and I cannot overemphasize the impor-tance of fitting the car to the driver for really maximum results. I personally find the seat too close to the steering wheel and there is not enough leg room.

The gearbox is excellent but I consider it dangerous to leave the present braking layout, with brakes dependent on engine,[45] as everybody misses a gear eventually, and if one is driving on the limit there is simply not time to re-engage a stalled engine to obtain brakes.

The engine power is much improved at low revs, compared to Barcelona but the car is more difficult to drive, or rather will take longer to learn to drive really fast, than if the power was available at lower revs.

Throughout the race the engine was unwilling to rev over 9000 and at times was missing slightly. So that the race had to be driven with this speed as the limit. In any case at over these revs the heat became unbearable, and increased in direct proportion to the revs. There was no question of driving the car with either skill or precision as concentration became impossible owing to the heat and fuel spray.

The gear ratio seemed correct for Silverstone and second gear was used on four corners.

The cornering and stability of the car are the present limiting factors in my opinion and a great deal must be done before they can be considered right.

I personally feel that I do not wish to drive the car in a race again until,
(A) road holding and steering have been considerably improved
(B) seating position and fitting of car to driver have received alteration
(C) timed tests have been carried out on a known circuit.

I fully realise that there was not time to go through all the above this last meeting and it was a very good effort that two cars were produced for the race at all. On the other hand I am certain that the car cannot compete in its present form and that it should not be raced again before thorough chassis (road holding) testing against the watch, particularly around corners timed, from the start of the corner to a point about 50 yards out of the corner.

This is where the car is losing time.

Drivers will require much time on this car before doing it full justice and every moment in the car is valuable, even if it is only running in or driving slowly.

Peter Walker hoped of his report that this kind of criticism was the sort of thing that was wanted and that it might lead to improvement and ultimate success of the car. On August 2, 1951, Alfred Owen replied to him, rather enigmatically:

We are pleased that your report was fortunately available for the Board Meeting which was held on Monday and we went through it in detail as a result of which certain decisions were taken. No doubt you will be hearing from either Peter Berthon or Raymond Mays...in the meantime...thank you for sending through the report which together with the comments of Reg Parnell have enabled us to deal with many of the criticisms upon which you were both agreed...

43. Lindley, the new Motor Industry Research Association (MIRA) test track then being developed near Nuneaton in Warwickshire.
44. Not the phenomenon of 'throttle lag' so familiar 30 years later in 1½-litre turbocharged Formula 1, since the V16 supercharger was directly mechanically-driven. This was carburettor lag since the SUs had no accelerator pumps – the reason why those who raced on Webers had an advantage.
45. A camshaft-driven brake servo being used, if the engine died, servo-assistance would fail.

The average lap speed was about five seconds per lap slower than the leading cars...

Clearly, the Council was no longer deluding itself...

MONZA '51 – TRIBULATIONS, AND TRIALS

On July 31, the Executive Council met in the *Welcombe Hotel* at Stratford-upon-Avon where RM and PB presented the drivers' reports upon Silverstone from Reg Parnell and Peter Walker (Walker's is reproduced in full elsewhere). Both had insisted "...roadholding and driveability must be improved, cockpit heat now 70 degrees Centigrade must be reduced, air scoops are desirable..." and pointed out that the suspension struts on Parnell's car had been fitted incorrectly, that wheel flap which was sometimes apparent might be improved by fitting shorter swing arms – centrepoint steering might improve controllability – the steering wheel should be further from the seat so the driver's arms could be straighter – recommended that the brake servo system should still operate when the engine was not running – Parnell wanted the knobs

on the back of the steering-wheel rim removed and the right-hand cockpit coaming lowered. General performance was "below average and the engines would not exceed 9,000rpm..." – hardly surprising in view of their scrambled assembly and preparation prior to the race.

It was agreed that a) wishbone link independent front suspension should be draughted as soon as possible; b) a new-type gearbox with the brake boost pump attached to it rather than to the engine should be fitted to car No. 3; c) cars Nos.1 and 2 should not be prejudiced by modifications; d) Stirling Moss should be given a drive as soon as possible; e) Ken Richardson should be given the opportunity to race later in the year; and f) "The Continental driver Snith [*sic* I am afraid – DCN] should be given a drive if possible while the cars are at Monza..."

At this range no-one can recall who the mysterious Mr Snith might have been, but the name intended was presumably 'Stuck'?

Cliff Mander reported that it was now hoped to build no less than 12 V16 engines in the following 12 months. No. 4 chassis frame was being built-up and over 75 per cent of the Bourne machine shop load was now car production. One car every six weeks might be possible once the projected programme reached its height.

It was agreed to enter cars for the Italian GP at Monza on September 16, in the Spanish GP at Barcelona on October 28 and possibly one car at Goodwood in between, on September 29.

Testing resumed at Folkingham and the engines were taken up to peak revs. The Council reported:

> Silverstone had taught us little or nothing in the engine department, but it did bring to light a number of steering and suspension points giving scope for improvement. These problems were duly tackled, with improved results...

PB reported that the lightest possible magnesium pistons had been made for the SU carburettors to overcome 'G' effect in corners, both carburettors were now tuned alike to secure some balancing effect of fuel head in corners, the air intake had also been modified to prevent pressurization. Improved needle valve assemblies had been machined for the float chambers and an overflow device fitted to minimize flooding. During Monza practice the float chambers would be rubber-mounted remotely upon the chassis frame, with flexible feed pipe connections to the carburettors. Testing indicated that all this had improved mixture control, eliminating the erratic pick-up due to mixture enrichment which had previously dogged the cars. Lucas painstakingly rebuilt the distributors to eliminate the slop which had closed contact-breaker gaps at Silverstone, and improved distributor arms were fitted to minimize backlash which had previously developed too quickly. New ignition harnesses were adopted with even wider-spaced leads, and Exide delivered larger – and still heavier – batteries to guarantee over 13 volts for a minimum three hours. Separate scavenge pumps were fitted to the supercharger oil drains, further reducing the amount of oil blown into the induction which PB still blamed for fouling the plugs. The car ran clean – until another major engine failure occurred at Folkingham.

It was on V16 engine 'No. 2' (Type 10/2) – Walker's Silverstone unit – and its No. 12 cylinder had hydrauliced, jamming its rod across the crankcase where it broke the crankshaft! Its heads survived, and its crankcase was salvaged by Rolls-Royce. PB's version of Tony's earlier story is that he had recognized "brown coolant stains...on the flame rings at a point between cylinder barrels...flame rings had reduced in thickness .010ins to .012ins... From this evidence it was diagnosed that hydraulicing troubles were also being caused through flame rings being insufficiently hard and squishing out through initial torque loading, permitting head to bounce on liner at high power finally leading to ingress of coolant to cylinders..."

Here was the key to a major breakthrough. Harder rings were promptly made and extra care taken in finishing mating surfaces (*vide* Phil Wilson, 1949?). Head stud torque was raised to 65 tons stress against 45. Special 90-ton studs were ordered.

Then a second engine, a brand-new one, reputedly seized a piston due to flooding, although Cliff Mander's contemporary production reports don't identify it. Improved fuel tanks were produced ready for Monza, a new asbestos sandwich bulkhead

with better sealing against the bodywork now insulated the cockpit from the engine bay and improved ventilation was provided around the pedal area. New front engine bearers were made, and after a rear axle radius rod had broken, all arms were modified with steel pick-up ends. Front-wheel centre point offset was reduced from 1.25in to 0.7in, which with new-type column UJs provided lighter steering.

The loss of one Silverstone engine and of the additional new one prevented adequate testing of the second car pre-Monza, but PB added: "Nevertheless the first car did considerable running...all modifications...made improvement. We left for Monza feeling that we had at least overcome the hydraulicing trouble which had cost us engines and dissipated our resources for so long."

The Council's report added:

> "But the fact remained that no effort of ours could speed delivery of the engine sets, and delays on this score – for which no blame attaches to our suppliers – meant that the spare complete engine prepared for, and taken to, Monza could not be bench-tested before the equipe's departure. In normal circumstances, of course, such an omission would be unthinkable..."

There was a driver problem, however, through lack of proper forward planning. Monza clashed with the RAC Tourist Trophy at Dundrod, where Peter Walker was committed to drive for Jaguar. Leslie Johnson tried the car instead. Aston Martin were willing to allow him to drive, and he actually offered to fly to Monza at his own expense to help. But after the usual confusion BRM ended up with Reg Parnell entered for one car, and Ken Richardson at last being given his long-promised chance in the other...although the RAC warned that he did not have the necessary full International visa for his competitions licence.

What followed was the usual BRM mixture of tragi-comedy and genuinely unforeseeable misfortune.

Tony: At the last moment Peter Haynes could not go to Monza due to the desperate illness of one of his children. The mechanics and I assumed I would deputise as Team Manager, as I seemed to have become accepted as part of the scene, but not by PB who said I was too familiar with the mechanics and would not be able to exert the necessary discipline. We ended up with a compromise: I would be in charge during the journey, but once we arrived at Monza, Ken, who was travelling out with RM in a works Ford Zephyr, would take over for race preparation. I would be Pit Manager.

Our cross-channel ferry could not enter Dunkirk harbour because the sea-lock gates had jammed. The ship had to return to England instead, while RM telephoned Dover from the Captain's cabin to book another crossing. We reached Dover in the early morning and then found it was impossible to return all the trucks on the same boat. Consequently we lost more than 15 hours and landed in France facing an all-night drive, our military schedule immediately in tatters.

Meanwhile, the seeds of the only BRM strike in history had been sewn before we left.

The company paid the mechanics' hotel bills, but in those days of strict currency control, arranging pocket money for

September 1951, the beleaguered BRM team's Lodestar transporters on the Dunkirk ferry en route to Monza, on the celebrated occasion upon which they found the Dunkirk lock gates jammed and embarkation denied. From this point forward the Italian Grand Prix foray was all downhill...

laundry, postcards home, etc, was tricky. The company secretary, Jim Sandercombe, was a nice man but he always tried to run things along military lines. He had a tough time interpreting decisions from the board, but I had managed to negotiate an allowance of 10s per day for the mechanics. I told them this had been arranged, but when we stopped in Lausanne and I applied for their 10 bob a head it was not forthcoming...

The next day we drove over the Alps through the Simplon Pass. The Commer workshop boiled its petrol and the Austin Lodestars their water. The Commer had been designed without Alpine passes in mind and on some of the tight hairpins it had to be shunted to and fro. In the tunnels we had to let its tyres down to clear the roof, then pump them up again at the other end.

Then we fell foul of the Customs. We'd left Calais in such a rush that our carnets had not been properly stamped. The Swiss were no bother accepting my argument that since officially we were not really there, the best way out was just to let us go! But the Italians became very suspicious. They told us we were wasting our time in any case going into the lion's den to face their Alfa Romeos and Ferraris. Eventually we sorted it out, with vast bundles of *Lire* changing hands, but after finding Monza without difficulty we couldn't find our destination – Villasanta.

I offered a small boy a 100 *Lire* note to lead us there on his bicycle and he promptly pedalled off into the distance. We never saw him again.

Older and wiser, the next small boy I asked, I tore the 100

Lire note in half, gave him one half as deposit and promised the other upon arrival...

RM had booked us into the *Hotel Marchese* in Villasanta, opposite the Monza Park gates on the far side of the Autodrome. It was pleasant enough, with large garages and a courtyard where we could work on the cars. The German teams had evidently stayed there prewar which was probably why RM had chosen it.

PB subsequently set down the Monza story like this:

REPORT ON PRACTICE AND RACE AT MONZA, 1951.

Pre-Official Practice.

A special practice was arranged for us on the Thursday for trying out our gear ratios on the circuit and for the official observation of Ken Richardson's driving – running in Parnell's car – High axle ratios were fitted to both cars. Both cars were running on English fuel brought over in the tanks. Both drivers complained of high tyre pressures which had been raised by Dunlop to suit the high speed characteristics of the circuit.

Ken Richardson was observed by the race stewards and accepted, and the R.A.C. telegraphed at midday asking for their official approval of his entry.

It was decided that the axle ratios were too high for the course and arrangements to fit the low ratio made on both cars.

Thursday, September 13, 1951 – unofficial Italian Grand Prix practice, Monza: Ken Richardson tried hard to fulfil RM's expectations and faith in his as-yet unproven abilities as an international-grade racing driver, but a missed gearchange and spin next day into the straw bales at Lesmo would finish his hopes of approval from the British RAC. Here on the porphyry stone setts at Vedano his as-yet un-numbered car shows off its new 10-slat radiator grille.

The best lap times were: Ken Richardson 2.2; Parnell 2.4.

First Official Practice – Friday.

Both cars completed axle ratio changes and practise in the afternoon, still using English fuel. Parnell's best lap was 2.2. The car appeared to be running well, but too much oil from the exhaust so that blower feed was reduced.

Parnell stopped after some 10 laps round the course. It was later found that the engine was in trouble. Ken Richardson ran into the straw bales on the *Lesmo* corner owing to being unable to engage third gear, with damage to the radiator, front end body cowling, steering arm and brake backplate. Richardson's car was repaired overnight, the steering arm straightened and it was crack tested by Alfa Romeo. The bodywork was repaired by Count Lurani's works.

Parnell's engine was found to have big end bearing trouble, and work commenced to change the engine for the spare overnight.

Second Practice – Saturday.

Parnell's car was not completed after the engine change; Richardson's car only was available. His best lap time – 2.4. The car was now running on Italian fuel and started misfiring at high r.p.m. after three or four laps. This state of affairs continued, and with new plugs, the car would run for three or four laps before misfiring. The remainder of the day and night mechanics worked on engine change of the Parnell car. Several snags were

encountered, entailing the making of new parts due to the spare engine being of the latest 1951 type.

At 10 p.m. the Automobile Club phoned for a meeting concerning Ken Richardson's permit, they having received a telegram refusing confirmation. Walkerley of the Temple Press was asked to attend as an official member of the R.A.C. Competitions Committee. We proposed withdrawing the Richardson car, but the Committee and Walkerley were very anxious that we should start both cars and proposed Stuck as available and the most experienced, with a number of Monza wins to his credit.

Stuck was contacted at 2 a.m. on Sunday morning and agreed to drive. A special practice was arranged at 7 a.m. for Stuck to be tried out in the Richardson car. Leslie Johnson telephoned from Ireland as arranged saying he was unable to arrive at the circuit before 9 a.m., and since this was after the latest practice time that could be allotted, and as he would have no sleep after his drive in the T.T., his trip was cancelled.

Race Day

Parnell's car was run in [by Ken Richardson] with the new spare engine as soon as it was light, at 6 a.m. The car stopped with engine trouble near completion of running in just as Stuck was ready to start his practise. Stuck did approximately 10 laps, the car missing slightly at high r.p.m. as before after 4 laps, returned a time of 2.4. The Parnell engine was superficially examined and blower trouble suspected. The cars returned to our garage for examination.

When Stuck's car was being pushed off the course, it

was noticed to be very stiff with a noise in the back axle, and the gear box appeared very hot. The car was taken to our paddock locker, filters, pipe lines, etc., were removed to check up on the trouble. After eliminating the possibilities, the trouble was finally diagnosed as a seizing needle bearing [Tony: slip of the tongue, plain bearing, needle bearings were the solution] on second and third gear, and although the car could be run on the seizing ratio only, the gearbox would seize completely if other ratios were used. No manoeuvre on the part of any driver could have caused this trouble.

At 11 a.m. these conclusions were reached, and it was reported that the spare engine in the Parnell car had failed with big end bearing trouble and was therefore eliminated.

The considerations now were:

(a) Could the gear box be removed from Parnell's car and fitted to the Richardson car so that Parnell could start in the race? The time available before going on to the grid for the start was 3½ hours.

(b) The mechanics were dead tired [having started to swap gearboxes nearly two hours previously] and much exhausted by the intense heat, but were willing to try.

(c) The job could normally be done in four hours, *provided there were no snags*.

(d) How much delay would be involved in getting the mechanics back to the hotel garage and then back on to the course with the gear box, as the traffic jam was now becoming intense at all entries to the circuit?

(e) If the change could be accomplished, what were the chances of the same thing happening to the other gear box?

Both gear boxes ran through Silverstone in identical condition, having been only examined, and these particular ratios not disturbed prior to Monza. This was new trouble and indications were that this high speed course had shown up a new weakness. It was therefore a very definite possibility that the other box would show the same failure during the race if started.

This defect was of a most dangerous nature since complete seizure would mean the selection of two ratios at once, which would immediately lock the rear wheels of the car. On such a high speed course with fast open bends, I considered the risk to drivers' life to be a serious possibility, and advised Raymond Mays and G.A. Vandervell[46] that the car should not be allowed to start. Work on the car was abandoned at approximately 11.30, when the team had a picnic breakfast in the workshop van. Post race examination showed that third gear had partially seized. After further running in post race tests on the course, the other gear box (ex Parnell's car) was opened for examination and found to be suffering from exactly similar trouble, though not quite in such an advanced condition of seizure.

Although the decision not to run was criticised by some not in possession of the full facts, it was the only one that could be made at the time and, as it transpired, it was the right one.

27th September, 1951   P. Berthon
                                    Technical Director.

PB/EP

46. Despite PB's inference here, when GAV found Tony Rudd around noon he was 'incandescent' with rage because he had heard of BRM's withdrawal from a pressman, and not from his 'employees' – PB or RM.

September 15, 1951 – Italian Grand Prix practice, Monza: Lovely subject for a scale model, the Latin organizers in Spain and Italy both favoured fancy race numbers on the BRMs around this period, viz this shadow style on Parnell's intended V16 'No. 1'.

Nearly 40 years later, Ken Richardson still blamed personal animosity from Col. Stanley Barnes – head of the RAC Competitions Department – for their refusal to let him start. Recalling his practice incident he explained: "The gear linkage used Mollart joints which had to be set-up perfectly to avoid free play. I used to check them myself, but that time I hadn't had a chance to. I was going into the first Lesmo corner and when I braked and changed down this freeplay made me miss my gear. As I declutched to try it again, the bloody engine died and of course if it wasn't running you had no brake servo. By this time I was going really quick, far too deep into the corner, so I just locked over and spun it. I almost got away with it, but although the spin had scrubbed off most of the car's speed before its nose came round one final time it just swiped the front suspension sideways against the straw bales…"

Tony: At Monza I was allowed to become more involved with the engineering, and in addition to Ken Richardson's moment at *Lesmo* both cars were far over-geared because – not for the last time – we had fallen into the trap of thinking that Monza was much faster than it really was.

I took the bent pieces from Ken's car to the Alfa Romeo factory that evening, where thanks to help from Count 'Johnny' Lurani they straightened them out. The following morning was hot and dusty and the cars were nowhere near as quick as we had hoped. Reg's engine then blew-up, running its big-end bearings which entailed another all-nighter to change the engine for the spare which had never actually run since its rebuild. And here we were not very bright…

We changed the engine and cleaned out the oil system, but forgot to clean the gauze strainer inside the car's oil tank and that triggered the final split with Tony Vandervell.

The following morning, Ken went out in the re-engined car and returned with its bearings ruined. Next morning we found the root cause of both failures had been jointing compound clogging the gauze strainer, and our failure to clean it of compound and debris after the first incident had been fatal.

When the press asked what was the trouble, RM quoted bearing failure, which was true, but nobody can expect bearings to survive without lubrication and the inference that something was wrong with Vandervell bearings – when there wasn't – utterly enraged Tony Vandervell who eventually resorted to law to get the statement corrected.

Then we had the Richardson/RAC drama and the decision to give Hans Stuck his car. Alfred Owen's Council report later explained:

…four days prior to the scheduled departure date, the Manager of the RAC's Competitions Department, in a private telephone conversation with Raymond Mays, suggested that a certain course should be adopted…to arrange for Richardson to make practice runs at Monza under the eye of the organizing club's official observers. Then, providing his handling of the car satisfied the Milan Club, Raymond Mays was to ask them to cable the RAC making known their approval and asking for the RAC's sanction to his driving to be immediately wired back to Milan.

This procedure was in fact followed to the letter, and the Italians' cable duly expressed complete satisfaction with Richardson's form. Their wire went to London on the Thursday, three clear days before the race, but the reply – flatly refusing sanction – did not reach Milan until the Saturday. Actually it was 9.30 on Saturday night that the news of the refusal was given to Raymond Mays by the Club officials…

RM, meanwhile, had admired the Austrian multiple European Mountain-Climb Champion and former Auto Union

September 15, 1951 – Italian Grand Prix practice, Monza: The equally ill-fated Ken Richardson car 'No. 2' with its slatted grille is wheeled away as the shadows lengthen. It will be tried briefly by Hans Stuck on race morning, and it will break… No BRMs will start in the Italian Grand Prix.

After the Italian Grand Prix BRM's team remained at Monza for prolonged testing. Here Dave Turner, Colin 'Gelati' Atkin, Cyril Bryden and Willie Southcott wheel out the still drum-braked 'No. 1' in its contemporary metallic pale green livery – fancy race numbers long-since removed – under the critical gaze of five local tifosi. The apparent effort demanded of four men merely to push the V16 is perhaps significant…

No. 1 driver Hans Stuck for many years, he was available at Monza and so RM made the much criticized but undoubtedly reasonable decision to offer Richardson's drive to him.

Back in the garages behind the Marchese we were told that Stuck would be driving next morning as he needed some experience of the car before official practice began. So both cars were sent out first thing, with Richardson testing Parnell's and Stuck in the other. The disconsolate Richardson ground his teeth as Stuck revved his BRM wildly leaving the pits, and drew away in a cloud of acrid clutch smoke. "You could smell it burning, all the way along the pit lane…" Stuck returned after his exploratory run, and it was then that his gearbox was found to be on the point of seizure…

By this time the mechanics had been hard at work for two nights and more days. They were hot and dreadfully weary. None was very experienced in foreign travel. Some had upset stomachs from strange food; most were sunburned. Tempers were understandably frayed.

Even so, as soon as we finished running, about 9am in the paddock lock-up, we had all set about what seemed to be the only logical thing possible, which was to take the undamaged gearbox from Parnell's blown-up car and put it into the Stuck/Richardson machine with its healthy engine for Reg to race.

Then RM and PB appeared, declaring their decision that the cars should not run. The danger of a gearbox seizure hurting someone was too great.

We had gone through hell to get the cars that far and were determined to see at least one start. There was a fearful row, but they were adamant. It was about 11.30am and the disgruntled mechanics marched off for a well-earned cup of tea dispensed by the Ferodo racing service caravan, which was always present at the Grands Prix as they serviced the leading Italian teams.

Some journalists saw the mechanics sitting there, and attacked them in print for drinking tea instead of putting a BRM on the startline! In the circumstances, this was desperately unfair and was *bitterly* resented.

Meanwhile, a journalist had told Tony Vandervell the news and he was stamping around the paddock even more enraged after finding the BRM lock-ups deserted and the trucks gone. The first BRM person he bumped into was me, and he gave me a severe going over, and then encountered Ken Richardson who was naturally disappointed and unburdened himself to GAV, which made the bearings magnate still more incensed! He was fit to burst.

The BRM mechanics watched the race from the pits. When our withdrawal was announced, the crowds hissed and whistled. I made them all remove their distinctive BRM overalls. We kept a pretty low profile…

That night, back at the Marchese, the mood was pretty mutinous. Nobody would listen to instructions from the Directors, then Reg Parnell appeared, sensed the atmosphere and ordered vast flagons of Chianti all round – and we enthusiastically drowned our sorrows. I vividly recall the foreman of the engine shop – Dave Turner – in such a shocking state that the only way he could get upstairs to bed was on his hands and knees, backwards.

We all had thumping headaches next morning. Then RM and PB arrived and told us that the race organizers were willing to take care of the hotel bill – on which Parnell had put all that Chianti – but since we had not started the race there was no start money.

They then told me we were to stay on at Monza for some serious testing because the circuit offered a genuine yardstick of relative performance against the latest Ferrari and Alfa Romeos. One car was to stay, attended by PB, three or four of the bachelor mechanics, and myself.

The damaged engines and gearbox were to be taken home and we would be supplied with parts from Bourne to keep the test car running.

Initially, Ken Richardson did most of the driving as Alfred Owen's October 30 report emphasized that his "...personal mileage on the cars greatly exceeds that of anyone else". But RM also invited his old friend Louis Chiron and Piero Taruffi to have a go, and even PB tried his hand and learned more about his car than he had absorbed in the preceding 22 months. Then RM finally invited young Stirling Moss to come out and drive it.

One good reason for BRM's troubles had always been the lack of a good analytical test driver. Amongst all those with a high mileage on the car the only one with worthwhile experience of a modern GP car was Reg Parnell – and that only briefly with the Alfa Romeo team in the previous year's British GP. Most of his V16 experience had been in the wet or under distracting circumstances. Ken Richardson had no real long-term idea of what to look for, nor of the direction the programme should take, and no experience of other contemporary GP cars. PB and Taruffi between them produced a list of shortcomings, but Moss' list would be even longer.

PB and Peter Knight of SU developed a method of setting the carburettor, using a pressure bottle adapted from a brake pressure bleeding kit, to avoid an apparent flooding problem on Monza's long, fast curves. This revised our method of setting 'the levels'. I had briefed the mechanics on this new method, but I was away from the garage when Ken Richardson arrived and advised them instead to do it the old way, which sparked an altercation between Ken and I. He went home, ultimately leaving the team, and I was advised that since I had contrived his departure I should look after the technical side as well as team administration and logistics...

We spent three or four days just putting the car into proper trim, while a typical diversion of the time was 'the affair of the fuel'.

At that time, the BRMs ran on a brew of 70 per cent methyl alcohol, a proportion of acetone, distilled water etc – plus some alkylate iso-pentane, which is a very high energy petrol, not to be confused with the oxygen-liberating additives like nitro-methane and nitro-benzene. It gave significant improvements in fuel consumption, and probably in power.

Taruffi introduced us to a very tall – 6ft 6in – Italian engineer, *Ingegnere* Bei, who hit the headlines in 1968 with a proposal for a Formula 1 safety car. It was suggested that the higher ambient temperatures of Italy affected this exotic fuel and perhaps created some of our carburation problems.

Bei's advice was very useful, and he put us in touch with an Italian company, unique in those days, which specialized in blending alcohol fuels. Its name was *Martelli e Zampatori*, and they were situated not far from the Alfa Romeo factory. We set off there in one of the Lodestars with two 50-gallon drums and myself, Bei and the driver Willie Southcott crammed into the cab. We had a language problem and we got lost. Eventually we understood from Bei we should follow one of the Milanese trams, so we did literally that...

When it went down the tree-lined centre strip of the dual-carriageway boulevards, we followed, bumping over the tramway sleepers. When a policeman held up traffic at a crossroad to wave the tram through, he was rather startled to see our black Austin Lodestar bumping after it. He could do little more than jump on his cap after we'd passed.

PB kept a remarkably comprehensive diary of the Monza tests, eventually circulated to the Trust. It gives a fine insight into the stresses within the team, while also recording his own impressions after driving the car (on October 3). Its main substance read as follows:

MONZA TESTS
REPORT No. 1.

Monday, 17th September, 1951:

Richardson car. Gearbox opened for examination and 3rd gear on input shaft found to be in advanced state of seizure. Parnell gearbox also examined and 4th gear found slightly seizing. Clearances checked and found to be low, so trouble believed to be lack of clearance possibly due to inaccurate positioning of differential bolt on assembly. Parnell gearbox reassembled with larger clearances and fitted to Richardson No. 2 car.

G.A. Vandervell came over from Milan in morning, saw cars and had lunch – Tony finds this hard to believe since GAV was so hopping mad on the Sunday and for months after he surely would not have gone anywhere near RM and PB – Raymond Mays left for London with North after Lunch. Alfa Romeo collected me where I spent afternoon with Allessio. [47]

Tuesday, 18th September, 1951:

No. 2 car – Richardson's – being completed. Saw Bacciagaluppi who said Auto Club might consider paying mechanics' hotel bill as per arrangement, but the advance of 500,000 *Lire* against starting money would have to be refunded. Pointed out impracticability of repaying this and would be illegal to suggest refunding in London. He agreed to discuss the position further with the Automobile Club. Is prepared to help with any further testing where required at Monza and would agree to using the course as long as we reasonably required, free of charge. Concerning drivers he suggested that Taruffi as an engineer and a Ferrari team driver would be a useful man for us to have. He agreed to contact him.

Car to course in late afternoon. Latest type carburetter [*sic*] springs fitted and carburetters [*sic*] tuned for Italian 'Esso' fuel now being used. New 51's gave good results for 7 laps, then missing and burbling set in.

Ken Richardson driving. Best lap time 1.59.6. Car pulling 11,600r.p.m. on pit straight and 11,400r.p.m. on back leg. Oil temperature 120°C, pressure 43lbs. sq. in., water consistent 103/105°C. Weather very hot. Driver complained bitterly of high tyre pressures. Struts changed in the evening back to Silverstone damping. High tyre pressures require higher damping.

47. **Dr Alessio – President of Alfa Romeo.**

Wednesday, 19th September, 1951:

Weather very hot. Car to course in morning. K. Richardson thought increased damped struts an improvement but complained of car wandering at speed. Further tuning of carburetters [sic] by Knight (S.U.) attempt to eliminate missing etc.

Taruffi called late morning saying he would be pleased to help and pointed out as he was a Ferrari team driver we must not ask him to give any information concerning the Ferrari and its performance. He showed us the Ferrari method of timing at the Monza track in 4 separate sections so that the car's performance could be seggregated [sic]. Also said Ferrari knew we were faster (considerably) than they on the straights but lost time on corners and twisty sections of the circuit. Taruffi stayed Lunch and drove car afterwards. The car ran well and cleanly for 3–5 laps on new 51 plugs. After, started missing and burbling. On new 53 plugs ran clean from 1–3 laps only before started missing. Taruffi did some 12 laps, best time being 2 mins. dead.

From this morning all laps are timed in the 4 sections using the Ferrari method. This is exceedingly useful and begins to show already where we are losing time. It is obvious from the figures got today that with the engine running clean, limited to 11,500 revs maximum, we are 2 seconds faster on the pit straight, but on the twisty sections of the course we are losing up to 8 seconds. Taruffi very impressed with engine performance and thinks rear suspension good. Considers steering to be bad and we were losing time due to lack of steering precision which does not permit car to be steered within a yard either side of the chosen line. Taruffi now in [sic, empty space left in report] for a few days, so contacted Chrion [sic] at Palace Hotel who came out for dinner. Changed complete ignition set at night with first engine ex Parnell car.

Thursday, 20th September, 1951:

Now getting very short of new plugs. All used plugs appear to have a browny-grey deposit which is unusual. Car exhaust pipes now clean and hot as those sand blasted, without trace of carbon. Beginning to suspect fuel contains some foreign matter that is depositing on plugs.

Car to track using best set of 51's. Richardson ran a few laps at reduced tyre pressures i.e. 40 front, 50 rear. Said car felt no different but times recorded show an improvement of 2 seconds on twisty section although overall lap time had not improved. Tyre pressure back to standard i.e. 46 front, 55 rear. Last new set 51's fitted for Chiron. 6 laps clear without missing. Attempts made to clean plugs and replace but in further running up to 16 laps, missing and burbling could not be avoided. Chiron kept driving to get to know the car. He was very impressed by the performance and liked the gearbox and brakes very much and thought that with practice and improvement to steering which he criticised, times

could be reduced to record lap. His best time 2 m. 10 s [48].

Decided to try change of fuel. Contacted Professor Speluzzi who sent an engineer by B.A.I. [Presumably dictation error, PB simply spelling out Bei's name, wrongly – DCN] to Milan with Rudd to have the fuel mixed by a small firm who were used to the requirements. As no Alkalate Isopentane available in Italy, decided to use a mixture containing 75% (of 99.8% Methanol), 10% (of Benzol containing 98% Benzine), and 7% of Acetone. This fuel should be kinder to engine on this high speed circuit and will require a 10% richer setting due to difference in calorific value. Fuel changed. Richardson did 2 laps slowly on the new fuel but very light throttle to check mixture, when car stopped with failed piston.

Friday, 21st September, 1951:

Engine removed – dismantled. Found that No. 7 Piston had 'washed'. With 'wiped' rings and heat signs on top land. Supercharger and induction manifold contained heavy red-brown deposit like sand. One flame trap damaged, quantity of elements missing and bits scattered throughout engine. Suspected piston failure due to continual misfiring on No. 7 cylinder but could find no evidence in ignition system etc to prove this. Ball bearings and remainder of engine in excellent condition. Heard Alfa's are due to test this afternoon and sent Rudd down to get some sectionalised times.

Saturday & Sunday, 22nd & 23rd September, 1951:

Engine built up with new pistons and liner No. 7 cylinder. Cylinder heads with flame traps from the spare engine (new engine) and supercharger from new engine.

Fuel system on car checked completely through, and considerable quantities of scale, rust and metallic particles removed from tanks, filters, liners and carburetters.

Sent Turner, Atkin and Southcott with Parnell car and damaged engine parts back to Bourne, who left 4.30 a.m. on the 23rd. Telegram from Ray asking me to contact Moss at Modena and use in further tests. 'Phoned Moss, agreed to come over when finished racing at Modena (Driving his works team HWM).

Monday, 24th September, 1951:

Car to track in morning. Richardson running on 47 plugs. All pressures checked – found O.K. and low [sic, means 'blower'] oil feed opened to 5 clicks. [Tony: We didn't do this, we had been running since Silverstone with the valve wide open, but this is PB's story!] Plugs changed to new 49's and running-in continued. Revs

---

48. For comparison, Fangio's *Alfetta* had taken pole position for the Italian GP in 1min 53.2sec; Farina's fastest race lap in a sister car was 1min 56.5sec, 121.49mph. Parnell's best official Italian GP practice time for BRM had been 2:02.2, Richardson's 2:05.6...

increased to 9,000 at high throttle. After 15 laps total, car stopped round course, further piston trouble evident. When car was pushed in further gearbox trouble noticed. Moss was anxious to return to England and agreed to come back and carry out tests during the following week. Cylinder head removed. No. 1 piston found to have clean plug pre-ignition hole in crown. Plugs carefully examined. Two further plugs found to have ceramic insulator broken off which had fallen down resting on earthwire. Believe we are suffering from inconsistency of plugs both 51's and 49's, though this amount piston failure might be due to over-driving on 49 plugs which is easily done on this circuit, but Richardson is used to running in and this has never previously happened.

Tuesday, 25th September, 1951:

Heard from Tresilian that crank of first failed engine now back in Bourne appeared correct to drawing and that failure was due to inadequate oil tank suction filter causing starvation at [high] r.p.m.[49] In view of this decided to strip engine completely, check through oil system. Also, stripped gearbox. Found 4th gear again seizing on input shaft. This trouble not entirely due to lack of side clearance as first suspected. On examination, obvious that oil flow into shaft was inadequate and at high input shaft r.p.m. oil was prevented in feeding through differential bolt to second half of shaft due to C:F.

Left instructions for new 3rd speed lay shaft gear to be fitted. All clearances to be increased to .007–.010. Engine to be stripped, thoroughly cleaned, faces, liners etc lapped and the engine prepared for assembly. Decided to return Richardson with spare engine (original engine fitted to Parnell's car) and other used spares now requiring replacement. Ambrose as 2nd driver. Richardson not pulling his weight having been unsettled by Parnell and G.A.Vandervell. Consider unwise to leave him here in charge in my absence.

Labour inclined to be fed-up with continual set-backs and some dis-unity in the camp. Got them together, thrashed out their problems which were minor, i.e. lack of spending money, personal requirements of clothes etc. They were also dissatisfied to continue the race arrangement of £1 per day and all found. Agreed that this would be dealt with on return and some allowance for overtime would be made. Left Rudd in charge of party with Aldridge as Head Mechanic, and Mrs. Berthon agreed to do their personal shopping.

Wednesday, 26th September, 1951:

Richardson and Ambrose left with van at 5 a.m. with sufficient food to get through Switzerland owing to lack

49. This fault had been identified at Monza on Monday 17th. The tank had not been returned, being cleaned instead by the crew in Italy. Tresilian's conclusion confirmed their findings. Tony: 'Inadequate' is an odd euphemism for 'clogged'!

of Swiss *Francs*. I left for 6 a.m. train from Milan to Zurich.

Saturday & Sunday, 29th & 30th September, 1951:

Arrived back late last night. Turner arrived 29th according to schedule. Engine ready to build up. New piston and liner No. 1 cylinder. Damaged hemisphere cleaned up, 2 new valves fitted. All valves checked for sealing with petrol. New filters fitted. Oil tank cleaned and filter checked. Found to be fairly dirty but not sucked in. Head and liners were re-lapped with set of new type plain rings. Gearbox ready for assembly with new gear fitted. Modified oil feed pipe and extension fitted so that total feed equals ⅛"dia. Bevel shaft feed 2¹⁄₁₆" holes. Feed to shaft through differential bolt 1³⁄₃₂" hole. Flow from pump increased by doubling area of suction hole.

Monday, 1st October, 1951:

Turner built up engine. Checked timing at 5 p.m. Heads torqued up O.K. Difficulty in fitting blower mods. However modifications completed to drawing omitting ¼" drain hole through case. Work going well and morale high. Hope car will be ready by Wednesday. Mechanics working to new schedule starting this morning as follows: 6.15 a.m. call, 6.45 a.m. breakfast (bacon and eggs), 7 a.m. commence work, 10.30 a.m. Rudd coffee or tea from workshop, 12 a.m. lunch, 1 p.m. commence work, 4.45 p.m. tea and sandwich each (included in pensions), 7 p.m. finish work, 7.15 p.m. dinner.

Mrs. Berthon has completed their shopping requirements and covered lack of clothing situation.

During this period owing to shortage of money it has been customary to buy their cigarettes and small personal wants and issue a personal allowance of 5,000 *Lire* per head on Fridays. Now Sandercombe has arranged a credit I have promised this will be a regular feature.

Received letter from Bank confirming credit of £500.

Rex Munday and wife for lunch. Anxious for us to try K.L.G. plugs. Arranged with Tresilian to sleeve set of old heads to take standard plug threads.

Engine complete and supercharger mounted this afternoon.

Tuesday, 2nd October, 1951:

Telegram from Alec Fraser to meet him Gianinos for lunch, but he did not turn up.

Gearbox and engine in car but not quite finished.

Mechanics packed up 6.30 p.m. – all very tired.

Tresilian phoned that Richardson delayed at Le Bourget with fuel but should make Rheims tonight. Rex Munday called evening to check on the standard plug hexagon but no good. Wired K.L.G. to make some special plugs quickly for trial here.

Saw Fangio and Farina but were both full of apologies that Alfa would not let them drive the car while they were under contract, but both were anxious to drive immediately after Barcelona, and Fangio would be prepared to make a special trip to England.

Wednesday, 3rd October, 1951:

Saw Bacciagaluppi re import of fuel. Confirmed Auto Club would do everything possible to facilitate. Thought it best to wait until Richardson arrived at Isella. No news of Richardson.

Car completed by lunch. Carburetters [sic] set up at best setting used so far on Italian fuel. Although would prefer to go straight on to known English fuel, decided to run-in on Italian fuel, it being filtered into tanks through chamois leather.

Taruffi called for lunch, enquired progress. Very insistent on bad steering characteristic. Went down to course and ran car 15 laps on 47 plugs. Completed running in 49 plugs. All pressures etc: checked, engine appears to be running. [?sic]

Running will now be delayed as we have no good 51 plugs though 3 sets only are coming out with Richardson and fuel.

'Phoned Tresilian in the evening to urge new steering box ratio and enquire progress on mods. arranged during my visit. My impressions after driving car on circuit as follows:
(1) Steering characteristic is chronic. Steering is not heavy, much too direct high geared, and too much backlash in system, and it amazes me that no driver has been able to tell us that the drift is worse when the front is in roll causing wheel patter and lack of adhesion.
(2) Consider roll bar far too heavy which is assisting the front end of the frame to twist about the back engine mounting.
(3) Find front tank movements due rubber mounting moves steering wheel considerably and causes driver to alter wheel position.
(4) Cannot find evidence of marked understeer on trail in corner changing to over-steer (break away) when using power.
(5) Rear of car has higher cornering power than front but consider movement in rear hub assemblies and radius arms should be reduced.

Chiron phoned that he is available at Monte Carlo and will come over if necessary the moment we require him. Explained fuel position.

Thursday, 4th October, 1951:

Mechanics spent morning in checking over car and refitting bodywork, as unwise to continue running on Italian fuel, decided to give mechanics half-day.

Had steering tracked up and checked over.

Richardson phoned at 9 p.m. that he was stuck at Domodossola and the Customs would not let him enter Italy without Fuel Import Licence. Contacted Bacciagaluppi who had already made application for licence to Rome, and had got Auto Club and Banca d'Italia to agree import. Thought delay would be about 4 days. Told Richardson to have fuel unloaded and locked in Customs store and to bring van and spares on for which paperwork was completed.

Raymond Mays wired saying Moss arriving tomorrow…decided tests must proceed particularly as Moss arrives today and asked Zampatori to make up 400 litres of 75/18/7 fuel checking ingredients and taking special care. Ready for collection tomorrow.

Rudd took Mrs. Berthon to catch a train in Milan and meet Moss whose aircraft was 3 hours late and he returned here 6.30 p.m.

Moss said that Parnell had done his best to stop him driving the car and tried to get the B.R.D.C. agreement that nobody else should drive until modifications had been made and that he, Parnell, was satisfied that the car was good enough. Moss said that Leslie Johnson had countered Parnell's suggestion and had advised Moss to come out here.

Tresilian phoned to say that second blower appeared to be clogged with mixture of sand and castor oil. Considered possibility of somebody having put sand in fuel tanks, but think it likely the trouble is due to the use of dirty barrels by the fuel company. Car had fuel system drained and the new Zampatori fuel filtered into tanks through chamois leather. Carb. setting richened about 10% and car taken down to track.

Using new set of 49 plugs Moss went out and ran with very light throttle to get to know the car. After 12 laps car stopped round course obviously in trouble. Examination showed that another piston had gone, this time No. 16 with the same small pre-ignition hole in the crown. Plug examination showed definitely faulty plug together with 2 other plugs in engine in serious trouble. No question that 49 plugs we have out here are a faulty batch and decided to impound remainder.

Moss very pleased with his run in the car and although limited to 9000r.p.m. with very light throttle went round in 2.11 fairly consistently in these first few laps. He thinks the steering isn't at all bad but merely requires getting used to.

Car returned and engine removed.

Alfa running during afternoon and Moss was invited to try a car. He did 5 laps in their test car, fastest time 2.11. Later he said that the front end of the Alfa steering was much more solid and direct than the B.R.M. and the road holding particularly good and most noticeable at Pave corners. The engine had a lot of power at 5,000r.p.m. and it was very easy to get too much wheel spin but after that speed it did not appear to develop much more power up to 7.5r.p.m. and seemed to have a good deal less power than the B.R.M.

Sunday, 7th October, 1951:

Engine rebuilt with new pistons and liner. Checked timing at 7 p.m. after which engine complete and ready to be placed into chassis.

Guiadotti [sic][50] called lunch time and took Moss to

---

50. GianBattista Guidotti, team manager.

Como in the afternoon during which he tackled Moss on driving for Alfa next year.

Monday, 8th October, 1951:

Engine in chassis after a 6 a.m. start by lunchtime. Went to Milan to Bank – drew £200 which only just cleared *Marchesi*, fuel bills and immediate petty cash requirements. Car on track by 2.30. Richardson ran 20 laps very slowly on 47 plugs. Cleaned and tested set of 51's fitted. Moss took over to gradually progress speed. On using gradual throttle up to 9,500r.p.m. water temperature went off the scale and he came in with the system boiling madly. System checked over. Seemed O.K. Header tank refilled for further trial. After 3 laps same thing happened and car returned to garage. Ran engine with cylinder head return pipes disconnected but returning to header tank. At 8,000r.p.m. and above flow appeared very much reduced to 1–8 cylinder bank. Pump examined – found O.K. All pipework examined and apart from traces of Lisapol and Captax, system seemed alright. Thought possible that mixture was frothy causing air lock in 1–8 bank so had system thoroughly flushed out for retest.

Tuesday, 9th October, 1951:

Moss has to return Thursday latest to compete at Winfield. Sent Rudd Milan to arrange booking. Car at track early and with 51 plugs and any attempt to use performance; water system rocketed up to 120°C. Returned to pub, removed radiator and fitted spare. Both radiators reversed flushed in examination and found to be full of rust scale which was blocking up the cores. It seems these aluminium radiators are very sensitive to becoming blocked up and we must in future make water system entirely of aluminium.

Car returned to track after lunch. Moss continued running. Water temperature now well below 100°C with throttle. Running continued with increasing speed and after some laps returned to pit saying engine felt to have lost all its performance. [It was the] Richardson engine and it was apparent that something seriously wrong with supercharger. Car returned, supercharger removed. Rotor shaft seized solid and although were unable to strip the supercharger here, it appeared as though the rear ball bearing had seized. Spare blower fitted. Suspect modification fitted previously for better control of ball bearing lubrication is scavenging oil from delivery side of bearing so preventing flow through the bearing.

Morale getting a bit low and although we are learning a great deal about the car, Moss returns day after tomorrow at mid-day so there is little time left before he leaves to get results and a good lap time would be worth a great deal to us all at the moment.

Wednesday, 10th October, 1951:

Mechanics tired this morning, so allowed them start late. Tresilian arived from Milan at 9 a.m. and wired Allen, Rolls-Royce, my suspicions on the supercharger oil modification asking him to do some careful tests on the rig, so that this persistent supercharger oiling trouble which we have now had with us for a year, can be ironed out for good.

Car down to track about 1.30. Blower oil feed opened to 8 clicks to ensure adequate lubrication. Moss did considerable amount of running throughout the afternoon increasing speed continually and what is really important succeeded in getting his time down through the twisty section of the course to somewhere near the Alfa times.

Persistent missing and burbling continues when full throttle is used and can only be avoided by using sets of brand new plugs which run clear for 3–5 laps, then the cycle starts all over again. This missing is stopping Moss really being able to use the performance and not giving him a chance to reduce his time on the straight. Nevertheless, pulling not more than 11,000r.p.m. due to missing he has reduced his time to 1–57.4. If we can get the engine to stay running absolutely clean for 10 laps and pulling the revs it should be on the straight, it should reduce his best straight time by over 2 seconds. Moss is quite certain he can get the car round as it is in 55 seconds and I believe him because so far he has carried out everything he said he thought he could do. Moss is extremely keen and watches the times on the sections of the course with great care and when he says he can take 2 seconds off on any particular section; he goes out and takes 2 seconds off. He is also one of the few drivers who comes back and gives pressures, temperatures, and information without being bullied into it.

Running continually to dark without any success, to eliminate the misfiring and burbling.

Held a general discussion in the evening and put it to everybody that if we could eliminate this missing, we could really begin to make progress, and anybody might put their finger on the trouble.

We have on many occasions run clean. The 2 cars to Silverstone with Bira and Walker were noticeable for this. The running done at Folkingham prior to leaving for Monza on this same car was also conclusively clean which led us to believe that we had got rid of this trouble with the problem of hydraulicing. We have been right through the carburation range and from this point of view the engine has appeared to run very well...[*after eliminating carburation and sticking valves PB continued:*]...So, rather unwillingly, we can reduce this trouble theoretically to ignition. All the usual checks were made, all the leads are found to be deteriorating badly and the rubber is cracking longitudinally. Doubtful leads are replaced and we decided to carry out some definite tests tomorrow to try and locate this trouble. A further quantity of fuel ordered and collected this afternoon... The engine installation completely and carefully checked over and although we would like to make some ignition changes for trial, there [are] no spares available here.

Booster gauge fitted to car and a set of new 53's reduced to .009/.010 gap (standard gap .012–.015).

Thursday, 11th October, 1951:

To track at 9.30. Moss driving. Last new set of 53 plugs fitted and the following run made:
(1) Driving on boost gauge only, ignoring r.p.m. using maximum of 20lbs boost and running through range. Engine ran perfectly clean 5 laps.
(2) Repeated (1) but using a maximum of 30lb boost ignoring r.p.m. and driving on boost gauge. Engine ran clear for one lap and then light and spasmodic missing became persistent. 5 laps.
(3) No. 1 test repeated exactly. Engine ran nearly clear with very slight missing. 5 laps.
(4) No. 2 run repeated with last new set of 51 plugs. 5 laps. Results exactly as (2).
(5) Close gap 53's fitted and No. 2 test repeated. Engine missed badly first lap but ran absolutely clean and clear for a further 5 laps.

On 7th lap Moss came in and said that the engine felt incredibly rough. Car returned to garage, examined and appeared superficially O.K. Valve gear checked etc. Found O.K. Blower removed and the bob weight on No. 1 throw of the crank found lying in the sump it having showed [sic ploughed?] through an oil filter casing when breaking away from crank. Examination showed that the crank web had 2 old cracks in the corners of the bob weight groove. Checked the stress in the web. Found to be ridiculously small at about 2-tons per sq. in. at maximum r.p.m. It would seem that added to the original cracks the continual missing has probably assisted the failure. The total running this car has done on the course to date is just under 800 miles and this engine was the original Walker engine that ran through Silverstone.

Raymond Mays phoned and told position.

Tony: As PB's report so clearly recalled, when Stirling Moss arrived it was like a breath of fresh air…

He brought a completely new approach to BRM testing. He was able when driving to apply part of his incisive mind to controlling the car while another part recorded everything that happened. His sensitivity was staggering…particularly this Thursday afternoon of that series when he came into the pits and said he suspected something was wrong with the engine, it had "…a little tremor".

We ran it up, all 16 cylinders seemed fine, its oil pressure was perfect, but he insisted he would not drive it until we had found the problem. Its valve gear proved normal, no broken springs, and since it was an exceedingly difficult engine to strip we were reluctant to do so without what we felt was good reason.

However, the standard strip procedure started at the bottom of the crankcase and worked upwards, and when we eventually removed the oil filters we spotted slivers of what proved to be magnesium from the sump, just a little more than we would expect. We removed the supercharger and 'hey

presto' one of the tongued and grooved crankshaft balance weights had come adrift and was lying there…

The engine was only some 5 per cent less balanced than it should have been, but Stirling had sensed it. This gave me immense faith in his ability…

PB's log continued:

Friday, 12th October, 1951:

Decided to return half the team immediately. Railway tickets arranged for Tresilian, Turner, Richardson and Ambrose and returned on the 5.15 train Saturday. As crank position looked fairly hopeless, phoned Raymond Mays and suggested that Tresilian should go straight to Rolls-Royce to see whether they would help and assemble 2 cranks really quickly. I felt that everything should be done to continue the tests as we have not had an opportunity of trying any of the modifications to steering, front suspension etc for which parts are now nearly ready but the delay on a crank or an alternative engine must decide the issue.[51]

Saturday, 13th October, 1951:

We had an official deputation from Alfa who asked if they could examine the B.R.M. in the garage as they had now decided to go ahead with a new edition of their 12 cylinder engine [Alfa had actually been racing eight-cylinder cars but at the time were perpetuating this fiction of a confirmed 12-cylinder F1 programme – DCN] …for the next 2 years. As the engine was now out of the frame I had to put them off saying that we had to carry out a complete routine examination of the car and for this purpose it had been dismantled.

Decided to strip the car for complete examination which work the 3 remaining mechanics here could carry out…

Tony: Looking back on those first Monza tests, although *Martelli e Zampatori* blended a new fuel for us amidst great ceremony, I doubt it made much difference. In later years when we switched to BP, Beveridge Rowntree – who was probably the greatest expert on alcohol fuel blending – advised us to revert to the old faithful '80-10-10' mix, and the engine went just as well, or as badly, dependent upon one's viewpoint.

51. The engines damaged during these Monza tests were as follows:
    'No. 3 (Type 11/3)' – first failure, heads removed and swapped with those from 'No. 1 (Type 11/1)'. Main parts of 'No. 3' scrapped comprised three con-rods, two pistons, three cyl liners, two valves, one crankshaft. Rebuilt and returned to Monza. 'Blew up' again at end of testing, late November and returned in car, frame 'Mark 1/2'
    'No. 4 (Type 20/1)' – second failure, scrapped seven con-rods, three pistons, three cyl liners. Damaged crankshafts from these two engines were uncoupled by Lucas and sent to English Steel to investigate potential salvage.
    'No. 1 (Type 11/1)' – third failure (crankshaft balance weight) saved from further damage as described in text by Moss' mechanical sensitivity. Thrown weight had actually cracked upper wall of crankcase lower half, but damage was repairable.

Taruffi's division of the circuit into four separately-timeable sections had gone like this: from the bottom end of the pits, the car could be timed from the moment it came into view from the *Curva Vedano* until it vanished around the *Curva Grande*. One then timed the interval before it reappeared on the back straight, which provided its time through the *Roggia* and *Lesmo* corners. It could then be timed down the back straight. This enabled us to tell whether we were losing time through the corners or down the straights. The V16 did both, but more so through the corners!

While awaiting spares from Bourne, we watched other activities at the *Autodromo*.

We found an ally in a character who I think worked as a groundsman at the circuit. In return for a drink and our waste engine oil, he proved a mine of information. He was always after *"Olio"* so we christened him 'Olio', or 'Oily'. He would appear at the Marchesi in the evening and indicate that Alfa Romeo would be testing next day. We would go to our lock-up and try to time their cars as a baseline comparison, while Alfa's people did their best to obstruct us.

Eventually, I slumped in the transporter pretending to be asleep while Willie Southcott sat on the pit counter smoking. When he waved his cigarette I pumped the stopwatch, so we recorded Alfa's times. Soon after, we timed Ferrari too. Out in the woods we marked a shorter stretch to check maximum speeds…

This pleasantly academic interlude was punctuated by the overhaul of our pit gear and practising high-speed refuelling. With Lorna Berthon's help, gearbox fitter Cyril Bryden had bought himself a flashy pair of bright ox-blood Italian shoes, of which he was inordinately proud. One refuelling practice flooded the garage, after which Cyril walked away with only his shoes' uppers still on his feet, the soles having bonded themselves irretrievably to the floor…

But, of course, Moss was the revelation. Until he had proved himself in Europe through 1950 driving John Heath's Formula 2 HWMs, the older Brooklands brigade had dismissed him as being "just another young Cooper 500 maniac", but in the HWMs he had really shone amongst very serious company at some daunting venues.

RM had first invited him to try the BRM at Folkingham on July 17, 1951, Stirling recalling: "I couldn't get much idea of the car on the track, but I did learn how much power it had. As I couldn't do much with it there, I suggested they should take it to Silverstone or Goodwood, where I could make some comparisons."

RM had agreed – of course – but no such tests took place, although Stirling was offered a contract on the spot. He had said he would think it over: "There was a vast difference between that car and any other I had ever driven…most noticeably the power. When the throttle was pressed down even at high speeds and in top gear, the whole car shuddered with a frightening surge of power. It was enough to cause wheelspin at speeds equal to most other cars' top speed. There was a very strong sensation of 'G' pushing my head back against the headrest and when I put on the [grabby] brakes I was jerked forward against the wheel…"

On August 26, Stirling had returned to Bourne for a long discussion with RM and PB. He had explained how he preferred to drive only British cars, so the BRM was his only competitive possibility for Formula 1. RM offered him a drive in the Spanish race at Barcelona, which he accepted. Next day Ray issued a press release, adding that Moss had agreed to drive the BRM in all its races in 1952, which was news to Moss…

In fact, he would never sign a BRM contract.

On September 18, after the Italian GP debacle, RM had written to him:

"We all feel that extensive Monza tests are the one thing that the BRM has needed for a long time. Unfortunately, for various reasons, including shortage of parts, this has not been possible. Further, we attach so much importance to the continuance of these tests, that we feel that such tests must take priority over all racing this year. All being well, our intention is to remove the 'bugs' from the BRM at Monza, and then settle down to building a team of three cars, with one or two spares if possible, in readiness for next year…"

Stirling's times at Monza had seen a best of 1:58.8 against Farina's Grand Prix lap record of 1:56.7. But the BRM refused to rev above 10,500. On day five, he had seen 11,400rpm on the straights before the engine faltered again. At the end of the series he penned his own report on the car which he issued to the Council on November 21, after discussing his findings with PB, RM, Tres and Tony. Characteristically, he pulled no punches.

THE MOSS MONZA REPORT

All the following remarks are based upon facts and findings and not theories.

1. The real difficulty in handling this car springs from the fact that it becomes unbalanced very easily, i.e., when it is put into a drift or slide. No sooner has this begun than the car gives a flick sideways, in a small but troublesome oversteer; this characteristic is made worse if the surface is bumpy.

2. The car has a dangerous trick of understeering excessively on a trailing throttle which, although undesirable, is sometimes unavoidable. This was found to decrease if the anti-roll bar was made thinner, or completely done away with.

3. The car's handling definitely improved a lot in the wet if the anti-roll bar was removed, but when tried in this condition in the dry it was bad. When a very thin anti-roll bar was fitted, the cornering in the dry on slow (up to 70mph) bends was improved over the thicker bar; but when it came to fast curves (over 120 and up to 165mph) a high-pitch patter developed and the other bar was found superior.

4. On fast curves the front of the car drifts out too far, showing that the wheels do not grip sufficiently. This makes it difficult to steer the car accurately while drifting.

5. On watching the front wheels closely while cornering, I found that they wobbled sideways, as well as the usual up and down suspension movement. This wobbling was apparent on the track rods as well as the wheels and, although considerable, no judder whatsoever was felt at the steering wheel, pointing to the fact that there must be considerable play in the

layout. In actual fact I found that one could move the steering wheel 5" to 7" without the car's direction being affected. While the car was on ramps I turned the steering wheel 10" with only 1" movement of the road wheels.

Could a rack and pinion steering be tried?

6. With the driving position as it is now, the steering ratio is too low, as proved by the fact that one's arms get tied up before a correction can be effected. This fault may be corrected when the driver has more room between himself and the steering wheel.

7. The driving position is bad because:

a) The driver is much too close to the wheel.

b) Brake pedal and throttle are too far apart; this could be corrected simply by turning the brake pedal pad round.

c) The seat back is too erect and I think it would be more comfortable and a better layout if it was leant back 5 to 10 degrees more. The padding round the shoulders is very good but I should like a little more in the small of my back and stronger sides to the seat. Pedal distance is excellent for myself.

8. I think the rear end of the car is excellent, also the brakes.

9. The top gear seemed to be about right for Monza, as far as I could judge. It would be an advantage if 3rd gear was lowered a bit so that both Lesmo and the Pave could be taken in this gear. 4th could be a fraction higher, I think, but until we get the car's road-holding improved it is difficult to say what speed one can get round the Curva Grande in that gear.

This remarkable report, emphasizing much of what both Parnell and Walker had already described, hit PB and RM like a brick. Certainly it should have made the Trust members demand just what had been going on during the car's interminable 'testing' at Folkingham, since it was so clearly still unraceworthy.

At the time, the science of roadholding was not understood. It would be many years before BRM learned how to play with camber-change and toe-in adjustments, wings were a world away and the car was effectively non-adjustable, even if the engineers had understood at that time how to adjust it.

Don Badger, the very able Dunlop technician, had been there, but about the only thing the team could do was to juggle tyre pressures while he tried different compounds, and neither could cure the car's fundamental problems.

It was surprising, however, that Moss should have described the rear end of the car as "excellent" as when PB drove it he had noticed that the beautiful fabricated sheet duralumin radius arms which located the de Dion back axle were flexing under power. They would subsequently be replaced by much less attractive but far stiffer welded-up tubular steel radius rods.

When Stirling complained about the steering Tony remembered having read in *The Autocar* how Freddy Dixon had blocked a front wheel on one of his Rileys against the chassis with a couple of short wooden baulks and had then turned the steering wheel to check lost motion remaining in the system.

Tony: When we tried it, it was shattering to find we could move the steering wheel through 90-degrees without disturbing the front wheels at all...!

The old recirculating-ball steering box was mounted on a cast aluminium chassis pillar, which we discovered was moving all over the place. The steering arms were also bending, and so were the front suspension's beautifully-machined Porsche trailing arms. The cast aluminium arms which contained the little needle roller bearings on which they articulated also bent a little, and it all added up to startling free play. We fitted an extra steady bracket to brace the steering box, which was changed to a similar worm-and-nut type with 22:1 gearing. The steering box and column UJs were adjusted to reduce backlash to a minimum. And all this reduced free-play to about two inches at the steering wheel rim...

A replacement engine and gearbox were sent out, this latest type 'box incorporating a brake booster pump. This ensured servo assistance so long as the car was rolling, regardless of whether or not its engine was running.[52]

Meanwhile, 'Oily' had hung around, trying to scrounge fuel for his moped. We kept explaining it was special racing fuel. I think he understood, but he also coveted some of our spark plugs in their beautiful trays and clearly could not understand why we refused him, particularly since we had so many. He didn't appreciate they were the specially-made ⁹⁄₁₆in BRM thread which would not fit his moped. Eventually, overcome by cupidity, he stole a couple.

Of course, when he screwed them into his moped's cylinder head he stripped its threads, and he arrived next day alternating between tears and rage. I think he'd finally got the message.

In all we stayed at Monza for 10 weeks. At one stage we reverted to fuel blending to find more straightline speed and a party travelled out from Bourne with 500 gallons of British fuel in one of the transporters. The Italian Customs were startled by the idea of 500 gallons of duty-free fuel. They didn't know what to do and so ushered the problem away to their HQ at Domodossola. Unfortunately the crew of the lorry missed the Customs office in the town centre and were stopped at a road-block outside. Their excuse that they had missed the turning was rejected and they were jailed...

We winkled them out two days later, but the Customs held the fuel for a week. I eventually drove up to Domodossola to collect it, armed with an enormous wad of 10,000 *Lire* notes, and then discovered they wanted me to pay extra on the barrels. By that time I'd had enough, so we broached one of the barrels and started to empty it down the Customs office drains. They couldn't have the fuel, but I was willing to give them the empty barrels. They hastily back-pedalled, and we departed with the fuel.

52. The BRM Type 15's original drum brakes were unusual in having three trailing shoes. Conventional practice preferred leading shoes which employed drum rotation to increase the clamping force of shoe against drum. The problem with such a layout was that once the drum had started to lock it was difficult for the driver to reduce braking effort and so brake accurately. A hydraulic servo – as on the BRM – would exacerbate this insensitivity. The Girling/BRM trailing-shoe design, therefore – with its natural tendency to unlock the drum – obviated this effect. Tony Vandervell was sufficiently impressed during 1951 to have a set of Girling/BRM brakes available for his *Thin Wall Special*.

Running recommenced at Monza, in the wet, on October 31. The brake fluid reservoir emptied itself after two or three laps, and we found the new transmission-mounted Plessey pump had dumped its fluid into the gearbox. The pump required opposite-hand rotation! We then found that with a correct-rotation pump fitted, reversing the car sucked fluid out of the front brake system. The old gearbox and engine-driven pump were refitted…

The aluminium radiator cores continued to block with rust scale, so the 'least blocked' core was selected and fitted.

As the weather deteriorated, Monza became a very different place. The *Lesmo* curves were slick with wet leaves, and incessant rain and flooding cost a full week's running. Many drivers and engineers came by to offer advice, one being Ruggeri of *Scuderia Milano* fame, who had produced the highly-supercharged Maserati-Milan, and who propounded many ideas.

Stirling had returned, but he could only sit about or run to keep fit. After floods struck the Po Valley, and fog then blanketed the region for days, we had a final engine failure on November 12 and two days later finally left for home.

The journey which followed could fill a book on its own, with roads washed away, the trucks having to take to the railway line in one place, more Customs troubles and – in France – the mobile workshop breaking a rear spring after hitting a 'level' crossing at prodigious speed. The impact also broke all kinds of kit through the Commer's floorboards.[53] Our battered convoy finally limped into Bourne after one of the most staggering journeys I have ever had, with the trucks on their last legs. And when we broke the Customs seals to open the doors and look inside we found absolute chaos…

We each drew our accumulated back pay, then slept for about 36 hours.

I went off to London, bought myself a new Aston Martin – which would not be delivered until February '52, the day of King George VI's funeral – and ended up at the racing mechanics' annual dinner in the *Park Lane Hotel*.

There, two very eminent Jaguar drivers – Le Mans winners no less – saw some Park employees with a large lorry pumping

out drains, whereupon by removing a cover on one side of the lorry they amused themselves watching the water being pumped out of the drains and clean through the lorry to cascade down the other side back onto the road. Then they were arrested.

On November 20, PB summarized overall Monza findings: the new steering box and reduction of backlash had eliminated steering wander and dart, but a new 'box was required with a ratio of 18 or 19:1. The modified rear hub/radius arms assembly had "completely eliminated tendencies to wander and to run round bumps…general stability at high speed shows great improvement". He confirmed that "the most serious defect in fast cornering is due to insufficient torsional rigidity in the frame…with the present mounting the engine gives no support to the frame…". He intended to eliminate the front spring operating lever on the inner end of the top front swing-arms to provide more direct control, and to produce a more rigid front stub axle assembly using a steel back-plate for planned new disc brakes…

Girling had produced their original car-system disc brakes – derived from aeronautical experience – for use in the BRM in the autumn of 1951. They featured a large-diameter thin steel disc with chromium-plated working surfaces, which was ingeniously mounted upon a centre Duralumin drive system intended to absorb differential expansion under the inevitable temperature variations of normal use. These brakes had a D-section caliper with six circular friction pads, each *c*.1½ inches in diameter, to be clamped against the disc by individual hydraulic pistons pressurized from a common piped circuit. The calipers were mounted directly above the hub. When applied to the BRM Type 15, these disc brakes were boosted by a powerful engine-driven servo pump circulating hydraulic fluid around the system. When the driver hit the brake pedal he closed a bypass valve, preventing fluid circulation and so building up pressure within the master cylinder. It housed a further floating piston which in turn pressurized the hydraulic circuit fluid which then compressed the wheel cylinder pistons against their related pads and the disc sandwiched by them. The prototype system was to be fitted to one of the BRMs back home at Folkingham, ready for serious evaluation early in the new year.

Meanwhile PB's Monza summary continued: – Three broken engines were attributed to big-end bearing failure (two in the Parnell car), all on "new-delivery Mark IA crankshafts". This was traced to oil starvation "which appears worse near the centre of the crankshaft and improves towards the ends". Three pistons had failed due to pre-ignition caused by 'dud' plugs, and another had picked-up its rings "caused by 'rubbish' in Italian fuel". Two rocker pads had portions broken off, a new single-piece steel rocker being developed on the test-rig at Bourne. The only supercharger with modified lubrication system ran a roller bearing, while another returned as being suspect "…apart from being clogged with Italian fuel 'rubbish' proved to be mechanically sound…".

The pre-Monza carburettor mods were successful, ignition and plugs generally quite the reverse. The drum brakes were "good and consistent", having run 900 miles before drums and linings were replaced although the drums "were heavily crazed".

"Although tyre sizes are in balance [for] wear", PB

---

53. This mobile workshop had been fitted-out at the expense of the Midland Automobile Club, organizers of RM's favourite hill-climb at Shelsley Walsh.

On December 10, 1951, Jim Sandercombe wrote to MAC Secretary Leslie Wilson to comment on the truck's performance: The Monza trip had totalled 2,418 miles, fuel consumption 9.6mpg, oil consumption had been negligible while the best day's run had covered 620 miles, Cannes to Abbeville. The workshop had assisted in three complete engine strips/rebuilds, five gearbox strips/rebuilds and one complete car strip/rebuild – "Quite a number of bushes and similar components were turned up on the lathe and one car was given a paint respray." Sandy reported that "Fangio inspected it personally…and described it as *'Atelier Formidable'*…". Its ventilation was poor and its interior temperature rose too high in hot climates while the generator caused considerable vibration and was to be converted onto paraffin to save expense – during the 10 weeks at Monza it had run for some 120 hours. Finally: "The riding comfort is extremely good and the vehicle drives and handles well. The radio is a great asset; the B.B.C. programmes could be heard right down to Monza and in fact, the details of the General Election Broadcast were heard by our mechanics there…"

(On October 25–26, Churchill's Conservative Party had toppled Clement Attlee's Labour Government; 321 seats to 295.)

considered, "…the front sizes must be increased in section to increase the cornering power of the front. Dunlops sent out 18x5.50 tyres…but wheels must be obtained to try 17x6.00. Present front tyre size 18x5.25…"

No bodywork or chassis troubles had occurred although "rear axle Hooke type joints showed sings of wear; this is due to poor seals which permit lubrication to be flung out…".

Five years later similar problems would beset another, more raceworthy breed of BRM, but at the gearbox end, not the wheel end, as here…

1952 – TIME RUNS OUT

Time is a remorseless enemy, and by the end of 1951 BRM had simply squandered too much of it. When the CSI met during the Paris Salon on October 2–4, the delegates discussed possible replacements for the contemporary Formula 1 after the end of 1953. The British representative to the CSI, Earl Howe, argued – largely on BRM's behalf – for a continuation of the current Formula. But its provisions for 1½-litre supercharged/4½-litres unsupercharged racing cars had survived since 1948 and derived in fact from a class first adopted 10 years earlier still. Despite the support of Daimler-Benz's Alfred Neubauer – who also had an interest in perpetuating 1½-litre Formula 1 – Howe was resoundingly out-voted.

Agreement emerged instead for a change to 2½-litres unsupercharged, with forced-induction engines tied right down to just 750cc. This new Formula was to take effect from January 1, 1954. Until then, the intervening two seasons would give interested manufacturers time to design, test and develop suitable cars. For BRM this meant that at most their V16 had just two seasons' Formula 1 life left to it.

However, after the team's failure to guarantee entries during 1951 the immediate short-term future of Formula 1 was already in jeopardy for lack of competitive support.

Alfa Romeo, having only narrowly salvaged World Championship success from the new 4½-litre Ferraris in 1951, were talking about complete withdrawal in 1952. At first they declared they might compete "only in short-distance events" which would leave only BRM to oppose the well-developed and very fast and powerful Ferrari 375s. But since BRM had won itself a well-deserved reputation for non-appearance, race promoters believed Formula 1 would be a complete Ferrari walkover, opposed by nothing more than obsolescent and unreliable privately-entered Maseratis, Talbot-Lagos and ERAs. Few Continental race promoters saw great spectator attraction there.

During the winter of 1951–52, the French organizers in particular then met to discuss their plans. In mid-January 1952, the British weekly, *Autosport*, ran the headline: "BOMBSHELL FROM FRANCE! Wholesale Switch-over to Formula 2". It reported:

> Rumour has turned to fact. Every singe [sic] race of Grand Prix status in France this season will be for Formula 2 (500cc S and 2000cc U/s) machines, while it is expected that Belgium, Holland, Switzerland and

Germany will also limit their Grands Prix to this category… This announcement must be a severe blow to the sponsors of BRM and if other countries follow the lead of the French the fate of the existing Formula 1 may be sealed even before the start of the 1952 season…Raymond Mays told [us] that he was most concerned about these developments, as it is the intention to run a team of BRMs in every possible Grand Epreuve…

Yet French influence within the CSI had indicated – furthermore – that by common consent World Championship status could be accorded to a Formula 2 series if insufficient F1 events were held. Obviously, this would deny World Championship racing to BRM, and Raymond Mays was understandably horrified.

The project which had occupied the past six years of his life seemed about to collapse, its very foundation crumbling into dust.

He cabled and wrote to every race organizer whose plans remained unclear, assuring them he could guarantee BRM entries if only they would stand by Formula 1. He claimed that in future no manufacturer would ever again take the risk of building a racing car if race promoters were to ignore precedent and arrange their Grands Prix "…for any Formula they fancied…".

His hyperbole was wasted on most race organizers, even those with whom he had enjoyed such friendly relations in the past. Compared with full, potentially competitive – and cheap – Formula 2 grids, the attractions of the too-often delusive BRM proved eminently resistible.

To Ray's horror, even Desmond Scannell of the BRDC announced that the Club's International Trophy race at Silverstone on May 10 would be run for Formula 2 cars, and that "a decision" had yet to be taken over the British GP there on July 19.

Scannell had in fact approached BRM in December regarding potential entries in the Trophy race, but Alfred Owen had been unable to indicate what the position might be. Now, regarding the British GP, Scannell crystallized the fears of race organizers throughout Europe and pressed for confirmation of whether or not "…a B.R.M. team will be available to compete in this race if it is run as a Formula 1 event". He added a sting in the tail: "If the answer is in the affirmative, then perhaps you would also let me know if, in your opinion, B.R.M. Ltd. would be prepared to furnish satisfactory guarantees that the team would turn up both for official practising and the race?"

Pulling no punches, Scannell continued: "Now that Alfa Romeo have definitely decided not to race this year, the B.R.M. is left as the only potential rival to Ferrari supremacy. Therefore, if a Formula 1 Grand Prix were staged and B.R.M. team failed to appear, the organizers would inevitably incur a loss of many thousands of pounds, for the public would not be interested in watching a Ferrari procession.

"My personal view is that no Club…can be expected to take the risk of organizing a Formula 1 event unless:
1. B.R.M. cars publicly demonstrate within the next few weeks that they now have the requisite speed and reliability to put up a showing against the Ferraris.

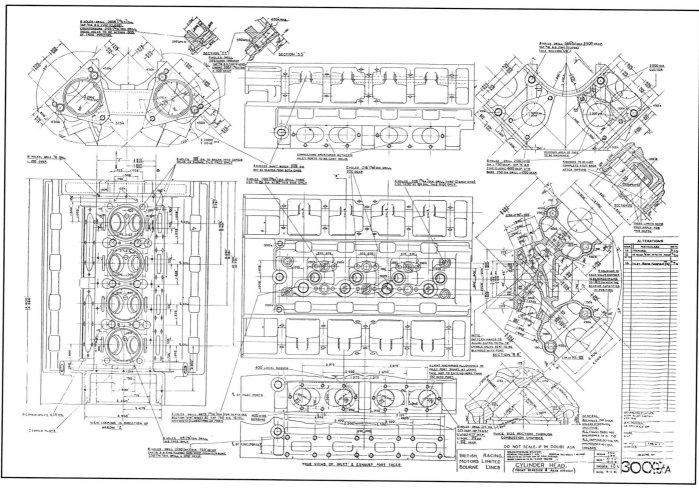

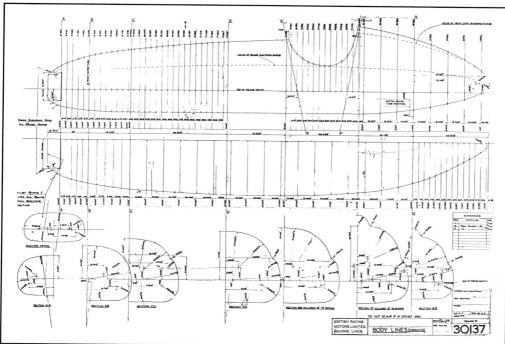

Above: Originated on April 22, 1947 upon 'Automobile Developments Ltd' headed drafting paper, this primarily Aubrey Woods-drawn cylinder head design for the V16 BRM was updated here under the 'British Racing Motors Ltd' title on April 9, 1951.

Left: Very few of the original V16 drawings have survived in good order after years of neglect in damp storage at Bourne. These detailed body lines for the 'production' Mark I were signed-off on February 28, 1950. Painstaking curve radii are specified on the cross-sections.

Above right: Ringing the changes – the 1951 open-nosed body form for the Mark Is took shape during the preceding winter. This original on cloth has been damaged – lower right – by damp.

Right: This badly frayed drawing appears to be all that survives of Tony Rudd's original concept for the 1954–55 V16 Mark II or Project 30 'sprint car'.

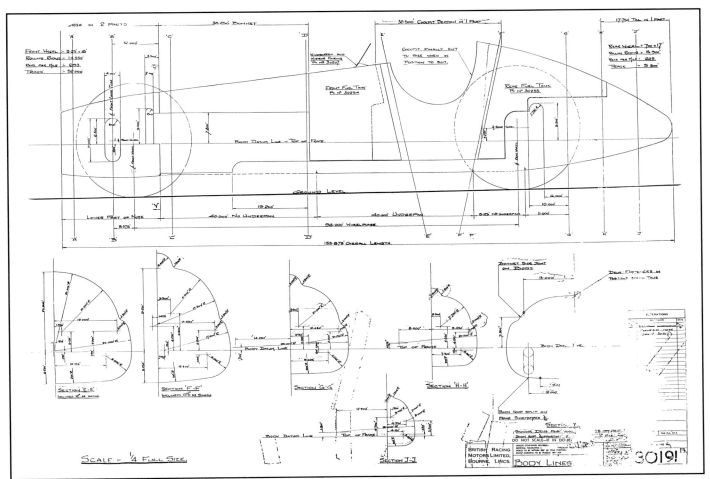

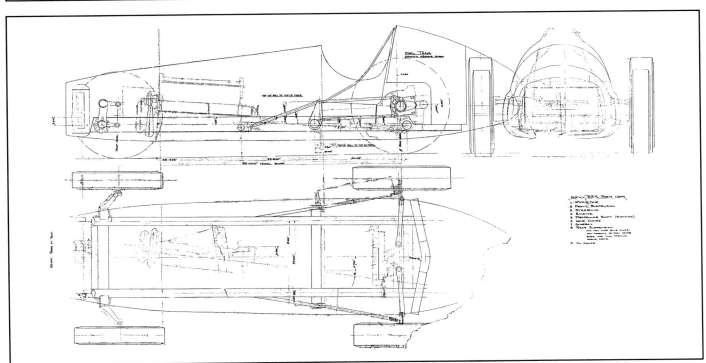

2. B.R.M. Ltd. must agree to pay very substantial damages should the team fail to appear both for practising and the race...

"...This is a personal opinion but I am convinced that unless action is taken on the lines indicated, there will be no important events organized this year in which the B.R.M. can compete..."

Owen declared his confidence that the cars "will offer serious competition this year" and that "...there are earlier races from which the performance may be judged...as a sporting gesture I am sure my Board would agree to put up an amount equal to...the Organisers' B.R.M. starting money...".

Thereupon, Scannell pointed out that British GP regulations had to be finalized three to four months in advance, pre-empting the "earlier races" cited by Owen. He snapped: "I am of the opinion that a guarantee of B.R.M. entries cannot be expected to carry any weight. What is wanted is proof that the cars are now sufficiently reliable and fast and will start and finish. These are, in my view, essentials which must be publicly demonstrated forthwith." He also warned that "...your Board should bear in mind that Enzo Ferrari is a very shrewd man. He is obviously aware of the current trend and may decide to sell his 4½-litre cars. Certainly, he will be well placed to do so for a team is now in the Argentine... The remaining cars are racing at Indianapolis[54] in May in the 500 miles race...you will have to convince not only the race promoter but also Ferrari that the B.R.M. car can provide a serious challenge in Formula 1 Grands Prix."

Owen rightly responded that: "Actually Formula 2 racing would suit Ferrari best, since he would have no competition. None of the British cars in this section have nearly enough potential performance..." – but, crucially from the organizers' point of view, there would be plenty of them...and full grids provided spectacle.

BRM's ability to start and finish GP races could not be publicly demonstrated, nor was it.

On January 18, 1952, Ray released this notice to the press:

BRM Ltd announce that it is their intention to compete with a team of cars in all Grand Prix races, including the British, and in any International Formula 1 events that can be fitted in. With reference to recent conjecture and proposals about adopting Formula II, we have had no official intimation of any such negotiations...

Motor Sport commented:

In spite of 'official proposals' having by-passed

Bourne, it seems that BRM may not have much 'fitting-in' to do! Alfa Romeo is expected to enter only for short-distance races and Ferrari may not bother to enter for our 'local' Formula 1 events, so it is now too late for the BRM to prove itself a world-beater. Their only hope of retrieving some of their lost prestige is to win every one of the few races still open to them. If Mr A.G.B.Owen can flog this unwilling horse sufficiently for it to do this – and we sincerely hope that he can – then BRM may prepare with confidence for 1954. If not, they might as well give up trying to make racing cars.

At Bourne and Folkingham the French bombshell seems to have bounced off the BRM personnel's oft-tested armour plate. They were beavering away to perfect their cars. So – what if there were some problems with the foreigners, never mind, RM, PB and the other 'higher-ups' would sort it out. Meanwhile they just buckled-down to improve their world-beater.

On January 31, 1952, Cliff Mander issued a typically verbose Production Report – tacitly highlighting equally typical design confusion. He recorded the general position as follows:

The redesigned front suspension design has now been considered as not the most suitable design. Drawing for another design with plain bearing instead of needle and roller type have been rushed through and three to four more sets of parts practically completed. Frames for the first two cars have already had the necessary brackets made and welded to the frame. It is, however, agreed not to proceed with the alterations for the new suspension to any further frames until after the first two have had an actual road or track test as the feeling at the moment is that the new design front suspension may not after all be necessary. The reason for this is stated to be due to the greatly increased rigidity given to the front of the frame by the new front engine bearer plate which may, perhaps, give the improved steering required and with the old type of front suspension...the rest of the modifications, as indicated by the late Monza trials, are proceeding fairly well but the previously mentioned changes will prolong the original completion times of the first two cars...

Of the first three V16 engines, their various spectacular ailments had resulted in two being completely rebuilt, 'No. 11/1' being on the test-bed at that time and 'No. 11/3' in chassis No. 2 at Folkingham. Mander warned that '11/3' had not been run on the test-bed and should be run-in there before powering the car either at Folkingham or in a forthcoming return test-programme at Monza. The third engine, '20/1' – first of the improved series – was in pieces awaiting replacement crankcase studs before it could be reassembled. Its crankcase had also been found to be porous. The fourth engine, '20/2', was awaiting completion due to late con-rod delivery from Austin Motors, and of the crankshaft which was in the Lucas tool room for final coupling. Its head casting was also porous and repair was in hand.

The fifth engine, '20/3', was as yet just a collection of part-machined bits, again with porous heads. No rods were

---

54. Alan Hess, PRO for the Austin Motor Company, had recently completed a publicity stunt demonstration run at Indianapolis in an Austin A90 Atlantic. On February 27, 1952, he telephoned RM at Bourne to suggest that BRM should enter the Indianapolis 500-Miles Speedway classic. Ray contacted Owen advising against entry "particularly now that we have so heavily cut down our programme of cars". At his request, Owen wrote a letter appreciating Hess' idea, but regretfully rejecting it on grounds of impracticability. Possibly – just possibly – the centrifugally-supercharged BRM would have been well-suited to 'Indy'...

available but Lucas had the crankshaft halves. Engine '20/4' existed merely as machined cylinder heads collected from Standard on January 30. Crankcases were due mid-February. Neither rods nor crank were yet available. Engines '20/5' and '20/6' "…are now the last two that Standard Motors propose to machine… It is, therefore, considered that our engine programme be limited to this total of eight engines". It was considered wise to add three extra sets of rods and a pair of spare crankshafts.

Four gearboxes were available, two originals without the brake servo pumps and two new-type with them. Machining of the fourth 'box was about to begin at Austin Motors, who had promised to machine five new-type to make a final run of seven V16 gearboxes in all. Mander cautioned: "…we shall have to use these as carefully as possible…"

The car position he revealed was that No. 1 – using frame Mark 1/2 – and No. 2 – using frame Mark 1/3 – were due for completion mid-February. No. 3 – frame Mark 1/4 – had been set aside pending front suspension trials.

George Gray had completed all bodywork save final trimming and car No. 4 – frame Mark 1/5 – was in hand at Bourne. Rubery Owen's R&D Department at Darlaston was quoted as being "well forward with the first of the new type bolted up frames". Mander voiced doubt on this new design since "…the front cross member, which is now machined to close limits, would not have the new steering box bracket welded to it without serious distortions which would almost certainly mean the scrapping of this part…The sixth car has the second of the new type frames and I have asked R&D to withhold completion of the front cross member until we have a decision as the welding of the steering box bracket…" In fact, no V16 cars would ever be completed with these bolted-up chassis frames…

Clearly, with a programme including six cars, eight engines and seven gearboxes, BRM planned an all-out Grand Prix season very much in the Daimler-Benz mould so revered by RM and possibly PB. But in view of the news from Europe and slender finances, this would never happen.

On February 9, Francis Howe wrote to Ray commiserating over the wholesale change to Formula 2, and enclosing a card from the Secretary of the *AC Torino* in Italy, who was "definitely staging an event for Formula 1 cars…on the 6th April. He is most anxious to secure your entry."

This was RM's first intimation of an event upon which the future – or failure – of Formula 1 would hinge, and around which Ray would almost blindly tip the balance.

On the 29th of that month he confided bitterly to Howe "…there is now nothing further that I can do to influence the course of events regarding the British Grand Prix, but, if the decision does finally go in favour of Formula II, I have the absolutely certain feeling that history will condemn it as an outright betrayal of all those public-spirited individuals and concerns who have poured out their efforts and resources on the B.R.M.'s behalf over these past years…"

Against this background, in a Trust board meeting at the Royal Hotel, Sutton Coldfield, on February 8, the Directors decided to compress the build programme to maintain the three existing cars plus existing engine parts, sufficient only for five assembled units.

Stirling Moss, Peter Walker and Leslie Johnson were discussed as being prepared to test drive for the team, and W.K. Hartley replaced Jim Sandercombe as Trust Secretary, 'Sandy' being awarded a silver salver for his efforts in that position, while continuing to perform his duties at Bourne.

There, meanwhile, Tony Rudd was learning more of BRM's problems…

The shortage of parts and material meant we could not pursue a proper development programme. The philosophy was: 'If it hasn't broken, leave it alone…' We couldn't run an engine flat-out or for a long period on the test-bed because of restrictions in the cooling and exhaust systems there, even if we had had sufficient engines to risk. The shortage of engines and gearboxes restricted car development and the very idea of running a Grand Prix distance on test was still unthinkable.

The shortage of cash was BRM's most fundamental problem. When RM had set out to seek support and sponsors, £10 a week had been good money. In 1946, £50,000 would fund a Grand Prix team for a whole year. By 1951, inflation had crippled the value of money, and BRM's complex car required double the man-hours per year development that the Trust could then afford. This is proved by the fact that in 1954, when the appropriate number of man-hours had finally been expended on the V16's development, it did run reliably, and very fast indeed.

Had funds been available to have crammed all those hours into one year early on, instead of spreading them thinly over four, the cars could have been as competitive in 1951 as they eventually became in 1954, and so they should have won races – had all our other problems been dealt with at the same time…

But into 1952, any such thoughts were idle, and initially we all concentrated upon completing the lightened disc brake car for a new test series at Monza. If things went well there, it was planned to race in the Turin GP on April 6. A drum brake car was to be present to provide baseline comparison during testing, and potentially a back-up for a race entry at Turin.

Meanwhile, PB had decided that the drivers were being disturbed by seeing their strip tachometer whistle round to 12 and 13,000rpm. So he had the instrument marked into coloured bands instead of numbers, starting white, then green and finally red. The driver was meant to keep the revs in the green band as much as possible, since that was where the power lay, while the red should be avoided at all costs.

Unfortunately, the crib sheet for all this got mislaid, and when we finally went testing we realized that 'the red' did not begin exactly at 12,000rpm, while 'the green' *might* have begun at 8,000rpm – or was it 9,000? A conundrum indeed…

Stirling came up to Bourne to try the car for size and to be available to test the new disc brakes that winter. Late one night we were talking in the *Angel Hotel* – where I lived and where Stirling was staying – when PB telephoned to say he was in the policeman's house at Ropsley village, just nearby. Could I pick him up? Stirling came along for company as the countryside was blanketed in dense fog. After reversing into a signpost we finally discovered PB wearing a blanket like a kilt, warming himself by the constable's fire. He had missed a corner in the fog, shunted his Vanguard and while seeking help had fallen in the village pond…

A FORWARD VIEW BY PB – Spring 1952

Through the winter of 1951–52 the motor racing world was digesting the CSI's announcement of the new 2½-litre unsupercharged/750cc supercharged Formula 1 due for 1954. At Bourne, Peter Berthon chewed over the published regulations and eventually penned a well-thought-out memo for the Trust, considering not only a possible replacement for the V16 cars, but also their own short-term future.

In this six-page document he analyzed first the 'General Considerations' of the Formula change, observing:

> A new formula invariably brings a wave of optimism for new participants but history shows that once would-be newcomers have realized that their production units are totally unsuitable and that considerable money, time and resources are necessary, the number of potential competitors eventually sorts itself out to the consistent few...

He reasoned that since contemporary experience showed race promoters to be more interested in minimizing costs while maximizing entries than in perpetuating the premier class...

> Although it is a handicap on design, any new design therefore must be capable of meeting either [Formula 1 or 2-litre unsupercharged Formula 2]...

He believed that under the new Formula 1:

> ...although half the power would be initially expected, it is possible to produce cars with the very similar acceleration and cornering properties of those of the present Formula I and eventually engine development and attention to aerodynamics, which is bound to follow, will restore the maximum speed level. To offer serious competition a car... would have to start in 1954 with not less than 250h.p. and a maximum starting line weight of 1200lbs, and must be able to run 200 miles without pit stops.
>
> During the life of the Formula, engine development will quickly push the power up to 300b.h.p...the most profitable method of improving general performance being to concentrate on the conditions under which the car is travelling slowest and taking the most time.

PB then considered the obvious potential supercharged 750cc BRM – but not merely the V16 halved – observing:

> The changes in relative capacities put the supercharged 750 to a greater disadvantage than present Formula I and since engine capacity can only be truly rated by the amount of air it consumes, the following gives an indication of the scale of such disadvantage.
>
> This means that the supercharged engine for the new Formula I will have to show an improvement of 12% to obtain equal performance and in the case of the present Formula II (when suitably modified), 25%
>
> Eight cylinders of the present B.R.M. engine would give the required capacity and as the engine must be as short as possible, in the interests of overall weight, it would have to be a V8 at 90°. Such an engine would produce 250h.p. and by pursuing present technique would be pushed up to 300

with a probable maximum of 350. While a few common parts of the existing engine...would be usable, completely new castings, crankshafts, camshafts, gears and superchargers would be required.

> A new smaller supercharger would present problems and present efficiencies would not be realised, due to scale effect... Due to the necessity of pursuing still higher r.p.m. up to 15,000, engine weight would be about two-thirds present engine, or 315lbs.
>
> Fuel consumption will get worse as performance is pushed up, but assuming similar consumption to the present engine, pro-rata, the car would require a tank capacity of 50 gallons for 200 miles, which means 400lbs starting line weight of the car. Similarly the weight of the cooling systems could not be reduced pro-rata since air speed would be lower and for 300h.p. the cooling system would have to [be sufficient to] cope with 400h.p. For sheer maximum horsepower the supercharged engine would be difficult to beat, but Ferrari has demonstrated very clearly that it is not maximum horsepower that wins races but only produces technical headaches.

Regarding the unsupercharged 2½-litre option he then reasoned:

> ...Such an engine will be shorter overall than the supercharged edition, would be lighter by virtue of no supercharger, or drive, considerably lighter and simpler ignition, no reduction gears in output drive. The estimated weight would be 250/260lbs.
>
> Transmission would be lighter, due to the better torque characteristics of the unblown engine and requiring less gears. Oil and water systems show weight savings on the supercharged edition and fuel required for 200 miles could be reduced to 25 gallons or one-sixth of starting line weight.

Significantly:

> ...The reduction of 2,000c.c. capacity, present Formula II, in the order of 20%, is practicable though would give away some weight.

He then realistically examined BRM's contemporary capabilities:

> In considering a new racing car, we must profit by our experience, and careful consideration of our history and the present car show (a) that the available resources control the speed with which we manufacture, develop, alter and achieve success, (b) that the present car, although still technically superior to those of competi-tors, has failed because it is too complicated and costly to be developed in time with the resources at our disposal.
>
> [It has around] 4,000 component parts...90% have been made outside. [Since] the capacity for outside manufacture is rapidly diminishing...we must in the main consider a design that can be handled with much reduced facilities. Further, it is doubtful if the financial resources during the period of design and construction would be on the previous scale, and with constantly rising cost it is a fundamental that any new design we consider should be economical and simple, even to a slight extent at the

expense of performance. This is a must with all future racing.

One of our present serious limitations is a question of labour, equally we can only afford to design what can be built, maintained and developed with the labour we have got. The design proposals then are for a type of car that can be basically reduced to less than 2,000 component parts of which at least 50% can be made with our own facilities. This means that the total parts to be placed out would be reduced by 70%.

Deciding therefore in favour of the unsupercharged 2½-litre engine alternative, he concluded with the following:

Recommendations:
We have considered alternative schemes for some months and Tresilian has done considerable detailed work investigating the various problems. As a result of this, we recommend a simple, economical design of car with a minimum of components and where the foremost consideration is light weight. The engine to be a 6-cylinder V at 120° with a bore of 84mm and a stroke of 75, to run within the accepted piston speed range, i.e. 9,000r.p.m. Such an engine would be very short, i.e. about 15" over cylinder blocks, and have high efficiency and low mechanical losses due to few cylinders and bearings and come well within the engine weight required. The cylinder head technique to be based on the known and proved water cooled edition of the racing Norton engine I did for them some while ago [which, ironically, would provide the basis of Tony Vandervell's ultimately World Championship-winning rival Vanwall!]. With present day accepted M.E.P's., this engine should give immediately 250b.h.p. and should be readily capable of producing 300h.p. plus with development.

Immediate policy:
Work has already started on layouts for a 6-cylinder engine and Tresilian and one draughtsman are now spending full time on it. We feel strongly that if the Board accept this recommendation, Drawing Office work and manufacture

should be pushed ahead as rapidly as possible in an attempt to have the car running early next year...[1953].

Then turning to the V16 programme he pointed out that:

...At the present time all resources are harnessed to the production programme of 6 cars, 8 engines and 7 gearboxes for the present car.

Although Raymond Mays is doing his best to persuade Automobile Clubs promoting Grand Prix races to stick to Formula I for this year, the fact has got to be faced up to that it is unlikely that there will be more than 3 events available for our cars this year and possibly less rather than more. Whilst he may to some extent save the immediate situation from the B.R.M. point of view, it is fairly certain that there will be a swing over to Formula II or the new Formula I next year. To have a new car ready seems the best possible argument for continued support. We feel that in view of this the present programme is excessive and in the interests of financial economy the present programme should be considerably reduced to a basis of having a few cars, which we can prepare properly with labour available, rather than having a number of cars we can't handle. We recommend that the three cars at present existing only be built and beyond the provision for reasonable spares for these three cars, all orders and outside work be cancelled as soon as possible with the exception of castings from Standard and Austin, crankshafts and conrods, which are required to bring our old and repaired engine sets up to a proper state for racing.

As the bulk of the modification work arising from Monza is now completed, Drawing Office capacity would become available through reduction of the present programme and some manufacturing capacity might be diverted to components for a new car.

With the impending demise of the British Motor Racing Research Trust, PB's proposed unsupercharged 2½-litre V6 BRM would never be built, and in fact very little work was done upon it but long-term, Stewart Tresilian had an even more economical alternative upon the stocks, as we shall see...

On another occasion that winter I was returning to Folkingham in the snow, having just collected Stan Hope from Bourne. Stan was senior amongst the panel-men seconded to BRM from Motor Panels in Coventry to speed progress when George Gray had become overwhelmed by bodywork demands. Portly and bespectacled, Stan was both well-educated and a very fine craftsman, and he prided himself with some justification on being the local strong man. We had collected one of the 168lb gearboxes from the upstairs engine shop in the Malting. When there was some difficulty with the hoist, Stan had simply picked up the gearbox and carried it triumphantly down the stairs. Apart from going red in the face, neither Stan nor the stairs seemed to suffer any ill-effect. We had loaded it into the back of my fabric-bodied Austin Seven, and then with Stan and myself both well wrapped-up against the cold we had set off for Folkingham.

On one of the many snow-covered ess-bends, the Austin entered a sensational 20mph skid, punctuated by a terrific thump against a gate-post. This impact launched our gearbox

straight out through the fabric side, into a bramble thicket.

Once we had finally come to rest, it took us half an hour to find the gearbox, twice as long for me to talk Stan into reloading it into the car and then even longer to get him to ride any further if I was intending to drive. The Austin now looked very Bahamas, in the snow, with a roof but neither sides nor doors.[55]

Delivery delays – far more serious than this one – slowed completion of the cars until on March 8, the scheduled departure date for Monza, we were still not quite ready to go with just one drum-braked car – the disc-braked prototype was to follow. Stirling Moss and new recruit Ken Wharton were to do the driving.

Panics began as soon as we winched the drum-braked car

55. This long-suffering Austin Seven passed eventually to Jock Milne, the BRM project's broad Scots caretaker at Folkingham. The panel-bashers there fashioned him an aluminium bodyshell for it, prolonging the poor thing's hard life...

Stirling Moss' second series of Monza BRM tests began on March 17, 1952 with the disc-braked car. Earlier (on October 4, 1951) he had paused for the camera while sampling this drum-braked V16 for the first time on a serious circuit. Reg Parnell had tried to talk Moss out of driving the car – Leslie Johnson had encouraged 'The Boy' to do so... His most immediate finding was that its driving position was far too cramped, irritatingly "prewar". By the time he returned to Monza for the later tests, some – but by no means all – of his many criticisms had been answered.

into the transporter, when we realized that my beautiful winch system had one fundamental fault. Its guide pulley neatly amputated the oil pipes beneath the car's sump as it came aboard. After suitable modification, we set off in company with the mobile workshop, going the long way round through the south of France as the Alpine passes were still snowed-in. In Reims we stopped to cash some travellers cheques. While crossing the road I looked the wrong way and stepped straight into a cyclist's path. He came off second best, being carted off to hospital for attention, while I was interviewed by the *Gendarmerie* who seemed to think I'd suddenly rushed out and attacked him.

Under way again, we made good time before reaching the frontier post at Ventimiglia. Fuel was cheaper in France than Italy so we topped-up our tanks before passing into the no-man's land between the two Customs posts. There we discovered that the fuel transfer pipes on the mobile workshop had been dislodged, 50 gallons of precious fuel gushing down onto the roadway towards the Italian post. We stemmed the flow by isolating one tank on the changeover tap and stuffing rags into the other. Meanwhile Willie Southcott, who was driving the other transporter, kept tugging at my sleeve and saying: "Come and look at this" while I kept shaking him off saying: "Don't bother me just now Willie".

When I finally went to see what ailed him I was horrified to find that, in backing the transporter out of the stream of leaking fuel, its very fierce clutch had caught him out and he had slammed back against a kerb. The tail of the truck was left jutting out over a cliff, 100ft above the sea, and the car inside had burst from its tethers so that its tail was bulging out the truck's rear doors. Only the two set-screws which held the door catch were preventing our beautiful BRM from taking a swan-dive into the sea...

The Lodestars were notoriously jerky in drawing away. It was clear that one more jerk could lose the car, so we tied rope round the doors while I vowed that our next transporter would have a side-access door so that should such an incident

ever happen again we could at least get to the car inside. Eventually we sorted it all out, and the Italian Customs waved us away, probably believing that we would flood them with petrol – not for the first time – had they proved difficult...

Once at Monza, we found that our car's beautiful long tail had been quite badly crumpled. I had some pretensions as a panel beater, and managed to straighten out most of the damage and Gordon Newman resprayed it in the garage that night. When PB arrived next morning and asked what kind of journey we had had, we assured him it had been trouble-free. We then wheeled-out the car, to find in daylight its tail was clearly a different shade of green from the rest; somehow, we got away with it...

We had left Bourne on Wednesday, March 12, Stan Hope and Dave Turner following with the disc-braked car[56] that Saturday, March 15. Moss drove most of the time. We were rather disappointed when he reported that the modifications seemed

---

56. The drum-braked car was 'No. 2', fitted with engine '20/2' (new-type with re-machined crankcase halves and latest design crankshaft) and gearbox 'Mark 1/3' (old-type without brake pump), and with PB's new front engine mounting, Burman steering 'box and modified fuel tanks. The disc-braked car – similarly-modified – was 'No. 1' fitted with engine '11/3' (old-type with original-style crankshaft) and gearbox 'Mark 11/1' (new-type with brake pump).

In the absence of a permanent test driver – following Ken Richardson's dismissal – RM had driven the drum-braked car at PB's request at Folkingham on March 11. Since it was tailored to Moss' "comparatively slight physique" Mays found himself "unduly cramped...in particular, insufficient fist-to-lap clearance..." but writing to Alfred Owen he declared (perhaps predictably):

"I was more than impressed with the terrific improvement from when I last drove the B.R.M. The steering is beautifully light, and the road holding, taking into consideration the very bad surface at Folkingham, I thought good. I took the car up to over 170mph along the straight, and the steering was very positive at this speed..."

New recruit Ken Wharton had also driven some acclimatization laps at Folkingham. He "wisely did not attempt to run before he walked...but the form he showed fully justifies the decision to invite him to Monza".

to have done nothing to improve the unpleasant handling. Actually, this was predictable; since we really knew nothing of the factors which decide road-holding we had not – in fact – done anything which could have improved it. This impression did not find its way into PB's official report. However, Stirling observed that the engine and gearbox were better and that the new disc brakes – when they worked – were fabulous.

On March 18, during the first week of this new Monza test period, Walter Hill – who had become Honorary Organiser of the British Racing Motors Association supporters club – compiled his Report for Branch Secretaries, detailing: "so far as present knowledge takes us, the 1952 races in which one or more BRM cars are to compete: …i) June 1st, Albi GP, (ii) June 7th, Ulster Trophy race, Dundrod; (iii) June 22nd, Grand Prix of Europe, Spa; (iv) August 2nd, *Formule Libre* race at Boreham, Essex; (v) September 7th, Italian GP, Monza; (vi) October 26th, Spanish GP, Barcelona…the British Grand Prix at Silverstone on July 19th is still in the melting pot [with RM trying his damndest to sway the BRDC against Formula 2] because, despite the clear lead given by the Royal Belgian A.C. in adopting Formula 1 for the European G.P., most important road race of the year, it is known that many influential B.R.D.C. elements still incline towards Formula 2 for Britain's own G.P. …"

The German GP on August 3 was also still in doubt, although the Italian GP was "expected to be a Formula 1 race, and there has never been any serious doubt about the Spanish G.P.…."

Regrettably, the Swiss had decided to adopt Formula 2 for their GP at Berne "…which robs B.R.M." wrote the optimistic Mr Hill "…of a race over a circuit which would have admirably suited the cars' characteristics. In a most regretful letter to Raymond Mays, Robert Braunschweig, editor of the Swiss *Automobile Revue*, says:

I think the British press is responsible for this to a large extent. When they published their piece about the Swiss Grand Prix being a Formula 2 race, no decision at all had been taken'. This illustrates in a very striking fashion the great harm that can be done when wishful-thinking journalists give premature rein to rumours of their own concocting. If the British G.P. too should be 'lost' to B.R.M., much of the blame will belong in the same quarter.

By the time Hill circulated this report on April 2, it was accompanied by a covering letter explaining that possible participation had been considered in the Valentino GP at Turin on April 6 "…but I can now say officially that B.R.M. will not participate in that race…".

This – in retrospect – suicidal decision was based upon RM's typically star-struck admiration of the reigning World Champion, Juan Manuel Fangio. As early as January, 1952, while Alfa Romeo dithered over whether or not to withdraw finally from Formula 1, Fangio was actively looking for another berth. He was still at a loose end when Desmond Scannell contacted him through Eric Forrest Greene, the Buenos Aires-based importer of British quality cars, including Rolls-Royce and Aston Martin. Scannell was organizing the

BRDC's Formula 2 International Trophy race at Silverstone, and offered an HWM drive there. Fangio was considering it when RM made contact, also through Greene, of Juncal 462, BA, to offer No. 1 status for the season with the BRM Formula 1 team…

Initially they talked of Fangio test-driving in England in late February, then postponed the date until mid-March when "…the modified 1952 BRM" would be ready.

Ray was totally mesmerized by this chance of signing-up the reigning World Champion. His interest in and experience of motor racing had always been primarily as a driver. He believed a team existed largely to provide star drivers with the tools to perpetuate their star status.

Cables flurried between Bourne and Buenos Aires. Greene explained that Fangio remained unsure of Alfa's plans. Despite having been unhappy with their "…perpetual wrangling and indecision…before each race" it was still thought possible that Alfa might send two cars to BA for the inaugural meeting on General Peron's new municipal Autodrome.[57] Greene suggested that Fangio should be offered 50 per cent of the starting and prize money, either full travelling and living expenses or a fixed expenses payment each month, plus a small retainer fee, which "would help negotiations as Alfa Romeo have never done anything in this respect" apart from giving him a new road car.

On February 22, Greene complained that many people were trying to influence Fangio against the British BRM:

The Italian colony here is a very strong one…of the motoring fraternity 99% are Italians… He [Fangio] right from the beginning, has tried to stick to his original decision but I think his friends have been in touch with Italy practically every day…

Greene found an ally in 'Pancho' Borgonovo, Competitions Director of the *Automovil Club Argentina*, which had backed Fangio for years.

We pointed out to him that it was he who was going to drive and not his friends [and] he agreed that I should cable you this morning his final decision.

Greene's cable read: "FANGIO AGREES TO DRIVE FOR BRM FOR 1952 SUBJECT TO SATISFACTORY CAR TRIAL. WRITING AIRMAIL TODAY. CONGRATULATIONS."

His letter explained that Fangio would be free to fly to England following the two Argentine races and two in

---

57. The new *Autodromo 17 de Octubre* in Buenos Aires' *Parque Almirante Brown* was duly inaugurated with a 30-lap *Formule Libre* race on March 9, 1952, followed by a second there on March 16. The busy South American series then continued with the Uruguayan *GP de la Commission de Turismo* and the Piriapolis GP on March 23 and 30. Fangio won *all four* of these events in his ACA-entered 2-litre supercharged Ferrari 166FL *America*.

Subsequently, the great Anglo-Argentine enthusiast Eric Forrest Greene shared an Aston Martin DB2 with Carlos Stabile in the BA Autodrome's inaugural 1,000kms World Sports Car Championship race on January 24, 1954, when, after 14 laps, his car overturned and caught fire. Police in the immediate vicinity were reportedly reluctant to attempt any rescue, and tragically he sustained fatal burns.

Uruguay between March 9 and March 30, so: "…the week commencing the 30th March and ending 5th April he should be in England". April 6 had already been confirmed for the Formula 1 Turin GP in Italy. With so few cars available, BRM could not possibly prepare an adequate mount for Fangio to try in England if they were also to confront Ferrari in the race around Turin's Valentino Park. Something had to give. Would it be Fangio's test-drive, or a race start in Turin?

As a bonus, Greene also offered Jose Froilan Gonzalez's services as a second driver:

> …as although he can drive for either Ferrari's or with the new Gordoni [*sic*], from the Argentine point of view it would have been magnificent for both of them to have driven for B.R.M.

Ray received this letter on February 29 so he had more than a month in which to consider the pros and cons of Fangio testing for BRM in England, or preferably at Monza, which could enable the team to race at Turin. Unfortunately, Greene took great pains to point out that Fangio was sensitive about testing this British F1 car at Monza on his recent employer's home-ground.

The March 18 Trust report mentioned that Fangio:

> …is expected [to] arrive in this country on or about April 2nd – four days before the Turin race – It had been hoped for him to carry out his tests at Monza, but for personal reasons he prefers to run at Silverstone.

The report continued, rather cynically:

> Every confidence is felt that Fangio, after trying the car in its current form…will be as keen to sign as we are to have his services. If, however, the negotiations should fail for any reason, it is felt that Wharton may well develop into a promising substitute. Everything is therefore being done to foster cordial relations with Wharton…

The British Hill-Climb Champion, Ken Wharton, was at that time sharing test driving at Monza with Stirling Moss, who was considering Ray's latest offer of 50 per cent of starting and prize money, plus £500 retainer for the year.

This second Monza test period was not as well-recorded as the marathon post-Italian GP session, but PB finally found time to include it in his 'TECHNICAL AND DEVELOPMENT PROGRESS REPORT' of May 20, 1952, which in part read – rather optimistically – as follows:

MONZA

Tests commenced on Monday, the 17th March with the disc brake car with Stirling Moss. It was apparent in the early stages that the handling of the car was much improved, particularly on the twisty section of the course through *Grande* and *Lesmo* corners and with the new carburettor arrangements burbling had been overcome.

Considerable development work was carried out during the first week on the disc brakes with gradual elimination of the troubles experienced…

Suspension and damping characteristics were varied to find the optimum settings and although Dunlop had let us down with the new wide base front rims, 18x5.50 tyres were tried on the old rims with improvement. As expected from static development tests…the change of front strut position was found unnecessary and as it meant spending considerable time on finding the optimum strut settings this change was abandoned for other development work.

The new type of Lodge plugs (modified 53) proved satisfactory but in view of the fact that No. 16 cylinder tended to run weak, it was decided to change the fuel to a mixture giving a higher latent heat value and would enable an overrich mixture to be used more readily without burbling.

When Moss started lapping at speed it was found that the main oil pressure dropped dangerously low although this engine was provided with the new separate camshaft feed pump.

Porous castings were suspected and the engine removed from the frame and half crankcases separated. It was found that the case faces were very poor, permitting considerable oil leaks. The lower half was machined by a local firm to take rubber ring type seals and the oil system tested statically. Some porosity was found and a temporary repair effected.

During this period Stirling Moss left to run in the Charbonnieres Rally for Jaguar and the drum brake car was put on test with Ken Wharton, who had arrived by air.

After completing running-in, Ken Wharton improved his driving technique with the car considerably, and was beginning to use some power, when No. 16 piston failed. A new piston was fitted, fuel and settings changed to the same as the disc brake car and further running by Ken Wharton produced good times round the Pave corners until further engine troubles put this car out of action.

On examination it was found that No. 16 cylinder liner had never made the joint on the cylinder head, due to the fact that the spigot ring was considerably over sized and the cylinder head was too badly damaged to continue running. Poor inspection and poor fitting are the reasons for this failure.

Moss returned to continue tests with the disc brake car but was never able to put in any really fast laps, due to either a wet track or continual locking of the rear wheel brakes, which had proved a persistent trouble, but was eventually overcome.

Approximately 800 miles running was carried out on this car and apart from lack of oil pressure, which was eventually much improved, the engine ran cleanly with good power and free of burbling and backfiring the whole time.

Unfortunately, towards the end of the testing period when the suspension was properly adjusted and the brakes [were] consistent and reliable, bad weather and a wet track prevented Moss from seeing what times he

March 1952 – Monza testing: PB sits and thinks in the disc-braked prototype car during BRM's second prolonged series of tests at the Milanese Autodromo. When he drove the car he identified flexure in the rear radius rods. Willie Southcott and Tony Rudd look on. Note the tail cone panelling and tail tank detail. From this angle, front hub, wheel-rim and tyre sizes look strangely insubstantial.

could do. Nevertheless, on the section of the track between the *Grande* and *Vialone* corners he consistently reduced his last winter's times by 2 to 3 seconds. Round the Pave section he was consistently one second faster but Ken Wharton, although slower round the Vialone section, was able to get through the Pave on an average half second faster than Moss. Had Moss had a clear run on a dry circuit, he is quite confident he could now get round in 1min. 54secs. or better.

Moss and I went over to Turin to see the course and met the organisers who confirmed the starting money they had offered to Raymond Mays by letter. We confirmed there was a possibility of running only one car and this was doubtful, dependent on the tests then being carried out at Monza and also final arrangements for testing in England with Fangio and Gonzalez who were coming to England specially for the purpose.

Gregory [sic, should be 'Gregor'] Grant [returned with Moss] and created rather a difficult situation. He made the point that the Turin race on April 6th was the first Formula 1 race in the 1952 season and if B.R.M. did not appear, it would understandably have an effect on the availability of No. 1 races during the season and also, as Moss had done tests and donkey work for B.R.M. it was only fair that we should give him an opportunity of running in the race as we were on the spot and a finish would give him an advantage for the B.R.D.C. Gold Star. Moss was rather wrath [sic] to forego his share of the starting money.

After a number of telephone conversations with the Chairman and Raymond Mays it was decided to return the team forthwith to maintain the arrangements made with Fangio and Gonzalez.

The Monza tests showed that the winter modifications

had proved entirely successful and that we had mastered the bogey of burbling. It was also apparent that we had to tighten up considerably at home on inspection, engine build and individual testing of engine components…

Tony: The BRM was the first really high-speed car to use disc brakes and during these initial Monza tests both Girling and ourselves were learning about them. Girling's engineer Redmayne was present and when the brake pedal went soft he quickly found the cause.

Play in the wheel hub bearing was allowing the wheel, and therefore the attached brake disc, to lean slightly under cornering load. The caliper clasped the top of the disc so that as the disc leaned, it pushed back the pads and pistons in one side of the caliper. This movement simultaneously separated the pads from the disc on the other side of the caliper, so that when the driver subsequently applied the brakes, the pedal would sail down someway in taking up the slack before the pads began to bite.

This phenomenon became known as 'knock-off'. Obviously it was more sensible to mount the caliper at hub level, around the disc's neutral axis of tilt, but in those days disc brakes were fresh from aviation where one tries not to indulge in high-speed cornering on the ground. If you do, then you have more pressing problems than knock-off…

Redmayne introduced a crafty little device like a spring-loaded non-return valve to prevent fluid passing back up the line to the caliper until a pre-set pressure had been exceeded. This maintained pressure within the caliper as the disc leaned, so that as the pads and pistons were pushed back on one side, those on the other moved out to follow the disc surface. Knock-off as a problem was replaced by high fluid temperatures.

Generally, the car ran well on test, Stirling lapping in 1:57s. I also had a very brief go, but we then encountered the oil pressure problems described in PB's report. When not driving, there was very little for Stirling to do, and he amused the Italians immensely by running round the Park to keep fit.

A Milan workshop machined the sump for us. Unfortunately there was quite strong anti-British feeling in Italy at the time over Trieste (the 'Free Territory' on the Adriatic created after the Second World War and disputed violently between the Italians and the Yugoslavs); rioters were overturning and burning British cars. The machine shop went on strike and when I arrived in the Lodestar to collect the sump – with Stan Hope riding shotgun – the pickets turned ugly and tried to capsize the truck with Stan inside. Fortunately, a tram came by, they stepped back, and we got him safely into the factory.

On another night, Redmayne and Vic Barlow of Dunlop, returning late from a trip into Milan, found the Monza Park and hotel gates locked, so they slept in their car. Early next morning Stirling hit a hare or fox in the woods near *Lesmo*, smashing the car's nose. The mechanics had taken the wreckage back to the garage behind the hotel, and were hosing the inside of the Lodestar to remove the gory fragments when Redmayne awoke to see it all – and instantly assumed the worst…

Apart from all the oil pressure problems, both cars ran well, but due to our confusion over the tacho colour scheme we had no precise idea how engine rpm compared with the previous year's test series. RM eventually arrived with the code which showed the relationship of colour to rpm, but on his way down a garage mechanic had topped-up his beautiful new midnight-blue Bentley's windscreen washer bottle with battery acid in mistake for distilled water and by the time he reached Monza the coachwork was in a rare mess…

While Stirling and PB visited Turin to inspect the Valentino Park course for the Grand Prix, and PB was talking starting money with the organizing *AC Torino*, we were now convinced of our cars' promise, and believed that if they could run reliably they would – in disc-braked form – have a marked advantage over the big Ferraris. We settled down to prepare

one car for Turin.

A worthwhile showing there by BRM should certainly have given Ray ammunition to convince other race organizers of our ability to fulfil race entries and to support Formula 1. The ACT had offered £1,500 starting money for one car, and Ferrari had agreed to run their latest 'Indianapolis'-style V12 cars for Ascari, Farina and Villoresi.

In England, into that first week of April, it remained unclear exactly when Fangio would appear. Then on Wednesday, April 2, the Monza crew received the message from RM: "Bring the cars back to England at once for Fangio to try…"

We argued. We tried to persuade RM and the Trust to let us race at Turin and then rush the cars home non-stop. Let Fangio come to Monza, better for him to try the car on a circuit he knew well, or simply let him wait until after Turin. But all our arguments fell on deaf ears.

Stirling was *livid* – even more so when he heard that Gonzalez was coming as well as Fangio. We simply could not defend our management's decision to him.

By Thursday mid-day, three days before the Turin race, we had packed for the long trek home. We arrived in Bourne on Sunday, April 6, while the Ferraris were enjoying a walkover in Turin and significant Formula 1 finally lay down and died…

We had again defaulted on our entry; even if it had not been filed officially we had certainly been geared-up to go. Subsequently in his report of May 8 to the British Racing Motors Association, Ray explained:

In view of the various press reports…that there was a division of opinion about running at Turin I must say that, when all factors, which included the condition of the cars following the tests at Monza, and the date of Fangio's arrival in England, had been taken into account, Peter Berthon and I were in complete agreement that it was impossible, much as we regretted it, to enter one car at Turin. We knew that…our cars were not in a position to do themselves full justice at

March/April 1952 – Monza testing: Moss cornering the prototype disc-braked car on the porphyry setts in the double turn before the pits, then known variously as the Vedano Curves or the Curva in Porfido. When the high-speed track was built here in 1954–55 the foreshortened road course's Curva Parabolica – which survives today – inherited these corners' function and the grubbed-up setts resurfaced areas of the paddock.

Turin, and troubles rectified since the return to England would have caused retirement... In these circumstances it would have been madness to risk [Fangio] coming all that way and finding no car in a fit state to prove its worth. Moss' disappointment, as I say, was understandable, but it can hardly be denied in the light of subsequent events the decision taken was the right one. We wanted Fangio, and we owed him the courtesy of a car ready for tests...

In fact Ray had completely misjudged the relaxed and always gentlemanly Argentine, who later remarked that if only he had been told of the clash of dates he would quite happily have changed his plans to fit.

M. de Harlez of the *RAC de Belgique* had irately tackled Ray after Turin, RM protesting that "no entry had ever been made" for the Italian race while confirming that "we hope to have three cars with you for the Grand Prix of Europe...having, of course, complete priority...".

He also assured Enrique Perez Sole of the Pena Rhin in Barcelona that three BRMs and possibly four would be entered for his scheduled race, and pressed Bacciagaluppi at Monza to confirm that "...your September race [the Italian GP] will be for Formula 1 cars". But none were impressed, and the Pena Rhin event was simply cancelled.

BRM's defection from the 1952 Turin GP certainly proved to be one of the most fateful decisions in motor racing history, for it changed the entire course of Formula 1. Thereafter, no race organizer would risk building a major Formula 1 race around BRM versus Ferrari. Even the Belgian and Italian races were subsequently run to Formula 2. Ferrari didn't mind – his 2-litre car was by far the best F2 around, so he won either way. But although Tony and many of his team-mates felt that passing-up the Turin GP had been the wrong decision at the time, with hindsight he doubted if it had much real effect upon BRM's story: The truth was that, at that time, we could never have stood the pace of a full season's Grand Prix racing, and perhaps if we had embarked upon such a programme BRM would have vanished for good that year. But this incident certainly alienated Stirling Moss, who never really trusted BRM ever again.

OF FANGIO, AND FURTHER FAILURE...

Upon the team's return to base, the disc-braked car was hurriedly prepared for Fangio to test-drive at Silverstone on Tuesday, April 8. PB reported:

> ...it was noticed that the cast-in oil gallery in the lower half crankcase was split. The engine was removed and the lower half crankcase changed. The car went to Silverstone early Tuesday...and in continuous rain both Fangio and Gonzalez tried the car. The engine was not running properly...tending to misfire at high r.p.m. and it was afterwards found that three cylinder head holding down studs had pulled out of the crankcase. Both

The BRM V16s' original tailor-made Girling drum brakes were of three-leading-shoe design. They were beautifully crafted, each drum cooled by peripheral finning and 10 large drillings in its outer face. The pioneering disc brake system developed by Girling through the winter of 1951–52, which replaced the complicated drums, presented greater development problems, but once they had been overcome offered great – if still not trouble-free – advantage.

Fangio and Gonzalez were delighted with the car's performance, the brakes, and particularly its handling in the wet. Fangio agreed to sign up the same evening...

RM was thrilled to see these truly world-class drivers at last sampling the BRM.[58] They were accompanied by Borgonovo of the ACA, by Eric Forrest Greene and by a Senor d'Amico from the Argentine Embassy. Ray – rather romantically – told the BRMA:

> There was something unforgettably dramatic about the whole atmosphere of that wet and overcast afternoon at Silverstone. Of course, nobody – not even Fangio – could hope to give the car anything like full throttle on a streaming track, from which great blades of water were flung up into the air from each wheel as he explored his way up the straights in a series of tail-slides alternating with lightning corrections. The superb confidence of his cornering – considering just how frightening the conditions were – was something that had to be seen to be believed. He was particularly anxious to find out how the new Girling disc brakes would behave under these conditions, and lost no time in making experiments...on two or three occasions he found himself running into corners considerably above their 'natural' speed...Fangio simply put his brake on – hard! – halfway round the corner. The result of these highly unconventional tactics was this: instead of the car spinning like a top...it glued itself more firmly to the line the Champion had chosen and ripped through the turn under perfect command.
>
> ...Watching him work on the section between Copse and Stowe corners...I think I can fairly say that few drivers

58. In his book ***BRM*** (Cassell & Company, 1962), co-written with the late Peter Roberts, RM describes Fangio's first test-drive in some detail as having taken place at Folkingham. This was not so – the wet Silverstone test came first, Folkingham next day before the press.

Tuesday, April 8, 1952 – Silverstone testing: First acquaintance – no man could possibly have appeared more relaxed despite the challenge of thumping the BRM V16 around the rain-drenched circuit than Fangio, wearing the crash helmet demanded by new FIA regulations which within weeks would save his life...

Left: 'Pancho', Il Cabezon, 'Pepe' – Jose Froilan Gonzalez answered to each of these, but generally liked his driving to speak for him – here taking his turn to unleash the V16 on one of the remoter reaches of off-season Silverstone.

would have gone through that leg any faster in the dry. For two-fifths of the distance within my visual range he had the car at angles of at least 35 degrees to the direction of travel, yet one could tell that he was completely unruffled. Then he handed over to Gonzalez, who is of course the lap record holder...Gonzalez motored with a good deal lighter toe, but, on completing his session, loudly seconded Fangio's vote of confidence...

While the Argentine party celebrated with RM and PB, Tony and the crew discovered the leaking cylinder head which explained that top-end misfire. In consequence running for the press next day at Folkingham was kept to a minimum.

Ray recalled the World Champion's first laps at Folkingham like this: "I took him round...in a Zephyr. Then he got in the BRM and shot away, straight up to 11,500rpm as though he had driven the car a score of times. We waited for

Above: It's a deal — the delighted RM feels his controversial advice to the Trust to recall the test team from Monza has been justified by Fangio's agreement to drive for BRM. Gonzalez is joining too. Below: Ever accessible, always the gentleman, the World Champion signs his autograph for Alfred Owen's schoolboy second son, John.

what needed improving on the car and how he thought it could be modified, we were startled when his interpreter said: "Are you not satisfied with his driving? Has he not gone fast enough for you?" We said: "Oh no, fine" and so on and then Fangio asked: "If you are satisfied with the times why do you want to interfere with the car? If the car does not go fast enough and you are not satisfied with it then you fire the driver and find a quicker one."

To us, this was really a startling approach, but both Fangio and Gonzalez were signed-up. They repaired to *The George* in Stamford, where hung a painting of the giant Daniel Lambert. Glancing at Lambert's waistline, Fangio nudged Gonzalez, nodded down at Pepe's midriff and they both roared with laughter. Colin Atkin was at Eastgate House when Fangio first visited. He was impressed: "D'you know, he *bowed*!"

Although the March 18 report had stated:

> In preparation for the Fangio visit both the cars have been provided with special adjustable seats giving ranges of movement in two directions. Slightly shallower scuttle tanks have also been put in hand, to permit increased up-and-down adjustment in the steering column...

when pressed, Fangio admitted to being handicapped by 'the Moss driving position', and asked for the steering wheel to be raised, a separate bucket seat to be made and footrests provided. This new bucket seat was mounted higher than the propeller shaft, so he could see out better — which obviated any need for the car's expensive and complex angled engine and transmission system which had enabled the driver's seat to be lowered in the first place...such was the price of association with genius!

Meanwhile, Moss told RM he was still prepared to drive for BRM, but in fact he would never sign his contract. A press release to announce his signature was never issued.

After the brief Folkingham run, the disc-braked car's suspect engine was replaced, as Fangio and Gonzalez were keen to try the car in the dry back at Silverstone. Unfortunately, after Fangio had completed some running there on Tuesday, April 27, it began to rain. In its later laps his new engine began to run erratically, lubricant from the main oil galleries having seeped into the coolant. This was the third time this particular V16 had failed despite four separate sealing treatments to porous castings. Even so, Fangio had lapped the 'inside' Silverstone circuit in 1:45 — this course being considered 3 seconds per lap slower than the full Grand Prix circuit.

him to come round again. He did not appear. We were, naturally, worried. We jumped into cars and went to investigate. He had taken a bad right hand bend too fast and run on to the grass. Unfortunately the grass concealed a wooden sleeper on which the car had 'spiked' itself, smashing an exhaust pipe and manifold.

" 'I'm sorry', said Fangio. It took us three hours to mend the car, then Fangio completed his test... Within a few laps he was getting round Folkingham four seconds quicker than anyone had done before!

"Fangio was the first man who was complete master [of the BRM]. Fangio treated it like any other car. So long as he was comfortable and could see out of it, it seemed not to matter to him what he drove."

Tony recalls that at Silverstone, thanks largely to Stirling, the car handled rather well in the wet. When we asked Fangio

REAL RACING AT LAST?

The Albi GP now became the target, deep in southern France on June 1. But somebody within the Trust had rashly promised the Prime Minister of Northern Ireland that no fewer than three BRMs would start in the Ulster Trophy race at Dundrod on June 7 — the Saturday following Albi...

On May 6, Cliff Mander reported:

> All four engines run by Fangio and Gonazales [*sic*] in

Left: Wednesday, April 9, 1952 – Folkingham: Ken Wharton had had brief experience of the V16 at Monza before reporting at Folkingham to meet Fangio and Gonzalez, fresh from Silverstone – and the World Champion had managed to wipe off an exhaust system. Here Ken has just dropped the clutch and smoke puffs from the exhaust stubs, behind the front wheel. Transport mechanic Maurice Dove, soon press-ganged onto the race team, Jack Davis of Girling, Colin Atkin and Arthur Ambrose do the pushing.

Below: An embarrassed Fangio has just explained his Folkingham misdemeanour. RM and newcomers Dick Salmon and Maurice Dove (left) see the funny side. Maurice had served in the Far East as a National Serviceman, guarding Japanese war criminals for trial and many for execution. Both entered the race team after acting as BRM transport mechanics.

the April tests gave very good performance before the porosity set in too severe for safety without risk of damage. All engines have therefore to be stripped completely and all castings subjected to special sealing.

Engine '20/1' was running on the test-bed, the other five units then extant all being dismantled. Four complete gearboxes were available, plus one lacking only its outer casing due any day from Austin. The Girling disc-brake car was stripped in preparation for Albi while its drum-braked sister was readied to accept discs. The third car, wearing bodywork by Motor Panels of Coventry, was due to be completed in time for the Ulster Trophy but would have to use drum brakes since a third set of discs was not yet available.

Engine '20/2' was running-in at Bourne ready for the existing disc-braked car and simplified new exhaust systems were on-stream to improve both cars' ground clearance after Fangio's Folkingham misdemeanour.

Engine '20/2' ran extensively on the Bourne dyno on Sunday, May 11, but during the lunch-break next day it was sitting silent on the dyno when one of its 100-ton tensile strength cylinder head studs suddenly snapped. The stud was replaced, but a second then snapped in similar circumstances – engine stationary and nobody present in the Test House. These broken studs were examined with grim perplexity while Les Bryden's machine shop rushed through an emergency batch of less-brittle 65/75-ton tensile studs, in EN25V material, not heat-treated.

Owing to a drawing-office error, these new studs were too short when engine '20/3' came to be assembled, so a replacement set then had to be rushed through. Insidiously, with an impetus all of its own, the stage was setting itself for another BRM debacle…

Meanwhile, the disc-braked car had been found to be in generally excellent condition during post-testing strip down, apart from two bell-cranks in its gearchange mechanism having been slightly bent, apparently due to "forcing gear

Relieved to see the funny side, Juan Fangio and the spherical, bull-strong, wide-as-he-was-tall Froilan Gonzalez, RM and Ken Wharton all admire the crumpled V16 exhaust system which the World Champion had ripped off against a Folkingham runway light.

changes", and slight picking-up in the differential "probably due to excessive wheelspin coming out of corners…".

Fangio test-drove the drum-braked car at Folkingham on the weekend of May 10-11. He was very happy with his new bucket seat and the altered steering wheel position provided by the latest scuttle tank. In 15 laps he lowered his time to 1:38 – over 10sec faster than any other driver. This car then began conversion to disc brakes and preparation for BRM's first race of 1952…

Could Albi possibly become BRM's glorious first of June?

Moss had a clashing engagement that day, driving a C-Type Jaguar in the unique sports car Monaco GP, so Ken Wharton instead made his debut as BRM's reserve driver, accompanying Fangio and Gonzalez to the French circuit. To take advantage of the Ulster Automobile Club's good starting money at Dundrod for the following weekend, it was arranged for a Silver City Airways Bristol Freighter to collect the team from Toulouse after the Albi race and fly direct to Belfast.

On May 20, PB compiled a remarkably frank Technical & Development Progress Report for the Trust Board, which included the following revealing paragraph:

Throughout the last few months, apart from the continual heart breaking trouble of disgraceful castings,

we had no mechanical engine trouble whatever. Quality of engine build is extremely poor and there is little control of proper routine tests and checks and control of sequence of build operations to avoid continual dismantling. The enormous waste of time in building engines with hopelessly porous crankcases, in water and oil systems, could have been avoided if the tests that have been laid down were rigidly adhered to. The first of the new type crankshafts which Lucas produced through a week-end need never have been lost if the usual elementary precaution of clearing grinding swarf from the crankshaft oilways had been adhered to.

He added:

Even now it does not seem to be understood, one good engine will win a race for us and 6 or 7 engine sets thrown together merely get us into trouble…

RM and PB knew the *Moto-Camping-Club Albigeois* well from ERA days prewar, and the Secretary, M. Vedel, wrote to Ray early in May:

We have upheld, in spite of all others, the Formula 1. We have heard that certain races, fearing the non-appearance of the B.R.M., have decided to abandon this Formula. For ourselves this question has never arisen. We have given our word and we are confident that you will keep yours…

BRM did.

Tony: The long drive down into southern France was quite uneventful. Upon arrival at the very fast *Les Planques* public road circuit we unloaded the Austin Lodestars and wheeled out the cars. The 'No. 1' car was the recently converted machine which Fangio had driven so quickly at Folkingham,

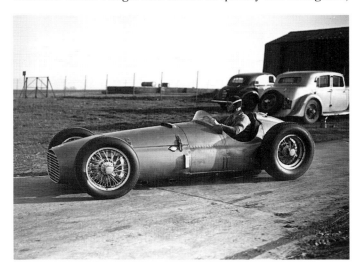

Raymond Mays very seldom drove the V16, preferring to leave most of the testing to Ken Richardson during 1950–51. Here at Folkingham RM heads the prototype 1952 disc brake car out of the BRM compound onto the team's perimeter track-cum-runway test circuit.

The linen wind-helmeted Juan Fangio pondering what he would recall ever after as having been "the most fantastic car I ever drove". PB looks on in dark glasses, the caravan in the background providing his temporary Folkingham residence until his family flat could be completed in the control tower here.

using engine '20/1' – the other was the original disc-braked 'No. 2' car with engine '20/2' installed. I was just checking them over for transit damage when I spotted water weeping from a head on one engine. To my horror, as I reached down to wipe the water away, a holding-down bridge piece, and half the retaining stud, fell away in my hand.

From that instant, Albi '52 became a nightmare…

The stud had clearly failed either as the engine cooled down after its previous run or somehow during the trip. It was a recurrence of the Bourne Test House failures on '20/2'. In fact, while the studs on that engine had been replaced by the new

65/75-ton steel type, the suspect 100-ton tensile studs had been left undisturbed in engine '20/1'. Tony and the mechanics now found that four 100-ton tensile bolts had also been left in '20/2'.

At Bourne, four men then worked through Wednesday afternoon, right through that night and until Thursday midday to complete a full set of replacement 65/75-ton studs, Clarrie Brinkley flying out with them in a charter 'plane which departed Folkingham at 1pm Thursday, to arrive at Toulouse at 7pm.

Tony: As we tried to remove the old studs so several broke

Cordiality – RM in debonair mood tells Argentine radio listeners of BRM's regard for Fangio. The brothers Luis Elias and Manuel Sojit travelled everywhere with the ACA drivers, broadcasting live race commentaries for the folks back home. Left to right, this group includes Maurice Dove, Dick Salmon, PB, Gonzalez, Fangio, the tall Stewart Tresilian (dark glasses behind Sojit), Tony Rudd and Alfred Owen's PRO, A.F. Rivers Fletcher.

With the world's finest driving talent signed-up and ready to race, V16 development continued apace in the Bourne Test House, but Formula 1 had been overtaken by the FIA's decision to open its Drivers' World Championship instead to Formula 2. What Colin Atkin was working on here, for PB and Tony Rudd, had outlived the class for which it had been created…

and threads stripped. We concluded that some of the 100-ton studs were too fragile to risk removing. The mechanics were right up against it once again. The heat in the garage was extreme and we took it in turns to play a hose on the roof to cool it down. Sanitation was also primitive and conditions generally became most unpleasant.

Once the engines were equipped with as many 65-ton studs as we could fit, Fangio and Gonzalez began practising, whereupon overheating proved so bad in the hot sun of the Midi it seemed we would be lucky to see them survive even 10 race laps…Our one consolation was that while the cars were running, they were *very* quick…

Alone during first practice, Fangio lapped in 2:55.0 – 114.3mph – to shatter his own Maserati lap record of 3:06.7, but any attempt at sustained running was curtailed by chronic overheating. Something mysterious was going on inside his engine – '20/2' – which we could neither trace nor cure.

In second practice, Gonzalez drove Fangio's car round in 3:02.4 before spinning harmlessly and then Ken Wharton trundled it round for a few familiarization laps before it overheated again, this time badly damaging '20/2''s cylinder heads.

We had a terrible panic cutting extra cooling louvres into the top of the nose cowl, with Fangio, Gonzalez and their retinue pitching in beside us with the tin snips. I'll never forget the power-packed Gonzalez lifting panels between finger and thumb as if they were featherlight when in fact they were anything but…

The night before the race, Tony set off for Toulouse Airport to collect a freshly-assembled spare engine – '20/3' – flown out from Bourne. According to Tresilian's Test House report it was "the best engine for power curve and max. H.P. we had yet completed…" but it had 100-ton head studs which were about to be replaced when the urgent call came for it from Albi. As a precaution against stud breakage in transit, they were eased from the standard 450lbs torque to 250lbs, with instructions

to the race team to re-torque them pre-race.

This engine weighed 500lbs, it had been shoe-horned into a wood-and-fabric DH86 Rapide biplane and Tony's main memory of the sweating French loaders struggling to extract it became the sound of their feet popping through the aircraft's wing fabric.

One of the most time-consuming parts of an engine change, or even a head change for that matter, was the struggle to replace the exhaust manifolds. They were retained by some 64 special nuts, every one inaccessible. The easiest way to do this was to run the car over an inspection pit, and when RM, PB, Fangio and the interpreter decided to hold a counsel of war beside the car, they didn't realize that two mechanics were in the pit beneath it, until a purple face appeared around the engine and demanded: "Why don't you do something [several expletives deleted] useful instead of *gabbing*? Grab this set of spanners!" – whereupon Fangio and the interpreter readily pitched in to help.

June 1, 1952 – Albi Grand Prix, *Les Planques*, France – 34 laps, 189.15 miles

Although the two V16s started on the front row of the grid, faced mainly by the private Ferrari 375s of Louis Rosier and Chico Landi, a flock of elderly Talbot-Lagos and a mixture of Maseratis and Gordinis, the race was indeed an – at least promising – BRM disaster. Fangio raced with engine '20/1' while the new spare '20/3' with its eased head studs had blown water from its exhaust pipes when we started it at dawn on raceday.

We had hastily fitted new flame rings, refaced all joints and satisfactorily pressure-tested it before Gonzalez took it into the race.

Fangio built a long lead despite lapping some 16sec off his

Left: May 30, 1952 – Albi GP, Les Planques: Fangio driving the V16 BRM for the first time in anger during practice on the fast road circuit in southern France. Note the unlouvred body with its heavily riveted scuttle tank and the latest upswept side exhausts to enhance ground clearance after Fangio's experience at Folkingham.

practice pace. Gonzalez had made a very slow start, getting away at the tail of the field, before hurtling through to second place behind his team-mate after only three laps. In the process he set a new lap record in 3:06, 107.65mph, but after six rumbustious laps he stopped at the pits, the fresh engine '20/3' sizzling furiously and billowing smoke and steam to the great excitement of the French firemen. Its heads had nearly melted…No. 2 piston crown was holed and No. 1 cylinder head hemisphere had a large opening burned or blown through its flame-joint ring to the waterway. Several other hemispheres were also cracked or burned away between the sparking-plug orifice and the two valve seats. But not a single stud had broken!

On lap 15, Fangio went past the pits with his car spewing out water. Next time round he retired with its suspect engine boiling – sure enough, one of its remaining 100-ton cylinder head studs had snapped.

Rosier and Landi finished 1-2 in their private Ferraris, and

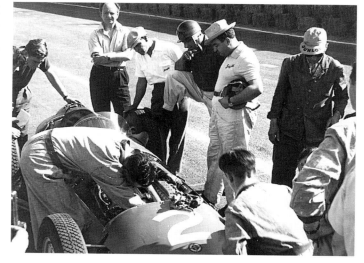

Above: 1952 Albi GP practice. Pensive Argentinians look on as Fangio's overheating V16 is investigated; Tony Rudd (extreme left), the worried RM and Dick Salmon (by the car's nose) await the verdict.

Left: 1952 Albi GP. Back in the garage, Gonzalez glances up from watching his V16's preparation. Its exhausts are yet to be refitted. Note the enormous scuttle tank, distinctive chassis structure alongside the engine bay, and the cross-braced twin-tube radius rods by 'Pepe''s knees, which replaced the original dural channel sections after Monza stiffness testing.

Above: 1952 Albi GP. Under the biggest umbrellas BRM could find to provide relief from a roasting sun, the hastily louvred V16s stand ready for the race.

Right: 1952 Albi GP. For ease of comparison this shot of Maurice Dove, Willie Southcott and Dave Turner with local help wheeling one of the disc-braked V16s out for practice shows their unlouvred spec as delivered fresh from Folkingham. The ad hoc modifications in a desperate attempt to cool the troubled engines are obvious.

Left: 'Moleskin 'Arry' presides on the entirely al fresco Albi pit counter, tousled and dog-tired, relaying his intentions to Ken Williamson — recalled by most BRM men today only as 'Flo-Joe' — and to the decidedly dehydrated looking Dick Salmon.

Below: Informal meal for "the higher-ups" at Albi, PB and RM, with Fangio being entertained by the perennially star-struck Lorna Berthon.

we now had to refit both BRMs with repaired engines and get them to Dundrod in time for the Ulster Trophy, six days later.

The broken engines returned to Bourne by road, while after a struggle we finally took off from Toulouse at 4.45am on Thursday, June 5, for the 800-mile flight to Belfast. The noise and vibration of the Bristol prevented sleep although we snatched an hour on the grass at Hurn while the 'plane was refuelled. It finally touched-down at Nutts Corner at 11am that day.

Fangio's Albi race engine – '20/1' – had been revived with a replacement stud, but in retrieving the broken stud-end a crankcase tapping had been damaged. After practising briefly at Dundrod this engine was removed and its undamaged heads were used to revive the cooked Albi practice engine '20/2'.

Meanwhile, engine '20/4' had been sitting almost complete at Bourne, but removing its 100-ton head studs proved exceedingly difficult and delayed its completion. By working non-stop, it was hurriedly assembled by Tuesday morning, June 3, and there was no chance even to check it adequately – much less run it up on the dyno – before it was despatched to meet the Albi team in Belfast. Since it had not been run-in it was to be used there only as a last resort.

June 7, 1952 – International Ulster Trophy, Dundrod, Northern Ireland – 34 laps, 252.11 miles

In Belfast, the team set-up shop in Jasper Johnstone's Clarence Engineering Co works off Donegal Street. Colin Atkin had travelled over with Tres and RM's young friend, Peter Romaine.

Tony: We split the team into two shifts and worked round the clock to rectify the overheating, assisted of course by the dank Ulster climate. Moss replaced Gonzalez for his BRM debut race, but we only managed one serviceable car [late] for practice on the Friday evening and it wasn't running at all well because its supercharger was a later type and the tired and inexperienced mechanics had incorrectly connected its volute oil drain.

Fangio still clocked 88.99mph on only his fourth lap against Taruffi's 87.25mph in Vandervell's brand-new *Thin Wall Special* Ferrari with 24-plug V12 engine. Moss then managed a couple of slow laps before the car expired and we took it back to the workshop to change its engine.

The reconditioned V16 had arrived from Bourne to go into Stirling's race car, and at first light on race morning RM ran-in Fangio's fresh engine at Aldergrove Aerodrome. He then drove one BRM and Moss the other up to the circuit, arriving behind the Northern Ireland Prime Minister Sir Basil Brooke's open Austin A40. Moss was worried.

In his brief practice laps, he had found Fangio's BRM feeling far more dangerous than at Monza, despite actually handling better. The problem was the narrow Ulster circuit, composed merely of everyday country roads, hemmed-in by tall hedges and banks which emphasized the car's tendency to wander on the straight. This hadn't bothered him at all on the wide open expanses of Monza, or Folkingham, but Dundrod was an altogether different proposition.

On arriving at the workshop that morning, Moss recalls he was shown to what had been Fangio's car, while the World Champion had Moss' nominated car with the fresh engine – '20/4' – installed. Stirling had agreed in advance to such a change, he was happily No. 2 driver, but what irked him was that nobody told him anything had been changed. The car had his seat installed and wore his number, but he recognized the difference immediately, and was miffed by the secretive manner in which the swap had been made. A new radiator had been fitted to minimize overheating but in the race the header tank relief valve jammed open allowing the system to eject all its water. Having missed official practice, both BRMs started at the back of the grid. Moss later told the story of the race like this:

"When the starter held up the 30 seconds board I put the

June 7, 1952 – Ulster Trophy, Dundrod: Moss in his mac arrives having driven his BRM out to the course from the team garage in Belfast. Considering he had only briefly driven Fangio's mount in practice, he has never been justified in his sincere belief that "BRM switched cars on me". He can only mean that his race car was not that which he had tested so thoroughly at Monza... Note all the cooling mods from Albi the previous weekend.

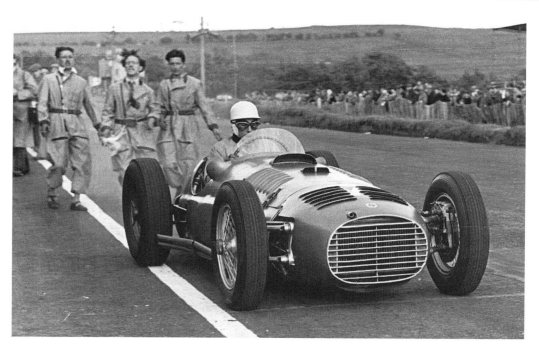

Below: In contrast, Fangio, by the mechanics' estimation, "gave it a real Go" in 'No. 1'. Here he is doing just that, apparently quite unfazed by the V16's queasy handling and straightline wandering on Dundrod's narrow everyday country roads.

clutch out and selected first gear. I always do that earlier than strictly necessary to make absolutely sure I'm in gear when the flag drops. There was about 10 seconds to go when the clutch began to take up and the car began to creep. There was nothing I could do about it as I had the clutch hard down. I had to heel-and-toe…to hold the car still…finally had to put the brakes on quite hard and of course just as the flag was about to fall the clutch burned out and the engine stalled.

"I looked across and saw that Fangio had stalled his engine on the line too, seconds before the flag fell. So when the field roared away in a cloud of spray we were both left there. The mechanics rushed out and push-started us, and we screamed off…

"My clutch was slipping badly and [Fangio] quickly lost me. When I came round the left-hand corner before the hairpin bend I came across Fangio facing me, going backwards…he'd had to take evasive action when 'Bira' – in the OSCA – went through the hedge…

"By the end of the first lap, apart from the bad clutch – which didn't really matter so much as the gearbox was so good – I hadn't even got full revs and the engine was boiling again…on the second lap…the gear lever knob came off in my hand…we were both having trouble getting round the hairpin…we had to slip our clutches.

"After the second lap I came to the pits with chronic overheating…they told me to keep going…" but finally "…they pushed the car away after my fourth lap".

Tony: In the pits we had tried to fix the header tank relief valve but when we tried to remove it the whole device had seized in the tank, and fearful that we would tear the whole thing out of the tank we tried to hold it with a collection of adjustable spanners, for which we were pilloried in the press for not having the proper tools. There was no way of getting it out since it had apparently been damaged during the Albi experience.

Fangio lay third behind Taruffi and – ironically – Hawthorn's

1952 Ulster Trophy: Lap 1 at the Hairpin, Moss locks over 'No. 2' having just been confronted head-on as he rounded the left-hander in the distant background by team leader Fangio's 'No. 1', which the World Champion had spun avoiding 'Bira''s crashing OSCA. The roadway was too narrow for Fangio easily to turn the long BRM around between the banks, so here he's coasting backwards in neutral down to the Hairpin to resume his race. But next day – after an overnight dash to Monza – the dog-tired Fangio will crash his F2 Maserati, break his neck and miss the remainder of the season.

2-litre Formula 2 Cooper-Bristol, but his BRM's exhaust note sounded flat and its tight new engine refused to rev above 9,000rpm. Eventually, after 25 laps, he pulled in. We diagnosed fuel starvation. And it was – the main fuel filter was blocked.

We subsequently found a precipitate which looked like cotton threads in Esso's racing fuel. This material eventually clogged the entire system, and had it not been for that problem Fangio felt confident he could at least have held the lead for a while.

As it was, Taruffi won in Vandervell's *Thin Wall Special*. Alfred Owen, Trust Chairman, was present in person, and he was not at all impressed…

Moss wanted nothing further to do with BRM. On June 11 he wrote to RM:

> Since my return from Belfast, on 8th June, I have given the matter of my position in the B.R.M. Team some considerable thought. You will recall that in our early talks…I made it a condition of my agreement that I would consent to drive the car subject to my approval of its handling capabilities.
>
> I have reluctantly decided that I no longer wish to remain a member of the B.R.M. Team, and would rather that you found a replacement… I shall not be returning the contract…but would like, however, to wish all concerned with this ambitious project the best of luck and success in the future.
>
> Kindest regards to all, together with my deep and sincere thanks for your kindness.

He told the crew later that the car had many good points and for races at Monza or on wide-open circuits like the English airfields it had potential, but for road racing on confined and narrow circuits it frightened him…"and I don't want to drive a car that frightens me…".

Owen subsequently met him at the *Welcombe Hotel*, Stratford, and felt he had talked him round, and as late as June 25, RM wrote to tell him:

> …we are entering two cars for Silverstone on July 19th and for Boreham on August 2nd. One car to be

driven by you and the other, in the absence of Fangio…by Gonzalez…

In fact Stirling remained unmoved – he would never race the V16 again.

Meanwhile, Fangio had been booked to drive a Formula 2 Maserati at Monza the day after the Ulster Trophy. He had intended to fly out that evening with 'Bira', but after his first lap accident 'Bira' had flown out alone. Fangio then took a scheduled flight with Rosier as far as Paris, drove with him down to Lyons and then – still unable to find an available flight to Milan – borrowed the Frenchman's car to drive himself overnight direct to Monza. He started the Italian race clearly fatigued in his ACA Maserati A6GCM. In his own words: "I arrived at Monza at 2, started the race at 2.30 and was in hospital by 3…". He had suffered a monumental accident which broke his neck and put him out for the rest of the season. [59]

Tony: When we had a chance to sit back and reflect upon the Albi/Dundrod period it was clear that within the space of 10 days or so we had gone from arriving at Albi in considerable optimism to leaving Dundrod with our tails well and truly between our legs – deep, deep back into the depths of despair…

Alfred Owen was dismayed, telling Donald McCullough – not altogether fairly in view of the fuel precipitate problem:

> …with five days to get from Albi to Dundrod and change the engines completely in the two cars…this resulted in just bad work. Neither of the two cars at Dundrod should have failed. Both were caused by just rank bad maintenance. To let Fangio's car go into the race without the filters being cleaned was shocking…and with regard to Stirling Moss's car it is better to leave it as a closed book.
>
> While I appreciate the view that the car has become a joke in the minds of the Music Hall star and certain

---

59. This incident persuaded the CSI to move towards banning drivers from competing in two major races on two different circuits within the space of 24 hours. Sixteen years later this same regulation would upset BRM plans, again at Monza.

members of the Press it has entailed much development work (and discovery). The world is always hard for pioneers but even if we fail I am sure history will record that we tried hard to succeed in spite of what some people imagine and would like to say.

At Bourne, PB diagnosed the cause of the Albi overheating as too-small radiators. Tony disagreed but was shouted down, and no attempt was made to investigate any further. Fangio's latest '20/4' engine had survived 25 laps at Dundrod and was considered "a very good one".

On inspection, Moss' hapless '20/2' unit was found to have one head cracked at the plug holes, therefore becoming scrap, while the head sealing rings showed darkening, a sign of possible gas leakage causing overheating. Its crankshaft bearings were also very tight indeed, and it was found that two big-end bearing caps had been refitted the wrong way round during the general chaos. Some little-end bearings were also tight, possibly due to overheating. An extensive rebuild began to salvage most of this unit, in the course of which its block was then found to be porous and so was despatched for impregnation.

The cars were immediately modified with enormous new radiators, plus all the associated larger pumps and piping which that entailed, and requiring an unsightly new nose-top blister to help accommodate them. The hastily-cut Albi louvres remained, some more were added, and two cars were prepared – in what would effectively prove to be their definitive form but their last in metallic pale green livery – for the British GP meeting at Silverstone on July 19.

Desmond Scannell of the BRDC had followed his Continental peers in adopting Formula 2 to qualify the British GP for World Championship status, but back at the start of May – when de Harlez of the Belgian Club had announced the *GP d'Europe*'s change-over to Formula 2 – Walter Hill of the BRMA had lobbied Bourne to press *The Daily Express* to squeeze a *Formule Libre* event into the BRDC's May Silverstone meeting, which the newspaper sponsored. This proved impossible at such short notice, but Tom Blackburn, General Manager of Associated Newspapers, subsequently pressured Scannell into including a special 103-mile *Formule Libre* supporting race in his British GP meeting in July, largely to give BRM a run. In addition, *The Daily Mail* backed a combined F1/F2 race in the West Essex Car Club meeting at Boreham Aerodrome on August 2.

PB remained highly sceptical of Scannell's motives, confiding (wrong-headedly) to Alfred Owen:

It has been our firm belief that the Scannell anti-B.R.M. campaign and the promotion of Formula II for Grand Prix races, would probably come unstuck before this season was through. We were well aware that Formula II…would prove a pathetic spectacle… In spite of our failures, there is still a strong following for the B.R.M…no doubt that if we show fast lap times and stamina in the next few races, there is going to be a demand for the cars to appear in the main races which the race organisers will find difficult to ignore.

Scannell already sees the 'writing on the wall', and is preparing a back door in the form of this 100-mile race, but he is still approaching us with his old tricks of suggesting little starting money and *that* only to be decided when the cars appear in official practice…

By June 25, RM had test-driven the ex-Fangio Dundrod car at Folkingham and that afternoon Gonzalez took it out to explore cooling performance with its new enlarged radiator. He had arrived with the front of his loaned Standard Vanguard stove-in. Tony: When I asked what had happened he explained that on the country roads on the way up to the airfield he'd

July 17, 1952 – Formule Libre Trophy, British Grand Prix meeting, Silverstone: An uncharacteristically grimly reflective RM seated in 'No. 2', in which Ken Wharton is about to make his team debut. Now the British Grand Prix is for Formula 2, and the V16s can only face Ferrari in this supporting race. Equally thoughtful are mechanic Gordon Newman and (beyond) prewar Auto Union Chief Engineer Prof Dr Robert Eberan von Eberhorst, postwar of ERA, Aston Martin, Jowett, etc…

1952 Libre Trophy, Silverstone: Geoffrey Goddard's classic shot of Gonzalez hurling his BRM 'No. I' round Silverstone. Eventually he leaned so far out of the window that he 'fell out'. Below: Gonzalez limping his battered 'No. I' through Woodcote Corner after hurtling off through the wickets at Stowe Corner and having a timber stake removed from the car's damaged radiator and steering. In practice this pale metallic-green BRM had its new nose-top blister coded yellow (Wharton's was red), and white race numbers were applied direct upon body colour. But officialdom insisted on black-on-white discs for raceday.

hit a pig. Its owner appeared almost immediately and pronounced it dead and after considerable excitement conveyed to Gonzalez that it had been the future mainstay of his family and persuaded him to part with £50! We went to see the farmer and won a rebate of at least £20 which we returned to Gonzalez, much to his delight. I lived in the village pub in those days and about a year later the local pig killer presented me with a joint of pork which he felt I ought to accept, since it was apparently the pig which Gonzalez had run down! It had evidently survived to oink another day. When I next saw Gonzalez I told him this story, and thereafter, if we ever visited a restaurant together, he would always make a point of ordering pork for me.

Meantime, Ken Wharton was called-up for his first BRM race in place of Moss, and all eyes turned towards Silverstone…

July 19, 1952 – BRDC *Formule Libre* Trophy, Silverstone – 35 laps, 102.45 miles

Ferrari had entered Luigi Villoresi in an 'Indianapolis'-type 375, while Piero Taruffi reappeared in Vandervell's *Thin Wall Special*, both using unsupercharged 24-plug 4½-litre V12 engines.

Below: After taking over Ken Wharton's 'No. 2', 'Pepe' rampaged back into the race, as here, after passing 'Chico' Landi's private Ferrari 375 Camelli and shortly before 'The Pampas Bull' uprooted the hapless V16's gearchange.

Gonzalez's modified BRM, with engine '20/4', damaged its nearside-rear hub bearing and the hub itself at Folkingham on the Wednesday before the race. The quickest means of repair that night was to transfer the entire de Dion assembly from the 95 per cent-completed 'No. 3' car. Wharton's, meanwhile, used engine '20/2' – he drove it round Folkingham in 1:42 that Wednesday – and then during first Silverstone practice on the Thursday, Gonzalez set a new unofficial lap record at 97.57mph and on Friday confirmed his BRM on pole position with an even faster record lap of 1:47.0, 98.48mph, against Villoresi's best of 1:49.0. Wharton's best time was 1:53.0, which equalled Taruffi's, so the four-strong front row of the starting grid was arranged BRM-Ferrari-BRM-Ferrari – exactly what Formula 1 enthusiasts had ordered...

Taruffi and Villoresi led from the flag while both BRMs made typically slow starts, being overwhelmed by the 'Bira' OSCA, the private Ferraris of Rosier and Landi, and others. But by the end of that opening lap, Gonzalez lay second behind Taruffi with Wharton sixth. By lap 5 Gonzalez had closed to within 4 seconds of the *Thin Wall Special*, but the Stewards had in fact penalized Taruffi 30sec for jumping the start, so the BRM was actually holding a comfortable 26sec lead.

Ignorant of this true situation, Gonzalez really pressed on until, as he entered Stowe Corner on lap 8, he spun wildly and ploughed through the marker-hurdles there. His car's vast new radiator was ruptured by a stake and its steering bent, and the chubby Argentine driver limped it into the pits, stopping *en route* for marshals to disentangle the stake from its steering. At the pits, he was quivering with rage when he fell from the cockpit and Tony guessed what he wanted without recourse to the interpreter: I gave him the flag to signal Wharton in.

He nearly hit Ken over the head with it as he went by in third place, but Ken came straight in knowing what he was expected to do. Just as he started to get out he gave the throttle a jab to avoid stalling. Gonzalez misinterpreted his motives, thought he was about to take off again and just dragged him bodily from the cockpit before cramming himself in and rocketing off, all the while cursing loudly in Spanish...

Whether that car was faster than his original we have no way of knowing, but he certainly drove it faster!

The change-over had cost 20sec, and after 15 laps – with Villoresi and the penalized Taruffi dead-level on elapsed time, Gonzalez was 49sec behind but closing fast. As Taruffi established a clear lead despite his 30sec penalty, it became clear that Gonzalez would catch the slowing Villoresi for second place. Three times – twice in his first car, and significantly once in Wharton's – he lapped at 1:49.0, 96.67mph, though Taruffi equalled this new record. Then on lap 33 the BRM was suddenly overdue...

Eventually it toured into sight, slowly heading into the pit-lane and Gonzalez stepped out regretfully. Its gearbox bevels had broken and the pudgy Argentine's electrifying drive was over...

By this time the team really needed to achieve something concrete, but at least at Silverstone the cars had shown real speed and some staying power.

Autosport's editorial the following week declared:

> Although the B.R.M. failed once again, the Bourne people are to be praised for a plucky attempt to overcome their jinx...Gonzalez's tremendous bid with both cars was as exciting as anything ever seen on the circuit.

Gregor Grant added:

> Disappointment at Gonzalez's last-minute retirement was not exclusive in the BRM pits, the crowd showing considerable sympathy for Bourne in their latest failure. May the pendulum of luck swing BRM's way at Boreham a fortnight hence.

But the old adversary, *Motor Sport,* offered a harsher perspective. Its report admitted:

> Gonzalez…thrilled everyone present with a stupendous attempt to retrieve B.R.M.'s precarious position. He drove like one possessed, spectators and marshals alike waving him on. Regardless of the wheel-flap out of corners, refusing to give way to anyone, he screamed round the course…

This stirring overture was then countered by:

> Let us…face a few facts. Due to the noise of the V16 engine, Gonzalez seemed to be going like an atom-bomb. Actually, he proved that his limit in both B.R.M.s was exactly that of Taruffi in the old Ferrari…which had something not quite right about its suspension. The atom-bomb was elsewhere, in the gearbox, which couldn't face less than 100 miles of this sort of racing. B.R.M. have found the driver but cannot produce a worthwhile racing car…if Ken, holding third place, had been left alone, he would almost certainly have finished third, without having to push the frail machine as Gonzalez had to, to regain that position, to ultimately burst…

Back at Folkingham it was decided that the Wharton/Gonzalez car's gearbox had stripped its input bevels' teeth: "…due to insufficient strength in the washers and collars which are used to take the thrust load to the ball thrust bearings. Unfortunately the gearbox casing has, by reason of this gear breakage, been damaged to the point of scrapping…".

On strip-down, that car's engine – '20/2' – was found to have broken several teeth from its duplex gears output shaft, "possibly caused by…the general shock to the transmission when the bevel drive in the gearbox failed…".

The fatal damage sustained by Gonzalez's original car was confined to its holed radiator and a fractured track-rod end ball pivot pin, new and stronger pins being promised by Lockheed for Friday, July 25.

All this was unknown to Alfred Owen when he wrote to 'Sammy' Davis, former Bentley Boy-turned-Sports Editor of *The Autocar* – and also consultant to the Boreham organizers – on July 24:

> Frankly…Gonzalez was responsible…for both B.R.M.s being out of action. On the first he came into the corner too fast…and in the second instance he jammed the gear selector. Actually the car could have been driven in fourth gear where it was jammed to the finish, as the

jamming was cleared in fairly quick time and I gather from Ray it was only Gonzalez's brutality which caused the jamming…

Although the cause might have been identical, Cliff Mander's report quoted above – and dated two days later – better understood the effect, which had indeed been terminal.

The Boreham race meeting was sponsored by *The Daily Mail* and the same cars were prepared at Folkingham, but it had now been decided to repaint them so they would not show dirty finger marks so easily. Tony: Lorna Berthon chose the new colour, which was known as 'Dark Lust' – for 'Lustrous' – 'Green', and provided you remembered to shake the tin I quite liked the metallic dark green finish.

Aubrey Woods: "RM had really hated the original pale green BRM colour, and at one stage I believe he tried to have British racing colours changed to dark blue, because he always loved blues. The Trust had chosen the pale green metallic colour which we'd used through 1951 – I think that was the first time we'd seen metal flake in paint – and then Dockers kind of added some dark blue to it." Only the blower air intake 'snout' above the new radiator cowls survived, for this one race, in the old pale metallic green on Wharton's car, while Gonzalez's was painted white.

Boreham provided the last significant event of the season open to Formula 1 cars. The team suffered its usual all-night sessions, and when the crew returned to their village pub for breakfast the landlord's huge dog refused them entry… situation normal for BRM…

'No. 1' car was assembled with early engine '11/4' and new-type gearbox '11/1' installed, while 'No. 2' car carried engine '20/2' with gearbox '11/2' – ex-Wharton/Gonzalez, Silverstone, resurrected with a casing supplied for what should have been the team's sixth transmission. Both cars ran disc brakes.

The Boreham perimeter-track circuit combined very fast open curves with a long uphill straight. It was potentially much faster than Silverstone, and practice began there on Thursday, July 31. Villoresi reappeared in the works 'Indianapolis' Ferrari 375, taking pole position at 103.45mph. Gonzalez ended up second fastest at 101.69, flanked by Landi's Ferrari (99.09) and Wharton (96.26) – but Vandervell had demanded more start money for his *Thin Wall Special* than *The Daily Mail* would underwrite, so it did not appear.

August 2, 1952 – *The Daily Mail* International Trophy, Boreham Aerodrome – 67 laps, 201 miles

On race day, drizzle began which became a downpour during the first half of the main race. RM later reported:

> Anybody's guess was as good as anybody else's as to…rain stopping and the track rapidly drying out. Depending on which guess one chose…we had the alternatives of fitting new rear tyres or using part worn ones. If…the surface would be awash throughout, the second course would be the right one; it is axiomatic that water-cooled and 'lubricated' tyres last better than dry

August 2, 1952 – Daily Mail *International Trophy*, Boreham: Wonderful scene as 30 assorted Formula 1 and 2 cars take off on the rain-slick aerodrome surface, Landi's Ferrari 375 leading away from Rosier's sister car (right), eventual winner Luigi Villoresi in the factory Indianapolis Ferrari 375 (left), the wheel-spinning Gonzalez (25), slithering Wharton (26) and long-time race leader Mike Hawthorn's giant-killing Cooper-Bristol (behind Villoresi). Moss is next up on the nearside in the bulky one-off G-Type ERA-Bristol.

Left: Ken Wharton battling on through treacherous puddles in the repainted dark lustrous green 'No. 2' after Gonzalez had crashed 'No. 1'. The nose-top blisters introduced over the new outsize radiators at Silverstone were still colour-coded the same way.

ones, and furthermore partly worn casings present a considerably flatter surface to the road than new ones.[60]

Our guess, however, being that the weather would clear up, new covers were fitted, giving relatively poor traction. This guess proved to be the right one – up to a point…

As the flag fell Gonzalez's BRM hung fire with terrific wheelspin on the streaming startline while the Ferrari 375s of Villoresi, Landi and Rosier led away. One report read:

> Gonzalez is not using his head. In his efforts to come to the front he is making the BRM go all over the place, sliding this way and that as he tries to conquer wheelspin and keep the car straight… It is only a matter of time before Gonzalez either shunts someone else or leaves the circuit. He chooses the latter course; after tailing Rosier on lap three as they come up the pits grandstand straight, he hurls the BRM into Hangar Bend at an impossible speed and comes through backwards in the throes of the great-grandfather of all slides…the car quits the road abruptly in a shower of straw and mud, scattering spectators in all directions and finishing up as a badly-battered BRM against someone's parked motor-car. It was tragic for Bourne, but it was entirely the fault of Gonzalez…

Wharton seemed completely out of his depth, largely due to his disc brakes grabbing unpredictably. While Mike Hawthorn's modest little 2-litre unsupercharged F2 Cooper-Bristol led all the Ferraris in the wet, it actually lapped the BRM twice. The press made much from this fact – such as:

> Contrast between the elaborate BRM workshop set-up and the converted bus used by Coopers was most marked…The BRM debacle was complete when Wharton retired with gearbox trouble after 61 more or less humiliating laps…

According to BRM's records, Ken had actually completed only 58 laps when his 'No. 2' car's rebuilt transmission again stripped its bevels. Despite having been: "…rebuilt with greatly strengthened supporting collars and sleeves for the end thrust bearings taking the thrust load from the input bevels…it is found that the stronger collars and sleeves have proved capable of supporting the thrust to the bearings

without failure, but nevertheless the input bevel gears have failed, stripping off the teeth of both gears…".

RM publicly attributed this second successive bevel-gear failure to poor heat-treatment, but really it seemed that: "the new design gearbox casing, made to incorporate the brake pump, is not so strong at the bearing housing for the bevel gear as was the old type casing. This…would account for this only happening with this new type gearbox."

The damage to Gonzalez's battered 'No. 1' car was confined mainly to its bodywork, repair cost being estimated as £500–£600 "if the front fuel tank is repairable – if not, a further £450 will be claimed for cost of a new tank…".

DEFEAT

This Boreham debacle almost completely negated BRM's strong showing at Silverstone.

Five days later Sammy Davis offered these very perceptive and fair observations to Alfred Owen in a letter from his home in Waldens Park Road, Horsell, Woking. In fact the experienced old veteran was hitting the nail right on the head:

> It is the project which matters and what I say is an endeavour to help. I agree the car is probably faster than its rivals but I think there is a possibility it has characteristics which are unsuitable to modern racing…I think the car is undesirably difficult to drive… Now it is always possible to blame drivers and certainly you did not have the right men for Silverstone and Boreham…
>
> Now comes the difficult part. My distinct impression is that the best drivers are unwilling to drive the B.R.M. not because of the car but because they do not feel they can trust the management and do not like the set-up or the method of preparation.
>
> This has been so for years even in the days of the E.R.A… If you can get Moss to talk you will find that he is definitely sure he was double-crossed. The other good British drivers are all chary of going near Peter and to a certain extent Ray remembering what happened before and the trouble with Cook. Uninstructed opinion is that the whole thing is run not as a business but as a game out of which comes a good living in the best of circumstances for those concerned but not the drivers. [Regarding Government or SMMT backing] …certain enquiries [by them] among the racing world has resulted in a good deal being said that would have been better unsaid because of the active dislike for the people concerned that I have mentioned already.
>
> Yet Ray's ideal is high and his enthusiasm great and he has no intention whatsoever of creating a feeling of which he is probably entirely ignorant.

Davis was often regarded, even then, as a waffly old buffer, and although his words accurately defined the situation, Alfred Owen largely dismissed them.

Donald McCullough was still, however, a valued friend. He wrote of Boreham:

---

60. This of course contradicts modern knowledge, with slick tyres for dry conditions, or deep-treaded tyres to ensure drainage and prevent aquaplaning in the wet. RM's account was contradicted by an Alfred Owen letter to S.C.H. Davis, 15-8-52: "No tyres suitable for wet weather [were] available to us, and secondly the tyres we had were brand new and the pressure was too high, but in this respect I am told very definitely that the Dunlop people were sitting in the pits and utterly refused to let our staff reduce the pressure although they saw in the Ferrari pit the tyres were considerably reduced in pressure when the weather was so wet."

He added that "Gonzalez was broken hearted over the fact that he had been driven off the course…" presumably by Rosier whom he was attempting to overtake at the time of his departure if not from the straight and narrow, then from the sideways but secure?

I am afraid it was final evidence that either the car is not good enough or the organisation is ineffective. There is a great temptation to feel that we should be well advised to cut our losses... But as I see it, there are two arguments in favour of carrying on:

(i) we have at least set up the machinery for pooling resources to produce a racing car...

(ii) owing to the fantastic amount of public interest in the car, it is now only necessary for any comedian to mention the B.R.M. to bring the house down. This is humiliating for all of us, but at the same time it shows the extent of public interest in the country and if we can once start to win, the car will become the biggest box office draw in motor racing.

Owen convened a board meeting on August 14 to discuss the future, and next day he circularized supporters as follows:

THE BRITISH RACING MOTOR RESEARCH TRUST

15th August, 1952.

Nearly two years ago, the whole structure of the Trust and its operating Company was re-organized and financial support received, partly dependent on the attaining of success in racing. It is felt that having once more nearly used up those funds and not having achieved the success hoped for, we should take stock and ask ourselves "What is the next stage?". Let us, therefore, sum up the situation as we see it.

1) That the cars, whilst overcoming many technical difficulties, are still not fully developed...with lack of competition in Formula 1 events which has shortened the life of that Formula, there seems little justification for completing further costly development.

2) The project has relied in the past two years upon a hard core of large scale backing. There are positive indications that such support is no longer available...due to lack of success in racing and a certain lack of confidence in our activities with our limited technical facilities.

3) In view of the above points, it is not possible, as it stands, to develop cars to conform to the new Formula I ...and it is felt there is no point in developing Formula II cars.

The assets of British Racing Motors Ltd are held by the B.R.M. Trust. The Executive Council of the Trust which by nomination is also the Board of B.R.M. Ltd, feels reluctantly bound to recommend to the Trust the sale of the assets of the Company and, if this cannot be achieved, the closing down of its activities which would entail its winding up...

...We regret that these recommendations should have to be made, as there seems ground for believing that we should soon be demonstrating in actual races good performances – we had hoped to win for Britain in a Formula Grand Prix, a success not achieved since 1923 – but that is impossible now.

We make or offer no excuses for not having attained our goal and simply point out once more that we have no right to carry on beyond our resources. A General Meeting has, therefore been called...

– at the *Welcombe Hotel*, Stratford, at 10.00am, on September 4.

Meanwhile, following a suggestion by Robert Walling of *The Evening Standard*, RM had reacted to Mike Hawthorn's sensational performances in Bob Chase's privately-entered Cooper-Bristol by inviting the tall young man from Farnham to test a BRM at Folkingham, on Sunday, August 10.

He suggested that if all went well Hawthorn could drive a BRM in the forthcoming *Libre* race at Turnberry in Scotland, two weeks later. Coincidentally, Tony Vandervell offered him a rival drive there in the *Thin Wall Special*.

Mike Hawthorn recalled: "I went up to Bourne to try the BRM first. I met Mays and Berthon and got into the car; they pushed me off. But it was no use – it was incredibly quick, the acceleration was fantastic, but every time I came to a corner and went below 8,000rpm, the power went right off. You would come out of the corner with the revs down and as you accelerated it would just fluff and burble; then, suddenly, as you reached the 8,000 mark the full power would come in with a bang and you had a job to hold the car straight. At over 8,000 revs it really did motor, but the steering was nothing to write home about. I made the mistake of doing my first lap without earplugs and that nearly shattered my eardrums. The noise was incredible. I told Mays that I had got to try the *Thin Wall* first and then I would let him know...".

He chose to drive Vandervell's Ferrari at Turnberry, and through GAV would join the great Italian works team for the following season. Ray, however, reported to the BRMA:

> ...Young Hawthorn looked and was right at home in the B.R.M. from the first moment he stepped into the cockpit and, after eighteen or twenty laps of this far from billiard-table circuit, said he was delighted with its handling and road-holding. His times confirmed this good opinion.

Turnberry was merely a National meeting, open only to holders of British competition licences, so Gonzalez could not run there. Despite Reg Parnell having publicly criticized BRM the previous year, when explaining why he no longer wished to drive for the team after the Monza fiasco, he now accepted Ray's offer to replace Gonzalez, alongside Ken Wharton, at Turnberry. Perhaps the appearance of a complimentary article by-lined to Parnell in the August 10 issue of *The Sunday Express* was not pure coincidence?

August 23, 1952 – *The Scottish Express* National Trophy, Turnberry, Scotland – 20 laps, 34 miles

The Scottish Car Club's short aerodrome circuit at Turnberry on the Ayrshire coast was quite bumpy, the faster cars becoming airborne in some places. Mike Hawthorn set fastest practice time there of 1:16, 83.36mph, in the *Thin Wall Special* with Ken Wharton's disc-braked BRM 'No. 2' – using

August 23, 1952 – National Trophy, Turnberry: Mike Hawthorn (dark helmet and bow tie) elected to drive Vandervell's ThinWall Special rather than a BRM here in Scotland, and he has vacated the car to ensure the feverish BRM crew have time to repair a minor fault on Reg Parnell's newly-assembled 'No. 3' on the grid. Wharton waits quietly in 'No. 2' (race number 52) while Ron Flockhart completes the front row in ERA 'R4D' (48), which he has bought from RM. Right: Parnell and Wharton steal the lead at flagfall as Hawthorn's sportsmanship is poorly rewarded by a gearbox full of neutrals...

engine '20/3' and ex-Gonzalez car gearbox '11/1' – next quickest, one second slower. Parnell was giving the brand-new 'No. 3' BRM its race debut, using engine '20/4', old-type gearbox 'Mark 1/2' and drum brakes. This car was actually based upon chassis frame '1/4' and had been completed at snail's pace employing many salvaged components from the now discarded original prototype 1949/50 'Test Car', frame '1/1'. That original frame had itself long since been employed as the basis of a body-builder's buck – and the balance of evidence is that it was eventually scrapped.

On the startline, one of the high-pressure fuel lines running across Parnell's engine now split. Tony: We cut a piece of rubber hose to slip over the split and were still working on the car, jubilee-clipping this repair, as start time approached. Mike Hawthorn was alongside in the *Thin Wall* and, seeing our feverish activity, he strolled across and simply said: "Take your time, they can't start without us", and just stood by apparently unconcerned, watching while our repair was completed.

Once we had restarted Reg's engine, Hawthorn said: "Right, let's go racing" and sauntered back to his car.

His reward for this super gesture was then to be stranded on the startline, unable to find a gear, while Reg rushed off into an immediate lead with Ken second!

Reg's gear-knob then came away in his hand, and he waved Ken past to take the lead while retaining second place, changing gear with the bare lever. Ken looked set fair to head a BRM 1-2 finish until a proprietary steering-ball – not the

BRM-made steering arm itself – broke on his eighth lap approaching Maiden's Corner. Fortunately he wrestled his car to a halt without hitting anything.

Hawthorn retired, and so 'the BRM' had scored its third race win, and in every case the victorious driver had been Reg Parnell...

An enthusiastic Scottish crowd mobbed Parnell and his car, and in the hotel afterwards RM stood the elated mechanics a decent meal and a drink with the tolerantly teetotal and equally happy Alfred Owen footing the bill. He wrote about Turnberry to a friend:

I was always extremely keen that we should give Reg Parnell an opportunity as virtually he is the only driver who has managed to keep the B.R.M. on the road and complete its course...it was only his personal good judgement after taking the lead and not over-driving the car which was popping badly at speed which enabled the car to finish. The filter and the pump were full of dirt but whether the responsibility is Esso or B.R.M. I do not know but apparently this mixture with high alcoholic content deteriorates when stored and Esso state that B.R.M. have been holding this petrol far too long whilst B.R.M. state that Esso have only just delivered most of it. I am of the opinion that there has been laxity on the part of B.R.M. in mixing old and new petrol. Any way we won and the victory was a great personal triumph for Reg Parnell who was virtually unable to

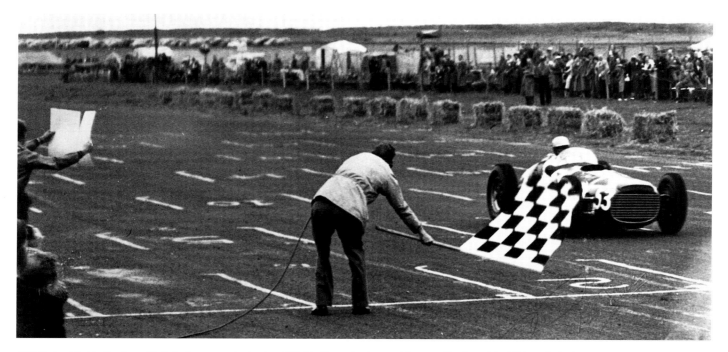

1952 National Trophy, Turnberry: 'Uncle Reg' stammers the victorious BRM 'No. 3' past the chequered flag – notching his and the BRM team's third outright victory, and over the longest race distance yet. At Folkingham, in essence, each V16 had a senior mechanic with a two-man floating support crew – ex-RAF Halton apprentice, Fairey Battle air gunner Jack North in charge of 'No. 1', ex-Tank Corps/REME Sergeant Gordon Newman 'No. 2' and Maurice Dove 'No. 3'.

move from his car for at least an hour after he won…

Autosport commented on Reg's win and Ken's failure for BRM:

> This adds up to a wonderful choice of ammunition for both the 'give them another chance' school and the 'drop them in the sea now' fraternity…
>
> No one can deny, however, that when the BRM goes it is a magnificent car to watch and I count it as one of this season's most thrilling experiences to have seen and *heard* two of the cars go roaring down the home stretch at Turnberry…

However, *Motor Sport* remained implacably derisive, and for those with the eyes to see, chillingly realistic:

> Let us debunk any idea that Turnberry was the turning point in B.R.M. fortunes. Mike Hawthorn…was experiencing serious gearbox trouble, but before his retirement lapping in 1min. 16secs. whereas the best B.R.M. time was 1min. 17.6secs. This was slower than Hawthorn's best Formula II lap in the Cooper-Bristol![61]

61. This sentence is very misleading, *Motor Sport*'s contemporary high standards slipping badly. Hawthorn actually won the Turnberry F2 race in a Connaught A-Type, not his usual Bob Chase-owned Cooper-Bristol. Strangely, amongst the Turnberry meeting reports in the specialist 'comics' – *Autosport, The Motor* and *The Autocar* – none published fastest-lap data for any race other than the National Trophy, but Hawthorn's best practice lap in the Connaught that weekend was reported as being 1min 20sec, actually 2.4sec *slower* than the BRM.

In this race of 35 miles Wharton's B.R.M. fell out after less than 12½…while Parnell's finished with a broken gear lever and suffering from noticeable fuel starvation. Its speed was 79.5mph and Gaze's pre-war 2.9 Maserati was always about 300 yards behind the B.R.M. in spite of possessing very tired brakes. There was, in fact, no modern opposition at all to trouble this sick B.R.M. of Parnell's…

It is not surprising that the B.R.M. Trust has at last thrown-in the sponge and has offered the B.R.M. concern for sale…Raymond Mays' idea was an excellent one, but his ability to put it into practice was, like the cars which he fathered, not so hot.

Upon strip-down at Folkingham, it was discovered that Wharton's Turnberry engine had lost a small piece of No. 16 cylinder liner spigot, broken at an undercut. Parnell's winning engine had suffered similarly, but in this case the broken pieces were found loose in the cylinder where they had badly mauled both the piston crown and the cylinder head…little wonder that Alfred Owen had observed the engine 'popping badly at speed'. Redesigned liners with a small radius instead of an undercut at this point were ordered 'rush' from Brico; there were still two race dates remaining on the team's makeshift 1952 calendar.

But meanwhile 35 Trust members attended the Extraordinary General Meeting on September 4 at the *Welcombe Hotel*.

After Alfred Owen had made his introductory comments and various minor queries had been settled, J.R. Moore of Speciality Instruments proposed, and Denis Flather of W.T. Flather Ltd seconded, a motion "to sell the business of British

Racing Motors Limited as a going concern…". This and six more subsidiary motions were carried unanimously. A month was allowed for offers to be made for the cars and equipment. Only offers from British buyers were to be considered, and the use of the title 'BRM' would not be permitted. Raymond Mays was to recall: "We did not want its name dragged into disrepute." He was asked to value the cars, and as there would soon be no races for them he could only suggest their scrap value – around £500 each.

How that must have stuck in his throat…one's heart cannot help but go out to him. For all his faults – his blindness to his own and his closest associate's selfish shortcomings, his lack of application, his blind priority to place his and PB's convenience above the team's best interests – the great project which had dominated so much of his life was collapsing around him…£500 – scrap value.

But during the month that this offer was open, the three V16 BRMs were entered for the final Goodwood International, Gonzalez returning to accompany Parnell and Wharton, Fangio still being *hors de combat* recovering from his Monza injuries.

For the Goodwood meeting, 'No. 1' car was equipped with engine '20/1' and repaired gearbox 'Mark 11/3'; car 'No. 2' used engine '20/2' and gearbox '11/1'; and car 'No. 3' carried engine '20/3' and gearbox 'Mark 11/2'. This latest car had also been converted onto disc brakes to match its older sisters and its engine was described by Cliff Mander as: "…giving the best performance of all…running up to 13,000rpm without misfiring!"

Tony: We had been bothered for some time by a peculiar power loss accompanied by the odd exhaust note which Tres had christened 'burbling'. It took a few laps' running to develop, and had recurred after the fitting of the larger radiators. It could be cured temporarily by changing the plugs. Carburation adjustment could alleviate the problem, but not eliminate it.

Gonzalez, Parnell and Wharton had all test-driven at Folkingham and Gonzalez was very pleased with his 'No. 1' car though he was unable to try 'No. 3' as it wasn't quite ready. Subsequently, RM drove it "in final testing and adjustments in order to get the ultimate". Mander reported to Owen:

> I may be proved wrong but it is my feeling that we really have, in the first and third cars, two cars capable of winning in both the Goodwood races…

This was his last BRM Production Report, as he was being recalled to mainstream Rubery Owen duties at Darlaston.

For Goodwood the cars were using a very low gear ratio and one of the engines began burbling while RM was testing it at Folkingham. Tony: We played around with all kinds of carburettor needles. We used to make our own from quarter-inch diameter blanks supplied by SU. After a few needle changes and adjustments, RM came in to report the problem cured and said he was seeing "…an honest 12,000 at the first intersection". Soon after, I noticed the mechanics looking puzzled and found that in error we had fitted a blank needle – nothing more than quarter-inch bar!

The engine simply should not have run, since its mixture would have been over 50 per cent weak, but in fact it had run very nicely… So we fitted the next-best needles and all three engines subsequently ran well at Goodwood. Our brows were furrowed.

During practice there, the front nearside piston in Parnell's engine burned through. This was not unknown, and gave us further food for thought. It was possible to change this piston – and only this piston – with the engine still installed in the car. The head and supercharger had to be removed, and then the piston and rod could just about be withdrawn through the supercharger opening. The law of maximum cussedness never normally worked in our favour, so why should it always be this piston which burned?

We duly fitted a replacement and ran it in by jacking-up the rear wheels in the wash-bay of our garage in Chichester, playing a hose on the radiator, and running-up the engine in first gear. When we started up, a fishpaste executive opposite had just got a long-distance telephone call through to Edinburgh. He was not pleased.

September 27, 1952 – *Formule Libre* Woodcote Cup, Goodwood – 5 laps, 12 miles

For this event the three much-louvred, dark green BRMs lined-up on the front row with Gonzalez and Parnell sandwiching Vandervell's *Thin Wall Special*. Hawthorn had crashed his Cooper-Bristol at Modena and was in hospital, and Dr Farina was driving GAV's car.

Ever since the fuel filter clogging at Dundrod the BRMs had been fitted with an enormous fuel filter in the cockpit, between the pump and the carburettors, holding about a gallon. The drivers had to switch-off the fuel on the grid to prevent flooding and then switch on again before restarting. Wharton had switched off on his way to the grid so his engine cut by itself, having emptied the filter bowl, as he arrived. It took time to refill the filter by pushing the car, and when his engine refused to restart at the two-minute signal the mechanics pushed Ken halfway to Madgwick Corner before giving up and wheeling it off onto the inside verge to sit it out. Fortunately Gonzalez more than compensated for this latest very public BRM failure by winning easily from Farina – who made a bad start – with Parnell third, 10sec separating the two BRMs.

And while accelerating out of the chicane on its last lap, the *Thin Wall* stripped its crownwheel, leaving Farina a non-starter in the main event.

September 27, 1952 – *The Daily Graphic Formule Libre* Goodwood Trophy – 15 laps, 36 miles

Despite the *Thin Wall*'s absence, the ear-splitting din from the three V16s on the front row – Wharton's having now been easily revived – electrified the crowd and simply deafened the thin opposition ranged behind them.

Gonzalez and Parnell ran 1-2 throughout, while Wharton had to displace Alan Brown's cheeky Cooper-Bristol – with which had made a catapult start to snatch an initial lead

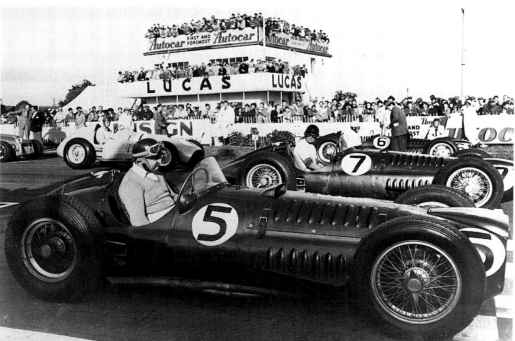

September 27, 1952 – Woodcote Cup, Goodwood: From 1952–54 a tremendous Formule Libre rivalry evolved between Tony Vandervell's ThinWall Special Ferrari as driven here (far side) by Dr Farina, and the BMRRT/Owen Racing Organisation BRM V16s such as 'No. 3', equipped since Turnberry with disc brakes, and entrusted here to Froilan Gonzalez – who will score its second consecutive race win. The third followed later this same afternoon in the Goodwood Trophy, for which 'Pepe' lined-up alongside Wharton's 'No. 2' and Parnell in 'No. 1' – and they achieved BRM's only 1-2-3 race finish.

towards the first corner. Ken got by starting the second lap, and the BRMs bawled round thereafter first, second and third.

Never mind the opposition – standing beside the track Dave Turner loved every moment of it: "I'd built all of them engines and there they were really letting rip and sounding just fantastic! After all we'd been through, and all the rubbish thrown at us for years, I reckon that Goodwood race with the BRMs first, second and third like that was one of the proudest moments of my life…".

Reg set fastest lap, at a record 1:35.6, 90.38mph, but his car was burbling noticeably almost throughout. He was intent on showing his worth against Gonzalez and it's doubtful if his new piston enjoyed much running-in. He finished with the engine boiling, but he finished – and BRM had achieved that rare motor racing distinction at any level, a 1-2-3 result.

Alfred Owen had left Goodwood before the race but confessed to Donald McCullough it had been: "…very pleasant to find no last minute rush. The cars, some hours before the race, were in their pits with tarpaulins over them and beyond warming up there was nothing further to be done. I think this impressed the crowd quite considerably… Unfortunately…I had to return to West Bromwich for a Presentation of the Colours to the West Bromwich Battalion of the Boys' Brigade but I listened in to the B.B.C. commentary. I think it made me travel all the faster, because I arrived at West Bromwich with but three minutes to spare – not too bad scheduling for a 150 mile trip…".

The only problem was, of course, that 15 laps round Goodwood was nothing like Grand Prix distance.

Two of the cars were then prepared and taken to Berwickshire for the Winfield Joint Committee's[62] season-closing meeting at Charterhall Aerodrome.

October 12, 1952 – *The Glasgow Daily Herald Formule Libre* International Trophy, Charterhall, Scotland – 40 laps, 80 miles

The Scottish organizers had offered generous start money to attract all three BRMs, but Gonzalez had returned to South America so the team fielded only Parnell and Wharton to face Farina in the *Thin Wall Special*. Yet it was BRM-reject Peter Walker's Cooper-ERA which led away from the start until Bob Gerard caught him at the first corner in his ancient, but beautifully-prepared prewar ERA. Both the V16s had started gently, permitting Farina in the *Thin Wall* to hurtle past them both and take the lead from Gerard. Parnell's car then retired with transmission trouble, Farina retired the *Thin Wall* and Ken Wharton's BRM was left in grim pursuit of Gerard and the ERA. *Autosport* reported:

Time and again the snarling B.R.M. closed up, only to fall back at the bends. Gerard was cornering at a remarkable pace… Eventually Wharton managed to edge past but Gerard never let up…Wharton had to go all out to hold off Gerard. Just when a B.R.M. victory seemed likely, he spun off the road and the veteran E.R.A. swept ahead and stayed there till [*sic*] the end…

With only two laps to run, Ken had spun due to a grabbing front brake – he recovered to finish second, 5.4sec behind that embarrassing, bright green other product of Bourne – Bob Gerard's ERA; and with that event – and this ironic result – the BRM project in its original form had run its course.

THE SALE

On Tuesday, October 14, 1952, at 10.00am, a Trust board meeting was convened in Alfred Owen's dark-panelled boardroom at Darlaston. He resigned both as Chairman of the Executive Council and as a Trustee since he had made an offer to buy. Bernard Scott was elected to replace him and all the offers which had been received were discussed in detail.

Messrs Stephens, Champion & Slater, valuers, of Birmingham, reported on BRM's sale both as a going concern and full-sale:

> Bourne plant and machinery, going concern £18,710 – full sale £14,110.
> Cars and spares, going concern £30,500 – full sale £14,700.
> Total, going concern £49,210 – forced sale £28,810.

Seven offers had been made.

Leslie Johnson's ERA Ltd offered £13,000 but he was mainly interested in plant, not the cars and their spares.

Newman Industries Ltd offered £8–£10,000 for the plant, machinery, office furniture and fittings, material and transport. Champion Electric Corporation offered £15,000 for the going concern.

A Mr N.F.C. Smith wanted just one car.[63]

Oliver Hart offered £1,000 for three cars and R.R.C. Walker £1,500 for one car, plus one spare engine, other spares, relevant records and logbooks and a complete set of drawings. Decades later, Rob Walker observed: "I had never had any faith in the BRM. My offer was just taking the mickey." As couched, it doesn't look that way…

But the final and only all-embracing offer came from Rubery Owen, whose board was prepared, under Alfred Owen's leadership, to assume all BRM assets and liabilities as a going concern for £23,500 from November 1, 1952, including all service agreements with both PB and RM. Tony Vandervell

---

62. This organization combined the competition interests of the Berwick & District Motor Club, the Lothian Car Club and the Hawick & Border Car & Motor-Cycle Club. "And…", according to former ADL draughtsman John A. Cooper, then sports editor of *The Autocar* "…a very good job they made of it…".

63. This rather mysterious offer is mentioned in some surviving Trust documents, not in others. It probably was not a serious bid, and it was omitted from the agenda document for the October 23 EGM in London at which the successful purchase proposal was finally selected.

had made it clear he would only be interested if nobody else made an offer.

The Trust accountants reported that cash in hand or available totalled £6,311 and that estimated liabilities were a nett £22,934. Prize monies had yet to be received from Goodwood and Charterhall and "£4–500 may yet be received from the insurance claim accruing from Boreham…". Expenses for Goodwood and Charterhall raised some eyebrows – totalling £1,474 alone, and this merely for such minor events. Clearly, anybody contemplating racing the cars abroad was going to be faced with prodigious expenditure by contemporary standards…

The Executive Council unanimously recommended acceptance of the Rubery Owen offer:

> …for the following reasons:
> (a) It is the best that has been received.
> (b) It is the only offer that will ensure that the liabilities of the Trust are met.
> (c) It is the offer which is most likely to ensure in some way the continuity of the work and the (continuing) use of the accumulated experience of the project.

A full Extraordinary General Meeting was then convened at the Royal Thames Yacht Club, in Knightsbridge, London, at 3.00pm on October 23. Only 21 attended. David Brown proposed and F.M. Sayers of Lodge Plugs seconded a motion that the Rubery Owen offer should be accepted, and it was. Donald McCullough and J.C. Hopcraft moved a vote of thanks to Mr Owen "for taking over the project and continuing the work", which was also carried unanimously. A discussion followed on the desirability of continuing the name 'BRM' and Flather and Brown moved: "That the present three B.R.M. cars only should continue to be known by that name". This was agreed and the Chairman, Bernard Scott, declared the meeting closed…

For RM, Alfred Owen's purchase: "…was in complete accord with my own wishes. I had in the past often told him that I would like to see him as the sole owner of the BRM. He had more faith in the project than any of the others and I knew that the car was more likely to succeed under him than anyone else."

As the legal people set about the winding-up process, funds remaining in the Trust's account were donated to the Motor Agents' Benevolent Fund.

To the staff at Bourne and Folkingham, Rubery Owen's purchase was greeted as a positive move. They were to become Rubery Owen's 'Department 31 – Engine Development Division – Bourne' and Owen's long-term objective would in part be for them to develop, manufacture and supply proprietary racing engines (and perhaps gearboxes too) for customer sale. At least BRM would now be answerable to only one chief, and with a clear policy and fixed budget the team could now properly plan ahead. The change was almost universally popular at Bourne and Folkingham.

On October 24, the day after the Royal Yacht Club meeting, RM wrote to Alfred Owen:

> Needless to say I am delighted that things went the way they did…The best thing is for Peter and I to prepare a proposed plan of action for your approval, incorporating the main points such as:
> a) Suggested staff that it will be necessary to keep,
> b) Plans for the new Formula car,
> c) The people to whom to write to ask them to leave their equipment here,[64] and
> d) Plans for the running of the existing B.R.M. cars in certain suitable events next year.

News of the sale was immediately released to the press, John Cooper in *The Autocar* commenting:

> So that is that; the end of a project of which nobody ever questioned the excellence of the idea, but the faults of which lay in the execution rather than the conception… It is announced that no publicity will be afforded to any new activity until the engine, or whatever it may be, is developed and ready for racing; this, too, is a move in the right direction, for much harm was done in the early years of the B.R.M. by ill-advised and premature publicity.

DEVELOPING THE V16

As the dust began to settle at Bourne and Folkingham following the Rubery Owen purchase, Tony Rudd was informed that he was to inherit test and development duties on the V16s which would continue to race through 1953. Stewart Tresilian had performed this role, but he had for some time been concentrating upon alternative research in planning a future 2½-litre Formula 1 BRM for 1954. Jack North – the senior chassis mechanic – left and Gordon Newman was promoted to Chief Mechanic overall as Tony would not be able to spend so much time at Folkingham.

---

64. The equipment in question was mainly plant provided on loan, such as the Bourne Test House dynamometer from Heenan & Froude, the Ford V8 slave engine there from the Ford Motor Company, and various machine tools from Archdale & Co of Birmingham.

There seemed an interesting future ahead…

Tres had been employed for many months on a consultancy basis, initially part-time before, at Alfred Owen's recommendation, his position at Bourne became full-time. But while RM and Rudd thought much of the tall, enthusiastic Cornishman, others seemed to have 'put down the poison for him'.

A few days after Rubery Owen took over, Alfred Owen himself visited Bourne. Tres told him he could no longer work for PB, and gave his reasons. Owen was in a spot; he could not fire PB, they had a row and Tres left that day, telling Tony Rudd what had happened. Obviously he remained on the payroll for an appropriate period and wound up his affairs by mail. In January 1952 Owen confided to Bernard Scott of Lucas: "Unfortunately Tresilian is still not filling the position of Development Engineer because Frank May and many of the draughtsmen will not work under him… Frank May told Ray and Peter and myself that if ever he had to accept Tresilian's instructions he would walk out and so would a good percentage of the draughtsmen. We still, therefore, have not found an official position Tresilian can occupy. The problem seems to be that Tresilian has an unfortunate way with him or Frank May thinks he has every right to be Development Engineer…". Tony: I am surprised to read that others detested Tres; none of the draughtsmen I knew did. He did not suffer fools and incompetence gladly. AGBO had received some highly coloured information from somebody. Tres went on to a very senior position in Bristol-Siddeley Aero Engines, in charge of helicopter engine design.

That June then saw Frank May resign as Chief Draughtsman, effective July 31. Having done so much for seven years to bring the BRM project to fruition, he moved on within the motor industry.

Tony: Having inherited the V16 development programme from Tres, I also fell heir to a lengthy string of as-yet unanswered questions posed by the unit's erratic running and performance.

Tres had gone far towards sorting out the engine's fundamental development problems with PB, but there had really been far more than one man could possibly cope with since he was becoming very involved in initial planning for the 1954 engine, and since he was still technically an outside consultant.

He had a wife, Nan, and a growing son, Nicholas, to support, and he had wisely refused to commit himself totally to BRM. So he operated instead as a consultant engineer, maintaining a home in the New Forest to which he returned most weekends.

On January 5 Tres wrote to Owen:

> With regard to the 2½-litre engine…design drawings of the complete engine, off which the details will be made, will be complete by the end of January. Detailing is hardly started, as we have also been finishing off chassis design drawings. Detail drawings of the experimental single cylinder engine will [also] be complete by the end of January. Many are already complete, and I have started talks with Sandercombe as to who are to be our suppliers…

Throughout his time with BRM, Tres had had to compress a vast amount of work into a normal working week. He was, however, a superb engineer. He had provided a sound foundation upon which the team could now build. The apparent lack of development progress on the V16 that far should take into account all the other work he had to do.

Tony: Tres had laid to rest the myth that the incredibly high power output necessitated such extremely high spark plug voltages that the spark could jump from one plug lead to another, this having been blamed for all the early major blow-ups. There is on file a report by Tres in the autumn of 1952 when he measured voltages and found they were in fact quite low – around 12–15kV – which was sufficient in normal atmospheric conditions only to jump a gap of about ½–⅞in. With the plug leads normally spaced this would pose no problem at all.

Laurence Pomeroy in his technical writings subsequently perpetuated this myth concerning the V16, and somebody should have pointed out that the plug fires before incredible cylinder pressures are generated because otherwise these pressures cannot be created. The engine had a relatively low compression even though it was highly supercharged, and the cylinder pressure at which the spark occurred was not much greater than those on later petrol engines – around 400–450psi – so there would have been no danger of 'buckling con-rods' and general mayhem from this cause.

There had been the fearful spate of head stud breakages at Albi, possibly magnified by efforts to make a tight joint between the head and the liner to prevent coolant entering the bores.

The true cause of the massive engine failures had in fact been the sealing ring between head and liner, which deformed due to the blowpipe effect once the joint opened.

Under full load, the liner settled slightly, allowing the head joint to part and permit coolant to blow into the bore where it created a hydraulic lock. This was what made con-rods buckle and break, and general disintegration to ensue.

Liner construction and general design were similar to the Battle of Britain version of the Rolls-Royce Merlin aero engine – not the later variants – so it was logical to approach Rolls-Royce and use their head-ring material. This nearly, but not quite, cured the trouble. When it reappeared it was never in such catastrophic form. The joint would merely blow slightly under maximum power, which would pressurize the header tank and cause overheating. The leak was hardly ever great enough for water to flow into the bore against cylinder pressure so there was no repetition of the early hydraulic-locking.

Once everybody became obsessed with head sealing, the first idea was to screw down the heads just as tight as we could, increasing loading and therefore strength of the holding-down studs. This naturally began to pull studs out of the crankcase. This was overcome by using bigger threads and then exotic stud materials such as Vibrac. I suspect Frank May may have had a roasting from Tres over Vibrac stud failures. If the joint is collapsing the last thing you do is to use a higher tensile stud to hold it together because higher tensile means less elasticity, and the same amount of settling means the tension in the stud is far less. Also a higher tension in the stud might have caused it to resonate like a bowstring. It should have had an anti-vibration collar to stop this.

After the overheating disasters at Albi and Dundrod, and the fitting of enormous new radiators and ever bigger water pumps with swept-forward impeller blades, the engines would still overheat, pistons would seize or burn, and it was very difficult to persuade the engine to run cleanly. We engaged in incredible rituals changing carburettor needles, changing the levels and even blanking-off the supercharger air intake, all in an effort to prevent the carburettors flooding.

The resident SU engineer would often walk away shaking his head sorrowfully at the various theories being propounded. He was convinced there was nothing wrong with his carburettors, it was that 'blank-blank' engine. He was even more horrified by BRM's administrative systems.

Now, in the winter of 1952–53 it was quite an exciting proposition to be able to run a V16 on my own on the test-bed. The Bourne cell was very small, quite well silenced, but of course this meant that free movement of air in and out had to be excluded. Air was brought in therefore through a duct from the roof, but in inadequate quantity. Exhaust gases were vented through underground water-cooled pipes to the traditional vertical silencers. Water was injected into the pipes quite close to the supercharger, but the back pressure produced was always considerable which rendered power readings rather inaccurate.

When I first started testing I was unaware of the power we should be recording. I could read the load on the dyna-mometer, but one arrives at bhp figures by dividing the load shown by a calibration factor stamped on the dyno data plate, then multiplying by the rpm indicated at that moment.

However, PB's obsession with security had led him to remove the data plate and hide it. Eventually I was given the factor by Perkins Diesel in nearby Peterborough who had a similar dyno and H&F later confirmed it. Once PB became aware I knew the constant, he surrendered the plate, plus the formula and slide rule he had made to calibrate the engine's output, and to correct it for ambient conditions inside and outside the test cell.

In fact, it was not until a couple of years later when the dyno was removed to Folkingham that I found he had based his calculations on a ratio of 0.512:1 between crankshaft and output shaft, whereas in fact this ratio was 0.519:1. That's quite a difference, and it actually *increases* the engine's true power output.

PB's restrictions on security grounds meant that nobody was allowed in the test cell when an engine was running, other than himself, RM, Tres and subsequently myself, and the two senior engine build personnel, Dave Turner and Willie Southcott.

My first engine runs were pretty hair-raising. The dyno was electronically controlled and this equipment failed. We ran up an engine with the control console removed so we could see what was happening. This allowed us to see straight down the carburettor intake and we saw what Tres already suspected, that above 9,000rpm the carburettor's pistons and needles came to full lift and the needle levitated itself right out of the jet.

This explained the burbling and why the solid needle blank had worked so well during pre-Goodwood testing. If the needle was clear of the jet, its shape became irrelevant. I got three bollockings from PB over this: one for talking about it to the

engine shop, a second for risking the Dyno electronics running without the cover plate and a third for not spotting it sooner.

I also found that occasionally one cylinder would fade out.

The exhausts which had been glowing cherry red in the general test-cell gloom at around 9,000rpm would suddenly fade to black. Amidst the general uproar in the cell there was no other way of telling that this had happened, apart from the dyno load dipping slightly more than one-sixteenth. To lose one cylinder in four might be a disaster, but losing one in 16 is not so noticeable. There really seemed neither rhyme nor reason to this problem, but it appeared to affect rearward cylinders more than those at the front.

One pointer was that the engine would begin to overheat around 8,000rpm and that water-jacket pressures fluctuated as temperature rose. I managed to obtain a venturi calibrated for a 1½in pipe which we could insert in the water system to measure the water flow as a difference between the heights of two mercury columns. We discovered immediately that water flow was breaking down. So we stripped the engine and began a pretty thorough investigation.

We rig-tested the water pump and discovered that its swept-forward impeller vanes, which greatly improved water flow, would actually stall when asked to pump water aerated by steam bubbles at any engine speed of 8,000rpm or more. Below this point the pump was just incredible – in fact it would have done justice to a fair-sized fire engine!

Meanwhile, our dyno running had also seen the engine spitting back violently through its carburettors whenever we tried to exceed 10,500rpm. This would frighten the deafened tester out of his remaining wits. I suspected the 5ata boost pressure that we were using was blowing the inlet valves open when they should have been shut.

While waiting for new water-pump impellers to be produced to avoid the stalling problem, we had a good look through the engine and found varying stages of distress evidenced by all the valves, seats, guides and pistons.

Notes of January 14, 1953, show that every exhaust seat was blowing to some degree, matching scores were found on valve stems and guides and the valve seats were also scored, vaguely matching the valve-scoring. Nos. 1-8 cylinder bank had the worst seats, particularly on cylinders Nos. 2-3-4-5-7, whereas No. 4 valve and guide were not scored, and although No. 8 seat was quite good its valve stem and guide were very bad. I felt I was on to something...

The inlets were also intriguing. Every one had been blowing, with carbon across the seats, and No. 14 valve spring was broken.

Once cleaned and reassembled, the inlet valves would hold paraffin in their combustion chambers, but there was considerable scoring between stems and guides and evidence that they had been blowing when the engine was running.

Turning to the pistons, we found that the clearance above the top rings was about 4-thou more than top limit allowed. Clearly we had located a massive ring-wear problem. The piston manufacturers tackled it in a most thorough manner, advising us to revert to cast pistons though we might encounter a strength problem across the gudgeon pin bosses. The forged piston, although strong, was prone to heavier wear.

We then instituted dimensional checks on drawing limits

for everything.

At this point I began to wish I had not started the hunt.

Clearly, much of the problem derived from sticking exhaust valves. And the inlets must have been staying open as well – it was the only way to account for them blowing. I felt sure the supercharger pressure had been blowing them open, but everyone else said this was rubbish. Anyway, applying the works air-hose to the inlet manifold proved sufficient to blow them off their seats!

We then realized that all valve heads had been reground at least once; all the valve seats had been recut and reshaped many times, and the heads had never been re-seated. So some valves were as much as 10-thou too deep into the head when checked against the drawing tolerances.

Valve spring platforms had been re-machined when worn, the collets were worn and bedded-in, and then I found valve springs way down on poundage. The V16s were suffering simply from chronic dimensional errors and the effects of a long hard life.

Once we restored a test head to as-new condition we achieved a valve seat load of 80lbs, but even then 60lbs air pressure in the manifold would cause a slight leak. We readjusted dimensions and put packing pieces under the spring platforms. Using the old camshaft test-rig to run-in the valve springs we were certain they would now hold a seat pressure of 65psi. There was nothing scientific about this figure; it was the most the works air-line could supply…

Relative to the 56psi boost (at 10,000rpm) we were then using, this improvement was probably sufficient. We tested each set with paraffin in the combustion chamber. One bubble was sufficient for rejection.

The exhaust problem was different. Here there was no external pressure to blow the valve open. Over-large clearances could allow carbon to enter the guides and cause the valves to stick, and at that point I gave up, put the bits in a box and went for the weekend to Derby to see my friends at Rolls-Royce.

They arranged to chromium-plate 20 of the inlet and exhaust valve stems, recalling how this had worked on civil Merlin engines.

They suggested I should hardness-check the piston crown, as this would indicate overheating which might bother the valve seats and would also give me an idea of the heat path down the engine. This research really shook me.

The hot pistons were at either end of the engine.

Consequently, I presented the evidence to PB, and proposed a full rig test of the cooling system, plus material changes for the valve guides and announced that I had sent a set of valves to Rolls-Royce.

The wrath of heaven burst upon my head…

I had breached PB's carefully erected security screen. We would read the whole story in the press next day. The opposition would have the stuff tomorrow. No way would he allow *any* changes to be made. I managed to suggest that Rolls-Royce's security was far better than ours and operated to protect the national interest. He cooled off, and suggested I could at least have taken the evidence to him rather than immediately to my friends in Derby. He agreed on chromium-plating, to new guide material and to re-

inspection of everything.

In fact, BRM had some very fine inspectors, complete with view-room and excellent equipment. An elderly inspector named Horace checked every new part to the nearest tenth of a thou – 0.0001inch – Gerry Edwards, the Chief Inspector, was very good on layouts such as chassis, and the third was an ex-RAF air gunner known as 'Flash' Gordon.

As a result of the ensuing witch hunt, half our engine material was scrapped, while an enormous salvage programme commenced, regrinding slightly bent valves with chromium-plate rebuilding of the stem, Brightrayed seats and so on. They were better valves than ever, and more expensive.

Working from our piston hardness tests, we now set up a cylinder block and one head with its water pump on our test rig and measured coolant flow through the engine, and particularly around each cylinder.

Here, at last, we discovered that at low speeds the water passed from the pump into the middle of the cylinder block, around the centre pair of cylinders and then away, leaving no flow at all around the cylinders at each end. At 6,000rpm there was no flow around Nos. 1 and 2, and Nos. 7 and 8; most flow around Nos. 4 and 5 and a trickle around Nos. 3 and 6. At 10,000rpm, water was flowing around the end cylinders but at just a fraction of the rate around those in the middle.

This at least could be easily fixed. We made up spring rings with projecting buttons, which we slipped into the waterways inside the block to restrict flow along it. We tested and modified the system until from 5,000rpm all the way up to 12,000 there was even water-flow around the entire engine. Flow was measured with the traditional bucket and stopwatch.

The test rig in those days was at the top of the stairs above the chassis build shops, outside the engine assembly shop. The operator stood on a box and directed the considerable jet of water into the bucket while I applied the stopwatch. Few BRM employees escaped a soaking from that well-aimed jet.

We made new outlet pipes with beautifully graded tapers so the water flow was sorted-out but not impaired. By this time it was the end of March 1953, and the new impellers and cast pistons had been delivered and we were ready to rebuild the engines.

The Goodwood Easter meeting was looming dangerously close. We ran what I thought would be the first definitive unit, taking it up to 10,000rpm at about half-load, collecting data and measuring water flows.

Our revised pump impellers still didn't take kindly to steam in the system, and so we measured the amount circulating by collecting the coolant in a 20-gallon drum hanging from a spring-balance. In theory, if the drum contained 10 gallons – as it should have done through the position of the inlet and outlet connections – then it should have weighed roughly 100lbs. But it did not; nothing like…

Using glass water pipes, and dye in the water, we could see streaks of steam and air trapped there. With help from Rolls-Royce at Hucknall, we then adopted a centrifuge which separated steam from water and sent the steam into a condenser header tank where it could condense out, water then being returned to the eye of the water pump. This was of course the now traditional 'shunt' water cooling system.

At this point – at last – the engine began to run quite

happily and consistently up to 10,500rpm and delivered well over 500bhp – going as high as 525 – and then there would inevitably come a thunderous 'BANG!', the engine would windmill almost to a standstill, and then pick up again…

Some of the main diffuser bolts which passed right through the supercharger casing into the main block would inevitably be broken and we then had to return the supercharger casing to Rolls-Royce for reconditioning. They would report back that it was distorted. Obviously there had been a major flashback in the induction.

This was very surprising. Flame-traps were fitted to make this in theory impossible. We ran the engine on stub exhausts and found that mixture distribution was very bad, the end cylinders, front and rear, on the left bank were too rich as were the middle cylinders on the opposite bank. This indicated that the blower was centrifuging some of the fuel out, which went to the front of the left bank where it bounced off to the middle of the right bank and then back to the left rear. We tried a diffuser in the front of the manifold, with no effect, but a three-diameter trunk pipe suggested by R-R made a 75 per cent improvement. I had to curtail this line of development as open exhaust runs took some time to set up, and invariably resulted in an engine failure.

When we put one engine into a car – despite this problem, since we needed to test some winter chassis improvements – we were again surprised to find the engine running cleanly and powerfully right up to 11,500rpm and beyond!

Ken Wharton did some of the driving at Folkingham, and he reported the engine was transformed.

He described it as "Gutsy", and it seemed the flash-back was a test-bed condition created by the red-hot exhausts. We could just take a flash reading with the engine in the test-cell on the car exhaust system at 10,500rpm, but within seconds the cell – even with its doors wide open – would fill with choking fumes. We then had to leave the engine idling for about five minutes until temperatures and conditions returned to tolerable levels, and only then could we flash it back up to 10,500 to see if the reading was repeated. Such a performance wasn't really practical.

When we took the engine up to 11,000rpm, the poor thing ingested hot exhaust fumes which proved too much for it – four pistons failed simultaneously, hot oil showered down on us from the test-cell ceiling and it all became a shambles. It was amazing the engine was not more seriously damaged…

Finally, on February 22, with everything on top line, electric fans and their cables everywhere including the open doorway, we tried again with engine '20/3' on stubs, letting the engine idle (at 5,000rpm) to clear and cool the test-house atmosphere for at least two minutes between each power check, and even longer between 10,500 and 11,000rpm. Then, having got a reading, greatly daring, we tried for 11,500. The needle had just steadied, showing over 600hp, when there was the usual bang and shower of oil, with a minor fire from the hot stubs. The air intake temperature was nearly 40°C. Even then I suspect that what the bulb thermometer was telling us was history. Only two pistons were holed but several more were not far off.

However, the new racing season was upon us – our first as

part of Rubery Owen – and it was in this state of tune that we set off for Goodwood, on Easter Monday, 1953…

RACING THE OWEN V16s – 1953

In anticipating the British motor racing season of 1953 there was undeniable relish amongst the average British enthusiast for the prospect of Alfred Owen's BRMs locking horns with his old adversary Tony Vandervell's *Thin Wall Special* Ferrari. In many ways this formidable car had become more Vandervell Products than Ferrari, and its first confrontation with BRM under new 'Owen Racing Organisation' management came at Goodwood…

April 6, 1953 – *Formule Libre* Chichester Cup, Goodwood – 5 laps, 12 miles

Rain sank the new Owen Racing Organisation's chances in this preliminary sprint, both Reg Parnell and Ken Wharton fighting a losing battle against wheelspin in chassis 'No. 1' and 'No. 2' respectively. Superstitious, often tetchy Ken had insisted upon driving the car Fangio normally drove. Since Reg didn't mind either way he had his wish. Yet neither could catch the Swiss Baron de Graffenried's Formula 2 Maserati on the wet track and Wharton was actually hard-pressed by Ron Flockhart in RM's old ex-works ERA, 'R4D', while Parnell's engine sounded woolly and he could do nothing to catch Flockhart and had difficulty keeping ahead of Tony Rolt's Rob Walker-owned Connaught…

Ken made a desperate final attempt to catch de Graffenried but the BRM merely crept out of the chicane with its rear wheels spinning furiously, allowing the genial Swiss to win by 0.8sec at the line. Ken set fastest lap at 1:46.2, 81.26mph, while Flockhart finished third and Parnell a somewhat disgruntled and distant fourth.

Tony: I stood by the trackside spectating with Mr Owen who asked me to explain just how de Graff's unsupercharged 2-litre Maserati with less than 200 horsepower could be blowing-off our sophisticated V16s with nearly 600.

I explained that in the wet you could only use the power the tyres would accept and transmit. I thought de Graffenried's Pirellis would probably accept more than our old diamond pattern Dunlop R1s in these conditions and as 'Toulo''s Maserati was probably half the weight of the BRM, they had much less work to do to make it accelerate. He did not seem to believe me, but asked some penetrating questions and he certainly absorbed what I said and stored it away for future reference…as we would discover.

April 6, 1953 – *Formule Libre* Glover Trophy, Goodwood – 15 laps, 36 miles

For this main race of the day, on a drying track, the BRMs faced Piero Taruffi in Vandervell's *Thin Wall Special* and de

The Goodwood circuit witnessed some of BRM's most spectacular ups and downs, providing ammunition for both the marque's most avid fans and those who have forever rubbished everything the Bourne team did. It was certainly a happy hunting ground for the V16s, witnessing eight of their race wins, 1950–55. In 1953 the Easter Monday meeting saw Ken Wharton and Reg Parnell face Taruffi in the ThinWall, and Ken win the Glover Trophy, while September saw Fangio's farewell as a team driver, giving best to Hawthorn in Vandervell's Ferrari 'special'.

Graffenried's impertinent Maserati. Wharton started from pole and led into Madgwick Corner after making one of the best starts ever in the V16. He was pursued by de Graffenried, Taruffi and Parnell until lap four, when the *Thin Wall* boomed past the Swiss Maserati to take second place. It was not on form, however, and as Gregor Grant reported:

To the sound of loud cheers, Wharton crossed the finishing line to win the fastest-ever race run at Goodwood, with an average speed of 90.47m.p.h. He had broken the lap record five times, finally cutting it down to 1min. 33.8secs, 92.21m.p.h.

Taruffi finished second, 6 seconds adrift. Alfred Owen and Tony Vandervell – who had been standing side-by-side watching the race – shook hands, swapped congratulations and commiserations, and BRM had partially settled an old score…

Reg Parnell had retired his "ropey-sounding" car on lap four when its supercharger quill-shaft had sheared, a piece which we made with a hole down the middle for the blower oil feed. It had probably been over-stressed in one of the monumental test-bed backfires and some detail design changes were subsequently made to improve reliability in this area.

Back at Folkingham, one car was prepared in time for a return trip to Charterhall on May 23, after which all three were to race at Albi the following weekend, May 30. Ken Wharton would drive at Charterhall, while at Albi he would be No. 3 to Fangio – recovered from his Monza crash the previous year – and Gonzalez.

The team really had some more old scores to erase there, but to Tony's dismay he found in testing after Goodwood that the engines had had enough and the old misfiring and burbling problems had returned. It was apparent that after some 100 miles' running exhaust-valve guides were beginning to carbon-up, the valves consequently would start to stick and blow, so the engine lost power. What caused that distinctive burbling note was the charge continuing to burn down the exhaust pipe. Another sign was if all the soot was burned off the inside of the tail-pipes to leave a pale grey, almost white, colouration.

Tony: When Fangio encountered this effect he would come in, pull my head close to his in the cockpit and purse his lips, imitating the burbling noise in my ear. Many years later, long after his retirement, he would do this whenever we met, then roar with laughter amidst much back-slapping. He well remembered the BRM burble…

These tell-tale signs immediately meant heads off, ream-out valve guides, clean valve stems, re-set and reassemble. The engine would then be restored sufficiently for another 100 miles or so, which was not good enough because the Albi GP comprised a 55-mile Heat and a 100-mile Final.

We tried rubber seals on the valve guides but they made the valves stick – the very problem they were intended to cure. We raised spring-loading until we began to wear the rockers away, and this increased life to at least 100 miles.

We then succeeded in measuring temperatures at the bottom end of the valve guide, at its middle and at its top end. This provided a clearer picture of clearances required and so we made a tapered valve-guide bore, believing that the necessary clearance was much less at the top – where both guide and valve-stem ran much cooler – than at the bottom. We also reasoned that if oil couldn't get down the guide, then it couldn't burn-on and carbonize there. This idea seemed to work, but it was far too difficult and expensive to produce, and exceedingly difficult to restore in the field. We then tried crushing back the top of the guide with a roller – not very effective – and eventually evolved a double-diameter guide with the top 5⁄16in or so smaller in diameter than the rest. This effectively scraped carbon deposits off the stem. Carbon would pack into this area where we could clean it off relatively easily. This took us to a life of around 180–200 miles, which might just be sufficient.

I was also very keen to tidy up the engine's external oil pipes and to prevent oil being blown from the breathers. With around 4ata boost, blow-by – excess pressure within the

cylinder finding an escape route downwards past the piston rings – was a considerable problem. The poor rings had little chance, some boost pressure always entering the crankcase and venting through the breathers.

By fitting four 1¼in-diameter chimney stacks, with half-moon baffles, we dispensed with 27lbs weight of catch-tank, breather-pipes etc, and during this work we also discovered that the cambox oil scavenge pipes didn't work.

The gear that drove the cambox scavenge pump ran in the front of the cam-cover, and by fitting a little Perspex window there we saw on the test-bed how the gear swept oil *away* from the pump. The camboxes must have been running nearly full of oil, so we fitted gravity drains into the sump and removed the pump completely. The pressure relief-valve plug, on the side of the crankcase where a cross-drilling to the valve emerged, was the obvious place to drain the oil to.

I had long suspected the sleeve-type relief valve of sticking open, and now we discovered this was so. Consequently, we then fitted a disc-type relief valve on the end of the main oil gallery, scrapped the sleeve valves and drained the camboxes through external piping via the relief valve ports.

It was interesting that although all four camshafts were fed through only a 0.18in hole that it still demanded two ⅞in pipes to drain the oil away! But minimizing the amount of oil in the camboxes considerably alleviated the valve-stem carbonization problem.

Then came our third trip north of the border…our second to the aerodrome circuit near Kelso, with the return trip to Albi scheduled for the following weekend.

May 23, 1953 – *The Glasgow Daily Record Formule Libre* Trophy, Charterhall, Scotland – 20 laps, 40 miles

Ken Wharton drove the lone BRM entry, chassis 'No. 2' with its engine '20/2' modified as above, driving gearbox '21/2'. The team's high hopes seemed fulfilled in practice when he lapped the bumpy little Berwickshire airfield circuit in a record 1:24.8. Ominously, however, Ron Flockhart from Edinburgh forced old 'R4D' round only 0.7sec slower. Bob Gerard joined this pair on the front row of the grid and from the start it was Flockhart who took an immediate lead, followed by Peter Walker's Cooper-ERA, Gerard and then Wharton – who quickly rushed through into second place.

After four laps Flockhart's ERA led Wharton in the BRM by 5 seconds but in one more lap Ken closed the gap to less than a second. But rushing into Toft's Turn history repeated itself, Ken had a front brake grab and – to the crew's disgust – he spun like a top. After a long delay he rejoined seventh and despite setting a new lap record at 1:24.8, 85.7mph, he could finish no better than third, Flockhart winning from Gerard in their obsolescent ERAs.

Tony had a working party waiting at Folkingham when the car returned home: We overhauled the engine's top end and prepared it for Albi. When the engine ran it ran quite well, but it had ingested a lot of dust during its spin.

Raymond Mays' movement document for BRM's return to

October 11, 1952 – International Trophy, Charterhall: Ken Wharton looked set to win this Scottish aerodrome race only to spin while leading. In the May 1953 meeting here he spun again. Both times it was an ERA which benefited and won – Gerard's in '52, Flockhart's in '53.

Albi records that all three of the Lodestar car transporters plus the Commer mobile workshop were to leave Folkingham at 10am on Monday, May 25, bound for Dover and the night crossing to Calais. Tony Rudd, Jack Heward and Dave Turner crewed the workshop KVP 362, while the three Lodestars respectively were ETL 483 with Gordon Newman, Colin Atkin and Stan Hope, ETL 615 with Dick Salmon, Maurice Dove and Arthur Hill, and the oldest KOM 257 with Willie Southcott, Ken Williamson and Cyril Bryden. RM ended the document with the following paragraph:

It is emphasized that this is the first occasion that the Owen Racing Organisation has been represented overseas, and it is hoped that everyone will conduct themselves, at all times, in a manner in keeping with this obligation.

May 30, 1953 – Albi Grand Prix, *Les Planques*, France – 10-lap 55.63-mile (F1) Heat, 18-lap, 100.14-mile Final

M. Francois Flad's race at Albi was organized as a combined Formula 1 and 2 event, with a preliminary 10-lap heat for the F2 cars followed by a second 10-lapper for the Formula 1 entry. There were nine F2 entries and ten F1s, which were headed by the three BRMs for Fangio ('No. 1'), Gonzalez ('No. 2') and Wharton ('No. 3') who faced Ascari's factory Ferrari 375 in its latest, long-wheelbase, developed 'Indianapolis' form and Farina in Vandervell's *Thin Wall Special*.

Fangio qualified on pole for the heat, lining up his car most carefully on the right side of the track where the surface was quite dusty, reasoning that this would enable him to spin the wheels easily and so punch the car away – once the tyres gripped – at near maximum torque. Ascari was on the centre of the narrow 3-2-3 grid's front row, with Gonzalez on the outside, and Wharton and Farina behind.

During practice, all three engines had run quite well. Fangio pointed out the tell-tale signs of burbling in his, so the crew removed its heads and reamed the valve guides. Tony: I

gave it a shake-down run at first light, and knowing what was coming tried to give it as much throttle as I dared on the bumpy, narrow, steeply-cambered, tree-lined road. It seemed fine. The others were running well – so well in fact that Albi was to reveal that perhaps BRM had too much horsepower rather than not enough!

In first practice Gonzalez's car ran five laps, then two more before bursting a 17-inch rear tyre.

Next day on 18-inch rear wheels and with the front struts re-pressured to 330psi this car completed seven more laps without further tyre trouble but required a supercharger change for the race.

Fangio led from the start. He clocked 2:58.2 on his standing lap and two laps later had broken Ascari's Ferrari, which retired to the pits, followed soon after by Farina. With their main opposition gone the BRMs looked secure and sounded fabulous, but on lap four according to published reports – but lap six according to BRM's chassis log, Gonzalez came in with his car's nearside rear 17-inch tyre in an extraordinary state…

It hadn't thrown its tread so much as stripped the covering from its sidewall and tread area complete. His stop to have the wheel changed left Fangio and Wharton leading Rosier's private Ferrari 375, winner the previous year. Fangio had set a new lap record third time round of 2:52.3 – 115.56mph – and when Dick Salmon and Maurice Dove had trouble push-starting Gonzalez's car – since the enlarged radiators fitted in 1952 had left no provision for external electric starting – he lost 90 seconds and rejoined sixth. Fangio and Wharton completed the ten laps comfortably first and second, 1min 11.5sec between them, with Gonzalez eventually finishing fifth.

Fangio recalled: "I left Ascari and Farina way behind and broke the lap record. It was the most fantastic car I ever drove – an incredible challenge in every way…".

Fangio and Wharton naturally headed the line-up for the combined F1/F2 18-lap final – after his stop, Gonzalez's average speed in the Formula 1 heat had been slower than some of the F2 cars in their's so he was buried back on the fourth row. The BRMs were fitted with 18-inch wheels for this final, and loaded with 35 gallons of fuel.

Rosier led into the first corner, but by the end of that

opening 5.5-mile lap Fangio was fully 2 seconds ahead. Wharton had tucked onto his tail and by lap seven the V16s were hurtling round 1-2-3 – "a stirring sight" as one reporter put it. But next time round, Wharton's nearside rear Dunlop was in ribbons and he lost 47sec while it was changed, falling to fifth. Fangio's nearside rear tyre stripped similarly at *Mon Plaisir* and he went glancing along the roadside bank but charged on towards the pits.

Fangio, the fatalist, thanked his luck: "I was in the lead and accelerated out of the village at the end of the circuit along the narrow straight, lined by dozens of enormous trees, on the way back towards the corner opening onto the short pits straight. Now I don't know why I did it, but something about braking into the previous corner must have felt strange, because I pressed the brake pedal in the middle of the straight,

and it flopped straight to the floor – I had no brakes at all. If I had not tested the brakes like that I would next have needed them entering the tight final right-hander before the pits and the trees on the outside there – *whoooo*! [he arched his eyebrows and flung his arms wide] This *biiig*!...The brake caliper was displaced...no brakes. My luck, you see?"

Tony: We found his left rear brake caliper choked with pieces of rubber from the tyre failure, and the hub was cracked. It seemed as if the rubber jammed between the disc and hub was more likely to blame than scraping the bank.

This left Gonzalez leading from Rosier and Wharton until lap 12, when 'Pepe' stopped with his offside rear tyre stripped – and Ken was missing...

He had crashed very heavily indeed on a 140mph right-hand curve entering a lazy ess-bend in the outward section

Left: May 30, 1953 – Albi GP practice, Les Planques, France: RM's vindication of the V16s. He steers Fangio's 'No.1' back towards the paddock, Dove and Salmon pushing. Denis Jenkinson of Motor Sport (check shirt) talks with Rivers Fletcher while the aldermanic figure of Stan Hope (specs and attache case) paces home... Stan came to head car build at Folkingham. An educated figure, he claimed to have been an actor in the late '40s and was Willie Southcott's equal as a key player. Immensely strong, he later burst in upon RM hosting a VIP visit to the racing shop, with a chassis under his arm, shouting "'Ere, Bagwash! Where d'you want this bugger?".

Below: May 31, 1953 – Albi GP F1 Heat: Tension mounts – Fangio and Ascari settle their goggles – Arthur Hill and Gordon Newman (right) tend Gonzalez's BRM. Farina in the ThinWall (3).

Right: 1953 Albi GP. Starting lap 2, F1 Heat – Fangio's V16 showing a clean pair of heels to Ascari's works Ferrari 375, which will break in the attempt to close. Fangio has set up 'No. 1' for the second right-hander exiting this brief pit straight to head out into the country, towards St Juery. At the apex the V16 will be sliding and he will exit on full noise in a typically V16 series of incipient side-swipes… PB and Tony Rudd (overalls) stand out on the pit lane.

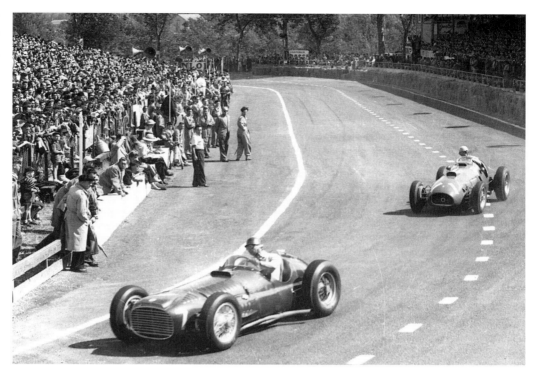

Below and centre right: The first tyre failure – Dove, Salmon and Rudd stare in dismay as Gonzalez flaps 'No. 2' into the pit lane, its exhaust smashed by flailing rubber. Tony directs as the rules prescribed, Dick and Maurice change the wheel. At right are Cyril Bryden, Vic Barlow of Dunlop and Gordon Newman.

Above: It's Fangio's turn for the left-rear tyre to strip its casing, passing Vandervell's pit on his way to BRM's. Behind him is Vandervell mechanic Cyril Atkins, to become BRM Chief Mechanic in the '60s. Right: The win – Fangio's 'No. 1' led the F1 Heat throughout from pole position and broke the lap record.

THE 1953/54 PROGRAMME

In keeping with RM's lifelong policy of always consulting his friends, Laurence Pomeroy of *The Motor* had been asked confidentially to research possible approaches to the new 1954 Formula. On May 28, 1953, comparing at great length the theoretical potential of 2½-litre unblown engines versus 750cc supercharged, he concluded:

> ...there is likely to be little difference between the weight and power output of these two types, and any superiority attained by the unblown engine must be paid for by having at least six and preferably eight cylinders. Both engines have about comparable possibilities of development along lines already explored and both are capable of considerable expansion by the use of turbines in the exhaust system. [This nearly 30 years before turbocharged engines became successful in Formula 1! – DCN] The successful use of such a device would be dependent upon considerable time and money devoted to research, but granted these factors the benefits would be greater in respect of the supercharged type than they would of the unsupercharged engine, irrespective of whether the turbine were used to drive the supercharger (if fitted); geared to the crankshaft; or independently geared to the rear wheels...

Showing off his spectacular appetite for duff gen, 'Pom' reported:

> There is good reason to believe that Mercedes-Benz will in fact race a six-cylinder 750cc supercharged engine with some form of turbine auxiliary...[in fact they raced an eight-cylinder 2½-litre unsupercharged engine with no form of turbine auxiliary]...and it is known that Ferrari are developing a supercharged 750cc engine...[which they did not, developing an unsupercharged 2500 instead].

In order to restrict necessary new design work, to utilize existing experience and existing stock, 'Pom' finally flew in the face of PB's intelligent early '52 analysis of the way ahead by recommending development of a supercharged 750cc V8 based upon one-half of the existing V16-cylinder design, using two-stage Zoller supercharging at up to 60psi boost.

On June 22, Peter Berthon finally issued his detailed 'Recommendations for Development and Racing Programme Winter 1953/54 and 1954 Season' for Owen's scrutiny. It read in part as follows:

1. EXISTING B.R.M. CARS

Since the Grand Prix Formula changes at the end of 1953 season, there will be no first class races available for existing Formula I cars. There will, however, be Formula Libres [*sic*] short-distance events, particularly in Great Britain. The courses used are all slow average type, for which the B.R.M.s were not designed and not suitable in present form.

As we shall not have a Formula I car available during the 1954 season, it is important to keep the existing cars running for the following reasons:
(a) To maintain public interest in the marque.
(b) To maintain the support of accessory firms.
(c) To keep our drivers together for the new car.
(d) To maintain the value of the present cars.

In spite of the fact that B.R.M. cars have been able to establish record lap times on the short circuits, they must be improved to retain winning form. It is therefore recommended:
(a) That 2 cars be rebuilt in a lightened, shortened form, with altered weight distribution. The existing proved components to be built up on a new single tube frame, ancillary equipment to be simplified and long distance equipment omitted.
(b) The 3rd car to be retained in existing form as a spare. It may be of interest to attempt some International records during 1954.

Design work for (a) is completed. The first car to be modified is the crashed Albi car, and availability has been promised for the October Goodwood meeting.

Engines are now giving adequate power with much improved reliability and no further development work applicable to the 16-cylinder engine only is proposed...

---

heading away from the pits before the village of St Juery. RM recalled: "I had heard Ken talk to Fangio before the race asking him what gear he took this corner in. Fangio said: 'Fifth', and Ken said: 'I have been taking it in fourth'. Ken worshipped Fangio. He followed Fangio's example – quite rightly – and began taking the corner in fifth, but he had not quite mastered it in fifth and the crash came...".

His car had actually run wide, launched itself off the roadside bank, fortunately dropped Ken neatly into a well-cushioned roadside ditch, and then bounced upside down and almost totally destroyed itself against a brick wall, ripping off the left-rear wheel, demolishing the tail and severely distorting its chassis frame '1/4'. Wharton emerged miraculously with nothing worse than bruises and shock, but the car was a write-off with only its engine and gearbox and some minor parts salvageable, and then only after considerable repair work.

Contrary to many contemporary and subsequent reports,

the accident had not been caused by another tyre failure, for all four were found intact at (or near!) the scene.

Gonzalez was left to regain a minute on the leader, Rosier in his private blue Ferrari, with only six laps to go. Gonzalez ripped 9 seconds off the deficit in one lap but the French veteran was kept well-informed by his pit-crew and paced himself nicely to the finish to beat the sole surviving BRM by 31 seconds...

BRM had been defeated, but had at last showed solid form in genuine Continental road racing before the hammer had fallen from a most unexpected quarter.

Tony: Dunlop had been very twitchy about tyre conditions at Albi in the inevitably hot weather so we had taken 18-inch as well as the normal 17-inch wheels and tyres. PB and Dunlop were undecided which size to use and I had unloaded our entire stock behind the pits, much to PB's disgust.

The cars raced on 7.00-17 and 7.00-18 tyres, and after experiencing trouble in the F1 heat on 45psi inflation,

2. NEW FORMULA I (2,500c.c. Unsupercharged or 750c.c. Supercharged).

We have a design for a 4-cylinder 4-valve 2½-litre engine with novel bore/stroke ratio. A single cylinder test unit of similar design is in the throes of manufacture.

Further consideration shows that the good features may be offset by the bad:

Good Features.
(1) Reasonably short overall length and low weight.
(2) Simplicity and possibly lower cost than a multi-cylinder.
(3) Ease of service and maintenance.

Bad Features.
(1) Very high piston acceleration which is the present limiting feature of the B.R.M. 16-cylinder engine performance.
(2) Impossibility of securing compressions higher than 11–1.
(3) Poor combustion chamber shape with long flame travel and high surface volume ratio.
(4) Loss in volumetric efficiency generally associated with a 4-valve head.

It is thought that these features of the design can only be overcome by the use of a different valve gear. We have designed a new type of valve gear which is basically simple and employs known technique and lends itself admirably in overcoming the limitations of the short-stroke high-speed large-bore engine. A wooden model is being completed and a design for an inter-changeable head is being produced for the single-cylinder test unit...

Stewart Tresilian had schemed out this four-valve-per-cylinder 2½-litre engine as a 'homer' and had initially offered it to Rodney Clarke of Connaught while BRM was eyeing more complex ideas. The four-cylinder was now far towards being adopted by BRM instead. In its 16-valve cylinder head it was a very advanced design, but PB had simply jibbed at the prospect of developing the bugs out of such a design. Consequently he had schemed an alternative two-valve-per-cylinder arrangement, maintaining gas flow volumes by the use of inordinately large ports and valve heads. This is the "new type" of valve gear mentioned above. He continued:

To summarise – Owing to lack of direct information on high-output unsupercharged engines, we would not recommend pursuing the 4-cylinder design without considerable experience on the single-cylinder test unit...

He explained that over the previous two years considerable progress had been made with the supercharged V16 and that BRM now understood better:

...the technique of high-supercharged high-speed engines. The B.R.M. engine is now a long way ahead of any other supercharged engine in power output for weight against capacity...

Half the existing B.R.M. engine arranged as a VEE-8 using accessories and components that are proved and already exist would give immediately 250/300b.h.p., sufficient to match the 2½-litre engines over the next 2 years...development on a 750c.c. version should show steady increase up to a possible 400b.h.p... The most difficult feature of this engine will be in the provision of superchargers. Although Rolls-Royce may help officially or unofficially with an Axial Flow design, an alternative arrangement is essential.

The alternatives are Rootes [*sic*], Zoller type, or Centric. With the former 4 stages will be required, with a mixture of Rootes and pre-compression type 3 stages, while 2 stages of Centric or Zoller would suffice with some sacrifice of volumetric efficiency at the lower speeds...

Designs for a gearbox, front and rear suspension, chassis frames etc were completed some while ago. These require revision to accommodate either type of engine...We believe the design of a 750c.c. engine will be completed with detailed component drawings by the end of September...

The famous BRM tendency to over-optimism was once more shining through...

pressures were raised to a full 70psi for the final in an attempt to stabilize matters and keep the compound attached to the carcass.

RM described the problem in restarting Gonzalez after his tyre-change in the heat like this: "New radiators had no provision for the use of starting handle or electric starter motor, and the only way of starting the car was to push it. *With Gonzalez in the cockpit it weighed one ton two hundred pounds.* [My italics – DCN] The rules allowed only two mechanics to help. They were hardly moving the car. Gonzalez leaped out...and threw his weight behind it too; the car fired, he jammed himself back in and was away...".

Ray remembered Albi '53 to his dying day as the V16s' redemption.

"The sight and sound of those three green cars leading the International field, first, second and third left a vivid impression on all the 350,000 who cheered them that day at Albi. This was the climax of all our hopes, our sleepless nights and the work of our dedicated band of mechanics...".

At the time, Gregor Grant was moved to write:

The magnificent show put up at Albi last Sunday by the three B.R.M.s will not readily be forgotten...The sight and sound of F1 Grand Prix machinery tearing round the fast Albi circuit was unforgettable and the B.R.M.s may well have justified any claims to being the fastest cars ever to race since the big-engined Mercedes...Juan Manuel Fangio pulverized the lap record – a record which may remain until such time as powerful supercharged machines reappear in Grand Prix racing...

Objectively, their performance would have proved more had the works and Vandervell Ferraris survived, and – moreso – had they only reached this pitch of development three years earlier...

Albi, 1953: The downside – Ken Wharton was tremendously fortunate to escape virtually unscathed from the violent somersault which wrote-off 'No. 3', demolishing the car's rear end and bending its chassis like a banana. The missing left-rear wheelrim was retrieved with its Dunlop tyre still intact. This was driver error…

Below: 'No. 3''s excised tail fuel tank was left resting on its front end behind the wreck, the oil tank on top. Note the de Dion tube, oil-streaked transaxle sump, ruined exhausts and once full-length undershielding. Even the brake disc is buckled…

After the Esso fuel contamination problems of Dundrod and Turnberry the previous year, Alfred Owen had been approached by Shell with a more attractive fuel contract. The team now benefited from the vast experience of Beveridge Rowntree – the acknowledged expert in high-energy fuel brews – and the V16s now ran on Shell No.1 fuel – 80% methyl-alcohol, 10% acetone and 10% benzol instead of the exotic 70% alcohol, alkylate isopentane mix, and were by this time all delivering a genuine 585bhp at 11,500rpm.

Tony: We had made two or three test-bed runs recording this figure with an open exhaust before air pollution within the cell and irate local residents forced us to shut down.

After Albi, several early BRM backers contacted Alfred Owen, typically Robert Bache of Geo. Salter & Co, who wrote warmly:

> Congratulations on having at last established that the B.R.M. cars are, as you have always believed, the most outstanding Formula I racing car ever produced. It is most disappointing that tyre trouble robbed you of the victory you deserved… Having proved that your faith in the vehicles has not been misplaced, I hope that you may have many more victories.

Owen confirmed Bache's view that: "tyre trouble robbed us of the first three places in the final. The cars in the heats certainly showed that they were considerably faster than the Ferraris and…for once in a way, the papers were sympathetic to our trouble."

On June 10, Evan Price of Dunlop was on the defensive in an Albi *post mortem* meeting with RM and PB at Fort Dunlop. Price reported:

> The evidence shows that the failures have occurred due to heat, and the pressure increases which were tried, ranging from 45lbs to 70lbs, had no appreciable effect in reduction of tyre temperature, which indicated that

conditions other than those in the tyre were responsible for the heat generation.

The complete stripping of the sidewall rubber "seems to indicate the presence of high atmospheric temperature round the tyre". It was concluded that hot exhaust gases were being ejected direct onto the tyre from the out-turned side exhausts and this combined with the dynamic loads being applied by the heavy and powerful cars and the high ambient temperatures at Albi that day had created conditions which the tyres could not survive. The circumstances of Ken

Wharton's accident were explored and it was confirmed that his shunt was due neither to a thrown tyre tread nor to tyre deflation, but to driver error.

BRM's next public appearance was in an Isle of Man demonstration by Reg Parnell during the BRDC's British Empire Trophy in Douglas on June 18. The car used was Gonzalez's Albi mount 'No. 2' with engine '20/2' and gearbox '11/3'. Reg completed six laps in practice and four in demonstration.

Tony Rudd made the trip with Dick Salmon and Maurice Dove, and when Reg experienced trouble with his works Aston Martin DB3, all three pitched-in on the night before the race to help the Aston mechanics...not a universally popular move, for Ken Wharton was driving a rival Frazer Nash!

Next day Parnell won the Trophy race from Wharton and he invited the three BRM men to "stop by at the Farm [his home at Findern, just south of Derby] ...on your way home."

Maurice Dove: "We were carrying the car in one of the Austin 3-tonners, so on the way back from Liverpool Docks to Folkingham we stopped for tea at Reg's place. He was pleased as punch with his win on the Island and just as we were about to leave he said: 'Hang on a minute, I've got a present for you', and he came back with a piglet from his piggery!"

Dick Salmon: "We drove home with the three of us in the cab, Maurice on the nearside with the piglet down by his feet in the footwell. But the exhaust ran just under the floor there, so the footwell got very hot and the piglet became very restless. Eventually Maurice ended-up nursing it on his lap, with its nose out the window. I'll never forget stopping at some traffic lights where the pig stuck its snout out the window and oinked just as a couple walking past were reading the lettering on the side of the van, obviously thinking 'Coo look, there's the BRM'. You should have seen their expression change; they must have thought that's the ugliest mechanic I've ever seen...".

Tony: We had hoped to demonstrate our new-found performance the following month at Silverstone in the *Formule Libre* race accompanying the British GP. On July 11 at Folkingham 'No. 2' was tested for 15 laps using modified suspension balls and revised dural radius-arm brackets to lower their chassis attachment point to give what is now known as 'anti-squat' to help our deplorably bad traction. Everything seemed fine, but at Silverstone we made a hash of preparing Fangio's car, a disaster for which I bore the ultimate responsibility...

July 18, 1953 – *Formule Libre* Trophy, Silverstone – 17 laps, 49.76 miles

In practice Fangio in chassis 'No. 1' broke the joint Taruffi/Gonzalez 1952 lap record with a time of 1:46.0 – but this pole position lap was very much an 'arms and elbows' affair, overshadowed by Farina who on four separate laps was consistently and smoothly only a second slower – a narrow margin in those days – in the *Thin Wall Special*. Since BRM had only two cars left, Gonzalez made way for Wharton to join Fangio on home soil, his car filling third spot on the front row

June 1953 – Reg Parnell was highly regarded by the BRM personnel and brought considerable success to the team. But as a driver he gave way to the younger Ken Wharton and could never hope to match the Argentinians. Dick Salmon and Maurice Dove enjoyed his company, and he provided them with the BRM pig...

with Mike Hawthorn's new 2½-litre four-cylinder Ferrari 625 outside him. Wharton had run 'No. 2' off the road in first practice on the Thursday, complaining of the brakes locking.

Tony: Fangio's engine carboned-up its exhaust-valve guides in practice and, fully confident now, we had a working party ready to whip off the heads, ream out the valve guides and reassemble. The whole operation ran like clockwork, but for one small thing...

We had available for each engine a spare set of head joint rings, varying in section, to match each unit. Each ring, around 0.100in thick, had been carefully lapped and labelled to suit the intended cylinder of its particular engine. In case of accidents, we always included a spare unlapped ring of the thickest dimension among each set so there were 17 in all for each unit hung on nails on our garage wall in Brackley. This careful planning was typical of Willie, whose idea and work it was. But when we finished re-assembling Fangio's engine there were no rings left on the wall. Clearly, one cylinder must have been fitted with two rings...

When we filled the engine with water, about 4am, with the plugs removed, water gushed from three of the four plug holes of one head. By the time I reached the scene the head had been removed. I was told two rings had been fitted by mistake, but it was clear to me that only the thicker, 17th unlapped ring had been fitted. Even so, it had forced the liner down on its seat in the crankcase, causing permanent deformation. We carried spare extra-thick joint rings against emergencies, but they were about .008in thicker than we needed, and took ages to lap down. While this was going on I conducted, to no avail, a witch hunt, to find who was responsible for all 17 rings having gone from the board. I suspected – and still do – that Willie was intended to be the fall guy for what began as a genuine accident, because my high regard for his skill and integrity was obvious, and I had been pushing to make him test-house charge hand.

An attempt, which nearly succeeded, was made to convince RM of the two-ring story when he arrived about 11am on his way from Stratford-on-Avon. By now the car was nearly finished, so I was sent to the circuit to set up a mini pit at the entrance to the pre-race marshalling area. RM had

July 18, 1953 – Formule Libre Trophy, British Grand Prix meeting, Silverstone: Fangio making the most of an unfortunately fudged-up job with 'No. 1' – unable to improve upon second place behind Farina's ThinWall Ferrari. The good-luck horseshoe apparently came from a wedding cake, and greatly appealed to Ken Wharton, who subsequently insisted upon 'Fangio's car' in the maestro's absence...

decided, with little justification, that the only way to get the car to Silverstone in time was for him dramatically to drive it there along the main Oxford/Northampton road. He enjoyed every minute of it, while the police fortunately looked the other way.

When he arrived at the circuit, my team filled the fuel tanks, checked the engine over and fitted hard racing plugs. Dunlop had provided special tyres with only 4mm of tread instead of the usual 7mm in an attempt to avoid a repetition of Albi. All this time, Fangio had been patiently waiting, easily the calmest person present, and he climbed aboard in good time for his warm-up lap.

Hawthorn made the best start but Farina was through into the lead by Stowe Corner, and on lap two Fangio took second place from the 2½-litre Ferrari, but could make little impression upon the leading *Thin Wall*. Fangio was reportedly handicapped by a locking rear brake but all he ever said to me was that the engine seemed slightly rough, was down on power and got very hot as the race progressed, so he eased off. After Hawthorn retired, the race became a procession with Farina lapping ever faster and Fangio leaving Wharton behind. Farina broke the lap record on lap three – at 99.41mph – and then set the first-ever 100mph race lap of Silverstone fifth time round, taking a 9sec lead over Fangio with Wharton a further 8sec behind. The *Thin Wall* won comfortably, from the BRMs adequately second and third, but Fangio's engine was out of water and absolutely on its last legs

at the finish.

While the cars had been practising at Silverstone on the Friday before raceday, half a world away A.R. 'Dick' Messenger, organizer of the Auckland International Grand Prix Inc, wrote to Alfred Owen from Selborne Chambers in O'Connell Street, Auckland, New Zealand as follows:

> ...I suggest that it would be a grand bid for British prestige and the greatest individual boost for the British motor industry as a whole if one or more cars could be sent on what would be almost demonstration runs in New Zealand and Australia...my organisation has the most important race in this part of the world. The distance is 210 miles on a road type circuit devised from the runways and taxiways of Ardmore [65] aerodrome. Prize money totals approximately £4,000, *Formula* [sic] *Libre*. We are in negotiation with Mr. Ken Wharton and are prepared to pay travelling expenses, freight on his car and starting money as well... In addition to the big

65. Just postwar, Auckland area racing enthusiasts had used a circuit on remote Seagrove Aerodrome on the southern shore of Manukau harbour. It became unavailable when Auckland University set-up a physics research centre there. In February 1953, negotiations with the NZ Civil Aviation Department and Ministry of Defence had finally won permission for the Auckland Car Club to use Ardmore one day each year for motor racing. Interested clubs would later be granted permission for more meetings on shorter circuits there.

event at Auckland there is another event at Christchurch...and there are several in Australia. All these carry starting money so that the final figures may finish with a credit...in my opinion the actual monetary return would appear trivial when compared with the overall and lasting benefit that would accrue to the whole British motor industry... I sincerely hope that the difficulties of sending a car will not be insurmountable...

So the seeds were born of BRM's first InterContinental foray, in the New Year – 1954.

Meanwhile, after Silverstone, while early work on the 2½-litre Formula 1 programme began to occupy ever more time at Bourne, the V16s ran in seven more races at five meetings, commencing with the USAF Trophy at Snetterton.

July 25, 1953 – Aston Martin Owners' Club *Formule Libre* race, Snetterton – 15 laps, 40.65 miles

This meeting, sponsored by the 3rd US Air Force, started badly with the death in practice of Ulster privateer Bobbie Baird after he had rolled his sports 4.1 Ferrari at Riches Corner. Otherwise it was a bright summer's day on which Ken Wharton starred for BRM.

Having reported the preliminary races, Gregor Grant of *Autosport* wrote:

> Then came the moment for which everybody had been waiting. A series of ear-splitting banshee wails from the direction of the paddock heralded the presence of the B.R.M. Team manager Tony Rudd warmed up the 16-cylinder motor, while every available camera in the paddock area was levelled on the dark green machine...

Ken started on the outside of the front row, flanked by Flockhart in 'R4D' and Tony Rolt in Rob Walker's Formula 2 A-Type Connaught. While the F2 car was dropped in third place, Ken was able along the straights to draw away quite easily from the 2-litre supercharged ERA. He clocked 1:48 on lap two, for Snetterton's first official 90mph lap, and soon after left the lap record at 1:47.4, 90.50mph. By lap 10 the BRM was 10 seconds clear of the ERA and Wharton eventually won by 20.8sec, having averaged 88.79mph.

July 25, 1953 – *Formule Libre* USAF Invitation race, Snetterton – 10 laps, 27.1 miles

This poorly-supported race closed the USAF meeting, with only five starters as the majority of trailers and transporters had long-since been loaded-up and left for home. This time Ron Flockhart kept 'R4D' closer to the BRM's shapely tail, equalling Wharton's fastest lap of 1:48 until, after seven laps, the 2-litre supercharged engine began to falter. Leslie Marr's

Connaught took second place from the ERA on the final lap. Ken had averaged 87.79mph, but victory over a 2-litre unsupercharged Connaught, a sick prewar ERA, Wyatt's Frazer Nash and Ted Whiteaway's prewar BHW special "which still continued to spray its unfortunate driver with rusty water", was hardly what the BRM's creators had had in mind...

This objective and negative view should be tempered, however, by the now successful BRM's quite genuine popularity at the time. In British terms, as Gregor Grant accurately observed:

> Without a doubt, the Alfred Owen car is the greatest spectator attraction motor racing has ever had; people will travel miles merely to hear that fantastic exhaust note...

For many it mattered nothing that the BRM was beating feeble opposition in insignificant races – it still provided a terrific spectacle, accompanied by that wonderful noise...and above all it really was the British Racing Motor, in the metal.

Development still continued, 'No. 2' being fitted with a new-type de Dion on August 7, ready for another Scottish trip in company with 'No. 1'.

August 15, 1953 – *The Daily Record/Newcastle Journal Formule Libre* Trophy, Charterhall, Scotland – 50 laps, 100 miles

Ken Wharton enjoyed a strenuous but highly successful day at Charterhall in 'No. 1' where in nearly two-and-a-half hours behind the wheel he not only won the *Formule Libre* race in the BRM, but also the equidistant Formula 2 event in his own Cooper-Bristol.

Reg Parnell was present to drive the second BRM, but during practice a rear brake locked-on and he half-spun, broadsiding at around 100mph off the aerodrome course to crash backwards against a barrier. Reg was unhurt, but the car sustained considerable body damage and was a non-starter.

Giuseppe Farina bettered his existing lap record by no less than 3 seconds in the *Thin Wall Special*, which had been fitted with Goodyear-designed disc brakes since its previous outing on the Berwickshire circuit. His time of 1:21.8 – 88.08mph – compared with Wharton's 1:24.4 in the BRM and Flockhart's 1:25.4 in the ageless 'R4D'.

After early rain the course dried for the F2 race which Wharton led throughout. Despite threatening skies rain held off during the later *Libre* race, in which Farina took an early lead from Wharton and Moss' short-lived Cooper-Alta. The *Thin Wall*'s hard exhaust note softened with ignition trouble, enabling Wharton and the BRM to catch up and pass. Farina eventually retired, while Wharton not only won from Rolt's Connaught at 82.7mph but also lowered Farina's lap record, leaving it at 1:24.0, 85.71mph.

On August 29, Ken Wharton demonstrated BRM 'No. 1' at

Left: July 25, 1953 — USAF Trophy, Snetterton: Ken Wharton in 'No. 1' set the Norfolk aerodrome circuit's first 90mph lap in holding off the aggressive Ron Flockhart's ERA 'R4D' which Ken himself would eventually buy for hill-climb use.

Below left: August 14, 1953 — Formule Libre Trophy, Charterhall: Cheerful group with the boss' Bentley, Wharton in the winning 'No. 1' with its horseshoe (which was sometimes swopped to the sister car to persuade Ken he was OK, it was Fangio's) and mechanics Dove and Salmon with RM — one of the faithful Lodestars beyond.

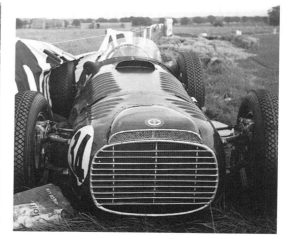

Above: Reg Parnell 'dropped' 'No. 2' in preparation for this his last BRM outing and broadsided it into the Charterhall aerodrome barriers. Damage was too severe to allow it to race. Team-mate Wharton became BRM's only starter, and won.

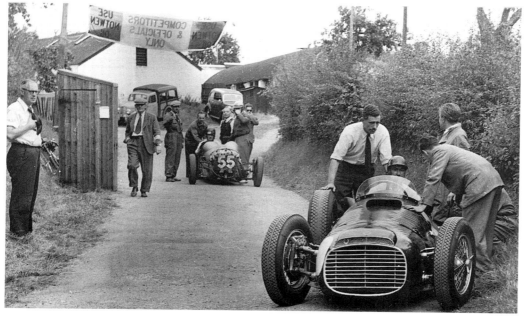

Left: August 29, 1953 — Shelsley Walsh demonstration: Wharton at the height of his relationship with BRM, about to hurl 'No. 1' at the steep little Worcestershire 'climb, the car tended by Gordon Newman (wearing tie), Maurice Dove (hidden) and Willie Southcott.

Right: September 26, 1953 – Woodcote Cup, Goodwood: Wharton ran second in this five-lap sprint before spinning here at the chicane. Tony Rolt, driving Rob Walker's A-Type Connaught, managed to avoid the BRM but crashed the Connaught heavily into the barrier protecting this photographer

Below: Sheer precision – Fangio only ever won one race on British soil – the 1956 British Grand Prix for Ferrari. Otherwise almost every car he drove here gave trouble. This September Goodwood meeting saw him unable to catch Hawthorn's ThinWall in the Woodcote Cup and then he retired from the feature Goodwood Trophy – the last of his seven races for BRM...

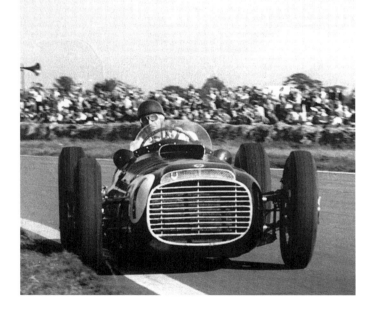

Shelsley Walsh as a gesture of thanks to the Midland Automobile Club for their long support of the original project. Unfortunately, the meeting was marred by heavy rain, nobody could better 40sec climbs and Ken – as reigning British Hill-Climb Champion – set BTD in his ERA at 41.82sec, and flailed the highly unsuitable BRM up the steep little hill in 49.84. During dry morning practice, however, he had left the BRM's mark indelibly on the hill with massive wheelspin away from the bottom Kennel Bend and out through the central Esses – clocking a quite remarkable 37.97sec, barely a second outside his climb record.

The major Goodwood International followed:

September 26, 1953 – Woodcote Cup, Goodwood – 5 laps, 12 miles

A beautiful, crisp autumn day dawned for the season's closing meeting at the Sussex circuit, and the two BRMs were fielded for Juan Manuel Fangio – 'No. 1' – and Ken Wharton – 'No. 2' – confronting Mike Hawthorn in the *Thin Wall*.

During practice Ken complained of "no power at the top end" so engine '20/2' was replaced by '20/1' for the race. The team experimented with alternative five-stud and R1 tyres, and Ken would run five-stud in the Woodcote Cup and R1s in the Goodwood Trophy later that day.

Roy Salvadori won the preliminary Madgwick Cup race for Formula 2 cars in a Connaught, breaking the shared BRM/*Thin Wall* outright lap record from the previous season. It was Vandervell Products' turn to stage a last-minute panic arrival, the *Thin Wall* having broken its engine during practice the previous day, which required an all-night rebuild. The car was hustled onto the grid with just 30 seconds to go, Hawthorn initially lining up alongside Moss' Cooper-Alta on the second row until Stirling gestured him through to his rightful place at the front. Mike had the *Thin Wall* projecting a yard beyond the line when the starter dropped his flag regardless, so he took off with terrific wheelspin and led away through Madgwick Corner, leaving the rest of the field for dead.

Salvadori was running second in his Connaught until an oil pipe parted, allowing Wharton through, hotly pursued by Tony Rolt in Rob Walker's Connaught, then Fangio. But braking for the chicane on lap three Wharton spun and Rolt – taking evasive action – ran wide in the narrow chicane itself and crunched into the concrete barrier on the infield. Hawthorn careered round to win handsomely, from Fangio

A QUESTION OF TRUST

Halfway through the Owen Racing Organisation's first season of competition with the BRM cars, at 4.30 in the afternoon of Friday, June 19, 1953, the committee of the British Racing Motors Association – the BRM supporters' club – met at Automotive Products' Leamington Spa offices.

Present were A.C. Burdon, Walter Hill, Captain John Hopcraft, H. McPhillips, G. Rivers, N. Riddihough and Bernard Scott, with Rivers Fletcher and E. Tinto in attendance. In Donald McCullough's absence as Chairman, Walter Hill presided.

This meeting's primary purpose was to consider what legal steps were necessary before the BRMA could throw its full support behind the Owen Organisation's continuing efforts with BRM. After reserving future expenses funds (including potential winding-up costs) it had prepared to donate what money it could towards the new season's racing activities. Out of some 1,400 members circularized, 46 per cent had returned their voting cards, amongst whom 96.73 per cent were in favour of continued support of the project under Owen's stewardship. Consequently, £4,000[66] was donated on the BRMA's behalf to the Owen Organisation in support of contemporary and future BRM racing activities.

Soon the BRMA's title would be changed to the Owen Racing Motors Association – ORMA – and under that name it would continue to co-ordinate enthusiast support for future BRM operations...

Meanwhile, on Wednesday, July 15, 1953, the Executive Council of The British Motor Racing Research Trust met at 10.30am at The Royal Thames Yacht Club in Knightsbridge, London.

Bernard Scott chaired this meeting, with Alfred Owen, Captain Hopcraft, RM and Jim Sandercombe all present, PB absent and J.R. Muirie, H.L. Pryce, P. Derek Warren and W.K. Hartley all in attendance.

There was considerable discussion regarding the continued use by Rubery Owen of the BRM name. Minute No. 5 of the Trust GM of October 23, 1952 was cited as stating that only the three V16 cars then extant should continue to bear that name. It was agreed that the Chairman would write to all Trust members to gauge their reaction to the Owen Organisation being allowed to apply the BRM name to cars other than those three Project 15 V16s.

It was also agreed that the sum of £70,044 advanced to British Racing Motors Ltd during the 11 months ended October 31, 1952 should be written-off, and the meeting heard that the total of the Reconciliation Statement connected with Rubery Owen's purchase of the assets of British Racing Motors Ltd had amounted to £22,287 against the maximum estimate of £23,500. RM then proposed that formal approval be given to the accounts of the BMRRT presented for the 11 months to October 31, 1952. Alfred Owen seconded the motion, which was carried unanimously. There being no other business the Chairman declared the meeting closed. After a pleasant lunch, those present and in attendance variously bade their farewells and then went their separate ways, out into the scurry and bustle of Knightsbridge on a summer afternoon.

The business of The British Motor Racing Research Trust was at an end...

66. By 1993 values the figures involved here are: 1) the £4,000 donated by BRMA to ORO = no less than £54,500!; 2) The 1952 advances to BRM Ltd of £70,044 written-off by the BMRRT = over £958,800; 3) Rubery Owen's purchase of the assets represents a final value of over £305,000 against the maximum estimate value of over £321,600...

and Wharton. But the margin was immense – Fangio 23.2 seconds behind in just five laps, and Wharton another 12.2sec back. Hawthorn's race average of 92.11mph equalled Ken's previous lap record, while his fastest lap was a new record for Goodwood including the chicane – 1:32.0, 93.91mph.

Tony: We were invited to protest as Hawthorn had been over the line when the flag fell. We declined, saying it was not the way we wished to go motor racing, and so did Fangio who said: "Mike won by much more than the advantage he had on the line." He told me he suspected his gearchange had been slower than usual...

September 26, 1953 – Goodwood Trophy – 15 laps, 36 miles

The BRMs framed Hawthorn and Salvadori's repaired works Connaught on either side of the front row, with Fangio on pole. Hawthorn led again through Madgwick on the opening lap, and tore away to win as he pleased from the BRMs once Wharton had displaced Salvadori for third. Fangio's BRM 'No. 1' was falling away from the *Thin Wall* because the Argentinian was finding it increasingly difficult to select gears. On lap nine he stopped briefly at Woodcote, searching around for a gear, and three laps later he came into the pits to retire. Hawthorn meanwhile went from strength to strength,

ultimately lapping in 1:31.4 to raise the lap record speed to 94.53mph and win by 3.4 seconds from Wharton in second place. Ken had decided by that time that 'No. 2' was over-geared, and when inspected back in the paddock its input bevel oil seal was found to be moving and leaking.

On the following Monday, RM wrote to Owen:

I was bitterly disappointed on Saturday, and I know you felt the same...in spite of the fact that both Fangio and Ken Wharton broke the old circuit record many times, we were still not fast enough for the Ferrari in its very high compression sprint tune. (Incidentally, it did blow up in the paddock as the car entered it after the race.)...

He also asked permission to approach Herrington, of High Duty Alloys, to have much-needed new cylinder heads cast – they were required to keep the V16s racing.

One more British meeting remained that season, at Castle Combe the following weekend...

October 3, 1953 – *Formule Libre* Castle Combe – 15 laps, 27.6 miles

The media had christened this 1.84-mile Wiltshire circuit 'The Goodwood of the West' and a large crowd assembled on a sunny autumn day at the old grass aerodrome primarily to watch Ken Wharton in his customary BRM 'No. 2', equipped again – as at Goodwood – with engine '20/1' and gearbox '21/2'.

He started from pole position and simply won as he pleased from Bob Gerard's ERA – 28.8 seconds behind – and Horace Gould's Cooper-Bristol – just 0.8sec further back.

Cyril Posthumus reported for *Autosport*:

> Peace reigned over Wiltshire again as Wharton cut his engine and came in to receive the victor's laurels from Mrs. K.R. Maurice, Secretary of the Meeting and owner of the land on which the circuit lies. The good lady, however, came too close to the B.R.M.'s hot exhaust pipe, burning a large hole in a nylon stocking. 'Oh well! Something to remind me of the day the B.R.M. came to Castle Combe', she said…

Ken Wharton always went well when he felt he held all the cards, and that day he broke Bob Gerard's existing Castle Combe lap record, set with the ERA, leaving it at 1:13.8, 89.77mph. Even so he had driven around a handling problem, since 'No. 2''s right-front strut had failed and the right-rear

was found to be way down on pressure. The radiator was also found to be leaking…

Regardless, the Owen Racing Organisation's maiden season of racing the BRM V16s had seen them make 21 starts in 11 events – including Heats – finishing 17 times, winning seven, and adding six second places, three thirds, one fourth and a fifth.

After that Castle Combe finale, RM invited Ron Flockhart – who had driven Ray's old ex-works ERA 'R4D' so well in *Libre* events – to try a BRM during a Ken Wharton track test session at Goodwood.

Both V16s were available, but Ken was unwell on the Tuesday and arrived instead next day. PB split the circuit into four – using Monza experience – and Vic Barlow of Dunlop timed every lap in four portions. Ray wrote:

> Flockhart arrived with his father and had quite an amount of running, and for a newcomer to the B.R.M. I must say he showed very great promise. In his few laps he spun the car off the road, but fortunately no damage was done, and he was out again within an hour after the car had been 'spring-cleaned'…

Right: What Sunday in the '50s was complete without the lunchtime BBC Light Programme's Billy Cotton Band Show, "Wakey Way-KAY!!"? Bandleader Billy Cotton tries a V16 to RM's great amusement, with Ken Wharton, left. Between 1937 and 1939, Bill Cotton had driven the ex-Dick Seaman ERA 'R1B' in 18 events. It was maintained for him by W.E. 'Wilkie' Wilkinson, who would join BRM in 1961…

Below: October 3, 1953 – Hastings Trophy, Castle Combe: What the mighty had come to… By the end of 1953 the old Formula 1 for which the V16 had been designed was completely moribund, and ORO found itself running the cars against such thin and obsolescent fields as this – Wharton bound for a win in 'No. 2', from Rolt's hastily patched up Walker Connaught behind, and the ERAs of Bob Gerard (64) and Graham Whitehead.

Ray was very attracted to the handsome, fair-haired young Scot and he added: "…we *must* attach much importance to Flockhart, and *his future*, because I am sure he is our best bet, and a very nice fellow at that. I particularly wish you to see Flockhart and his father…".

Owen would subsequently agree to RM signing-on Ron as a driver, and a between-races salesman's job was arranged for him in one of the Organisation subsidiaries, the Charles Clark car dealership in Birmingham. I am assured that, as a well brought up – indeed rather prim – young man from Edinburgh, Flockhart hadn't a clue of at least one reason for RM's extremely attentive interest in his well being. When a more worldly-wise friend jokingly advised him to "watch out", and Ron asked the reason why, he was simply *stunned* by the explanation…

Through that mid-summer Tony and the team had completed a little more test-bed work on the engine but the winter of 1953–54 would see the Test House at Bourne finally vacated – due both to its inherent inadequacy and to an increasing chorus of complaint from townspeople. Quite apart from the familiar muffled but nagging scream of a V16 on test the increasing numbers of TV sets in neighbouring homes had magnified local opposition. Spasmodically appalling blizzards of TV interference had been blamed upon the multi-cylinder engine's unsuppressed ignition demands!

Engine testing was now to be conducted instead at Folkingham, in the remote aerodrome's former Fire Station building. The Owen Racing Organisation was on permanent 28 days' notice from the Air Ministry there, so total removal from their fenced-off compound and its assorted buildings had to be possible at all times within 28 days. Consequently, the Bourne drawing office had to design a bolt-down removable dyno installation which could be removed within this time limit should Defence requirements dictate. It was not designed to cope with the V16 – all eyes looking forward to the 2½-litre P25…

With more refinements to the exhaust and water systems and development of a lightened oil cooler arrangement for the new Project 30 Mark II 'sprint cars' (which had been under construction, with considerable delays, throughout the autumn following the Owen/Rudd conversation at Easter Monday Goodwood), Tony's V16 test team also discovered that if they kept revs below 11,000 they could avoid any valve-sticking problems.

Having improved distribution, they reverted to the original manifolding, and by the end of that 1953 season the BRM Type 15 V16-cylinder engine was at last – after eight years' often agonizing design and development – truly raceworthy…

ENTER 'THE SPRINT CAR'

From July to November, 1953 the prototype lightweight Mark II V16 'sprint car', using numerous components salvaged from Wharton's chassis 'No. 3' Albi write-off, was being built at Folkingham after an uncertain start while PB and Alfred Owen had wrangled over whether it should be built at all, who by, where and how, because PB maintained it would only delay the new F1 car programme.

Tony: Alfred Owen had both authorized PB to proceed with a new Grand Prix car design for the forthcoming 2½-litre Formula and had also recalled our discussion at Easter Monday Goodwood on power-to-weight ratio. He now initiated work on a lightweight version of the V16 for *Formule Libre* racing, which became BRM's Project 30, and with PB committed to 2½-litre research, it became my baby…

By this time my solution to every problem was to ensure that everything was made exactly as the designer intended and to make everything more and more rigid. I thought that suspension should be soft, but that the structure upon which it reacted should be absolutely rigid.

Project 30 became virtually a backyard special as Bourne's resources were concentrated largely upon 2½-litre design. When building his Aston Martin special, Tony had been forced to take Accles & Pollock's minimum-batch quantity of oval-section 5in x 2.4in tube and had plenty left. This was sold to BRM after PB exploited the fact that he was unlikely to find a buyer anywhere else.

He recalls: The new sprint car's wheelbase was to be 8ft 0in instead of 8ft 6in and we had to build it at Folkingham without the aid of the design office in Bourne. We had a very old drawing-board set-up in a long single workshop at Folkingham and as fast as I drew the new chassis so Stan Hope and his gang put it together, only one stage advanced from the traditional chalk marks on the garage floor method…

There was a general belief in those days that only supermen could weld racing car chassis. Ferrari and Maserati certainly gave the lie to that, but we had not noticed. Rubery Owen despatched a superman of their own to us, named Maurice Cradock, and he came over when there was enough welding to be done to make the trip worthwhile. He really was a super welder. This became apparent when we made the first Mark II front crossmember which was virtually a series of lightening holes welded together.

We had made up a punch and a flanging tool and cut the front and rear faces out of a very large crossmember, punched and flanged the holes inwards and then made top and bottom strips to wrap around it. They were then punched and flanged as well, and Maurice welded-up the entire assembly with virtually no distortion. It was a wonderful example of the welder's art.

This strong yet light crossmember incorporated bearing tubes for needle-roller bearings and into these tubes we then pressed the hard tracks from the cast aluminium suspension pillars of the Mark I cars. After planning to incline them at 1 degree to give negative camber, which would have meant expecting the roll bar to work with 2 degrees of bend in it, (which it did not seem to mind in our rig tests), it suddenly dawned on me that all we had to do was to space the lower arms further out to give us quite a wide variation of camber adjustment. Out of deference to Stirling Moss we also fitted Morris Minor rack-and-pinion steering and although the rack was considerably shortened we utilized its inner ball-joints etc for ideal steering geometry.

By locating the rack quite high we managed to get away with only one true UJ in the steering system. Where the column passed over the supercharger we needed a little flex and there we inserted spring-steel strips, slightly star-shaped, to give a little plunge and angularity. Certainly, when complete, this system felt much better than the Mark I cars' and there was virtually no play in it at all…

At the rear we made a large triangulated lever to link the air struts to the suspension, articulating the inner end of the strut direct onto the top of the gearbox so that each strut reacted on its twin and the gearbox absorbed the loads. I was not very bright at the time, but when we completed the geometry of the air-strut movement relative to wheel movement, despite my best efforts, we had a falling rate system. That is, the load on the strut proportionately decreased the further the wheel rose.

This is diametrically opposed to what one should require but since the air-struts themselves had a diabolically high rising-rate due to the air heating-up inside them, they compensated for my error by themselves!

We then adopted a one-piece de Dion tube with welded ends which was located by twin parallel radius arms on each side. By putting the whole thing under a hydraulic press and giving it a fearful squeeze we produced 1-degree negative camber and about a ¼in toe-in for the rear wheels. Bending the tube like this lowered the rear roll-centre about half-an-inch. We did not realize it at the time but this one-piece de Dion tube

was being used rather as an anti-roll bar.

When the new car was completed it was around 400lbs lighter than the Mark I and retained most of the diabolical wheelspin characteristics. Being much lighter it was also very much quicker away from the corners. Fuel in its 40-gallon tail tank was concentrated above the rear suspension, and drivers reported that the new car was not too bad when the tank was full, but decidedly hairy when it was running light! I did most of the test driving in this car, softening the rear suspension considerably and finally fitting smaller, wider front wheels and tyres. I did most of this in a wet autumn in intervals between trying to stop the ram air pressure generated by forward speed from blowing the fuel out of the float chambers, and emerged firm in the belief that racing drivers were sadly underpaid and definitely needed the protection of a trade union…

Initially, an in-car engine start-up date of October 25 had been the target for the first Mark II – to become known as V16 chassis 'No. 4'. This slipped into late November, but finally the car was completed in time to test at Goodwood on November 30.

We had been about a week late, but no-one seemed very interested. Then we had a monumental row over which I nearly walked out.

Confident in all we had done to the new car's cooling

March 1954 – Folkingham: Rudd's baby – the prototype V16 'sprint car' – Mark II 'No. 4'. As originated with Tony's small radiator, the Mark II's bonnet had no air exit apertures at all. In theory they needed c.5% greater area than the radiator intake to accommodate enhanced volume through heating. Tony was approaching the correct area by trial and error with the four oval holes seen here when he was forced to fit the huge Mark I radiator…

He had intended the small-radiatored Mark II's nose to curve smoothly into the bonnet profile to clear magnetos and engine-top water manifolding. Louvring would stiffen the slightly domed bonnet, which had to be made right first time, hence methodical progress towards that goal. RM and PB's insistence upon fitting the larger radiator destroyed this aim.

system, I had used the original small radiator to save weight, space and money. In fact the size and shape of the front crossmember had been determined by the outline of the small radiator, so confident was I. RM came up to look at the car after it had been painted and said to PB: "Peter, the radiator is much too small!" In vain I produced all my data, pointed out that 40 per cent of its area was blanked off to get the engine warm enough for a November day, but all to absolutely no avail...

PB ordered new radiators that were about 10 per cent larger in area, which meant a new nose, more money and more weight. The air intake calibration had to be done again. The whole incident must have wasted about three weeks and

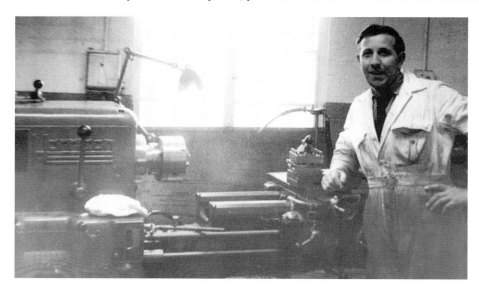

The BRM compound at Folkingham aerodrome was quite well-equipped and it was there that the cars were built, developed and prepared using components delivered from the main design and machine shop facility in Bourne. PB remained wary of permitting photographers into the place, but here's a selection from c.1953. Left: Race mechanic/lathe operator Maurice Dove was nicknamed 'Mo the Mangle'. Here's Mo, and that's his mangle...

Below: Snap shots of V16 car 'No. 1' stripped in the Folkingham race shop – backed by Maurice, Dick Salmon, Willie Southcott, Gordon Newman and 'Flo-Joe'. Willie nicknamed Gordon 'Bagwash' as an insult, but it stuck, 'Humphrey' following from his leisure dress and since he was a notorious lady killer. For 1954 he became Chief Mechanic, and one evening retorted to Willie "Sir Bagwash to you", and then impressed everyone with his sprint for tools at Goodwood as Wharton starved his V16 into silence on the grid. Consequently he ended up as "Sir Humphrey MacDonald Bagwash, TGIP" – for "Thank God I'm Pure". Gordon Newman was known as 'Baggy' for short...

cost over £6,000 (in 1953!). Even on hot summer days we subsequently used to run with half the radiator blanked off, which infuriates me to this day. PB would not argue with me, just refused to listen to my engineering logic or look at my data. He had the larger radiator drawn at Bourne, and when it arrived it was sent to Folkingham with an instruction to stop all testing and fit it immediately.

But Owen's intention had been to have the second surviving Mark I cannibalized to produce a second Mark II ready for the new season, and on December 3, PB wrote to him complaining that since one car plus spares was on the high seas *en route* to New Zealand and the other was on a promotional tour as an exhibition car, with bookings until January 29:

> …the point arises that unless this work on conversion can be got on with immediately it will clash severely with the building of the new 2½-litre cars early in the New Year.
> As you have sanctioned the production of a second sprint car, would you confirm that we should go ahead…

Owen wrote in one margin of PB's 'Rubery Owen & Co Ltd – Engine Development Division'-headed letter: "Only if the first showed promise & was faster than the 'standard' car", while in the other he scrawled (concerning the exhibition car): "I think much good work can be done without it for the exhibition car is virtually only a shell." His formidable senior secretary, Miss Polly Ramsden, would then interpret these remarks in letter form for AGBO's signature, and next day at Bourne PB would receive his orders in rapid order…

Now for 1954 there was the prospect of an all-new breed of 2½-litre unsupercharged BRM, plus the lightened, shortened P30 V16 Mark II, and also experience for Bourne of a Grand Prix car made in Italy… It would be a busy year, and it would begin with Ken Wharton racing a V16 some 12,000 miles from home – in New Zealand…

1954 – AUTUMN OF THE V16s

The Owen Organisation had growing interests in New Zealand which provided the promotional reason behind Ken Wharton's works entry in the New Zealand Grand Prix at Auckland, North Island, and a follow-up outing in the Lady Wigram Trophy race at Christchurch, South Island.

BRM chassis 'No. 2' was shipped on the *SS Port Nelson* on November 24, 1953, due to dock in Auckland a month later, on Christmas Eve. In preparation for the trip, the often demanding Ken Wharton complained to Owen that the two assigned mechanics, Gordon Newman and Willie Southcott:

> …seem to have done nothing to fit themselves for tyre and wheel-changing…[while] the success of the B.R.M. in Auckland is going to depend on our capacity to change tyres quickly in the pit…

Alfred wrote to Sandercombe at Bourne:

I understand our man Rudd was actually able to change wheels in about 30 seconds and this should be a target for our men in New Zealand to achieve…!

For Gordon Newman and Willie Southcott the adventure began at 8am in Bourne, when they caught the bus to Peterborough. This was followed by a train to King's Cross, London, to report to KLM's Sloane Street office at noon, a bus to Heathrow and then a 5pm flight to Amsterdam, thence to Auckland via Sydney, Australia. They had a worldwide letter of credit with them, value £130, comprising 50 per cent of 15 weeks' wages (£60), expenses at £3 a week (£45) and an extra £25 for contingencies. The New Zealand Grand Prix at Ardmore Aerodrome was to be run on January 9, and the Lady Wigram Trophy race on the RNZAF base at Christchurch in the South Island was on February 7, with sundry exhibition dates in between.

January 9, 1954 – New Zealand Grand Prix, Ardmore Aerodrome, Auckland – 100 laps, 210 miles

Ken Wharton – his BRM using engine '20/2' – brought the 70,000 spectators to their feet at the start, immediately bellowing into the lead from fellow-Briton Peter Whitehead's 2-litre V12 Ferrari and the Australian Stan Jones' single-seater *Maybach Special*. Within the first five laps he had lapped most of the field and at quarter-distance he held a 37 seconds lead over Whitehead in second place. Ken was caught out on one lap at the hairpin and spun, but continued after a push-start, which was permissible under the local regulations.

Rain then began to fall, and he eventually came into the pits after 44 laps to refuel and change a wheel. This stop cost 44 seconds and permitted Jones to take the lead. The damp track then lopped 2–3 seconds off the BRM's lap times, but after seven more laps Wharton had repassed Jones to regain the lead.

As Peter Greenslade reported:

> Then, on lap 60, the Bourne jinx reared its head. Coming down the main straight, vapourized brake fluid suddenly streamed from the front brake cylinders of the B.R.M. Looking as though it was on fire, the car slowed down and came into the pits. Repairs were impossible so the front brake pipes were disconnected and from then on Wharton drove with rear brakes only, and his gearbox. He gradually dropped back through the field, but kept going in what must have been one of the greatest drives of his career to bring the B.R.M. home fifth and to complete the longest race in the car's history…

Stan Jones was eventually declared the winner from Horace Gould's Cooper-Bristol after a considerable controversy over the true positions since everybody's lap charts seemed to differ.

The aerodrome perimeter track surface had broken up progressively as the race wore on, producing flying grit which

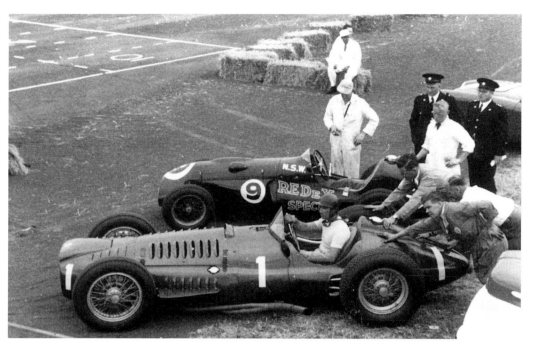

had lodged in one of the BRM's disc brake calipers, preventing the piston returning fully and so causing the brake to overheat through constant friction, eventually popping off a brake hose union and letting the fluid gush out onto the hot disc. Grit had also been ingested by the supercharger intake but such problems had been budgeted for, and Newman and Southcott replaced engine '20/2' with the spare '20/3' complete with another late-type blower ready for the Christchurch race four weeks later, after a long series of Owen Organisation promotional functions.

February 7, 1954 – Lady Wigram Trophy, Christchurch, NZ – 48 laps, 100.8 miles

During practice on the 2.1-mile South Island aerodrome circuit, Wharton easily achieved pole position with a time of 1:23.0 in the re-engined BRM. Flanking him on the front row of the grid were to be the steady Peter Whitehead, the English-based Australian Tony Gaze's blown HWM, and local man Freddie Zambucka's prewar Maserati 8CM.

Whitehead made the best start, but the BRM led by the first corner, clocking 1:32.6 for that opening lap. Wharton was said to be exceeding 150mph on the back straight: "…taking a perfect line through the corners, blue smoke lifting from his back tyres as he accelerated out of them…" reported Peter Greenslade. Just after half-distance Gaze displaced Whitehead to run second before making a 31sec pit stop to refuel and change a rear wheel. "It looked as if a B.R.M. was really going to win, for it was clear that Wharton was not stopping for fuel or tyres. Suddenly, however, the ear-piercing note of the B.R.M. began to sound decidedly unhealthy, and Wharton came past his pit gesticulating and tapping the top of his crash helmet. Nevertheless he stayed ahead until the 42nd lap when

Whitehead flashed by and the B.R.M. came into the pits. The bonnet was lifted, quickly replaced, then Wharton was on his way again, now third... Momentarily the B.R.M. seemed to regain proper tune, and Wharton put in one lap in 1min 21.8sec...

Whitehead won from Gaze: "But where was the B.R.M.? The unhappy Bourne car had slowed to a walking pace and finally came to a stop.[67] Wharton jumped out and slowly pushed it the last quarter-mile to receive the flag for third place just after the fourth man – McMillan's Alfa Romeo – went into his last lap...".

This long-distance venture had not quite proved to be the prestigious demonstration ORO had hoped... The car was shipped back home on the *SS Karamea,* due to dock in London on April 7. Ken Wharton flew home via Hawaii from where he wrote to AGBO thanking him for the opportunity to drive the BRM in New Zealand, while Gordon Newman decided that New Zealand was such a pleasant country he would eventually settle there...

Back home there was a considerable panic – typical BRM – in preparation for the opening Goodwood race meeting on Easter Monday, April 19.

On March 1, engine '20/1' had been installed in the new No. 1 Project 30 or 'BRM V16 Mark II sprint car'. This engine's ancient cylinder heads were sub-standard and regarded as unraceworthy, and after testing the engine was scheduled for overhaul by March 16. The heads from the cooked Christchurch race engine '20/3' were, however, expected to be serviceable, and were earmarked to be transferred once they arrived in port. Engine '20/2' on the ship had no known defects, but would certainly require inspection, overhaul and testing, but Bourne expected to turn it around in seven to 10 days after receipt. Engine '20/3' ex-Christchurch was expected to be in poor condition and certainly required a major overhaul, so would not be usable at Goodwood. 'No. 20/4' engine required a supercharger gear bearing housing, due March 14, and also lacked raceworthy heads.

Cylinder head castings to latest spec were due from High Duty Alloys and the inventory report demanded:

> Thorough tests should be carried out before racing... The engine position at the moment is almost entirely controlled by receipt of N.Z. parts. Without these parts we cannot have even one engine available until just before Goodwood and that with new, untested, heads.

Meanwhile, the No. 1 P30 sprint car was effectively ready to run, while the chassis frame for No. 2 was not yet welded, target completion date being March 3.

On the 13th of that month, Ron Flockhart test-drove the Mark II prototype at Folkingham. This car was variously referred to as both 'Mark II No. 1' or 'Mark II Chassis No. 4' in

the works records, while its sister Mark II would be referred to equally as 'No. 2' or 'Chassis No. 5' – all rather confusing until one gets the hang of it.

Flockhart totalled 30 laps that day at Folkingham, but the car's fuel tank split and the engine briefly misfired above 10,500rpm. Next day, in seven more laps running, the fuel tank split again and a brake pipe failed. Two weeks later, on the 27th, Wharton drove 15 laps until the car's gearbox mounting failed, and on April Fool's Day a Silverstone test session was aborted due to magneto failure after just one brief lap. Three days later, at Folkingham, Flockhart tested some ex-NZ plugs for five laps, "popping at 10,500", three more laps were sufficient to split the tank yet again, and after rear damping had been increased and 16-inch wheels fitted, running totalled 29 laps.

On April 6 another trip to Silverstone with Wharton yielded 16 fruitful laps in which the front damping was improved, and on the 16th a pre-Goodwood shake-down at Folkingham saw Flockhart cover 10 laps in the Mark II and 22 to acclimatize himself to the hastily re-prepared ex-NZ Mark I 'No. 2', freshly retrieved from London Docks.

The trip south followed, for BRM's opening race of 1954 and for Ron Flockhart's debut as a BRM team driver and teammate to Ken Wharton.

April 19, 1954 – Chichester Cup, Goodwood – 5 laps, 12 miles

During Goodwood practice on Saturday the 17th, Wharton gave the new Mark II an auspicious debut, setting fastest practice lap at 1:35.0, 90.95mph, but No. 2 piston failed after only seven laps running and had to be replaced. In the dark on the Sunday night, Tony Rudd ran-in the repaired engine, using the runways of Ford airfield. This process was terminated after he had 'popped' most of the runway lights with the Mark II's stub exhausts. Flockhart drove the old Mark I to set second fastest practice time in 1:35.8, completing 18 laps without mechanical fault, merely asking that the seating position be improved.

On the Monday morning Wharton completed three laps "special practice" to complete running-in the Mark II's new piston, and while the Chichester Cup developed into a three-cornered battle between Wharton – in misfiring troubles as the magnetos were again acting-up – Roy Salvadori (in Syd Greene's new Maserati 250F) and Reg Parnell's Ferrari 625, the unfortunate Scot was crowded out at Madgwick Corner on the opening lap, he spun and could only rejoin last, having lost 25 seconds.

Salvadori, always an aggressive racer, made a last-minute lunge to overtake Wharton at the chicane on the final lap, but the Owen machine streaked away, displaying astonishing acceleration almost matched by the Grand Prix Maserati. They finally finished less than half a second apart, with just over a second separating them from Parnell in third place. Flockhart was fourth after haring back through the field, and sharing fastest lap with the three leaders at 1:35.6, 90.38mph.

---

67. Engine '20/3' had in fact seized and 'No. 1/4' quarter cylinder head was subsequently condemned as scrap. The lower crankcase half was saved by a 'reduxed' patch (one secured by the new 'redux' epoxy resin adhesive treatment, e.g. Araldite, while the upper half was considered salvable by deposition of aluminium around the butchered areas and re-machining lower spigots for the liners. Rolls-Royce were approached to perform this repair.

April 19, 1954 – Glover Trophy, Goodwood – 21 laps, 50.4 miles

Wharton and Flockhart swapped cars for the feature race, Ken taking back the Mark I and Ron inheriting the new Mark II in which he started from pole position, Wharton alongside him, then Rolt's Connaught and Parnell's Ferrari. Poor Rolt was so deafened by the BRMs blipping alongside him that he over-revved his own engine while waiting for the flag to fall. It was feared that the Mark II's magnetos, for which Lucas had not yet modified any more drives so there were no spares, would not last the race, and certainly would not have recovered from their first-race maladies.

Flockhart led for the opening lap until the magnetos reached operating temperature and began to misfire so

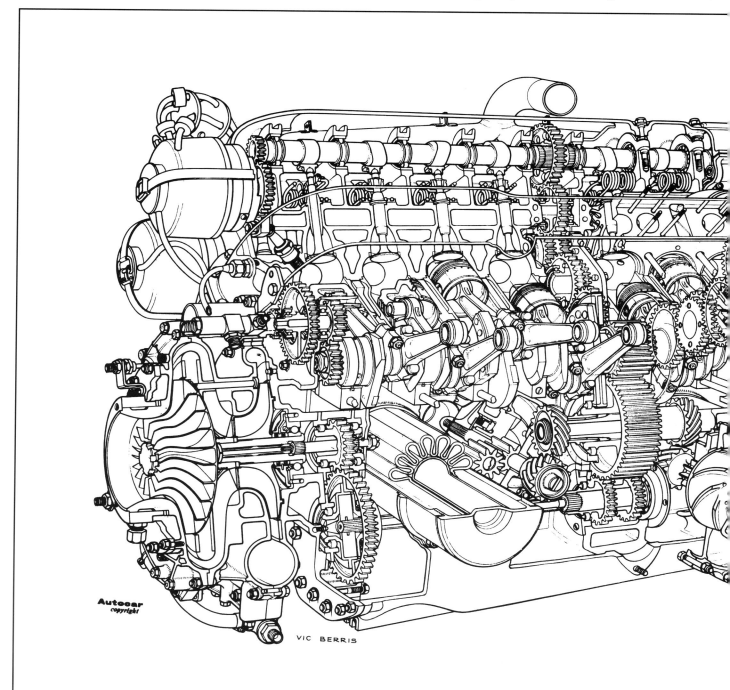

Autocar
copyright

VIC BERRIS

Wharton blared by. Parnell retired on lap three leaving Salvadori in the new 2½-litre six-cylinder Maserati 250F to duel with Wharton. There was little love lost in this battle, and while Wharton maintained a margin of about a second, the 250F's efficient drum brakes and lighter weight made it the braking equal of the BRM on discs. By lap 19 Salvadori was frustrated and angry at what he regarded as Wharton's constant baulking. His Maserati's nose had been hovering

around the BRM's shapely tail for lap after lap, until rugged Roy decided he saw an opening on the entry to Lavant Corner.

Wharton 'slammed the door' on the green Maserati, the cars touched, the BRM half-spun and was immediately rammed violently amidships, just abaft its right-front wheel. Salvadori bounced away, off onto the verge, his Maserati stalled and sadly crumpled around its nose.

The impact merely punted the BRM back straight and Wharton drove on to complete the final lap with 'No. 2' handling oddly and a huge dent in its side. He took the chequered flag to win by a clear 40 seconds from Kenneth McAlpine's Connaught, while Leslie Marr's sister car in third place was followed home by Flockhart's badly misfiring Mark II, fourth.

Wharton and Salvadori shared fastest lap at a rather poor 1:37.8, 88.34mph, and the incensed Maserati driver's entrant, Syd Greene of Gilby Engineering, lodged an official protest against Wharton, claiming the BRM driver had deliberately baulked his man much of the way. The protest was considered by the Stewards, but rejected, BRM being confirmed as winners of the Glover Trophy with what proved to be a written-off car!

To add insult to injury, engine '20/5' actually broke a connecting rod due to hydraulic lock after the race had ended, and in stripped form it then went straight into the No. 2 Mark II chassis as a mock-up slave unit during the new car's completion. The lower-half crankcase of this engine was damaged beyond economic salvage while: "The upper-half crankcase may be a possible salvage…but as main bearing studs have repeatedly failed in this engine and it has several doubtful liner lower faces, particularly No. 11, it is suggested that this crankcase is discarded. No. 5/8 1/4 cylinder head is scrap, as it is holed through No. 6 cylinder…"

The right-side chassis rail of V16 Mark I 'No.2' had been stoved in several inches by the Maserati's attack, and the frame was so distorted it was judged to be beyond economic repair. Consequently, after the loss of 'No. 3' at Albi, only one Mark I then survived, car 'No. 1', based upon Rubery Owen frame 'No. 2'…

The national Snetterton Spring meeting followed on April 24, Flockhart having the Mark II 'Chassis No. 4' 's engine destroy itself due to hydraulic lock after seven laps of pre-race testing at Folkingham the previous day.

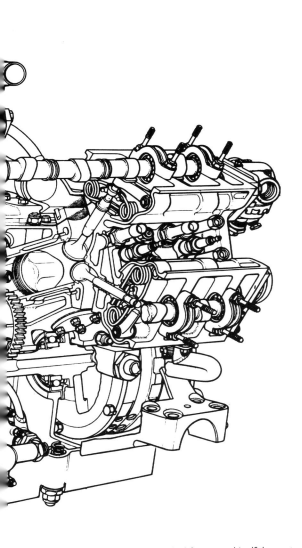

The V16-cylinder BRM engine in its final form proved itself the most powerful Formula I engine for its size ever built until the advent of turbocharged 1½-litre FI in the early 1980s – no mean achievement for the Mays Project, but full development had, agonizingly, come too late for the Formula to which it had been built.

April 24, 1954 – Aston Martin OC Spring Snetterton *Formule Libre* – 10 laps, 27.1 miles

It had been expected that Salvadori would reappear in Gilby's Maserati to confront Flockhart in the Mark II, but the Italian car defaulted, still being under repair after the Goodwood collision. Left to face a thin *Libre* entry, Ron cheerfully told the press: "It's a pity – but when you bring the bulldozer, they expect you to push over the molehill…".

After fuel-flooding problems with its hastily-fitted replacement engine '20/2' during five laps of practice, the Mark II cleared its throat in time for the race and by the end

Left: April 19, 1954 — Glover Trophy, Goodwood: Ken Wharton and Roy Salvadori — driving Syd Greene's new Gilby Engineering-entered Maserati 250F — locked into the terrific duel which ended on the entry to Lavant Corner on the final lap, when the cars collided.

Below: Ken Wharton, brown helmet, yellow shirt, bronzed and brawny arms, hammering 'No. 2' through St Mary's S-bend during its final race. Note the spilled-fuel burn attacking the paint on the tail.

Left: Having been T-boned amidships by Salvadori's Maserati, Wharton's BRM bounced straight, and he was able to drive on, down the Lavant Straight, round Woodcote, through the chicane and here past the chequered flag. Thus the 1954 Glover Trophy became one of the few races ever to be won by a written-off racing car — for 'No. 2' was beyond economic repair...

April 19, 1954 – Glover Trophy, Easter Monday, Goodwood: Having driven Mark I 'No. 2' in the afternoon's earlier Chichester Cup, Ron Flockhart took over the new Mark II 'No. 4' for this main race. Dove (left), Salmon (right), Rudd and PB (back to camera) are more relaxed than Ron. The Mark II's original special motorcycle magnetos had to be replaced by larger ones which, due to the engine being angled within the frame, demanded a huge louvre hump over the left-hand inlet mag. The right-hand mag had more room, but PB insisted it should have a matching bulge "as otherwise the bonnet will look stupid…".

of the opening lap already led Gould's Cooper-Bristol by almost the length of the pit straight. Flockhart equalled Wharton's 1:47.4, 90.50mph, lap record on both his fifth and sixth laps before setting a new mark at 1:46.8, 91.01mph, on his seventh.

Retirements left only six cars running, and Flockhart finally beat Gould by 50.6 seconds. It all seemed highly inconsequential in such a minor meeting, but at least the hard-worked BRM mechanics had another win to relish on their way home, plus a modest share of the bonus and prize money earnings.

The fuel tank split at a seam, yet again, on the penultimate lap. Ron kept his finger over the leak like the little Dutch boy. This incident led to the development of the BRM tank mounting system employed for the next five years whereby a rubber-clad steel tube was passed through another tube welded in to the tank, to provide both some flexibility and vibration damping.

By this time what was now Rubery Owen's 'Engine Development Division' at Bourne was well down the road towards seeking its own commercial work to underwrite the race programme, but manager Jim Sandercombe's monthly reports were low-key, detailing hours spent on Raymond Mays' favoured new cylinder head conversion – drawn in the Maltings office – for the Ford Zephyr saloon, together with Bowser fuel pump metering units commissioned from the same source. In January 1954, for example, the drawing office was engaged in work on the single-cylinder test engine for the new 2½-litre project, related Formula 1 chassis, the Ford conversion and the Bowser programme.

Since Stewart Tresilian had finally left the company for Bristol-Siddeley at the end of February the previous year –

May 8, 1954 – Formule Libre, Ibsley: Ron Flockhart on his way to winning this rare New Forest aerodrome race in Mark II 'No. 4' – fitted with the long-tailpipe exhaust system which simply slipped over the even more ear-splitting stubs employed at Goodwood and Snetterton. Interestingly, no Mark I had ever employed stub exhausts; they were difficult to arrange over the chassis without excessive back pressure. The simplified Mark II frame facilitated the use of stubs, but some circuit promoters would object… Performance was little changed.

1953 – and Tony Rudd's involvement with engine development in addition to his duties supervising racing car engineering at Folkingham, PB felt the need for high-grade assistance (partly to cover for his continuing absences) in charge at Bourne. A year later, in February 1954, 'Sandy' happily reported the re-appointment of "an assistant for Mr. Berthon…in the person of Mr E.G. Richter". The somewhat eccentric but brilliant backroom boy who had played such a major role in the creation of the V16 was due to rejoin the team at Bourne on May Day, only to decline the offer subsequently, whereupon PB approached another key former employee – Frankie May. Eventually Richter would return, for another brief period with BRM.

Meanwhile, the team followed up their Snetterton appearance with an entry for the West Hants & Dorset CC meeting at the short-lived Ibsley Aerodrome circuit near Ringwood, in the New Forest, using a 1.99-mile version of the circuit there. Flockhart tested the Mark II "without snags" for six laps at Folkingham on May 5, then off to Ibsley…

May 31, 1954 – Aintree '200': Peter Collins leads into Tatts Corner in the inaugural (and only) anti-clockwise Aintree International – his ThinWall Special leading Flockhart's Mark II, Parnell's Ferrari 625, Salvadori's Maserati 250F and Wharton (centre) in the new 'No. 5'.

Below: During the '200' Final, Flockhart spun 'No. 4'. Fuel slopped from the car's flapping fuel cap has stripped the tail paintwork.

August 14, 1954 – Formule Libre, Snetterton: The torrid outing in which Ron Flockhart spun three times and lost 128sec, here trying hard to recoup lost time in the battered Mark II 'No. 4', running stub pipes.

May 8, 1954 – West Hants & Dorset CC Ibsley *Formule Libre* – 15 laps, 31.35 miles

Once again it was Flockhart and the BRM against a motley cross-section of indifferent motor cars, yet Ron's 18 laps of practice ended with a damaging spin through the straw bales in which the car's front wheel, tail and fuel tank were buckled and bent. Temporary repairs were made for the race, in which the car – using long-tailpipe exhausts in place of the stub pipes deployed at Goodwood and Snetterton – led from start to finish, winning from the *Ecurie Ecosse* C-Type Jaguar sports cars of Jimmy Stewart and Ninian Sanderson. Jimmy had a younger brother at home in Dumbarton, named Jackie…

Ron won at 83.48mph and set fastest lap at 87.39.

BRM's running log for the season owns up: *"FIRST – New Lap Record – No opposition."*

On the following Thursday Flockhart was detailed to carry out a 100-mile test run at Folkingham to test modified magnetos, offered by Lucas as a solution to the frequent failures, but after 21 of the required 37 laps the magneto failed and the test was abandoned. Next day both driver and car completed the distance successfully, at an average of 98.4mph, to demonstrate the nature of Folkingham's circuit.

On Wednesday, May 19, the second Mark II, 'Chassis No. 5' in BRM's V16 series, was given its shake-down test over 10 trouble-free laps there, and that afternoon one of the ageing Lodestars rumbled off towards Liverpool to deliver it to the opening ceremony of Mrs Mirabel Topham's new 3-mile motor racing circuit, laid down around the perimeter of her Grand National horse-race course at Aintree.

The inaugural meeting was to be held there on Saturday, May 29, and the course was unusual in being lapped anti-clockwise. During this preview function on the 20th, Ken Wharton won the toss of a coin with Reg Parnell to open the circuit in the brand-new Mark II, completing five quick laps after which Flockhart also put in a couple.

Both Mark IIs were then prepared with stub exhausts for the Aintree race, Flockhart testing 16-inch wheels at Folkingham on 'No. 5' and even running 10 laps anti-clockwise to acclimatize himself to mainly left-hand turns.

He completed 30 laps in all that day and on the 27th he ran both Mark IIs briefly before Wharton put in 10 more serious laps in the later car.

May 29, 1954 – BARC *Daily Telegraph* Aintree '200', Liverpool – 17-lap, 51-mile Heats, 35-lap, 105-mile Final

Unfortunately, Mrs Topham's inaugural Aintree meeting was marred by continuous rain. During practice both BRMs ran in the wet, Flockhart clocking 2:17.0 in 22 laps and Wharton 2:19.2 in 26 against Peter Collins' dry-track pole time in the evergreen *Thin Wall Special* of 2:5.8. Ron reported no snags while Ken complained that his new car's gearchange was "difficult".

The rain fell faster from a leaden sky for Heat One in which Wharton's new Mark II proved a real handful on the flooded surface. While Collins pounded away into an ever-increasing lead, Parnell's Ferrari, Jean Behra's nimble little Gordini and Moss' new Maserati 250F ran wheel-to-wheel with the slithering BRM until the *Thin Wall*'s Ferrari engine began to splutter. Parnell caught and passed Collins on lap 10, Behra's engine stammered onto five cylinders and Moss finished third, some 8 seconds clear of the BRM, Wharton explaining – quite reasonably – that he had taken no risks at all in the rain.

Flockhart fielded 'No. 4' in Heat Two, leading Salvadori's Greene Maserati all the way on a rather drier surface to win by 3sec. Salvadori set fastest lap during his pursuit and pressed Flockhart hard, but the determined young Scot kept his head and drove very sensibly to score another race win for BRM, albeit merely in a heat.

For the Final, Parnell then lined-up on the left-side pole position from Flockhart, Salvadori and Collins, Moss flanking a rather disgruntled Wharton on the second row. As the rain eased and the circuit dried still further, Collins led into Tatt's Corner from Parnell, with Flockhart third, Salvadori fourth and Wharton fifth. Under acceleration out of the corner Flockhart powered into second place but could do nothing to prevent Collins drawing out a 21-seconds lead in five laps, with Wharton third behind his young team-mate and being hard-pressed by Moss.

Flockhart spun on lap six, rejoining eighth, Moss took second place from Wharton, and on lap eight Behra passed the BRM, Parnell following through next time round. Flockhart began to gain ground while Wharton, looking blacker on every lap, fell away to be overtaken by his team-mate. On lap 15 the *Thin Wall* spluttered past with Moss gaining relentlessly. Parnell was third and behind him Flockhart was slowing, being caught and passed by Gerard's Cooper-Bristol to an enormous and ironic cheer from the dank grandstands. On lap 20 Moss was less than 3 seconds behind Collins, and the *Thin Wall* headed for the pits. Flockhart was duelling wheel-to-wheel with Gerard while on lap 22 Wharton retired with the new BRM's front brakes locked on, glowing red hot and smoking.

The *Thin Wall* did one more slow lap before retiring and Flockhart just managed to defend his third place to beat Gerard by 1.4sec at the line, finishing 1min 44.2sec behind Moss' victorious – and modern – Maserati 250F. This margin was no real disgrace considering Flockhart had lost 1min 30sec in his early spin.

The routine of Folkingham preparation and pre-race testing – generally by Flockhart – then appearances in minor British *Formule Libre* races, continued through the remainder of the season, these V16 activities dovetailing with more serious events, related elsewhere, involving the Owen Racing Organisation's own new Maserati 250F – and intensive work upon the all-new 2½-litre four-cylinder Grand Prix car which was gathering pace in the new Folkingham build shop.

June 5, 1954 – Whitsun Trophy *Formule Libre*, Goodwood – 15 laps, 36 miles

This Whit-Monday Goodwood meeting saw Ron complaining of increasing brake pedal travel and decreasing brake efficiency after 22 laps practice in 'No. 4', whereupon Ken Wharton took over for four quick laps to report: "No snags – the brakes seem OK to me." After 25 laps in his own car – 'No. 5' – he had changed his tune: "The brakes are losing efficiency."

Wilson McComb reported the race like this:

> ...the start...will long be remembered by those who saw it. Collins was in pole position on the inside of the front grid, with Wharton beside him and Flockhart on the outside. All three shot away with immense acceleration...Wharton fighting furiously against wheelspin in the middle, but getting into Madgwick ahead of Collins and behind Flockhart. However, he lost his place to the Thinwall before the lap had ended, and was also overtaken by Salvadori (Maserati) at Lavant Straight on the second round.
>
> It seemed that the Thinwall had the edge on Flockhart's B.R.M. ... After two laps he had closed in on Flockhart, to wage a terrific duel until, on the fifth round, he succeeded in getting past...then drew comfortably ahead...
>
> Wharton's B.R.M. stayed firmly in fourth place...

Collins's fastest lap was at 93.30mph, impressively close to Hawthorn's Goodwood record of 94.53mph with the same car.

Flockhart finished 15 seconds behind the *Thin Wall*, and fully 42.6sec ahead of Wharton, who complained: "N.S. rear strut failed – not substantiated...". The Smethwick driver was not doing much this season to impress his team.

Alfred Owen was unimpressed by yet another defeat at the hands of Vandervell's *Thin Wall Special* and said as much to RM. There was a huge difference in style between the devout, aldermanic, mild-mannered Owen and the autocratic, impatient, feisty Vandervell. John Cooper of Cooper Cars was on good terms with them both – indeed he was designing an F1/F2 chassis for GAV's new *Vanwall Special* – and he recalled how at these British race meetings: "There'd be Old Man Vandervell up at one end of the paddock with the *Thin Wall Special*, his Maharajah's caravan, champagne and smoked salmon; and Alfred Owen down at the other end in his crumpled suit, waistcoat, watch and chain, with his BRMs, a flask of tea and a cheese sandwich...".

In response to AGBO's disappointment at this latest Goodwood defeat, PB wrote to him on June 22, explaining:

> It tends to be rather misleading when comparing lap times achieved last year with those achieved recently, because the course is quite a bit slower, which Freddie Richmond[68] said is due to subsidence between Fordwater and Lavant.
>
> The fastest Thinwall time, as you point out, was achieved by Mike Hawthorn, who lapped in 1 minute 31.4 seconds. In the same event Fangio lapped in 1 minute 32.15 seconds (in September 1953).
>
> Gonzalez, according to my records, in 1min 32.8secs; and Flockhart's best lap was in practice for this year's Whitsun event in 1min 32.8secs.
>
> The Thinwall is rather faster than it was last year; and I would say that Collins handles it as well as Mike Hawthorn, so that on straight comparison there is a deterioration of 1.2 seconds.
>
> Although Flockhart is not yet in the same category as a driver as Fangio, he was able to lap as above within .45 seconds of Fangio's best time. I am afraid Ken is outside the comparison range as he rather tends to try only when he is holding all the cards.
>
> ...It would seem that the Mark II car is about 1 second per lap faster than the Mark I; but this is still not good enough, as the results show.
>
> As regards maximum speed on Lavant Straight: This will be improved with a higher gear ratio and more so by better air ducting to the carburettors, as we now find there is some starvation at high r.p.m. This will be overcome with reducing and retuning the carburettors.
>
> From [Flockhart's gearchange sequence]...it is

---

68. **Freddie Richmond – Duke of Richmond and Gordon, owner and creator of the Goodwood circuit upon his Sussex estate. As the Earl of March he had achieved considerable success as an enthusiastic MG driver, prewar.**

obvious we are losing considerable time round the St Mary's and Lavant corners because the gear changes on two occasions come right in the middle of the corners. To help this we are altering the ratios so that third gear can only be used on this leg of the course and are increasing the performance around 7,000 engine revs, which is the lowest engine speed used on this section in that particular gear, and at which speed there is presently insufficient torque for re-acceleration.

I think these alterations should enable an improvement in lap times of up to 2 seconds to be made…

Owen had asked if his Organisation's Eaton two-speed axle device could be applied with advantage to the BRMs: "…We cannot use [it] because our axle unit and gearbox are designed as a whole," replied PB.

During the following weekend Ron Flockhart and Tony Rudd seized the chance to test their theory that using lower rpm in the gears would reduce wheelspin. It took them some time to sell the idea to PB – while RM and Wharton *never* accepted it. On June 28 PB reported:

The times prove conclusively that, using the higher overall axle ratios, and not using high r.p.m. in the lower gears, enables the time when accelerating from 60m.p.h. over 800 yards to be reduced by two seconds. Our acceleration from 100m.p.h. is better than that of the lower speeds. This is due to wheelspin, which the driver does not feel, due to the smoothness of the torque and the system in general, until it has reached a really large amount, which then causes loss of direction and stability…

A table of the tests carried out by Ron Flockhart on June 26, 1954 read as follows:

Rolling start, *Car No. 4*, 6,200 R.P.M. in 2nd gear; *Car No. 5*, 6,000 R.P.M. in 2nd; *Ratios, Car No. 4*, IIIb, with high 2nd. *Car No. 5*, IVb, low 2nd.

CAR No. 4

	DISTANCE (yards)				
	0	200	400	600	800
Time (sec)	0	5.0	10.2	12.8	15.4
	0	4.4	10.2	13.0	15.0
	0	4.4	10.0	12.8	15.0

Changing up at 11,000r.p.m. floating to 11,500 in top gear during 600 to 800 section. Test terminated.

CAR No. 5

	DISTANCE (yards)				
	0	200	400	600	800
Time (sec)	0	5.2	9.8	–	14.2
	0	5.0	9.6	12.4	14.0
	0	5.0	9.6	12.2	14.0

Changing up at 11,000 – not quite peaking at 800 yard mark.

	DISTANCE (yards)				
	0	200	400	600	800
Time (sec)	0	5.4	10.0	12.6	14.6
	0	5.2	9.8	12.4	14.4
	0	5.2	9.8	12.4	14.4

Changing up at 10,000. 5th gear 11,800.

	DISTANCE (yards)				
	0	200	400	600	800
Time (sec)	0	5.2	9.4	11.6	13.8
	0	5.0	9.4	11.4	13.6
	0	5.0	9.4	11.4	13.6

Changing 2/3rd at 9,500; 3/4th at 10,500; 4/5th at 11,000. 5th gear 11,500.

	DISTANCE (yards)				
	0	200	400	600	800
Time (sec)	0	5.0	9.4	12.2	14.6
	0	5.0	9.4	11.4	13.6

5th gear 12,000 lifting. Air intake orifice doubled in area.

The Shelsley Walsh hill-climb was to be held on June 20, and on the 17th there, Ken Wharton made three runs in a Mark II, clocking a best of 37.8 seconds after his front brakes had locked on the second climb. The V16 was not used in public, Ken running his ex-Mays, ex-Flockhart 'R4D' instead to lower the historic 'climb record to 36.58 seconds, with former owner RM looking on, misty-eyed in nostalgic admiration.

The V16s' first public outing since Whitsun Goodwood came at Snetterton in August, pre-race testing at Folkingham comprising 25 laps for each car, punctuated by a bad flat-spot below 7,000rpm, magneto trouble and a failed camshaft bearing, only one car – chassis '4' – making the trip for Flockhart to drive.

August 14, 1954 – West Essex CC *Formule Libre*, Snetterton – 40 laps, 108.4 miles

The West Essex Car Club ran quite a major *Libre* event which renewed the old Owen-BRM/Vandervell-*Thin Wall* rivalry.

In Friday practice Flockhart lapped in 1:45.0, reproducing identical times on three separate laps, 0.8sec quicker than the big 4½-litre Ferrari – first blood to BRM! However, in his total of 17 laps he found the brakes fading badly, and detected a developing flat-spot in the engine…after which Saturday simply was not his day.

No fewer than 14 non-starters decimated what should have been a 29-strong grid and Collins made a phenomenal start to lead throughout. In his wake, Flockhart was quite unable to close the gap and on lap seven 'No. 4' hurtled off the road as the brakes misbehaved. Calling at the pits to check damage and refasten the loose bonnet, Ron ripped back through the field to recapture second place, only to be lapped by Collins 18th time round, and immediately career straight onto the grass at Riches Corner. Marshals manhandled the car back onto the course, and Flockhart limped back to the pits with the engine refusing to run clean.

Its distributor cap had cracked, it was replaced and Ron rejoined yet again, charging harder and faster than ever to finish a distant third, three laps behind. Considerable damage had been done to the car by all this; he had lost 128 seconds in spinning and was not a happy chappy by the end of that day…

He had the opportunity to redeem himself, and the team, at Castle Combe two weeks later, the Lodestar's trip to Wiltshire being preceded on the 26th by a now customary pre-race shake-down at Folkingham: "No snags – 3 laps."

August 27, 1954 – Bristol MC & LCC Hastings Trophy *Formule Libre*, Castle Combe – 15 laps, 27.6 miles

For BRM's return to the West Country, Flockhart was entrusted with 'No. 5' – the second Mark II, remember – but in his first 10 laps of practice its engine ran roughly with the carburettor flooding. Once the float levels had been corrected he put in 12 more laps during which he set fastest time of 1:16.4, well down on Wharton's 1953 record of 1:13.8.

Horace Gould's Cooper-Bristol beat the hesitant BRM into the first corner, but Flockhart out-accelerated the little 2-litre car to lead until lap seven, when the BRM was caught by none other than Bob Gerard in his Cooper-Bristol. The Combe's straights were just too short for the BRM to demonstrate its huge power advantage, and with the brakes again undermining Ron's confidence and magneto trouble causing misfiring and engine hesitancy he was overtaken on lap 10, and could only finish second – beaten by 0.4sec. They shared fastest lap at 1:15.0, 88.32mph.

The team log commented: "Complained of brakes and misfiring magneto – both substantiated."

Back at Folkingham, 'No. 4' had been rebuilt following its Snetterton damage, and when Ron tested it for 13 laps on September 2, he reported: "It's never run better." With rather more confidence then, the car was taken north of the border for Flockhart's first BRM drive on his native soil…

September 4, 1954 – National *Formule Libre*, Charterhall, Scotland – 20 laps, 40 miles

In practice at Charterhall, Ron completed 20 trouble-free laps, clocking 1:21.0 three times to underline his consistency and putting in one very fast lap at 1:20.4, 2.6sec inside Farina's Charterhall best with the *Thin Wall* and 3.4sec faster

than Wharton's official BRM record. This looked quite promising, but…

A.N. Ford's *Autosport* story told the sad tale:

> On the starting grid for the *Formule Libre* race, the ear-rending sounds of the B.R.M. filled the air and one could only hear Salvadori's Maserati very faintly. Down came the starter's flag and 200 yards later there was a deathly silence. No B.R.M.! The Bourne brachytypous [*sic* – search me, DCN] had the appalling luck to catch up a tiny stone in its fuel system which jammed a carburettor piston and resulted in the car's retirement. The dismay of poor Flockhart knew no bounds…

The Greene Maserati broke an oil pipe, and Bob Gerard won yet again in his Cooper-Bristol.

Fangio visited Folkingham on September 13 and drove the Mark II 'No. 4' for 10 laps, using the new lower rpm change-up technique to clock a best time of 1:39.0 and averaging 100mph for his last seven tours… This was the last time he drove a BRM. It was evidently a memorable sight, the multiple World Champion driving a Mark II when contemporary for the first, last and only time.

The running log then includes the following entry:

> 20.9.54. GOODWOOD, TYRE TEST – RON FLOCKHART – Mark II, No. 4. – 17 laps.
> Car hit turnip heap and driven away. Engine stripped for inspection and removal of turnips.

Three days later, in practice for the 24th's Goodwood International, Flockhart and Wharton ran both Mark IIs, the Scot in 'No. 4' achieving a best of 1:34.6 in his 20 laps, while Wharton clocked his best of 1:33.8 after 13 laps in the same car. Ron was still unsure of his car's brakes and reported "some increase in pedal travel". However, this meeting really saw a sign of changing times as the Goodwood Trophy feature event was for current 2½-litre Formula 1 cars and the V16s were relegated to what was now a very minor *Libre* race over less than half the distance. The Owen Maserati had been entered for Wharton in the Goodwood Trophy, but its oil pump failed in practice so he was to concentrate upon the *Libre* event alone.

September 24, 1954 – BARC *Formule Libre*, Goodwood – 10 laps, 24 miles

Ken led Collins' inevitable *Thin Wall* and Moss' Maserati from the start, and on the charge into Woodcote Corner towards the end of that opening lap Flockhart found himself off-line in trying to recover lost ground and 'No. 5' spun off onto the grass verge to damage its front suspension in a hidden gulley.

With one car thus having failed to complete a lap, BRM's honour depended entirely upon Wharton, but almost simultaneously 'No. 4' 's engine began to misfire, and Collins swept by and away to another comfortable win. At least Ken was able to maintain a 3.6sec cushion over the duelling Moss

(Maserati) and Hawthorn (Formula 1 four-cylinder *Vanwall Special*) to finish second, still misfiring badly.

The final meeting of the season remained to complete the Mark IIs' maiden season, in preparation for which Wharton tested both cars at their Folkingham lair on September 30, reporting no snags after 11 laps in 'No. 4' and two stints of five and nine laps in 'No. 5'.

October 1, 1954 – BARC *Daily Telegraph Formule Libre*, Aintree – 17 laps, 51 miles

Practice saw Moss' F1 Maserati fastest overall with a best time of 2:3.6, with Wharton next quickest in 'No. 4' on 2:4.2, Collins' *Thin Wall* 2:4.4 then Flockhart's 'No. 5' on 2:4.6. Wharton had been troubled by locking brakes throughout his 22 laps and a new set were fitted for the race. Flockhart was slowed by No. 16 cylinder cutting out, but completed 24 practice laps.

Moss won the feature Formula 1 race, then lined-up again in his private but by this time works-supported 250F on Aintree's left-side pole position, even though the Aintree circuit had now been reversed, cars lapping conventionally clockwise.

Wharton, Collins and Flockhart were ranged alongside the young Englishman's 250F, and ending lap one the BRMs lay 4-5, Flockhart ahead of Wharton. Second lap, Collins was increasing his lead, Wharton and Flockhart having swapped places. Moss closed on Collins, Wharton displaced Harry Schell's 250F for third place, but out at Cottage Corner the Franco-American tried to take the place back and the two cars collided heavily – the Maserati having to be abandoned out on the course while a furious Wharton limped his battered V16 back to the pits to retire, its left side badly dented.

Out front the *Thin Wall* began to crackle and bang, and Collins retired on lap 10, leaving Moss to win comfortably from Sergio Mantovani's sister factory Maserati and Flockhart a distant third in an ailing BRM, beset by Sintox cracking on No. 3 plug and spasmodic carburettor flooding.

1955 – TWILIGHT: FAREWELL TO THE V16s

Into this final season of BRM V16 *Formule Libre* racing, the Maltings machine shop in Bourne and the race and assembly shops at Folkingham were awash with work on the new 2½-litre Formula 1 car programme, while the Owen Maserati 250F was keeping the race team occupied at significant international level.

In effect the V16s' appearances – restricted as they were entirely to home events – served to keep the BRM name prominent before the British public, and gave the BRMA/ORMA faithful a continuing – and still deliciously ear-splitting – cause to support.

None of the events they contested was particularly long or arduous, the biggest challenge being provided by the 60-miler

at Aintree in August. By this time the V16s were mechanically very reliable, certainly in such modest races. The Mark II cars were by this time well understood and as adequately 'sorted-out' as they would ever be. The V16 programme of 1955 was run on a low priority. However, motivated by the input and inspiration of a new driver with *Thin Wall* experience, Tony Rudd modified several features, primarily the geometry of the linkage operating the rear air strut to reduce the rear suspension rate, which according to Peter Collins made a major improvement. This work, carried out by the racing shop, tapered off as the Maserati and then the new car took priority. Even a majority of the project's faithful supporters regarded the cars with a kind of fond nostalgia – "The old BRM's running at Snetterton on Saturday. You coming?"

In addition, the drawing office and machine shop at Bourne were both increasingly involved in commercial work, including the Raymond Mays Ford Zephyr cylinder head conversion and the Bowser fuel pump metering project. Clarrie Brinkley was running the Bourne works while Jack Heward had been assigned to Folkingham to progress bought-out component deliveries. In the midst of all this activity – with the 2½-litre programme at fever pitch and the single-cylinder test engine, blow-ups occurring much faster than the machine shop could replace them – Peter Berthon hurt himself badly.

It was on the night of February 15–16, 1955, and he was driving his issue Ford Zodiac in his customary manner – 'bull at a gate' – returning from his London home (by this time in Hallam Mews) to his company flat in the former control tower at Folkingham. He simply fell asleep behind the wheel and careered off an icy road to ram a tree near Peterborough. He would be out of action for some months.

Meanwhile, during the 1954 season, Peter Collins' handling of Vandervell's *Thin Wall Special* had deeply impressed not least the BRM V16 drivers beaten by it, but also RM and Alfred Owen himself. Ray, of course, became a great fan of the fair-haired, blue-eyed, motor trader's son from Kidderminster, and urged Owen to take him on for 1955. Negotiations were surprisingly involved, but Peter Collins made his debut for BRM at Goodwood, on Easter Monday. In truth, the V16's irrelevance was emphasized by the only two events open to it that day – one of seven laps, the other a handicap of only five…

April 11, 1955 – BARC Chichester Cup, Goodwood – 7 laps, 16.8 miles

Collins drove the later Mark II 'No. 5', having set fastest time of the entire meeting in practice, at 1:33.0. Car 'No. 4' had been run in practice but encountered brake trouble, despite having just been fitted with a completely overhauled system by Jack Davies of Girling after its brake problems at Aintree in the closing meeting of 1954. This work had included rechromed discs, new pads, some salvage work on the hard-pressed calipers and overhauled master cylinders. However, in practice at Goodwood the master cylinder again gave trouble, so it was removed and despatched to Girling for investigation.

With PB out of commission Tony Rudd had explained to RM what the race team could and could not do. It had never been the intention for Ron Flockhart to run a car in the race, and RM wholeheartedly agreed 'without a murmur'.

Tony: Even after the V16 cars became sufficiently reliable and well-developed we were not in any position to mix it with the opposition, really to demonstrate the cars' braking superiority – which they undoubtedly had – due to continuing disc brake difficulties. We had problems with boiling fluid, vapour locks, flares on the ends of Bundy piping pulling off, dirt in the system and chromium-plate coming away from the discs. The early system had been too insensitive when the servo pump was driven from the engine. We had moved it to drive from the road-wheel side of the gearbox in 1952, so that the faster the car travelled, the more servo-assistance it had, which was much more sensible than using engine rpm. But towards the end, poor Ron Flockhart kept finding his brakes were inconsistent at one end or the other and he would often spin off. Whenever we dragged the car back for examination we could never find anything wrong and this led to some fierce disputes with Ron suspecting that nobody believed him.

Above: April 11, 1955 – Chichester Cup, Goodwood: Photographer John Ross' lovely shot of BRM newboy Peter Collins ready to make his debut for the team in Mark II 'No. 5' on the Easter Monday grid.

Left: Collins hammering 'No. 5' through the difficult undulating S-bend at St Mary's, showing off the long-tailpipe exhaust system upon which the Mark IIs were standardized for 1955. Save for continuing brake bothers, they were effectively only brought out and dusted off between races – Folkingham concentrating upon 250F and Type 25 preparation and development. Only seven entries were made for the V16 'sprint cars' in five race meetings this final season.

We were 'Piggy in the Middle' trying to convince Girling there was a problem we could not reproduce. There were several such inconclusive incidents. Girling even fitted two master cylinders, completely changing the method of operation, but to no avail. Some five years later we abandoned the servo altogether, and brake problems were greatly reduced. There has to be a clue there, somewhere...

Pre-Goodwood '55, Davies had inspected 'No. 5''s brakes at Folkingham and had pronounced them fit "for 100 miles only". Two days later, Tony was giving the car a 3-lap shakedown at dusk when he lost its rear brakes: We had no choice but to fix it ourselves – a defective seal, which caused a major upset with Girling. When Girling's Competitions Manager, Charles Russell, heard that BRM had overhauled the system on their own he contacted Owen, disclaiming all responsibility for any future failure, due to inadequate opportunity to inspect and test. On Easter Saturday at Goodwood he finally inspected 'No. 5''s system, gave his verbal approval and Peter Collins went racing in it...

Peter lined up on pole position flanked by Don Beauman's Connaught, and the two modern Maseratis of Salvadori and Moss. He promptly took an immediate lead and neither Maserati 250F could make any impression as he punched the V16 Mark II around the undulating circuit in impressive style, eventually to win this brief sprint by 5.4 seconds from Salvadori in Syd Greene's Gilby Engineering Maserati. Peter's fastest lap was timed at 1:34.4, 91.52mph. The brakes seemed fine...

April 11, 1955 – BARC Easter Handicap, Racing Cars, Goodwood – 5 laps, 12 miles

Running in this meeting-closing handicap event – a poignant reminder of prewar Brooklands practice from the era in which the BRM project had been so firmly rooted – Collins turned out again in 'No. 5'; prey to the handicappers' axe. He naturally had to start from scratch, hurtling through the backmarkers amongst a field which included Bob Gerard's Cooper-Bristol, Roy Salvadori's Maserati 250F and the Connaughts of John Young and Don Beauman, eventually to finish fifth, all but catching Beauman on the finish line. This time out he lowered his fastest lap to 1:33.0, 92.90mph…fast, but still well short of the lap record.

The Whitsun weekend then saw the V16s racing at Snetterton on the Saturday, the Owen Maserati at Crystal Palace on Whit-Monday. The Norfolk event saw both Mark IIs fielded, for Collins and a somewhat disgruntled Flockhart.

May 28, 1955 – West Essex CC National Spring Snetterton *Formule Libre* – 10 laps, 27.1 miles

At Snetterton, Collins retained the later Mark II 'No. 5' and Ron Flockhart reappeared in 'No. 4', the Scot miffed by the attention being lavished upon newcomer Collins so early in the season. For some reason grid positions for this *Libre* race were decided by ballot rather than by practice times, which produced a bizarre front-row line-up flanking Collins with the Lister-Bristol sports cars of Noel Cunningham-Reid and Archie Scott-Brown, Bill Smith's C-Type Jaguar, and Jim Russell in 'Nobby' Spero's ancient ex-Whitney Straight/'Bira' Maserati 8CM, dating from 1933–34.

Collins and Flockhart made the best of the start, but Salvadori's 250F displaced Ron during that opening lap and he began to fall back. Collins was clocked at 1:42.2 to set a new outright lap record of 95.1mph, but on lap seven, screaming down the straight – merely separated from the parallel main A11 road by a grass verge and hedgerow – Collins dived left to pass outside Cunningham-Reid's Lister under braking into the hairpin. At that moment Cunningham-Reid had just glimpsed the BRM in his mirrors and ducked left to give Collins the inside line…The cars collided side-to-side, a Lister knock-off hub cap burst a BRM tyre and 'No. 5' spun to rest in a cloud of rubber smoke, out of the race.

Salvadori drove on to win in the Greene Maserati, with Flockhart 14.4 seconds adrift, in second place, and complaining that the brake pedal travel necessary to produce the same deceleration varied considerably. In any case, when Tony Rudd inspected the cars after this outing he found that "the rebuild of the brakes on 'No. 4' did not appear… satisfactory, and those on 'No. 5' had covered a considerable mileage and were suffering from wear and tear…".

The newer car was subsequently fitted by Jack Davies at Folkingham with new discs and overhauled calipers, its master cylinders were overhauled, and after a Collins track test the system was pronounced 100 per cent fit. A faulty front caliper was then replaced on 'No. 4' and its brakes fettled "for at least 300 miles". Its rear discs required replating, but during this inspection the engine was found to have been damaged beyond immediate repair – which consigned the entire car to the redundant store.

Meanwhile, immediately after the Whitsun outing, RM wrote to Owen:

> The week end racing as a whole was a great success. a) Collins drove the B.R.M. magnificently at Snetterton and it really was bad luck when this car which he was lapping pulled across in front of him, and the collision occurred. He would have been an easy winner, but it is most gratifying to know that he broke his own Thinwall Ferrari lap record by just on 1½ seconds…

– but he still had not signed his ORO contract!

Ray went on to ask Owen's permission to order V16 pistons, liners, valves, valve guides and springs, plugs, tyres, 5th speed gears, float chamber needle valves, magneto drive gears, stub-axles, prop-shaft ends and another SU carburettor:

> …if this car is to continue running in any *Formula* [*sic*] *Libre* events in this country, to be driven by Collins or Flockhart, and if these cars are to be kept runnable, both for the present and immediate future for possible record attempts…

Into June, Owen was pressing Jim Sandercombe to research ways of minimizing the number of new spares required to keep the V16s running, but added:

> The most important thing is we have got to keep these cars on the road. It may be that this coming winter we shall make some determined effort on various speed records in America, and there must be no doubt about the availability of spares for the purpose…

Back in 1952 Donald Campbell had approached Owen, wanting to install a BRM V16 in his father's old Water Speed World Record-holding boat, *Bluebird K7*, but the approach had been deflected – no engines spare, no funds, no time. Now Peter Collins had expressed interest in tackling class world records in a suitably modified car at Bonneville, and thought had gone (briefly) beyond that, to a lowline, slimline Land Speed Record contender.

Such dreams remained just that – sadly; but the Campbell *Bluebird* and Bonneville factors would combine with Owen's multi-million-pound support in 1960 for a wheel-driven 400mph LSR bid.

On Sunday, June 5, 1955, the prototype new four-cylinder 2½-litre BRM Type 25 chassis '251' ran for the first time under its own power on the sadly deteriorating and increasingly pot-holed test circuit at Folkingham. In fact its always loose and crumbly surface was now in such a state that surfacers Bristowe's Travis Ltd of Grantham were called in to fill the worst of the holes. Eleven days after the P25's first run, Eric Richter returned to the fold, rejoining the Bourne staff.

May 28, 1955 – Formule Libre, Snetterton: Collins' definitive Mark II 'No. 5' setting fastest lap before his sudden side-swipe collision with Cunningham-Reid's sports Lister-Bristol – an ever-present danger of Libre racing. The long exhausts were heavy and fouled the Loadstar loading ramps, so were only fitted – about a three-minute job – on arrival at a circuit. While splash guards were easily fitted and removed on a Mark I, the Mark IIs had a double-skinned side panel forming part of the air duct to the oil cooler and tank. Once fitted, their guards stayed put.

Unfortunately he was by this time a sick man, his health failing, and he would be absent for long periods in hospital.

One BRM character having returned, another departed – Dave Turner leaving the engine shop at Folkingham for a quieter life with Mirlees-Blackstone, the diesel engine manufacturer, in Stamford. Then, in August, after a 10-week break, the sole surviving active V16 Mark II – 'No. 5' – reappeared, in anger, at Snetterton.

August 13, 1955 – West Essex CC *Formule Libre*, Snetterton – 25 laps, 67.75 miles

Peter Collins in the lone BRM faced strong opposition from Harry Schell in one of Vandervell's new Formula 1 Vanwalls, fresh from winning the feature National Benzole Trophy 25-lap Formula 1 race from ex-BRM team-mate Ken Wharton's sister car, Moss' Maserati 250F and Jack Brabham's rear-engined Cooper-Bristol 'Bobtail'.

Otherwise, apart from Salvadori's 250F and ex-BRM Grand Prix driver Peter Walker in the unrelated Rob Walker's dark-blue Connaught, the field was weak. Schell led, Collins' car broke a half-shaft joint at the wheel end – not the notorious inboard pot joint – on the opening lap, Schell's went out soon after, and following a minor collision between them Walker won from Salvadori. It was BRM's poorest showing in years…

After Snetterton the complete de Dion assembly from the already retired Mark II 'No. 4', was removed and grafted onto the stern of 'No. 5', using new brake discs clasped by the existing calipers from that frame. It was then despatched to Liverpool in one of the Lodestars, in company with another bearing the prototype new Type 25…

September 3, 1955 – BARC *Daily Telegraph Formule Libre*, Aintree – 17 laps, 51 miles

After the defection of the brand-new 2½-litre car in practice for the *Daily Telegraph* Trophy Formula 1 race, Peter Collins applied his full attention to Mark II 'No. 5' for this supporting *Libre* event. The field was thinned by 10 non-starters before the warm-up lap, on which John Young's Connaught broke its engine to become yet another defaulter.

At flag-fall, Collins rocketed into an immediate lead from Gerard's Cooper-Bristol, while Salvadori broadsided at Melling Crossing and lost much time sorting out the Greene Maserati on the trackside lawn. When Gerard's hitherto almost totally reliable Cooper-Bristol broke a valve on lap 13 the fast-recovering Salvadori inherited a distant second place, and with only six cars running, and Collins being shown "Easy" signs from the BRM pit, the Mark II won a meaningless race very easily, having averaged 85.20mph – the fastest of the day, as was his fastest lap at 2:4.0, 87.10mph.

As PRO Rivers Fletcher's *ORMA Bulletin No. 11* irrepressibly reported to enthusiastic members of the Association:

Peter Collins drove the old V16 in the *Formula [sic] Libre* race, and it went really magnificently. Even the most hardened racegoers were thrilled with the way he flung it round the Aintree circuit. It had a runaway victory, but even so an exciting one, purely on account of the terrific way the old car goes. Collins lapped…very considerably faster than any other car at Aintree that day and only 4secs. slower than the Mercedes record. [Only?]

V16 swansong – October 1, 1955 – Empire News Trophy, Castle Combe: Here on the opening lap Ron Flockhart in 'No. 5' briefly leads Harry Schell's latest Formula 1 Vanwall which will soon nip by and pull out a winning margin of 50.6sec in the 20 laps… Les Leston lies briefly third driving Stirling Moss' own grey Maserati 250F.

The works' race history of the BRM V16s was now almost at its close, and it seems strangely apt that their swansong came in the *Empire News* Trophy race, at Castle Combe, where Stewart Tresilian and his wife Nan were then living, in the prettiest village in England. They came to see the team before the race.

Chassis 'No. 5', the youngest and last of the 16-cylinder cars, was race-prepared for the final time at Folkingham, and then, in company with the Owen Maserati, it was borne away to fight its last battle, on the Wiltshire aerodrome circuit…

October 1, 1955 – Bristol MC & LCC International *Empire News* Trophy *Formule Libre*, Castle Combe – 20 laps, 36.8 miles

Peter Collins was entered in the feature Formula 1 race in the Owen Maserati 250F, leaving Ron Flockhart to make only his second appearance of the season for BRM, in the Mark II. Harry Schell was driving the 2½-litre Vanwall and although Flockhart led initially in the V16, as Cyril Posthumus reported:

> …he could do nothing about Mr Vandervell's Formula 1 machine and its Franco-American pilot. Nor, on this occasion, could the redoubtable Bob Gerard practise his habitual sport of B.R.M.-hunting…

The story which Raymond Mays had launched 10 years earlier, in 1945, had finally run its course, and perhaps to some degree the old adversary, Tony Vandervell, had had the last laugh…

This swansong works outing for the V16 occupied just 25min 47.4sec of Ron Flockhart's time as he finished second, 20.6 seconds behind Schell's victorious Vanwall. And then the disappointed, white-helmeted Scot swept off the circuit, blipping his way back into the grassy paddock and his gloved right hand reached forward for the mag switch. A brisk flick of the wrist abruptly stilled the centrifugally-supercharged V16 engine's ear-splitting exhaust blast. The ringing ears of onlookers could relax and 'No. 5' entered a long, long slumber as its hard-worked mechanicals cooled, contracted, and settled…

Alfred Owen's RAC entrant's licence for 1955 – last year of BRM V16 competition – one item of ephemera auctioned by Christies' over 25 years later…

DEPARTMENT 31, PROJECT 28 AND THE 'RAYMOND MAYS' FORDS

During the winter of 1952–53, when Rubery Owen's 'Department 31 – Engine Development Division' was created at Bourne by Alfred Owen's takeover of BRM, he wanted it to underwrite BRM's continuing race programme with a range of commercial work.

PB and RM noted the demand for Bristol's production six-cylinder engine in Formula 2 tune. At that time they were both running Ford Zephyrs as their company cars, and PB began to analyze the production six-cylinder engine's potential as a customer racing engine.

Ford's 1,508cc 'EOTA' series Consul four-cylinder and 2,262cc 'EOTTA' series Zephyr six-cylinder engines – introduced in 1950 – were both modern overhead-valve, over-square units. PB investigated revving his Zephyr six unit faster, raising its compression ratio, enlarging its standard cylinder head's siamesed ports, and providing three carburettors.

After a meeting at Bourne on February 16, 1953, RM reported to Owen that for potential F2 use, although these modifications "…have proved successful and reliable…it is evident that to obtain equivalent power, or even greater power, than known units such as the Bristol, most of the standard Ford engine would have to be redesigned. The cost of this would probably equal the designing of a new engine…".

Meanwhile, Ray's own garage business – Raymond Mays & Partners Ltd (his partners being PB with Lance and Constance Prideaux-Brune) – had operated on the ground floor of the Maltings building before finding a permanent home in new premises on the opposite side of the Spalding Road, where it was managed by Henry Coy as a supplier of Rolls-Royce and Bentley cars, and – according to its letter heading – as "*Specialists in high speed tuning, car and motor cycle sales and repairs…*".

Ray's report to Owen now declared that the prohibitive cost of an adequately modified Ford Zephyr-based F2 engine would apply equally to a sports-racing version, so he recommended instead that "…the most suitable use to which these experiments could be put would be to market a modified conversion of what has been done, for Zephyr owners to purchase…the main point against this is that…Ford owners or distributors and agents could carry out these modifications themselves, once they had inspected an original modified unit. Therefore there is little or no commercial value (for) Engine Development Division at Bourne…". However, since the test units had proved successful: "…Peter Berthon considers that the best answer…would be for Rubery Owen to manufacture and market a simple new cylinder head…interchangeable with the standard Zephyr head (which) could be marketed through Raymond Mays & Partners Limited, and possibly through Ford distributors for resale…to try out the market. Raymond Mays & Partners could offer to carry out the conversion of existing Zephyr heads (as has been done to Raymond Mays' and Peter Berthon's engines) and this would effectively act as Stage I…".

He added: "To gain the full benefit of the increased power an overdrive is essential. To enable this to be tried out it was arranged that the two existing Zephyrs, of Raymond Mays and Peter Berthon, should be converted, and…" – stretching the elastic too tightly this time – "…it was also agreed that Mr A.G.B.Owen and Mr Raymond Mays should personally bear half each of the cost of these two conversions. Peter Berthon considers that this should not exceed £250 in total…".

Alfred Owen queried this 'agreement' with right-hand man Glover – also present at the meeting – and he scribbled across the minutes "Not to my knowledge". Owen then corrected RM by deciding that the price of these company car conversions "should be retrieved out of sales of heads & included in price to be charged to clients".

Conversions were initially offered for the standard Ford iron heads on the contemporary Ford Zephyr six-cylinder saloons then the Ford Consul four-cylinders. Three SU H4 carburettors were applied to the six, two to the Consul's four-cylinder. The Zephyr head was skimmed at Bourne to raise compression from the standard 6.8:1 to 7.6:1 while 60-thou off the Consul head gave 7.7:1. Combustion chambers and the enlarged and reshaped ports were highly polished. Double valve springs were fitted and new Servais straight-through silencers mated to the standard Ford manifolds.

The Autocar tested these 'Raymond Mays' conversions in September 1953, commenting upon the modified Zephyr's "remarkable display of top gear flexibility and acceleration…". Braking was unimpressive (!) but above all "top gear acceleration between 50 and 70mph is particularly improved…". The testers warned that the standard three-speed gearbox's top gear would be irritatingly low for long-distance Continental work but was "not exasperating" on British roads. Fuel consumption driven hard was "under 20mpg" while "driving really hard but without wasting fuel unnecessarily the car yielded 22mpg".

The four-cylinder Consul was better geared than the Zephyr. Fuel consumption ranged from 22-23mpg driven hard to 33mpg cruising. "Unlike conditions for the Zephyr test, wet roads were encountered with the Consul and some care was necessary on corners…". I bet.

The triple-carburettor Zephyr conversion was priced at £75, the twin-carburettor Consul kit £60, against respective new-car prices of £771 15s 10d and £686 2s 6d. One problem was that the new carburettor arrangements intruded upon battery space, so it was removed to the boot. Unfortunately the combination of voltage drop and higher compression then made these Mays-converted cars unwilling to start.

Meanwhile PB progressed design of an entirely new aluminium cylinder head to provide the Zephyr with six de-siamesed individual ports. When casting quotations were received, the West Yorkshire Foundry's was lowest, at £12 a time plus £2 10s for inlet manifolds, minimum batch 200. This minimum may have proved unacceptable – it appears the West Yorks quotation was not accepted and a 50-minimum alternative prevailed.

Bourne's total unit cost approached £16 17s, Mays & Partners adding all fittings and the expensive hand-made sand-cast SU carburettors. While the standard siamesed-port Zephyr conversion required three, this new P28 head carried just two SU H6s, swept up at 45 degrees to allow the battery's return to the engine bay.

In December 1953, PB reported that a sample casting of the new head was imminent and asked Owen if the firm could provide him with a new Zephyr of the latest type – the high-compression, better-equipped Zephyr Zodiac having just been launched. Its standard compression of 7.5:1 (against the basic Zephyr's 6.8:1) enabled it to run on premium grade fuel, adding three horsepower for 71bhp at 4,200rpm. PB wanted this new car "on which to develop the conversion, the car to be supplied through Raymond Mays & Partners on special terms…".

The draft agreement between Raymond Mays & Partners and Rubery Owen states that this new six-port alloy head was initially

May 7, 1955 – Production Touring Car Race, BRDC Silverstone: As prelude to Peter Collins' F1 win in the Owen Maserati, Ken Wharton's spectacular 'Mays-headed' – and Mays-blue – Ford Zephyr won its class and placed fourth overall behind the dominant Jaguar Mark VIIs of Mike Hawthorn, Jimmy Stewart and Desmond Titterington. Note RM's favourite number '17'...

to be marketed as 'The Owen Head'. But RM prevailed, and 'The Raymond Mays Headed' Ford Zephyr would become perhaps the best known 'go-faster' British saloon of the 1950s.. Rubery Owen was to sell the P28 heads to RM&P at a fixed figure including an RO profit margin "in the order of £20". After RM's company had deducted costs of carburettors, extra parts and fitting, the remaining profit was to be split with Rubery Owen. This residue's precise amount – together with the actual numbers of conversions sold – would become a bone of future contention...

The P28 six-port cylinder head was cast in aluminium alloy. Two separate cast-iron exhaust manifolds fed Burgess or Servais silencers. Overdrive was recommended, on second and top gears, to provide in effect a five-speed transmission, together with uprated Armstrong rear dampers and 'anti-fade' brake linings. Top speed in overdrive top was around 95mph, and minimum fuel consumption c.21mpg. Upon its eventual launch in November 1954, conversion price (excluding overdrive) was £100 "plus £5 for fitting".

Acceleration through the gears from 0–30mph took 5.6sec in the 1953 triple-carburettor, standard-head Zephyr and 5.9sec in the Consul. The first six-port heads now provided 0–30mph in 4.0sec. 0–60mph times were respectively 17.4sec for the triple-carburettor Zephyr, 23.7sec for the Consul, but a contemporarily shattering 13.2sec for the six-port head car. Top gear accelerations included 50–70mph in 11.4sec (triple-carburettor Zephyr) and 12.4sec (twin-carburettor Consul) against 7.4sec 40–60mph for the six-port. The alloy-head car also covered the standing-start quarter-mile in 18.9sec against a standard Zephyr Zodiac's 21.5sec.

Saloon car racing was absolutely in its infancy at that time, only the BRDC's *Daily Express* May meeting at Silverstone providing a prominent platform. Their annual 'Production Touring Car Race' proved perennially spectacular and often hilarious, and in the 1955 meeting – in which Peter Collins'

Owen Maserati won the Formula 1 race – the 25-lap Production Touring Car event saw Ken Wharton broadsiding his way home a sensational fourth overall in the demonstrator Mays Zephyr, JCT 17. This registration included the superstitious RM's favourite number – *vide* his telephone number 'Bourne 17' and later cars, DCT 17, CTL 17, etc.

Wharton beat Harold Grace's Riley to win the 2,001-3,000cc class after a tremendous battle "in a car that even with its modifications costs under £1,000...". BP advertised his success as proof of the efficacy of "*New BP Super – A Platinum Processed Motor Spirit*". Peter Collins was sufficiently impressed to ask if he could drive JCT 17 next time out. RM was delighted but had to ask Peter "...do you know of any suitable events?". One emerged in the West Essex CC International at Snetterton on August 13 – a 10-lap handicap. Having retired his V16 Mark II on the opening lap of the *Libre* race, Peter was then given a 45sec start over the scratch Aston Martin DB2/4 but could not stave off Dick Steed's Porsche Super (which started 15sec after him). *Autosport* reported: "Collins certainly drove that Zephyr, and disproved theories that these cars suffer from tail-end breakaway when cornered very rapidly. The Mays version appears to have all the road holding in the world...". Collins won his class. Rallying provided greater opportunity for customers' cars.

In March 1956, Ford launched their series 206E Mark II six-cylinder Zephyr, enlarged to 2,553cc, and a 'Raymond Mays' head was tailored to it at Bourne. The standard production engine had a compression ratio of 7.8:1 and developed 90bhp at 4,400rpm with peak torque of 137lb.ft at 2,000rpm. The modified six-port Mark II Mays head was again cast in aluminium, with austenitic cast-iron valve seats shrunk in, oversized Silchrome inlet valves, XB alloy steel exhaust valves and uprated single valve springs. Alternative compression ratios were offered, 8.75:1 for premium-grade fuel, 9.2:1 for 100-octane. The 8.75:1 version was claimed to provide 127bhp (gross) at 4,750rpm, the 9.2 132bhp. A high-lift, long-overlap race camshaft was also available, offering 145bhp. The standard Ford pistons and bottom end were considered perfectly capable of handling these increases in power and rpm. Peak revs of 5,500rpm were recommended, but in testing and racing PB claimed 6,200rpm in relative impunity. Peak torque was claimed to be as high as 154lb.ft at 3,000rpm.

Ford offered Borg-Warner overdrive as a Mark II optional extra. It was recommended for the 'Mays' conversions along with the 4.1:1 Consul back axle ratio in preference to the Zephyr's normal 3.9, better to exploit the extended rev range. At 5,500rpm this gave 97mph in direct-drive top, or 101.2 in overdrive (although *The Autocar* testers considered 105mph a true top speed). This Mark II Zephyr conversion cost £135 (without fitting).

It offered 0–30mph in 3.3sec, 0–60mph in 10sec and 0–90mph in 25.5, and covered the standing-start quarter-mile in just 17.6sec. In comparison the Austin-Healey Hundred sports was 0.3sec *slower* 0–60mph, and just a tenth-second faster over the quarter-mile. But it cost £1,063. The Mays Zephyr performed even better against the 3.4-litre Jaguar XK140, which was a whole second slower 0–60, and only two-tenths faster over the quarter-mile for £1,598...more than half as much again. Nor could the Jaguar carry six adults and their luggage!

This Mark II conversion showed its paces in the Oulton Park Gold Cup meeting of September 22, 1956, when Ken Wharton ran his own Mays-modified Zephyr 511 GHK in the 10-lap Manchester Motor Trades Luncheon Club Trophy race for production cars. Ken hurtled round to finish third – first saloon home – behind Tony Brooks in Rob Walker's awesome Mercedes-Benz 300SL ROB 2 and Ivor Bueb's Jaguar XK140 Fixed-Head Coupe. According to one report, Wharton "...led the saloon car class throughout...handling and sounding like a Formula 1 car". Rubery Owen made much of this success in the Conversion's promotional pamphlets.

Through the late Fifties, many motor sporting stars drove Raymond Mays Zephyrs – Colin Chapman accepted one as his fee for sorting out BRM's handling in 1957 while the great Archie Scott-Brown's was distinctively painted in dark green/ bright yellow centre stripe Lister-Jaguar livery.

The basic Ford 206E six-cylinder engines remained on line until 1962, and the Raymond Mays heads were updated to keep pace. An effectively cut-down four-cylinder version was also introduced for the Mark II Consul and subsequent Zephyr 4 Mark III. From as early as 1958 marinized Mays-headed Consul and Zephyr engines were used in Fenn & Wood, Moonfleet and Dowty Turbocraft boats.

The go-ahead British Racing & Sports Car Club organized its inaugural British Saloon Car Championship in 1958, Jack Sears taking the title in his Austin A105 Westminster with Jeff Uren fifth overall but second to Sears in the 1,601-2,700cc class in a Zephyr he had tuned himself.

For 1959, Uren approached Ford and RM for the tools to win the Championship. One, possibly two sealed engines were assembled for him at Bourne overseen by Willie Southcott, with modified combustion chambers, high-lift camshaft and triple Weber carburettors. Uren won the Championship, Ford began to regard competition seriously and these engines provided the inspiration for their new Competitions developments in 1960 and a whole series of International rally entries, culminating in special engines used on the works Fords, plus Reliant Sabre Sixes and Sabre Fours tackling such major events as the Monte Carlo and Alpine Rallies.

Meanwhile, Ken Rudd used the heads in a whole range of Stages on the Ruddspeed AC Ace and Aceca sports and GT cars, Basil van Rooyen in South Africa ultimately extracted 220bhp from his Mays-headed Zodiac Mark III racer, the Cheshire police used them on their M6 patrol cars, and the converted engines also powered examples of the Britannia, Fairthorpe Zeta and variously obscure specialist sports and GT cars.

On April 22, 1960, a young New Zealand enthusiast – James H. Ganley of Hamilton – wrote to "The Competitions Manager, Raymond Mays Ltd", explaining that "...the racing team for which I am manager is running a Mk 2 Ford Zephyr, fitted with one of your light alloy heads...driven by Ivan Segedin, finished the season third in the New Zealand saloon car championship, despite competing in only three (qualifying) races...".

He asked advice and PB replied that the best step forward "would be for us to send you out a special Mark II head...a big improvement on the old Mark I which has long since been obsolete...Generally both valves and ports are larger. The head shape is slightly different to give more turbulence and better breathing, and the internal water flow has been improved. The compression ratio is approximately 10.6 to 1...For competition work we normally use H6 SU carburettors, 1 3/4", and with a 'bunch of bananas' type of exhaust system, approx. 165bhp is available...3 dual Webers would increase the maximum bhp to 175/180bhp. These are very expensive and only put extra bhp on the top with little improvement, coupled with poor fuel consumption, in the mid-range. We have available a special camshaft with high lift and wider angles, which we only recommend for use on very special engines, fitted with special con rods, etc., for high rpm. Using standard con rods it is not advisable to exceed 5,500rpm for any length of time, otherwise you will certainly break a con rod bolt and wreck the engine..." (a rather different tale to those of 6,200 safe rpm told in 1956...).

PB recommended that Ganley should fit "1) Special Mark II competition head fitted with 3 H6 SU carburettors. 2) 'Bunch of bananas' exhaust system. 3) H.&G. pistons, with increased clearances. 4) Lead-Bronze Indium shells in big ends and main bearings. 5) Balanced rods and pistons. 6) Balanced crank with lightened flywheel. 7) Large capacity sump with radiator, Tubes in bottom. 8) Additional large capacity fuel pump. 9) 3-inch propeller shaft and joints" – because "at the torques involved the standard propeller shaft joints are too small" – while in addition he recommended for the car's chassis and suspension "1) Ford Disc Brakes – available approx. 2 weeks. 2) Export hard front and rear springs. 3) Special front damper units, 'Silverstone' dampers for rear. 4) Anti-Tramp bar and rear axle. 5) Special anti-roll bar...".

Twelve years later, Department 31's would-be client – James H. (Howden) Ganley – would become a BRM works driver.

These later heads carried cheaper die-cast SU carburettors at a 30-degree angle, while triple-Weber manifolds were also developed. It appears that RO Raymond Mays head production ceased in 1962, but residual stock kept the programme afloat for several years more. Casting quality was "not brilliant", where cracks might have been re-sealed with melted Bakelite in the '50s, Araldite took over into the '60s, and while skimming might salvage a warped head, repeated skims would push compression to 12 or 13:1 whereupon replacement became the only cure – the original head was only good for scrap.

Project 28 never generated enormous revenue, but some 7-800 heads were produced, providing RO's Engine Development Division with useful commercial income – and RM himself with a few years more as a marketable motoring 'name'.

PART THREE

Interlude...

July 4, 1954 – Grand Prix de l'ACF, Reims-Gueux: disappointing debut of the brand-new 'Owen Maserati' – '2509'. Ken Wharton locks the car as delivered from Modena into Thillois Corner – a standard-wheelbase, customer-specification Tipo 1 250F, with the much-louvred small body, early-style engine bay dry-sump oil tank – note filler cap – bevelled twin-exhaust tailpipes, Borrani wire wheels and standard Maserati drum brakes.

THE ITALIAN JOB

Here we must retrace our steps a little, to return to the winter of 1953–54 and a period in which Ken Wharton had performed quite nobly for BRM and was enjoying a most cordial relationship with Alfred Owen, although rather greater distance existed between him and RM, PB and the boys in Lincolnshire. Some got on with him, Rudd was one who did not.

This Midlands garage proprietor and all-round professional driver left nobody in any doubt regarding his achievements, his letter heading – "Ken Wharton – Hume Street, Smethwick, England, Business telephone: SMEthwick 0613; Private: Hagley 2292" – announced him as 'Trials Champion of Great Britain 1948–49–50', 'Hill Climb Champion of Great Britain 1951–52', 'Record Holder of Shelsley Walsh, Prescott, Bouley Bay, Col Bayard, Craigantlet, Rest and be Thankful, Lydstep, Boness'.

He had a highly developed financial sense, and rather strangely remained more remote from the team than any other driver. Perhaps this was insecurity, for his ability clearly did not equal that of most of his BRM team-mates. He was superstitious and could be temperamental. He had a very attractive girlfriend, and on one occasion when she appeared at a meeting wearing an elegant feathered hat it ended up being worn by any BRM mechanic who had to work beneath an oily car...

But after his exploits for BRM, including his lucky escape at Albi for which perhaps Owen felt personally indebted, Ken Wharton was most anxious to assure himself of a full season's employment in 1954. It was clear that Bourne's efforts were now concentrated upon the new 2½-litre car, and that the out-of-Formula V16s had become mere makeweights which could maintain a team presence in the few national *Libre* races open to them. But there was little money to be made from a seven-lapper at Goodwood or a 10-lapper at Snetterton...

Just as in 1949, when Tony Vandervell had pushed BRM into running another manufacturer's car – the first Ferrari 125 *Thinwall Special* – to gain experience while their own V16 approached completion, now Ken urged purchase of one of the latest 2½-litre Maserati 250Fs from Modena.

An undated document – probably from October 1953 – survives in which he made this proposal direct to Alfred Owen, explaining that since:

> ...the new Formula cars will not be ready until the 1954 season has commenced, I have given serious thought to some form of programme that may bridge the gap, and at the same time reduce the delay in producing and testing the new car...one must consider the... maintenance of fitness and skill, of the drivers. With this in mind I would put forward the following suggestion.
>
> Once the new car is complete, the amount of time dissipated in trials and testing will occupy considerable time. If only a method could be employed where a known Formula I car could be used, as a guinea pig, and the engine used to test the B.R.M. chassis, and the chassis used to test the B.R.M. This would in my opinion reduce by 50% the time required to develope [*sic*] the new car.

> It is essential that the drivers continue to race as soon as the season opens, and I am quite naturally concerned primarily with my own position. In view of these circumstances I submit the following suggestions.
>
> A new 2½-litre Maserati to be purchased immediately, subject to satisfactory trials at Monza before acceptance. As you know I am not over-burdened with wealth, but would willingly contribute £1,000[69] towards the cost of this car, or if possible a little more, in fact all I possibly can afford.
>
> With regard to the general arrangements I would suggest that the car be entered in Mr Owen's name, run and controlled by him, in it's [*sic*] entirety, but that I should take part in the choosing of the events in which it should run. With regard to finance, Mr Owen to take 90% of the prize money, 50% of the starting money, and 75% of the bonus money. The other portions to be retained by myself. As and when the car was sold I to receive pro rata my share of the figure for which the car is sold, relative to my £1,000.
>
> The car should have a spare engine which in turn could be a slave for the B.R.M. also a 2 litre engine so that 2 litre races carrying good prize money could be entered.[70]
>
> Mr Orsi Director of Maserati is readily agreeable to giving all possible help in this matter, which would undoubtedly prove valuable assistance to B.R.M.

Owen set Ken's proposals before RM and PB, indicating that he would concur if they felt the idea could work. PB was keen to study Maserati's contemporary practice as closely as he could, and what better way than to run such a car from Bourne? He was, however, in a cleft stick. He could not admit that the new F1 might not appear until far into 1955, so he expressed instead deep suspicion of Wharton's suggested race programme, observing: "He seems to pay more regard to the possible starting money potential of the car than to the practicalities of adequately preparing the car between events...", but on AGBO's say-so negotiations began with Maserati to place an order. PB agreed to differ and made it clear he wanted nothing to do with the car whenever it should arrive.

No other manufacturer – apart from Ferrari, who was offering a few 2-litre *Tipo* 500s updated with enlarged engines in *Tipo* 625 form – was offering fully-fledged F1 cars for purchase. The Maserati was a far more comprehensive redesign of a 1952–53 2-litre F2 concept than the Ferrari, and it became known that amongst customers already queuing for them were Stirling Moss, Syd Greene of Gilby Engineering – whose car would be driven for him, as we have seen, by Roy Salvadori – Louis Rosier, 'Bira' and several others.

Into January 1954, purchase details were being ironed out

---

69. This **£1,000 offer represents a value by 1993 standards over £13,600, quite a substantial sum for any such established driver to invest in his own employer's new car.**

70. **Strange comment. The 2-litre Formula 2 class expired at the end of 1953, 2½-litre Formula 1 then standing alone for two full seasons (1954 and 1955) until in 1956–57, a new 1,500cc Formula 2 was developed.**

THE OWEN MASERATI – MODENA MODIFIED

In September, 1956, during much in-house agonizing over how rigid a rigid chassis need be, Tony Rudd wrote an internal report which included the following description of his development work on the Owen Maserati, carried out largely through the previous winter:

> In its original condition the suspension and handling characteristics of the Maserati were criticized by most drivers, although the type of car enjoyed a very good reputation from the suspension angle. Our car had, of course, been lightened – and gave more power and used different wheels and tyres when compared with other cars – also there was a certain amount of driver prejudice, e.g; the first test on this frame…showed it to be alarmingly flexible – comparisons with photographs of the prototype frame showed that the prototype had additional bracing tubes. During a visit to the Maserati Works, enquiries were made why these additional bracing tubes were omitted, and were informed that failures occurred of the upper frame tube immediately in front of the tubular structure carrying a flameproof bulkhead. This was thought to be due to a sudden change in stiffness.
>
> Measurements were taken with dial test indicator to ascertain the maximum deflections in bays, etc, and the torsional deflections per foot run plotted to see if any part of the frame was stiffer than others.
>
> It was found that the upper tubular structure moved over sideways relative to the lower structure by a reduction of .6" on the diagonal of the rear crossmember. 1" diameter 18 SWG tubes were inserted in the crossmember in the form of an X – this made a great improvement, and increased the overall stiffness from 200lbs ft per degree to 256.
>
> It was still apparent that the upper and lower structures moved independently; it was impossible to cross brace the centre crossmember, as the large clutch casting was located in the centre. Cross bracing further aft was prevented by the presence of the driver and forwards by the engine.
>
> The approach of making the upper tube structure torsionally stiff and relying on the lower structure being tied to it at frequent intervals, to give the whole frame stiffness, was then tried.
>
> Maximum linear deflection occurred around the scuttle structure, so it was decided to stiffen this structure as giving the most benefit; also it was at this point where the structure had maximum depth. The instrument panel mounting tube 17.5mm in dia. was replaced by .875 dia, braced backwards with .750 dia tubes, which were on to the cowling tail tube at the bulkhead, and were carried as far forward on the side tubes as the carburettors and exhaust pipes would permit. Two .500 tubes also ran from the junction of the .750 tubes with the .875" dia instrument panel mounting tube forwards, and met in the centre of the bulkhead hoop, triangulating the structure.
>
> This produced a considerable increase in stiffness to 400lbs ft per degree.
>
> We found, however, on checking deflection per foot run, that a disproportionately large amount of deflection was taking place immediately in front of the bulkhead; short .875" dia. gusset tubes were added between the upright and horizontal tubes, reaching as far forwards and inboard as space limitation would permit.
>
> A final check on linear deflection indicated that the upright tubes carrying the front shock absorber mountings were being twisted – these were removed and tubes 25% greater in diameter substituted. The final frame had a stiffness of 450lbs feet, more than double, and weighed 144lbs as compared with 138lbs before modification.
>
> The handling of the car was vastly improved, and appears to have superior handling on slower corners to the latest Maseratis, and is equal on faster corners, while still enjoying the advantage of being 8% lighter…

between RM and Omer Orsi, son of Maserati's industrialist owner Adolfo Orsi and Managing Director of the company. Orsi made a firm offer of a suitable car – then known only as 'Offer No. 42' – to the Owen Racing Organisation on January 11, 1954, RM having specified that delivery should be completed no later than April, although Orsi insured himself by carefully inserting the words: "…subject to unforeseen circumstances" in his confirmation.

An irrevocable letter of credit had to be established for payment to the *Banca Commerciale Italiana* in Modena, for the Sterling equivalent of 9-million *Lire*.

In February, RM was confirming details of spark plugs required "for the 2½-litre Grand Prix Maserati car which you are producing for Ken Wharton", 14mm long or short-reach? He was about to approach Lodge for suitable supplies, and also requested information on wheel and rim sizes "because of taking the matter up with Dunlop".

The necessary import licence for the new car was received from the Board of Trade on February 17, permitting application for the letter of credit. Lep Transport were briefed to collect the car, via train/ferry service. Alfred Owen himself wrote to Orsi at 322 Viale Ciro Menotti, Modena, advising:

> …we do consider it essential that he (RM), Mr. Peter Berthon and Mr. Ken Wharton visit you before the car is packed for shipment so that they can have the advantage of your kind instructions on the operation and handling of the vehicle…

This was a courteous era, and both Alfred Owen and Omer Orsi were courteous businessmen.

The letter of credit was valid until April 17, 1954, but as Maserati struggled to complete sufficient 250Fs to meet demand they missed their target dates. Unused to the ways of Italy, of Italians and of Maserati, great fuss and flurry ensued within ORO, all manner of paperwork being necessary to extend the letter of credit until the car's completion.

To support this new programme, RM also ordered from Maserati on ORO's behalf two spare wheels, two con-rods complete with bearings, six 'intake' valves, six exhaust valves, 18 assorted valve springs, two pistons, a set of piston rings and a pair of gudgeon pins, Maserati agreeing an all-in price of £100.

On February 18 Maserati confirmed the invoice price of: "1 'MASERATI' type 250/F racing-car. Formula 1. Complete with 4 wheels with tyres, 2 bare wheels as spares, 2 back axle gears and tool bag – At the price of…£5,200 0s 0d".

It was to be despatched when ready, "by us by rail truck direct to your address in London", which was Rubery Owen's Kent House office, in Market Place, Oxford Circus. Owen hastily put them right, having the car reconsigned through to Bourne.

By March 9, Lep Transport had arranged shipping with Maserati's agents, Saima of Milan and Modena, and Orsi advised that the car should be ready for testing at Modena *Aerautodromo* on or around April 25.

On April 17, ORO finally received confirmation of its new Maserati's chassis serial: "…we would mention that the car intended for you will bear the following numbers: Engine 2509, Chassis 2509…" – no mistaking which of the two was the more important to the Italian mind…

But April 25 came and passed and still there was no sign of '2509''s completion. Finally, on May 21, RM received a telegram from Orsi advising the car would be ready for test in Modena on Saturday, May 29, but Ray had to reply:

> Most unfortunately it will be impossible for Mr Ken Wharton to come to test the car at Monza on that day because he is driving in the '200' Scratch race… at Aintree.

He suggested an alternative date, at Monza, one suspects because the hotels were familiar to him, and rather better.

PB and Ron Flockhart, who was to do the acceptance driving, finally flew to Milan on the Sunday after the Aintree race, spending a few days at Modena and accepting delivery of their brand-new Grand Prix car. Arthur Hill, who was to be the car's mechanic, brought it back to Folkingham in one of the Lodestars. With Owen's approval PB ordered an additional spare engine, agreeing a price of 3.5-million *Lire* with Orsi, and since he had clearly had his ear to the ground regarding early factory and private-owner experience of racing the new cars in Argentina, where Fangio had won the season-opening Grand Prix, at Spa – where Fangio had won again – and in other non-Championship events, he inquired on June 22:

> We are most anxious to fit the later type of gearbox input bevels for the French Grand Prix at Rheims [*sic*]. Would you please arrange for your mechanics to bring a selection of different ratios of this new type…so that we can pick them up and fit the appropriate ratio before the race…

He also offered BRM's full team facilities for Maserati's works team use during their appearance at Silverstone in the British GP the following month. But within days the tone began to change.

On June 25, RM to Orsi:

> On inspecting the spare parts that came with the Maserati, which arrived safely, we notice that the gear-box input bevels 14/20 have been used previously and are

in very poor condition… I feel sure that we may have your co-operation in this matter, and your help when we arrive in France with our new Maserati…

'The Owen Maserati' was run for the first time at Folkingham on the 25th, driven by Tony Rudd, who was impressed by its roadholding and handling but not so much by its very heavy brake pedal. Next day a 'proper racer' tried the car, not Wharton at all but resident test-driver Ron Flockhart. He adopted a 7,000rpm rev limit and completed 15 laps trouble-free. The car was then reloaded into its transporter and set off for Reims in the care of Arthur Hill, Maurice Dove and Tony Rudd. The ORO team was about to make its Continental race debut with a car not of its own manufacture.

July 4, 1954 – Grand Prix de l'ACF, Reims-Gueux, France – 61 laps, 344.76 miles

In his peerless *Motor Sport* report, Denis Jenkinson described the Owen Maserati's debut on the first day of practice, June 30, like this, after commenting on how the new Mercedes-Benz streamlined F1 cars with their straight-eight fuel-injected engines:

> …set the pace of the French Grand Prix and overshadowed all other competitors…from the word Go.
> There were only three other cars out for this first practice, an H.M.W. [*sic*]…Salvadori with the Gilby Engineering Maserati and Wharton with the Rubery Owen Maserati, the latter all new and shiny and being run in its first race.

He observed that: "The two Maseratis were running well…", but BRM's people were just hiding their grief quite well.

In reality their new engine had run very rough, its exhaust camshaft had failed and the propshaft was out of true. Ken completed only seven laps, his best time of 2:49.0 being exactly 10 seconds slower than Fangio's fastest in the glistening new Mercedes.

For second practice next day:

> The B.R.M. Maserati did not turn out this time as a bent prop-shaft had shaken everything loose the previous day as well as having a worn-out camshaft.

RM, not to mention Ken Wharton, whose idea it had all been, were far from amused and Maserati *Direttore Sportivo* Aldo Lugo had his ear well and truly bent by them.

After Ken had covered four laps on the old camshaft just to qualify, Lugo seconded a couple of works mechanics to fit a new one into '2509''s engine.

Ken lined-up on row seven of the grid, 16th fastest, and as Fangio, Karl Kling and Hans Herrmann put Mercedes-Benz's new mark on Formula 1 racing – with Gonzalez's stumpy *Squalo* four-cylinder Ferrari keeping them honest – "Wharton was not happy with the Owen Maserati, the prop-shaft still causing a terrible vibration…". Its engine was running rough on its 'new' exhaust camshaft which ultimately failed and the prop-shaft remained wildly out of true. The factory record indicates he retired "on 19th lap, due excessive vibration. Propshaft out of truth again – in 10th place".

The storm burst around Lugo's head…

Back at Bourne on July 8, RM wrote to Omer Orsi, first thanking him for an invoice concerning the spare engine ordered by PB while in Modena, and then expressing himself bluntly, to ensure no mistake in translation:

> Frankly we are so disgusted with the performance and appalling lack of reliability of the car we purchased that we have little interest in acquiring any more liabilities at the moment. The camshaft business is quite disgraceful, since the engine had extremely little running before it went to Rheims [sic], and having completed only 10 laps during the race, the camshaft which you sent to Rheims [sic], and which was fitted by your mechanics, is in a worse state than the one it replaced. The prop shaft is equally unsatisfactory, and after only 10 laps racing has caused a complete breakdown of the clutch output shaft and its bearings etc. The fuel tank split at its bottom mounting point, again with next to no running at all. Other things that have happened to the car include the steering box mounting brackets and clutch casing brackets which have broken… The sump bolts were found to be finger tight only when the car arrived here, and the performance of the engine has at all times been pathetic, and well down not only on the works cars, but on the cars you have supplied to the better private owners.
>
> We paid the very high price you asked without question to acquire a car for the purpose of keeping Ken Wharton in Grand Prix racing for this season, and apart from losing some of the races through very late delivery…it appears to be one of the worst you have ever turned out.
>
> Quite frankly, we understand the difficulties in making racing cars, but there is no excuse for shoddy components and poor workmanship, which have obviously been put into this car to scramble it together in order to deliver it and collect the money.
>
> We insist that you personally look into this whole matter and give us reasonable satisfaction by supplying spares immediately, together with the other require-ments asked for in our telegram of today's date…Yours Sincerely…

Ray's telegram to Lugo, listing spares required to repair the car, began:

> Car extensively damaged after 10 laps running at Rheims [sic] STOP Must have immediately following spares to rebuild for Silverstone STOP…

and ended:

> Please dispatch mechanic immediately as arranged bring all parts with him wire arrival London airport and

we will meet STOP You must make a serious effort to get this car running satisfactorily for Silverstone present performance and reliability are a disgrace to Maserati – Raymond Mays…

No pussy-footing there!

Orsi and Lugo responded by despatching mechanic 'Dan' Ghelfi – who had a strong Brooklyn accent – plus parts, to work alongside the BRM lads at Folkingham over the period of the British GP. When first run on the Bourne test-bed, after Dan's rebuild, everyone was shattered when the Maserati engine gave only 208bhp! After some panic phone calls to Modena, recarburating and so on, it was persuaded to deliver 222bhp before it was put back in the car ready for Silverstone.

July 17, 1954 – RAC British Grand Prix, Silverstone – 90 laps, 263.42 miles

On July 15 Flockhart tried the rebuilt Maserati for six laps without snags at Folkingham before it was taken to Silverstone, where that afternoon Wharton completed 17 laps, decided it was wrongly geared and clocked a best time of 1:54 compared with Gonzalez's Ferrari best of 1:48.

RM and Alfred Owen had Flockhart's interests at heart and in order "to keep this very promising young driver" in practice, Ray arranged for him to be nominated as reserve driver for 'Bira', who had entered his own private 250F but was feeling unwell with a developing bout of malarial fever. This arrangement would have a far-reaching effect upon the Owen Maserati story…

Heavy rain swept the aerodrome circuit during Friday practice, Wharton completing 10 laps before changing to 6.50-section rear tyres to find no improvement in another six-lap stint. Flockhart drove a similar distance without trouble, but Ken's best of 2:12 again compared poorly with Fangio's 1:58 in the Mercedes, which he was finding difficult to place on the slick circuit, with its barrel-lined corners.

For the race, Ken started from ninth-fastest place on row three and he eventually finished eighth after a 73rd-lap pit-stop to change hard plugs after developing a misfire, exacerbated by the driver switching off each magneto in turn in a misguided effort to identify which plugs might be affected. He had been running seventh and lost 105 seconds in this stop, finishing four laps behind the victorious 'Pepe' Gonzalez.

Meanwhile, 'Bira' had qualified with an identical time to Wharton's on row three of the grid, and after 20 laps was running 13th, 7sec behind Ken. He was feeling increasingly unwell and the prospect of completing the long 90-lap race persuaded him to tour into the pits on lap 42, handing his car to its reserve driver – RM's nominee, Ron Flockhart.

Perhaps anxious to set times decently comparable to Wharton's in '2509', Ron hurled himself into the race on a still slightly damp and treacherous track, and almost immediately got into a vicious slide at Copse Corner; the blue Maserati bucketed sideways across the bumpy verge, clipped the spectator safety bank, reared up – and rolled.

It was quite severely damaged, its chassis bent, and an

acutely embarrassed Ron Flockhart was fortunate to be winkled out from underneath unhurt. There was some discussion at the time as to whether or not a broken de Dion tube – a recognized 250F weakness – might have initiated this incident, but it could have been broken on impact as the car bounced off the bank.

Mechanic Ghelfi eventually flew back home to Italy on July 25.

On the 23rd an exhaust camshaft, new 14/20 and 13/18 bevels, a dozen large inlet valves and valve seats, a set of clutch plates and a pair of prop-shaft UJs had been ordered from Bourne, significantly, plus crash spares including a de Dion tube, half-shafts, steering drop-arm, steering links and track rods, two king-pins, and the lever and outer pivot pin for the left-hand lower rear wishbone.

Ghelfi returned on the 29th with parts in his personal luggage, including a pair of bevels, the prop-shaft UJs, even the Trident badges for the nose and steering wheel – totalling £17 excluding bevels…

Immediately after the British GP, 'Bira' had expressed his vexed astonishment at the damage inflicted by ORO's recommended driver upon his valuable Maserati. It became a straightforward question of who was going to pay for it to be repaired on the traditional basis of all borrowed racing cars – 'You Bend It, You Mend It'.

Apparently – for no paperwork record whatsoever appears to survive to record the happy compromise agreed – ORO exchanged the virtually as-new Owen '2509' for 'Bira''s bent '2504', and when 'The Owen Maserati' reappeared with all its '2509' number tags welded or riveted firmly into place, it was really the repaired shorter-wheelbase 'Bira' car with BRM's original engine and gearbox installed. Conversely, the Prince's '2504' with which his mechanic Reg Williams set off to Caen four days later, was in fact the French and British GP Owen car fitted with 'Bira''s own engine and gearbox, repainted in his blue and yellow livery, and now bearing his chassis serial.

There was one major snag in all this, which the boys at Bourne did not appreciate at the time the deal was done. 'Bira''s car had been one of the very first 250Fs to be delivered – reputedly the works prototype – and it used an early 7ft 3in wheelbase, which during early factory testing had proved rather too nervous to handle. Consequently, later versions like the original '2509' had had a 3-inch longer wheelbase, which made a considerable difference and provided the stable platform which became the front-engined/rear-gearbox 250Fs' greatest single attribute. 'Bira' had got the better of the deal…

PB viewed the 250F purchase entirely as Alfred Owen's baby "…to keep Ken Wharton happy". To him it was nothing but an unwarranted distraction from the real job in hand, which was to complete development and production of the new 2½-litre BRM, and so he had placed the programme entirely in Tony Rudd's hands.

So it was under Tony's direction that, after the British GP, the replacement (and extensively repaired) '2509' was modified to carry Dunlop light-alloy disc wheels in place of the hefty and flexible standard Borrani wire-spoked type and Dunlop disc brakes.

Dunlop had made most aircraft disc brakes during the war and held the master patents. While a Girling system had been developed on the V16s from 1952, Dunlop discs had shown their value on the C-Type and D-Type Jaguar sports-racing cars through 1953–54. When ORO began to lay out the Type 25 car, Dunlop had proposed a package deal in which the new 2½-litre BRM would feature their duralumin perforated disc wheels, their tyres and their disc brakes too. This gave ORO the opportunity to work with the originators, who made a suitable contribution to team funds.

Tony: The discs for the Maserati were made in Dunlop's aircraft department. They really appealed to me, beautifully made and bearing the hallmark of proper aeronautical engineering practice. While Girling had preferred to use slightly higher line pressures and a relatively soft, benign pad material which was not too hard on the discs but suffered a fairly high wear rate, Dunlop used a fierce pad, lower line pressure and were harder on the discs.

Harold Hodkinson was their engineer in charge, a big, strong, dogmatic personality who would only see things blindingly white or jet black. He seemed absolutely indestructible, he would work with us 'til it became too dark to run the development car around 9 at night, would then retire to the village pub with the mechanics and consume copious amounts of beer, and then jump into his development XK Jaguar, return to Coventry at an incredible rate, organize people to work all night on a modified brake set and then be back with us at first light next morning to run it.

One problem involved the attachment of pads to the hydraulic cylinders. Dunlop preferred a light rubber solution. To replace the pads you just broke them away from the pistons. Unfortunately, at the temperatures the Maserati began to develop – since it was a relatively reliable and good handling car capable of being driven faster around a circuit than the V16 – the rubber solution would fail. There was inevitably a certain amount of taper wear in the pads and so they used to rotate under initial application and grab, which Ken Wharton hadn't liked one bit. At Barcelona, for example, the problem had become quite bad, but that was one of the few races where we had little technical back-up from Dunlop. Willie Southcott, our engine specialist, was there and he couldn't see why we were mucking about with rubber solution and suggested we just Araldite the pads in place. This we did, and once cooked by the high temperatures generated it later nearly drove the Dunlop chaps mad trying to get the assembly apart!

The 250F's exhaust tailpipes were considerably shortened to latest factory specification and the engine was rebuilt and coaxed up to 238bhp. The bodywork was resprayed in what Jenks would describe in his forthcoming Swiss GP report as "olive green" – in fact standard BRM metallic green in place of Maserati's interpretation, which had disappeared under the 'Bira' blue…

Tony: After the unhappy experience at Reims, we had discarded Maserati's standard and rather primitively-made prop-shaft whose imbalance had created such destructive vibration problems, and had made our own most beautiful replacement. Essentially the 250F had reasonably effective suspension geometry and a good reputation for roadholding, far superior to the contemporary Ferrari, and probably the Mercedes-Benz, too, whose power it could not match.

Having now lost our original long-wheelbase frame to find

ourselves instead with what had been 'Bira' 's early type, when we came to fit our exquisite new prop-shaft we found it was 3 inches too long, which is when the difference in wheelbase between the two cars first came to our notice. When I laid the problem before PB and RM, on the basis that since they had got us into this, they should get us out, PB told me to move the engine forward rather than make a new prop-shaft, which had probably cost as much as the chassis! This brought me the hard way face-to-face with racing car polar moment of inertia problems.[71]

With Dunlop disc wheels and brakes plus a BRM-made Elektron (magnesium alloy) body, the shorter car weighed some 110lbs less than the original '2509'. We easily talked PB out of going down Maserati's nitro-methane-fuelled route on the grounds that the tank might not be big enough and persuaded him that light weight was the card to play. We toyed around with the engine's breathing, which probably paid greater dividends than the possibility of adding nitro-methane to the fuel brew, which would have increased fuel consumption so much we would have required a very heavy fuel load on the startline. As it was, with Dunlop disc wheels and disc brakes and that much less weight of fuel the Owen Maserati emerged probably one hundredweight lighter on the startline than its sisters.

On August 22, Wharton completed a 14-lap trouble-free test with the car, proving disc brakes at Folkingham before the new modified '2509' – tended by Arthur Hill, Dick Salmon and Tony – was despatched to Berne for the Swiss GP. Ken Wharton had always troubled Tony and the mechanics with his apparent suspicion that not everything was being done in his best interests. Now Tony lived in mortal fear of Ken discovering that the modified car was in fact 'Bira' 's early short-chassis frame "with the built-in oversteer".

Tony: This I felt would mean that once Ken found out about the car he would want nothing more to do with it on the grounds that whatever we did to the thing it would have "the most appalling oversteer". The truth was that while the 228cm so-called medium-wheelbase 250Fs had a nice, comfortable degree of inherent understeer, the shorter 223cm type which we had ended-up with thanks to the Flockhart incident had a mild degree of inherent oversteer.

Ken also had a substantial bee in his bonnet about the performance of Pirelli tyres, especially in the wet, a view that most drivers, including Moss shared. Dunlop did not produce the 'R4' which broke Pirelli's dominance until May the following year. Moss was in the forefront of prodding Dunlop, but was invariably publicly loyal and helpful to them.

August 22, 1954 – Swiss Grand Prix, Bremgarten, Berne – 66 laps, 240.25 miles

In 12 laps during first practice on this very dangerous and demanding circuit, Wharton clocked 2:48 against Fangio's 2:41 on a wet track. Next day, in heavy rain, with the course even more dangerous, running 37mm carburettor chokes and

August 22, 1954 – Swiss Grand Prix, Bremgarten, Berne: Ken Wharton's race debut with the much-modified, different-chassised, definitively 'Owenized' version of '2509' was punctuated by this early tangle with Sergio Mantovani's works 250F. Ken continued – greatly detuned. The car by this time is the ex-'Bira' short-wheelbase interim frame and body, reassembled at Folkingham with ORO's engine, transmission and running gear, Dunlop disc brakes and wheels and resprayed 'BRM green'.

Pirelli tyres, Ken completed 15 laps. Flockhart then took over for experience, but could only complete three faltering laps, one at a time, between stops to change oiled plugs.

By the time the mixture had been weakened Ken could only squeeze in one final lap before it became too dark for safety.

On raceday, Ken ran sixth in the opening stages while Fangio and Kling led for Mercedes from Moss' private but works-supported 250F. In the race, the BRM log reads:

> Involved in collision with Mantovani on 4th lap; dropped from 6th to 11th. Lost 31secs; finished sixth – 2secs behind Mantovani; 26secs behind Mieres. Best race lap 1:44.8; fastest Fangio 1:42.2.

Wharton was not a very aggressive driver, and mixing with Mantovani and Musso who were the second-string works drivers and a real cut-and-thrust pair it was hardly surprising he should come off second-best. Jenks reported on the later stages that: "…the Rubery Owen Maserati was sounding as healthy as at the start". This would be the car's best performance that year, but what a pity Wharton had tangled with Mantovani's factory car early on, for the experience on that slick and treacherous surface had clearly detuned him.

Tony: Apparently, after the race Ken persuaded RM to run the car in the Italian GP at Monza 15 days hence. The plan, quite logical, was to send the car direct to Monza from Berne,

71. **'The dumb-bell effect'** – a short-shafted dumb-bell with its weights close together will be easy to spin in the hand, and the direction of spin can be changed abruptly with little effort. A long-shafted dumb-bell with the weights far apart offers more inertial resistance against spin being induced, and when one attempts to reverse the spin-direction quickly there's a good chance of breaking a finger. As originated with the main masses of engine and rear-mounted transaxle gearbox mounted just within the wheelbase, the 250F was a well-balanced car inclining towards a high polar moment as a compromise between directional stability and nimble readiness to turn into a corner; with those masses more widely separated, relative to the wheelbase, some of this nimbleness would be lost, and the car would be less willing to respond readily to directional inputs. Masses further apart indicates a higher polar moment of inertia; masses closer together imparts a lower polar moment of inertia, improving the 'swervability' factor…

one day's drive, drawing on the Maserati works for spares to overhaul it. We were a very fragmented party at Berne – RM, Ron Flockhart, PB and his daughter Jacquie. RM came to the pit for a few minutes each day, Ron for first practice, then we saw neither again. Nobody came to our garage at all.

On the Monday morning after the race, I went to see RM as instructed at the *Bellevue Hotel* at 10am to collect money for the return journey, and to confirm that the original plan to re-import the car into England still stood. He seemed distracted, but confirmed the plan, handed over the money and we set off home.

The Maserati had been imported "under Treasury Direction". This meant Rubery Owen had registered it as a development vehicle, essential to their business, exempting it from import duties, which were heavy in the mid-'50s. The only snag was that someone from Rubery Owen's finance department then had to meet us at the port of entry with a mass of new papers each time we brought the car into the country. We would specify the ferry that we would arrive on – it worked the first time – and the formalities only took about an hour to clear.

Other teams who had paid the duty could whistle through customs with their carnets, saving valuable time and probably more money in the long run. This time there was no-one to meet us when we arrived on the specified night ferry from Dunkirk, we had to hang around from 6am until 4pm and then we were stopped by the police for exceeding the 30mph limit which applied to all lorries in those days. So, it was after midnight when we got back to Bourne, with none of us in the best of humours.

Next morning (Thursday) I was summoned to Bourne to face an extremely irate Alfred Owen, who had been dragged from his annual family holiday at Cromer by an equally furious Ken Wharton, demanding to know why the car was back at Bourne and not at Monza! I told him I knew nothing of the plan to go to Monza, made it worse by saying it was now too late to overhaul the car and get it to Italy anyway, and had a moan about the stupid paperwork system. I suspect I carried the can for this incident for ever. My relationship with Ken – which had already suffered from my heat-of-the-moment outspoken criticism of his stupidity in races ("Leave the thinking to me" I had told him) – entered terminal decline.

In fact RM had been distracted that morning in Berne since for one very rare moment he had succumbed to his innermost self and had been reported by a hotel liftboy for importuning. This potentially disastrous slip attracted the wrath of the rigidly red-necked Bernese police and only after great diplomatic activity and the intercession of Ray's similarly-orientated Swiss friend, Count Jacques de Wurstemberge, was the entire matter hushed-up and resolved.

On Monday, September 20, tyre testing for '2509''s appearance in the closing Goodwood International, Ken completed 36 laps, including a best of 1:35.4 with power in hand, when a half-shaft UJ was found to have too much play and the others were not much better. RM telegrammed Modena:

> Have broken two half-shafts in Maserati on test. Car running Goodwood Friday and Saturday. We are sending

Flockhart by air tomorrow Tuesday morning…

Sure enough, Folkingham go-for Flockhart played courier, flying out to Milan and back to collect two half-shafts and UJs complete.

Colin Atkin, who had already spent, and was to spend, many more long hours working on the Italian engine at Bourne, said: "It was all face-fitting – no head gasket so that if both surfaces weren't just perfect it would leak. I spent many a night scraping it in, to and fro…". But the problems continued. Back at Goodwood for practice on September 23, Ken managed only three untimed laps before the engine seized and '2509' had to be scratched. The tip of a valve spring had broken off and jammed the oil pump's gears, which broke. Ken did not notice the disappearance of oil pressure and the engine needed a new crankshaft. Tony's opinion of Ken Wharton diminished further…

An entry was then made in the Championship-qualifying Spanish GP at Barcelona, scene of the V16's first Continental foray four years before. Ken was again nominated driver.

On October 13, Tony wrote to Maserati confirming that Ghelfi had been asked to ensure a spare magneto would be taken to Barcelona for ORO, and suggesting its cost should be offset against that of valve forgings obtained for Maserati from a UK supplier. The new crankshaft was of the latest type, and they managed to swap the spare connecting rods for those suitable for the new crank. Tony: During the rebuild, fired up by Dan telling us the new crank would cost some 4bhp through increased friction losses, we had managed to stoke up the power to 248bhp.

October 2, 1954 – Spanish Grand Prix, Pedralbes, Barcelona: ORO's return to the Catalan course four years after the V16s' Continental debut there – an unhappy Wharton grimaces towards the pits, just apprised of his Owen Maserati's true provenance… convinced it is unmanageable. Windborne litter posed a major problem at this last significant Spanish Grand Prix for 14 years – '2509''s radiator intake is partially blocked…

Right: 1954 Spanish GP: The definitive Owen Maserati at Pedralbes displays its interim-type body, dominated by that long rear fuel tank and tail cowling, shapely splash-guards and Dunlop disc wheels with three-eared centre-lock knock-off fixings. Note balance weights bolted through two of the smaller drillings on the right-rear. There's one clearance blister over the carburettor intakes, the other over the gearchange. The oil tank has now been moved.

Below: Effective high-tech – the Dunlop disc brakes and light-alloy wheels adopted on '2509' were developed in parallel on Jaguar's works D-Type sports cars, which won the year's Reims 12-Hours race. Note 5.50 x 16 diamond-pattern Dunlop Racing R1 tyre, and how this car gleamed… Moss' private 250F would become similarly Dunlop-wheeled and disc-braked.

October 24, 1954 – Spanish Grand Prix, Pedralbes, Barcelona – 80 laps, 313.19 miles

This was really the last nail in the coffin of Ken Wharton's BRM career.

Tony: During practice he claimed the car was nothing like as fast as the works cars down the straight. PB, who said he had only come to see the debut of the new Lancia D50s, suggested it was because the works cars loaded the same French-brewed BP fuel that we were using with 5% nitro for practice. This was hard to prove. Alf Francis and Stirling had had plenty of experience of the stuff with the Cooper-Alta. There was no trace of its characteristic smell. If it was true, they would have had about 10hp more than us.

Maserati's chief mechanic and tester Guerrino Bertocchi was then persuaded to try the car, which of course he was keen to do since he wanted to see if its disc brakes gave any advantage, and whether or not the ORO-tweaked engine gave more power than the works' since his two junior drivers had apparently been bashing his ear about it ever since the opening laps at Berne!

Bertocchi tried the car and reported there was nothing wrong at all. It merely seemed a little twitchy, but he put this down to its funny aluminium disc wheels compared with the works' Borrani wires. Ken was still not satisfied, and then – perhaps intentionally, perhaps innocently – 'Bira', who was very indignant because PB wouldn't let him have any of the team's surplus fuel, spilled the beans and Ken discovered the provenance of his chassis. 'Bira' had merely asked how he liked its short wheelbase?

The result was total disenchantment, and from then on Ken simply didn't try with it.

After a pit-stop in the race – for a chat and a rest according to Tony – he finished eighth, six laps behind Mike Hawthorn's winning *Super Squalo* four-cylinder Ferrari on a bad day for Mercedes-Benz, whose cars all suffered problems. At one stage Ken had been placed as high as sixth, but '2509' ran roughly towards the end and showed little sign of being truly competitive despite its many modifications.

1955 – '2509''s SECOND SEASON

The end of 1954 saw the parting of the ways between Ken Wharton and ORO, even though he remained on relatively good terms with RM (but not with PB who was particularly 'anti'), and he would continue to drive his 'Raymond Mays'-headed Ford Zephyr quite successfully in production car racing.

For Formula 1 Ken joined Tony Vandervell's new Vanwall team, while former Vandervell driver Peter Collins joined ORO.

On February 7, Ken – as yet then unattached to Vandervell – wrote to Owen reporting that he had spent the previous Thursday at Bourne with RM and PB and had been:

> …most impressed with what I saw of the new car and the progress that had been made with it. I must say it really looks the part and I hope that in the very near future I shall have the pleasure of a drive in it.

He had discussed prospects for staying with ORO and explained to Owen:

> As you know, due partly to the small number of events in which the B.R.M. ran, and secondly due to the…small starting money, I had a very bad year financially. This also applied of course to the Maserati where in all instances…I paid all my own travelling costs including air tickets…and did not receive a great deal of remuneration in return, so therefore it is essential that we arrange something as soon as possible so that I know exactly where I stand before the season commences…

Regarding the Maserati:

> …I am deeply conscious of the fact that you spent a considerable amount…and it is my earnest desire to help in every way possible to redeem much of this cost, and for that reason I would suggest that a slightly more ambitious programme be arranged so that travelling could be cut to a minimum by coupling together a series of Continental events where the starting money is invariably good. For instance, the Goodwood Meeting on Easter Monday April 11th cannot bring any great return in the way of prize money and the starting money will be equally small. On the other hand, the Grand Prix of Pau takes place on the same date and will carry considerable prize money plus a handsome starting fee. Shortly after this comes the Grand Prix of Bordeaux, which is little more than 100 miles from Pau…

and much more of the same…

His suggested programme included eight more events than PB's, who commented that:

> …Ken's letter has an accent on his financial side of motor racing and so naturally wants to collect as much starting money as possible. We feel that his approach to running at many events and rushing the car to races every weekend for maximum starting money gain will do neither Rubery Owen or himself any good… From our point of view it is important that the Maserati goes well and is driven well as we are extremely anxious…to use it as a yardstick against the opposition which we will have to face with the new car.

His amended target fixture list included only seven events, Pau "(if possible)", May Silverstone, the Luxembourg GP, Albi, and the French, British and Swiss GPs.

On February 21, 1955, the "Basic Programme – Maserati", was expounded as follows:

> The Maserati has been promised to Dunlops by the end of this month for tests of an improved tyre. Mr. Badger is pressing for this. In addition it was planned to convert the Maserati to S.U. fuel injection. The first race is planned for Easter – which is effectively six weeks from now.
>
> The labour force is stretched to the limit on the

B.R.M. P25; and, to meet the above three commitments, it will be necessary to withdraw at least three men and occupy the test-bed at this critical time for nearly a fortnight.

> It is suggested that the proposal to convert to fuel injection be shelved, as the original intention of gaining experience is lost as we are now at an equivalent position with the B.R.M.s; and we learn from S.U.'s that they are only getting 235 b.h.p. from Moss' engine, whereas we get 248 h.p. from ours on Weber carburettors.
>
> Secondly, we could suggest to Dunlops that, as Moss' car is already in their possession for the fitment of disc brakes, they may care to carry out the tyre tests with his car, particularly as it should be ready before ours, and he has greater experience on Maserati's with Pirelli tyres. We could lend them wheels and similar items to assist. This would give us much more time to prepare the Maserati for its first race and would possibly free one man for work on the B.R.M.
>
> In addition, if the first race at Easter could be cancelled, this would give us an extra month, by which time the first Type 25 B.R.M. would be running, and the labour position less acute.

Through the early months of 1955 ORO's management had continued to haggle with Wharton, RM offering him: "…a retaining fee of £500 for the 1955 season's racing. Shell are not terribly interested in the Maserati, pinning their hopes and faith on the new BRM…". He suggested Shell would not pay more than £25 bonus for each Maserati start.

But Ray was also negotiating with the cheerfully slap-happy, irritating – and potentially brilliant – Peter Collins. Alfred Owen insisted it would be wrong to sign-up the boy with an exclusive retainer, since ORO clearly would not have the new Formula 1 car available for him, perhaps until the end of the season. A scrupulously fair man in all his dealings, Owen told RM that perhaps Collins ought to be allowed to stay with Vandervell, and the BRM overture should be withdrawn? However, Peter was keen to accept and ultimately agreed the same terms as Wharton the previous season.

In March, Peter, with his motor dealer father Pat Collins MBE, had visited Folkingham to test-drive one of the Mark IIs. RM discussed terms but Collins' outlook was decidedly 'me first' or simply irresponsible, for without either team being told, he was negotiating simultaneously with Vandervell, who wanted to run his new F1 'Vanwall Special' cars in 1955 with the all-British driver duo of Mike Hawthorn and Peter Collins. GAV had gone so far as to enter two cars for them in the Pau GP before learning that the latter had in fact just agreed to join the Owen Racing Organisation.

While Pat Collins had tried to talk up the potential fee his son would be paid to drive for ORO, it had eventually emerged that there was a clash between the young driver's existing oil company ties (with Esso for fuel, and – strangely – Castrol for oil) and BRM's obligation (with Shell). Collins was also tied to David Brown's Aston Martin company for sports car racing, and the Feltham team had prior claim to his time.

The problem of duplication immediately arose in preparation for Easter Monday Goodwood, as Esso flatly refused to release Collins to run the Shell-backed V16 Mark II. On April Fool's Day – perhaps fittingly – Collins wrote to RM requesting that his Mark II should be run on Esso fuel and Wakefield oil, receiving a suitably dusty answer:

> …utterly impossible. We have been under contract to Shell for a considerable number of years…

Collins was advised to get a grip and sort out his own affairs. While this was going on, Wharton was offered £500 as a retainer and 50 per cent of all starting and prize money earned in the Maserati. Ray was clearly hedging his bets.

Eventually, on March 31, 1955, Alfred Owen – using his standard signature style 'AGBO' – had written to Collins at his home, Shatterford Grange, Nr Bewdley, Worcestershire, agreeing that:

> …we pay you a retaining fee of £500[72] for this year…and that the acceptance of this fee guarantees that you will not drive any other Formula 1 or *Libre* racing car during the 1955 season without obtaining our consent in each case. Obviously this in no way affects your sports car arrangements with Aston Martin… The above fee is to include your tests of the new Formula 1, 2½-litre B.R.M., but any reasonable out-of-pocket expenses in this connection with [*sic*] be paid. This expense allowance also applies to any other events in which you may drive for us… As soon as the new B.R.M. is ready to compete in a race and we have therefore two motor cars, i.e. one B.R.M. and one Maserati, you will have the opportunity of driving one of these two cars… I am sure all concerned hope that your association with us may be long and successful…

This £500 retainer was identical to that which ORO had paid for 1954 to Ken Wharton, and he would be paid the same again for 1955 since both RM and Owen felt beholden to him, despite the fact that Ken had just been 'aced out' of his team seat by young Collins, fully 15 years his junior. However, come April 29, Owen would write abruptly to RM:

> I have not heard from Wharton other than your telephone call to the effect that he has been entered twice for Silverstone and what the *Sunday Express* said about him was apparently true with regard to him being linked with the Vanwall. If he wishes to drive for the Vanwall we have no further need of his services for the BRM…

Ken Wharton thus became an ex-BRM team member.

On May 3, Pat Collins visited Owen at Darlaston and after their meeting approached Esso and Wakefield to confirm that Owen would be 'loaning' the 250F to be entered by Peter in nominated national events that season, this in return for their permission for him to run the car as a Shell-backed ORO entry at International level. They had sent telegrams of approval, and it was confirmed that starting money for those events

would be paid by Peter to ORO.

Next day Ray wrote very frankly to Ron Flockhart at Charles Clarke & Son, Chapel Ash, Wolverhampton:

> My dear Ronnie,
>   If you are to be any use in the future you must at least keep your eye in on a Formula 1 car in addition to testing the new 2½-litre BRM. Owing to Ken Wharton having left us we have to try to strengthen the team. For some considerable time it has been Mr.Owen's wish to obtain the services of Peter Collins… I want to be completely frank with you. It was felt that on occasions your performance with the B.R.M. did not come up to our hopes. I agree that you had certain troubles with the brakes, but those other incidents and the fact of the unfortunate mishap to Bira's Maserati at Silverstone did somewhat shake our confidence. However, I am sure I am voicing Mr. Owen's opinion that you are to be given further opportunities…

Ron had been trying to obtain an Austin-Healey for sports car racing, and Owen agreed to pull what strings he could with Donald Healey at The Cape, Warwick. In fact Healey had approached Owen concerning the possibility of obtaining a version of the new 2½-litre BRM F1 engine for sports car use. He was politely advised there was no chance…

Cooper-Bristol privateer Horace Gould – the garage owner from Bristol – inquired if the old Mark I BRM might be available for him to drive, but he was turned down – Bourne had no spare facilities to prepare it. The hill-climber Tony Marsh, of Dursley Hall, Stourbridge – who had caught Ray's eye – was invited to visit to try one of the old V16s: "…don't come until after Peter Berthon has recovered from his injuries…".

On April 13, 1955, Tony had been requesting correct front and rear track dimensions and king-pin offset for the 250F from Maserati. Then, after having made his auspiciously victorious debut for ORO in the V16 Mark II at Goodwood on Easter Monday, Peter Collins' next outing followed a month later in the BRDC May meeting at Silverstone, this time behind the wheel of the distinctively disc-wheeled Owen Maserati.

May 7, 1955 – BRDC *Daily Express* International Trophy, Silverstone – 60 laps, 175.61 miles

The BRDC's entry list for their major non-Championship F1 race of the year was weakened by the non-appearance of works Maserati and Ferrari support, and it was really left to the privately-owned 250Fs to make a race of it. They did just that…

In Thursday practice Roy Salvadori clocked 1:48 in the Greene Maserati, a time which Mike Hawthorn equalled next day in the fuel-injected Vanwall. *Autosport* ironically observed of the Vanwalls:

> These cars show great promise, but were clearly not *au point* for Silverstone, the mechanics working busily and constantly before race day in a manner reminiscent

---

72. This £500 retainer fee in 1955 represented over £6,440 purchasing power at 1993 values.

May 7, 1955 – BRDC International Trophy, Silverstone: Peter Collins' maiden race in the Owen Maserati brought its only win – a great tonic for the ORO team and vindication both for the car's purchase and for Collins' signing, ex-Vandervell. In the absence of the Italian works teams, the Trophy race became a duel between the British-prepared 250Fs of Collins, here in '2509', and Roy Salvadori in Syd Greene's more standard Gilby Engineering-entered Maserati '2507'. The Owen Maserati took the lead for keeps on lap 33…

of the B.R.M. equipe in recent years. In ironic contrast, that self-same equipe had the Owen Organisation's Dunlop disc-braked G.P. Maserati in excellent trim for Peter Collins, the latest of the long line of drivers they have employed. He clocked 1min. 51secs. (on R1 tyres but in the new Dunlop compound) during Friday's rain. Stirling Moss did 1min. 50secs. in a rather shaky Maserati (on R4s), while Jack Fairman achieved an encouraging 1min 51secs with the prototype aerodynamic Connaught, gaining a front row start with Salvadori, Hawthorn and Moss…

Fairman's unexpected pace bumped Collins back onto the inside position on row two, from where he made a superb start – on brand-new, virtually unscrubbed R4s which Tony had obtained at the last moment after invoking Dunlop MD Evan Price's help – and shot through between Hawthorn and Salvadori to lead briefly before Roy characteristically stole the advantage into Copse Corner.

The two green Maseratis began a spectacular duel, with Jack Fairman driving perhaps his best race in the Connaught streamliner in third place, and setting a new F1 record at 1:49.0, 96.67mph. He improved this time soon after, while unreliability struck much of the field, both Vanwalls making stops – Hawthorn's for good.

Fairman's throttle eventually fell apart, but meantime Collins – having got the measure of the new R4 tyres – finally caught and passed Salvadori on lap 23, only to be repassed entering Copse, on the exit to which Roy ran wide so '2509' ducked past him yet again. It was a rare duel which really held the enormous crowd enthralled.

With a record 98.48mph lap, Salvadori regained the lead which he held for the next six laps until, on lap 33, Collins retook the lead and began to pull away. Peter explained he was quicker round Club and "…had more squirt up the hill to Abbey, ditto Becketts and the straight".

Wharton – who had fought hard to win his class with the works Mays Zephyr in the supporting production car race – was out again in the second Vanwall after a long delay in the pits when he made the mistake of attempting to unlap himself from Salvadori on the outside entering Copse Corner. Roy seldom took prisoners on an aerodrome circuit, and Wharton found himself suddenly on the far verge, crashing through a concrete-based corner marker which broke his car's de Dion tube, ruptured its fuel tank and triggered a huge fire from which the ex-BRM driver was lucky to escape with just nasty burns on his arms and neck.

Collins was left to pace '2509' to the finish while Salvadori apparently settled for a safe second place – the two 250Fs finishing 39 seconds apart after just under two hours' fine racing. They shared fastest lap, a new outright Silverstone record, at 1:47.0, 98.48mph – the Owen Maserati had won at last, and Peter Collins had proved himself capable of winning at premier level, albeit in the absence of first-class factory opposition.

He was delighted, as was John Wyer of Aston Martin, who had kept ORO's lap chart. Peter took the mechanics to the beer tent to celebrate, inviting everyone to admire his still spotless overalls, saying it must be the first Maserati to finish without an oil leak!

May 30, 1955 – BRSCC London Trophy, Crystal Palace – Aggregate result of two 12-lap, 16.68-mile Heats

At this Whit-Monday meeting on the tight London parkland circuit, nobody could touch Peter Collins in the first heat in '2509', which with its disc brakes proved eminently better suited to the course than Salvadori's Greene car. Towards the end of the heat, Salvadori's engine began to sound rough, but he finished second, 8.2sec behind Collins after just 14 minutes' racing. Collins' fastest lap was timed at 1:08.4, 73.16mph.

Heat Two was another walkover, with Salvadori's rough-running engine blowing up on lap three and Peter pacing himself easily to win at 70.38mph – compared with 71.47 in Heat One – from Gerard's Cooper-Bristol, 2sec behind. Fastest lap this time was in 1:09.8, 71.69mph, and Collins and the Owen Maserati had won outright for the second time in two outings.

The car ran minus its tail cone after a mildly damaging practice spin. But any racing car which wins is beautiful…

The far more serious business of a full-distance World Championship-qualifying Grand Prix race followed; the British and European GP at Aintree.

July 16, 1955 – RAC British Grand Prix, Aintree – 90 laps, 270 miles

After problems in practice,[73] Collins qualified 23rd, on the back of the grid, with only Jack Brabham's privately entered rear-engined Bobtail Cooper-Bristol slower.

With the car repaired, he ran a spirited fifth before retiring after 30 laps with connecting rod failure. One of the new rods had split down the centre from a forging seam, like a split pin. He had pressed Hawthorn hard in the works Ferrari before out-braking him into one of the tighter Aintree turns on lap 13. Ten laps later '2509' was closing rapidly on Musso's factory 250F and Piero Taruffi in the number four Mercedes. By lap 26 Peter was within 5sec of Musso and 7sec of Taruffi, but then Musso responded, closing on Taruffi's silver Mercedes, with Collins right on his tail all the way. Then the rod broke, and '2509' was out.

Gregor Grant enthused about Collins passing "eight cars from his last place on the starting grid…" and singled-out his drive as one of the brightest features of the race, which Moss won from Fangio to head a Mercedes-Benz 1-2-3-4 demonstration finish.

October 1, 1955 – Bristol MC & LCC International Avon Trophy, Castle Combe – 55 laps, 101.2 miles

This event, run so soon after the new BRM Type 25's race debut at Oulton Park, saw ORO scratch their original entry for the four-cylinder car and substitute the Maserati, for Collins, instead. He faced Harry Schell's works Vanwall, Walker's Connaught, the literally evergreen Gerard Cooper-Bristol and three sister customer-spec 250Fs driven by Louis Rosier,

73. The practice problem had been a repeat of September Goodwood, 1954: the tip had broken off a valve spring, evaded the wire gauze added to prevent a repetition, and had jammed the oil pump drive gears, partly seizing the engine. It was rebuilt using in part spares drawn from Maserati. Failure had occurred early on before Collins got the hang of the car and circuit, hence his poor lap time. He was told to take it easy early in the race, as a new piston had been fitted.

July 15, 1955 – British Grand Prix, Aintree: Classical grace – Collins pushing '2509' hard in ORO's home event, catching Luigi Musso's works Maserati by lap 29 without quite being able to pass it as both closed upon Taruffi's Mercedes-Benz, which finished fourth. Then clutch failure sent Collins coasting into the pits. Note the car's distinctive straightline twin-pipe exhaust system.

Horace Gould and Roy Salvadori.

Schell led from start to finish. Peter made a poor start in fifth place having had very little practice as the cylinder-head joint blew while Tony was giving it a shake-down run at Folkingham, which meant Colin Atkin and his men had yet another session scraping and sliding the head to and fro on the surface plate. He powered past Gerard, Walker and Gould to run second behind the Vanwall until unlucky lap 13, when the ageing Maserati's de Dion tube broke. This had always been an Achilles' heel of the Maserati design, and in truth the ORO crew were quite surprised it had survived so long… As they parted Peter told Tony that he was leaving at the end of the season and hoped to join Ferrari. He gave as his reason that he could not stand RM, who never told him the truth. Tony, whose father had just died suddenly, and was about to depart on a fortnight's holiday, was sworn to secrecy.

The Maserati was then repaired back at Folkingham and taken to Oulton Park on November 12 for comparative testing against the new Type 25, where Moss wanted to try the new BRM to decide his destination for the following year, Mercedes-Benz having just withdrawn from racing. He had also asked Vandervell to send a Vanwall for comparison and although the circuit was wet beneath the trees in the woods it was a fine, dry day.

Stirling took one look at '2509' and said there was no point in driving it – he knew what a 250F was like around Oulton.

While he drove the Vanwall and the BRM, Collins circulated in the Maserati, clocking a best of 1:55.6 in 12 laps, against the official lap record – standing to Moss' factory 250F – of 1:55.0. PB's internal report observed that this showed:

> …that this car, although 3 inches shorter in the wheelbase than the standard car, is as good as the latest works car driven by Moss during the Oulton Park race.

With RM increasingly desperate to finalize driver contracts for the forthcoming season – Collins up to his old tricks of keeping all his options gaping wide open – Moss was clearly more interested elsewhere, but still gave BRM a fair crack of the whip, asking to test the Type 25 again against Connaught and Vanwall at Silverstone.

Meanwhile, Mike Hawthorn and some other promising British drivers were invited to test for the team at Silverstone on Thursday, December 1. The Maserati accompanied both Type 25s then extant and, with weather fair and track 100 per cent wet with large puddles, '2509':

> …was run continuously through the day, and all drivers tried the car, including Hawthorn and Collins.
> The fastest time was returned by Hawthorn in 1:55.6secs. Of the new drivers, Ivor Bueb was obviously the most promising, who steadily reduced his lap times. Fairman was erratic, although put in a fairly fast lap. Tony Marsh was out of his depth… Nevertheless, he reduced his lap times consistently. Both Ivor Bueb and Tony Marsh have never previously driven a Grand Prix Formula I car…

Against Hawthorn's '2509' fastest of 1:55.6, Fairman

managed a 1:59.8 on his eighth lap (and spun off the road on his ninth), then later clocked 1:58 in a five-lap stint just before dusk fell. 'Ivor the Driver''s 10 laps culminated in a 1:58.6, while the inexperienced young Tony Marsh's best was a cautious 2:06.4. Next day Collins drove seven laps with a best 1:58.4 and Bueb completed 11 laps towards the end, studiously keeping out of Hawthorn's way in the Type 25 and achieving a best of 2:02.

A week previously Ray had written to Owen about the Type 25 and the driver conundrum in preparation for 1956:

> All this week has been extremely hectic with continuous Silverstone tests with Moss and Peter Collins. The car has behaved amazingly well on the whole, and whether Moss and Collins drive for us or not we have learned an enormous amount of very valuable data…

Highlighting the driver problem:

> The question of Moss and Collins driving is becoming very difficult. Moss is out for the World Championship, and although he favours British cars, he puts his World Championship first, and for this reason I rather feel he favours Maserati. These cars have been running three years, and Moss quite rightly considers that they are developed to a higher degree of perfection than the English cars, but we are still awaiting results.
> In the meantime, as drivers mean so much to us next year, I am endeavouring to contact Fangio and Hawthorn because we simply must not be left high and dry. The position today has never arisen before in the history of motor racing. In 1939 there were something like 15 drivers who one could truthfully say were world-ranking, whereas today there are only three or four…

In December the news broke that Peter Collins had joined Ferrari. RM, December 13, 1955:

> Dear Alfred,
> According to the papers today Peter Collins has signed with Ferrari. This is shattering news for us, because all along in discussions with Peter alone, with his father alone, and both together, I have always repeated that you wished Peter to continue to drive for us, and that irrespective of who else drove, you were ready to sign him, on terms to be mutually agreed.
> It has always been understood by all of us, and I know by you, that Peter would be with us this year, and the first intimation of anything different was when Mr Collins told me he thought Peter would like to drive in the same team as Stirling… Quite honestly I am surprised, but I must say that Bryan Turle of Shell-Mex has always warned me that you could not rely on Peter's word.
> …it is simply vital that we have Hawthorn… Terms to Hawthorn, who I do know has not much capital for his garage business, mean a great deal…

That same day, he wrote to Tony Brooks…the young dental student-turned racing driver who had just sensationally won the Syracuse GP, beating full works Maserati opposition, in a B-Type Connaught.

Collins wrote in self-justification to Owen – copied to RM – from Bewdley on December 16:

> I would have liked to have told you myself I have signed with Ferrari but unfortunately the press have beaten me to it – from Italian sources…I feel it will be very helpful to me to have a season's racing as number two to Fangio. This will also mean there will be two British contenders for Championship honours.

RM responded, surely too cooingly in the circumstances:

> Peter Berthon and I received your letter dated 16th December. We were pleased to receive this, because quite frankly we felt very disappointed, after our close association, to have the first intimation from the papers. After all, I am sure you will realise that we all had very much banked on your being with us in 1956, and it is a great disappointment that you have decided otherwise.
>
> I note that you have decided to sign for Ferrari, and that you will be driving behind Fangio as Number 1. I am sure you could not possibly drive behind a better driver, nor a nicer man. May I wish you every success.
>
> It is kind of you to say that you would be happy to place yourself at our disposal for testing purposes in between events…

But when he received Collins' letter Owen snapped back:

> I do not think you were as frank with us as you ought to have been, especially as we trusted your good faith implicitly… I should have thought that World Championship honours would have been much more worthwhile if British drivers competed in British cars…

He had already written to Hawthorn at his Tourist Trophy Garage business in Farnham, Surrey, after a Type 25 test failure at Silverstone:

> I thought you would like to know that the engine blow up when you were driving was traced to a definite cause, and this was in no way your fault. On this particular engine we had one or two experimental bits and pieces in the valve mechanics, and Peter's theory on this has now been proved. Incidentally the engine in the other car has now done nearly 1,300 miles, without any new bits and pieces whatsoever…I will let you know as soon as the two cars are ready for test again, and in the meantime please understand that we have every wish for you to join with us for next year…

By this time the Owen Maserati seemed virtually redundant since the Type 25s were up and running, showing immense promise despite posing new problems almost every day. The 1956 World Championship season was to open with the Argentine Grand Prix, and as Mike Hawthorn was engaged to lead the ORO team into 1956 – and Basil Putt, ex-Connaught,

became new Team Manager – it was arranged for them to make the long trip with '2509' for what would become Bourne's first World Championship race start since Silverstone '51, virtually as a private entry tended by the most skeletal of skeleton crews.

The team would find Hawthorn living up to his image as an extrovert who enjoyed practical jokes and wild parties, but very much with his established friends – not with new acquaintances, outsiders, strangers. To BRM's people he seemed extremely tense and highly strung, a closed, tetchy personality, and it was certainly his misfortune to drive for the team at a time when stupid errors of preparation and in some cases of design were to dog their every move…

Hawthorn recalled: "It was obvious the [new] car was not going to be ready for the Argentine races, so I suggested they send out the Maserati… It was rather prone to oversteer with a full tank and switch to understeer as the fuel was consumed, but it was quite a nice little car…"

PB to Owen, January 3, 1956:

> I have contacted Reg Williams [Bira's ex-racing mechanic] and he is willing to undertake the trip to Buenos Aires with our car…I spoke to Mike Hawthorn last night. He has made no arrangements with the race promoters and prefers that Ray deals with it entirely. Ray has wired the Automobile Club in Buenos Aires… In the meantime Putt has started and he is dealing with provisional bookings for Hawthorn, Williams, and the car…

Owen was concerned that Ray should obtain financial support for the trip from "Shell and others" and then ORO's low-key two-race Argentine odyssey began.

As time was short, Basil Putt had arranged to fly the car there – at a cost of £1,500 each way – while he, Hawthorn and Reg Williams flew out separately on: "…a tourist flight in an elderly Constellation which rattled and rolled; there were no hot meals – only coffee, cocoa and thick sandwiches – and we decided it was a thing to avoid if possible…".

January 22, 1956 – Argentine Grand Prix, Buenos Aires Autodrome – 98 laps, 237.85 miles

In hot, dusty Buenos Aires the target time in practice was Gonzalez's 1:43.1, 84.9mph, set in 1954, and the local racing press were hugely impressed by the old Owen Maserati's braking power which was described as "a revelation, streets ahead of the opposition". Hawthorn described his race tactics as being: "…to last out and wait for the faster machines in front to blow up". He worked his way unobtrusively into seventh place in the early stages, ahead of Collins, who was making his Scuderia Ferrari debut.

Local polo star Carlos Menditeguy was leading for Maserati since Fangio's Lancia-Ferrari was in trouble, from Moss' sister 250F and Castellotti's Lancia-Ferrari. New team-mate Luigi Musso, ex-Maserati, was flagged in to hand over his car to the

World Champion and on lap 42 Menditeguy's surprising drive ended when, perhaps predictably, he crashed.

Moss' engine went sour while leading, Fangio inherited victory and at a late stage all the retirements saw Hawthorn running third in '2509', which is where he finished, lapped twice by Fangio and Jean Behra's second-placed works Maserati, but scoring four valuable World Championship points.

Autosport's correspondent declared: "Hawthorn upheld the British colours most brilliantly. It is, of course, regrettable that he could not do so with the B.R.M., but it is to be hoped that we will see the little green cars from Bourne next year. Stirling Moss told me he was most impressed by the way the B.R.M. had performed on test, and said he thought it was probably the fastest Grand Prix car today, but the steering was imprecise as the front end tended to lift…"

A follow-up International race completed this brief Argentine *Temporada* tour, at Mendoza, up country… Hawthorn called it: "a pleasant little city which is a centre of a large wine-growing area in the Andes. We flew the 600 miles or so in a well-worn DC4 and during the flight someone remarked that there was a lot of oil streaming back over the wing on his side; then someone else swore he could see petrol leaking, so we all trooped over to have a look. Immediately somebody else announced that the same thing was happening at the other side, so we all rushed to see. Goodness knows what the pilot thought…but he got us there safely…".

February 5, 1956 – Buenos Aires City Grand Prix, Mendoza Autodrome – 60 laps, 156.01 miles

The Municipality of the City of Buenos Aires and the *Automovil Club Argentino* co-organized this wildly misnamed F1 race, nearly 650 miles away from the Argentine capital on the new Autodrome which had just been completed with private subscription. The venue was high and hot, at some 2,200 feet in the Andes, and all the Maseratis seemed particularly badly hit by carburation problems.

Fangio, Castellotti and Musso dominated the race in their Lancia-Ferrari V8s until the latter crashed spectacularly – but without injury – in a left-hander just beyond the startline. Behind all this, Hawthorn was delayed by steering trouble in '2509', eventually finishing second-last, ninth, six laps behind the winner – Fangio of course.

"I found that my steering was becoming rather vague…the car was lurching from side to side, and would sometimes leap across the road when going into corners; I pulled in and we found the bracket which holds the steering column on the dash had fractured…"

Jackie Greene, son of the late Eric Forrest Greene who acted as intermediary between RM and Fangio in 1952, had been a great help to the visiting 'temporary' ORO, and had supplied "some of his boys to help in the pit, but we did not get very highly organised in the time available. No complete lap score was kept, so our people did what so many other people do – nipped along to the Maserati pit and asked Ugolini" – Maserati's new team manager, having replaced Aldo Lugo.

After these far-away exploits, the Owen Maserati returned to England abandoned, redundant, now unwanted, being surplus to requirements in Customs bond at Heathrow as it was still under 'Treasury Direction'. The record attributed to it included four outings in 1954, being placed sixth and twice eighth, although only the latter pair of outings – in the Swiss and Spanish GPs – had really involved this particular ex-'Bira' machine. 1955 was its best season, when with its ORO-stiffened chassis it contested four events and won the two it finished. Then had come the brief Argentine foray at the start of 1956, two races, a third at World Championship level, and ninth. It was the Lincolnshire team's best yet.

The Australian driver Jack Brabham had just completed his first season in the northern hemisphere, making his Formula 1 debut in the British GP at Aintree in the rear-engined Cooper-Bristol special which he had assembled at Surbiton in John Cooper's workshops. He had shipped the car home for the Antipodean summer season and had won the Australian GP with it before finding a buyer and emerging with sufficient funds to return to England for 1956.

The future three-times World Champion recalled: "I thought the 250 Maser was the best car around and I was carried away by having a few pounds in my pocket. Stirling Moss' own car had also raced through the previous season on Dunlop disc brakes and went very well and I was negotiating to buy it through Stirling's manager, Ken Gregory. We'd almost reached a deal when I returned to England and went up to the Moss farm at Tring to see the car.

"I found then that its disc brakes and other good bits had all been removed and the standard wire wheels and drum brakes had been refitted. Ken and I fell out over that so the deal collapsed. Then somebody told me that the Owen car was up for sale.

"I was pretty dim in those days, the money was burning a hole in my pocket and I went to see the car, it looked very nice and although there wasn't time to try it I bought it on the spot.

"Only afterwards did I discover that BRM had it in the country on temporary export papers which had by that time expired, and if I wanted to race it in England I'd have to pay purchase tax on it which amounted to about twice what the car was worth. The only way I could race it in England would be to take it out of the country and then re-import it on new papers.

"I eventually loaded it into an old Commer transporter I'd just bought, and I drove it down to Newhaven for the Channel Islands ferry. There it was craned across onto another boat returning within the hour, the paperwork was sorted out and so I started racing it, and found it was totally clapped out."

He was black-flagged from his debut race in it – at the Silverstone May meeting – for dropping oil; subsequently he was stung by Maserati on a Modena engine rebuild, but he managed to finish third in the low-key Aintree '200' and the Vanwall Trophy at Snetterton. Tony: The people handling the Maserati's sale had been supposed to warn any intending purchaser that it was normally given an engine strip and overhaul every 500 miles and it had just done over 800. The mechanics and I were horrified when it appeared at Aintree, still without an overhaul. Willie was deputed to go and warn Jack Brabham, as we were not quite sure what deal had been done. Willie reported that Jack had said he was going to take it easy. Even so he finished third behind Tony Brooks. We were not surprised when the engine blew up at Silverstone, during its fourth race without an overhaul. It was then rebuilt by the Maserati works using standard parts. They kept our special cylinder head and camshafts, and in the process it probably lost some of the performance we had gained.

Brabham's season was rescued for him when John Cooper offered a works drive, and later in the year Jack avoided running the 250F "…in case it spoiled my chances of keeping the Cooper drive the following year"!

That winter he took two Coopers and the Owen Maserati down-under for the Tasman season,[74] and he eventually left the 250F in New Zealand, where builder Gavin Quirk from Te Awamutu finally bought it. From Quirk the old car was then sold to chicken farmer Lenny Gilbert, and from him it passed to a teenaged newcomer named Chris Amon, for whom the car was rebuilt by local specialist Bruce Wilson.

Eventually the Owen Maserati was retired from NZ Gold Star competition to be retained by Amon's mentor Len Southward, who displayed it in his motor museum at Kapiti,

North Island, where it is still preserved as I write these words. It is a vital link in the Owen Racing Organisation/BRM story, the car which bridged the Formula 1 gap between V16 and Type 25 1954–56, which maintained the team's presence within the premier class during that period, and which brought them a rare – and much needed – taste of Formula 1 victory.

74. The tragedy of this trip came during the New Zealand Grand Prix meeting at Auckland's Ardmore Aerodrome circuit, where Ken Wharton had raced the V16 in 1954. This time round, the 40-year-old English journeyman driver had qualified his John du Puy-owned Maserati 250F on pole position for the afternoon's GP, but in the supporting sports car race he was driving his own Ferrari 750 *Monza*, leading Brabham's Cooper Bobtail, when he entered the left-hand curve leaving the Clover Leaf far too fast; the always tricky Ferrari broadsided into a straw bale barrier and flipped, somersaulting several times. Ken Wharton, who had had such a long relationship with BRM and ORO, was thrown from the car onto the concrete apron forming the pit road, sustaining severe head injuries, to which he succumbed, just over an hour later, in Auckland's Middlemore Hospital.

TONY LAGO, THE 'LE MANS TALBOT-BRM' AND THE 'TALBOT-FORD'

On March 20–21, 1956, RM and PB visited their old acquaintance Major Antoine 'Tony' Lago in Paris, where Ray had been fitted for his one-off drive in the prototype Talbot-Lago *Monoplace Centrale* before the 1939 French GP, and where Peter Berthon had been working when the *Wehrmacht* had invaded in 1940.

In reporting this 1956 visit to Alfred Owen, PB explained how the French Government had taken effective control of *Talbot Darracq SA* due to its heavy debts. They had then run it "with a steadily increasing turnover until two years ago, when M. Lago re-acquired control…"

Its range of luxurious and expensive 4½-litre road cars had been costly to produce and difficult to sell, thanks both to their obsolescent, basically prewar, design and punitive French taxation. On re-assuming control, Lago had scrapped them but kept sufficient material going through to cover the spares requirements, "as there are still some 27,000 of these vehicles on the road".

He'd had a modern twin-overhead-camshaft 2.5-litre engine designed, but lacked the finance to build it. PB reported: "Tooling is now completed for a modern light tubular chassis; also for the first production body, which is a very attractive sports 2/3 seater Coupe. ..This car is now running on initial production with a new 2½-litre four-cylinder engine, derived basically by using four cylinders of the old 4½-litre engine, with an alteration in bore and stroke. This engine is claimed to give 120bhp at 5,000rpm which figure appears optimistic to me and M. Lago admits it is not a successful engine…"

PB, however, was impressed by the "simple but good design" of the new chassis frame and attractive bodywork: "Raymond Mays had a chance of trying one of these cars and found the road holding and general driveability to be excellent…we both feel that this vehicle rather better engined and with more power would sell well up to the quantities M. Lago proposes initially, i.e. 150/200 a year…

"Since their market lies in the sports and high performance car class M. Lago considers that some initial prestige publicity

derived through sports car racing is absolutely essential to his sales policy…(he) proposed to run one sports coupe body and one open sports 2-seater at Le Mans this year; but since his present engine does not give sufficient power to make the attempt worthwhile he is anxious to secure two engines for this event giving towards 200bhp…The cars are required to have a maximum of 150/155mph."

PB and RM offered, and Lago agreed to accept, "…two of our racing engines, suitably arranged to run on the fuel specified at Le Mans, with provision for dynamo, starter and means of adaptation to the gearbox they use". PB proposed that Bourne should take care "of the installation and event point of view and preferably loan him an engine for this purpose…the whole arrangement being subject to an order of 200 for his first twelve months output of a productionised edition; price to be agreed…"

A production version of the P25 Formula 1 engine had been investigated by the Bourne DO, envisaging a cast-iron unlined crankcase, and wet-sump lubrication. An alloy head was to be 'cheapened' by use of 'non-fill' valves, straightforward camshafts etc, suitable for 6,000/6,500rpm. Manufacture of 4/5 per week was envisaged… ho hum… or so PB said.

A 'Le Mans Replica' version of the proposed Talbot-Lago was to be fitted with a Lago *Grand Sport* Coupe body to sell at £2,600 and compete with the latest Mercedes-Benz 190, which was then selling in Paris at £2,750. Maximum speed of this road-going version was to be around 130mph – which would require 160–170bhp.

In writing this pitch for Owen, PB even professed a willingness "…to curtail our own racing programme (so) we could put two engines for this purpose in time (cars…" – for Le Mans – "…have to be completed on or before July 1st for examination purposes). In view of the necessity of limiting our expenditure at Bourne and promoting commercial work, I recommend that some part of our own racing programme be sacrificed in favour of promoting this business…".

But Lago also required an engine for his standard sports coupe and a four-seat sports saloon and PB declared this was "…more difficult, as the maximum selling price has to be in the neighbourhood of £1,500 and our 4-cylinder could not be got low enough in cost for the quantities involved."

Lago – who must have been dreaming – told his visitors that a thousand engines per year would be required and PB told Owen "…even with very considerable tooling it is doubtful whether the cost of our production version of the 4-cylinder could be got low enough.

"I therefore proposed that we supply the 2½-litre Zephyr/Zodiac 6-cylinder engine, fitted with our Conversion Alloy Head, which, with a small amount of development, could be got up to the power required. This engine is very smooth and quiet and could be got into the price range required."

At that time Bourne had a stock of 100 castings to provide an initial supply. PB had a spare six-cylinder prototype engine of the old Mark I 2,300cc size. "M. Lago has agreed that this capacity will be satisfactory for an initial trial".

Time was of the essence and PB urged Owen: "If you feel the scheme worthwhile and are prepared to sanction at least the initial moves, I feel we have an excellent opportunity of setting up the type of business we so badly need here at Bourne in becoming engine suppliers to the Talbot Company."

It was plain that in the time available – and in face of the P25 valve problems encountered at Monaco that May – there was no chance of BRM engines being provided in time for Le Mans. Lago, however, had hedged his bets. Even as RM and PB were visiting him, his two 1956 Le Mans *Barquettes* must in fact have been under assembly, already designed around the Maserati 250S six-cylinder engines they used in the 24-Hour classic that July.

Still the possibility of a 'Raymond Mays'-headed 'Talbot-Ford' survived, although that summer saw Rubery Owen investigate the affairs of *Automobiles Talbot Darracq SA*, of 33 Quai du General Gallieni, Suresnes (Seine) and not like what they found: "A credit of Frs: 4 million as requested appears to be high and sound guarantees should be sought…".

Still prospects seemed sufficiently promising for PB to spend more time in his rented flat in Paris and on November 8, 1956, he wrote to Owen:

"…the Talbot business is not going well, and they are not selling sufficient cars to make the business pay. As far as I can elucidate the reasons are:-

"1) That Lago is persisting in making his car with a right-hand drive steering, which the French people and the other Continental people do not like.

"2) His 4-cylinder engine is a poor unit being too rough and having an inadequate performance.

"3) The selling price of £2,700 in France is much too expensive and should be basically a £1,500 car.

"He has a complex concerning the 6-cylinder engine because it is basically a Ford engine, and he feels that any association with the name of Ford in France would be derogatory to his sales. I have continually made the point to him that if he will use this engine, which is a good deal better and cheaper than his own and seriously set about getting the price down, and the car has good performance for its value, it cannot help selling in the relatively small quantities he requires to make it pay (15 a month).

"He has agreed to fit a 6-cylinder engine and gearbox into his chassis for trial and I think he is manoeuvring to persuade us to loan him this engine on the same basis that we loaned the original Mark I type, that he only put on the test bed. Frankly, I think he should pay for this unit…The engine could be ready for despatch by the end of this week…"

The Mays head's 45-degree downdraught carburettors would not fit beneath the Talbot's bonnet line and PB promised to investigate horizontal carburetion, but on November 5 Tony Lago complained to PB at Bourne:

"I got your telegram reading as follows 'Having engine repaired for despatch. Are gearbox and overdrive required. Please write.'

"I am sorry to say that I am absolutely upset. I thought that you were in production with this engine which you talked so much about but I find out now from your telegram that you have only got one engine and that it has got to be repaired before you send it to me.

"Let me be perfectly frank with you and I hope that our friendship will make you forgive me: It is not the question of fitting the 4-cylinder engine or anything else in my car that keeps me back but that I do not want to embark in making the car fitted with an engine that you might not be able to supply after…

"Look at the time that we have been talking about this thing: it is over a year and we spent a lot of time and money designing and making wooden patterns just to do nothing.

"If your firm is prepared to supply me with a new 6-cylinder Mark II engine, complete with gearbox and overdrive so that I can put it in my car and test it properly and can guarantee me in writing the date of delivery and the quantity they can deliver, I am prepared to go on. Otherwise, I am dropping the matter…I must know immediately whether I can count on regular deliveries or, otherwise, I must buy an Italian engine or make a new one of my own…"

He concluded: "So, excuse my letter but I thought that it was necessary because I am arriving to a point where I cannot waste any more time unless I want to see Talbot closing down…

"With kindest regards to Mays and yourself…"

While PB and RM had kept Alfred Owen abreast of developments – possibly in good faith but quite possibly just to show good faith in seeking commercial return for BRM – Tony Lago's car company was actually in deeper trouble than the British suspected. Through 1955–57 he sold only 54 of his new 2500 model with the T14LS four-cylinder 'Lago Baby' engine… They could never match the contemporary performance of the Alfa Romeo Giulietta nor the Lancia Aurelia yet cost more than the Ferrari 250 *Europa*! In 1957 Major Lago did turn to an outside engine supplier – but it was BMW, not BRM – adopting the Bavarian 2,476cc, 138bhp, light-alloy V8 for his Lago *America*. But only 12 of these cars would be completed, and after Simca absorbed Talbot in 1959, they built five final cars with the V8 Simca Vedette side-valve engine – perhaps the ultimate indignity for the one-time *Grand Marque* – even worse, one suspects, than being 'tainted by Ford'?

PB eventually moved out of his Paris flat and had Phil Ayliff break his return trip from one GP to load some sealed crates into the mobile workshop for return to Folkingham. But at Dover he fell foul of HM Customs: "I had carnets for everything but PB's mysterious crates, so the Customs officer opened them up and three of the first four were packed with gin! I eventually got away with paying £250 cash in Duty which I then claimed back on my expenses. I never did hear how Berthon explained that one…"

A decade after this abortive Talbot project a French car would run at Le Mans with BRM power – but that's a different story, to be told in Volume 2.

PART FOUR

The Type 25 BRM

BRM's day of atonement – September 14, 1957 (seven years after the V16's debut debacle) – BRDC International Trophy, Silverstone: Jean Behra driving the old prototype of this new breed of BRM, '251', in its latest 1957 form, to head a team 1-2-3 whitewash – albeit of an indifferent field...

A NEW BREED OF BRM – PROJECTS 25 AND 27

Stewart Tresilian was largely responsible not only for the original conception and design of the BRM Project 25 2½-litre four-cylinder engine, but also of the compact P27 – or Type 25 – car intended to carry it into battle.

Tresilian's original engine design had emerged at the end of 1952 around the time of Rubery Owen's BRM purchase. He had produced a homogeneous concept of car and engine combined, its essence being the complete antithesis of the original V16 in that it was all as small, compact and simple as possible, with the arguable exception of his projected 16-valve cylinder head for the four-cylinder engine.

In his final months at Bourne, Tres had supervised the detailing of the power unit, PB likewise the gearbox with Alec Stokes, and Tres had started Aubrey Woods on the chassis concept.

Aubrey: "Tresilian had succeeded in selling the idea of simplicity in place of complexity. It was very attractive to Alfred Owen, and especially to his brother Ernest, who was a dry old stick, but who had his head screwed on!" – but who generally disapproved of BRM and refused to have anything to do with it until the early '60s. "PB took to it, but decided four valves per cylinder was going too far when you could do the job as well with two. I think that decision was made partly in pique, at being up-staged. He was prepared to take Tresilian's four-cylinder – but not to take it *all*. We first built a four-valve, single-cylinder test engine, then PB proved his two-valve alternative on it..." Colin Atkin and Willie Southcott assembled this test-rig unit: "Tres was over-ruled by PB, and when it started breaking his oversized valves Tres" – by then long-gone – "was saying 'I told you so...'" Certainly PB would not have risked entering a theory argument with Tres; he knew he would lose.

In his four-cylinder design Tresilian followed a theory which would regain currency in the late 1970s of placing balance weights where there were loads on the crankshaft and main bearings where there were no loads. Consequently his concept featured only four main bearings, with an enormous balance weight where there should conventionally have been a fifth or centre main.

To fit this engine into the car he placed its camshaft-drive timing gears at the back of the unit so they could be quite big there within capacious housings without compromising the lowest possible bonnet line.

PB would later plan to use SU direct port fuel-injection, and in Tres' very neat crankcase layout there were three matching flanges at the front permitting magnetos – or a central injection pump – to be attached as convenient, and Tres intended to do a great deal of single-cylinder test-engine work to decide the optimum spark plug position. Tres wanted to run on carburettors until the engine was sorted, and designed it with carburettor flanges.

There was one plug mounting situated between the valves and one at each extremity of the inlet and exhaust valve intersection. It was not necessarily intended that they should all be used, but this was a reasonable provision for subsequent

Folkingham aerodrome, July 1955: Tony Rudd testing '251' as first completed, with unpainted tail-finned bodywork. There was no cooling scoop for the single rear disc when first run. Tony positioned it using war-surplus pitot instruments, and a test scoop was then Dzus-fastened into place, permitting easy change. Tony would get into more trouble with PB over published photographs of something new or non-standard than for anything else, yet usually the picture had been taken by visitors being shown around by RM, and at his invitation. "I could get away with it when RM appeared in the picture – it was the ones without him or sometimes which Rivers had taken which did the damage..."

development.

The bore and stroke dimensions finally selected were 102.8mm x 74.93mm, displacing 2,491cc. This stroke/bore ratio of 0.728:1 provided a piston area of 51.52 square inches, greater than any rival contemporary 2½-litre F1 engine. High Duty Alloys Ltd cast the one-piece aluminium crankcase-cum-block, which was then finish-machined in the BRM machine shop at Bourne. The sump was a separate magnesium casting. The four-main-bearing crankshaft was in Nitralloy, and all bearings were Vandervell lead-indium, 2.375in diameter in the front and intermediate positions, while the rear main bearing – against the timing gears – was 2.5in diameter.

The connecting rods were beautifully machined from solid forgings, and incorporated four retaining studs for the big-end cap to provide an extremely robust and stable bottom end. Floating gudgeon pins, retained by circlips, were used in conjunction with bronze-bushed little ends. In initial form, cast pistons were fitted, with tall domed crowns incorporating large valve-clearance pockets. There were three piston rings, the bottom one being a dual oil scraper.

The cylinder head was cast in RR53 aluminium alloy, featuring hemispherical combustion chambers with inserted valve seats, and in original form that provision for a choice of three spark plugs. Each overhead camshaft ran in five white metal bearings and operated the two valves per cylinder via massive fingers. The inlet valves were a gigantic 2.4 inches in diameter, the exhaust valves 2 inches.

On the left-hand side of the crankcase, driven from the back of the gear driving the outermost magneto, was a most ingenious oil system assembly, comprising an oil-pump relief valve, scavenge pumps and oil filter connected into the various oilways. The oil tank would eventually be schemed by Tony Rudd at Folkingham in December 1954, sited under the exhausts on the left side of the engine bay, with an aviation-type oil cooler plugged into its top. This placed the very thin-gauge aluminium tubes of the cooler in direct contact with the oil swirling around through the tank, and since cooling water passed direct from the water pump through this cooler before returning to the engine block, so oil heat was rejected into the water which was then cooled by the conventional nose-mounted radiator cores. The objective was to reduce drag to a minimum. The nose radiator inlet was very small, with two water cores divided by a large box-section central duct which fed cold air direct to the injection system.

Tres had also considered side loads within the crankcase and adopted transverse bolts passing clean through the main-bearing caps to clamp the entire assembly firmly together. The water pump was on the front of the crankcase, and the fuel pump at the back above the clutch.

The unfortunate weakness of this design was, of course, its cylinder head gasket. Although he provided four main studs and two inverted studs per cylinder to hold down the head there was a major sealing problem – everything was too flexible.

Tres had originally conceived the chassis with air-strut suspension *a la* V16 mounted within a large-diameter tubular front crossmember, where the Lockheed struts would support bottom wishbones, with outriggers or towers on top for the shorter top wishbones. At the rear he planned to link the air struts direct to the bottom legs of a forward-facing de Dion tube at a point where a bottom radius rod linked into the hub.

When PB reviewed what Tres had done in the spring of 1953 – in effect design a ladder frame of large-diameter tubes – PB told Tony he thought it would present welding problems and be too heavy. No-one, except perhaps Tres, who could do this sort of sum in his head – and he was not telling – had taken the trouble to calculate how much it would weigh. PB was taken aback when Tony told him about 50lbs, but that it would not be anything like stiff enough. In view of AGBO's directive that he was to prove the engine first, the chassis design was put on the shelf.

After Tres had left ORO in January 1953, PB decided, probably correctly, that the air struts would work happily in most planes except truly horizontal as in that position there was no way they could purge themselves of air.

PB's stressed-skin monocoque construction for the P27 chassis was influenced to some degree by a remarkable sports special which had made its public debut in September 1953. This was the Killeen K1, which had been built by sometime Jensen engineer Tom Killeen for his friend Jack Newton – of 'Notwen Oil' fame. Killeen had accumulated experience of aeronautical monocoque structures while repairing damaged RAF airframes during the war. Jack Newton had asked him to create a sports-racing car of superior power-to-weight ratio in March 1950, and its design had been completed that November. The car was then assembled around a chassis fuselage featuring three more or less evenly-spaced transverse hoops in eighth-inch T-section steel, supporting six top-hat-section longitudinal steel stringers. These basic formers were then united and triangulated by a fully stressed 16-gauge Hiduminium alloy skin, secured by snap-head rivets. Tubular formers created the scuttle and cockpit surround, while front and rear cockpit bulkheads at the second and third lateral formers were provided by Plymax diaphragms. With front suspension and rear axle suitably suspended from this stressed-skin structure, the Killeen K1 was powered by a bored-out 1,476cc MG engine, and it weighed barely 10cwt.

Unfortunately, its slimline fuselage left the wheels exposed beneath cycle-type mudguards, which cost the car's top speed dear against enveloping-bodied sports car class rivals, despite its use of a blown Perspex windscreen and generally sleek and compact lines. Jack Newton campaigned it from 1953–56 while Tom Killeen sought to 'sell' the monocoque chassis idea to industry – the Owen Organisation included.

But his efforts to patent the concept all effectively failed against interests which were simply "…too big, too rich", while late in 1954 – just before the Owen Maserati left for Barcelona – he demonstrated the car to PB and Tony Rudd at Folkingham.

Tony: It looked rather like the special postwar Le Mans HRG, with a vaguely oval body section and brief mudguards. Its body was lined by neat rows of blue rivets – aircraft coding to show the grade. Its panels were curved in both directions, not just bent, so whoever had actually made it really knew what they were about as the material had to be normalized before it would stretch to curve in two planes. It really was beautifully made and any loss of stiffness through the holes necessary to install its engine, and the driver and passenger, was recouped by a very carefully-shaped deep transmission tunnel rather like a Lotus Elan – the whole idea was years ahead of its time.

I spent an afternoon testing it and was totally entranced. It felt totally rigid, with extremely soft suspension, and it handled like a dream. One uphill curve at Folkingham demanded a major back-off in the V16s; it was a nervous undertaking in the 250F, but in the Killeen you could just charge through there absolutely flat-out. The car had a profound effect on me and launched me on my stiffness crusade…

Tony was not alone in being so impressed. The Killeen confirmed PB's interest in stiffening his basic new P27 frame with a stressed-skin monocoque centre-section, but to protect the Owen Organisation from any potential patent suit Alfred Owen had his Research Department investigate numerous precedents to Killeen's work and PB wrote to him on November 26:

> …I do not feel that this type of construction would be of value to us… As you know, we construct very few cars, and most of our designs are arranged so that we can modify, repair, etc, very quickly; and I feel strongly that with a stressed-skin type construction this end would be entirely defeated…

One can imagine Killeen's frustration, therefore, when BRM's Type 25 finally emerged with its stressed-skin centre-section in 1955. He subsequently conducted a lengthy correspondence with the Owen Organisation which extended right into the early 1960s, while Alfred Owen's lieutenants assured him that no patents had been infringed and that Killeen had no case to answer…

Tom Killeen remained a prophet, without honour – and his K1 a terrific little car.

PB started again. He reasoned, probably correctly, that the damping system in the horizontal air struts might not work, although the late 1956 scheme with pivoted rocking levers he produced had them virtually horizontal. His design had front and rear crossmembers of body profile – lightening holes welded together, like the front of the Mark II. These sections helped support near equal-length upper and lower front wishbones, which were to be aligned effectively parallel to place the roll-centre just above ground level. The original rear suspension layout was retained, and the de Dion tube was located centrally by the traditional sliding block in a guide channel on the front of the gearbox casing, which in this car hung outboard behind the crownwheel-and-pinion. No provision was made at this design stage for a front anti-roll bar – largely on the basis that the car had been so beautifully designed it surely would not need one… This assumption was incorrect.

The chassis scheme that finally emerged was a hybrid structure with four main steel tube longerons, the lower pair 2 inches in diameter, the upper 1.5 inches, joining the front and rear crossmembers and spaced 20 inches apart in plan and 12 inches vertically. A 0.75-inch square tube cross-braced the longerons, bent to body profile as appropriate, with holes for rivets and 0.5-inch diameter holes opposing them to give access to the riveting dolly. In best Bourne Drawing Office tradition, about 20 per cent of these were not accessible. A double-skin elektron bulkhead separated the engine from the driver and provided considerable much-needed stiffness. Thin steel strips with alternating lightening and rivet holes were tack-welded to the longerons and an aluminium body skin was welded to them, joining the two front and rear cross-members. All this created a semi-monocoque hybrid structure with the four 1½-inch diameter chassis tubes stiffened by permanently attached stressed-skin panelling.

Although its design was roughly contemporary with Malcolm Sayer's and Bill Heynes' work on their D-Type Jaguar sports-racing car, with its stressed-skin monocoque centre-section, it pre-dated the more truly stressed-skin Colin Chapman-conceived Lotus 25 by almost a decade.

The new Project 27 frame's nearly flat under-pan was formed in elektron, but where double curvature was required the panels were formed in half-hard aluminium with soft aluminium rivets. It was about two years before Tony and Alan Ellison, the new body shop charge hand, developed a technique of annealing elektron so it could be rolled and shaped, by applying an oxy-acetylene flame to one side and watching soft soap blacken on the other to indicate when they had reached the right temperature. Tony Rudd tested the first frame for torsional stiffness in December 1954 without its fuel tanks and was appalled to find it was no better than the Maserati at 480lbs/ft per degree. PB and the Bourne DO then devised fuel tanks fashioned from very light-gauge steel, the finished item being skewered upon thin-gauge 4in-diameter tube passing right through the middle. This tube was then supported at one end against the rear engine-bay bulkhead, and at the other end to the crossmember carrying the rear suspension. It also plugged into the chassis frame and carried the front attachment for the radius arm locating that side of the de Dion tube. Though a very light-gauge structure, this overall assembly proved fairly heavy, but moderately improved the stiffness to around 800lbs/ft per degree deflection.

There was a very small hole provided up front into which the engine could be inserted, a neat letter-box slot on one side through which a mechanic could reach the brake fluid reservoir, and the cockpit opening in the middle "for the man"

FOLKINGHAM – BRM HEARTLAND

As Folkingham was now reaching its peak, as regards people working there and number of cars built and running, a description of ORO's set-up at the airfield is appropriate. Stan Hope reigned in the Salopian building, which was some 80 feet by 25, with home-made wooden benches all down one long side. Entering the only door at one end you would first find an open space originally intended for a newly-completed car to stand on its wheels for suspension-geometry setting up. Some 25 feet into the shop was a large structure made from two long pieces of 10 x 8in planed rolled-steel joist, bolted to cross-pieces, and set level on the concrete floor. Further planed 8 x 6in cross-pieces were bolted and dowelled to the main members with structures to carry the various suspension, engine and gearbox mounting points of the chassis to be built upon there. Stan reverently called this "the Jig". Along the opposite wall from the benches was the hydraulic press, the pipe-bending machine and the welding plant. Thanks to Peter Spear some of the myths and mumbo jumbo about welding had been dispelled and there was a first-class welder in residence, Alf Martin ('Flash Alf').

At the far end one would found the sheet metal workers (bashers) under Alan Ellison with their paraphernalia of hammers, leather bags and rollers plus some wooden body formers. Alan's two main supporters were Bill Wilcox, who generally made exhaust systems, and Danny Woodward, who welded-up the aluminium fuel tanks. Alan himself formed and welded-up the body panels but they all had a hand in this operation when required.

The original racing 'shop under chief mechanic Gordon Newman, soon to be replaced by Phil ('Corporal') Ayliff, son of RM's Vauxhall-Villiers mechanic, housed the completed cars. It was slightly smaller, the cars, generally minus wheels and resting on build stands, were arranged in echelon with space for four of them. Each bay had a bench and a large-wheeled metal trolley onto which the car was stripped, the pieces washed, inspected and crack-tested, ready for rebuild. At the far end was a 5-inch Jackson centre lathe manned by Maurice Dove ('Mo the Mangle') flanked by an inspection table, two pillar drills and the crack-test facility.

Jock Milne, the Geordie caretaker, had built a 6ft-wide extension along the bench wall of the 'shop which was on the side of a slope, so the extension was about 18 inches lower than the main building. At the door end was a small office which housed Tony Rudd's drawing board and the telephone, and in the following year came the airflow rig.

Alongside the racing shop was the old airfield fire station which now housed Willie Southcott's domain – the test-beds. Inside the main door on the left was the Ward Lennard set, a combination of variable speed electric motors used for rig testing oil and water pumps. On special occasions it powered the pot-joint rubber rig, desmodromic valve gear and injection pumps. To the other side of the door lay the electrical supply and switch gear for the site, and Willie's work bench.

Through a partition on the left one would then find the control gear for the Dynamatic – the engine on test, the Dynamatic dyno itself and the Ford Zephyr donkey engine used for starting and motoring tests. Parallel to this brake stood a smaller Heenan DXP 2 water brake for the single-cylinder with either a Ford Consul or later an Anglia donkey engine. At the far end a roller-shutter could be raised, exposing a government-surplus Gipsy Major aero engine complete with propeller. When power testing or engaged in exhaust development, the door would be opened, this roller shutter raised and the Gipsy run at about 1,000rpm to send

Folkingham Aerodrome: (Left) from the 1945 War Office location plan; (Right) as used by BRM, 1949–1960; *1* – The BRM Compound; *2* – 'Bira's gearbox mounting failure, 1951, and ACR's V16 fire (burst scavenge pump), 1952; *3* – First P25 timing gear failure; *4* – Fangio's exhaust-shedding spin, 1952; *5* – Skid pad, 1956; *6* – Run-off used in 1959 brake testing; *7* – "Everybody spun here!"; *8* – ACR's 1959 Type 25 high-speed spin; *9* – ACR's V16 Mark II high-speed spin; *A* – Test House, post-1960, today Hall & Fowler (arrow towards Folkingham village); *B* – Aslackby lane past Klingoe's farm where Gonzalez hit the pig, ACR's Austin 7 ejected a V16 gearbox in clobbering the gate post, and Phil Ayliff 'lost' the BRM works bus on snow – lane accessed A15 to Bourne.

The wire-fenced BRM Compound at Folkingham: *A* – Former aerodrome 'Building 362 Radar Workshop'-turned-BRM Build Shop; *B* – Panel-bashers area; *C* – Set-up area; *D* – 'The Jig'; *E* – Workbenches (see also in Racing Shop); *F* – 'Bldg 355 Crew Briefing Room'/BRM Racing Shop; *G* – 'The Lathe'; *H* – Toilets; *I* – Offices, 1950–55; *J* – Lean-to 1958–60 (Tony Rudd's office); *K* – Airflow rig; *L* – 'Bldg 354 Floodlight Trailer & Tractor Shed'/Engine Test House, 1954–60; *M* – The Dynamatic (above), single (below); *N* – The Ward-Lennard set; *O* – Stores, incl. PB's garage (lower end); *P* – 'Bldg 353 Signals Apparatus'/Engine Shop, 1954–60; *Q* – 'Bldg 351 Control Tower'/PB's flat; *R* – Jock Milne's place; *S* – ACR's caravan office, 1955–58; *T* – PB's caravan, 1950–54; *U* – Jock's vegetable patch; *V* – Gate used only for racing fuel and coke deliveries; *W* – Coke stock (heating stoves and external flues are marked in Racing & Build Shops); *X* – Fuel dump.

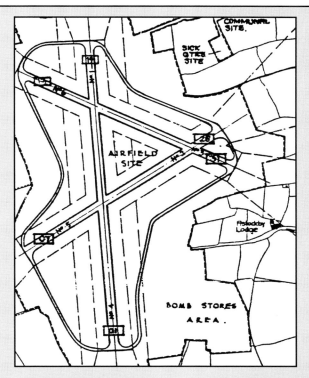

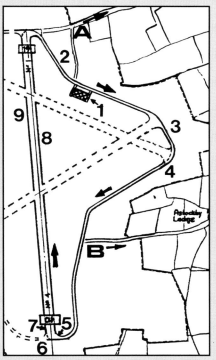

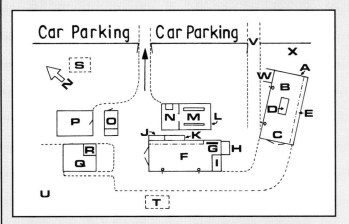

a howling gale through the entire test house.

Across the yard stood a collection of three small garages knocked into one, which had become the stores. Behind them stood the Control Tower, the upper floor of which was converted into the Berthons' flat. Jock Milne and his cats inhabited one room on the ground floor. To the east of the Control Tower stood another square Salopian building housing the engine build shop, under Colin Atkin, with crack-test equipment and air compressors in lean-to additions.

At times some 35 people worked at Folkingham, most of them brought up from Bourne in an aged ex-London Transport bus driven by Len Reedman, who also looked after the transporters and workshop lorry which lived in a Bellman hangar the other side of the track.

It became standard operating procedure for Tony Rudd to draw the chassis in consultation with Stan and Flash Alf. He had been warned about superimposed welds by them both. Raw material, sheet steel and tube were drawn from the stores and made into chassis. Wishbones and so on were made by Dick Salmon and his team in Stan's build shop. Bosses and simple fittings were produced by Mo on his mangle (centre lathe). More sophisticated parts came from the Bourne machine shop, via the stores. PB and Stan insisted that the completed frames were sent to Bourne to have all the suspension pick-ups finally machined on one of the big boring machines there, despite Tony's protests that the frame's contact with the road was through flexible rubber tyres which Dunlop fitted to the wheel-rim by hand, without any measuring equipment at all. The chassis then had its suspension fitted and was next mounted on trestles in the 'bashers' area with a mock-up engine installed, and piped up for oil and water systems, while Alan and his men fitted the skin.

At some stage a crisis would arise and the part-finished car would be moved into the racing shop for completion, brakes etc. A proper engine would arrive having been tested and then checked over back in the engine shop. The complete body was sent to Bourne, to the local undertaker, to be painted, or more often his man would come up late at night and repaint such panels as he could lay his hands on. Finally Tony would run the car for a few laps before it was sent to a race or test session, sometimes at Folkingham.

Only if machining had to be performed at Bourne would prints be made of Tony Rudd's original drawings, otherwise they were stored in a cupboard in the build shop, which explains why many chassis layouts for the V16 Mark II, the tube-chassis Type 25s and 57s no longer exist. Through the 1950s the Folkingham site was in many ways the true heartland of BRM.

while the tail could be detached to expose the rear-mounted fuel tank. The nose cone was also removable, providing easy access to the radiator, steering gear and the ignition system.

Tony: It was halfway to being a monocoque in the later Ferrari tradition, with four interior foundation tubes, and all its diagonal stiffness came from the overstressed skin and from the sheet aluminium bulkhead. Had we known better we would have made those bulkheads in duralumin and spread the stresses. As it was, still fresh from the aviation industry, duralumin was a material which had to be riveted with coloured rivets from refrigerators, we didn't know how to bend it and shape it, and most definitely not how to weld it. Consequently we made a lot of trouble for ourselves by using ordinary commercial half-hard aluminium to skin the thing.

We also made life difficult for ourselves – in order to maintain the best possible stiffness within the structure – by making the hole into which the engine dropped as small as possible, in common with all the other access holes…

The car would prove itself a claustrophobic skin-scraping nightmare to work on.

PB's gearbox – drawn and detailed by Alec Stokes, who was destined to become BRM's dedicated transmission specialist, and one of the country's leading 'gear men' – was a four-speed with reverse, carrying a conventional cast guide on the front of the casing to locate the de Dion tube's slider block. This was quite traditional in those days, but it was unusual for the de Dion tube to be sited ahead of the gearbox, between it and the driver's seatback. It was also unusual to see the input entering the bottom of the gearbox with a pair of change-speed gears there to enable quick ratio-changing before the drive entered the main gearbox section.

Rear suspension was also by Lockheed air struts derived from V16 experience, and these of course proved the source of another of the car's problems.

The back of the gearbox, right from the outset, also carried another controversial feature – the single, longitudinal-axis rear disc which became known popularly as the 'bacon-slicer'. As with so many controversial features, the thinking behind it was very simple.

Since the weight distribution of the car was about 50/50 front/rear, it was assumed that under heavy braking some 70 per cent of the load would be carried by the front wheels, leaving only 30 per cent on the rears. Thus it seemed logical to have two brakes outboard in the wheels at the front sharing the load 35 per cent each, and one on the back of the gearbox at the rear, to handle the remaining 30 per cent.

Once the team and the various brake suppliers sorted out the basic problems of too-high rubbing speed and inadequate cooling and fully appreciated how this system worked – which took far too long – this arrangement worked quite well on the front-engined cars.

The team's Morris Minor-based rack-and-pinion steering system was housed within a work of art – two magnesium castings joined by a paper-thin duralumin tube, unlike the Mark II which had used the same rack-and-pinion in a casing hogged from a solid lump of duralumin.

The finished car would weigh only 1,085lbs when first completed, not bad at all considering its 46-gallon fuel tank and the hefty engine plus a massive five-speed gearbox. Wheelbase

was to be a mere 87 inches, which made the new 2½-litre BRM the tiniest Formula 1 car of its time. It was to be really minute, and very light, and very powerful…and very troublesome.

These cars have passed into modern history as the BRM P – for Project – 25s. In fact the BRM 'P25' classification strictly referred *only* to the 2½-litre engine and all related engine items. The chassis then powered by these engines – and the gearboxes through which they drove – came under Project 27 and they would have their individual chassis numbers stamped into the instrument panel cross-tube – under the steering column on the original-series semi-monocoque cars, '27/1'. Tony Rudd recalls referring to the cars at the time as '271' or '272' etc to differentiate them from engines '251', '252' and so on. But quickly a year prefix was added to the engine numbers – e.g. '2581' in 1958 – and the 2½-litre car series was completed with chassis '256' to '2511'. However, contemporary records apply '25' chassis numbers even to the early 'Overstressed-Skin Special' cars and refer to them when assembled and running as the *Type 25* and *not* P25. P25 has become an accepted term of reference only in modern times, long after the cars had finally retired from active service – and although this author is after all largely responsible for having popularized the vague 'P25' tag through many years of magazine articles and other books, the '251', '252' etc style will be used here and the series are Type 25s, not P25s. Sorry about that…

Meanwhile, as we have seen, into the winter of 1952–53, Stewart Tresilian had become increasingly disenchanted with the Bourne set-up in general, and the personality clash between himself and Frank May in particular. He told Alfred Owen exactly what he felt about it all and declared that he could not continue to work under such conditions.

It was arranged that he would stay on a week-to-week basis until February 28, 1953, at the latest.

Alfred Owen, uncharacteristically, mistrusted Tres, and instructed Sandercombe:

> …to see, as Manager, that Mr. Tresilian responds…by putting forward 100% effort during the month. I have a fear that he is treating the whole matter in a supercilious, lighthearted manner, with the attitude that as he is going in the near future there is no need to make any great effort…

He continued:

> I understand, too, that the engine that has been designed is covered by certain patents Tresilian has taken out in his own name prior to his employment at Bourne, and I think we ought to know where we stand with regard to this matter before he leaves our employ.

'Sandy' duly researched Tres' British Patent No. 669349 of April 22, 1949, which claimed primacy to:

> (1) A four-stroke poppet valve engine of not more than .75 to 1 stroke bore ratio and having at least two inlet valves; (2) As claim (1) with at least two exhaust valves; (3) As claim (1) or (2) with an overhead camshaft in a tunnel in the cylinder head; (4) As claim (1), (2) or

(3) with a Scotch crank;[75] (5) As claim (4) with opposed pistons and Scotch crank…

There were further associated claims involved, including "A four-stroke engine of not more than .75 to 1 stroke bore ratio, with two inlet valves and Scotch crank", a similar engine with two inlet valves per cylinder, and with overhead camshaft in a tunnel in the cylinder head; and one with two inlet valves and camshaft in the crankcase.

ORO took patent advice on Tres' protection: "None of the separate ideas disclosed by this patent is novel, every feature having been used either alone or in conjunction with some other subject matter of the claim; but the use of the Scotch crank with opposed pistons may be novel. Engine designs have been so varied during the last 50/60 years that it is doubtful whether any claim can be sustained."

Around the time of Tresilian's departure, in the drawing office on the upper floor of the Maltings, Aubrey Woods was keeping a scoreboard of former ADL/BRM employees: "I had drawn up a number of tombstones, which were pinned to the wall, with names and dates; 'Died' if they'd given their own notice or 'Assassinated' if they'd been fired…"

Before the split, Tres had completed his single-cylinder test engine, and had started to run it. There were two major problems. Its flywheel regularly dropped off and for some reason its cylinder head gasket would continually fail. Tony believed this was because its head was cast in aluminium bronze – "a slightly misleading material".

PB commenced running the engine in 1953 under similar conditions of obsessive secrecy to those in which he had originally run the V16. He quickly concluded that its cylinder head-joint problem was insoluble, and he redesigned the head to accept a Wills gas-filled ring against which the cylinder liner could be screwed into place to nip it tight and form quite an effective seal. This work also led PB into adopting an alternative valve layout, dropping Tres' experimental four-valve-per-cylinder design and instead employing only two valves – one a very large inlet and the other a fairly large exhaust.

The original single inlet valve was quite conventionally shaped and became known at Bourne and Folkingham as a 'Nail' to distinguish it from a later design which had a very large concave radius on the underside of the valve head and which at high rpm and under high loads would prove liable to distort.

The single-cylinder engine was run extensively with this and quite early in the development process it was found necessary to fit the rocker with a return spring additional to the hairpin valve springs to reduce valvegear loadings.

It was around this time, in the winter of 1953–54, that BRM's Test House in Bourne really aroused strong local complaints.

Consequently, the big Heenan & Froude Dynamatic testbed was uprooted and removed to the old aerodrome Fire Station at Folkingham, along with the much smaller waterbrake for the single-cylinder test unit.

As previously mentioned, under the terms of BRM's

Folkingham-site lease from the Air Ministry, any equipment which BRM installed at Folkingham had to be capable of removal within 28 days' notice should the military need to re-activate the site. This meant that all the dynos and the Ford Zephyr donkey engines for starting the test units, motoring them over, etc, were mounted upon what looked like an enormous narrow-gauge railway, comprising parallel lengths of massive 10in x 8in rolled-steel joists, welded into a rigid frame. They merely sat on the concrete floor with the complete installation of oil and water heat exchangers and instrumentation bolted-up and wired into the mains. This masterpiece was largely Willie Southcott's handiwork, and it was to his enduring credit that it was in commission and working well so soon after the move.

The old abandoned exotic Test House at Bourne became little more than a storeroom and occasional workshop. Ironically, its end wall, pierced with fan holes for the ventilation system, is one of the old works' few structures to have survived into the 1990s, backing the car park which is there alongside the Old Maltings site today.

PB continued his development running – usually in the dead of night – at Folkingham, normally with one or two assistants, Colin Atkin and Willie Southcott prominent amongst them. For a long period the new two-valve head seemed no more successful than the four-valve. Throughout 1954 there were major blow-ups and major rebuilds and nobody seemed to know why or could suggest what might be happening.

The test unit breathed through a single SU carburettor, and PB had decided not to become embroiled with the intended fuel injection system until the carburetted unit seemed to be running properly.

In early-February 1955, Tony Rudd was sent to Modena to see what improvements Maserati were offering their private owners that season – very little, he found. On his return to Bourne he developed a shocking cold: I was in bed next day, when my wife of six months [Pam Carvath – a cousin of RM] suddenly burst in to tell me that Peter Berthon was in Peterborough Hospital, having been badly injured in a road accident in the small hours of that morning.

It was February 17, 1955, and as RM reported to Alfred Owen that day:

He has broken his jaw in three places, has abrasions on his face, a damaged chest, where the steering wheel hit him, and one very bad ankle [and] he has lost practically all his teeth…

In Peterborough Memorial Hospital his jaw was wired and a collapsed lung successfully reinflated. There was a spectacular scene when Mrs Lorna Berthon arrived to visit him only to be refused admission by the Matron who said they already had his wife – Mrs Berthon – in the next ward with fairly severe injuries. Before he was moved to Mount Vernon Hospital, in Northwood, Middlesex, where his torn and battered face was – in his own words – "put together again", RM wrote a letter to Owen purporting to be from PB upon his return home to Hallam Mews on March 2:

I'm very sorry to be away just when the results of our

---

75. Scotch cranks are complicated devices intended to obviate sidethrust upon engine pistons by effectively eliminating the conventional con-rod, replacing it instead with a complex sliding pin and block mechanism.

August 29, 1955 – Folkingham: ORO publicly unveiled the new BRM Type 25 on the forecourt of Raymond Mays Ltd's garage on Spalding Road, opposite the Bourne Maltings. Here the newly completed launch car – the second built, but first to be raced, chassis '252' a.k.a. '27/2' (see text) – is about to be loaded for its short trip to Bourne. Its startlingly compact build and fine finish impressed a sceptical press. Note low-sided cockpit, bonnet extending into exhaust coaming, neat front suspension cowls, Dunlop disc wheels and tyres, rear brake cooling slot in finless tail redesigned from prototype '251' form, and divided radiator cores flanking central carburettor air intake duct.

efforts are beginning to materialise…Ray is bringing Peter Collins round for a few minutes at teatime…he'd rather sign with you for this season if you can offer similar terms. As I believe he is the best of the young British drivers we should sign him up immediately & run him as & when we can. He has seen & understands our car position…

PB would suffer a series of relapses, including pneumonia arising from the collapsed lung, and it would be at least four months before he was anything like fit again. Tony: Hearing of the accident I left my sick bed and having picked up the threads went to see RM as requested. He had just returned from visiting PB and said he would be out of action for some time. I recommended that we should scrub the plan to convert the Maserati to fuel injection, and try and get out of a Dunlop tyre test programme which had been proposed. I said we should not try and run the V16 at Goodwood Easter meeting. This did not go down so easily, so we compromised on one car, driver unspecified. It was agreed I would make completion of the single-cylinder programme top priority, and RM undertook to find PB's notes, which he thought were still in the wrecked car. Build of the main engine was to run in parallel, and the car not far behind. We parted with mutual expressions of goodwill and co-operation. For the whole time PB was out of action RM was very supportive, and providing I

Right: Low-down on the new Type 25 showing its twin radiator cores divided by central carburettor intake duct. The tyres are Dunlop's latest R4s. Dunlop did not make R4s in the V16's rear-wheel sizes, neither did they produce the right-size old five-stud R1s in 1955 compounds. Peter Collins badly wanted to try the V16 Mark II on the same Pirellis which the rival ThinWall used, but trade ties prevented this.

Below: Type 25 launch – Raymond Mays Ltd, Bourne: Engine bay of car '252' examined by press and Owen Racing Motors Association (ORMA) members, showing off the P25 engine – a cultural and conceptual opposite to the ultra-complex centrifugally-supercharged V16 launched at Folkingham less than six years previously...

kept him informed down to the last detail, every day, could not have been more helpful.

The notes didn't seem to explain why the engine kept blowing up, although he clearly suspected that a valve was striking the piston at high rpm. If this was indeed the cause, clearly the valves were not following the cam profile, or else something was distorting.

The single-cylinder unit's overhead cams were run by timing chain rather than by the complex gear-train which would appear on the finalized four-cylinder. We were already into the second year of the 2½-litre Formula, and although BRM had virtually completed their new car the engine for it was nothing like ready because worthwhile information had yet to emerge from the single-cylinder programme.

At this time I was running the car build shop and the Maserati and PB's accident piled a big extra load on me. But having just got married I didn't have any girlfriend problems

and it became really one of the most enjoyable periods of my BRM career...

After returning from Barcelona at the end of 1954, a new 60ft-long shed[76] had been erected in our compound at Folkingham and we had erected the jigs for the new frame in there and arranged for the transfer of several skilled people from Rubery Owen and the Group's subsidiary body-making company Motor Panels.

By this time, following his experience of the Mark II V16s and subsequent work on the Maserati 250F, Tony was confident he "knew a bit" about roadholding and how it could be achieved. But for him the '2½' was to provide an appallingly rude awakening.

Its steering geometry as originally built was disastrous. It toed-in about half-an-inch on the Dunlop gauge at the extremes of bump and droop: Once the chassis' front end was together complete with its wishbones and steering, I went through the motions of lifting the car up and down without its air-struts fitted to check the camber change and toe-in at the wheels. I found to my horror that all kinds of dreadful things happened. They toed-in at full droop and waved about all over the place on the way to full bump. There had obviously been a fairly classic blunder in the location of the steering rack and the track-rod lengths. We sorted this out by trial and error, and then began to test the frame for torsional stiffness.

It wasn't very good, as already related.

All this had been reported to Peter Berthon before his accident and it was then that he designed the steel fuel tanks to reinforce the frame. They were in fact a waste of time and contributed nothing significant.

---

76. This used the concrete base of wartime aerodrome building '330' and was a prefabricated steel agricultural affair manufactured by Salopian, another of the vast Rubery Owen Group's varied satellite companies, which produced a wide range of farming equipment. When Reg Parnell had been driving the V16s for the team he would haggle over assorted fees and bonus payments in both cash and kind, at one stage taking a Salopian baler in lieu of cash for his farm at Findern, and on another being paid with pig farrowing equipment. Not too many 1990s Grand Prix drivers breed pigs...

We then got to work to find the optimum exhaust pipe length, trying 2in, 2¼in and 2½in OD pipe. The best length we found was something like a 20in long inlet pipe with its 2in SU single carburettor actually suspended by wire from the Test House roof, where it drew in its air from an open window.

On one Sunday morning we got an engine run which indicated that the complete four-cylinder engine should produce around 270 horsepower. We had set ourselves a target of 275 so we were perhaps better-placed than Coventry Climax, who had abandoned what was actually a very good 2½-litre four-cam V8 engine solely on the strength of propaganda then issuing from the Italian racing teams. Maserati told everybody their 250F gave 250bhp, and since the Ferrari was about as quick everybody assumed it had at least similar power, while Mercedes were obviously ahead of both. It seemed obvious that if you didn't have 100bhp per litre you needn't turn up. At least we had first-hand experience of the Maserati – in the form delivered, after some work to get it up to specification, we saw 235bhp. With much work we got it up to 255–260.

I evolved a routine of running the car build during the day, spending an hour or so in the drawing office feeding them information from the rig tests of the growing prototype chassis, looking at the gearbox being built, and then, when everybody had gone home at around 8pm, Willie and I would run the single-cylinder which he had rebuilt during the day.

I decided that if we progressively ran the unit to higher rpm, stripping and inspecting it at various rpm levels *before* it broke, we might learn what we desperately needed to know – the reason for its persistent failures…

So we ran it only to 5,000rpm the first night, Willie Southcott stripped it next day and it all looked perfect.

Next night we ran it up to 6,000rpm, and this time when Willie stripped it there, sure enough, were the tell-tale marks on the piston crown, revealing where the valves had touched. The marks were not in the cut-out provided to ensure clearance, but at the sides.

At that time it was traditional for a high-performance engine to have a hemispherical head with a fairly large included angle between the valves, something like 40 degrees either side of the vertical. Of course, at near Top Dead Centre, when the valve was starting to open or had not quite yet closed, there was a cut-out provided in the piston for the valve-head to pass into without contact.

I had some half-formed theories that the shape of the piston was actually masking the gas flow, but I knew precious little about it at the time and we had no facilities to investigate, so it remained just a theory.

All this time, of course, we were also racing both the Mark II V16 and the Maserati. We were doing quite well with them, so everybody's morale was sustained and we could put up with the incredibly long hours necessary to keep it all running. It was very rare for me to get home before midnight, and a Saturday evening off consisted of leaving Folkingham at 9 o'clock, an early Sunday evening probably meant knocking off at 7. But that was the only way to do it all and the wonderful morale and spirit of BRM people – so often remarked upon at the time – was never more evident than then. Everybody really believed we were working on what would be a better car. By juggling the clearance between the block and the crankcase on the single-cylinder test unit, using a 15-thou inserted shim plate, we were able to increase clearance within the head. This of course reduced the compression ratio, but not by a lot because we could also enlarge the valve-to-piston clearance by adjusting the timing, but I didn't want to confuse ourselves by altering too many things at once.

Finally, having increased the valve/piston clearance from 30-thou to 72-thou (inlet) and 50-thou to 90-thou (exhaust), the engine was able to run faultlessly to its designed speed of 9,000rpm – and to keep on running.

When we felt we had at last got the single-cylinder situation under control we had that very good win with the Maserati at Silverstone in May, which confirmed to us that 275bhp was an ideal target.

We would subsequently discover the car could lead races with only 240bhp, but we neither understood nor digested the lessons from all this…

Having got the test-unit to run reliably and powerfully, PB was sufficiently recovered, after a series of operations and plastic surgery, to see me. I took all the data down to show him in the Mount Vernon Hospital, and he agreed we were at last ready to commit the rest of the engine. The prototype unit was nearly complete, but I had delayed giving the OK to make more castings until we were sure from the single they would need no major changes.

Of course, the prototype car had been completed some time before.

The gearbox had been completed quite early in the piece, along with the propeller shaft, and by about Easter 1955 the whole car was sitting on its wheels waiting for the engine. The instant we had the all clear from the single-cylinder we built the main engine, and the first signs of the trouble which would dog the P25 throughout its life then began…

We had terrible trouble obtaining valve springs of the right poundage and the right fitting. The plan from square one had been to use SU port-type fuel injection. The prototype unit was assembled and placed on the bed at Folkingham.

We motored it over with the Zephyr engine at the other end of the rig, to ensure oil and water were circulating OK, while we set up the pilot injection system. Stirling Moss was also working with SU's on it. It had a kind of vernier arrangement with a spring-locking device on the back enabling us to adjust mixture strength with the engine running. It sensed the manifold depression and would have been quite satisfactory for a passenger car.

We started the engine running after a little difficulty. One key factor was a little disc mounted on top of the unit with a tiny hole – perhaps 20-thou – which was a bleed intended to permit vapours from hot fuel to escape and to de-aerate the pumping unit. It was possible to achieve a certain amount of tuning with this, and one very protracted weekend we couldn't persuade the engine to run at all because we had forgotten to fit the disc at all, so all the fuel was bleeding away – unnoticed.

However, once the engine was running, because of its very large inlet ports and enormous induction system it gave very good power on the test-bed, particularly at high rpm. We were soon seeing over 260bhp at 8,000 and I decided the last 15-horse could wait for the second engine which we would build-up rapidly.

The prototype engine was installed in the waiting prototype chassis, and one Sunday in June, PB returned to Folkingham, still in a wheelchair, and we managed to start-up the new car and I drove it for 19 laps, not exceeding 6,000rpm. It was very impressive in many ways.

GROWING PAINS

As far back as February 1953, Alfred Owen had confided in Walter Hill, of the BRMA:

New engine designs are finalised and certain parts have been ordered and we are testing out a single cylinder, prior to going ahead with the complete unit. No engine will be available, of course, until 1954… What I have stressed to Peter is that all concentration must be on the engines, as there are plenty of chassis builders who are clamouring for an engine to put into their chassis, and our whole thought should be centred on the engine and not the chassis. This can follow if the engine is so good that it requires a particular chassis for it.

As early as December 1953, PB was talking to Joe Wright of the Dunlop Rim & Wheel Co, of Foleshill, Coventry, about wheels and disc brakes, primarily for the new Type 25, but also for the Maserati 250F, exploring:

…the possibilities of using Dunlop disc brakes on our new Formula 1 car together with a new type of hub and light alloy wheel assembly which would supersede the rather heavy Rudge Whitworth arrangement… As regards the rear brake we believe that a single transmission brake operating through the differential can be perfectly satisfactory.

He went on:

The crownwheel and pinion reduction indicated on our drawing is 4.75:1 which means that when using 16 x 6.00 tyres a disc speed will be 8,500r.p.m. at 150 miles an hour. At this figure the disc mean surface speed is around 14,000ft. per minute. Actually very little braking occurs at these speeds…we find that real braking does not occur much over a road speed of 120 miles per hour, which will give a disc speed of 6,750r.p.m. or a mean surface speed of 11,200ft. a minute…

We estimate the torque needed at the rear disc to be to the order of 150ft. lb.

Concerning the light alloy wheels and method of central mounting we believe the peg drive arrangement…to be light and sufficiently robust…

Bets were hedged by a parallel approach for disc brakes to Mr Kinchin of Girling, but the Dunlop deal would go through. Development dragged through 1954 before taking its spurt

in the spring of 1955 as the prototype chassis and a sister were approaching completion and Tony Rudd and Willie Southcott at last began to make some sense of the single-cylinder test engine, although by that time a prototype design had already been finalized for short-term production.

It had been hoped that the prototype P25 engine would have been ready to run on the bench by March 7, then ready for car installation on the 21st. In fact that prototype engine '251' did not make its maiden dyno run until March 21 and it subsequently had to be stripped for modification in the light of single-cylinder experience. By April 4 it had run three hours under its own power, and on that day Tony reported:

The delays in delivering the engine to Folkingham were mainly associated with the valve gear; for example, although the valve springs were received within a few days of the promised date, they were found to be first in the wrong material and, secondly, malformed; and it was necessary to select the best of these malformed springs to run in the engine…

He confirmed:

Construction of the second chassis should have reached the stage that assembly of the second car can commence around April 15…ready for body work.

However, No. 2 inlet valve had broken at the collet location, Tony's failure investigation concluding that the valve had been scored by the collets, which did not mate properly with associated pieces. The score then acted as a stress raiser, producing a fatigue failure. Finish standards were improved, the first engine rebuilt with collet tapers matched to their carriers and each set marked accordingly, and Racosine was used as an anti-scuffing agent. Bench running recommenced, and by the 15th seven hours had been completed, at up to 5,000rpm, and much was being learned. For example, there was considerable oil splash from both breathers above 4,000rpm. Oil flow to the camshafts had been increased, which could have been to blame, an inlet rocker box drain pipe being made up accordingly.

Owen had pressured PB to have a pilot layout drawn to mate the new P25 engine to the 250F chassis, just in case. Bourne machine shop manager Clarrie Brinkley provided Owen with an analysis of all the outstanding Project 25 programme parts in May, creating in the process a major explosion by the lay preacher's civilized standards. He angrily minuted Mays:

I am rather disturbed at the whole situation. I only wish I had laid the law down very much more strongly about our going for an engine to begin with and fitting this into a standard chassis as a start off, developing the chassis later when we were sure that the engine was right.

Now we have done exactly the same as we did with the original B.R.M., in fact we have got many new ideas to co-ordinate in the first car and it may be that teething problems and modifications are likely to prevent us from making any show this year…I am very disappointed that the original intention and request was not kept to by Peter at Bourne…

RM fought Bourne's corner, highlighting the flaws in AGBO's case:

> …taking into consideration this is a new engine of entirely new design, the amount of troubles and modifications have been extremely small…modifications of connecting rods, oil coolers, etc. must inevitably follow wherever a racing engine is built…the connecting rod failure which necessitated the rods being stiffened only occurred after 40 hours (running).
>
> As regards fitting this engine in a standard chassis…no chassis could be purchased other than something like a Maserati or Ferrari, minus the engine…In any case, our new chassis has in no way held up engine development. In fact the chassis has been and still is, waiting for the engine to be installed.
>
> I do feel that in this case we have brought the two along side by side, and actually the chassis has beaten the engine by a short head…

Owen accepted this defence but added, with 20:20 foresight:

> My chief concern would be to find that having developed the engine and got this into running order, we then spent a lot of time making the chassis roadworthy. You will appreciate that on the original B.R.M. …the road-holding qualities on our early chassis left a lot to be desired.

Just two days after he had dictated these words – on June 5, 1955, the prototype BRM Type 25 chassis – strictly speaking '271' since it was a Project 27 structure but to become known in BRM-ese as '251' – turned a wheel under its own power for the first time at Folkingham, driven by A.C. Rudd, with Peter Berthon – wheelchair-bound – looking on.

In its original form the car ran unpainted, its body skinning in bare aluminium, its tail cowl featuring a rather ugly raised fin while its cockpit was high-sided with wrap-around Perspex windscreen. Engine '251' was fitted with the SU injection system, and the car was equipped with Dunlop disc brakes, a servo pump being run from the centre of the single rear disc on the back of the gearbox. It had a 7ft 3in wheelbase and 4ft 0in track, and its air-strut suspension was direct-acting on the front wishbones, while at the rear the system incorporated small wishbones and links with a slide-located de Dion axle. As first completed, '251' ran a one-piece propeller-shaft.

As Jim Sandercombe's 'Department 31' Engine Development Division report for the months of April and May 1955 – but also covering the first days of June – later recorded:

> Since that date a programme of modifications has been started both on the engine and on the chassis, but it is thought that the initial tests show some promise. The second Project 25 engine is now available for testing. *Project 27* – The second chassis of the new Formula is now under construction…

During this initial testing an immediate 'drivability' problem was highlighted with the fuel injection system. The induction air intake between the nose-mounted split water radiator cores fed into a 4in diameter trunk alongside the engine, from which four 18in long ram pipes drew air into the ports. Inside the trunk was a single throttle butterfly.

Willie Southcott christened this assembly *'The Queen Mary'*, and when everybody pointed out that the real ship had only three funnels he declared he never could count anyway. But this system provided the first major Type 25 problem.

By the time the driver opened the single throttle butterfly at the front of the *Queen Mary* and the fuel injection reacted some way behind it, the car had rolled perhaps seven or eight lengths. This throttle lag made the engine feel completely unresponsive. It all felt fine along the straight, and once it gathered speed it would go very fast indeed. But delayed throttle response made it very difficult to drive as quickly through corners as should have been possible.

Tony: We made a device which fired chalk at the road when the driver pressed the throttle pedal down, and another device marked where the torque actually increased. This confirmed the driver's impression that it took seven or eight car lengths, which made it impossible to steer the car on the throttle, never mind the acceleration lost.

Consequently, we sank the *Queen Mary* and put four separate throttle butterflies up against the engine with a kind of improvised accelerator pump. But nothing we did for the injection system reduced its throttle lag by more than half.

This was completely unacceptable, so we reluctantly abandoned the SU fuel injection and ordered instead some 48mm-bodied Weber carburettors. The first engine's carburettors were hung from the chassis in rubber, connected to the engine by metal dumb-bells about 4in long, with 'O'-rings each end. They reduced power to a little over 240bhp, but the torque was good, throttle response was almost instantaneous and the new car had suddenly become the extremely lively proposition we had always intended.

But another problem we had encountered was its diabolical vibration. The entire car would vibrate in concert with the engine. This vibration was so intense that rivets chattered loose and it was possible to rev the engine while sitting stationary in the yard at Folkingham and watch all the rivets rotating quite rapidly in their drillings…

I blamed some of this vibration on the single-piece propshaft, which I had never liked the look of, and persuaded a not-very-fit PB to replace it with a two-piece shaft with conventional universal joints. He wanted to remove the clutch from the back of the engine and mount it on the chassis beneath the driver's seat. As at that time I was the driver I point-blank refused to sit on top of a fast-rotating clutch, so that idea was deadlocked. We finally adopted a two-piece propshaft which was fitted in July – while the track was widened slightly to 4ft 2in – and we plunged into a great deal of balance work…

One fascinating – and rather salutary – discovery from Tony and the team running the car extensively in the wet involved cooling arrangements for the single rear brake, revolving on the back of the gearbox. ORO's design team had appreciated that being enclosed by bodywork, masked by the gearbox ahead of it and probably absorbing considerable gearbox heat, the brake would demand a lot of cooling. Tests were run as early as July '55, using air-speed indicators and pitot heads taped to the body to find a high-pressure or high-velocity region to locate a scoop or duct to direct cold air onto the disc. They had innocently cut a hole in the extreme tail to permit airflow past the disc and would end up with a neat intake duct by the driver's right shoulder, feeding through a 'bird's beak' funnel clasping the disc where it emerged from the caliper. This arrangement seemed to work well until somebody noticed after a wet-weather run that autumn, that more air, water, muck and rubbish was being sucked *in* through the tail vent than was being blown in through the forward-facing shoulder intake! All this grime would then zoom out of the low-pressure area within the driver's cockpit opening, leaving him very damp and uncomfortable with the dirty face and goggle-protected Panda eyes so classically typical of the 1950s racing driver…

By this time – autumn 1955 – Alfred Owen was becoming increasingly restless. Fortunately, Bourne and Folkingham had a face-saver in the good contemporary racing record of the Maserati and the Mark II V16s. Poor PB's accident had been a potent delaying factor, but as Tony recalls, Owen was repeating his famous phrase that "…we were always promising him 'Jam Tomorrow'…"

RM invited Stirling Moss and his business advisor, Ken Gregory, to visit Bourne to see developments, Ray trying desperately to massage the Mercedes-Benz works driver, fresh from victory in the British GP at Aintree, into joining BRM for the following season.

Finally, in August, a very defensive press statement was prepared for distribution from Bourne. It read, apologetically:

> The new Grand Prix Formula I B.R.M. will be entered for its first race at Aintree on September 3rd, 1955…The prototype car was first run on test about two months ago, but it is by no means yet fully developed, although at this stage the engine gives comparable horsepower with contemporary designs….In announcing their new car, the sponsoring firm, which is Rubery, Owen & Co. Ltd., Darlaston, wish to make it quite clear that the B.R.M. is not in any way a national project….Rubery, Owen & Co. Ltd. is the parent firm in a very large industrial organisation comprising some 40 companies, and because of this some people have thought that almost unlimited money and engineering resources are placed at the disposal of the motor racing section. Such a supposition is totally incorrect…The first consideration of the parent company must be to see that the firm is run on a sound commercial basis with profits ploughed back in…for its development and security. The economics and taxation of present day industry make it impossible to place more than limited financial and material resources at the disposal of motor racing. The establishments at Bourne and Folkingham are quite small, and…a part of their time is devoted to commercial work which brings in a financial return and helps to pay for the racing.
>
> Our principal competitors abroad are in an entirely different and much more favourable position. Even the smaller Italian firms have infinitely superior resources … The fact of the matter is that none of the large motor manufacturers in Great Britain produces Grand Prix racing cars, so it must be left to those with smaller resources to do the best they can.
>
> …The sponsors of this car are most anxious not to create the impression that there is any possibility of its making a momentous first appearance. It is naturally hoped, and believed, that eventually this car will put up a good show, but it…must go through a large process of gradual development in racing.

The lessons of the V16's over-inflated prior propaganda had been well learned…

On August 8, Ron Flockhart tested the prototype – chassis '251' – at Folkingham, and reported as follows:

> *Steering*: Too light – no centre comeback.
> *Gearchange*: Too much lever travel, back, forwards and across gate.
> *Gear Ratios*: 2nd and 3rd too low.
> *Seat*: Mid. back too hollow – no support.
> *Engine*: Good – roughness no worry. Smoother than 2-litre Connaught.
> *Windshield*: Too near wheel.
> *Brakes*: Good – but pedal drooping when hard on.
> *Rear Suspension*: Holds on well when in a corner, but inclines to oversteer when car put into corner.
> *Front Suspension*: Very Good.

He drove the car again on the 14th, reporting:

> General handling greatly improved – balance front to back better. Steering comeback better; quite positive and no tricks. Car now stable and runs straight at speed. Reverse gear still jamming up. Clutch pedal too much movement when fully out and appears not freeing properly when gear changing – cannot get gears cleanly. Rev. counter no good – flicks over range. Rear end tends to fidget when accelerating hard over rough surface and occasionally on braking. Brake pedal, flaps sideways, otherwise brakes appear satisfactory. Pedal block in wrong position and wants extending over whole pedal area. Throttle pedal too heavy and travel a little too long. Seat as before – suggest slotted backrest. Cockpit temp: – O.K. Windscreen angle must be slightly increased. General tinware and bonnet not secure – and very rattling. Left footrest required.

Three days later, August 17, it was Peter Collins' turn. He commented:

> *General*: Suspension is good on rough surface – front inclined to patter across fast corners.
> *Steering*: Shade too light – would like some comeback – otherwise perfect.
> *Gearbox*: Sometimes difficult to get third from second. Occasional lag in clutch taking up.

Brakes: Brakes perfectly adequate – juddering noise from rear when braking in neutral.

Performance: Acceleration very good and very progressive, and power easy to use through corners.

Pedals: Left foot rest required; like hanging throttle and half horseshoe (pedal shape) – proper block for heel.

Windscreen: More side protection.

Steering Wheel position: Perfectly O.K.

Steering Wheel: Requires rim of less diameter (now too thick).

Seat: Requires more rake, less roundness in back, more support for backside, and longer squab.

Exhaust: Too much heat in cockpit; requires shroud.

Cockpit ventilation: O.K.

Drip groove round scuttle.

Alfred Owen wanted ORMA members to be shown the car before its first public appearance, but RM and PB were paranoid about it being impossible to "keep out the Press" on such an occasion, in fact they were "…in favour of doing the thing properly and asking the Press to come along as well. As things stand…we have definitely promised members that they will be shown the car before it races, and it is going to be very difficult indeed to get over this promise…[we] should be given as much notice as possible of your intentions to run the new car anywhere at all, because when you do so, we have just got to decide on what to do about showing the car to members beforehand…"

The second car, '252', was completed with the second engine installed late in August, its sleek body panelling painted – as was '251''s by this time – in BRM's dark lustrous green livery, while the original finned tail-cowl of '251' had been replaced on '252' by a neater, more subtle design with a modest centreline headrest spine.

This second Type 25 also embodied several other improvements. Its Weber-carburetted engine was mounted 1½ inches further forward than '251''s, it had a two-piece propshaft from new, and its Dunlop three-disc brake system used an engine-driven servo instead of the gearbox-driven unit on the prototype. Its cockpit sides had been cut down low to give the driver more elbow room while a cut-down frameless Perspex 'aero screen' replaced the wrap-around moulding as used on '251'. Wheelbase and track matched '251''s, while PB's very elaborate original steel fuel tanks had been abandoned in favour of detachable diagonal bracing tubes in the chassis' side bays, which were located by fitted bolts and skewered entirely new aluminium pannier tanks shaped rather like pillow cases.

The undertray – like '251''s – was a permanently attached stressed panel, providing frame triangulation in plan, while also being shallow-spooned to possess considerable inherent torsional stiffness. Then the stressed-skin scuttle and bulkhead structure, of course, provided a major crossmember, being extended forward to the front crossmember frame and rearwards as far as possible to provide a torsionally stiff chassis overall.

But where the prototype car's basic tube structure, with stiffening panels, had been welded-up from 18-gauge T45 tube – presenting a stiffness of 225ft/lbs per degree deflection for a weight of just 62lbs compared with the Maserati 250F's 138lbs in similar state – this new car was different from '251'.

Its tubular base frame had been welded-up by Maurice Cradock from 17-gauge T45 tube because 18-gauge stock was unobtainable at that time. Its new alloy fuel tanks weighed 19lbs per side against 36lbs each for '251''s steel originals. The weakest point in these frames was just behind the instrument panel where the prototype's scuttle structure had developed numerous cracks after Flockhart and Collins – and Tony Rudd too – had been flogging it around Folkingham.

Consequently, a light tubular reinforcing structure was being designed for frame three. If it proved effective – as it would – both frames '251' and '252' would be modified to match.

This change stiffened the chassis and provided a good fuel system, with five tanks – a relatively large 18-gallon one in the tail, two small tanks alongside the driver's seat and the two larger tanks beside his legs. They were accessible via detachable side panels. Even so, the Type 25's fixed panelling earned the cars the nickname 'The Over-Stressed Skin Special' at Folkingham.

On August 29 the latest car was shown to invited pressmen at a modest launch function held in Raymond Mays Ltd's new car showroom opposite the Maltings, in Bourne. Then, after a brief shake-down at Folkingham, this light, low, lithe new car – the second Type 25 built, note, not the cracking-up prototype – was wheeled up the ramps into one of the transporters, where it was carefully chocked and tethered down before the Lodestar was driven off towards Aintree.

The day of BRM's debut in 2½-litre Formula 1 was dawning at last.

THE TYPE 25 GOES RACING…

Peter Berthon's internal ORO report on the new 2½-litre BRM's public debut told the tale as follows:

AINTREE MEETING – September 3, 1955
2½-litre Car (Type 25)

The new car was completed and prepared after the Press Meeting at Bourne on Monday, the 29th October [*sic* – meant 29th August!]. Difficulties with the installation of the carburettors and defective welding on the oil tank delayed the running in of the car until the Thursday morning. As it was a new car, it was run in carefully by Rudd during the day and, after adjustments, was run around the circuit by Peter Collins. He completed 5 laps at racing speed and felt that the car was satisfactory, and in all respects up to the standard for road-holding and performance of a prototype.

A fractured brake pipe, due to a badly-made flare, was found and the car did not run any more.

During the test period with Flockhart and Collins, when the [prototype?] car was driven hard for two or three laps, oil was gradually piling up in the sump, as it was not being scavenged properly and came out of the main engine breather.

The centre of the sump was altered prior to this car's

first running; and during the running in done by Rudd and the 5 laps at racing speed by Collins, it appeared perfectly satisfactory as no oil was thrown out of the breather.

At Aintree, on the Friday morning, when the car was unloaded and being looked over, it was found that a further brake pipe had fractured through a bad flare. This was changed while Peter Collins practised the 16-cylinder.

When nearing the completion of his second practice lap with the 2½-litre, Peter Collins spun off on the grass just before Tatt's Corner, uprooting a number of posts. He finally extracted the car from the grass and drove it back to the pits.

It was found on examination that the scavenging problem still existed and oil had been thrown out of the engine breather, covering the right-hand side of the car and right-hand rear wheel with oil. This had caused him to slide on the first left-hand corner after the swerves. It is evident that, although the scavenging seems satisfactory for a course of the Folkingham type, it is not satisfactory for a very twisty circuit, where a number of sweeping corners come one after the other as at Aintree.

With the semi-stress skin construction we are using, the crumpled panel work on the side of the car did not look too serious; but when examined it was found that all the panel work had been badly twisted across the stiffened centre section of the car, and most of the rivets broken or started; and as this seriously affects the torsional stiffness of the car, I did not consider it safe to run again without a complete check-up and proper repair, which we could not undertake there.

After the short drive at Aintree, Peter Collins remarked that the road-holding seemed extremely good through the corners, and acceleration out of the corners appeared a good deal better than that of the 16-cylinder.

RM tried hard to put the best gloss on their new car's debut, to Owen:

I do think Peter should be given credit for having produced such a light and such a beautiful little chassis…we have a potential winner if only we can lay down a careful policy and act upon it.

AGBO to RM, in agreement, but:

…at the same time I would remind you that a lot of money has been spent on this development and one must expect to see a return…times are not easy financially and the amount expended of something like £70,000 in the past 12 months is a big drain on one's profits. We must watch every penny we spend and economise in every way possible if we are to get the cars in racing trim in as short as possible time. It is no use spending money wildly on weekend work as it will just drain our resources away…We have always been prone to last minute efforts at high costs. We must not in fact try to improve the cars further in any way with these costly alterations, weekend work etc…

The engine oil scavenging problem was addressed by adding a false oil compartment beneath the exceptionally shallow sump. A changeover butterfly valve system was made up and connected between the two outlets and the scavenge pump inlet. The pendulum weight operating this valve would obviously be subject to the same acceleration and deceleration forces as the oil in the sump, thus switching the scavenge to whichever end the oil had gathered in.

In this trim '252' was tested at Oulton Park on Friday, September 9, where this weight system proved insufficiently sensitive. Extra weighting made the valve spindles more sluggish in operation, while through corners G-load on the weight system held both valves open!

Flockhart drove that Friday afternoon, and again next day, when no more than two laps could be completed before the sump filled, oil pumping from the breathers while oil pressure zeroed since none was pumping around the engine's vitals. Ron spent more time watching his gauges than driving hard, clocking only 2min 20sec at best.

On the Sunday, a suction-valve system was made to replace the weighted affair. With the throttle open, the scavenge pump was connected at the rear of the sump, throttle shut then created intake manifold vacuum, which flipped the valve system to scavenge from the front.

When running recommenced on Monday this system showed a slight improvement, but only for three full laps before breathing and pressure loss occurred. Flockhart meantime got down to 2:05, complaining that the suspension was inadequately damped for the bumpy Cheshire circuit. When air-strut damping was raised, rear end adhesion was lost. The team trailed back to Bourne early Tuesday morning.

At Folkingham the car's oil pump was rig-tested, which showed that when alternately opened to oil and then air, as in the car when running, it required a recovery time of 5 seconds, clearly demonstrating the need for two scavenge pumps. Over the following weekend an extra pump was cobbled together from V16 parts. Since at that stage the engine was running with two spark plugs per cylinder rather than Tres' precautionary three, an unused drive on the engine's front timing case was now adapted as a drive for the additional oil pump, which was then plumbed to the forward sump outlet (the existing pump being connected to the rearward one). Now, instead of having a scavenge pump just over 1½ times the capacity of the pressure pump, '252' had something like 2½ times the scavenge capacity.

Its suspension air struts were then modified to provide a lower spring rate by increasing the air volume with an air cylinder screwed into the inflation valve threads, while rebound damping was increased to a damping ratio of 3:1.

Oulton Park was again available on September 19, when Peter Collins – fresh from driving for Aston Martin in the Golden Jubilee RAC TT at Dundrod – completed 35 rapid laps completely free of oil scavenging problems. His average speed was higher over 25 laps than the last Oulton Park F1 race average and his best lap was 1:57, just 0.2sec outside Moss' record in a works Maserati 250F.

PB reported:

The suspension showed a definite improvement; but

as it is evident that our suspension alterations are on the right lines, further modifications to decrease effective spring rate and increase damping factor ratio, would show still improved road holding…Collins' opinion was that the steering ratio is slightly too low for such a twisty circuit; but we have an alternative ratio which should correct this…

Car '252' was then hastily readied for the start of practice for the Oulton Park Gold Cup race, two days later. Top and third gear selector forks in the gearbox showed evidence of rapid wear. Top and third gears showed heavy pitch line loading. The bottom front wishbone ball retaining nuts were also wearing too fast, permitting hammering in the ball seats. One prop-shaft UJ showed signs of overheating due to the male portion of the joint running out of true. Since the latest Oulton test session with the improved suspension set-up had seen Collins pulling 140mph between Esso and Knickerbrook corners a higher top gear was fitted, permitting 140mph at 7,500 engine rpm. Both engines '253' (installed) and '252' (spare) had been rebuilt and the car was finally reassembled and complete in the early hours of Thursday the 22nd, the team setting off immediately for scrutineering and the 2.30pm start of Oulton Park practice.

However, Peter Collins was soon in the pits there complaining of fluctuating oil pressure. The tank level was found to be low. It was topped up. After three more laps he came in again, same problem, but this time the engine was also running rough, breathing out oil and not scavenging properly.

With sinking hearts – "Why does this always happen in public?" – the car was removed to the garage and its engine removed. Its No.1 big end was in distress, the adjacent rod and crank blued. The pipes between the sump and suction side

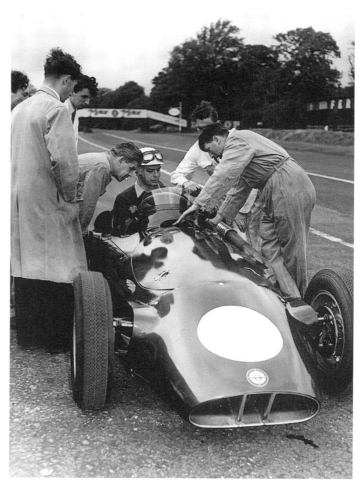

Above: Friday, September 9, 1955 – Pre-debut race testing at Oulton Park: Ron Flockhart in '252' – repaired from Aintree practice damage – tended here by Folkingham bodybuilder Allan Ellison (left foreground) – a "superb, intelligent and inventive panel-basher", later to found his own prosperous company and to become a magistrate – and mechanics Reg Smith, Willie Southcott (cigarette), Gordon Newman (white overalls) and Arthur Hill (like 'Baggy', a former Tank Corps Sergeant, nicknamed 'Hill, A.', often rendered 'Hilly', and who habitually wore his service beret).

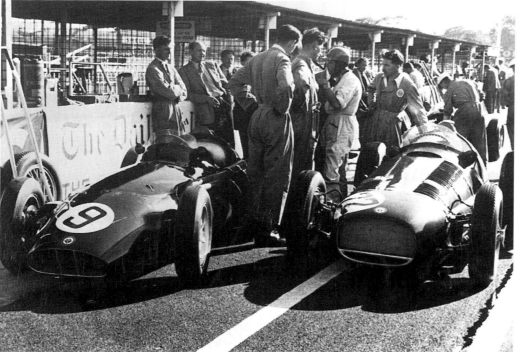

Left: September 2, 1955 – practice for the Aintree international: A rare photo indeed of '252' – race number 9 – ready to run on the Liverpudlian pit lane, with the small figure of Peter Collins standing between Gordon Newman and Dick Salmon, fresh from V16 Mark II 'No 5', ready for the Libre event. The new F1 car is about to blow oil over its rear tyres, crash mildly and become a non-starter.

of the rear scavenge pump had been "very badly fitted" so that the sealing 'O' ring had been pinched partly out of its recess, hampering flow.

The spare engine was fitted overnight and a new scavenge pipe and facings made up for the rear pump.

Collins just made the final 45 minutes of Friday practice, but after a few laps he reported low oil pressure, 50psi at best. Sent out again he completed just one lap and was at full throttle on the second, just having changed into top gear, when the front prop-shaft broke, the engine hit astronomical revs, and he hit the mag switch, coasting to rest on the grass verge…PB:

The engine must have momentarily gone up to at least 10,000rpm. That evening we found the inlet valves had stretched .020 to .030, due to hitting the limiters…but all valve gear looked satisfactory…so clearances were readjusted and apart from this the engine seemed quite satisfactory.

The prop-shaft breakage was traced to a fatigue failure starting from the main cross locating pin:

All other prop-shaft joints were working and…the method of cross pinning was unsatisfactory. The design of tube and ends were originally for a welded assembly; but this had to be abandoned as the tube supplied proved to be of non–weldable quality…the assembly was made with one main cross pin, with the ends swaged out, causing an area of high local stress. A completely new prop-shaft was built up overnight, with ends and tubes tinned together, and retained by means of three small taper pins per end.

When the oil pump was removed more sloppy workmanship was revealed:

…the by-pass valve had been assembled incorrectly, the camshaft by-pass valve being changed over with the main relief valve. This accounted for the low oil pressure.

Checked and corrected, the engine was reassembled and the car finally race-prepared.

September 24, 1955 – Mid-Cheshire MC Gold Cup, Oulton Park – 54 laps, 161.09 miles

Due to inadequate practice, Collins' starting position was at the rear of the grid; and after a good getaway, he passed through the field, and in 10 laps reached second place [wrong, third – DCN] but had to slow up to come into the pits, and was immediately re-passed by Musso. At the pits, he complained of no oil pressure and that the engine felt very rough; and, in consequence, the car was withdrawn.

In contrast with PB's bald internal report as above, *The Autocar*'s read:

Peter Collins' drive in the new B.R.M. – brief but very impressive while it lasted – left the big crowds at Oulton Park feeling that perhaps Britain may yet produce a Grand Prix car…Hawthorn (Lancia), who was suffering from tonsilitis and not in his true form, had, together with Castellotti, been passed first by Musso (250F), and then by the B.R.M. 'This', said the crowds, 'is terrific' – the B.R.M. in third place and leading a couple of Lancias, a Ferrari, Maseratis, Vanwalls and a formidable field of 2½ and 2-litre Connaughts. But it was not to last…At one stage Collins had been closing his distance behind Musso and it seems that, once the lubrication troubles that have dogged the car have been cured, it will be good.

At Folkingham on the Monday morning an *in situ* engine check seemed satisfactory so the car was started.

It was found that the oil pressure gauge had broken; and with a new gauge fitted the oil pressure was normal in every respect.

The new four-cylinder engine's phenomenal vibration had merely shaken the indicator needle off its spindle! Peter Collins could have continued his attack upon the leading works Maseratis of Moss and Musso at Oulton Park, but…

The car felt rough when driven, but it appeared to come from the gearbox and not from the engine…one tooth had broken off the top ratio output gear…the car had run a few laps in this condition, and no further teeth had broken off, which is remarkable, although heavy pitch line indentation was apparent. This failure seems to have been caused from a grinding crack, which extends halfway through the root of the tooth at one end.

It is evident that the gearbox gears tend to be overloaded and that the lubrication is inadequate. Steps have been taken to increase both gearbox pressure and scavenge pump sizes; and further gearbox gears that are ordered will have an improved tooth form, together with a twenty per cent increase in face width. These modifications will reduce the pressure load and stress in the root of the teeth…

Note how unsparing Berthon was in this report, made specifically for Alfred Owen's information. Precious little 'con' is evident in this one. The Chief Engineer was simply telling it as it was.

To prevent a recurrence of the instrument failure, all gauges were then placed upon a subsidiary panel, rubber-mounted in the dash.

The propeller-shaft arrangement was also redesigned, a one-piece type being produced with a ball centre steady bearing carried in a large co-axial rubber bush. The mechanics developed a setting-up trick at Folkingham which involved half-filling a freshly-assembled car with fuel, and then squatting in the driver's seat to tighten the bush-locating bolts, thus perfectly aligning the prop-shaft with the frame in the normal running condition. Tony had some misgivings about all this: although it worked quite well and

September 24, 1955 – Oulton Park Gold Cup: Tony Rudd with the new '252' – its race debut imminent – on the Cheshire circuit's pit apron; Tony Rudd, Reg Smith, Arthur Hill and Gordon Newman baby-sitting – this latest BRM was the tiniest car in contemporary Formula 1...

solved our prop-shaft problems, the vibration was still there...

In fact the Type 25's vibration became something of an obsession with Tony at Folkingham, particularly as drivers would complain bitterly of the steering wheel and column, the cockpit coaming, screen and mirrors, *everything*, all buzzing furiously in concert with the chunky four-cylinder engine's high rpm. He eventually borrowed a vibration inciter from Rubery Owen's Research Department and by experimentation, rubber-mounting the steering column and so on, the driver would eventually be insulated from the worst excesses of the P25 engine's high-frequency 'buzz'.

A QUESTION OF DRIVERS – 1955–56

Immediately after the brand-new BRM's promising but so frustrating race debut at Oulton Park, extensive tests continued on the P25 oil pumps. The system proved unsatisfactory, leaking badly between the main oil pressure camshaft feed and blow-off valves and from the bearing seal between the pressure and scavenge pump bodies. Both existing engines were rig-tested for internal leaks, at temperatures around 120°C. These proved the gallery pipe seals were inadequate and revealed leakage past the main bearing cap studs. Oil seals were improved and modified oil pumps were fitted.

The causes of valve stretching were investigated and when the Terry valve springs were double-checked it was found they had 'set down', permitting the collets to strike the limiters at high rpm, stretching the soft valve stems, which were also found to be sticking in their guides and limiters. Why were the valve stems soft? "...valves are normally nitrided on the stems; but recent supplies have been made in the soft condition due to late deliveries" – a batch had been accepted without benefit of the lengthy, 96-hour nitriding process.

At Folkingham, the Owen Maserati and the last active Mark

II V16 were prepared for their last British race outings at Castle Combe and work had begun to modify the prototype '251' into a raceworthy machine, fitting a new body like '252''s with cutaway body sides, a brake servo pump driven from the inlet camshaft for a new disc-brake set by Lockheed, a larger radiator, and replacing the original steel side tanks with the latest tube-skewered aluminium 'pillow cases'.

With this work under way, '252' was prepared for testing by Stirling Moss, whom RM was beseeching to try the new car with a view to joining ORO in 1956. New pneumatic-strut valve blocks were completed to offer increased rebound damping, raising the car's rebound-to-bump damping ratio to 4:1.

Oulton Park was again the test venue, on November 3. PB reported:

> The track was 90% wet, very slippery in places, due to leaves, etc, on the course. Visibility poor – tendency to rain. Ron Flockhart did some preliminary running and recorded the best time of 2 mins 20 secs.
>
> STIRLING MOSS did a run of 10 laps and a further run of 12 laps – best time 2 mins 11 secs. As it started raining quite heavily, Moss did not wish to continue so the tests were terminated.

Back at Folkingham a tendency for the clutch to stick was investigated. Its drive plate was found to be badly cracked, a new clutch was installed and "the car prepared and held ready for Moss, and weather...".

At Oulton again on November 12, both the Type 25 and the Owen Maserati were available for comparison, but the ORO crew had a surprise awaiting them as they:

> ...found on arrival that Moss had also asked Vandervell to send a car so that he could make comparative tests.
>
> Weather reasonably fine – track wet in the woods.

Moss would not drive the Maserati as it has a central throttle pedal, which he considers dangerous [Tony Rudd insists this contemporary reference is wrong, his Owen Maserati had a right-side throttle pedal. I'm staying out of it! – DCN].

Moss tried the Vanwall and B.R.M. and Peter Collins came up for the tests and he took the Maserati round.

Although the Vanwall was running satisfactorily in the early stages, it eventually started misfiring and was finally packed away with valve gear trouble, having caused damage to a piston – notch one for BRM!

Moss did approximately 25 laps in the Vanwall, it being the light sprint car (i.e. minimum fuel tanks used in the Castle Combe Formula race) and returned a best time of 1 min 54 secs dead.

Moss ran a total of 42 laps in the B.R.M. and during the tests insisted on tanks being filled to see how the car handled for the fuel [phonetic mistranscription? Should read 'full of fuel'?] – The best time returned was 1 min 52.2 secs – the course still being about 20% wet. Moss estimated that under dry conditions he could lap at least 2 secs faster. Existing record lap was 1 min 55 secs – although in official practice…Hawthorn, in a Lancia, did 1:53.4.

Moss concluded that the B.R.M. was extremely fast, but took a lot of concentration to drive at this speed, particularly on the straight, which is extremely bumpy. Moss now required additional testing…and nominated Silverstone.

Chassis '252''s leaking oil filter had been replaced by a spare, but its engine seemed rougher than hitherto and the clutch was suspected since it represented the only recent change. Sure enough, it was badly out of balance, and PB bearded Lockheed to tighten-up their procedures. ORO was still placing too much trust in outside suppliers and repeatedly fell victim to an outlook which maintained: "They are good suppliers and if it comes from them we should not have to inspect and test it again…" Such misplaced – almost idle – confidence repeatedly shot BRM in the foot.

Meanwhile, the work was progressing to modify the prototype and as yet unraced chassis '251' to match '252''s specification (in all but frame tube gauge) and fit it – unlike '252' – with Lockheed disc brakes, the younger car running Dunlops.

The differences between these systems, and their manufacturers, were as much philosophical as mechanical. As these parallel development programmes for the BRM Type 25 would develop, ORO's people found that Lockheed's two Freds – Ellis and Bothamley – were far more open to suggestions and new ideas than was Dunlop's naturally rugged and dogmatic Harold Hodkinson. If he approved of a new idea, once he had thought it out, he would support it wholeheartedly. If not, he would totally dismiss any discussion as a useless waste of time. In contrast, the two Freds might say: "We doubt if that will work, but we'll try it and see."

Their Lockheed disc system offered a different approach to Dunlop's generally more familiar design. Each Lockheed disc was clasped by a swinging caliper containing just a single big hydraulic cylinder on one side, and large rectangular pads.

One half of the caliper had no hydraulics in it at all, just a pad – while the cylinder and second pad were in the other half. A linkage system was provided to correct misalignment and although slightly more prone to taper wear they really had a similar servo system to Dunlop's with only detail differences. Lockheed's discs were cast iron with a larger area so local heating was not so intense.

The major remaining difference between '251' and '252' would be that the prototype car's engine mounting remained 1½in further back than its younger sister's.

On November 22, '252' – now known within ORO as 'the Dunlop brake car' – was presented at Silverstone where Moss had arranged to test it that day against Vanwall and the B-Type Connaught to guide his contract decision for the coming season.

PB reported:

The B.R.M. was exactly as had been run in previous tests at Oulton Park. He completed 25 laps…best time 1 min 50.2 secs. Best time on Vanwall – 1 min 47.8 secs; best time on Connaught 1 min 51.6 secs.

The Connaught blew up…Moss had his press party that evening, he had to leave for London, so that test was suspended.

Moss said that generally, although the car was considerably faster than the other two [sic], it was much more difficult to drive in the wet conditions…

Flockhart drove the Lockheed brake car ['251'] continuously to bed in the brakes and returning finally a best lap of 2 mins dead.

Having learnt [sic] nothing…we decided to stay over and continue…next day and arranged for Peter Collins to come over.

November 23rd

Track nearly dry; some puddles but drying with sun and wind. Overnight we reduced rebound damping on front…Collins…returned 1 min 47.2 secs (official track record 1 min 47 secs dead).

…the front seemed to lack movement under acceleration. Collins complained that the car was difficult to hold on acceleration out of the corners and at speed. 50lbs of ballast was strapped to the front cross members [on the front axle line] strut pressures brought into line to give correct static positioning and…Collins returned…1 min 46.2 secs on our timing; 1 min 45.8 on the Track Manager's timing.

Collins said the car was very much better – much less fidgety and more stable…although still tended to twitch on acceleration out of corners.

The Lockheed brake car, unballasted, with rear [ward!] engine position was brought into line re damping…Collins put in a number of laps…best 1 min 49.2 secs. Collins left for London to see Moss and report to him the improvements we had made.

Flockhart continued with the Lockheed brake car… 1:56 dead. Running was concluded due to a brake pipe fracturing.

Both cars ran satisfactorily throughout the tests.

Collins hoped he could persuade Moss to return and

try the car again before making his final decision and, in consequence, we stayed at Silverstone.

The next day, 24th November, Moss flew up. Unfortunately the weather was bad; it rained continuously throughout the day.

With the Dunlop brake car his best lap time was 1:58.8...he insisted he tried the car with Pirelli tyres, which Peter Collins had brought up with him from London....best time 1:58.4; the Dunlop tyres were then replaced...best time 1:58.6, showing little or no difference between the two makes of tyre, under the full wet conditions.

Continual trouble with Lockheed oil filter...three were changed – all leaking in the sealing joint ring after some laps running...

Cars returned to Bourne.

Moss had very little to say about the car, but agreed that an improvement had been made. It was then quite apparent that he had little intention of driving a British car, and that the main object of all the tests was to provide reasons for driving foreign...

...concluded Berthon, bitterly.

Beyond soft-stem valve wear in both engines they proved quite healthy when stripped, and the new-type prop-shaft was particularly satisfactory. But the driver problem for 1956 was becoming acute – late November and still nobody signed.

Despite PB's frustrated censure of Moss for clearly preferring to "drive foreign" – in fact rejoining his 1954 team, *Officine* Maserati – Stirling wrote to Owen from his home at 20 William IV Street, London WC2, as follows, on November 21:

It is extremely difficult for me to write to you this letter and convey what I am trying to say. I know that

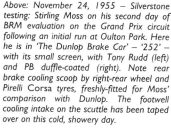

Above: November 24, 1955 – Silverstone testing: Stirling Moss on his second day of BRM evaluation on the Grand Prix circuit following an initial run at Oulton Park. Here he is in 'The Dunlop Brake Car' – '252' – with its small screen, with Tony Rudd (left) and PB duffle-coated (right). Note rear brake cooling scoop by right-rear wheel and Pirelli Corsa tyres, freshly-fitted for Moss' comparison with Dunlop. The footwell cooling intake on the scuttle has been taped over on this cold, showery day.

Left: 'The Lockheed Brake Car' – '251' – with tail body cowl removed, together with the exhaust tailpipe, exposing its welded aluminium fuel tank and the single rear disc brake's air-cooling shroud, trunk-fed from a right-side external tail scoop. The left-rear suspension's Lockheed air strut is visible; note low-mounted rear anti-roll bar, and detail inside that right-rear Dunlop wheel. Tyres are Dunlop R3s. Note close-set instruments, four-spoke steering wheel – and no Hawthorn in sight? He would test drive this car the following week.

The Silverstone tests – November 23, 1955: Peter Collins asked for more weight on '252''s front end. Arthur Hill obliges, clipping 50lb of lead onto that fabricated front bulkhead. The nose cowl's reinforced and riveted rear edge is visible on the tarpaulin, bottom right. Note divided water radiator cores with exit ducting to direct hot air away through the front suspension bay.

Right: Peter Collins prepares for his turn at the wheel as Moss steps out. He will not be rejoining BRM. Looking on (left) is RM in his familiarly sombre undertaker's overcoat, PB's duffle coat just visible (right). For many years Silverstone testing was based here in 'the layby' at the old pre-1952 start site, opposite Luffield Abbey Farm (background). Remember – this was a fateful stretch of road for BRM… Below: The loneliness of the long-distance test driver – and in such conditions results were limited. Collins in '252' pluming through the puddles past the farm. In eight months time this car will be destroyed right here.

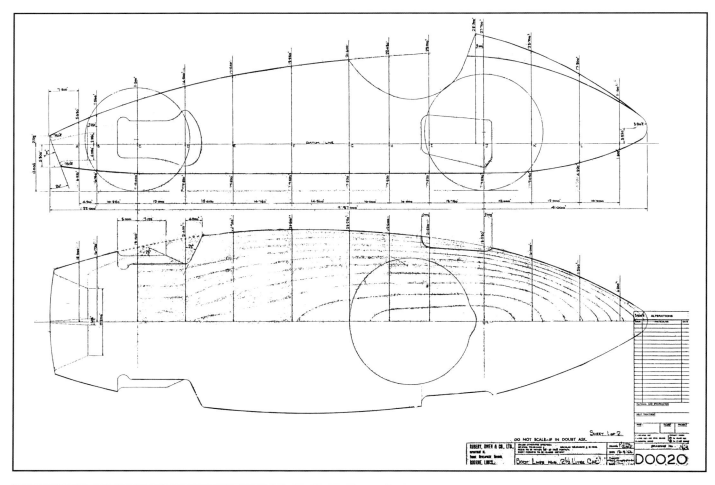

Above: As early as August 19, 1954, this body line drawing was completed for the new Formula 1 Type 25 — without a tailfin in sight…

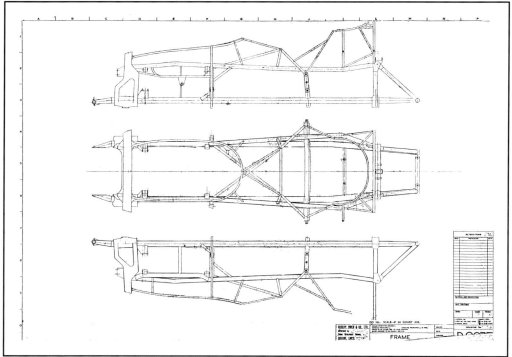

Left: Under the skin — with its stressed panelling around the cockpit area — the new Type 25 was based upon an essentially four-longeron tube frame. This is an early — undated — study of the general tube-chassis form employed for the first five cars, chassis '251'–'255' built 1955–57.

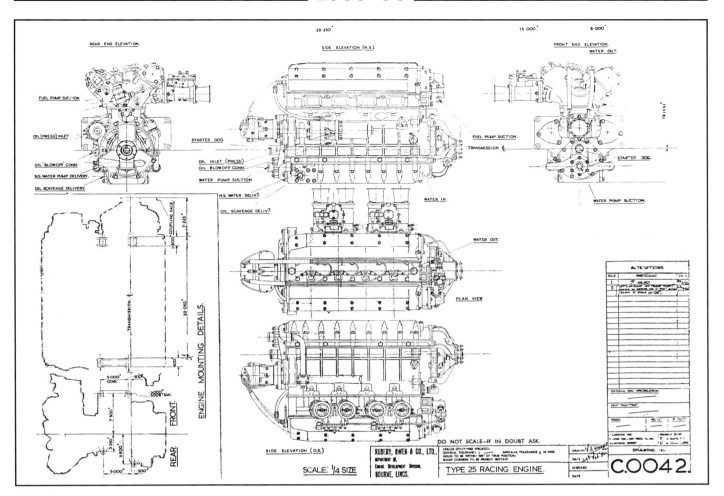

SCALE: ¼ SIZE

RUBERY, OWEN & CO., LTD.,
Department 25,
Engine Development Division,
BOURNE, LINCS.

DO NOT SCALE—IF IN DOUBT ASK.

TYPE 25 RACING ENGINE.

C.0042.

Above: Aubrey Woods' fine artistry depicts the P25 engine as of February 27, 1956. In retrospect Tony Rudd cites driving the camshafts from the loaded (clutch) end of the crank as the design's Achilles' heel. Tresilian's original idea had been to keep the front end low for an optimum bonnet line, but the drive-gear clearance humps were tiny "and not worth the trouble". Had drive been from the crankshaft nose, crank flex affecting the cam-drive gears could have been minimized. "PB cherished the belief that the more a piece cost the better it was, so he was wedded to grinding gear teeth profiles. This was fraught with danger…even Rolls-Royce only ground gears when absolutely necessary…" And BRM often found out why…

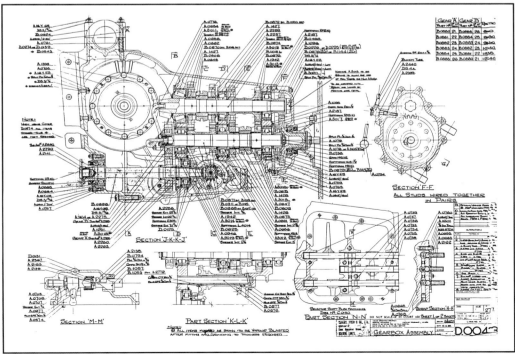

GEARBOX ASSEMBLY D.0043

Right: Alec Stokes became BRM's transmission design specialist. This drawing of August 17, 1955 details assembly of the brand-new four-speed P27 gearbox for the new Type 25 — complete with 'bacon slicer' disc brake on the tail.

you are aware of the various tests that I have had the pleasure of carrying out this week with the Vanwall, Connaught and BRM and also in Italy with the Maserati.

The first thing I must say is that I have listened to many people and have tried to remain impartial, at the same time favouring driving a British car. But after many hours of consideration I have come to the conclusion that I shall drive for Maserati this coming year…

One can sense Owen's disappointment, for by this time Moss was clearly Britain's best and of genuinely world class, but Stirling was also a lifelong car enthusiast and he continued:

I do genuinely feel that in this car you have the most potential Grand Prix car in the World and I do feel that in another 12 months the small problems will be ironed out if the car is continued at the present rate of development…the engine is wonderful but its reliability will have to be improved…more problems with the chassis because troubles are always increased when one has very high power to weight ratio.

He closed:

…I hope that my decision not to drive with you next year does not mean that BRM will not continue flat out with the development programme because I do feel this would be a great shame for a car with such potential… Whenever I am in England if there is any advice I can give to you towards setting the car up to the position where it can beat foreign opposition then I will be pleased to do so…

Owen replied:

Just as it was difficult for you to write the letter so it is hard for me to reply and say how sorry I am that you find yourself unable to drive the BRM next year for the reasons you give. It is very kind of you to write in somewhat glowing terms especially about its engine, and that if we can overcome the instability at its front then you seem to be satisfied about its future possibilities…

By that time RM had already contacted Peter Collins' great friend and rival Mike Hawthorn at his Tourist Trophy Garage business, East Street, Farnham, Surrey. The tall flat-capped, womanizing hell-raiser had won two World Championship GPs for Ferrari in 1953–54 before enduring a difficult 1955 season, split between Vanwall and Ferrari in Formula 1 and the Jaguar sports car team. He had won at Le Mans, but was vilified in some sectors for his unfortunate involvement in the disaster there which had left more than 80 dead.

Mike was anxious to join a British-based team, enabling him to run his garage business in Farnham, following the death of his father Leslie in a road accident at Whitsun 1954. The BRM team had thought highly of him ever since he had raced against their V16s in Vandervell's *Thin Wall Special*.

He agreed to try a car at Silverstone, so the Dunlop car – '252' – was prepared for him as it had last run there. The Lockheed brake car, meanwhile "…was ballasted with 60lbs on the front crossmember to bring it into front weight line with the Dunlop car. Strut pressures were altered accordingly." Peter Collins was in attendance, while RM had arranged for Ivor Bueb, Jack Fairman and Tony Marsh all to try the Owen Maserati during this test session:

SILVERSTONE TESTS, December 1st, 1955

Weather fair, strong wind; track 100% wet with large puddles: …

The best times recorded in the Dunlop car were – Hawthorn 1 min 58 secs. Collins 1 min 59 secs.

Hawthorn in the Lockheed car got down to 1:57 but Collins was not as fast on this car. Collins insisted that the Dunlop brake car particularly was not as good as when he had previously tried it (in the near dry), although no alteration whatever had been made; and both he and Hawthorn agreed that the Lockheed car was easier to handle, although Collins was actually slower than with the other car.

Collins had a further run on the Dunlop car…did not better his 1:59…stopped round the course with gearbox trouble, which resolved into no drive in top gear.

The Lockheed brakes were beginning to give trouble, as on the front the calipers were rubbing the discs…As dry weather tests were essential, it was arranged to continue the following day…overnight the front discs on the Lockheed car were reduced to give adequate clearance.

Next day: Course 100% wet with puddles. As Hawthorn was officially testing the '56 Jaguar Le Mans type car, our running was delayed until after mid-day, when the course was still wet, but most of the larger puddles had been cleared up.

The Dunlop brake car was not available due to gearbox trouble; but the Lockheed car was run consistently by Hawthorn…rear rebound damping reduced…1 min 57 secs.

Running was terminated in the late afternoon with engine trouble on this car. The cars returned to Bourne.

Hawthorn's reaction to the car generally was that it was extremely fast, but difficult to drive under wet conditions, particularly on accelerating away from corners, as the back tended to come round, he considered, far too easily, even allowing for the fact that the power to weight ratio was a great deal better than with any previous 2½-litre car he had tried.

Post-test inspection then revealed stripped teeth on top gear in the Dunlop-braked '252', and severe engine damage in the Lockheed-braked '251': …cylinder head and crankcase being a 'write-off'…the soft valve stems having picked up very badly at the top of the valve guides and travel limiters, so that several of the limiters had been riding up and down with the valve stem, causing the valve springs to break – one inlet valve with both springs broken had the head knocked off by a piston causing the final mishap.

After this salutary lesson, all soft-stem valves were despatched for nitriding while a small quantity of hard-stem inlet valves had at last arrived from Motor Components. The original cast-iron inlet valve guides were also changed for aluminium bronze, offering better anti-scuff characteristics.

A former Norton engineer named E.G.R. Welch had joined ORO briefly, and he recommended use of a 'tulip' valve shape which had increased power significantly when applied to the motorcycle unit. The valve head would, of course, be heavy, but this could be minimized by making it hollow and sealing it with a welded-in disc which became known as 'the penny'. These new tulip valves provided an extra 5-8bhp on the test-bed, but they were difficult to make, deliveries were slow and as the 1956 season began they were in very short supply.

All this work contributed to a '1956' engine spec for a new assembly series of P25 units which would be numbered '2561', '2562' etc, compared with the original 1955 '251', '252' style.

Amongst driver comments the greatest complaints had been that the clutch pedal was too heavy, the steering a shade too light "…and all drivers complain there is too much movement in the gear change, fore and aft and side to side across the gate…movement is being reduced on all cars".

Chassis '252' 's engine had now exceeded 2,000 hard miles, but: "The most serious of the drivers' complaints is the question of handling", but wet weather had robbed the team of any dry circuit test time whatsoever.

Meanwhile, pondering on these Silverstone test sessions, Tony appreciated that the V16-originated air-strut suspension medium had too much internal 'stiction' for the ultra-light Type 25 it was now supporting. PB authorized testing which began at Folkingham to find how strut stiction varied with movement and also the cars' precise centre of gravity under varying conditions of fuel load and driver weight, to enable weight transfer to be properly calculated. He reported:

> This will show whether we still have suspension at minimum weight conditions… Apart from fidgetiness on the front end, there is a marked tendency towards oversteer on the rear end. The geometry of both the front and the back have been checked with the greatest care; and we are quite certain that neither of these effects are due to inaccurate geometry. However, it seems important to resolve the problem of the front end first, which should make any back end trouble more apparent, and the causes easier to trace.

Test results showed that due to high weight transference from front to rear under flat-out acceleration, the front suspension ran out of spring movement "hence the car remained in effectively a stiff-legged attitude until the rate of acceleration decreased. This gave rise to a lack of steering that drivers had referred to as a 'twitch'."

The V16-derived Lockheed air struts were clearly too large in capacity for the lightweight new contender. Tony: It dawned on us that while the suspension was cold the roadholding was horrible. It was not until the air in the struts had warmed up that it became bearable. We had to set up the struts cold at a pressure which left the car sitting on its bump rubbers, but as it ran and the air within the struts warmed-up so pressure

increased and the car would rise up to its normal ride level rather like a Citroen DS.

I did a number of experiments forcing the suspension up and down against a known load. There was a difference of between 60 and 80lbs between the wheel rising and falling. I plotted a curve of suspension movement against known load, then removed the load and in theory the two curves should have followed, but there was a huge difference in places, and this was obviously loss within the air struts. So I conducted a campaign to get rid of them.

This was handicapped by the ultra-light 2lb struts being much admired by PB. But while they had operated reasonably well on the one-ton V16 they were showing their limitations on the half-ton Type 25.

So initially, as PB recorded:

> A hook-up arrangement was made using an additional pull off steel spring which exerted its maximum load at full rebound, and practically no load at static…overall effect being to reduce the rebound spring performance by approximately 100lbs per wheel.

Tony: Suspension and steering theory and the science of setting-up a racing car was a black art in those days. There was nothing like the published works available which there would be just 10 years later, and there were really only two people in Britain who seemed to understand it – David Hodkin, who had just left the postwar ERA concern, and Colin Chapman, of Lotus Engineering. Hodkin published an IME paper entitled *The Nature of Steering* which I avidly devoured and applied to the 2½-litre and evolved theories which fitted the known facts. Sadly, I used them to condemn the air struts whereas in fact they told us the geometry was dreadful.

It was therefore decided to concentrate upon suspension improvement. Tony advocated a transverse leafspring with enormous bump rubbers like the 250F. PB preferred torsion bars. They shared dark suspicions about the rear roll-centre. That at the front was some 5in above the road, but due to the sliding block in the de Dion system the rear roll-centre was something like 9in higher.

Meanwhile, the shattering news had broken that Collins had just signed – unannounced – with Ferrari. RM reached agreement with Mike Hawthorn to replace him and Alfred Owen also wrote to Mike upon Ray's insistence (December 13, 1955):

> Dear Hawthorn,
> I should like to say that it is my personal ambition to produce a Grand Prix car driven by an Englishman to win the World Championship for your country. If you should join with us I can assure you that all possible will be done in an endeavour to meet these ends, and I feel sure that your association with BRM will be a happy one…

After expending so much care on nurturing the coy Peter Collins, Owen had been appalled – and the lads in Lincolnshire deeply dismayed – when the first they heard of his joining Ferrari was when they read about it in the national press.

Running tests were resumed at Silverstone with Hawthorn and the find of the 1955 season, C.A.S. 'Tony' Brooks…

Slim, serious, dedicated and a quite brilliant if then inexperienced driver, Tony Brooks had just made his name when invited to handle one of the money-strapped Connaught team's B-Types in the far away Syracuse GP in Sicily on November 1. There he had simply run away from a full-strength Maserati entry, and had achieved for Connaught what RM, PB, Owen and all BRM supporters had craved so long – he had scored the first all-British victory in a premier-Formula Continental race since Henry Segrave and Sunbeam had won at San Sebastian in 1924!

Ray had contacted Brooks at his Dukinfield, Cheshire, home almost immediately he returned from Sicily, and he had agreed to test drive for BRM alongside the established star – Mike Hawthorn.

1956 – IF AT FIRST YOU DON'T SUCCEED...

The old year had closed with continuing attempts to complete some sensible track testing. At Silverstone on December 29–30, little running was achieved due to continuing rain, but "Hawthorn remarked that the front end was very much improved, but now the front end was behaving the rear end showed a marked inclination to oversteer in accelerating out of corners. Tony Brooks lapped in similar times......and liked the handling of the car, and on the whole thought it easier to drive than the Connaught with which he won at Syracuse... it is generally agreed by drivers that the overall car performance is extremely good".

Meanwhile, the Lockheed-braked '251' had been out of service since its Silverstone engine failure, and it was now modified at the rear to carry a clever form of swing-axle independent rear suspension which PB hoped would work, and was patentable. It "appeared to give the advantages of the present successful Mercedes system, coupled with a low roll centre".

It was very similar to designs adopted later – c.late 1959 – for the E-Type Jaguar and Lotus 18. It used fixed-length half-shafts with UJs at each end which comprised the upper link of the suspension and located the wheels laterally. Lower location was by a massive 'N'-shaped link which carried the hub, formed the lower wishbone and also pushed the car along, its forward extension preventing the rear wheel toeing-in. This system retained the air strut 'spring', but "the snag was that in those days we didn't know anything about jacking loads, which on this system were fearful...".

The engine from '252' went into '251' while the strutting arrangement was altered with a linkage to exploit the rapidly decreasing strut movement against wheel movement, with a high strut compression ratio enabling full rebound loads to be reduced without impairing spring bump performance.

Continuing wet weather permitted only three car tests before the end of January 1956. Brooks drove PB's swing-axle car in the dry, with icy patches, at Folkingham, and cut BRM's lap record there from 1:43 to 1:41.6. But Tony Rudd has vivid memories of Brooks rounding sharp corners with the car's outer rear wheel almost tucked right under by jacking load:

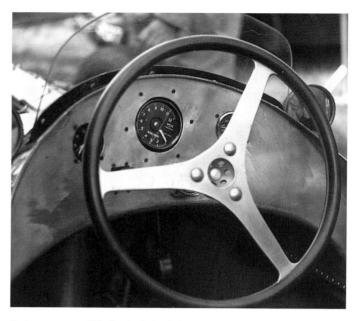

Dash arrangement of 'The Dunlop Brake Car' – '252' – was simplicity in the extreme, with abbreviated Perspex windscreen, oil pressure, tachometer and combined water and oil temperature gauges – distinctively different from the wider-screened, wider-spaced layout on 'The Lockheed Brake Car' – '251'.

Had we made it two or three years later we would have been on to a good thing. Unfortunately, we didn't know enough about suspension systems and jacking loads and abandoned it.

PB merely admitted: "The rear end appeared remarkably good on slow corners, but has a tendency to step out on fast ones under acceleration. This is believed due to considerable change of camber on the rear wheels in roll."

Meanwhile, the final set of first-series 1955-style engine castings had been built up into a new engine, which first ran on the Folkingham dyno at the end of December. It accumulated 20 hours running under full load, continuous refinements achieving 15–20 per cent extra power from 4,000 to 8,000rpm and developing over 270bhp. Importantly, after eventual strip-down no replacements were required. It was reassembled and installed in the Dunlop brake car – '252'.

A virtually identical new car, '253', was also being completed at Folkingham into April 1956; 7ft 3in wheelbase again, fitted with Lockheed brakes and with the carburettor air intake feed drawn from the centre division in the radiator intake. These two cars were then prepared for ORO's first home race of the new season at Goodwood.

April 2, 1956 – BARC Richmond Trophy, Goodwood – 32 laps, 76.8 miles

The newer car for Hawthorn wasn't ready in time for Saturday practice, so he drove '252' instead and qualified third fastest on the front row of the starting grid, slower than Moss' Maserati 250F and Archie Scott-Brown's B-Type Connaught, but ahead of Bob Gerard's B-Type. Tony Brooks qualified in the same car, which he would be driving on raceday so his

Right: ORO's convoy outside the pub at Goodwood; Arthur Ambrose heading for the Commer's cab, the Austin Lodestars behind. While it may have appeared that BRM had an army at most races, many (not here) were hangers-on, while lack of pit passes and budget inhibited useful numbers. RM would corner passes for friends while suggesting team supernumeries "should wear overalls and talk their way in" or "should hide in the transporter". Finally, someone's girlfriend was apprehended crossing the track at Monaco, wearing a brassard issued personally to RM. BRM came close to exclusion from the Grand Prix! Peter Spear reported in detail to AGBO. "Things became easier thereafter…"

Below: A powerful thirst for work; race mechanics are all the same – great pals Dick Salmon and Maurice Dove show what their right arms are for while ex-RAF Corporal Phil Ayliff outdoes them both…

time should have been the one which counted, leaving Hawthorn to start from the back of the grid. But RM worked a flanker with the organizers, who believed what was primarily Mike's car had been driven by Tony, thus relegating him instead to starting from the back row, although it would be Mike driving a different car on the Monday.

Of the race *Autosport* reported:

> Hawthorn's getaway was electrifying and into Madgwick the B.R.M. led narrowly from Scott-Brown and the Maserati…through the Chicane in a tight bunch, still with the compact little B.R.M. ahead – by inches. Then Scott-Brown sprinted past, and so did Moss, while Tony Brooks in the second B.R.M. now began ripping through the field in support of Hawthorn.

In fact Hawthorn had had his car jump out of top gear while tearing down the Lavant Straight, revs soaring and a valve just tipping a piston crown, with little effect. Tony Brooks ran sixth duelling with Salvadori's venerable Greene Maserati only to suffer a fuel pump failure, retiring after nine laps. On lap 16 Moss displaced the irrepressible Scott-Brown as the Connaught's brakes were weakening, and next time round the Alta-engined British car's crankshaft broke on the

fast approach to Woodcote Corner, and Archie skated off onto the verge, out of the race.

This left Hawthorn secure in second place, but with nine laps to go – disaster. Mike told the story like this: "The car was becoming a bit difficult to hold and suddenly, while I was doing over 100 m.p.h. near Fordwater, it started to slide. Correction had no effect and the car spun round in the road while I held on tight. Then I felt it hit the earth as it left the track and I knew it was going to overturn. I must get out. I let go of everything just as it pitched into the air and I felt myself being thrown out. There was a split second of panic as my ankle jammed between the seat and the chassis. The car was cartwheeling over – quite slowly it seemed – and I knew I must break free before it landed again or I should be finished. Suddenly there was a feeling of utter relief. I had broken free and was alone in mid-air. It was quiet and I seemed to be floating in space, defying the law of gravity. Then came the bone-jarring shock as I hit the ground.

"I got my breath back after a few moments, but there was a sharp pain in my ankle as I tried to stand. I sat there rather dazed, trying to figure out what had happened.

"The car was some distance away badly crumpled, with its wheels in the air. But there were only three wheels. One of the front wheels had been torn off as it landed after the first somersault…I was certainly lucky for I was the only survivor in three crashes that day…"

Autosport reported that "the offside rear wheel broke away and the car overturned", to the ORO executives' mortified rage! Years of suffering BRM brickbats had stretched their skins thin and sensitive… But this was demonstrably untrue.

The Type 25's transmission half-shafts were, of course, articulated to accommodate changes of angularity as the suspension rose and fell, plus alterations in length as the geometry of wheel movement on each end of their linking de Dion tube obviously differed from the swinging arc described by the half-shafts around their inboard ends, attached to the chassis-mounted final-drive.

BRM had adopted the traditional pot-joint method, employing a large cylinder each side driven from the final-drive, with two deep slots cut into it, in which slid two sturdy

bronze blocks revolving upon a wrist-pin which passed through the half-shaft's inboard end. At Goodwood, a rubber sealing gaiter retaining lubricant around this sliding pot-joint at the inboard end of the right-side half-shaft had split, permitting the lubricant to centrifuge away. The joint had then heated-up as it dried, until it finally seized, locking the suspension under load and causing the instantaneous flick-oversteer which had projected Hawthorn broadside onto the plough...

Fortunately he had escaped virtually unhurt, the car was not too badly damaged and between them they had put up the fastest standing-start lap ever recorded at Goodwood in 1min 35sec, and Mike's best flying race lap of 1:30.6 was only 0.2sec outside Moss' new lap record with the fuel-injected Maserati 250F.

At least the BRM Type 25 was clearly competitive...and in only its second race, too.

ORO's investigation of the failure which could so easily have killed Mike Hawthorn took some time, and in the interim the pot-joint lubricant-retaining boot which had split was replaced by assorted new joint covers leading temporarily to a very small rubber gaiter, sealed by fitting over PTFE-impregnated toughened bushes running on the shaft itself.

Rubery Owen's Research Department now became involved in investigating the original boot failure, which brought its head, engineer Peter Spear, into close contact with BRM racing affairs. Tony: Peter Spear, Director of Research, Rubery Owen, had first come on the scene in early 1953 when AGBO brought him along on a visit to Bourne. AGB told us the newly appointed Spear was there to help with his facilities and contacts, and was not to interfere unless we asked for his help. He did go a little further in a 1954 conversation with me, saying that with 40 major companies in the Rubery Owen Group he

needed someone to advise him on engineering matters.

However, by 1956 the battle lines had been drawn between him and PB, who looked upon Spear as a "spy and trouble maker" and had warned me to watch my step. He never missed a chance to emphasize Spear's inexperience and lack of knowledge of motor racing, especially of engines. Spear was extremely sensitive to jibes about lack of experience. He was younger than I, and over 15 years younger than PB, and took elaborate precautions to ensure no-one at Bourne ever found out. For his part he zeroed-in on PB's lack of academic

Above: April 2, 1956 – Richmond Trophy, Goodwood: Mike Hawthorn rips '253' into an immediate lead, clipping the apex here at Madgwick as he briefly leads Archie Scott-Brown's Connaught and Moss' ultimately victorious fuel-injected Maserati 250F.

Right and below: Goodwood infield – not so badly damaged as it looks by Hawthorn's 23rd-lap roll, the brand-new '253' was rapidly repaired. Autosport reported the car's offside-rear wheel had broken away. ORO were incensed – Gregor Grant published a correction the following week.

qualifications. He had considerable metallurgical knowledge and rubbed this in hard. I never was quite sure whether he had the level of AGB's confidence and freedom of access he claimed. He and PB were evenly matched. I had learned enough company politics at Rolls-Royce to realize I was in a very exposed position. I was accused of providing Spear with damaging information by PB, and by Spear of covering up for PB and RM. But there is no question that during the period covered by this volume, Spear personally, and his department, made a valuable contribution, which far outweighed the time-wasting in-fighting he caused.

Where the pot-joint investigation was concerned, the Research Department's high-speed photography techniques would eventually isolate the cause of the Goodwood failure. Polished areas had been found on the car's frame tubes and adjacent gearchange linkage as much as 3 or 4 inches clear of the pot-joint. They seemed inexplicable. Now high-speed photography of the boot running at anything above 1,500rpm – representing 150mph road speed – on Folkingham's Ward-Lennard test rig revealed all the oil or grease collecting in one lump, stretching out the boot into an enormous gumboil which then flailed around in unison with the rotating joint, ready to chafe and burst against any obstruction. This

Cause of the Easter Monday accident – the racially un-self-conscious Rubery Owen Research Department of 1956 dubbed this 'The Nigger's Knackers Photograph' – all the pot-joint boot's grease centrifuges out in one blob on the high-speed test rig...

triumph of laboratory investigation produced what Peter Spear imaginatively – if somewhat insensitively – referred to ever after as "the nigger's knackers photo".

On Saturday, April 7, ORMA members were invited to Folkingham to meet 'their' team and inspect the new car. Over 700 attended, meeting RM, PB, Tony Rudd and Basil Putt, while Mike Hawthorn flew himself in at the controls of his Fairchild Argus light 'plane. Tony Brooks – the erstwhile

dental student – more prosaically drove himself up at the controls of his Standard 10...

Tony Rudd warmed-up one of the cars and both team drivers then completed some rapid demonstration laps around the test circuit. Two weeks later, fitted with interim pot-joint covers, two cars were prepared for the non-Championship BARC 200-Miles race at Aintree, in Liverpool, and were tested briefly at Silverstone.

Mike Hawthorn: "I did a few laps in Brooks' car first and then went out in mine. I had only done a few laps, and was just coming into the straight before the pits when things happened so quickly I literally did not know what hit me. The bonnet had come off, hit me in the face, smashed my visor and almost knocked me unconscious. Dazed and groggy I somehow managed to stop the car, although I nearly lost consciousness...it turned out that the bonnet was not the one belonging to my car; it had been put on by mistake and did not fit properly. My luck was in, because if it had come round at a different angle it could have taken my head off..."

His cut face was dressed at Northampton Hospital, where the doctor wanted to stitch it, but Mike refused. He did a few

Above: Saturday, April 7, 1956 – ORMA members' day at Folkingham. Mike Hawthorn demonstrates 'their car' on the perimeter test track after flying himself up from Fairoaks, Surrey, and landing on the '2,000-yard runway'. In contrast to the established Grand Prix and Le Mans-winning superstar, his team-mate Tony Brooks had motored up in a Standard 10...

Left: Some 700 ORMA members attended that day. Here with '252', RM mingles (left), Tony Rudd, Tony Brooks, mechanic Reg Smith, Mike Hawthorn and Gordon Newman (right). Several fitters were seconded to the Race Shop for Type 25 production and some won a trial as race mechanics. "Most saw the light and left" – but one of the best was Reg Smith, who made a speciality of painting bodies and coined the description of the original P27 oil system as being "like a cheap Japanese toy..." He later set up a garage business specializing in high-performance cars.

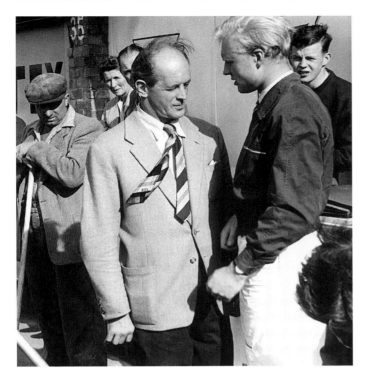

A grimmer mood behind the Silverstone pits – Mike Hawthorn was never a man to keep his feelings to himself; PB bore the brunt of some fearful tongue lashings when things went wrong – as they often did on Hawthorn's cars through the troubled spring of 1956…

more laps back at Silverstone on the old fighter pilot principle of flying again immediately after a bad fright, and then set off for Farnham, probably pondering his wisdom in having joined this crazy team…

Meanwhile, at Folkingham, chassis '251' was being lengthened and rebuilt as a 7ft 6in-wheelbase 'Hawthorn Special', tailored to accommodate the strapping six-footer's long legs. The car was equipped with rocking-lever air-strut front suspension (see later), Connaught link de Dion location, a short ram air intake for the carburettors, and would uniquely carry low-level rear-axle after-fairings along each side of its tail.

April 21, 1956 – BARC International Aintree '200', Liverpool – 67 laps, 201 miles

In practice at Aintree, Hawthorn's best with '253' was 2:04.0. "The B.R.M.s were very fast and the brakes were powerful, but they were still not very happy in the corners." His car's front brakes seemed erratic. The system was re-bled and evidence suggesting fluid vaporization was found in the pipeline to the rear caliper. As practice lasted only 40 minutes there was no further opportunity to test the car.

Back at the garage, PB discussed the problem with Lockheed's rep when it was found that his people had fitted a non-return valve in the rear caliper line to facilitate bleeding. With the BRM system that valve created back pressure as the

fluid warmed-up, which then held the brake on, to rub continuously. This accounted for the overheating and fluid vaporization. The guilty valve was removed and an air scoop fitted to the tail, directing air onto the caliper hydraulic cylinder – just in case.

The *ORMA Bulletin No.15's* race report then described how, on raceday:

> Archie Scott-Brown led initially followed by the two B.R.M.s but Hawthorn soon came by to take the lead. Hawthorn entered the 4th lap in first place but suffered a complete brake failure at Anchor Crossing. He managed to run off the circuit safely and toured to the pits where the car was retired. Brooks then took up the chase and driving beautifully took the lead after 13 laps when Scott-Brown's Connaught retired. At this stage in the race [he] appeared to have the legs of any of the other cars, but towards the end of the race the brakes started to fail and Moss started to close up with his privately entered Maserati…eventually driving without any brakes at all (Brooks made a hurried call at the pits) nothing could be done…Moss sailed past into the lead and Brooks, still driving almost brakeless, went on to finish a magnificent 2nd, a lap behind.

Hawthorn: "I made a good start, but left my braking rather late at one corner and was so busy concentrating on holding the car straight that I did not have time to change down. By the time I had got the lower gear in, Archie Scott-Brown had whipped past. I managed to get past him again on the straight…However, he was pressing me hard when I tried to brake going into Cottage Corner [*sic*]. But there *were* no brakes; not only that, there was no pedal! I stamped my foot down again, thinking I must have missed the pedal, but all I succeeded in doing was catching my foot against the accelerator and I went careering off the road onto the open grassland."

As the team discovered: "I was in a towering fury as I motored slowly back to the pits and I did not spare anyone's feelings. We found that the clevis pin connecting the pedal to the brake gear had dropped out; apparently because it had no split pin to hold it…"

Perhaps amazingly, Hawthorn was to recall: "Despite all our troubles I still had great faith in the B.R.M. as I was convinced that its defects were curable in a few months of concentrated development work and I persuaded Mr. Owen to enter one car for me in the International Trophy…"

Tony: That brake pedal clevis dropped out because one of the mechanics – who was then banished from the racing team in consequence – had failed to fit a special circlip correctly, and not unnaturally Mike was very worked up about it!

PB's report at the time tells a slightly different story:

> [It] was due to a pin breaking in the toggles linkage in the pedal and the twin master cylinder arrangement. Unfortunately the remnants of the pin have not been found, so the matter is not proven…Lockheeds have agreed that their twin type master cylinder is not entirely satisfactory in this installation. We have

now…refused to use it for further racing, and they have agreed to use the Dunlop type master cylinder, which is a simple tandem arrangement without any linkage…it provides a safer system, since the servo will be applied direct to the rear brakes, so that in case of servo failure, the driver has front brakes available.

Tony Brooks' Dunlop-brake car – '252' – suffered a different problem:

> The rear brake pads were not retracting properly, as the trouble which we had with the Maserati… consequently, the pads were rubbing the discs continually, putting heat into the calipers. The hydraulic piston rubbers overheated and charred, causing a complete loss of fluid from the rear caliper (servo system) during the race. When he stopped at the pits…since he had front brakes under direct foot operation, but without servo, I permitted the car to continue. The caliper has been returned to Dunlops…

In the course of Dunlop's investigation with Mintex they identified the high disc rubbing speed as the cause of the problem (see PB's earlier letter to Kinchin). A reduction gear was added at the back of the gearbox to reduce the disc speed by about 35%, which incidentally dropped the disc some four inches closer to the road and limited the option of increasing disc size to increase brake capacity in later years. Ferodo, when approached by PB, confirmed that rubbing speed was too high. Why the lining manufacturers had not warned against excessive rubbing speed earlier is not recorded…

Whatever trust Hawthorn had ever had in ORO and their BRM car was being rapidly eroded. It would not recover, although when the car felt good and he was on form he certainly drove it rapidly. But after the bonnet incident and this brake pedal affair he then spent much time watching his car being finish-prepared in the race paddocks.

The Silverstone May meeting was being held on May 5, the Monaco Grand Prix – first European round of that year's World Championship – following on the 13th. Two cars – '251' and '252' – were prepared for Monaco, the third to provide a lone entry for Hawthorn at Silverstone the previous weekend.

May 5, 1956 – BRDC *Daily Express* International Trophy, Silverstone – 60 laps, 175.61 miles

Mike was again forced to fold himself into the cramped cockpit of the repaired short-wheelbase '253' for this outing, and despite being in considerable discomfort his best practice time of 1:43.0 matched Fangio's best in one of the works Lancia-Ferraris and put him on the front row of the grid. Both were bettered, however, by Tony Vandervell's two Vanwalls in their latest teardrop-bodied guise, making their debut in the hands of Moss (in a one-off drive since Maserati had not entered) and Harry Schell. Both had clocked 1:42s.

Rivers Fletcher's *ORMA Bulletin No.15* report reads:

May 5, 1956 – BRDC International Trophy, Silverstone: Hawthorn was cramped and uncomfortable in the standard-chassis Type 25s, but when they were on song he went like the wind – '252' here leads the race which had been won the previous year by his bosom buddy Peter Collins in the Owen Maserati. Mike will lead the first 12 laps and set fastest lap, but his engine's timing gears will strip and it will cut dead at Club Corner.

Fangio was first into Copse, but Hawthorn was already in the lead by the time they reached Stowe and the crowd in the grand stand there rose as one man to cheer. This happened again when Hawthorn came past the grand stand opposite the pits with a commanding lead. For 12 laps Hawthorn held a magnificent lead [but] by Club Corner the B.R.M.'s engine suddenly cut dead. A timing gear had stripped its teeth.

In the stirring but apologist style which had become so familiar during the V16 era, Rivers declared:

> None of us will ever forget those terrific opening laps of speed which must have contributed to Fangio's eventual failure in the works Ferrari.

He concluded:

> Stirling Moss went on to score a notable British victory in the Vanwall.

Tony Vandervell – the old hard-nosed adversary – had succeeded where ORO was continuing to fail. It must have hurt. But at least, while it lasted, the latest BRM was stupendous to watch – and to drive – and it was clearly as fast as both the new Vanwall and also the works Lancia-Ferrari V8s. Mike had lowered the Silverstone lap record to 1:43, 102.30mph, a mark which Moss subsequently equalled several times in the Vanwall.

Hawthorn was impressed: "At the start, Fangio went into Copse ahead of me, but as I came out of the corner in third gear I pulled out, put my foot down and just left him on acceleration. It shook me almost as much as it did him. The performance was absolutely terrific and I pulled away, putting in one lap in 1 min. 43 sec. to set up an official record at 102.3mph which was equalled but not beaten by the Vanwalls.

"I was debating how long I could stick it, however, for… I was in increasing pain from the cramped driving position. However, the problem was solved on the 13th lap. The engine cut and my race was over…

"The remarkable thing was that the car had showed performance equal to anything else on the track although I was holding the engine down to 8,000r.p.m., compared to the 9,000r.p.m. limit permitted at Goodwood…because a slightly heavier type of valve was being used…"

His engine had stripped the teeth off its No. 1 timing gear. Unfortunately, the engines up to then had been built with less backlash between No. 1 timing gear and the crank gear than the hot crankshaft bearing clearance demanded. PB developed a theory that Tres' four-bearing crank was writhing about, but with Peter Spear's help, the Test House had already acquired a Sunbury Indicator which had an adaptor for torsional vibration analysis, and this proved that the crank ran remarkably quietly. In fact when PB introduced a five-bearing crank in 1958 a similar test showed it moved *more* than the four-bearing crank. However, it took much longer than it should to adjust the clearances in the drivetrain, despite No. 1 gear location being made adjustable on eccentrics.

Immediately after this promising but delusive Silverstone outing, Hawthorn flew himself down to Monaco in his Fairchild accompanied by his friend Neil McNab, who would many years later head Texaco's Formula 1 sponsorship involvement. Their journey occupied three days with enjoyable stops in Paris and Lyons…but they were bound for a BRM debacle of the type not seen since the Italian GP disaster of 1951…

May 11–12, 1956 – Monaco Grand Prix practice, Monte Carlo

Denis Jenkinson outlined what happened to BRM as follows in his annual *Racing Car Review*:

Two cars were sent, with Hawthorn and Brooks their drivers, both cars now having Lockheed brakes, but from the very first moment of practice nothing went right and the engines just would not give their usual brilliant performance. [Their] exceptionally large bore was to enable a giant-sized inlet valve to be used, in conjunction with the proportionally large ports and carburettors, this breathing system allowing very high r.p.m. to be used. With the head of the valve being nearly 2¼ inches diameter, a solid forged valve would have been of unwieldy weight and would have limited the r.p.m., so in consequence the head of the valve was hollow and the open end sealed by a washer. Mechanically the system was perfectly satisfactory, but variations in combustion temperature across the head of the valve were critical. On the engines built for Monte Carlo the same type of valves were being used, but before practice was finished the valves had suffered distortion and the sealing washer had dropped out. In an air of despondency the team returned to England without even starting in the race,

and while observers were getting used to the B.R.M.s running into trouble, it was unusual to see them packing up without even making a show…

Tony: The Monte Carlo street circuit saw the engines spending a lot of time on the over-run with the throttle closed, and this caused valves to stretch and lose compression. Then eventually pieces came out of the valves. These tulip valves had proved extremely difficult to make so they were in very short supply. We had three engines at Monaco, one in each car plus a spare, and we had plenty of the old-type valves known as 'nails', but they tended to distort and lose compression.

We were staying at quite a pleasant hotel towards the Casino, not far from the *Chatham Bar*, but I only saw it to unpack, and then to pack again for the trip home. First practice began and soon both cars were in the pits with loss of compression.

Hawthorn: "I practised with the B.R.M. and it went very well, except for a slight delay in picking up after the Station hairpin. But suddenly the engine went woolly and we had to have the head off…"

Tony: When we removed the plugs they were battered, indicating something horrible had happened inside the cylinder. It was pretty obvious what that might be. We had a medical introscope which we inserted through a plug hole and sure enough there in each engine was one of the sealing pennies from the inlet valve embedded in the piston crown.

We changed the spare engine over to tulip valves before fitting it so Hawthorn could run in the second day's practice and repaired the least damaged of the other two units. We telephoned Bourne for other engines to be built-up there with old valves and flown out to us in a chartered De Havilland Dove. But by the end of second practice it was obvious we were not going to get away with it, and after a second all-nighter fitting the engines flown out from England we realized we were not going to be in the hunt in any case.

Hawthorn's best time was 1:49.3 and Brooks' 1:50.4 compared with Fangio's 1:44s in the pole position Lancia-Ferrari, or even the Vanwalls of Schell and Trintignant which comfortably managed '45s.

Tony: We looked pathetic, so the cars were withdrawn and those of us deemed vital to the engine operation piled into the Dove to be flown home that Saturday evening. It was a diabolical five-hour flight, the aircraft so noisy sleep was impossible, but it was what we all needed desperately…

Hawthorn recalled this debacle sympathetically: "We could have patched up the engines sufficiently to start in the race and collect the starting money, a dodge which is sometimes practised…but Raymond Mays acted with exemplary integrity. He told the organizers frankly that the cars could not last the distance, withdrew them from the race and paid me what I would have received as my share of the starting money."

The dismayed Tony Rudd subsequently – on May 16 – listed "Monte Carlo – Faults" for cars '252' and '253' in addition to the valve trouble.

They included: Cracking of the rear camshaft pedestal bosses on the inlet side of the cylinder head of Engine '2561' – a steady increase in sparking plug gap. Plugs which had done some 15 practice laps showed a gap increase ranging from .004" to .008" – oil leaks from the cylinder head to block joint,

May 11, 1956 – Monaco Grand Prix practice, Monte Carlo: '253' for Hawthorn and '252' for Brooks stand silent in the quayside pits, subsiding in terminal valve trouble, forcing BRM to non-start in their second consecutive World Championship Grand Prix – their first had been the Italian race four and a half long years earlier. In effect, only the Owen Maserati had kept ORO in Grand Prix practise…

particularly at the rear, although the magnitude of the leaks was nothing like as much as that to which we have been accustomed – two cases of oil leakage from the gearbox, No. 27/2 again leaked badly from the left-hand side pot joint, where it had been salvaged, No. 27/4 leaked from a porous patch between the brake reduction rear mounting flange and casting proper, painting with Araldite reduced the leak by about 50 per cent – needle roller bearing propeller shaft universal joint appeared to behave very well – brake trouble on No. 3 car appears to be associated with the master cylinder, as changing the cylinder cured the trouble for the few laps put in by Brooks on Saturday morning, 12th May, 1956 – variation in the calibration of the strut pumps, as the struts on both cars read about 8% lower when checked after running with one pump after they had been inflated with the other…the drivers only complained of one car's handling, although both were at fault, when the strut pressures on both cars were brought up to 190lbs on the gauge we normally use, there were no further complaints. Fuel pressure gauges were also in error, the method of clipping the pot joint rubbers was still ineffective – header tank relief valves were faulty on No. 2 car as twice they had to add nearly a quart of water, yet during second practice when the car covered the greater distance the water level remained constant. The French fuel checked at 19 degrees C showed a specific gravity of .762 as against .765 for fresh fuel checked at Folkingham at 14 degrees C. This seems to show that we need another check in addition to specific gravity. New starter shafts were required since the present type sheared through the first taper pin hole."

As an immediate valve problem palliative, some solid KE965 valves were made with a modestly dished head.

Obviously, they were extremely heavy so the stems were drilled and part-filled with sodium then sealed with a plug screwed-in, lightly welded over and then machined. These became known as the "semi-solid" valves, and their adoption reduced safe engine speed from around 9,000rpm to 8,000.

PB detailed Tony Rudd to investigate ways of compensating for the horsepower lost by adding nitro methane to the normal BPK 50/35/15 fuel mix of AvGas 2/methanol/acetone.

Ten per cent nitro was added initially, dyno runs showing an immediate 7.5 per cent increase in power without ill effects. Having lost very little at the bottom end of the rev range this was a useful gain in mid-range torque. Trying 15 per cent nitro generated a 10 per cent power bonus and it was not until 17.5 per cent nitro was added that power ceased to rise. But nitro-methane is heavy and its presence increases consumption, which means more fuel must be carried on the startline, raising the car's weight.

Tony Rudd tested one of the short-wheelbase cars on 7.5 per cent nitro at Folkingham and found it squatted so violently under maximum acceleration that its front wheels almost lifted clear of the road: You could swing the steering wheel left and right without really deflecting the car at all when accelerating flat-out in second gear at around 85–90mph!

In the aftermath of the Monaco fiasco, ORO's entries were cancelled for both the Belgian GP on June 3 and the French GP on July 1. The British GP became the next major target, at Silverstone on July 14, but partly to give Tony Brooks a little more experience and partly to test the brakes again on a notoriously punishing course, a lone prior entry was made in the BARC's National Midsummer Meeting at Aintree.

June 23, 1956 – BARC National Aintree '100', Liverpool – 34 laps, 102 miles

Despite the BRM entry for Brooks being promoted quite heavily by the organizing club, ORO gave such low priority to this event that their car was delivered to Aintree barely in time for Friday afternoon practice, direct from a morning test session at Silverstone.

Max Boyd reported what happened to the Type 25 for *Autosport*:

At first, it positively refused to start at all, despite all sorts of pushing and cajoling. Then, when it did, Tony Brooks put in three or four fairly slow laps, a faster one, and then the fastest of the day, in 2mins 4.8secs. But the engine obviously hated every moment of it, for it stretched a valve, and the car was taken back to Bourne, after a total elapsed time at Aintree of perhaps two hours…

Fastest time of the day was nothing to get excited about – there were only eight cars competing, the best of them Scott-Brown's B-Type Connaught, plus Horace Gould and Bruce Halford in their private Maserati 250Fs. The BRM entry was scratched.

The search had also been proceeding to produce an effectively cooled rear disc brake to replace the turbo-cased Dunlop original. Tony: We were working our usual 14-hour days and to give me somewhere to keep my papers and to sit and think, a rather derelict little caravan had been parked on the grass outside the workshop at Folkingham. One valuable contribution from Rubery Owen's R&D Department at Darlaston was that they would send me all the latest technical publications, and I was sitting in the caravan late one night in June 1956, turning over the patents page of *The Engineer* magazine in its old format, when my eye caught a patent for disc brakes on the Berlin underground railway. It featured a hollow disc with curved vanes inside it, so that as the disc rotated it circulated cooling air through itself. It's familiar today as the ventilated disc, but it was then a novel idea which struck me as being ideal for our single rear brake, so I erupted from the caravan crying 'Eureka' and waving the magazine above my head. We were to become involved in a great deal of comparative testing, Dunlop brakes versus Lockheed, and when we eventually went with the Lockheed brakes this ventilated disc idea was set before Freddie Bothamley – their brake representative, and Fred Ellis, his Chief Engineer, who thought it was a good idea.

The only argument we had was whether the internal vanes should be swept forward or back, or not swept at all. If swept forward it would pump a lot of air and consume considerable power. With straight vanes it would pump a little air and consume a little power, but there was the risk the disc would corrugate between the stiffening vanes, due to pad pressure. If the vanes were swept back they would circulate very little air, but require even less power to drive it round.

We had some help from Ferodo at Chapel-en-le-Frith in Derbyshire, who ran some mock-up discs on their test rig, and we finally ended-up with a very slight sweep back in the internal vanes. Peter Spear persuaded the Coneygre Foundry to cast the discs for us but they found it very difficult to achieve a standard at which the discs would not burst, so it became a long-term development.

Caravans featured large in BRM's occupancy of Folkingham Aerodrome. PB and Lorna had camped out in one before their flat had been completed in the former control tower, displacing caretaker Jock Milne, who took over the caravan instead with his colony of cats. The Berthons' daughter Jacquie would also be in residence when home from boarding school. A sunny summer's day at Folkingham could become quite diverting for the ORO mechanics: "Both Lorna and Jacquie were pretty spectacular, and they loved sun bathing, so sometimes you didn't know quite where to look – though neither of 'em seemed to mind us ogling…"

Jacquie laughed at the memory: "It's very natural for a mother and daughter to compete. Folkingham could be glorious in the summer, ghastly in the winter. We just made the most of the sun, the control tower roof was made for it, and some of the mechanics were very sweet…"

Work continued at Bourne to lay the valve-gear demon, and all three cars extant were race prepared for the British Grand Prix…

A FATEFUL RACE – THE 1956 BRITISH GRAND PRIX

The three BRMs at Silverstone were to be driven by Hawthorn (the lengthened '251'), Brooks ('252') and Ron Flockhart in the ex-Hawthorn rolled/repaired '253'.

July 14, 1956 – RAC British Grand Prix, Silverstone – 101 laps, 295.62 miles

Moss qualified his works Maserati on pole position with a best practice lap of 1:41 dead, a clear second faster than Fangio's Lancia-Ferrari, while Hawthorn set third fastest time on 1:43, a time equalled later in the sessions by World Championship leader (!) Peter Collins – fresh from consecutive victories for Ferrari in both the Belgian and French GPs.

Tony Brooks qualified only ninth fastest, on the third row, at 1:45 while Flockhart – rather disgruntled at being treated so much as third-string within the team – started from 17th spot, on the fifth row, with a best of 1:49.

While, as had become his habit, Hawthorn was watching his car's final preparation the night before the race, he told Tony he had developed a great dislike for the exposed prop-shaft spinning between his legs and demanded it be caged in case it should break loose.

Tony tried to explain: If we made a cage strong enough to restrain a broken prop-shaft it would be ridiculously massive and heavy, and the best thing we could do was to put retainers over the universal joints at either end, which was where it would come free if it failed at all, while leaving the centre shaft exposed. This really didn't appease him. He ultimately made it the basis upon which he asked to be released from his contract. Even so, he retained a soft spot for all the mechanics and would often stop by for a chat long after he had left us…

Gregor Grant reported for *Autosport*:

The drivers sat patiently in their cars: Fangio, inscrutable as ever; Moss looking grimmer than usual; Hawthorn very large in the tiny B.R.M.; Collins making himself comfortable at the wheel; Brooks completely calm and relaxed…Up went the Union Jack; cars started

to creep, and with a thrilling crescendo the field hurtled towards Copse…

Yes, there were two B.R.M.s in the lead, and the stands rose as the little dark green machines came round Woodcote. Hawthorn, Brooks, Fangio… Ron Flockhart's race did not last long: his B.R.M. went out with engine bothers on lap 2…

The two Bourne cars were right out there in front, with Juan Manuel Fangio and Harry Schell (Vanwall) in hot pursuit…On lap 8, Fangio slid off the course at

Left: July 14, 1956 – British Grand Prix, Silverstone: Tony Brooks' ill-fated '252' on the starting grid, Tony Rudd looking distant, Brooks alongside – Rivers Fletcher (extreme left), Alfred Owen (extreme right) perhaps looking for an encouraging word with Flockhart – mechanics 'Sheriff' Perkins (left), and Reg Smith (right). For these Silverstone meetings, the team based itself in Alcocks Garage, Brackley.

Below: BRM's most crucial race since 1951 begins well with another meteoric Mike Hawthorn start in his now modified long-wheelbase '251', Tony Brooks in the standard '252' also leaving the works Lancia-Ferraris and Maseratis for dead… Writing immediately after this event, enthused by the BRM's rousing early showing, RM's old friend Pingo Lester – who lived at nearby Green's Norton – urged AGBO to apply for Government subsidy, recalling Supermarine's Schneider Trophy project when, his letter roared, "Lady Houston's magnanimity, in the face of Government blindness almost amounting to planned fifth column inactivity, IN FACT, saved Britain…".

Right: 1956 British Grand Prix: Lap 8 – Tony Brooks, about to lose third place to Moss' Maserati 250F, was running fifth in '252' until lap 39 when his engine's throttle linkage parted and he stopped briefly out on the circuit…

Right: Lap 2 – Ron Flockhart stammers BRM's third-string entry, '253', towards the pits with timing-gear failure, Cesare Perdisa's works Maserati lining up to pass. This race marked the reappearance of '253' after its Goodwood inversion.

Below: John Ross was on the spot as Brooks stopped at Club Corner and took this remarkable shot of '252''s parted throttle rods being temporarily reconnected with a Biro taped-on as a splint. This jury-rig, directed by marshal John Appleton of prewar Appleton Special fame, enabled Tony to drive into the pits for further attention. The bonnet lies on the grass beyond, its latches open.

Beckett's, rejoining the race in sixth place behind Collins. Moss, going like the wind, had flown past Brooks and began to threaten Hawthorn.

It was clear the B.R.M. was faster than anything else on the straight. Hawthorn was timed to exceed 137 m.p.h. – nearly 3 m.p.h. quicker than any of the Ferraris.

With 10 laps gone, Brooks had retaken Moss into second place…[but he was repassed]…Moss took Hawthorn for the lead; Fangio had screamed past Brooks…Gradually Moss drew away from Hawthorn [who] was now obviously slowing. To the dismay of the crowd the B.R.M. coasted into its pit. Grimly silent, Mike took off his crash helmet and pointed to the back end…

Hawthorn: "My B.R.M. and Brooks's got away to a terrific start and I was soon well in the lead, shadowed by Tony. They were going beautifully and were certainly the fastest cars in the race… This went on for about 15 laps… Then I began to feel uneasy about the back end. There was a very slight change in behaviour which seemed to be getting worse. Moss came

1956 British Grand Prix: Catastrophe – remarkably quick-witted Asian spectator Ranjit Topa captured this dramatic photo-sequence of Tony Brooks' spectacular race exit in '252' when its hastily repaired throttle almost certainly jammed open on the entry to Abbey Curve. Here at the exit from this very fast left-hander (above) Tony has lost control on the far grass verge and '252' spins backwards across the track towards the spectator bank (foreground). Left: Cannoning off the bank the BRM's tail tank has been crushed, showering fuel ignites, and the car lands inverted opposite 'that Farm'. Tony has been thrown out onto the grass verge and is hidden by the foreground bank (left) as the marshal runs to his aid. The ambulance driver opposite has come forward as the fire takes hold. Spilled fuel burns along the trackside. The driver rushes back to his ambulance and pulls it across to collect the miraculously lightly injured driver as flower-pot men foregather.

The Abbey Curve crash, 1956 British Grand Prix. Above: Pyrene foam extinguishers had little effect upon the furious fuel fire which consumed '252'. The car's left-rear wheel rim has broken away from its 'bell'. Right: Impact damage to the tail is evident in this exhaust-side view of the incinerating wreck. Precious little could be salvaged. Burning paint chips scatter the roadway. Below: The Northampton Fire Brigade had finally to quell the blaze, large-bore hoses from their powerful pump littering the scene, shovels and brooms clearing the road of foam, water, ash and detritus. The ruined wheel rim leans against the wall. A stout rope was finally attached to drag the wreck bodily from the track. See how the undertray has been melted...'252' is history.

past, while Salvadori and Fangio closed up behind me... By now I was convinced that a drive-shaft oil seal had failed again, so I pulled in to the pit. At first glance the mechanics reported that all was in order but I refused to continue without a closer inspection and they then found that the oil seal had failed and another universal-joint seizure was imminent."

At 30 laps Tony Brooks was driving a customarily smooth and imperturbable race, comfortably fourth, splitting the Lancia-Ferraris of Fangio and Collins in the wake of Moss and Salvadori's Maseratis, which were running first and second.

But Tony had just been displaced by Collins and was running fifth on lap 40 when his car's throttle pedal suddenly flopped to the floor and the engine gasped onto tickover. Its throttle linkage had fallen apart.[77] He pulled off onto the infield end of the aerodrome runway at Club Corner where with advice from marshal John Appleton the parted linkage was located and jury-rigged with a Biro pen taped to the rods as a splint... This enabled Tony to rejoin and head straight for the ORO pit.

There, a more secure jury-rig was completed and after losing 9min 43sec Tony rejoined, intent upon retrieving the best possible finish for BRM in what had already been the longest Type 25 race yet. On this his 41st lap he survived only as far as Abbey Curve...

John Riseley-Prichard – sometime Connaught driver – was official Observer at the marshal's post there, and on August 11 he wrote the following to Peter Spear, explaining what he had seen:

> Until the time of his pit stop, Brooks was one of the few drivers who had not touched the grass verge on coming out of Abbey. I had particularly noticed that he appeared to be able to get through the corner 'flat', i.e. without lifting the throttle at all, and this had especially interested me because the B.R.M. looked absolutely steady on this corner whereas, in practice, I had noticed that it did not appear to handle well on some of the other corners.
>
> The accident occurred on the first lap after his pit stop; the track was dry, but the grass verge was still slightly damp from earlier mist and drizzle. I particularly watched Brooks' entry to the corner and was of the opinion...that he aimed for the apex of the corner a little earlier than usual; I was consequently not surprised when, on coming out of the corner, the car was obviously going to drift close to the grass verge on the outside of the track.
>
> The driver's instinctive reaction in these circumstances is to lift the throttle momentarily, but I did not discern any change in the exhaust note (as I expected) and the car touched the grass verge: I should say that the off-side wheels were approximately one foot onto the

grass verge momentarily. As I have said, the grass was damp and consequently more slippery than the track. The back appeared to break away very slightly and almost immediately the car spun viciously in an anti-clockwise direction. The spin took the car (still travelling at about 100 m.p.h. I should judge) across the track to the inside verge some 200 yards from the corner where it struck the protective bank and overturned; it was when the car struck the bank that the wheel detached itself. It was difficult to see exactly what happened after the car struck the bank because of the cloud of earth and dust, but, in any case, the car caught fire instantaneously.

> Fortunately it threw Tony out onto the relatively soft verge before whirling over, wrapped in glittering flame, to land upside down, back on the track surface, where its fuel load blazed for several minutes defying all efforts of marshals and firemen to extinguish it.
>
> Tony was picked up carefully and removed to Northampton General Hospital, where he was found to have dislocated his jaw, chipped an ankle bone and to be generally battered.

Riseley-Prichard concluded:

> 1) That the driver's line was slightly different from usual, but this could easily have been corrected by easing the throttle.
>
> 2) The trouble with the throttle linkage and Brooks' statement that the throttle was sticking after his pit-stop seems exactly to account for his failure to ease the throttle. I believe firmly that this was the proximate cause of the accident.
>
> 3) I am as certain as visual observation can be that there was no mechanical failure of the braking system or the rear axle assembly...

(as had been suggested in some quarters).

On August 2 Tony Brooks penned this description of the crash for Peter Spear, who had been briefed by an insensed Alfred Owen to investigate everything and anything involved in BRM's latest, very public, Silverstone disaster:

> I realized the jury-rigged throttle was sticky but it wasn't too bad until I entered Abbey at my normal speed, trying to catch up. Then I realized it had jammed wide open and I tried to take a tighter line to compensate, but just ran out of road...
>
> The car had previously broken the throttle and was repaired at the pits and on recommencing the race the accelerator was not closing properly and it was necessary to brake through the corner but Abbey Curve was normally taken flat but to stop a slight rear end twitch I eased the throttle which should have been sufficient to place the car ideally for exit from the corner.
>
> However, the car revolved rapidly and shot backwards towards the outside bank...which it hit and threw me out fortunately, and the car overturned and caught fire. In my opinion the throttle did not ease back at the

77. '252''s long throttle rod had fallen apart at the pedal end due to a fatigue crack caused by vibration. This failure may have been accelerated by the end fitting on the rod having been overheated when it was brazed during manufacture. This end fitting was a ball-joint as used by Rolls-Royce. This was the first failure experienced on any part of the throttle linkage on any of the Type 25 cars. A new end fitting was adopted subsequently, soft-soldered in place to avoid any danger of overheating the steel during assembly. The failed rod had been fitted to '252' in its March conversion to external ram air intake, and had run 852 miles since.

crucial moment, on corners of this type an immediate closure being essential…The car was taken through Abbey Curve on the correct line (as used on previous laps) up to the point of easing the throttle, and the corner was entered at the correct speed…

BRM's 1956 British GP record was thus mixed: three cars started; one led the race and two ran first and second; two cars retired due to mechanical failure; one car destroyed and driver injured due to mechanical failure.

Alfred Owen was boiling. He gave RM and PB a dressing down immediately post-race of which neither probably thought him capable.

On Monday, July 17, he put it in writing in a private letter to RM, plus a formal note to both RM and PB. This duplication itself speaks volumes of the differing regard in which he held these two, and the extra trust he still instinctively placed in Ray.

Of him, Owen demanded:

> I want to know if the car chassis is stable…and will stand up to a long race… I shall not be satisfied until I have some worthwhile assurance in this respect… I am sure there is far too much being hidden underground; we are in this thing together, and the more people know the more they are able to help; but if we are only telling [suppliers] half the story we cannot expect to get the correct answer… Whilst calling for detailed reports from Mr. Berthon, as you are aware, beyond a spasmodic effort no information whatever has been forthcoming… it seems everything has been run on a rule-of-thumb method; and as Mike Hawthorn said to me, the test drivers have been used as a human test bed.
>
> I have been more than dissatisfied at the stories emanating from Folkingham, that virtually half-a-day's control is lacking in the workshops there because Mr. Berthon does not put in an appearance until mid-day. It is not the slightest use working the other end of the clock if the staff and workpeople are lacking direction for the first four hours of the morning…
>
> I trust that I have made the position perfectly clear.

Acting upon Owen's specific instruction, Peter Spear swept into Bourne and Folkingham the following Sunday, meeting RM, PB and Tony Rudd, while, as he reported back to AGBO:

> Incidentally, Wing-Commander Lester [RM's friend Pingo] was present throughout the discussions… Apart from being polite I ignored this gentleman because my only knowledge of him is as the somewhat erratic inventor of a lamp bulb for car headlights. I do not know why Raymond Mays brought him along other than the fact that he was staying with Raymond Mays that weekend…

Spear informed Owen that his 'word' with RM and PB at Silverstone:

> …has had some effect. They certainly appeared much quieter than usual and much more willing to discuss matters of detail…Peter Berthon apologised to me for any impoliteness which he might have shown me in the past…I did make the point with him that both Mike Hawthorn and Ron Flockhart had expressed to me almost identical comments in that they were dissatisfied that having got out of the car, after risking their necks, and made various comments on the performance of the car, that neither Mr. Berthon nor Mr. Mays appeared to take any notice. I could quote both of them as saying that 'R.M. and P.B. disappear off into a corner and go into a huddle and do not let me know if my opinions are being taken into account or not'.

Spear was to arrange weekly monitoring meetings with RM and PB at Bourne, appointing engineer Hawkins from his office as what he grandly entitled "my Co-ordination Officer". Spear also recommended to Owen that one of the team drivers be present whenever possible at these meetings, to air his perspective…

Ron Flockhart had also unburdened himself to Spear, who was impressed with both the Scot's candour and his engineering and driving qualifications – perhaps particularly since he had just won the classic Le Mans 24-Hours race in an *Ecurie Ecosse* D-Type Jaguar. Ron's reputation had been rather blackened to Owen by RM and PB, and by the management of the Group's Charles Clark distributorship where he held his nominal post as a salesman and demonstrator.

Spear on Flockhart:

> He readily admitted without any prompting from me that he has been slack in his duties at Charles Clark…points out he doesn't look upon Charles Clark as being any kind of career for him and in view of all his other racing experience that he could be used in a much better capacity in the Owen Organisation racing activities. He pointed out to me the large number of successes he has had in recent months driving for Acuri Ocsse [*sic!* – *Ecurie Ecosse*] racing stable.

Spear recommended that Flockhart should be better employed:

> 1. As a test pilot at Bourne…2. I think he should be present at the weekly meetings… This might then help to give Mike Hawthorn a lot more confidence in the car also.

Interestingly, Spear reported that Flockhart rated his own driving capabilities as being:

> …good second class but not yet first class though he considers that he can become a first class driver with practice. Peter Berthon agreed with this summing up…

Owen now flatly decreed that the BRMs were not to race again until they had proved they could survive a 300-mile Grand Prix distance by completing such a run in testing without fatal breakage. He based this requirement upon an instant reaction memo from Spear, written on July 19, declaring:

I can see no fundamental difference between the development of a racing motor car and the development of any other mechanical product, but the general idea at Bourne is very different and orthodox principles do not apply. I consider that it is essential to freeze the design of the car irrespective of what are the rumours about other people's work. I do not like the present testing methods. As I see it, the car must be given simulated practical test conditions and it should be certain that, mechanically at least, it will last 100 laps...

Owen assured Mike Hawthorn: "We are literally going to get down to this matter and remove not only the pettifogging things that have happened, but also to assure ourselves that the chassis, the brakes and the struts are all fundamentally sound in design and provide every security to the driver..."

Mike had noticed skid marks on the entry to Abbey Curve which convinced him that Brooks had been victim of a similar pot-joint failure to his own. Riseley-Prichard subsequently pointed out they had been left by Cliff Allison's spinning Lotus 11 in the preceding Formula 2 race. Hawthorn subsided, still unhappy...

Mike Hawthorn was released from his contract. He had driven a works D-Type Jaguar again at Le Mans, then a sports Ferrari in Sweden, but his sorry 1956 season was then ended by a nasty shunt at Oulton Park when he rolled a Lotus 11, damaging his ribs and back badly enough not to race again that year.

Following three rubber pot-joint gaiter failures, all on cars driven by Hawthorn, rig tests involving these components were completed by August 3 when Tony Rudd reported his conclusions:

1) The race failure at Silverstone was due to oil collecting at the weakest section of the rubber, forming a bulge, which chafed on the gear change tube.
2) The failure during testing at Silverstone was due to the same type of bulge, although the rubber split through being overstressed before it chafed enough to burst.
3) The new type Andre Rubber, running inside out and secured to the shaft by rubber rings, has given the best results so far. Unfortunately under running temperatures failures will occur much earlier and some re-design is necessary to eliminate overstressing...

In September Tony conducted a series of torsional rigidity tests on the Type 25 cars' P27 chassis since it was remembered that any flexibility of the frame on both versions of the V16, particularly around the suspension attachments, had adverse effects upon the suspension performance since it introduced an undamped spring into the system.

Further, with different roll-centre heights front and rear, a flexing frame became part of the anti-roll system. The danger was that since welded chassis parts would be loaded by any bending of the frame tubes, the end stiffness of the frame depended upon weld penetration, and two visually similar frames might actually have dangerous differences in strength and stiffness.

His records showed that the first test of the short ex-'Bira'

WHAT WERE THEY LIKE TO DRIVE?

In response to requests from Peter Spear, backed by Owen's newly-asserted authority, on August 10, 1956, Ron Flockhart set down the following:

OBSERVATIONS ON THE HANDLING OF THE TYPE 25 B.R.M. – R. FLOCKHART

My first impression of the handling of the car since driving it last was that it was now quite stable running straight. My own preference would be for more positive steering ratio, however, provided this did not bring any undesirable characteristics in its train.

Braking into corners was straight, safe and adequate.

The performance of the car on corners, however, was not yet a high enough order in my opinion. Though not so marked as previously, the car still had a tendency towards an oversteering 'twitch' or 'jerk' just as the power was applied first when bringing the car into the slide or drift in the first third of the corner, and secondly during the final exit while accelerating out of the corner this tendency was again apparent. During the actual central part while a steady drift was being maintained, the car did handle in a reasonable, but I would not say perfect, manner. I felt that it should be possible to apply more power, and the drift should be more pronounced.

This oversteering jerk I mention was more apparent the faster the corner, and not so noticeable on slow corners.

Although I stood to watch this point specifically after I came out of the race on the outside of Abbey Curve, I could see no sign of it in either of the other BRM's [sic Hawthorn and Brooks]. However, during practice while following Brooks, it was quite evident that the BRM in front was behaving in an identical manner to the one which I drove.

I feel that good as the acceleration is away from a corner, it would be even better if this characteristic could be eliminated from the handling of the car and it were possible to apply full power earlier.

My final observation is that engine vibration appears to have increased to the extent of causing distraction and possibly adding to fatigue.

TONY BROOKS' VIEW

Tony Brooks had composed a similar but more extensive report while convalescing after his Silverstone shunt at his home, 8 Park Lane, Dukinfield, Cheshire.

He liked the car's straight line running but said:

During acceleration the car sits down at the back and cocks up on braking rather more than expected on a Grand Prix car... This difference during the transition between acceleration and braking does not make the car unstable, but I mention it in an effort to be complete.

Of low-speed cornering he observed:

Autumn 1956: In the bruised, witch-hunt atmosphere of the post-Silverstone period, experimentation to improve the Type 25's handling ground on at both Folkingham and Silverstone, mainly using Ron Flockhart as the ORO's resident 'test pilot'. PB deplored the cars' prodigal understeer – unsurprising behaviour with such excesssive front roll stiffness as apparent here on '251'. Much work remained to be done.

Full braking into the corner in a straight line is good as described. However it is essential not to enter the corner a shade too fast for a reason to be explained, and to avoid this there is perhaps a little time wasted in braking too early.

If the corner is entered a little too fast, the back breaks away rapidly and it is not possible to put the car in a four wheel slide and so lose speed and go smoothly through the corner. This manoeuvre passes unnoticed in a car that handles well and is essential to really 'motor race' a car, as otherwise it is necessary to keep much in hand. It is therefore necessary to go round the corner as smoothly and neatly as possible up to the point of sideslip only. To get round quickly therefore requires extremely precise judgement.

When pulling out of the corner using the throttle, once again one can only go up to the point of sideslip as the back comes rapidly round otherwise and is very difficult to correct, much more than a flick of the steering wheel being necessary.

When accelerating from the slow corner it is not possible to turn the power on and control the exit from the corner with opposite lock, this manoeuvre being required on hairpins and slow corners especially (watch Moss!)...

This tendency to break away at the rear is accentuated on a bumpy corner as if the reduced (momentarily) adhesion starts the back going out often uncontrollably.

However, on very slow smooth corners (Monaco and Aintree) the car understeers badly especially when the stiff anti-roll bar is fitted as at the last Aintree meeting. This low cornering power of the front only shows itself on really slow corners because it is only on these that the front wheels are turned appreciably... This understeering on slow smooth corners occurs on trailing throttle or putting the power on. I feel sure that the car has insufficient lock, both for correction and for tight corners...

On fast corners:

The sudden oversteering tendency is still there with or without the use of the throttle, the use of the latter causing the breakaway to be perhaps a shade more sudden, but correction and ease of the throttle is necessary to stop it. Drifting on a fast bumpy corner is impossible because of the initiation of the rear end breakaway. A smooth fast corner such as Abbey Curve is quite comfortable, but only the merest suggestion of drift is necessary, a sustained drift being impossible because of the basic oversteering characteristic. A smooth surface therefore only conceals the tendency up to a point, and a slight drift is only possible on this surface by having a slight quick opposite lock correction so it is not a true full blooded drift...

He voiced suspicions that the air struts:

...make it extremely difficult to get constant handling characteristics for comparative purposes...When Mike and I swopped cars in practice at Monaco, the car I got was steering very badly and yet a few pounds in the struts transformed it on the next day.

He complained of the sound waves from the latest short exhaust pounding badly on his left eardrum despite wearing plugs "and at certain revs appears literally to shake my head". While appreciating the need for a tuned exhaust length he virtually begged for this to be changed:

All the above criticisms appertain to the short chassis de Dion rear end car. I have only had two brief laps in the long chassis car at Silverstone and oversize tyres were fitted on the front, so I would rather not comment...

Clearly, there was much to be done before the drivers would be happy.

Owen Maserati's frame – the original '2509' was never tested – had a torsional stiffness of only 200lbs/ft per degree deflection over its wheelbase. This was increased to 450lbs/ft by development "with an appreciable improvement in suspension characteristics".

The Mark II V16's relative stiffness figure was 400lbs/ft per degree over a 6in longer wheelbase, and the Mark I's 340lbs/ft per degree over an 11in longer base.

The original P27 frame's stiffness test revealed the following:

(a) Bare frame – 225ft/lbs per degree
(b) Bare frame with engine – 256ft/lbs/deg
(c) Bare frame with engine plus steel side fuel tanks – 410ft/lbs/deg
(d) Frame, engine, tanks, undertray and stressed skinning – 506ft/lbs/deg
(e) 2nd frame – less engine, with light aluminium side tanks mounted on detachable frame triangulation tubes, original stressed-skin scuttle – 620ft/lbs/deg
(f) 2nd frame with engine in position – 642ft/lbs/deg
(g) 2nd frame as above, but after 1,540 road miles – 575ft/lbs/deg
(h) 2nd frame rebuilt with light tubular scuttle reinforcement and 16SWG bulkhead in place of 18SWG – 768ft/lbs/deg
(i) 3rd frame as above – 740ft/lbs/deg
(j) 4th frame as above – 758ft/lbs/deg
(k) 1st frame rebuilt 3 inches longer (18SWG tube – others 17 SWG) – 706ft/lbs/deg.

The front end of the frame under test had been rigidly tied down through its lower front wishbone pick-ups, its rear end supported upon its longitudinal centreline by a roller, beneath the rear wheels. Torsional loads were then applied by a lever attached to the rear suspension medium mounting, a load of 1,800lbs/ft being the greatest normally applied which deflected the Maserati frame fully 9 degrees! This deflection was measured by attaching light tubes laterally at 12-inch intervals along the frame. Their height above the base, measured before and after the load had been applied, and the differences in height relative to the length of the tube used, expressed the deflection in degrees.

The Type 15 and P30 V16 frames were only tested for comparison purposes, the Mark I giving 340lbs over its 100-inch wheelbase and the Mark II 400lbs over 94 inches.

Now a series of Silverstone tests were run, commencing on September 13 with Ron Flockhart assuming his role as 'company test pilot' in car '251' – "…90-inch wheelbase, engine 254, gearbox 27/4. Axle ratio 25 drives 22, with 8 x 38 bevels; 6.50 x 16 rear tyres, 5.25 x 16 front. Standard valve and ignition timing. Fuel BPK 10.

"The rear suspension had been revised to use a transverse leafspring – in place of the air-struts – with small Armstrong dampers, and it carried 130lbs ballast to compensate for the lack of a rear fuel tank" (making room for the rear spring).

Other modifications included new-type throttle rods, rubber-damped steering column, non-rotating pot-joint covers with nylon A100 bushes, reinforced front wheel flares, modified gearbox gear location and open-coiled valve springs. The engine

had run 210 miles since its last build, the gearbox 70 miles.

The previous winter's promising swing-axle system having been dropped, '251''s standard de Dion tube's centre-slide lateral location had now been replaced by a Connaught-type parallel-motion linkage which tied its left-rear hub to the chassis. The normal radius arms still supplied fore-and-aft control. A new press had been acquired for Folkingham, in which the de Dion tube was given a frightful squeeze to produce a fixed negative-camber setting for the rear wheels. This Connaught-type geometry lowered the rear roll-centre, while an anti-roll bar was also fitted. A short intake ram was riveted onto the right-side body panelling to feed the carburettor bell-mouths.

September 13 was dry and sunny, temperature 64°F with a slight south-westerly breeze across the main straights. Mike Hawthorn – rather reluctantly – was present. Ron did one initial lap before stopping to have the new four-spoke steering wheel repositioned to enable him to see the instruments adequately. He then ran a 10-lap stint, best time 1:50.1 sixth time round.

He complained: "The back end still skips out, rear end damping is poor." Examination of scratch plates fitted to show wheel (de Dion) movement revealed that the tube was bottoming-out on its bump stops when 4½ inches through its 5.6 inches of travel.

Bump damping was increased 100lbs/ft to 1,350lbs/ft while 5 gallons of fuel added.

In 10 more laps, Ron clocked a best of 1:47.8 and none slower than 1:49.4. He came in to report improvement, but the back end was still "skipping" and some rear-wheel patter had been experienced. The scratch plates revealed 3½ inches movement, still bottoming. Four gallons of fuel were added, damping increased to 1450 x 1450 and temperature paint was applied to the dampers.

Ron then went out on a third 10-lap stint, clocking 1:47.2 second time round, then with his times being signalled to him managing 1:45.8. He was reaching 7,900rpm on Hangar Straight and 7,400 just before Woodcote Corner. On his ninth lap he missed a gear entering Chapel Curve, he spun harmlessly and stalled.

Upon inspection, the car's right-hand pot-joint rubber was found to have split, and back at Folkingham it was decided that the gaiter was being trapped by screw heads securing the inner pot-joint cover as the axle rose and fell. "Rubber appears to be dragged into pot-joint either by reaction from reverse thread in nylon bush for oil sealing, or aligning action due to angularity of half shaft, or both."

Split distance-pieces were then made up to prevent the bushes moving inwards and permitting the rubbers to contact the screw heads. Front air strut damping was changed to 10 x 50, rear (Armstrong) damping to 1350 x 1350 and with other specs as before the car was returned to Silverstone next day, which was dry and dull, 62°F, with a strong south-westerly wind.

Flockhart's first 10 laps included laps six and eight at a best of 1:46.0, and he reported the suspension improved, but considered rear rebound damping excessive so it was reduced to 1350 x 1250. Four gallons of fuel were added, pot-joint cover temperatures taken (210°F LH/190°F RH) while the gearbox casing was also measured at 190°F!

In five more laps Ron got down to 1:45.6, reporting the car

improved and then handing over to Mike Hawthorn, still stiff after his Lotus crash at Oulton Park.

After one lap he stopped to report the water temperature gauge u/s. In four more laps he clocked a 1:46.8 before stopping abruptly at the end of his fifth lap. His face was grimly set as he came coasting into view through Woodcote Corner and wheeled to a halt beside the pit counter.

The car's throttle had just stuck fully open entering Abbey Curve… He was quiet, grimly quiet, the ORO crew left in no doubt he was seething that such a thing should recur.

Tony Rudd reported it was due to:

> …the screw holding No. 3 butterfly [in the Weber carburettor] coming adrift, letting plate slip sideways at full throttle, jamming throttles wide open – screw replaced, engine checked for internal damage, none found. LH rear wheel changed, tyre worn; all throttle securing screws peened over; 5 galls fuel added, water thermometer changed.

Hawthorn refused to drive again.

Flockhart ran 10 laps with a best of 1:44.8 on his fourth. When stopped, the LH pot-joint cover was at 230°F, the RH cover 210,°F, gearbox 200,°F and temperature paint applied to the rear disc showed 575°C. The engine had shown a steady 85psi oil pressure and maintained a comfortable 85°C water temperature. The car was returned to Folkingham.

There the right-hand magneto was found to be defective, the condenser hanging by its wire because its mounting had broken. Dampers were returned to their manufacturers, water pump and rail were modified to increase flow and the rear fuel tank replaced the temporary ballast. The nylon pot-joint bushes were replaced by a similar design in Tufnol APC and the rubbers secured by split Tufnol clips.

At Silverstone on the 18th – cold, dull, 64°F, gentle breeze – Tony Brooks drove for the first time since his Abbey Curve accident, stopping after his first lap to report only the rear two cylinders were working. The front carburettor's float needle valve had jammed.

This was corrected and he ran nine laps, his times a model of characteristically intelligent style: times of 1:46.4 on the first flying lap followed by '45.2, '44.8, '44.5, '44.8, '44.2 and finally 1:44.1.

He commented: "Better than any other BRM I've driven. Very good on smooth surfaced corners, rear end still slides on rough surfaces; oil pressure 65–70lbs; water 80°C. Car appeared very stable."

Roy Salvadori, ORO's old rival in so many races with the Gilby Maserati, was present, and he then took the Type 25 out for seven laps, clocking a best of 1:45.8 and reporting:

> Terrific oversteer, very heavy brake pedal, vibration felt in back of seat, very impressed by unobtrusive performance.

Three gallons of fuel were added and Brooks returned for a 10-lap stint, running faster and faster until last time round he was right down to a 1:42.6.

He then observed: "Halfway from previous car to perfection, windscreen needs lifting 1", bad buffeting, exhaust noise very uncomfortable, seat very awkward and uncomfortable, using 8,200rpm in 3rd gear between Stowe and Club Corners, 7,600rpm on straight. Engine did not feel as powerful as my car at GP" (this is correct). "Car can now be drifted."

Indeed, he had been observed drifting on full throttle at 15 degrees through Abbey Curve, but it was noted that the inlet rocker cover had burst above No. 1 exhaust rocker and was bulged above No. 1 cam. No. 1 inlet restrictor had broken up and No. 3 exhaust valve spring was broken. With a chassis and engine mileage of 605, 360 on the gearbox, the car was returned to Folkingham and completely stripped. A modification introducing hard valve restrictors would be withdrawn.

HERE WE ARE AGAIN – MONZA, 1956

After PB had won a protracted major battle with Peter Spear over the issue, the team moved to the drier climes of Monza to achieve Alfred Owen's strict 300-miles-without-breaking test target. Flockhart had recently finished third there driving a Connaught B-Type in the Italian GP so he obviously had a contribution to make. Tony Brooks and Roy Salvadori were also engaged to drive there.

At Folkingham the 'Hawthorn Special' long-wheelbase '251' was prepared with 47mm-choke carburettors tuned for 7.5 per cent nitro fuel with a fairly massive rear leafspring and Armstrong lever-arm dampers. Engine '2562' was installed and it featured the standard brake cooling system.

The second test car was to be chassis '254' – brand new – which shared '251''s long 7ft 6in wheelbase, but had what the mechanics christened a 'Howdah' – as on a working elephant – providing a high-sided cockpit enclosure which was Tony Rudd's contribution to drag reduction, offering the driver a more comfortable time. It had two nostrils in its screen base to convey air to the rear brakes, while the car used a softer traverse rear leafspring, co-axial Armstrong dampers, air struts at the front, anti-roll bars at both ends and had engine '251' installed. Both gearboxes had external adjustable oil jets to reduce the amount of oil churning within the gearbox. The half-shaft pot-joints had Tufnol bushes with return-groove oil seals.

On September 27, PB to Owen:

> The trip has been delayed one day and the crossing will be made on Friday night. Tony Brooks has agreed to be available at Monza during this week and Salvadori and Flockhart will take over the testing the second.

Concerning Mike Hawthorn:

> Frankly I do not feel that [he] is of any use to us in connection with the type of testing we are undertaking. His attitude, when he did a few laps at Silverstone the week before last, was extremely unhelpful, to say the least of it…The three drivers we have chosen are all serious-minded, intensely interested in improving the car, and will, I feel sure, give us their true views during this testing period. If Mike Hawthorn hears that improvements have been made, after the tests he will be

October 1956, Monza testing. Above: The recovered Tony Brooks is push-started in the latest car – '254' – wearing its tall new applique cockpit enclosure which the mechanics nicknamed 'The Howdah'. Left: Tony cornering '254' in the Curva Parabolica during the team's lengthy attempts to achieve Alfred Owen's minimum target of running a full Grand Prix distance, trouble-free.

more anxious still to try the car, and I think you will find him much easier to deal with in connection with the ridiculous financial demands he is making for next season.

PB and Tony Rudd finally set off for Monza in the former's much-modified Ford Zephyr. Because of PB's chronic back trouble, Tony was driving and he distinguished himself on a wet road south of Reims by ramming a tractor which exercised its *priorite a droite* too literally and drove out of a field right in his path.

The now battered Ford eventually conveyed them to the Monza Royal Park, where the mechanics were sorting out all the material brought down in the transporters.

Tony: When the fuel was delivered there was quite a scene because it had quite a different specific gravity to what we expected. It was some time before we cottoned-on to the fact that at 27°C it would of course have a lower specific gravity than we were used to in cold and draughty Lincolnshire!

After problems with water blowing out we ended up pulling the engine out of the new car and replacing valves and pistons and I darkly suspected we had a cylinder head joint ring blowing, so after some discussion the rig at Bourne was dismantled, loaded into a van and sent down so we could change joint rings on site there. It was beginning to look like a long session – perhaps as long as BRM's last there – with the V16 in 1952...

As running continued, with the problems outlined in the appended log, the test team eventually got down to a lap time of 1:43, which was really getting amongst Ferrari times, the Maranello team testing simultaneously. Then Tony Brooks had to return to England and Ron Flockhart arrived to take over.

Unfortunately, Willie Southcott was hospitalized. He had slipped off a loading ramp and broken his right leg badly. Colin Atkin flew out to take his place, in company with Peter Spear.

However, problems kept intruding and the situation was becoming tense with Spear on hand as Alfred Owen's witness to see the 500km/300-mile run achieved as demanded. It was

Spear's job to keep ORO honest...

Tony: We had been there a fortnight, which is a bit longer than the average practice session, and we hadn't even achieved 100 miles failure-free, never mind 300!

Finally, on Thursday, October 11, with one of the original series of engines – '254' – we tried the run. Ron made several stops but the car kept going. Eighty laps represented the required 500kms, but once that landmark had been reached PB became over-confident and said: "Now we've got it right, we'll keep him going" and sure enough on the 83rd lap No. 2 inlet valve dropped into the cylinder and did the engine a terrible mischief, but the car had completed 329 miles and Peter Spear had witnessed it!

That night we had a big party. The hotel we stayed at opposite the Park gates was like most Italian hotels in that it was common for a guest to take a lady – not necessarily his wife – to be entertained to dinner and other pursuits for a couple of hours afterwards. Amidst the general jubilation, Peter Spear decided to buy the wine and tried to explain to the waiter he wanted it charged to his room number.

It never arrived at our table and when two or three hours later he went to bed he was rather tickled to find the bottle of wine at his bedside – with two glasses.

Due to the nature of the hotel's trade, the sheets had to be changed frequently and were always freshly laundered. Unfortunately they would also be returned rather damp, and when PB didn't take kindly to sleeping in damp sheets he decided to air them by putting his bedside reading lamp down the bed to warm it. Unfortunately, he forgot one night and leaped into bed with the lamp down there and sustained some very nasty burns, cuts, and shock of both kinds!

Still it was a jubilant BRM convoy which returned to Bourne and Folkingham, but when the team took sober stock it was obvious that major problems persisted. The P25 engines' valve gear was still suspect, the Type 25's handling was still far from right, and a daunting amount of progress still had to be made...

THE MONZA TEST RUNNING LOG, OCTOBER 1956

Despite leaning over backwards here to reproduce BRM engineering reports in their entirety, the ORO test period running log for the 1956 Type 25 tests at Monza is too extensive to be included in full, having been compiled by Peter Berthon and Tony Rudd expressly to impress Alfred Owen with its thoroughness. What follows, therefore is a *precis*:

2nd October 1956 Temp 27°C – dull, dry, no wind. Running started 3.0pm. Driver C.A.S. Brooks. Using road circuit only.

(1) *Car No. 1* – 5 laps – best 1:49.5 – 7,700rpm on straight (172mph).

(2) *Car No. 4* – Big tail and cockpit enclosure – 5 laps – best 1:48.8 – 7,700rpm on straight.

(3) *Car No. 4* – Tyre pressures down from 40–45psi to 35–40 – 5 laps – best 1:48.5.

(4) *Car No. 4* – Tyre pressures reduced 5lbs – limited to one fast lap by Dunlop representative – 3 laps, 1:47.4.

(5) *Car No. 1* – Rear dampers reduced 100in/lbs on bump and rebound, tyre pressures 30–35psi – 4 laps – 1:45.4. Driver reports handling very much better, nearly as good as Silverstone; going through Vialone flat with ease, getting 7,800rpm down straight (174mph); brakes not very good, having to pump – oil 80psi water 75°C. Observers report car looks very steady, going through Vialone in centre of road as on rails; water noted blowing from header tank relief valve vent – along straight three-quarters gallon of water lost. Tyre temp LHR 78°C, RHR 75°C, pot joints still leaking.

(6) *Car No. 4* – 5 gallons fuel added, tyres 30–35psi – 5 laps – 1:46.3 – better but not as good as No. 1; back hopping out, steering not positive, engine not pulling well. 7,600rpm on straight, brakes very good.

TOTAL DAY'S RUNNING –Car No. 1 – 11 laps (40 miles)
Car No. 4 – 18 laps (65 miles)

3rd October 1956 20°C, dull, cloudy, some rain showers; no wind, Driver C.A.S. Brooks. Road circuit only.

(1) *Car No. 4* – Extra leaf removed from rear spring, new spark plugs, yesterday's (53s) were defective as gaps opened out. Tappets reset, inlets had closed badly. Header tank relief valve set to blow at 15lbs instead of 10. Tyres 30–35psi.
9 laps – 1:48.2 – No better handling, engine rough and unwilling.

(2) *Car No. 4* – 5 gallons fuel added, dampers reduced to Silverstone best (1250 x 1350), carb jets changed to

No. 1's settings, 220 x 240. 10 laps – 1:47.5 – raining, track slippery, driver reports big improvement all round, engine better but will not pull over 7,600. Observers report front slips sideways at Lesmo.

(3) *Car No. 1* – New brake master cylinder, header tank relief valve reset as No. 4, tappets closed slightly and were reset, tyres 30–35. 5 laps – 1:51.4 – raining heavily throughout. Handling not now as good as No. 4 particularly on slow corners, engine feels normal but only pulling 7,600rpm. Observers report front suspension appears better than No. 4. Lost 1 gallon of water. Pot joints still leaking.

(4) *Car No. 4* – Centre exhaust pipe section shortened. Track very wet. 8 laps – 1:49.0, no gain in rpm. Better than No. 1 on wet roads, has more understeer giving superiority to No. 1 on slow corners.

TOTAL DAY'S RUNNING –Car No. 1 – 5 laps (18 miles)
Car No. 4 – 27 laps (97 miles)

5th October 1956 22°C – dull, cloudy. Driver C.A.S. Brooks. Road circuit.

(1) *Car No. 4* – Damping increased to 17 x 50, steering column rubber mounted as No. 1. Semi-solid inlet valves, new piston in No. 2 cyl. 8 laps – 51 plugs, running in piston; heavy oil leak, scavenge hose blown.

TOTAL DAY'S RUNNING –Car No. 4 – 8 laps (29 miles)

6th October 1956 24°C – bright sunny, no wind. Road circuit.

(1) *Car No. 4* – Oil leak rectified and given pre-race check. 10 laps – 2:10.0 running in. Car hit pheasant, radiator badly damaged, replaced. All fuel tanks filled. New tyres all round. 33–37psi.

(2) 25 laps – 1:45.0. Clutch failure. Lap times controlled by pit at 1:46 (120mph average) – limited to 7,600rpm in gears, getting 7,500rpm in top. Driver reports "Car still has tendency to slip sideways on bump, and thus cannot be drifted through fast corners even yet, but is quite good on slower ones (NB fast corners taken at 155mph). Believes could lap in 1:43.0 or faster if allowed 8,500rpm in gears. Rear disc 600–650°C; Fronts 750–800°C. Ferodo on clutch plate had broken up, one plug faulty.

TOTAL DAY'S RUNNING –Car No. 4 – 35 laps
(126 miles)

8th October 1956 23°C. Driver R. Flockhart. Road circuit.
Car No. 4 – new clutch, rear caliper, full fuel tanks, driver instructed to get used to circuit.

(1) *10 laps – 1:50.0. Driver: "Seems much better than at*

Silverstone and better than Connaught for Italian GP – bump at Vialone and Grande threw car out of its line badly – Brake pedal does not feel positive – had lost ¾ gallon of water."

(2) *Car No. 4* – R3 tyres, full tanks, 2 laps spun at Curva Sud, engine difficult to start and blew water from exhaust.

2 laps stopped to report water 200°F. Believes R3 tyres better than R4s. No. 2 cyl split, several inlet valve springs broken.

TOTAL DAY'S RUNNING – Car No. 4 – 14 laps
(50 miles)

<u>9th October 1956</u> 18°C; cold, sunny. Driver R. Flockhart. Road circuit.

(1) *Car No. 1* – As before, semi-solid inlet valves, stops to prevent pot-joint Tufnol bushes sliding outwards on shafts. New piston No. 2 cyl. 10 laps – 51 plugs, running in piston, lost ¼ gallon water. Filled fuel, 10RLP plugs, new R3 tyres – attempted 300 miles run.

(2) 10 laps: Stopped to report sudden increase in water temperature. Driver reports very stable on R3s, but rear suspension not as good as No. 4. Header tank relief valve pressure increased to 20psi.

(3) 6 laps – 1:52.7 – water temperature high, lost 1 gallon, no external leaks. Relief valve outlet wrapped in cotton wool to check if water is lost this way.

(4) 2 laps, stopped at Grande – sudden external water leak, cork packing oil cooler to tank joint had burst due to excessive pressure. Inlet valve spring broken. No. 2 rear plug faulty.

TOTAL DAY'S RUNNING – Car No. 1 – 28 laps
(101 miles)

<u>11th October 1956</u> 22°C, cold, sunny. Driver R. Flockhart. Road circuit.
Car No. 4 – As before, engine '254' with previous '2561' engine's inlet valves.

(1) 10 laps R3 tyres, 53 plugs to settle new engine – 1:53.

(2) New R4 tyres, filled fuel, 20RLP plugs, sent out for 300 miles. Controlled from pit. 24 laps – oil leak in cockpit, cockpit cleaned out. No other action.

(3) 16 laps (40th) – more oil in cockpit, from rear cyl head – quart added as precaution.

(4) 15 laps (51st) – pre-arranged stop to change rear tyres, oil tank over-full, cockpit cleaned out, 8 gallons fuel added as precaution.

(5) 32 laps (83rd) stopped Curva Grande – No. 2 inlet spring broken, valve in cylinder, engine severely damaged.

Driver's face, shoulders, inside of tail covered with rubber dust. Average 118mph, several laps at 1:46.0, driver believes he would have reached 1:43.0. Car still unstable at Curva Grande, jumps off bump and comes down with back out (Connaught same). Vialone flat on right line only. R4s better than R3s. Handling change with fuel load not as great as anticipated. Engine smooth and lively, no vibration through wheel. Oil press. 80–85, water 160°F. Never exceeded 7,600rpm but felt would have pulled 8,000. Wonderfully stable on straight, more understeer would be beneficial. There is no question that No. 4 is far superior to No. 1 in handling and driver comfort, and is ⅔rds of way to perfection on road circuit.

Used 44 gallons of fuel, no water, oil tank still over-full i.e. consumption less than 1 quart, ¼ inch lining left on rear caliper.

TOTAL DAY'S RUNNING – Car No. 4 – 93 laps
(335 miles)

[MISSION ACCOMPLISHED – but testing continued]

<u>17th October 1956</u> 22°C. Dull, cloudy. Driver R. Flockhart. Road circuit.
Car No. 1 – Engine rebuilt with new seal ring to No. 1 liner, AGIP Corse 30 oil.

(1) 3 laps – brakes spongy, cutting onto 3 cyls, driver asked to note suspension reaction to bump.

(2) 2 laps – still cutting – rear spring deflects to absorb bump but car lurches when spring is returning to normal. Sent out for 1 lap and cut clean to localize cause of cutting out.

(3) 1 lap – No. 3 plugs oily – small piece of wood found in No. 3 slow running jet. Rebound damping reduced 200in/lbs.

(4) 2 check laps – driver reports vast improvement in suspension but engine rough. No. 2 inlet valve spring broken.

Car No. 4 – Extra leaf in rear spring ready for banked circuit. Engine '2561' rebuilt with new liner. Pitot heads fitted with ASI to find best position for tail ventilation exit, 18" aft of filler cap. Road circuit used.

(1) 1 lap, ASI u/s, search ASI read 50kts at 110mph indicating position of low pressure. Equipment removed.

(2) 8 laps – 2:10.0, dangerous deterioration in roadholding, car sent onto banking as this may be due to spring settings.

(3) 3 laps of banked circuit, best 1:19.0 – just as bad, car unsteady on straight, rear axle steers? Oil pressure flickers 95 to 65psi at 6,000rpm.

(4) 1 lap Road circuit to check oil pressure – normal. Vibration at constant 6,000rpm on banking causes resonant vibration. Extra leaf out of rear spring.

(5) 4 laps, Road circuit – 2:04.0, no improvement.

TOTAL DAY'S RUNNING –Car No. 1 – 8 laps (29 miles)
Car No. 4 – 14 laps road circuit (51 miles) plus 3 laps banking (8 miles).

18th October 1956 21°C. Dull, cloudy. Road circuit. Wind blowing up pit straight. Driver R. Flockhart.
Car No. 1 – Broken inlet valve spring replaced – new brake master cylinder.

(1) 2 laps – handling good but not as good as No. 4 at its best, brakes effective but pedal still spongy, engine loses one cyl on trailing throttle.

Car No. 4

(1) 1 lap – handling just as bad. Out again for observation.

(2) 2 laps – lost ¼ gallon water from header tank relief valve vent, water in No. 1 cyl, observers report LHR wheel jumping. Damper changed.

(3) 1 lap – Twice as bad, out again for observation.

(4) 1 lap. Observers opine may be front suspension.

Car No. 1 – Driver Roy Salvadori, road circuit.

(1) 2 laps – Crashed at Lesmo on wet patch under trees, nose cowling badly damaged, steering, suspension etc appears safe – temporary repairs made to nose.

(2) 4 laps – 1:52.6 – stopping lap would have been 1:51. Losing one cyl on back straight, plugs oily, AGIP Corse 30 oil drained, replaced by BP Energol Corse 50.

(3) 7 laps – 1:51.0 – cannot take Vialone flat, gets

7,000rpm on back straight against wind; 7,600rpm along pits straight, twitches on fast corners.

(4) 1 lap – driver reports excessive vibration, bolt broken in gearbox flange of rear UJ.

TOTAL DAY'S RUNNING –Car No. 1 – 16 laps (58 miles)
Car No. 4 – 5 laps (18 miles)

19th October 1956 22°C, Dry sunny. Driver R. Flockhart, banked circuit only.
Car No. 1 – using rear prop-shaft from No. 4.

(1) 3 laps – 1:15.8 – ride surprisingly good, car jumps after bump, has to use steering wheel to hold himself in, caught glove in open gear change mechanism; rebound damping increased 100lbs/in. Engine not very happy.

(2) 4 laps – 1:11.0 – better, 6,000rpm on banking, 7,000rpm on straights. Still bumping, original damper setting was best for directional stability but bumping was too severe. 1in Sorbo rebound stops made and fitted.

(3) 6 laps – 1:08.2 – no change, more used to situation, 6,800rpm on banking, 7,100 on straights, engine still not very good.

(4) 5 laps – 1:07.0 – more used to car, engine seems to have lost power; 3rd gear seized and dragging.

TOTAL DAY'S RUNNING –Car No. 1 – 18 laps (48 miles)

GRAND TOTAL – Car No. 1 – 293 miles
Car No. 4 – 779 miles

Cars and equipment packed and returned to England

CHASING THE CHIMERA – TYPE 25 DEVELOPMENTS 1956–57

While the top men at Bourne and Folkingham were all prone to project the image of motor race engineering as being a special and exotic discipline all of its own, since the Silverstone setbacks a more open wider-industry approach was perhaps appropriate. RM called-in Alec Issigonis of the British Motor Corporation – an old prewar Shelsley Walsh friend from the days of his *Lightweight Special* – and his colleague Major Alex Moulton, renowned respectively as creator of extremely advanced and good handling production car chassis and as a specialist suspension consultant. Even then they were sewing the seeds of their epochal Mini saloon car to be launched in 1959.

After some study of the BRM set-up and its unique problems, they told Alfred Owen frankly that in all their industrial experience they had never encountered anything

quite like Department 31 – the Engine Development Division at Bourne – which was "peculiarly managed and directed".

According to Spear they agreed with him that a design should be frozen, built, tested and raced without continuous changes of mind and direction before anything had ever been properly proven. This is unlikely – both knew that in racing if you stand still you are lost, and Moulton denied any such recommendation. They would eventually suggest centre-pivot transverse leafsprings to offer no roll stiffness. The car could then be trimmed by anti-roll bars, while spring and damper functions would be separated by deletion of the air struts.

But Owen's resolve had become quite steely; September 26, to RM:

There is no doubt that what we lack at Bourne is that determination to overcome problems in a consistent and planned fashion before we think of the next one.

I am determined Mr P. Spear is going to be the means of getting down to these problems and keeping all of us down to earth, for if we do not master them over the next few months then I say quite literally 'I shall wash my hands of ever thinking Bourne will achieve this' and I would prefer to pay some other organisation so much per year to get the outstanding 'bugs' out of the car and close Bourne altogether.

Yours sincerely

This chilling missive was copied to both PB and Peter Spear. Now everybody knew precisely where they stood...

Once the team had returned from Monza, a programme of 'Drivability Tests' was run at Folkingham and Silverstone. Tony Rudd reported:

FOLKINGHAM
Test No. 1 – 14th December 1956 – Driver Ron Flockhart. Dry, cold, dull, strong crosswind on straight – 7.00x16 rear tyres, 5.50x16 front.

6 laps – best 1:43 – using 7,600rpm, spun off outwards on 4th lap at first RH corner. Still not as good as No. 4 at best, but better than No. 1 car has ever been. The car has the same feeling of instability at the rear end, slightly reduced...It is still not an 'understeering' car but more stable when power sliding as distinct from drifting. Out of corners slightly more throttle can be applied and it can be applied sooner.

Test No. 2 – Same day – Raining hard, track 100% wet, very strong and gusty cross wind. Front attachment of radius arms lowered 1" on frame. No other change.

5 laps – 1:54.8 – Turned broadside twice, accelerating out of first RH corner – Big improvement...could let car slide to breakaway, and then recover. Never been able to do this before. Car more stable on straight, trace of 'twitch' in corners, but no longer 'fidgets'. An all-round improvement."

Before the next series, the front leafspring was removed, the struts replaced at 190psi with the internal dampers removed, separate Armstrong dampers being retained, as in the leafspring system, with matching settings. The fourth stiffest anti-roll bar was applied, as at Monza.

That day, while this work was being done in the old racing shop at Folkingham – new-car build occupying the new Salopian shed there – across the country at Dukinfield, Cheshire, Tony Brooks was sitting at a desk hand-writing a personal letter to Alfred Owen. He began:

Dear Mr Owen,
I am sorry to have to tell you that I shall be unable to drive for you next year in Formula I.

I told Ray Mays over a month ago that I had tried the Vanwall and was very impressed with the car, intimating that I would have to seriously consider the car for next season.

I have seen Mr Vandervell and I shall be driving for

him next year subject only to final permission from David Brown and agreement on some finer details concerning the contract...

He believed simply that:

...there are so many factors still unproven that even if the handling is better I cannot risk another 'lost' season in Grand Prix racing...I dislike having to leave B.R.M. and would be very pleased to think that we may be able to reach agreement once again at some time in the future.

The team had lost one of the finest of all British racing drivers – but he would return.

The painstaking, dangerous task of trying to make some sense of the Type 25 went on at Silverstone as, at Darlaston, Owen received Tony Brooks' letter:

Test No. 3 16th December 1956 – Flockhart – Track very wet, more slippery than on 14th. Rear suspension as Test No. 2.

7 laps – 1:51.6 using 7,600rpm. Front suspension felt firmer, steadier ride gave more confidence, hands off at 7,000 on straight. Still slight twitch at point of maximum roll. Rear of car seen to lift axle with it as it rises.

Test No. 4 Same day – Flockhart – Radius arms lowered further ½in to 1½in on frame. Track still wet.

6 laps – 1:50.0 using 7,600rpm. Further improvement, rear wheels need more damping. Still large amount of wheel movement observed, even more roll, pattering of inside rear wheel.

Test No. 5 – Same day – rear rebound damping raised to 1250 x 1450. Raining again.

5 laps – 1:54.0. Slight improvement, observers report pattering cured but axle tramp if anything worse on fast left-hand corners. Tyre pressures found incorrect due to faulty gauge, were 30F/34R instead of 27/32 as standard.

Test No. 6 – Same day – correct tyre pressures.

4 laps – 1:54.8 – Driver preferred higher pressures – car broadsided on straight after hitting pool of water.

Testing then took a break until after the New Year, when they resumed on the bleak expanse of Folkingham:

Test No. 7 – 3rd January 1957 – Flockhart. Track 80% wet but drying. Slight cross wind. Car '251' as for test No. 6 but with 28/36 tyre pressures. 5 laps – 1:49.6 – 7,600rpm in top, 7,000 in gears. Handling slightly worse, engine not so willing, not pulling under 6,000rpm – felt rough.

Test No. 8 – Same day – Tyre pressures back to 27/32. Felt handling returned to approximately as 16th December.

Test No. 9 – Same day – Car '254' but with increased

Above: January 1957 – Silverstone testing. Ron Flockhart was joined by Roy Salvadori in further R&D work using low-sided cockpit car '251' and the Howdah-equipped '254' seen here, tail cowl and tailpipe removed, revealing tank and disc-brake cooling shroud and trunking. Above right: Tank removal reveals the Type 27 four-speed transaxle, trunking from both sides of the car feeding onto both faces of the disc. The high-mounted rear transverse leafspring has replaced the original Lockheed air struts. By the end of the year, with small-bore rear caliper, braking ratio would be 37.5:67.5% front:rear.

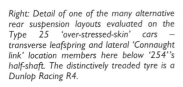

Right: Detail of one of the many alternative rear suspension layouts evaluated on the Type 25 'over-stressed-skin' cars – transverse leafspring and lateral 'Connaught link' location members here below '254''s half-shaft. The distinctively treaded tyre is a Dunlop Racing R4.

counterbalance engine. Tyres 28/36. 6 laps – 1:50.2 – Engine very smooth and willing. Feels as if it wants to rev its head off! Ride VG. Car feels taut and all in one piece. Corners well up to point then smooth slow breakaway which cannot be recovered. Definite oversteering tendency, car weaves on straight, slow rhythmic weave. Cannot place car within 3 feet. Brakes very good.

Test No. 10 – Same day – Car '254' – tyres reduced to 27/32. Not as good as test No. 9.

Both cars were then checked and loaded ready for a trip to Silverstone to continue testing.

Car '251' had the centre-pivot rear spring, radius arms lowered 1½ inches at the front end. Car '254' had the Monza suspension but for the radius arms being lowered 1in at the front. Roy Salvadori had been invited to join Flockhart, and on January 4 running commenced, with Silverstone 100 per cent wet, with puddles, the sky dull and overcast again, and the

temperature just 13°C. Car '251' was equipped with 7.00 x 16 and 5.50 x 16 tyres, '254' on 6.50 x 16s and 5.25 x 16s, both cars running 32/27 tyre pressures, front/rear.

Test No. 1 – Car '251' – Salvadori – 8 laps – Understeer very pronounced – goes straight on approaching some corners.

Test No. 2 – Car '254' – Flockhart – 7 laps – best 2:01 – Better on LH corners than on RH, very little warning of breakaway which is very slow, won't drift on throttle but understeers on trailing throttle. Engine exceptionally good, smooth, good top gear acceleration through range – 7,200rpm in top on straight.

Test No. 3 – Car '251' – Flockhart – 7 laps – 2:04 – Rear suspension too hard, too much understeer, car will go straight on at Beckett's where roll is an embarrassment – 7,000rpm only on straight, won't pull under 6,000.

Test No. 4 – Car '254' – Salvadori – 9 laps – Can use more throttle but unable to drift car, snakes slightly under acceleration, engine much smoother, pronounced rear end breakaway.

Test No. 5 – Car '254' – Flockhart – 8 laps – 1:58.6 (no comments recorded).

Test No. 6 – Car '251' – Salvadori – 5 laps – Brakes very bad indeed, engine feels rough.

The drivers agreed both cars were basically the same entering a corner, but No. 4, having better brakes, could be braked harder but weaved slightly under braking – in the corner '251''s understeer was too pronounced and roll embarrassing. No. 4 was better on LH corners than RH, accelerating away from the corners No. 1 would accept more throttle, although No. 4 had more power available. Along the straight No. 4 had by far the best ride and its engine was much smoother.

TOTAL RUNNING FOR DAY – Car No. 1 – 60 miles
Car No. 4 – 72 miles.

On January 7, PB wrote to Alec Issigonis at Flat 6, Linkside Avenue, Oxford:

My dear Alec...I do feel we have made very good progress, and got the car to a stage now where drivers are able to power slide through a corner with foot hard down and motor car under control.

While the separation of spring and damping rates has brought about an improvement on the rear of the car, the greatest improvement has been achieved by reducing the roll stiffness at the rear of the car. Still using the transverse leaf spring we have removed rollers, etc., and mounted the spring in a simple trunnion, and re-arranged the radius arms to permit some rear axle steer. While this achieves the desired result in the dry, it has produced a hopelessly understeering motor car in the wet... The answer appears to be a compromise... trying to control rear end roll...and to look after the difference between full and empty tanks. I am writing to Alex Moulton...on a further supply of rubber bump stops with different characteristics...

PB and Issigonis later met to discuss the conundrum at an old BRM watering hole...the *Welcombe Hotel* at Stratford.

At Silverstone again on January 10, the track was 25 per cent wet but drying fast, temperature only 9°C; cold, dry and sunny, a lovely winter's day, fresh after overnight rain.

Test No. 1 – Revs limited to 7,500. Car '251' – 7.00 rear tyres, 5.50 front at 32/27 – Flockhart driving – 6 laps – best 1:46.0. Brakes poor, handling very good indeed, engine opened up better, not as smooth as '254''s.

Test No. 2 – Car '254' – 6.50 rear tyres, front at 32/27 – Salvadori – 9 laps – 1:49.5 – Understeered, twitched entering Club, may have been change of camber.

Test No. 3 – Car '251' – Salvadori – 6 laps – 1:50.4 – Brakes very poor, more understeer than Car No. 4.

Test No. 4 – Car '254' – Flockhart – 5 laps – handling of Car No. 1 by far the best.

Test No. 5 – Car '251' – 6.50 x 16 and 5.25 x 16 tyres, fronts worn by use at Folkingham, 27/32 pressures. Rear damper settings reduced to 1250 x 1250 by changing dampers complete – Salvadori – 5 laps – best 1:48.0 – Pronounced understeer into Copse and Beckett's, ride more comfortable, handling slightly improved.

Test No. 6 – Car '251' – Flockhart – 3 laps, stopped. Nos. 2 and 4 inlet valve springs broken, engine was not right from start. Driver reports: Ride much improved.

Test No. 7 – Car '254' – Flockhart – Rear spring changed from 'No. 2' to 'No. 2 plus' in rollers 15" apart, reducing rear roll stiffness; spring rate 46psi per wheel. 4 laps – 1:48.7 – light failing. Better but not as good as No. 1.

Test No. 8 – Car '254' – Salvadori – 5 laps – 1:48.0 – Tends to twitch. Better than No. 1 at Maggott's, Copse and Beckett's. If twitch could be eliminated No. 4 would be the better car.

Ron and Roy agreed the cars were fundamentally the same entering a corner, No. 4 had slightly less understeer and a better ride, making the driver feel more relaxed; No. 1 was superior on faster corners since over-enthusiasm could be recovered, but its roll was still an embarrassment. Away from the corners No. 1 was superior, accepting more throttle, earlier. Along the straights there was very little difference between them.

Reviewing these test results and driver comments with the benefit of over 30 years' hindsight, it is apparent neither driver had much of a clue of what direction development should take. What ORO needed was an intelligent and experienced test driver with specialist chassis engineering knowledge...

One would, eventually, be found.

COMETH THE HOUR – COMETH THE MAN

Motor Components Ltd of Coventry eventually won the race amongst prospective Rubery Owen suppliers to perfect a method of manufacturing a hollow-headed inlet valve for the P25 engine whose sealing disc was at last welded into place in a trouble-free manner. With the engine basically reliable, ORO's heart-rending quest for truly raceworthy roadholding dragged on...

After the rather inconclusive test periods at Folkingham and Silverstone, it was clear that the Issigonis/Moulton-advised exploratory suspension changes had improved the Type 25's behaviour overall, without making either contracted driver – Salvadori or Flockhart – particularly happy, but of course Issigonis and Moulton had been asked how to identify

April 22, 1957 – Glover Trophy, Easter Monday Goodwood: First-lap exit for Roy Salvadori, completing his unhappy race debut for BRM as '253' – brakes jammed on – spins to rest at Woodcote Corner, narrowly avoided by Jack Brabham's works Cooper (left) and Archie Scott-Brown – recovering from his own opening lap 'moment' in the Connaught B-Type. Roy – not without justification – did not endear himself to ORO's mechanics by waiting until they arrived before very publicly kicking the newly rebodied car…

the Type 25's problems, not how to cure them…

Then in a final pre-Easter Goodwood test session – held at the Sussex circuit the preceding Monday/Tuesday – a new discovery left Tony Rudd – who by this time readily admits he fancied himself as a burgeoning suspension and handling expert – totally nonplussed…

Roy Salvadori had just declared that a set-up employing a front anti-roll bar and no rear anti-roll bar was the best yet. He then ran five or six more laps and described the car as being "just about as good", only for Tony to find – to his horror – that the anti-roll bar operating link was adrift on one side so Roy had in fact been driving a car with no anti-roll bars at all and couldn't tell the difference.

But Roy had just been signed-on as team-mate to Flockhart, who had done most of the testing and was particularly happy with the cars' handling. However, Tony suspected the Scot tended to drive round the problems and avoided being too critical in case it should jeopardise his place in the team.

Regardless, Flockhart had clipped 4–5 seconds off his previous year's lap times at both Silverstone and Goodwood, and now he was lapping the latter course at existing record speed, with Salvadori slightly slower. The Type 25's frightening earlier oversteer had become tamed into containable understeer and to some extent the crew understood how to vary this condition to suit any driver.

> PB: "Flockhart likes considerable understeer; Salvadori likes a neutral steering characteristic to a tendency to oversteer, and is able to lap in similar times; he has always felt that there is still something that does not give him absolute confidence to drive faster."

But troubles persisted with the Lockheed swinging-caliper brakes. Sometimes they grabbed and locked, other times they failed to work at all – the servo-assisted arrangement always seemed particularly sensitive, the brake pedal too often a feelingless on-off switch.

The first race of the 1957 European Formula 1 season, and ORO's comeback after Silverstone in July '56, was to be Easter

Monday at Goodwood, and during official practice there on Saturday, April 20, the track surface was coated with rubber and oil. Flockhart was driving '251' with centre-pivot leafsprings front and rear, trimmed out by anti-roll bars and retaining its low-sided cockpit. Salvadori was in '253', rebuilt with an integral stressed-skin Howdah-style cockpit surround – a finalized version of the detachable affair tried experimentally on '254' at Monza – and with centre-pivot transverse rear leafspring, co-axial Armstrong dampers and anti-roll bars fore and aft.

Both drivers recorded times 2 seconds slower than those achieved in testing and Salvadori was again deterred and worried by locking front brakes. He spun his car at the chicane, Jack Fairman crashing his Connaught in avoidance. A further half-hour's practice was run on the Monday morning, in wet conditions. Salvadori remained unhappy about the brakes despite Freddie Bothamley of Lockheed having stripped and modified them on the day of rest.

April 22, 1957 – BARC Glover Trophy, Goodwood – 32 laps, 76.8 miles

Both BRM drivers had a busy Easter Monday, driving in both the Formula 2 and sports car events for Lotus and Cooper respectively before lowering themselves into the Type 25s for the day's Formula 1 main event.

Moss and Brooks had qualified fastest in their two Vanwalls, Stirling on pole at 1:28.2 with Brooks 0.8sec slower. Archie Scott-Brown then squeezed his Connaught onto third spot on the front row with a 1:31.2, beating Flockhart's best, on the outside, at 1:32.6. Salvadori with 1:34.6 was sandwiched by the Connaughts of Stuart Lewis-Evans – with experimental 'tooth-paste tube' unpainted aluminium bodywork – and Jack Fairman on the centre of the second row.

But on the warming-up lap Salvadori's '253' had its brakes lock on and it required five men to push it onto the grid. Dan M. Glover – donor of the Trophy bearing his name – dropped the flag and the front row raced away into Madgwick Corner,

Moss leading towards St Mary's, where Scott-Brown ran off onto the grass and dropped to sixth. Hurtling down the Lavant Straight into Woodcote Corner, Salvadori's brakes locked again and he spun, and retired.

Completing lap two, Moss and Brooks led from Lewis-Evans' new Connaught, Scott-Brown, Fairman and Flockhart, two Vanwalls leading three Connaughts and only then the BRM. But Ron promptly spun at St Mary's, losing a place to Brabham's Cooper and next time round, same place, '251' spun again… BRM fortunes were going from bad to worse.

Vanwall had Brooks' throttle linkage break on lap four – fortunately without jamming open… Scott-Brown withdrew from his inherited second place, and Moss led Lewis-Evans until his Vanwall also broke its throttle linkage, at St Mary's. Lewis-Evans was left to win easily for the financially beleaguered Connaught team, from Jack Fairman, with Flockhart circulating as if on sheet ice in the sole surviving BRM.

Salvadori's front brakes had been rubbing on the warm-up lap. Bothamley had freed them on the grid but then they had locked again on the opening lap. With his three spins, Flockhart was unable to lap within 5 seconds of his previous best.

After the race Salvadori's front brakes and Flockhart's rear dampers were all changed. Back at Goodwood two days later, a full day's running was completed. The circuit remained greasy in places, both drivers still 2 seconds outside their previous best. Both cars completed over 300 miles without problems and both drivers confirmed they felt mechanically good and reliable. But testing ended with Flockhart and Salvadori at loggerheads, one wanting an understeering car, the other an oversteerer.

PB was now convinced that Flockhart had become acclimatized to driving around whatever demon might reside within the chassis, while Salvadori just could not come to grips with it, and was of no use in its eradication.

1957 Easter Monday Goodwood: Ron Flockhart settles himself into '251' – still with its 1956-style low-cut cockpit body in contrast to team-mate Salvadori's modified sister car '253'. Salmon and Dove prepare to push-start, Tony Rudd (right) in natty waistcoat. Standing by the unpainted 'toothpaste-tube' Connaught B-Type (right) which will win – driven by Stuart Lewis-Evans – is a youthful Mike 'Noddy' Grohman, who would move to Cooper and become Jack Brabham's chief mechanic in his back-to-back World Championship seasons of 1959–60. 'Noddy' became as much a pillar of Cooper Cars through their heyday as did Willie Southcott of BRM. Moving to Jack's own Brabham team from 1962, he almost literally worked himself to death, succumbing in February 1964 to a cerebral haemorrhage after yet another long day's labour. He was only 32.

Up at Leamington Spa, the Lockheed Hydraulic Brake Co Ltd's Fred Ellis took a long look at the front brakes removed from Salvadori's Goodwood car. An automatic adjuster spring in the nearside caliper was found to be broken, while the spring and rubber cups were jammed crosswise in the forward end of the master cylinder. The broken spring would have permitted the piston retractor springs to draw the piston back to its full off position, leaving excessive clearance between pad and disc.

The first brake application after this event would then have displaced much fluid, giving an exceptionally 'long' and soft pedal. This extra pedal travel then caused the front spring in the master cylinder to coil-bind and buckle, permitting its cup to skew and cross-bind within the cylinder. The rubber cup seal then extruded behind the spring cup, locking the spring in the coil-bound position, and rendering the front brakes inoperative.

Fred Ellis assured PB and Spear that both springs in the automatic adjuster and the master cylinder were being redesigned to avoid any recurrence.

Meanwhile, Tony: We had the performance curves of the latest Dunlop R4 tyre which was at that time in advance of the Pirelli, and our Chief Draughtsman, John Botterill, and I began to chart weight transfer in our cars with varying amounts of radial acceleration and braking. We put these results on a large sheet of paper, 36 inches top to bottom, 48 inches across, and covered it with columns of figures, then related weights on tyres and attitudes of tyres in camber and toe-in to produce cornering power curves from Dunlop to predict slip angles the tyres had to assume. And there it all was. The geometry of the front suspension was moving about so much there was no chance the driver could predict what the car's front end was going to do, while at the rear, because the roll-centre and the centre of gravity height so nearly coincided, nothing would happen. All this coincided with the aftermath of Goodwood '57, and when John Botterill and I had finished doing our 'football pools' as the mechanics at Folkingham christened them, all was revealed.

I consequently had several ideas for future development, but PB had a better one. He called in Colin Chapman…

'Chunky' was building his reputation as a chassis engineering genius with his Lotus sports and Formula 2 cars and had been called in by Tony Vandervell to redesign the Vanwall – with evident success. Now, what had been good for the old enemy was going to come to BRM's rescue.

Chapman visited Bourne and Folkingham on April 26 and on the 29th PB recommended to Owen that:

> …a third person [should] try the car, who is qualified as a driver and at the same time has ability in car engineering, and [I have] approached Colin Chapman, who designs Lotus cars, and was responsible for the new chassis and suspension on the Vanwall. He is a good driver and an intelligent and practical engineer…

He wanted to try the car at Goodwood:

> …as he knows the course so well and believed it to be the most difficult and demanding where roadholding is concerned.

THE CHAPMAN REPORT

Colin Chapman had twice driven the BRM, once at Goodwood and the second time at Folkingham, in May/June 1957 to form his own impressions of the car's behaviour, its good points, and its bad. The report he compiled for ORO was in two parts, and it read as follows:

Some Observations on the Handling
Characteristics of the B.R.M.

1. *Brakes*: There appears to be far too much brake effort on the front wheels and insufficient on the rear, which not only detracts from the overall braking performance, but tends to overload the front brakes to the point where locking up and consequent loss of control results. Pedal effort in servo seems very good, but in dead engine conditions the amount of pedal effort to produce any noticeable braking effect is quite disconcerting.

2. *Steering*: The steering is extremely light and lacks 'feel'. With the present pronounced understeer conditions, quite a lot of steering lock is required and it is very difficult indeed to feel exactly what point has been reached in front wheel adhesion by means of feel from the steering system as compared to other cars. The steering ratio seemed a little low.

3. *Suspension*: The car is extremely softly sprung and whilst giving a smooth flat ride in straight running conditions it does tend to wander considerably at speeds over 150m.p.h. (this was only experienced at Folkingham and may have been accentuated by wind conditions). There is considerable change of attitude in pitch between braking and acceleration and generally speaking the pitch frequency appears to be very low. In cornering conditions considerable roll is experienced and when pressed to the limit the inner front wheel appears to flap a little. This is probably the advanced breakaway on this wheel, as will be explained later. When in a corner the car understeers considerably, but this would not be objectionable provided sufficient power could be applied safely to help the car into a normal under-steering drift. Unfortunately, this is not so. The main trouble appears to lie in that it is extremely difficult to apply sufficient power to achieve this drift without suffering rear-end breakaway. Shock absorber settings may be altered in an attempt to ameliorate this, though it is felt by the writer that more than small adjustments are required. On entering a corner there is a decided initial roll oversteer which disappears once the car has attained a cornering condi-tion. It is felt that this is one of the reasons why the car is considered 'difficult' in corners. At the present time this roll lag is put down to (a) large roll angles which tend to show up any very slight deficiency in chassis geometry, and (b) the indeterminate effect of various elements of friction in the front and rear suspension systems as at present employed.

4. *Shock Absorbers*: These appear to be adequate at the moment, but as before stated, no extensive tests were made in this direction.

5. *Engine*: The engine appears to be completely trouble free judging from the considerable amount of running that has been done in test conditions of late without any major trouble. However, it is the writer's opinion, and this is only a personal opinion, that there is not as much power available as in one other Grand Prix car recently driven. [78] It is stressed that this is a private opinion and there are so many other facts to be considered such as handling smoothness, vibration etc. that not a great deal of weight can be assessed to this as against B.H.P. figures shown on a dynamometer.

The report continued...

Suggested method of treatment to attain the most rapid improvement in handling of the B.R.M.

It is the writer's opinion that there is nothing fundamentally wrong with the general concept of the present car when one considers things such as track and wheelbase of front suspension, type of rear suspension, weight distribution, height of centre of gravity etc. It is therefore considered a feasible proposition to effect considerable improvements in the existing design with some reasonably easy modifications to the front and rear suspension.

In view of the time factor involved the writer would prefer to modify one car immediately in every respect as enumerated below rather than substitute one at a time, individual modifications which may entail a whole season's testing...it is felt that an entirely different design approach to the problem of suspension and more in keeping with the writer's own principles of design and experience might bring results quicker than pursuing the present philosophy. I would therefore make my recommendations as follows:

Brakes: It is essential that the rear brakes be called upon to take their fair share of the braking effort. This means that the applied pedal effort to the rear must be increased...This may bring with it complications in the form of disc temperatures and accellerated [sic] pad wear and must be overcome by such methods as more effective cooling and increased heat sink capacity of the rear disc and increased pad depth if necessary. Secondly if some method could be devised to give better braking effort under dead engine conditions I feel this would raise the morale of the drivers as under the present system should the engine fail at the end of a long fast straight it is the writer's impression that it would be virtually impossible to stop the car in time to avoid a serious accident.

Steering: Considerably more feel is required in the steering so that the driver can estimate by means of the change in allignment [sic] torque the point to which road adhesion has been stretched and make corrections accordingly. To achieve this the more caster angle is required and also a higher steering ratio. A figure of 7° castor angle would be a good starting point instead of the

78. Significantly, this was the Vanwall.

April 23, 1957 – the Colin Chapman test drive, Goodwood: PB (left) wonders if this will all be a waste of time, Tony Rudd leans thoughtfully upon the fence – "What does he know about suspension theory that I don't?" – while Team Lotus driver Herbert Mackay 'Mac' Fraser (dark glasses) looks on as 'Baggy', 'Corporal Ayliff' and 'Mo the Mangle' push-start ACBC in Salvadori's latest-spec '253'. The car's new high-cockpit coachwork features a narrow bonnet, no longer extending to the exhaust-stack opening which is now entirely within a separate side panel.

present 3°. Similarly the steering ratio could be modified from the present 14–1 to about 10–1 or 12–1. In addition there is the question of Ackermann angle. It is the writer's impression that for a high performance car of this type the present Ackermann system must be adjusted completely and the steering arranged for the outer wheel to turn through a greater steering angle than the inner wheel for the highest cornering speeds to be achieved. This could be fairly easily accomplished by modification of the existing design of steering arm.

Suspension: It is felt that the suspension in general is far too soft and contains many indeterminate factors in the shape of friction in the front pneumatic struts, the rear pivoted leaf spring and the de Dion pot joints, etc. This springing system should be replaced front and rear within a frictionless type and preferably telescopic shock absorbers carrying coil springs… These units can be designed with[in] the next two or three days and the manufacture should be only…7 to 10 days… The suspension frequency can be increased considerably to the suggested figures of 75 cycles per minute in the front and 85 cycles per minute in the rear. Less emphasis can then be placed on roll-bars to achieve the desired weight transfer and just a small roll-bar can be used at the front to modify the understeer/oversteer characteristic of the car as required. At the rear it is considered imperative to eliminate the friction existing in the pot joints of the articulated de Dion half-shafts. These should be replaced by a ball bearing spline as already indicated and arrangements could be made to obtain a proprietary part for this at short notice….

Wheels: It is felt that a car of this weight can be considerably improved in the wheel and tyre specification.

Firstly the wheels are considerably oversize and therefore running at well below their design characteristics which have been assumed to be valid but need not necessarily apply because of the extreme de-rating of these tyres. It is therefore suggested that the tyre size be reduced to 500 x 15 front and 600 x 15 rear instead of the present sizes. If necessary tyre pressures could be increased to satisfy the tyre companies as to standing wave resistance, but some definite tests must be carried out on this question of tyre size…we are not to be dominated by irrational decisions made by the Racing Department of the tyre company concerned. In addition, and this is considered to be a most major point, either Avon or Pirelli tyres should be used in preference to the existing Dunlop. In the writer's experience it has been proved time and again that a Pirelli or Avon tyre will give 1 or 1½ seconds per lap over the contemporary Dunlop. At this stage in the game we cannot afford to throw away such major considerations as this for the sake of any established tradition…

…I would like to conclude with the statement that I would be most keen to see the development of this car carried through as soon as possible because it seems an enormous amount of time and effort has been spent by all concerned and if any other radical steps are taken all this work would have been wasted.

However, I would emphasise that I would like *all* of these modifications to be put in hand *immediately* rather than individually and incorporated one at a time…we do not have the time for research of this nature at this stage in the season.

Colin Chapman

His own cars had suffered similar problems with sudden breakaway, ditto the Vanwall when first run:

> This was traced in both cases to lack of wheel movement when rolled and weight fully transferred – the Vanwall was bad in the wet until they increased the rear axle bump by 2 inches.

Intrigued by Chapman's words of wisdom, Berthon then had the Type 25's axle movement checked and found that it was indeed restricted:

> Although there are serious space limitations we are increasing axle travel by 1½ inches and as soon as this is completed I propose running at Goodwood with Colin Chapman, and Salvadori to check his views…

What was more, Chapman was prepared to charge only if he could help – no fix, no fee. Alfred Owen knew it made sense.

On May 2, the latest high-sided cockpit, stressed-skin car '253' was returned to Goodwood, where Colin Chapman clambered aboard wearing his rather shabby blue overalls with BRDC badge sewn proudly onto their breast pocket, and his dark green crash helmet with clear plastic visor.

With PB and Tony Rudd supervising, the mechanics push-started their car, and Colin drove off into a series of fast and searching test laps.

At the end of that long day – again punctuated by brake problems – Colin returned to his home in Barnet, he studied his notes and pondered on his impression that the Type 25 was not nearly as bad as he had feared since a little free advice from him had already been adjusted into its set-up. He then scratched his head and, better than any other driver before him, appreciated the magnitude of the BRM Type 25 problem …and its possible solution.

Meanwhile, Peter Spear had continued to cast his own net of influence ever wider. He had been talking to that arch pragmatist, the charming John Cooper of the Cooper Car Co Ltd, whose rear-engined F2 cars had been going so well and were now – with interim 1.96-litre Coventry Climax four-cylinder engines bought off the shelf – being campaigned in Formula 1. John had helped create the original Vanwall F1 chassis for Tony Vandervell. Now he seemed to have developed a far less expensive way to go motor racing. This intrigued Spear, and on the evening of Chapman's test-drive at Goodwood a batch of Type 25 chassis drawings were mailed to John at his factory in Hollyfield Road, Surbiton, Surrey.

Alfred Owen had, of course, been kept abreast of this contact by Spear, who minuted him four days later:

> I am glad you told Mr Mays about Cooper because I was forced into telling Peter Berthon on the threat of semi-blackmail of drawings for Cooper…

The team was poised to return to the site of its previous season's first fiasco – Monte Carlo – and Spear added:

> I am very worried about the cars driving at Monaco. John Cooper has said, as I told you, with an understeer

May 12, 1957 – Monaco Grand Prix practice, Monte Carlo: The worst thing which can happen to any Formula 1 team is to present an apparently healthy car for practice which then laps too slowly to qualify. It is happening here to BRM as Roy Salvadori – completely detuned by doubts about '253''s troublesome brakes – cannot become one of the Monaco GP's classically exclusive '16 on the grid'. "Strangely enough, Flockhart had nothing but the highest praise for the brakes…" read a report to AGBO from "one of his spies…". Of course, the other great F1 team patron to rely upon such second-hand intelligence from the front was named Enzo Ferrari…

characteristic…Monaco can be a death-trap with the walls and water round the track…

One week later, tense with mixed anticipation and trepidation, ORO's Monaco trip began. The two laden Lodestars and the old mobile workshop rumbled down the pot-holed lane from their aerodrome lair – to head away southbound on the A1 towards the 11am Dover-Dunkirk ferry, bound for a rendezvous in Reims with PB to draw currency for their long journey…

May 19, 1957 – Monaco Grand Prix, Monte Carlo – 105 laps, 205.18 miles

The two high-sided Type 25s which Salvadori and Flockhart drove in Monaco GP practice that year were chassis '253' and '254' respectively. The lap time target there was Fangio's 1:44.2 pole position mark in the Lancia-Ferrari the previous year.

In Thursday practice both BRMs were beset by handling and brake problems, Flockhart working very hard, but Salvadori becoming quickly dispirited. The last thing one needs at Monte Carlo is an understeering F1 car with inconsistent brakes. He tried a 1.9-litre rear-engined works Cooper-Climax while his BRM was being adjusted, which left him even less happy, appreciating what he was missing through being contracted to ORO!

The Type 25s' Lockheed brakes were still grabbing. Flockhart spun at the *Tabac* corner before the pits, but kept it off the wall and was timed at 1:50.0 as he bravely carried on. Ron continued to flog around, as Denis Jenkinson reported, "…trying to make some sort of show for the B.R.M.s which were not only handling poorly but were not even going fast…"

Thunderstorms cleansed the course that night, but the roads were still wet when practice resumed at 6am next day. Of the four privateers vying for a place on the restricted 16-

strong starting grid both Horace Gould and Masten Gregory qualified in their Maserati 250Fs, with better times than BRM had yet approached.

Final practice on Saturday afternoon saw Flockhart, by great effort, achieving a 1:48.6 to qualify. Salvadori, however, toured round in 1:50s at best, joining Andre Simon, Luigi Piotti and Les Leston amongst the non-qualifiers.

Roy recalled how, after the binding brakes at Goodwood had ruined his public BRM debut: "Ray, as always, promised he would deal with it and ensure that Peter Berthon allowed only Lockheed to work on the brakes. It was, of course, all hot air, but Ray was so persuasive that I almost believed him!

"Monaco...is a circuit where complete confidence in the car is essential. As soon as I drove the BRM in practice, I became convinced that Lockheed had never touched the brakes and that BRM themselves had been playing with them. They were still sticking badly, but with the difference that they no longer stayed jammed on completely. This caused immense problems...at Casino Square the driver brakes to steady the car...and then accelerates hard down past the *Tip Top* bar. On this part of the course I became convinced that the engine was seizing, when in fact the brakes were still sticking from the application at Casino Square.

"This was happening all round the circuit...I was trying the brakes long before corners to make sure there was some braking power and my times were getting slower and slower...I lost confidence altogether because I thought the problem was with my driving and I failed to qualify..."

He had asked RM in the pits if the team had been playing around with the brakes but was assured they were absolutely standard, as supplied by Lockheed – which was substantially true, but Lockheed had been playing around with the system themselves.

Back at the *Hotel de Paris* – "it was ironic that BRM had provided me with superb hotel accommodation...in one of the most sumptuous hotels, and one of the most appalling cars I have ever driven" – he met a Lockheed representative who "confided, rather reluctantly, that BRM had modified the braking system and that he was not happy about the modification that had been made..."

When Roy angrily confronted RM, "Ray was more concerned about what he regarded as the Lockheed representative's breach of confidence. I decided to withdraw from the team immediately, but Ray urged me not to act hastily...I had insufficient confidence in the BRM to drive it really quickly and BRM were quite unable to keep their word. I withdrew from the team and returned the balance of the retainer of £2,500, after deducting a proportion to cover the two races at which I had driven..."

Salvadori, incidentally, believes to this day that Ron Flockhart "was a real hero" for staying on. Meanwhile, immediately after Roy's defection, Raymond Mays' briefing to Rivers Fletcher for the subsequent ORMA newsletter reveals the carefree manner in which he would always unashamedly polish the image of Peter Berthon and the team for public consumption: "Salvadori not being happy with the car asked to be released from his contract...Salvadori informed me that he had received the utmost co-operation from Peter Berthon and all the B.R.M. staff which he greatly appreciated..."

Morning rainstorms again swept Monaco on raceday, but the roads were drying and the skies clear as the start approached. Moss, Hawthorn and Collins all then crashed in the opening stages, leaving a straight duel between Fangio, dominant for Maserati, and Tony Brooks, second for Vanwall.

Flockhart's BRM circulated ninth in a duelling bunch including Gregory, Lewis-Evans, Trintignant, Scarlatti and Brabham. By 20 laps this battle had resolved itself into a trio, with Flockhart trailing Brabham's Cooper and Trintignant's Ferrari. Ron eventually ran fifth amongst the thinning field until, on lap 60, his engine stripped its timing gears while accelerating out of the *Gazometre* Hairpin along the curve behind the pits.

Meanwhile, Peter Spear was delighted with the finished 'Chapman Report', [as separately reproduced in full] for his R&D department at Darlaston had:

> ...reported last year that the struts were not too satisfactory and the point was proved when we carried out the various tests and showed the hysteresis effects. However, all this is part of the basic design background about which I have been complaining for so long.

But he lacked sufficient confidence in Chapman – just another motor racing 'engineer' – to appreciate Colin's priority recommendation that all changes be made simultaneously:

> My own opinion is that we did ought to try altering one variable at a time and replace the front struts first before we start altering the rear suspension...To be honest I was rather surprised with the information about tyres and wheels...

But on this memo to Owen of June 7, Spear had added in the margin regarding the point about altering one variable at a time: "I now know that this cannot be done easily..."

John Botterill felt rather upstaged by all this and left ORO, while PB and Tony Rudd agreed that the Chapman recommendations made sense. They would bring the BRM into parallel with the Vanwall, which was showing obvious potential in the hands of Moss and Brooks. Above all, deletion of the dreaded pot-jointed half-shafts in favour of a Ferrari-like ball-splined type promised to allow the Type 25's rear suspension real movement at last. Tony: When we thought about it we all shared a vivid mental picture of the cars rolling through a corner, and then staying rolled under acceleration as far as the first gearchange when the load on the pot-joint was momentarily relaxed, enabling it to plunge, whereupon the car would snap down onto an even keel again!

Colin's drawings had arrived when we got back from Monaco. He left the front suspension geometry alone, but specified an Armstrong telescopic damper with a coil-spring around it which fitted in the front suspension virtually in place of the original externally-mounted air-strut. For the back end he'd thrown out all our various location devices and had drawn a very simple Watt link arrangement, putting the rear roll-centre about halfway between hub level and the ground, and he recommended a simple coil-spring and telescopic damper layout. It took about three weeks to make

THE TARUFFI REPORT

Raymond Mays invited Piero Taruffi to sample a Type 25 and provide his recommendations for its improvement *a la* Chapman. This, as written, is the great man's report:

TECHNICAL REPORT ON A B.R.M. SINGLE-SEATER 4-CYLINDER 2500 – TEST ON THE CIRCUIT OF FOLKINGHAM

The tests have been effectuated on the days of 28–29th May, 1957.

Condition of Weather: Good – Windy.

Condition of the track can be considered moderate. The surface is not perfect, and in some places a little bumpy, especially in the straight, where is also a little dirty and variable in adherence coefficient.

For the getaway of a car, specially for the road holding, this track can be considered good.

The 28th May I have tested a car (Salvadori – Monte Carlo).

Observations on the behaviour of this car:

1) THE ROAD-HOLDING has to be considered poor. The car is affected from irregular movements, parti-cularly of the front parts; movements that oblige the driver at continuous correction.

2) THE STEERING seems too light and provides too little tendency to return. In the straight of the track the car does not run straight, but irregularly and rapidly deviate to the left, and especially on the right (may be the wind). This defect increases with the speed of the car and seems to be not affected appreciably from the acceleration or deceleration of the car.

Beyond the movement of the front part, I have noted an oscillatory horizontal movement transverse at the direction of the car. This movement moves transversely the driver in his seat. All this irregularity, damages the exact entrance on the corners specially those taken at high speed. This defect appears also some time on the central part of the curve and coming out, compromising the acceleration.

3) BRAKES: are very efficient, but too sensitive, and little variation of the pressure on the pedal makes them dangerous. This affect in a difficult way the driving, specially when the driver has to make changing speed. On this manoeuvre, the driver has not the support of the left foot at the movement of his body that has a forward push of the inertia forces. The ratio seem to be not correct. Brakes too much in the front (try with empty tank).

4) GEARBOX is good. Well geared and enough fast in changing speed.

5) ACCELERATION: Very good in comparison of cars of the same type. The curve of power of the engine seems progressive, specially beyond 3500 revolutions. The engine is also usable under these revolutions. The driver feels a sensible vibration due to the engine on the wheel, especially at engine speed of 5000–7000.

6) SPEED: Very good in comparison of cars of the same type. Regarding the characteristics of 5) and 6) – for have a more exact opinion should be necessary to effectuate timed test.

7) RELIABILITY: On all these tests the car has effectuated more than 200 miles driven as under racing conditions, the engine, and other various parts like in a race; nothing gave any trouble.

8) COMFORT OF THE DRIVER: A lot of dusty powder came in the cockpit. Seat is comfortable; try a more inclined front part of seat. The left pedal is too close at the gear lever change.

VARIATIONS DONE DURING THE TEST:

The defect most important of this car concerns the characteristic 1) and 2), regarding the road-holding. To reduce these defects have been done those following modifications (modification possible to do in a short time).

a) Increasing of the caster [*sic*] from, 3½° to 6°. Such modification has increased the feel of the steering and has produced a better return. The road holding in the straight is lightly improved.

(b) Increasing of the toe-in of the front wheel: No improvement.

(c) Decreasing of the ground moment of the front wheel from 2" to 1⅝": Worse impression.

The tests effectuated at point (b) and (c) could be not too exact because during them the forward suspension of the car is progressively become worse for defect of the springing or the damping system.

This observation is consolidated from a successive test effectuated in a second car (Flockhart – Monte Carlo), which is resulted to have an appreciable better road holding.

CONCLUSIONS The car has notable characteristics of speed, acceleration and deceleration. Has on the contrary a poor road holding. On accord to Eng. Berthon those noted defects of the road holding could be improved with modifications on the front spring system and at the rear system of the sliding joints. I agree with those modifications that could probably be the reason of the defects noted.

In any case, the car appears to me very well designed and built. For that I report that the defects noted can be and are worthwhile to be eliminated.

If these modifications should be carried out quickly the car should compete successfully in races.

30th May, 1957   PIERO TARUFFI

THE TARUFFI TESTS – PART TWO

TECHNICAL REPORT ON A B.R.M. SINGLE-SEATER, 4-CYLINDER 2500 – TEST ON THE CIRCUIT OF FOLKINGHAM

The Tests have been carried out on the days of the 26th, 27th and 28th June, 1957.

Condition of the weather and the track the same as the Tests on the 28th and 29th May.

Observations on the behaviour of the car:

1) ROAD HOLDING has to be considered as much improved. The irregular movement, particularly of the front that I observed in the previous test has been eliminated.

The car that had very much understeer is now quite normal. A little understeer at the constant speed becomes oversteer getting the power with high torque, specially in low gear. This oversteer is easily controlled.

2) THE STEERING seems to be improved and has now sufficient self-centring action. It was right to make a test with more castor.

In the straight the car still tends to wander slightly, but is much improved. The oscillatory horizontal movement is still affecting the car a little. This may be improved when the sliding joints are fitted.

3) BRAKES: These are still too sensitive and like in the precious test – dangerous. The front wheels are still locking, specially the right front, in comparison with the rear.

CONCLUSIONS: The car has now much more suitable characteristics for participation in races. The road-holding is quite good, and the handling is safe.

The first modification has to be directed to reduce the sensitivity of the brakes; and the second modification to try to add more understeer. With this modification it may be necessary to raise the ratio of the steering box.

The third modification to have the same power of the brakes when the engine is not running.

My point of view is that the car can run at the Race at Rouen with much improved chances of success than at Monte Carlo, specially for the big improvement that is brought about in the roadholding.

28th June, 1957   PIERO TARUFFI

---

the necessary bits and convert the cars…in time for the French GP at Rouen.

And while PB had recruited the new-wave genius of Colin Chapman, RM's idolatry of 'establishment Continentals' had led him to the hugely experienced *Ing* Piero Taruffi of long Maserati, Ferrari, Lancia and even Mercedes-Benz experience for a second opinion.

With new-found purpose, the pace accelerated at Folkingham. The two cars for Rouen – chassis '253' and '254' – were having new mounting brackets worked into them to provide new location and frame pick-up for the de Dion tubes and also for new top front wishbones. New layouts for brake cooling ducting and carburettor air intake were also demanded by interference from the new spring units. Springs had been made and delivered by Jonas Woodhead & Sons by June 20, and damper units were due the following day from Armstrong Patents. Ball-sliding joints were under way at Coventry Tool & Gauge, who were quoting 12 weeks' delivery. One pilot set was being machined at Bourne. RM to Owen, June 25: "The first B.R.M. with the modified suspension was started last night…As agreed, the moment the new car was likely to be ready I telegraphed Taruffi, and all being well he will be in Bourne sometime tomorrow, to carry out tests (again), I hope for the remainder of the week." Interestingly, Ray continued: "We telegraphed Colin Chapman at Le Mans asking him to contact Mackay Fraser with a view to coming back to England to try the car, because as yet a second driver has not been nominated…" (to accompany Flockhart).

Herbert Mackay Fraser was a dark, stocky and wealthy American racing driver with family interests in Brazil, who had made quite a mark for himself in British and European

racing in Ferrari and more recently Lotus cars. He was then driving sports and F2 cars for Team Lotus, and had been present at Chapman's Goodwood BRM test on May 2. He was a very popular, pleasant man, highly intelligent and with considerable potential as a driver. In effect he had come to BRM as part of the 'Chapman package' – Colin having recommended him to Tony in preference to Flockhart since he was 'analytical' and 'had no axe to grind'. While the cars were being prepared for Rouen he visited the race 'shop at Folkingham and perched himself quietly at the top of a step ladder, out of everybody's way, watching the mechanics assemble what was to be his car for the French GP.

For three days, June 26–28, Piero Taruffi returned to Folkingham to test-drive the revised Type 25, and he liked what he found.

Further engine development, still with 7½% nitro fuel mix, meant that no engine was signed-off the Folkingham test-bed below 285bhp (while the Vanwall gave 290/295bhp with an even fatter torque curve). The cars had gained weight, now approaching 12cwt against their original 10, and with the new ventilated rear disc braking was better balanced, so ORO set off for the July 7 race at Rouen in good spirits…

Tony: It was terrifically hot there, and even hotter inside our base garage, which was the transport department of the local BP oil refinery. RM took the hose from the car wash and spent much of his time spraying cold water on the roof for us. But he didn't know it was a pretty poor piece of hose with innumerable small jets issuing from various leaks, so the mechanics entertained themselves by persuading him to walk backwards until he stood over one of the jets…a minor triumph for them.

COOPER-BRM – THE FIRST CONTACTS

While exploring avenues to improve BRM's fortunes, Peter Spear developed quite a friendly relationship with John Cooper, whose rear-engined 1.9-litre essentially Formula 2 cars were at that time making their first tentative steps into the Grand Prix class.

John was engaging, informative and always faultlessly helpful. Where BRM's internal systemology was complex and paper-heavy – the Cooper Car Co's was practical simplicity incarnate. It's an obvious exaggeration, but in effect while at BRM everything was written down, recorded and reproduced with multiple copies, at Team Lotus records were kept on the back of an envelope, and at Cooper there was nobody who could read or write!

But this accurately reflects the degrees of bureaucracy within each company. And in terms of motor racing in 1957, each marque's success was in starkly inverse proportion to its systemology; Cooper on top of the pile, then Lotus, and BRM effectively nowhere, although in fairness Bourne was attempting to crack a far harder nut.

On Thursday, May 30, 1957, Peter Spear spent nearly five hours with John Cooper in his racing car works at Hollyfield Road, Surbiton. They discussed the possibility of John providing simple advice – a shoulder to cry on; the possibilities of contract work, Cooper for BRM; and the potential for a Cooper-BRM racing team, Bourne running Cooper-Climax F2 cars and maybe P25 engines in F1 Cooper-type chassis...

John's free advice was simple. "Ditch those bloody awful Lockheed brakes, and those oversized inlet valves in the engine, and those suspension air struts. What you want is a coil-spring independent rear suspension, or preferably a leafspring at the front..."

He felt there was little he could do for BRM on a contract-work basis, but urged Spear to promote a rear-engined car design, as Spear informed Owen:

> He thinks the real prospect is to mount the engine at the rear. He has gone into this, but there are more difficulties than he realised. In particular the gearbox is too low. A complete new gearbox arrangement would be necessary and magneto drives...

John was "diffident about the sort of co-operation he thought he would get" – obviously from Bourne and Folkingham – "but he would be interested in planning on the basis of being provided with an engine and gearbox and proper drafting facilities and full co-operation from Bourne. It would, however, be about six months before he could provide anything".

Spear then presented Point 4 in screaming capitals:

> IN JOHN COOPER'S OPINION THERE IS NOT MUCH POINT IN DEVELOPING A FORMULA 1 CAR ON THE PRESENT BASIS FOR NEXT YEAR AS HE CONSIDERS THAT THE PRESENT GRAND PRIX CARS WILL BE OUT-MODED NEXT YEAR BY CHEAPER VERSIONS AND PROBABLY OF THE PRESENT FORMULA 2 PRINCIPLE.

In this, John Cooper was absolutely right.

His basic recommendation was simply to mount the P25 engine and gearbox in the back of a very much lighter car, "running them at relatively low engine speeds where reliability would be guaranteed...".

He had told Spear that the Cooper Car Co's works F2 and sportscar team had made a small profit in 1956, but claimed he could afford neither the time nor energy to continue racing at such a pitch in future:

> He would be interested in negotiating on the basis of Cooper's providing a fully maintained team of Formula 2 cars to be entered by Mr. Owen with Cooper's officially in the background...under the control of the Owen Organisation and...the Owen Organisation to develop much further the present Coventry Climax type engine...

Spear concluded:

> I am impressed with John Cooper very much as a practical development man who is a very good mechanic... using proprietary components saves him an enormous amount of money. At the same time I would be a little worried as to what happened when a fundamental problem was struck... I should doubt if these are the people to go to for the solution to our existing problems. They have no real design facilities. I think that the whole question of redesigning the engine to go into a completely new car leaves something to be desired, but can be negotiated further... The question of a B.R.M.-Cooper establishment might well be worthwhile considering...

It would eventually happen, by a somewhat different route. Short-term, within a year of their meeting at Hollyfield Road, Spear would find himself congratulating John Cooper on his rear-engined marque's first two World Championship Grand Prix victories. The practical mechanic's approach was paying off...while BRM's was still failing to deliver.

July 7, 1957 – Grand Prix de l'ACF, Rouen-les-Essarts – 77 laps, 313 miles

Initially, Mackay Fraser took things very quietly to play himself into Formula 1 in '253', while Salvadori – now driving for Vanwall – was not as fast as Flockhart in his revised BRM – '254' – which gave the Bourne boys some satisfaction. While Fangio's Lightweight Maserati 250F took pole position at 2:21.5, Flockhart's best was 2:27.8 and Mackay Fraser's 2:29.9.

Tony: We had our usual crop of all-nighters, the principal problem being that now the rear suspension was so much more supple the half-shafts were required to articulate more and the pot-joint blocks overheated and suddenly we were back in all the early 1956 problems. We did all we could, but it was fairly obvious we wouldn't last the race. Some vigorous telephoning to Bourne and some pretty ingenious photography of Ferrari's ball-loaded sliding-spline half-shafts ensued. It was obvious they'd had similar problems, but had got round them.

'Jenks' of *Motor Sport* then reported of the opening lap:

> ...it was Musso who was leading...followed by Behra, Fangio, Collins, Schell and, of all things, a B.R.M. driven by Mackay-Fraser...

A V16 BRM BONNEVILLE PROJECT?

One interesting BRM might-have-been surfaced briefly on June 2, 1957, when journalist Dennis May – a great supporter and former ghost writer for Raymond Mays – wrote to Alfred Owen pointing out that following Connaught's recent closure:

> ...and the generally parlous outlook for (Grand Prix racing), there is naturally a good deal of conjecture as to how long B.R.M. will 'stick it out'...

Since MG were at that time putting the finishing touches to the first 1½-litre car to attempt four miles a minute – 240mph – record-breaking runs on Bonneville Salt Flats in Utah, USA, it:

> ...will obviously focus worldwide attention. If...it were to be immediately beaten by another British car...preferably by a spectacular margin – the latter project would reap a rich harvest of publicity 'on the rebound' so to speak.

And since the supercharged BRM V16 developed at least 150bhp more than the blown four-cylinder MG, May suggested that a suitably streamlined car could surely exceed 300mph, based upon a forward-drive, fully-prone driving position. May had suggested such an attempt to RM some years previously but was the time now ripe to go ahead?
May concluded:

> For all of us who have been cherishing hopes for B.R.M. for many years, it will be something of a tragedy if the marque dies without ever having achieved anything of historic importance...

This last struck home with Alfred Owen – reinforcing his own deep conviction that having set out on this hard furrow, he should continue to drive the BRM plough towards ultimate success.

Peter Spear was quite confident such a project could succeed but:

> If the present B.R.M. were being successful and if we were not losing so much money, then I think I would be enthusiastic... However...my general feeling is not to go ahead... I am about 60:40 against the idea. At Bourne, PB felt: With some special attention to the engine it might be possible to reach the 400 mile (per hour) mark, which is very near the world record irrespective of engine capacity... However, such a project would cost at least £20,000...

then adding with 20:20 foresight, but the wrong future solution to the problem thus foreseen:

> The other side of this...is that a 1½-litre Formula is almost sure to come into Grand Prix racing in the next change of formula, which will be within 2/5 years and...we have the only developed unit that would outstrip all comers on a sheer power basis...

Tony recalled: At Modena in September 1957, Peter Collins buttonholed me and gave a slightly different version. Peter claimed to have an arrangement with Vickers Aircraft Co and an un-named oil company, to build a Land Speed Record challenger. He hoped to used a V16, and wanted to know what power it would give for this purpose. I guessed 850bhp, reported to PB who was rudely non-committal but said that some time previously Elliott at R-R had told RM he thought with a modified blower and the right fuel a sprint version could in fact give about 850hp. I never heard any more.
RM then made the final contribution to (this) debate:

> ...as we are placed at the moment, with so much work to do on the existing 2½-litre cars, I think his suggestion...should be postponed for the time being...

And so it was...in perpetuity.

On lap three Salvadori slid his Vanwall on the fast bend before the pits, his Vanwall's oil filler flipped open and spilled some lubricant and Flockhart, right behind him, received the full benefit.

Robbed of all adhesion, the unfortunate Scot's '254' slithered off the road at high speed, slewed across the grass verge and plunged into a deep roadside ditch where it clouted a culvert, cannoned off and rolled. Ron fell out during these manoeuvres and was rushed to hospital, battered and bruised, and with his pelvis broken.

Meanwhile, 'Mac' Fraser was charging round in sixth place, keeping pace with the works Maseratis and Collins' Ferrari ahead of him and "making the B.R.M. really show its paces" as Jenks put it. Carlos Menditeguy caught and passed him, eventually, in another Maserati and BRM's new boy then became embroiled in a dice with Mike Hawthorn's Ferrari, this pair swapping places for several laps.

Tony: We were wondering how we could tell him he ought not to be in amongst that rough lot, when he fell back and pulled into the pits – on the cockpit side were the telltale dark oil spots indicating that one of the pot-joint rubbers had split, and as anticipated that was the end of it. But we returned home feeling very cheerful, because we now had a car with

roadholding, with good brakes, which was still quick on the straight and, what's more, Mackay Fraser was obviously a pretty good driver, too. Ball-splined half-shafts were imminent finally to remove the pot-joint problem, and the only debits were that Ron Flockhart was in hospital, and we had lost another car, for '254' was a write-off.

While painful and debilitating, Flockhart's injury proved not too serious, although full recovery would take some time. But tragically, the following weekend, Mackay Fraser crashed fatally at Reims, driving a stripped Lotus 11 sports car in the F2 *Coupe de Vitesse*.

On July 10, Colin Chapman hand-wrote a letter to Alfred Owen from *La Nourree*, Eden Roc de l'Ile-de-France, Villense-sur-Seine:

> Dear Mr Owen,
> I am pleased to confirm that there appears to be a certain amount of success with my suggested chassis modifications which have already been incorporated in the BRM. The car is now considerably faster (4 seconds a lap at Folkingham) & the drivers report improved handling characteristics.
> However, I would point out that I did call for all

July 4, 1957 – Lydd Airport, Kent: ORO embark on the Silver City Airways Bristol Freighter bound for the French Grand Prix at Rouen; car '253' for 'Mac' Fraser being manhandled up the loading ramp, with '254' for Ron Flockhart in foreground; RM, PB (foot on ramp), 'Baggy', Rudd, Salmon, would-be team driver Jack Fairman, Cyril Bryden – an ailing man on one of his last trips with the team – Arthur Hill and Dennis Perkins. Below: Flockhart in conversation in the Rouen paddock, his freshly rebodied and now coil-sprung '254' with recognition cross on the scuttle about to tackle its maiden race. It is wearing R4 front tyres, R3 rears. It became the shortest-raced Type 25.

modifications to be carried out at the same time if possible, & there is a damper in the retention of the existing pot joint in the final drive. Due to the greater suspension movement now possible, this joint is giving trouble again & it is doubtful whether the car would last a full length Grand Prix without danger of a partial seizure.

I have been asked by Mr. Raymond Mays to confirm these various points to you & to press for the manufacture of the special ball splined joints as soon as possible.

In the meantime…I have recommended the substitution of ordinary Hardy Spicer joints in place of the existing set-up as a temporary measure. Whilst it is doubtful whether handling will be much improved with the Hardy-Spicer joints, it will at least remove the dangerous situation.

I shall be pleased to give you a much more full report on my return to England.

Yours Faithfully,

Colin Chapman

Owen replied:

Thank you…for the considerable [*sic*] improved suspension which has made a radical difference to the handling of the car…

July 7, 1957 – Grand Prix de l'ACF, Rouen-les-Essarts: Ron Flockhart lost control of '254' on only the second lap, on oil spilled from the flapping cap of Salvadori's Vanwall. The BRM was tripped into a somersault by the concrete parapet of a culvert bridge further along this trackside ditch. Its front-end and rear suspension/frame damage left it a write-off. Phil Ayliff (closest) sat guard, recalling how Fangio in the victorious Maserati was the only man to accelerate consistently across the oil slick, dancing his car from lock-to-lock one-handed while acknowledging Phil with the other! "That's the day I became convinced he really was the greatest driver I ever saw…".

Below: Like a breath of fresh air, 'Mac' Fraser gave ORO new-found faith that their car had promise; here he is pre-race in '253' talking with RM – Tony and 'Baggy' Newman in attendance.

He added:

I am terribly sorry about the accident on Sunday to Mackay Fraser. It is a sad blow to you and to us and I am deeply sorry for his wife…

The important British Grand Prix was run at Aintree only one week after Reims, so RM cast around desperately for replacement drivers at very short notice. Archie Scott-Brown visited Folkingham to try one, but during his brief drive the brakes failed due to an hydraulic union having been left untightened. He survived somewhat surprised and, as Tony recalled: He was got at by his friends who assured him the car was dangerous and a driver-killer; look at Brooks, look at Flockhart, look at all the incidents Hawthorn had been lucky to survive…and he declined the rather doubtful privilege.

Ray finally arranged for Les Leston and Jack Fairman to appear for the team, expecting a lacklustre performance, and getting it.

Recommended for the drive by Colin Chapman, Mackay Fraser went great guns in his first Grand Prix amongst unruly company – here in practice he holds his BRM in tight through Rouen's downhill swerves, Peter Collins drifting behind him in the Lancia-Ferrari 801. 'Mac' – "that good guy" – has one week of life left…

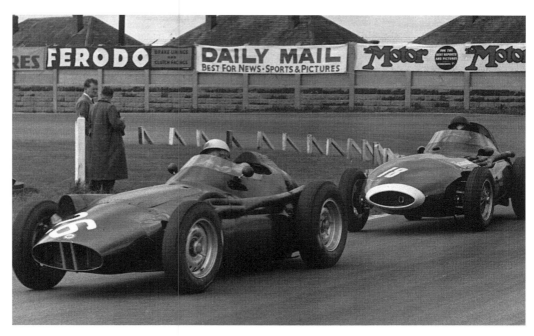

July 20, 1957 – British Grand Prix, Aintree:
Depths – British drivers in a British car won
a Grande Epreuve for the first time since
1923 – but former BRM men Moss and
Brooks did it in one of arch BRM critic Tony
Vandervell's Vanwalls. Les Leston – here in
'253' about to be lapped by Brooks in the
troubled Vanwall with which Moss had
started the race – and Jack Fairman both
had poor one-off drives for BRM. When
Moss saw Leston preparing to drive the car
in the paddock he remarked: "Saw the
advert in the evening paper, did you?". It was
difficult for BRM's men to appreciate the
joke.

July 20, 1957 – RAC British Grand Prix, Aintree – 90 laps, 270 miles

July 20, 1957 has gone into motor racing history as the dawn of the era of British domination since it witnessed the first *Grande Epreuve* victory by an all-British car and driver team since Segrave's Sunbeam victory at Tours in 1923. The winning car was, of course, the Stirling Moss/Tony Brooks Vanwall. In comparison, the BRM performance that day was one of the team's most dismal, yet its aftermath was of huge significance to the entire story of British Racing Motors. In ways beyond the Vanwall victory, the 1957 British GP was a major turning point in the fortunes of British motor racing…

The BRMs understeered too much in practice, any application of power ploughing the front end off line. Leston in '251' with interim roller pot-joint driveshafts was jabbing the throttle three to four times through the turns, which looked very jerky and untidy, but he emerged quicker than Fairman in his similarly modified '253'. Both cars suffered snatching brakes, Fairman at one stage skittering off the road and onto the grass at Anchor Crossing.

During the race Leston held up the two out-gunned little 1.9-litre rear-engined Coopers at the back of the field, until first Salvadori then Jack Brabham clawed their way past and left the BRM for dead once clear. Fairman was way behind after another off-road moment across the grass, circulating in company with Bonnier, Gerard and Bueb. At 47 laps Leston's engine failed and he retired at the pits and three laps later Fairman swished in with the other BRM trailing vapour from its exhaust. "Neither car had shown any speed capabilities and they had now lost reliability as well…" read one report.

Les Leston endeared himself to the mechanics by dumping two crates of beer in the back of one of the Lodestar transporters and saying cheerfully: "Never mind lads, you tried – have a drink on me."

As the deeply demoralized team packed away its gear and loaded their broken cars for the sorry trail home, Tony Rudd was called to the telephone: It was about 7 o'clock in the evening and it was RM summoning me immediately to the *Adelphi Hotel* where he was staying. He had just been talking to Jean Behra – the Maserati works driver – and Behra had an entry with the offer of a lot of starting money for a minor Formula 1 race at Caen the following weekend. He had been very impressed by the way one of our cars had behaved when he came up to lap it, and did I think we could prepare a car in time to make the trip with him as driver? We jumped at the chance. We whizzed the cars back to Bourne and prayed like hell that we'd have a pair of the new ball-splined half-shafts finished in time as there was no point in trying to race the car seriously without them if we had a driver of Behra's calibre in the cockpit…

CAEN 1957 – FIRST VICTORY

The first new ball-splined half-shafts were produced rather primitively in the machine shop at Bourne. The ball-spline tracks themselves were cut on the finest machine available there, but it could not handle a complete half-shaft so this prototype pair had to be bolted together from individually machined sections. These were built up on the Thursday night and fitted to '254', which Tony then tested briefly on the airfield and immediately found "transformed".

The car was then transported to Eastleigh Airport at Southampton and flown across to Deauville on a Silver City Airways Bristol Freighter. One transporter containing as many spares as could be mustered plus one of the old rubber-gaitered pot-joint cars – '253' – as a spare met the 'plane there – the idea being that if Behra should need to race the spare car

July 27, 1957 – Caen GP, Le Prairie, France: New heights – what a difference a week can make; BRM's great day as Harry Schell in '251' swops the lead with Jean Behra's ball-spline drive-shaft-equipped '253' – en route to the French Champion scoring BRM's maiden outright win in a Continental Formula 1 Grand Prix.

'Jeannot' Behra's infectious enthusiasm and readiness to share his accumulated knowledge and experience galvanized the entire BRM team. Above all, he told them as much about what was right with the car as what was wrong with it. This honeymoon period would wear off – but it was splendid while it lasted...

the lone set of ball-splined half-shafts would be transferred to it.

Tony: I drove down to Eastleigh with RM to join the flight that Thursday afternoon. He was a very nervous flyer and I must have been in high spirits because I spent most of the drive down regaling him with details of all the air crashes I went to in the days when I investigated accidents for Rolls-Royce. Around Newbury he was quite ready to turn back and abandon the whole trip... Then from Deauville it was getting dark and it was a hair-raising trip on a tow-rope at around 70mph into Caen. I couldn't even see the stop lights because the rope was so short.

We set up our base in one of the local garages and after some sleep next day went up to the circuit to practice. Behra liked the car and was going quite well when it developed a fearful vibration. Behra also had some decided ideas on how he liked his cars set up and he had us changing the castor angle and steering geometry, and against our normal 4 degrees castor he wanted 9 degrees! We did all kinds of terrible things to achieve so much, changed the toe-in, juggled the tyre pressures, but the vibration was worsening. It was clearly time to activate our contingency plan.

The spare car was fitted with the ball-spline half-shafts plus all Behra's steering and suspension set-up modifications. This work took us all night, punctuated by visits to a small cafe next door for fortification by coffee laced with Calvados.

We were just relaxing a little when RM arrived accompanied by Harry Schell and said he had just done a deal with the race organizers for the same amount of start money as Behra and we were to re-assemble the discarded car for him! After some argument – Harry was very persuasive – we agreed to try. We explained we hadn't traced the source of its vibration, but we suspected it was the prop-shaft.

The only possibility seemed to be that the prop-shaft had been somehow mis-assembled, and so it was all re-assembled upside down 90 degrees out of phase. I tried it up the road from the garage and it seemed much better, but not cured. Harry would have to start the race with it from the back row of the grid.

The French photographer Maurice Rosenthal was there

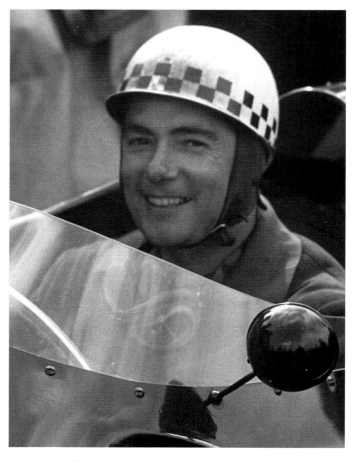

with a Lambretta motor scooter and Harry amused himself taking RM for rides around the circuit and all around the canals intersection just outside the garage and frightened him half to death.

There wasn't a great deal of opposition in the race – but it became a great day for us...

Historic moment – Jean Behra takes the chequered flag at Caen – '253' victorious…

July 27, 1957 – Caen Grand Prix, *Le Prairie*, France – 86 laps, 189.39 miles

Behra had easily set fastest time in the wet first practice session before clipping 4 seconds off the existing lap record on the second day. The President of the *AC Normande* and his officials were thrilled by the French Champion's efforts, news of which obviously boosted the potential gate come raceday. Consequently, they asked if the spare car could be raced by Trintignant. RM said: "No – it has been our intention only to race one car and the second is purely for training" but then Harry Schell – who had blown up his Maserati during practice – charmed RM and PB into letting him run the second BRM in place of his wounded 250F.

With no practice at all, other than two brief laps to warm up, with spectators and course-vehicles still on the circuit, Schell joined in the fun as Behra led away, Harry quickly charging through into second place in his wheel-tracks. Both drivers lowered the lap record continuously during the first half of the race, and to put on a show they then swapped the lead between themselves. Two lustrous green BRMs running 1–2 in a French Formula 1 race – this was almost the brief glory of Albi '53 revisited…

Of course it could not last. Schell – after 60 laps – retired abruptly when his hard-pressed engine threw a rod.

But crucially, Jean Behra drove on to win at a higher average speed than the previous lap record.

Glory be – after eight years' of active motor racing a BRM

had at last won a Continental Formula 1 event.

Immediately after the race RM – his voice quivering with excitement, telephoned Alfred Owen. Unable to contain himself he shouted into the mouthpiece: "Alfred! It's marvellous news! Jean won! Yes *won*! It was wonderful – the car has run perfectly. Harry Schell also led the race in our second car. We have had a little bad luck with it but the modifications have made all the difference!"

Tony: We were all tickled to death when he won. He then invited me to drive the car back to the garage complete with laurel wreath, and when I got in I discovered the gearchange rocking lever, supporting the universal joint where the shaft passed under the de Dion, had broken and he'd only got top gear left!

We had a tremendous dinner party that night during which Behra talked me into having a double portion of steak tartare, which caused me a terrible sleepless night.

But this race – despite us having no significant opposition – marked a tremendous turning point in the story of BRM because if a driver of Behra's reputation thought the car was good then there must be some hope. RM told me during lunch that he hoped to sign next day Jean and Harry for 1958. He did not see any sense in entering for the remaining Championship races, as neither they nor drivers of similar calibre were available. He mentioned Modena and Casablanca as possibilities and I suspect AGB may have talked him into trying to enter for Monza. But right there a deal was done for Jean to drive for us again in the International Trophy race at Silverstone, which had been postponed from its traditional

CAEN '57 – THE STRAINS OF VICTORY

After the Caen victory, back home at Folkingham, Tony Rudd's post-race strip examination of Behra's victorious BRM Type 25 – chassis '253' – revealed the following, as in his report dated August 6, 1957:

RACE DISTANCE: 186 miles
FUEL CONSUMPTION: Overall 8.2m.p.g. rear tank 9.05m.p.g.
7½% Nitro Methane.
OIL CONSUMPTION: 10 pints, heavy oil leakage from loose rocker covers.
WATER: None used.
TYRES: (Dunlop) R3 all round; 7.00 rear; 5.25 front. L.H. rear started 4.5mm is now 3mm = 1.5mm (wear).
R.H. rear started 4.5mm, is now 3.25mm = 1.25mm.
L.H. front started 4.0mm, now 2.0mm = 2mm.
R.H. front started 4.0mm, now 2.5mm = 1.5mm.
Finishing pressures 38 – 36 front; 39 – 39 rear.
Starting pressures 35 – 38.
BRAKES: Solid discs all round, large rear caliper with packing wear, L.H. front 0.15". R.H. front .015".
Rear .375 to .400", with taper wear, edge of caliper fouling top-hat section of disc.
PLUGS: (Lodge) Type 661, new for practice, centre electrode on No. 1 part missing; plugs look slightly rich.
ENGINE: Bearings good, free from foreign matter. Pistons good, look cool – no signs of pick up or contact with valves. Timing gears appear sound; 2/3 gear front ball race on verge of failure. .010" run out on oil pump drive shaft. Outer magneto condenser bracket broken. Inlet valve seats very good; exhaust tappets closed up 0 to .003". Oil pressure after race 80p.s.i. at 50°C. 5000r.p.m. All rocker cover nuts, new for race, at least 1 turn slack. Rest of engine in good condition.
FRONT SUSPENSION & STEERING: Springs had been fouling wishbone Castor 7½° geometry [from] .125 toe-in [rising] to zero.
FRAME: Crack in oil tank shroud, loose rivets around cockpit, L.H. rear bonnet fastener wearing badly, undertray sound, no indication of loose panel to account for 'flapping' noted from pit. Gear change bracket on frame broken, leaving only 2nd and top available; suspect material not suitable for welding – under investigation at R&D. Darlaston.
REAR SUSPENSION INCLUDING SLIDING HALF SHAFTS: All in good condition, very little brinelling of sliders – better than when stripped after practice, radial clearance now – L.H. .009" R.H. .005" – fit for further use.
GEARBOX: Sent to Bourne for overhaul – bevels very badly pluced [sic].
GENERAL: Oil gauge U/S, water thermometer U/S. Oil pressure pipe badly chafed on scuttle. Streamlines in brake and rubber dust show that rear louvre is ineffective – additional louvre required further forward.

6th August, 1957   A.C. RUDD

Meanwhile, Schell's car – chassis '251' – had worn all its tyres approximately 1mm, brake wear was .090in L/h front; 0.060 R/h front and .060 rear. Plugs were "about right" but, Oh the engine!...

No. 1 connecting rod cap broken from damage mark inflicted by spanner. Inlet valve seats poor – guttered. Inlet rocker cover loose, camshaft pedestal nuts loose, tab washers in position. Rear cam pedestal bridge in head broken away; stud and insert also broken. Engine severely damaged by rod failure – shows signs of over-revving by at least 500r.p.m. and also prolonged heavy vibration...

As on '253' the new front coil-springs had fouled the wishbones, and the rear roller-joint half-shafts just showed "faint blueing" on both sides, but no picking up nor oil loss. In the gearbox the L/h ZF stalk was broken at root of thread. Nut split-pin turned loose in pot joint. Bevels very badly plucked. The water gauge had broken, as on '253', there was less dust on the car's tail, but "streamlines show same pattern as No. 3." The roller pot joints – in their last race – were in good condition, "L.H. rollers just showing faint blueing; R.H. rollers blued but no pick up; bushes had been relieved – no oil loss."

Major changes which Tony recommended in light of the Caen experience included:

Connecting rod cap to be relieved and repolished to remove damage marks. Special spanners relieved where necessary. Detail redesign required on new rods. Gear change mounting on frame to be webbed to stiffen up, check material on all frames for cracks. Better instruments required... Investigate vibration...of mounting. Investigate... providing more responsive steering, i.e., more castor – means moving spring; more offset – means new wishbones, or larger section front tyres – means oversteer!

Additionally, Behra had recommended that gearbox ratios should be:

...3rd, 82½% of top for all circuits. 2nd, 65% of top for all circuits. For circuits such as Caen, 3rd should be 90% of top; 2nd 75% of top...

This was much more than just a simple win in a very minor non-Championship Formula 1 race. A great deal had been learned, and an impressive first contact made with both Jean Behra and Harry Schell.

May date to September.

This left us with about a month to prepare the engines, and to obtain the proper ball-splined half-shafts from the Coventry Tool & Gauge Co. They cost nearly as much as the cars for the machining accuracy and precision necessary to cut the splines and the 256-odd ⁵⁄₃₂in diameter bearings crowded around them was fantastic. They eventually proved to be so well thought out and so beautifully made that they would be used in our cars for several years and their probable cost in mileage terms was quite acceptable.

Four days later, a still brimming RM wrote to Behra at 2 Rue Chauchat, Paris 9:

My dear Jean,

This is just a short letter to say how thrilled Peter and I and all of us are over the win last Sunday at Caen. Also I should like to say how much Peter and I appreciated the great co-operation you gave us, and to say how really helpful this was.

We are most anxious for you to drive the car again at the earliest opportunity...I should like to confirm that we should like you to come and try one of our latest modified cars either towards the end of September or the beginning of October, and further, I wish to put in writing that Mr Owen, our patron, Peter and myself, would like you very seriously to consider joining us as our Number 1. driver for the 1958 season...

THE END OF THE BEGINNING – LATE '57

After the minor – yet for ORO so massively enervating – victory at Caen, entries were considered for the following World Championship rounds at Nurburgring and Pescara, but Ron Flockhart was still convalescing from his Rouen injuries, Behra and Schell had Maserati works team obligations to fulfil and no other top-ranking drivers were available. After the Aintree experience – despite both Les Leston and Jack Fairman having done their best for BRM at extremely short notice – there was no question of again employing makeweight drivers. In discussion with Alfred Owen – happy that his considerable (and arguably long overdue) team shake-up had had the desired effect at last – it was decided to cancel entries for both events and to concentrate upon further development work until September.

Since Easter 1956, ORO had had three BRM Type 25s more or less written off, and repairing and replacing them had strained resources to the limit. Owen had, however, authorized completion of another new car, and Phillips of Motor Panels in Coventry had agreed to loan three extra panel beaters to help complete it. The plan was for one car to be run in the Italian GP at Monza on September 8, subject to Flockhart being fit enough to drive. Two cars would then be

run in the BRDC International Trophy race at Silverstone – delayed from its traditional May date by the petrol-rationing aftermath of the Suez Crisis - the week following Monza, and both Behra and Schell had agreed to drive them.

On August 27, Ray to Harry Schell, at 65 Avenue d'Iena, Paris:

My dear Harry,

We are greatly looking forward to your arriving in England on September 11th....I had hoped to see you at Monza next week, but in view of the fact that Flockhart is not yet quite fit, after his accident at Rouen, we have cancelled our Monza entry...We have entered Flockhart on the third B.R.M. entry at Silverstone [which]...will be of the greatest importance to B.R.M. chiefly because it will be a Vanwall-B.R.M. battle. Incidentally [Ray again demonstrating his remarkable capacity for swallowing asinine tittle-tattle – DCN] is there any truth in the rumour that Fangio is driving a Vanwall at Silverstone?

Now as regards terms for the Silverstone race; you will appreciate that this race is not a full scale Grand Prix, but consists of two 45 mile heats and a final of 105 miles. For the B.R.M. you are to drive we shall receive £750, and we will pay you £400. In addition you will be paid 50% of any prize and bonus monies won. Further, your expenses to and from England, and your accommodation during your time in England, will be paid by the Owen Racing Organisation. We can pay your fee of £400 in French francs...so please confirm that you would like the £400 paid in this way.

Greatly looking forward to seeing you on 11th, and in the meantime my best wishes for Monza. Yours ever...

The twin letter to Jean Behra at the *Hotel Moderne*, Modena, that same day, advised: "For the B.R.M. you are to drive we shall receive £850, and we will pay you £500..." Otherwise the terms were identical to those offered to Schell, but Ray added: "We should like to enter for Modena on September 22nd, would you be free to drive a B.R.M. in this race?..." presumably as team-mate to the recovered Flockhart.

Ray's BRM/Vanwall battle at Silverstone evaporated since

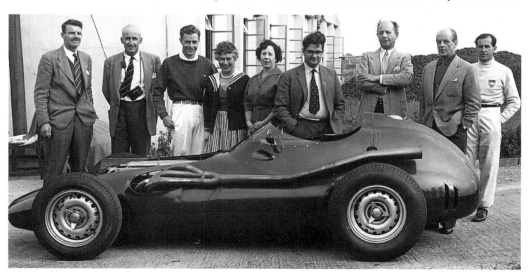

Folkingham: The ultimate configuration of the stressed-skin Type 25, 1957–58, backed by leading committee members of the ORMA 'supporters' club' – Elliot Russell (left) with Donald McCullough's Vice-Chairman Cdr Philip Shenton, RN (camera), Ron Flockhart, Miss Olive Beaumont, hard-working Association Secretary Mrs Molly Wheeler, Tony, RM, PB and – proudly displaying his BRDC badge – Rubery Owen's tireless PRO, Rivers Fletcher.

September 13, 1957 – BRDC International Trophy practice, Silverstone: Maximum effort by ORO, with PB, Behra, RM, Schell and Rivers Fletcher with Tony Rudd and cars '251', '253' and the latest – and last 'over-stressed-skin special' – '255' ready for the promotional battle, the team's three Lodestars providing the backdrop in the paddock behind the pits.

Moment of truth – flagfall for Heat One of the International Trophy sees BRM's only rival in sheer performance terms – the Rob Walker team's 1.96-litre Cooper-Climax driven by ex-ORO driver Tony Brooks – breaking its transmission on pole position, leaving Behra to take off and lead throughout. Flockhart, Masten Gregory's Scuderia Centro-Sud Maserati 250F (far right), Salvadori's works Cooper, Bruce Halford's 250F and Cliff Allison's Formula 2 Lotus 12 chase him here. Schell comfortably won Heat Two from pole in the third BRM.

Ron Flockhart in '255' finished second behind new team leader Behra in Heat One and third behind team-mates Behra and Schell in the Final of the 1957 International Trophy. BRM was one of the first teams to use white plastic stick-on race numbers, applied direct to their green base colour. Both the Silverstone and Aintree organizers objected, demanding "clear black numbers on white discs". At one point Tony Rudd as Team Manager dug his heels in and pointed out that British racing colours were green with white numbers, "ask the FIA"! A fair-sized furore was settled by compromise, as here, with black-on-white disc nose number, but the tail numbers were white direct upon lustrous green. BRM finally won the argument – see 1958...

Old Man Vandervell cared not one jot for these insignificant non-Championship British races upon which RM placed such great store. GAV was only interested in attacking the World Championship. RM was still obsessive about face, prestige, 'front' – especially before those he regarded as his audience, the British public. And of course he was convinced now that without top drivers any *Grande Epreuve* entry was a waste. Owen and ORMA both wanted to see home success for BRM. In stark contrast Vandervell couldn't care less what press and public thought. His racing team was aimed at his targets, to please him. Moss had just won the World Championship rounds at both Pescara and Monza, beating the Italian teams in their own backyard. GAV was happy and for him there was no need to race at Silverstone. His team's season was over, having been completed where it mattered, with victory in the Italian Grand Prix at Monza.

Tony: In truth at Silverstone our only real opposition would be Tony Brooks in Rob Walker's little rear-engined 2-litre Cooper-Climax, so that we could only really lose the race, there was nothing much to winning it. But we had to finish and we obviously had to break the lap record along the way…

September 14, 1957 – BRDC *Daily Express* International Trophy, Silverstone – Two 15-lap, 43.9-mile Heats and 35-lap, 102.44-mile Final

Chassis '251', '253' and '255' were prepared respectively for Behra, Schell and Flockhart.

The victory which followed, first, second and third for BRM, was described by RM as "a real tonic". Behra and Flockhart were first and second in Heat One, Schell first in Heat Two and then followed the hoped for 1–2–3 demonstration in the Final, while Behra's new lap record stood from Heat One, at 101.31mph. None of the cars gave any significant trouble during practice and the race.

Ray told ORMA members: "It is impossible to speak too highly of Jean Behra not only as a driver but as a man. Not only has he just the right touch for the B.R.M., but he also has a great flare for getting on with the mechanics and all the personnel.

"Of course we know there wasn't much opposition in the International Trophy, but who ever's fault that may be it certainly wasn't our's and there was no doubt at all as to the popularity of the win.

"Our hearts went out to poor Tony Brooks and Rob Walker when the Cooper failed on the starting line. What really bad luck after a splendid performance in practice. (We write feelingly remembering Sommer in the B.R.M. on the same circuit way back in 1950.)

"Having the effervescent 'Arree' Schell in the team was a lively experience. His fund of humour and jokes being apparently everlasting.

"Ron Flockhart's third place was particularly good in view of his very busy day. A win for Lotus in the small sports car race, another Lotus drive with the big sports cars and John Coombs' 2.4 Jaguar in the touring car race, quite apart from

the B.R.M. and he was barely recovered from his accident into the bargain…"

The non-Championship Modena GP was taking place in Italy the following weekend and two BRMs were entered for it. Tony drove down with Peter and Lorna Berthon in PB's Raymond Mays-converted Zodiac: It was the most odd trip in that we flew Silver City to Le Touquet, very nearly entered Paris but then diverted back to Reims. Meanwhile the Zodiac kept losing performance and gaining valve noise, but it wasn't until we had entered Switzerland that it dawned on me the special high-lift camshaft was wearing out. So the trip for me was spent resetting the tappet clearance to find a little more valve lift, and the further we drove the slower and slower the car went and we only just crawled into Modena, where a replacement camshaft was waiting, having been flown out for us.

September 22, 1957 – Modena Grand Prix, Italy – Two 40-lap Heats, 117.71 miles

Buoyed-up by their Silverstone demonstration, the team was running two cars at Modena for Ron Flockhart and Stuart Lewis-Evans – not required by Vanwall that weekend, RM had understood – to beard the Italians in their own den. This was a mistake. Flockhart arrived on the Friday with a message from Lewis-Evans that Mr Vandervell had refused to release him to drive for BRM, so Ray cast around and recruited the bearded, enigmatic and patrician Swede, Joakim Bonnier, as a last-second replacement.

The Modena *Aerautodromo* was a gruelling circuit, equally punishing for drivelines, gearboxes and tyres. The race was run in two equal heats, with the result being decided on aggregate of the two combined. Ferrari ran their experimental AvGas-burning 1,500cc F2-based Dino V6 cars with 1,983cc engines installed, which proved very competitive with the works 250Fs and left the BRMs well behind.

Flockhart's car failed after 63 of the scheduled 80 laps when the drive tongue to its fuel pump, driven by one of the camshaft gears above the clutch, failed and the car was retired by a component which the team could have changed in around two minutes…had they only had a spare available in the pits; which they did not.

Bonnier suffered a more exotic failure when a piece flew off the back of his car as it bellowed past the pits and a Ferrari mechanic brought it reverently to the ORO personnel, wrapped in rag because it was hot! Tony: We identified it as one of the universal joint bearing cups off a rear hub, and needless to say Bonnier didn't come round again and we found that the UJ driving flange at the wheel had broken off. It wasn't a particularly bright design.

We returned from Modena having learned still more. My head was full of ideas. Obviously Colin Chapman's mods had stopped the rot. He had pointed us in the right direction, the ball-spline half-shafts were a tremendous improvement, while having a top-line driver such as Behra who knew how a modern Grand Prix car really should handle also helped immensely.

At Modena we were troubled by the front of the car washing

September 20, 1957 – Modena GP practice, Italy: On what RM described as "a nasty, tight little course with a heavy strain on braking, engine, gearbox and back axle components..." the team fielded '251' for Ron Flockhart and the latest and last stressed-skin chassis '255' for newcomer Joakim Bonnier. Both would finish Heat One, but retire from Heat Two.

'JoBo' at speed in '255' on his way to a sixth-place finish in Heat Two of the Modena GP. The toned disc on the car's nose was – we believe – in yellow, the race number having been transferred to the other side on this unusually anti-clockwise course.

out in corners if the driver applied power, or if the car was decelerating. Behra said it was only right if you went round the corner on a neutral throttle, which of course you never do. I therefore retired to my drawing-board at Folkingham and with lots of lengths of black cotton, drawing pins and cardboard models of suspension, I drew a front end where the roll-centre remained relatively constant relative to the road and the roll-centre moved twice as far as the car's C of G did.

Berthon had gone on holiday following the Modena race, and it was not known when he was coming back. So I persuaded RM that we ought to make up this suspension since it was a step in the right direction. Appreciating there was no way we could contact Berthon for his approval, he thought it would be all right to forge ahead. I got Behra to back me up and also rang Colin Chapman to see if he liked the idea. Obviously he had been paid his fee and didn't have to help further – particularly since he was about to enter Formula 1 on his own account – but he agreed it was along the lines he had in mind to improve our car. I drew it out on my board at Folkingham and Stan Hope started making a new front end to graft on forward of the bulkhead, intended for the ex-Hawthorn long-wheelbase car – '253' – upon our return from our final race of the season, which was to be the inaugural, non-Championship, Moroccan GP at Casablanca.

Meanwhile, the lessons of Silverstone and Modena combined had been identified and analyzed. In PB's absence, RM reported both cars and engines had survived tests at Folkingham prior to leaving for Silverstone, then both Silverstone practice and race plus Modena practice, and as far as they had run before failure in 'GP' itself...

Gearbox '27/5' was found to have had no end plug in its brake disc gear oil jet, permitting a heavy leak. Reverse stop and selector springs were very weak in all gearboxes, drivers finding first or crashing reverse when seeking third. The gearchange on all cars was stiff and awkward, demanding a longer lever with bigger knob, located further forward. Nylon bushes were to be deleted from the gearchange because they swelled; needle rollers were to replace them permanently, bronze bushes in the interim.

There had been seven cases of condenser mounting failure, two magnetos had been wrecked. One magneto coil had burned out. The split between front and rear gearbox casing halves leaked heavily on all 'boxes. All gearbox bevels were found plucked. One 24–23 ratio-change gear set had plucked on the pitch line. There had been numerous cases of Lodge 661 spark plug gaps opening in service due to movement of the centre electrode. "In some cases, particularly cleaned and tested plugs, the electrode disappeared altogether!"

Engine oil consumption and leaks had been very heavy, unit '2574' 5 pints, '2573' 4 pints and '254' 7 pints at Silverstone. They all leaked oil from the back of the clutch, from the oil pump front cover. Engine '254' leaked from its head joint. Rocker covers leaked in practice.

There had been a gudgeon-pin circlip failure on '2573' ex-Schell, similar symptoms on '2574' ex-Behra, though not so advanced. At Modena low oil pressure was reported on '2574', unexplained. Inlet valve seats on all engines except '254' were "very bad", guttering and pitted, requiring re-cutting while the valves had to be re-faced.

Pistons were picking up at the junction of profiling on the skirts, and heavy loading was evident on the land between first and second rings. Semi-solid inlet valves in '254' had pulled badly through their collets, requiring replacement.

At Modena, there had been heavy taper wear on rear brakes. Car '255' had suffered a total brake failure when being tested at Folkingham due to hydraulic leak in the front caliper (the Scott-Brown test).

At Modena, engine '254' had suffered clutch slip due to broken clutch springs. One reconditioned clutch had been incorrectly assembled and had fouled the clutch cover on engine '2572'.

One fuel pump adaptor (Plessey) had failed through its setscrew counterbores – steel adaptor, with Allen screws to use smaller diameter centre bores required, with provision for 'O'–ring to reduce leaks at this point.

Car '251' had cracked its right-front brake caliper mounting. Front springs still fouled the wishbones at full bump despite .850in thick bump rubbers.

Grease sealing of the centre prop-shaft bearing was still ineffective, drying out after 100 miles. Rocker cover studs breaking off under nut when tab washered – several cases on both engines in the first heat at Modena – while the lip from No. 2 inlet valve guide had broken away on engine '254' and had passed through the cylinder, damaging both valve seats *en route*.

There is no doubt that BRM's performances were improving, but standards of preparation and fitting were still demonstrably, and in some cases culpably, 'variable'…

Now, in preparation for Casablanca, the French organizers of the race had urged RM to field a French driver, recommending Maurice Trintignant, who was duly signed-up for this one event as team-mate to Flockhart. Three cars were prepared for the trip, '251', '253' – destined to accept Rudd's projected new long-wishbone (as opposed to 'lightening holes welded together) front crossmember forepart – and '255' – one to remain as spare, the other two to be raced. On the Sunday afternoon prior to departure, Flockhart tested all three cars at Folkingham.

Spear noted: "He did a total of 35 laps and, to be candid, looked quite tired when he had finished…though Flockhart detected one engine – which has a slightly lower compression ratio – as having less power, in principle he could not differentiate between their handling and general performance…"

The cars were transported through France to Bordeaux

October 1957, Bordeaux dockside, France: En route to the non-Championship Moroccan GP, Casablanca. The one Lodestar to complete the entire trip dangles precariously as it is craned high onto the Ile de Bordeaux for the lengthy voyage to North Africa.

In Biscay bight – 'Hooray, up she rises' for BRM's entourage – left to right – Maurice Dove, Phil Ayliff, John 'Bilko' Speight, Roy Forman, Dick Salmon, Arthur Hill, Mick Vaughan of AP and Gordon Newman. No anti-roll bar was big enough for this ferry…

where they were hair-raisingly craned aboard a ferry for Casablanca. Mechanic Dick Salmon vividly recalled that voyage: "It was fine until we got out beyond the breakwater at Bordeaux when the ship immediately began to roll just unbelievably. We were later told it had been built as a Norwegian boat, for use in the fjords and around the islands, and had since been bought by the French ferry company. It was certainly out of its depth in the Bay of Biscay – it would roll through about 90 degrees! And we were on it for three days to Casablanca. Talk about a life on the ocean wave? They could keep it…"

Flockhart and Tony Rudd flew out via Paris, staying the night there before taking the onward flight. Ferrari's people shared the 'plane, including Mike Hawthorn, who was in one of his humorous moods and all our luggage became relabelled at Orly; if I hadn't seen him doing it, Lord knows where it would have ended up…

Trintignant, the dapper, moustachioed Mayor of the small French town of Vergeze, proved very easy to get on with, but he had fixed ideas upon how he wanted his car set up. Its seating position proved to be the vital feature, and once raised sufficiently for him to see out satisfactorily he expressed himself very happy.

BRM consequently enjoyed an easy practice period – by their standards – without too much trouble. Vanwall were there in force, but a vicious strain of Asian 'flu virus carved a swathe through the F1 circus, Moss, Hawthorn and Collins all being laid low by it.

October 27, 1957 – Moroccan Grand Prix, Ain-Diab, Casablanca – 55 laps, 261.45 miles

Trintignant in '251' qualified eighth fastest on the third row of the starting grid while Flockhart was 10th quickest, one row behind. Brooks put a Vanwall on pole with a best time of 2:23.3 while driving Moss' car, Trintignant took '251' round in 2:29, and Flockhart managed 2:30 in '253', while '255' was held in reserve.

The Saturday was a rest day, the Formula 1 circus having a visit arranged to Rabat where several drivers were received by King Mohammed V. The next day the King opened the circuit amongst great pomp and ceremony, and the race eventually commenced…

At 20 laps Behra led from Fangio for Maserati, with Lewis-Evans' Vanwall third and Trintignant's BRM fourth, Flockhart seventh and lapped. When Fangio spun and stalled on lap 24 he fell back to sixth, leaving Behra leading Lewis-Evans with Trintignant now third, holding that position to the finish, 1min 26.4sec behind Behra's winning works Lightweight Maserati 250F. Trintignant had covered 350 miles without major failure in '251' and Flockhart 170 miles in '253' before retiring.

Rivers Fletcher's ORMA report enthused:

October 26, 1957 – Moroccan GP practice, Ain-Diab circuit, Casablanca: New BRM driver Maurice Trintignant did a fine job for the team and won their considerable respect. Here he is in '251' ready for a push-start from Dove, Salmon and Roy Forman in between. Keith Ballisat of BP is looking on (dark glasses), Tony Rudd watches for traffic and there's RM in languid mood – cigarette between his fingers. Note the converging rivet lines on the car's flank edging its fixed-skin stress structure, the side panels to front and rear both being detachable.

Ron Flockhart ran respectably seventh in '253', following in Trintignant's wheel tracks for the first 11 laps at Casablanca. Detachable panels stand out in this shot as a paler shade against the darker stress-skinned area. The raised cockpit sides of these definitive 1957-spec bodies greatly increased stressed-skin area, which accordingly reduced stress levels within the skin, permitting larger access apertures closed-off by detachable panels.

The opposition was all there – the full Grand Prix circus in fact – Maserati, Ferrari, Vanwall, B.R.M. and Cooper… Let no one think that B.R.M.'s third place was achieved just because other cars fell out. On the contrary. Both the B.R.M.s went well right from the start – Trintignant and Flockhart driving faultlessly and doing battle with the Maseratis, Ferraris and Vanwalls from the fall of the flag. Flockhart's retirement was not caused by mechanical trouble in the excepted [*sic* – means 'accepted'] sense. He managed to collect a bird in the air intake and grit and bones from the carcass damaged the throttle controls. Needless to say Ron was much teased afterwards for 'chasing birds' instead of getting on with the motor racing.

1957 Moroccan GP: 'Trint' at speed during his highly competent – and cheering – drive into third place behind Jean Behra's victorious works 'Lightweight' Maserati 250F and Stuart Lewis-Evans' second-placed Vanwall. BRM '251' completed no fewer than 350 miles running during this North African race meeting.

Trintignant's driving has an immaculate quality. Very much like the person – neat and dapper. Of course the victory of a French driver, Jean Behra, was very popular with the crowds as was Trintignant's third place to another French driver.

Right at the end of the race we had some hopes of second place. Stuart Lewis-Evans on the Vanwall was obviously running out of fuel, but he just managed to cross the line before petering out, gaining another good place for the Acton cars.

Tony: Trintignant's third place earned us a big pot of prize money and he told us the car gave him no worries at all, which was a nice way to finish the season. I flew back to London next day in company with Tommy Wisdom, the motoring writer, and Dennis Druitt of Shell, and it transpired they had both served in Algiers during the war and they began reminiscing like nobody's business. The Customs man at Heathrow was quite pleased to see me because I think I was the only member of the returning party who didn't have a camel saddle. Back at Folkingham, aware that PB was taking a holiday after Casablanca and knowing from experience it was likely to be a long one, I plucked up courage and we cut the front off '253' and replaced it with the new set-up. Jean and Harry tried the converted car at Folkingham on November 18–19 when they both found it 1.5sec quicker. Jean described the improvement as "*nuit et jour*". When PB eventually returned at the end of the month, I thought I would be fired but he quickly calmed down.

I also reported on the results of the conversion from alcohol plus nitro fuel to AvGas, as required by the new regulations for 1958. Venerable engine '254' had gone from a maximum of 287hp with 7.5% Nitro to 272 on plain BPK alcohol mix with a significant loss in peak torque. Changing

Casablanca, 1957: BRM's equipe at the French organizers' prizegiving – Maurice Trintignant and his wife with the silverware, flanked by the BRM contingent (left to right) – Willie Southcott, Mick Vaughan, Phil Ayliff, Reg Smith, Maurice Dove, Gordon Newman, 'Bilko', Dick Salmon and 'Sheriff' Perkins – the quiet man so named after the high-heeled boots he wore, reputedly to combat injuries from a parachuting accident. He would become one of the most reliable lap-scorers in pre-computerized GP racing…

to AvGas then dropped us to 265hp, and I believed there was something in the exhaust system still to be found. This seemed to PB to be more important than my vandalism. He inquired about fuel consumption, which on the test-bed seemed about 18–20 per cent better. He told me to come up with a comparison which meant some part-throttle tests.

When I gave him the results a few days later, he said: "This means we can get away with 22 per cent smaller tank capacity". I showed him my sketches of a continuation rearwards of the new tubular front end with a detachable elektron skin and five skewer-mounted tanks. I was sent away to do some more sums, having been castigated for choosing five tanks when three would do. I argued that the rear radius arm thrust and reaction caused a problem. He told me to try for bigger tanks by the driver's knees, which I said would make for a fatter car. After a few days we came up with a compromise, with two small tanks each side of the driver's seat for really high fuel consumption races. Then he startled me by instructing me to make six such chassis two at a time! He then said: "Do not go blabbing to your friend Spear about this; RM and I are going to have quite a job selling this idea to AGB."

On November 14, Colin Chapman visited Bourne and Folkingham to review work on the new front end. RM to Owen next day: "Colin Chapman was in Bourne yesterday to have a look at the new front end of the car, which Peter has done, and which is now nearing completion on the test car…"

Typical Ray, the credit would *always* be Berthon's…

He went on to mention that Colin had "…raised the point of your agreement with him to supply him with a converted Zephyr" – in payment for his Type 25 suspension redesign and test driving – "…and he feels that the time is now here when he should have this… I should appreciate your confirmation that we may arrange for this to be supplied through Raymond Mays and Partners, and also your confirmation that it is to be paid for through the O.R.O. account…"

Taruffi had accepted £500 for his consultancy work, 'Chunky' just wanted the road car. In fact it would perform yeoman service in his hands – and probably cry itself to sleep

every single night… Colin was a storming road driver.

Meanwhile, RM had been negotiating vigorously with Behra, whose former berth at Maserati had evaporated as the company entered receivership and its in-house race programme was effectively shut down.

With the Type 25s' new front suspension apparently worth 1½ seconds a lap round both Folkingham and Silverstone, the team really thought they were at last on the right track. Behra and Schell were both signed ex-Maserati for 1958, and The Owen Racing Organisation was set to take BRM into the first serious World Championship race season of its *entire* history.

Considering that RM had composed his original White Paper in 1945, it had taken The Mays Project no fewer than 13 years to reach this point… Could it now succeed?

Wintertime work at Folkingham, 1957–58, saw trusty old stressed-skin car '253' stripped and its standard front-end replaced by a grafted-on multi-tubular structure designed by Tony Rudd to accept revised-geometry suspension. Memories dim, but it is possible wrecked '254' from Rouen may have been cannibalized as a mock-up for this development. Here (above) is the original-style heavily perforated fabricated front bulkhead, standard in stressed-skin cars '251' to '255' – note stressed-skin structure amidships with stiffening cross-bracing tubes on top of the footbox panelling. This compares with (left) Tony's new all-tubular forward frame grafted onto the existing stressed-skin centre-section of '253'. When Jean Behra tried this modified car he found its handling transformed…

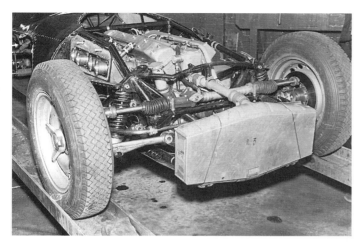

Clockwise from above: Folkingham developments for 1958 with '253''s new forepart now fully fitted with engine, steering, suspension and cooling systems; induction side of '253''s engine bay demonstrating how the stressed skin was riveted onto framework extending from the tubular base frame; exhaust side of '253''s engine bay showing the oil tank mounted low beneath a heatshield to protect it from the exhaust manifolding to be added above; throttle and brake pedals are visible looking forward into the car's right-foot well (the clutch pedal is in the left-foot well the other side of that clutch-house panelling). The body opening is defined by horizontal mainframe longerons top and bottom, rear suspension anchorages are on the vertical member between them, in-line fuel filter on undertray. Looking rearward into the car's left side, the transaxle casing, ball-spline loaded half-shaft, cooling trunking and rear disc brake detail are visible, with fuel tank underside top right.

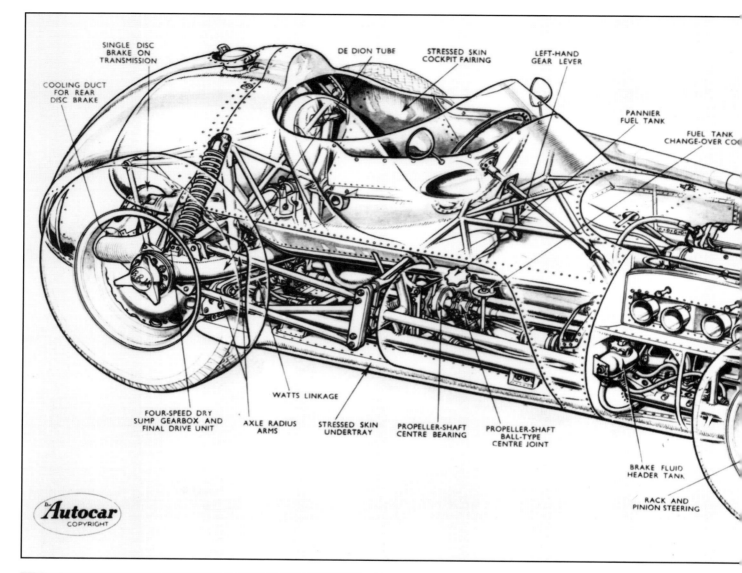

SINGLE DISC
BRAKE ON
TRANSMISSION

DE DION TUBE

STRESSED SKIN
COCKPIT FAIRING

LEFT-HAND
GEAR LEVER

COOLING DUCT
FOR REAR
DISC BRAKE

PANNIER
FUEL TANK

FUEL TANK
CHANGE-OVER COC

FOUR-SPEED DRY
SUMP GEARBOX AND
FINAL DRIVE UNIT

AXLE RADIUS
ARMS

WATTS LINKAGE

STRESSED SKIN
UNDERTRAY

PROPELLER-SHAFT
CENTRE BEARING

PROPELLER-SHAFT
BALL-TYPE
CENTRE JOINT

BRAKE FLUID
HEADER TANK

RACK AND
PINION STEERING

The **Autocar**
COPYRIGHT

*Left: A P25 engine ready for test in Willie Southcott's kingdom – the Folkingham Test
House with its rapidly dismantleable and removable dyno rig – during the winter of
1957–58. Here nothing would be audible above the bark of a running engine, but when he*

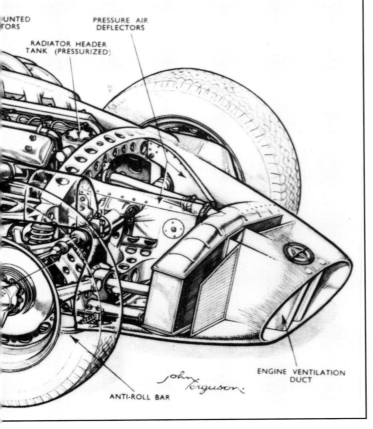

John Ferguson's Type 25 cutaway for The Autocar demonstrates layout of the 1957-spec stressed-skin design with its large-diameter four-tube base frame and wrap-around load-bearing skinning delineated by the rivet lines. Even at this stage in the Type 25's history, PB remained anxious that not too much information should be revealed in the press. Was he merely being stuffy or – judging by modern Formula 1 standards – was he far ahead of his time?

was working in a quieter shop all conversation would have to stop should an Alma Cogan number be played on the radio. Willie would brook no competition for her... Above and centre left: Grand Prix BRMs in their lair – a corner of the Folkingham race shop.

EARLY 1958 – FROM PROBLEMS TO PROMISE...

If Raymond Mays and Peter Berthon had expected Alfred Owen to be delighted with BRM's 1957 season they were quickly disabused of the very idea.

Despite that maiden victory with Behra at Caen and Trintignant's third place amongst strong opposition at Casablanca, during the Christmas break of 1957–58, Owen became increasingly unhappy as he reviewed the situation – and the team's expenditure...

Rubery Owen's Department 31 Engine Development Division at Bourne had been established to perfect racing engines and power unit technology for sale to outside customers. But not one cash order had yet been taken for the 2½-litre Project 25 engine. Having had contact with both John Cooper and Colin Chapman during the previous season, Owen appreciated that each was buying proprietary racing engines from Coventry Climax. In contrast, Bourne was no closer to selling anything more than the Raymond Mays-conversion Ford cylinder heads, and RM's private company was creaming off much of the profit from them...

In mid-January 1958, Peter Spear was again despatched to Bourne to put another squib under RM and PB. They had to realize this was the year in which all the effort, and all the investment, must at last show some tangible return...

Spear reported to Owen on January 20:

> I explained the situation in full, and although the initial reaction was that this was 'the same old story which they always went through', in the end I think Berthon and Mays were reasonably impressed. Certainly RM was chewing his fingers!

Spear had asked them to prepare schedules showing:

> 1 – The cost involved from July 1st if the whole of the Bourne project is cancelled immediately and all plant and personnel absorbed for other purposes or disposed of... 2 – Spending essentially no more money for the coming year and working to a reduced programme of cars, drivers etc... 3 – Assume that expenditure up to the end of December is approved and from January this year to work on a basis of £52,500 per annum on a January/December year, catching up later into Rubery Owen financial year. This would involve some further purchases and a very substantial reduction in personnel. The reaction of RM and PB was that if one halved the budget it would be necessary to more than halve labour and purchases, since with the reduced programme the incomings would also be reduced. The total staff and wages less bonuses for RM and PB, etc was over £79,000.[79] 4 – Any other ideas they may have such as

79. **This is the projected budget figure for 1958 which Tony Rudd was given when he took over at Bourne in April 1962, including rents and leases for the Maltings, Folkingham, RM and his Secretary's office, company cars, etc, covering not 'merely' therefore the racing plant, cars, team and operating costs.**

going out of racing for two years and running Bourne as a commercial unit only. I said this would never be accepted as in such an event we might as well bring everything to Darlaston and absorb.

Spear's squib was only half-effective as RM and PB knew that Behra and Schell were already signed-up for 1958. Owen himself had played a large part in the negotiations, meeting them both, and had endorsed the promises of new cars and engines for 1958. It was one of RM's most frequently used (and effective) defensive weapons that if the team was closed down, by the time the drivers had been paid off, and the rents and leases paid, for their legal duration, the money saved on materials and wages would not be very much more than the income which would be lost from sponsors (Shell, Dunlop, KLG etc) and from lost start money.

Evidently Owen believed that Vandervell was spending only £50–60,000 a year. RM and PB quite rightly dismissed the notion. They also pointed out – again quite rightly – there was no market for 2½-litre engines because the F1 displacement ceiling matched no other major class – American sports cars for example. They felt there was a better market for gearboxes but the profit there "is not worth the effort". Spear had been told by John Cooper that when he had approached PB to buy BRM gearboxes he was just turned away. Spear confided: "I think there is a fear of competition, but as you have said our engines could always be a step ahead…". They offered to ask for higher retainer fees from suppliers, but pointed out that ORO already drew more from Shell than did newly-dominant Vanwall from BP!

Spear added an amusing PS:

You may hold the record for the fastest from Folkingham to Wolverhampton, but I can now claim the slowest. It took me nearly 7½ hours on Sunday night with a broken throttle midway between Tamworth and Ashby!

Owen assured him:

The threat of cutting out Bourne was the only threat in the past that actually got anywhere. I made the same threat on Sunday when Raymond Mays telephoned me, so he must know…that if the expenditure was anything like the budget then we should cut Bourne out completely, and I feel it could be done at half the cost at Darlaston.

Owen also offered his Technical Director a word of caution for dealings with RM and PB:

Simply closing down Bourne is not today nearly as much of a threat as perhaps it once was because it has been suggested to me twice within the last year, if I wanted to get out of it, there were two or three other people interested.

Colin Chapman for instance put up a suggestion to me that he had a group who would be interested to take it over and he then tentatively suggested he was prepared to go up to £10,000 [nearly £120,000 by 1993

value]…there are quite a few of the sporting fraternity to whom Raymond Mays and Peter Berthon could go and perhaps have a period with them…

But still he lamented:

…why cannot we sell engines as Climax do. This was the reason why we called it the Engine Development Division but no effort whatever has been made to develop this idea…

But yet again he was mollified, and RM and PB survived.

Meanwhile, the new AvGas-burning F1 regulations had been applied, and in parallel the former minimum World Championship Grand Prix distance and duration of 500kms – 312 miles – or three hours, had been slashed to just 300kms – 200 miles – or two hours. The consequence of these changes was enormous…

Tony: Our old cars had had to carry sufficient fuel for 300 miles, around 40 gallons. This would not be necessary with the better fuel consumption offered by AvGas and with shorter races. From what we had learned we were confident we could build a much better and lighter car. PB had set me to work to design the completely new chassis embodying all we had learned through the previous season, while he went away to design a five-main-bearing engine which would finally lay our timing gear and cam-drive bogies since it would prevent the crankshaft writhing around as it had in the four-bearing units.

To comply with PB's instructions, given on the way to Modena, I took trusty old engine '254' – one of the original four-bearing units which developed 287bhp on nitro – and we simply converted it to run on petrol by changing its ignition timing, chokes and jets, whose size we calculated from the anticipated air/fuel ratios. With very little work it came up to 265bhp on AvGas on the old Dynamatic.

We believed that when we went to the new 1958 engines, which were to have better porting in addition to their smoother five-main-bearing cranks, that we would be looking at 275 horsepower – only 10 down from where we had been on nitro-laced alcohol.

Ignition timing optimization for AvGas fuel was easy on Willie's dyno set-up. I just held the engine at peak torque, around 6,250rpm, while Willie slackened the mounting nuts and twisted the magneto round until he saw the highest load on the dyno. He then knocked it back about 2 degrees and repeated the drill with the other magneto. When we ran the engine on the centre plug only, it needed some 3 degrees more advance than with the two outer positions. We then shut down, logged the precise timing and repeated this performance at 5,000 and 7,000rpm. Then, having obtained an optimum setting, we took a full power curve from 3,500 up to 8,000rpm.

When we ran on stub exhausts it seemed that we might need shorter primary pipes, but as we knew things might change with Bourne's new head – and the last thing they were likely to do was to keep the same exhaust port flange layout – we would be in for a new manifold anyway, and as I had ideas for a new system to suit the new car, we did not proceed any further. The engine looked good on strip, so we put it back together and took some part-throttle loops and explored choke sizes and valve timing, but what we already had seemed to work best. We converted the other engines, achieving similar results.

Aware that we would be losing some of the cooling effect from the 35 per cent alcohol in the fuel, we measured the heat rejected to oil and water when burning BPK, then AvGas. We found the heat to oil rather high on both fuels, but the increase of 18–20 per cent on petrol was about right. In the light of this we discarded the oil/water heat exchanger mounted in the oil tank, as it would no longer be big enough, and fitted instead a larger exchanger in the main pipeline from the radiator to the pump.

The heat to water was rather low on both fuels and the increase for petrol 12–15 per cent less than expected. This meant the existing radiator was big enough. I mentioned to PB that the engine was rejecting less than the theoretical amount of heat to water, and more to the oil. He said it was to be expected with such a large bore and short stroke, which made sense at the time. However, as the story unfolds it will be seen that, as usual, we had been presented with an enormous clue...

We also did a great deal of running with our Sunbury indicator which, despite its high sounding name, was really a fancy pressure-measuring device. The key to it was a battery-operated television or CRT. We could, thanks to Tres, screw a pressure transducer into the heads' unused plug hole and record instantly cylinder pressures on the screen. Being battery-operated, the equipment was not so affected by the ignition system. It was crude and clumsy compared with today's electronics, but 40 years ago it was the last word. We plotted pressure waves in the induction and exhaust system ready for our proposed new manifolding.

We heard rumours that Vanwall were having great difficulty converting to AvGas, which surprised us, as we had so little trouble. The Vanwall engine had been developed from the water-cooled Norton, in which PB and Richter had been involved, which ran on petrol, and should have had similar characteristics. I suspected that as they ran much higher amounts of nitro that we did – 12.5 to 15 per cent – they had been caught out by the power lost without it. I calculated they might well be down to 255bhp from this reason alone, in which case they *would* be worried.

We managed to make the first of the new spaceframe/detachable body chassis quite quickly and a second one followed – both true multi-tubular spaceframes in which only the underpan was riveted permanently into place. This new Type 25 design ended up almost twice as stiff as the original 'Over-Stressed Skin Specials' and was some 30lbs lighter...

There was then quite a wait for the new five-bearing, re-headed engines as there was a long lead time on the block-cum-crankcase castings and for the new crankshafts with their extra centre main bearing.

The first engine with its different induction system and five main bearings caused great consternation and dismay when after much effort it only produced a pitiful 245bhp. There was no time for much recrimination, even if there was plenty. New '256' was waiting for an engine to make its debut in the *Daily Express* Trophy race at Silverstone.

Meanwhile, the old stressed-skin cars '251' and '253' – the latter with its new tubular front end grafted on – were to provide Behra and Schell with their debuts as full-time ORO drivers. Even in their initial dealings, Tony had struck up quite a rapport with the French Champion: I enjoyed dealing with him because I could speak fairly fluent French. He came from Nice and I was told subsequently that I speak French with a southern accent, so we really got on well. He was full of ideas about what was needed on the car and really was the first driver ever to put across to me how the car was behaving and what should be improved in a way I could understand. What was even more inspiring about him was that from the beginning at Caen in '57 he told us what was right and good about our car, not only what was wrong and bad about it.

Unfortunately, at Easter Monday Goodwood, 1958, the bad would outweigh the good...

April 7, 1958 – BARC Glover Trophy, Goodwood – 42 laps, 100.8 miles

This was a peculiar race weekend from the moment it snowed heavily during Saturday morning practice. Race day eventually dawned overcast but dry, although the drenched paddock remained a quagmire, mechanics working frantically in the assembly area to wash-down muddy tyres before cars went out for their races.

Although practice had been a weather-affected farce, Moss qualified Rob Walker's 1.96-litre rear-engined Cooper on pole from Behra's BRM, with Hawthorn in a lone works Ferrari Dino 246 and Salvadori's works Cooper completing the front row. Schell lined-up his BRM on the inside of row two.

Moss was late arriving on the starting grid, and as the flag was raised his arm shot into the air – his engine had stalled. The Walker team's mechanics flung themselves upon the dark-blue car to push-start it, the flag fell and the rest of the field boomed off past them – Behra taking an immediate lead into Madgwick Corner from Brabham's works Cooper – off the second row – and Hawthorn's Ferrari. The red V6 car powered past Brabham into second place, but Behra was fleeing very fast in '253'. Sadly for BRM fans, there were Type 25s at both ends of the field, for Harry Schell struggled around that opening lap, dead last, grinding into the pit lane long after the rest had blared by. He bawled at the ORO crew: "It just won't go", but was sent back into the fray to try again...

Behra was rushing round in the lead, until near the end of lap four when, as *Autosport* reported:

> He arrived at Woodcote at a great rate, to find the brakes a little peculiar. On proceeding towards the chicane at a higher velocity than he would have liked, he was discomfited to find that he now had no brakes at all! As someone not familiar with Goodwood circuit, it seemed to Behra that he was hurtling straight towards the crowds packed on the right-hand side of the chicane – they are in fact well back out of harm's way – so he kept over to the left and the B.R.M. slammed into the brick wall at about 70 m.p.h...

April 7, 1958 – Glover Trophy, Easter Monday Goodwood: First corner, first lap – Jean Behra leading in '253' with its new tubular front frame and revised-geometry front suspension, tearing into Madgwick ahead of Jack Brabham's 1.9-litre Cooper-Climax, Mike Hawthorn's Ferrari Dino 246, Harry Schell's '251', Coopers and Connaught.

The unfortunate Frenchman – without seat belts, of course, almost a decade before their introduction into Formula 1 – was hurled forward against '253''s steering wheel, his thighs smashing up onto the dash-panel's lower edge, then back – with his seat broken free – to thump the remaining breath from his lungs against the cockpit back. The stricken BRM – its left-front corner crushed, the wheel and suspension ripped off, modified frame lozenged beyond repair – slewed to a crippled and steam-shrouded halt on the right-side verge.

Marshals and St John's ambulance men assisted the winded Behra from its cockpit, but after a few moments to gather his senses he was hobbling about painfully in the pits, insisting he should be taken not to hospital, but back to his hotel room in Chichester. RM prevailed upon him to go from there to the Casualty Department at Chichester Hospital, where X-rays revealed no fractures, although the top of his right thigh was badly bruised and his left knee had taken a nasty knock. He was treated and bandaged, ordered to rest in bed at the hotel for the next three days and a physiotherapist was called in for remedial massage.

Ray and Alfred Owen hurried down to the chicane the instant the race finished to examine the wreck, and the scene of the incident, Owen noting "two very clear blue marks on the roadway 10 yards from the chicane, which I was assured were marks made by Behra's car prior to his hitting the chicane…it was perfectly clear…the brakes had acted" – as they would under Behra's madly-adrenalized, and far too late, *in extremis* stamp upon a no longer servo-assisted pedal.

Hawthorn thus inherited the race lead which he maintained to the finish for Ferrari, while Schell had struggled round with a growing plume of bluish smoke following '251' until, after seven ever-slower laps, he trundled into the pits with the car's tail shrouded in acrid smoke. The single cheese-cutter disc brake on the back of its gearbox was glowing incandescent. It seemed that the Lockheed brake servo had again malfunctioned, wrecking BRM's hopes. On Behra's car the brakes had apparently jammed 'off', on Schell's they had jammed 'on'. His smoking BRM was pushed laboriously to the end of the pit lane, where a brief fire broke out and a brandished extinguisher at first refused to work at all, then burst, covering firemen and mechanics alike in foam. Yet another BRM outing had ended in near-tragic farce…

At 9.30 next morning the doctor called on Behra in his hotel room, and at 11 Peter Spear walked in, clutching an enormous basket of fruit from Alfred Owen and the Owen Organisation.

Spear reported:

> Both [Behra] and his wife were highly delighted with the fruit and seemed to appreciate the gesture very much. All he could do was talk about the cars! He explained that he was very pleased with the car itself which he considered 'perfect' as far as road holding and general performance is concerned. The only thing he is worried about is the brakes. In his opinion we should remove the servo…We can remove [it] quite easily, it will mean a different master cylinder arrangement… it would also mean that the drivers would have to press very much harder…or we would have to incorporate a more complicated mechanical linkage…

The Lockheed disc brake system's servo pump as used by BRM had variously been driven by either the engine or the gearbox to circulate pressure brake fluid. When the driver applied his brake pedal a piston within the master cylinder progressively shut off bypass bleed holes, enabling servo pressure to build up within the hydraulic brake circuitry.

It appeared that the master cylinder plunger had somehow been sticking, leaving the bypass bleed holes open in Behra's

1958 Easter Monday Goodwood – unhappy ending: Behra's brakes have failed entering the chicane on lap 4 of the Glover Trophy race – '253''s left-front is demolished against the apex brickwork, Behra – unbelted – cannons around within its cockpit; the ruined car ricochets off through the wattle fence, comes to rest on the verge and the battered Behra is able, miraculously, to step out with only minimum assistance.

case, and closed – so far as the rear circuit was concerned – in Schell's; or had it?

On the Wednesday, Spear and his assistant Ian Hankinson met PB and Lockheed's specialists at Folkingham, Hankinson explaining: "On examination of the braking system on Schell's car it was found the brakes were perfectly free until the engine was started up, when both the rear and front brakes came on without the foot brake pedal being applied. This indicated a fault in the master cylinder. [It] was removed from the car and dismantled by representatives of Messrs. Lockheed. A careful examination did not reveal any major fault that could have caused the condition that arose at Goodwood, although small particles of rubber were found. The master cylinder was reassembled after all parts had been cleaned, re-fitted to the car and the brakes bled. The engine was started up and the brakes did not come up. Mr. Rudd took the car for a short test and stated that the brakes were operating satisfactorily with no sign of any binding.

"Behra's complaint was that he had only slight braking when approaching the chicane at Goodwood, and this indicated that he had lost the servo assistance. This indicated some fault in the servo pump or in the master cylinder. The pump appeared to be satisfactory and no major fault could be found when the master cylinder was dismantled and carefully examined. Messrs. Lockheed have taken the servo pump, master cylinder and calipers back to the works where they propose to fit them on a rig…to reproduce the type of failure experienced by Behra."

He continued: "…there was nothing obvious that could have caused the brake conditions experienced" and added "…a new type of braking system without servo assistance and using two master cylinders inter-connected with a balance bar is to be supplied within the next two days…".

Owen asked: "Could our fitters have done anything at all to avoid the trouble that arose?" – had lack of adequate cleanliness in preparation introduced those rubber particles which might have fouled the systems?

S.M. Parker, of Automotive Products – the Lockheed system's manufacturers – wrote to Owen on April 16 to admit that "unfortunately" his engineers had found no abnormalities when they stripped and examined the removed systems:

> From the technical point of view, we would prefer to find a definite fault. [Behra's] might have been caused by a piece of foreign matter getting between the control faces of the valve…if you were retaining this system we should certainly suggest more positive filtration. On the Schell car it is clear that a number of laps were covered with a constant pressure on the brakes, probably of the order of 150–200p.s.i., and some obstruction preventing the foot or hand brake from returning to its normal 'Off' position seems to be the most likely cause.

Parker endorsed ORO's decision to remove servo assistance – "particularly on the grounds that the braking distribution is at present affected by stopping of the engine". Overall it was believed that Vanwall's rival Goodyear-patent disc brake system was inferior to BRM's Lockheed outfit in stopping distance, while Ferrari remained faithful to drum brakes and

the new little 2-litre Coopers and front-engined Lotus 12s were so light they did not require servo-assistance in any case. Since the latest BRM Type 25s under construction at Folkingham were to be lighter than the existing cars, now was clearly the time to abandon servo operation.

The terrier-like Peter Spear certainly defended the performance of ORO's mechanics at Goodwood:

> I do not think our fitters could have done anything to have avoided the trouble that arose…both cars had done a total of about 45 laps each on the Thursday and Saturday together and were taken to the garage by the transporter. On the Sunday (and I was present during all this) the only thing that was done to the brakes was to clear a slight foul on one caliper and to top up with fluid…only one car needed topping up anyway. The cars were then put back in the transporters and taken to the track…quite reasonable to have expected the brakes to carry on as they had been doing on the Thursday and the Saturday without trouble.

However:

> It is possible that Schell's trouble could have been caused by the fraying of the hand brake cable which runs underneath his heel pad. Mr Hankinson noticed this on the Monday. It was only apparent because the sides of the car were off and the heel pad had been removed. If this fraying had caused the brakes [to bind] on, and only a load of 10lbs is necessary, then it could have caused the trouble but one cannot prove it…a small modification has been incorporated to avoid [a repetition].

From a 1990s' perspective – or even from that of the 1960s or '70s – the possibility of a frayed handbrake cable being left in use on a Formula 1 works car surely boggles the imagination…

But Spear changed tack without further comment:

> It is very difficult to determine exactly what Behra's reactions were during the very short time in which he was in serious trouble. He was undoubtedly pressing very hard on the brake pedal and it is very likely that he was getting some 'un-servoed' brakes to the front of the car only…You state there was [sic] two very clear marks. If he was getting brakes on all four wheels…one would expect four blue marks. So this reasonably ties up…eye-witnesses [state] that they could not hear the engine note when Behra was in trouble. It would be possible then for the servo merely to be idling and not acting anyway. I do not know whether Behra himself had cut off the engine because of the impending accident…

Further to complicate the issue, when the wreckage of poor '253' was fully dismantled in the Folkingham race shop:

> …there was discovered in the gearbox, a broken lay-shaft. It is possible that this broke before the accident, although unlikely, but if it did it would mean that the

rear disc was not effectively coupled by the transmission with consequently no rear brakes anyway. However, Behra's foot should not have gone through the floor boards even under those circumstances because the caliper should still have been holding the disc which was still in position.

Behra was fit enough to test-drive at Folkingham on the Sunday following his violent accident, professing himself much recovered, though his legs remained sore and stiff. He was more bothered by chest and back pains, for which 12 X-rays had been taken on the intervening Wednesday. It appears he had actually broken several ribs when cannoning around '253''s cockpit in his dismounted seat...but he hid this diagnosis from his team.

More seriously for BRM's sustained development pace, PB had seen a specialist that same day. He had suffered increasing spinal pains ever since surviving his road accident three years earlier. Now he was ordered into hospital "...within the next three weeks" to have two vertebrae grafted together in his spine. Owen was informed that "...this will involve him being on his back for something like 12 weeks and subsequent exercises". Spear advised:

> It is absolutely imperative he has this operation... especially over the last few weeks he has been a very sick man. Over the last few days he has hardly been able to walk let alone drive a car...

In preparation for his supposedly enforced absence – Tony cannot recall him going missing at this juncture – one or two car entries were planned for the Aintree '200' and International Trophy at Silverstone, while construction of the new detachable-bodied spaceframe 1958-spec cars would press on with Rudd in day-to-day charge, and Spear visiting regularly "...to hold his hand in the technical sense". Tony: I don't recall seeing much of Spear at this time. If he had produced a hand it would have had a spanner or something stuck in it double quick. We saw very little of him in the spring of 1958 until Monte Carlo.

Peter Spear's involvement with the team was regarded with alarm by some of the mechanics. An often abrasive, rather pompous man, he was entirely confident of Owen's trust and support. His sometimes arrogantly expressed self-belief in an engineering superiority endeared him to few. But he made things happen, and provided a constant irritant – an impetus – which the race programme clearly needed.

It was entirely typical of the BRM family at Bourne and Folkingham to regard anyone from Rubery Owen at Darlaston as outsiders. While the men in Lincolnshire might squabble like cat and dog between themselves they tended to unite instinctively against such 'outsiders'. Equally, whenever BRM as an entity was attacked or criticized in the press or by rivals, both Lincolnshire and Darlaston factions would unite instinctively against the common threat.

Spear made the following recommendations for future BRM racing procedure:

> A.C. Rudd to handle all discussions with drivers on

technical matters and pre-race instructions.

The lap chart must be kept correctly throughout the race. Someone must be found to do this as Mr. Berthon normally does it. It is understood that Mervin White[80] is capable of doing it.

Senior mechanic Gordon Newman had somehow upset Spear – not difficult – who wrote:

> Newman tends to think he is the king pin in the pit. He should be in charge of the working party, in the pits with his men around him. He should not have the stop watch board outside the pits roaming around talking to his friends.
>
> One man must be responsible for all signalling and he will take his instructions from Rudd only...In motor races only two people must be on the ground. The driver comes in and says what is wrong...Rudd must then make decisions and give instructions to Newman who in effect tells the different teams of men what to do...Above all there must be no panic so that the men do not lose their heads...

and more in similar, to the modern eye patronizing, vein.

The conversion to non-servo brake operation further delayed new-car build, so two of the older 'over-stressed-skin special' Type 25s were modified for Behra to choose between at Aintree. Should he prove unfit to race, Ron Flockhart – himself not long recovered from the effects of his French GP crash at Rouen – would qualify both cars as reserve, but the intention was to race one entry only.

April 19, 1958 – BARC Aintree '200', Liverpool – 67 laps, 201 miles

Despite strapped ribs, Behra qualified '251' on pole at 1:59.8, 1.4 seconds faster than Salvadori's works 2-litre Cooper and 1.8 seconds quicker than Moss' Walker entry. Car '255' – nicknamed *The Vanguard* – had served as T-car during practice, driven by Flockhart, and publicly was announced as non-starting due to 'magneto trouble'.

The Coopers of Moss and Jack Brabham – the latter a works car, from row two – out-accelerated Behra, and Salvadori dived for the inside entering Waterways Corner, but the Frenchman slammed the door on him, hard. Out along the Railway Straight, the BRM's power told and Behra rushed into second place an appreciable distance behind Moss, the dark-blue Cooper and its lustrous green, front-engined pursuer sliding right-handed out of Tatts to complete that opening lap, with both works Coopers snapping at Behra's heels.

Moss was able to draw away at over a second a lap, while Behra pulled out a 3-second lead over Brabham by lap five. The Australian would rush up behind the BRM in the twisty infield section, then fall away along the straights. Behra was

---

80. **Mervyn White was a cousin of RM's, from the then well-known shoe-manufacturing family.**

May 3, 1958 – BRDC International Trophy, Silverstone: Ron Flockhart put in one of his most promising drives yet in the old, often-rebuilt prototype stressed-skin car '251' only to crash heavily at Copse Corner while avoiding Bruce Halford's Maserati, being re-started on the track in his path. This lovely shot highlights the stressed-skin-fuselage car's riveting and Dzus-fastened side panels, etc. One Dzus has popped and stands proud. Impact with the bank would pop Dzuses and rivets alike – and end old '251's career…

Halford's 250F has been pushed back onto the track from the grass verge, a Cooper zooms by to Bruce's right; Flockhart arrives, dodging between the 250F and the fleeing marshals, Wicken's Cooper set to follow him through: Ron was lucky that '251' did not overturn – but this wall-of-death ride distorted its (in any case) obsolescent chassis beyond economic repair.

looking unhappy; he lost second place, but then regained it on lap 16, repassing Brabham, but now fully 13 seconds behind Moss. On lap 27 the Walker Cooper's lead had grown to 17 seconds, but next time round Brabham emerged from Tatts Corner alone, and Behra followed slowly, trundling to a halt in the pit lane, clambering stiffly out of the BRM and explaining flatly that its brakes had failed again.

This time it was a mundane failure, but yet another thoughtless one. With the two standard production master cylinders fitted to Behra's car, the large BRM-manufactured rubber-mounted fluid reservoir, with one large outlet, could not be used. Two standard production Lockheed fluid reservoirs were fitted and the four-cylinder engine's notorious vibration had simply split the seam on one, the fluid had drained away and the pedal softened until it stroked clean to the floor with negligible effect. Behra had recognized the signs and rolled off his speed long before venturing irretrievably into danger…

New chassis '256' was completed soon after as the first 1958-spec car, with full spaceframe structure and – with the exception of a fixed undertray – all-detachable body panelling. It first ran about a week before the big Silverstone May meeting. It had been built originally with servo brakes, but the system was converted to non-servo after the Goodwood debacle, before it ran. Its oil-cooling heat exchanger was situated in the water pipe between radiator and pump. It would then be equipped with a short ram air intake during Silverstone practice.

Ron Flockhart had shaken the car down at Folkingham, reporting that it seemed "quite good", though not, perhaps, any better than the modified car '253'. Although it seemed "very smooth" without the vibration of the four-main-bearing

engined cars, he "…didn't think it had got much power".

He was quite right.

May 3, 1958 – BRDC International Trophy, Silverstone – 50 laps, 146.35 miles

Behra, of course, was to drive the brand-new '256' in its debut race, while a second entry had been made for Flockhart to run '251' in its final appearance, the old car also having been converted to non-servo brakes since Goodwood.

Behra then held the outright Silverstone lap record, at 1:42, 103.31mph, set the previous September in the last International Trophy race. But he had always been particularly finicky about his driving seat, and the first practice session at Silverstone for this 1958 BRDC meeting passed with '256''s seat being painstakingly adjusted to his absolutely precise requirements. The second session then saw PB, Tony and the crew listening patiently while Behra complained bitterly about bad carburation, diagnosed as vibration-induced flooding, and the recalcitrant new car was finally rushed back to Folkingham to have a remote rubber-mounted carburettor system similar to the 1957 standard induction system fitted.

Where the team's latest 1958 specification mounted the two twin-choke Weber carburettors direct upon the engine, providing a constant equal-length inlet tract, the preceding '57 system had taken a leaf out of Ferrari's book with their four-cylinder *Tipo* 500/625/553/555 engines by isolating the carburettors from engine vibration by rubber-mounting them upon the chassis frame, whence they were connected to the engine by a dumb-bell tract with flexible 'O'-ring sealing.

However, the original engines, designed for fuel injection, remember, had tangential ports entering at 80° to the crankshaft axis, which meant that each pair of ports were of unequal length. In contrast the improved 1958 head had been designed for carburettors so had 90° ports and solid mountings for the Webers.

The conversion to rubber mounting moved the carburettors outboard, lengthening the tract, which was corrected by shorter trumpets, but it meant cutting a frame tube out of the brand-new chassis and altering the body to clear, but this was all achieved by midnight. A more time-consuming task was then to arrange a throttle linkage with fulcrums in positions not affected by movement on the rubber mountings and more progressive as demanded by Jean Behra.

Tony: We finally got it all finished by about 5.30am, when I gave it five laps round the test circuit to settle it down, and we then rushed the car back to Silverstone. Imagine our dismay when Behra brought it in after only six or seven rather slow practice laps and informed us – in emphatic French – that there was something "diabolically wrong with the rear suspension – the car will not handle and just oversteers in all directions. What have you done to it?".

Fortunately we realized there was nothing at all wrong with the chassis. After all the modification work the only problem was that his seat was moving around! We jammed it firm with jubilee clips, rubber hose and suitable pieces of wood, and then he went out and simply flew, provisionally qualifying on the front row of the grid!

But he was still unhappy about the carburation and the lack of progressiveness in the throttle mechanism. So at the end of the session we carted it all back to Folkingham again for another bash at both.

Back at Silverstone next morning – race day – he then insisted upon running the car up and down the paddock to try alternative carburettor jets until finally we had to call a halt – we were running out of time.

Meanwhile, Ron Flockhart had been doing his usual obedient and quietly effective job, and the two BRMs eventually lined-up on the second row of the grid, with times of 1:42.4 and 1:42.6 respectively. But a sign of the times was that ahead of them on the front row were three rear-engined Coopers – Salvadori's on pole at 1:40.8, flanked by Brabham's sister works car with a 1:41.4, Moss in Walker's 2.2-litre car at 1:41.8 and then Peter Collins in the sole foreign works entry – the Ferrari Dino 246 – on the same time. Additionally, this race witnessed the first Formula 1 entry ever made by Team Lotus – Graham Hill's spidery little 2-litre essentially-F2 Lotus 12 having qualified only 0.2sec slower than Flockhart's BRM, and 0.4sec slower than Behra's…

As at Goodwood, Moss' Climax engine died when the flag was raised and he was left stranded at the start while the rest of the 33 starters – the field combining F1 and F2 entries – thundered away towards Copse Corner. Collins came screaming round to lead back past the pits at the end of the first lap, with Behra close behind, pursued by Flockhart and Masten Gregory's *Centro-Sud* Maserati 250F.

Behra closed onto the Ferrari's tail and began harrying Collins, eventually carving his way by on lap four and beginning to build an impressive lead. Already, on lap two, he and Collins had set a new lap record in 1:40, 105.37mph, and now the BRM supporters, basking in the spring sunshine around Silverstone, really began to enjoy the day…

For 10 laps the French star's lustrous green BRM boomed round in a growing lead, but on lap 11 Behra's head jerked back. His right-hand clutched involuntarily at his face.

The BRM slowed and faltered, then accelerated again, but ending the lap Behra shot into the pits and stopped.

Tony: A stone had been thrown up which had shattered one lens of his goggles. Since his TT accident at Dundrod in a sports Maserati – when the spare pair of goggles around his neck had been broken and the lens edge had sliced off his right ear, leaving him to wear a plastic one for the rest of his life[81] – he had steadfastly refused to wear spare goggles. Consequently, he had come hurtling in for attention and a spare pair.

It took me quite a while to swab the blood and glass splinters from his eye, and by the time he could rejoin he was back in 11th place. Behra began doing his best to make up lost time, but was showing signs of his dismay at having been robbed of a splendid first place ahead of Ferrari's finest. Eventually he managed to repass Graham Hill's ailing Lotus for fourth place on lap 37, and there he finished, behind Collins' Ferrari, Salvadori's works Cooper and – a hurtful one, this – Gregory's old Maserati 250F, built by Behra's previous employers…

Meanwhile, once the unfortunate Frenchman's goggles had been smashed and Collins had established his Ferrari in a handsome lead, Flockhart had been running second in '251', some 15 seconds behind, and under constant pressure from Salvadori, who eventually managed to nip ahead of the BRM in traffic. Ron then ran third – seeking to regain his place – until mayhem erupted at Copse Corner. Peter Collins had made a mistake…

His leading Ferrari slewed broadside, then spun onto the grass verge, but he kept its engine running and was able to rejoin after several seconds' delay, without losing his place. Bruce Halford then spun his private Maserati 250F onto the outside grass verge at the exit to the same corner, but this time stalled his engine. A band of marshals was attempting to push-start this heavy car as George Wicken's F2 Cooper came hurtling into the corner, about to be lapped by Flockhart, still in hot pursuit of Salvadori.

What followed became something of a *cause celebre* between BRM and John Eason-Gibson, the hard-nosed Secretary of the organizing BRDC. Two days later RM wrote to Eason-Gibson:

Flockhart was rounding Copse on the outside of Wickens' Cooper, making to overtake and just level with his rear wheels, when they both suddenly saw Halford's Maserati to all intents and purposes stationary on the track, surrounded by marshals. It was at a point on the exit to the corner which was right on the line

---

81. One of Behra's favourite party tricks when in polite British company was to reach up and remove his plastic ear, which he would then hand around, explaining proudly "Made in England…"

normally taken by fast cars. Wickens had to steer suddenly in order to pass the Maserati on the right, but in so doing, the rear of his car momentarily swung out and touched the B.R.M. This put Ron into such a position that he had the alternative either of going straight into Halford, or round him on his left on the grass. He made for the grass, but there were a number of people standing there watching Halford being pushed, and looking the other way, and in order to avoid knocking them down he had to make for the bank. This damaged the car and very nearly turned him over.

At no time during the few seconds taken by this incident did Ron see any warning flags being displayed; in fact eye-witnesses agree that the flag marshal had put his flags on the ground while Halford was being pushed. Nobody was exercising any proper control of the situation…the flag-marshal positioned before Copse Corner, Mr. R. Gibson-Jarvie,[82] admitted that it was impossible to see the marshal on the other side of the corner, or to see what was going on around the corner, partly because of the display of hoardings on the inside of the track at that point. During the incident in question he only put out his yellow flag when he saw a cloud of dust, but there is no evidence the flag was out before Ron went past: it is possible that the dust seen by Mr Jarvie was raised by Ron, who certainly denies having seen any warning displayed to him when he approached the corner.

Eye-witnesses agree that Halford's car was pushed from a perfectly safe place on the grass to one of extreme danger on the track.

Ray hoped that Silverstone marshals would be better sited, and better-briefed, in future, while pointing out that "the disastrous loss of the front of the B.R.M…is a most serious matter to us…".

Poor Flockhart was beside himself since this had been his first BRM drive of the new season, he had been well-set for a decent result, he had been confronted by a frightening, and potentially gruesome situation, and now he had crashed a Type 25 – perhaps most pointedly at the same corner at which he had capsized 'Bira''s Maserati 250F in 1954, causing a fearful fuss which, as we have seen, greatly scrambled the history of the Owen Maserati almost before it had begun…

Flockhart clearly felt the need to justify his actions, and after gathering his thoughts he sent a hand-written letter to Alfred Owen from Blunham House, Bedfordshire, on May 22 placing:

82. Bob Gibson-Jarvie was the Jaguar D-Type owning head of the United Dominions Trust finance house, prominent in motor car hire purchase and at that time poised to promote its own image as a Formula 1 and Formula 2 team sponsor – first with Colonel Ronnie Hoare[83] of Bournemouth Ford main dealer F. English Ltd as the United Racing Stable – and subsequently with 'Pa' Moss and Ken Gregory's British Racing Partnership to create the UDT-Laystall Racing Team of 1962–63.

83. Colonel Hoare would himself soon take over from Hawthorn's Tourist Trophy Garage Ltd of Farnham, Surrey, as British Ferrari importer under the company title Maranello Concessionaires Ltd.

The main responsibility for the incident…with the marshals who directed and pushed Halford's Maserati back onto the track on the blind side of Copse Corner, directly in the line of oncoming cars…The positioning of flag marshals was at fault…[both] are good and trusted friends of mine – Bob Gibson-Jarvie of U.D.T. and Basil de Mattos of Laystall Eng. – and they…had pointed out this lack of communication during the previous day's practice. I have had a word on this subject with John Eason-Gibson…but I'm afraid he is taking a somewhat unrelenting line.

From my own point of view, had those thoughtless marshals not been standing around between the Maserati and the safety bank I would probably [have] been able to steer the car through the narrow gap…

I was extremely disappointed as…despite driving a 1957 car [I] felt sure of repassing Salvadori into second place before the end…as the car was behaving very well indeed…

On June 5 the unbending Eason-Gibson – like Flockhart a serious-minded Scot – responded to RM:

I have been instructed by the General Committee (of the BRDC) to write you in the following terms.

It is clear from the evidence, that the Yellow flag was displayed 150 yards before Copse Corner, from the time Collins and then Halford spun, prior to Flockhart and Wicken passing that flag point. It is also clear that the Yellow flag was waved and remained out until all drivers had been shown it, and held motionless until Wicken and Halford had left Copse Corner and the track was clear.

It is unfortunate that expressions of opinion to should [sic] have created an impression contrary to the truth.

May I personally, and on a friendly level, assure you that there is no doubt that the above is justified, and I can only assume in the heat of the battle the waved Yellow flag was not noticed by Flockhart…

Interestingly, Salvadori had backed Ron's impressions of the incident to Peter Spear, who assured Owen that "no blame can be attributed to Flockhart…" and Owen subsequently wrote a brief but comforting note to his aggrieved team driver, who must have been feeling increasingly persecuted. In this respect, Ron's season would get worse…

Despite the disappointment and controversy of Silverstone, the BRM team returned home in some elation for their cars had run very competitively and reliably and had clearly been robbed of a decent result by circumstance entirely beyond their control. Vitally, Behra was in positive post-race mood. Tony: He told us not to be downhearted, the car was very good, and providing we carried out the list of modifications he gave us he guaranteed he would take the prize for the fastest practice lap at Monte Carlo on the opening day of practice there, the following week. And then, he told us, he'd spend the prizemoney by standing us the finest meal we'd ever had.

In time for the Monaco trip, the second new detachable-body spaceframe car '257' destined for Harry Schell was then completed, with non-servo brakes, short ram air intake and an otherwise identical specification to '256', and it was bedded-in at Folkingham before the transporters were loaded and the long – minimum two-day – drive commenced down to Monte Carlo. Only Behra's car had the full preferred chassis-mounted carburettor conversion, while Schell's was held back for the more vital modifications to be made to it, and was then rushed non-stop to Monaco by mechanics Gordon Newman and Phil Ayliff, using an open truck borrowed from Rubery Owen's Transport Department and arriving in time for first practice.

May 18, 1958 – Monaco Grand Prix, Monte Carlo – 100 laps, 195.41 miles

This was the first time a pair of spaceframe-chassised, detachable-bodied Type 25s had been fielded together, Behra in '256' and Harry Schell – back in place of Flockhart, as planned – in '257', while '255' accompanied these two 1958-spec machines as T-car.

First practice was held around the tight and confined street circuit on the Thursday, and Jean Behra was immediately as good as his word and set fastest time – at 1:40.8 – then simply sat on the pit counter and watched all his rivals shoot at it – a *completely* new world for BRM!

As Harry Schell went quite well, both setting-up his new car and trundling around in the old one, Monte Carlo – BRM's place of demons in previous years – seemed utterly transformed.

But right at the end of practice, the Bourne boys became a little too full of themselves and failed to keep a keen enough eye upon Tony Brooks in the Vanwall as he equalled Behra's

best time without '*Jeannot*' having an opportunity to respond.

Tony: That evening, instead of the usual late-night preparation session, Jean took us out to dinner in a restaurant on the outskirts of Nice built into the cliffs which he informed us had been torpedoed by the Americans during the war under the impression it was an enemy warship.

The cars did not run in the early-morning session next day, but out again that afternoon Behra clouted the wall at the *Tabac*, without serious damage. Brooks eventually denied Behra and BRM pole position, lowering his best time to 1:39.8, while Jean's Thursday best of 1:40.8 was good enough for the centre of the front row, flanked by Brabham's 2.2-litre Cooper on the outside at 1:41.0. Harry Schell qualified 12th, at 1:43.8, on row five, between von Trips' Ferrari and Cliff Allison's 2.2 Lotus.

There had been some minor panics with tappet clearances closing up, but otherwise practice had been spent tuning the new cars, adjusting braking ratios, roll bars, tyre pressures etc. The only dangerous problem seemed to be wavering oil pressure, otherwise everything seemed almost eerily to be going BRM's way…

On race morning Peter Spear handed Tony Rudd a formal letter from AGBO, copied all round, informing him that henceforward he was in charge of the pit, tactics and running the race – all well and good. But he was also to organize a formal pre-race check procedure, with each mechanic concerned signing-off for each operation. Tony ruefully commented that this was a bit too late, as the cars were just leaving the garage for the circuit…

At the start, Salvadori rocketed his Cooper through from the inside of row two, but arrived at the *Gazometre* hairpin far

May 18, 1958 – Monaco Grand Prix, Monte Carlo: Jean Behra tackled the entire Monte Carlo weekend with tremendous enthusiasm, confident of his new spaceframe car '256''s capabilities. Here he leads the Vanwalls of Brooks and Moss into the Tabac ending the opening lap, already drawing out a considerable advantage. But it would evaporate… Note the 'safety barrier' along that quayside…

May 25, 1958 – Dutch Grand Prix practice, Zandvoort: Tony Rudd and Jean Behra became very close during the French star's single season with BRM and both would want to renew the association come 1959. Here in the Zandvoort pits they pass the time of day…the French star's artificial right ear evident. Before donning his crash helmet he would hand the ear to Phil Ayliff, who would carefully wrap it in a clean handkerchief and pop it into his overall pocket. The drill when Behra got out of his car was for him to remove his helmet, offer his palm, into which Phil – like a surgeon's theatre nurse – would slap the ear for re-attachment.

too fast and ran wide, enabling Behra to lead out of the corner with Brooks' Vanwall on his tail and Schell's sister BRM seventh. While Behra set about building his race lead, Schell was beset and overtaken by a jostling trio of works Ferraris – Musso, Collins and von Trips.

Moss set fastest lap at 1:42.7, Hawthorn equalled it, Brooks lopped off another tenth of a second, then Behra a further three-tenths. Gradually – wonderfully – Behra's BRM was drawing ever further away from Brooks in the best-placed Vanwall, which was being threatened by Hawthorn's Ferrari Dino 246. To be heading all the works Ferraris, Tony Vandervell's "bloody red cars", was nice – but also to be heading the anti-BRM bearing magnate's own Vanwalls was probably nicer still for some in the team…

On lap 15 Behra improved Fangio's lap record of 1:42.4 with a 1:41.8 and on lap 18 Hawthorn took second place as Brooks' Vanwall engine began to falter and Tony eventually switched off and retired. After 20 laps Behra held a 5sec lead over Hawthorn, but he was having to brake ever earlier into the tight corners as his car's pedal softened, and the Ferrari rapidly closed, Hawthorn eventually barging ahead on lap 27.

Tony: Jean came in to report loss of brakes, and we found to our dismay that the flare on a piece of bundy pipe on the rear brake master cylinder had pulled off. With all our vibration problems it had been our rule that we would only use machine-made flares, but such had been the panic in final preparation that we had inadvertently used a hand-made flare and this was the one which had split. Then Schell came into the pits complaining of carburation problems.

After running seventh at 30 laps, one of his carburettors was flooding dreadfully, dousing two spark plugs and giving Harry a terrible struggle merely to climb the long hill up to the

Casino Square with the Type 25 spluttering and popping on two cylinders only. From the Square it was virtually all downhill to the pits, but Harry had lost a lot of time when he finally got there. It then took several laps to find a tiny sliver of *wood* jamming the float needle down. Once this was removed the car went quite well. At 60 laps Harry lay ninth, seven laps behind Trintignant's leading Walker Cooper. It was a hard, hot and mucky race, with oil, grit and brake dust coating the drivers. Gregor Grant reported in *Autosport* that "…Harry Schell continued to circulate, his face blacker than a Zulu warrior…". And thanks to retirements ahead he eventually finished fifth, real reward for perseverance and an object lesson in the value of never giving up when all seemed lost…

BRM had again completed a Continental World Championship-qualifying Grand Prix race, and had scored two World Championship points. Behra's defection from the race lead due to a preparation error had been a severe blow, but Schell's race finish was enormously cheering to the long-beleaguered British team.

Tony: I slept in the neighbouring hotel room to Harry's, and I clearly recall the terrific excitement when he had himself called early next morning to entertain the latest in his long line of exotic girlfriends. This was because after the race he considered he had given too much of himself in the racing car to do adequate justice to her – typical Harry…

Spear had attended Monaco as Owen's eyes and ears – leaning towards the team, one feels, in reporting:

> The race preparation and pit control were good, although there was some difficulty with the carburettors. There was plenty of room [in the pits]. The people present apart from Berthon, Mays, Rudd, the mechanics and myself were Schell's and Behra's wives, Behra's stepmother and father and his son, my wife and 'Robin', the mechanic from Peterborough who came down with Raymond Mays on a personal basis. Rivers Fletcher and his wife were present part of the time when they were filming. There were no hangers on in the pits…

– in fact there was very little room in the old Monaco pits on the centre strip between the roadway and the promenade before the modern swimming-pool complex was built and RM, Robin, Behra's entourage and Peggy Spear took themselves off before the start. Spear continued:

> Behra's car ran very well for the first 25 or so laps and his times were consistent. He retired with brake trouble. It was caused by a slight oil [*sic* – means brake fluid] leak under pressure in one union which gradually lost him pedal movement until during the last few laps his foot was on the floor-board. Schell had some carburation trouble and a little brake trouble as one front brake was running hotter than the other. This is rather a characteristic of the circuit on our brakes and is not a fundamental thing to worry about. It was felt generally that Schell could have driven a little faster in this race, and Behra was a little disappointed with him.

Tony: Harry was in effervescent mood after the race and

took PB, RM and myself to dinner at a restaurant in Nice old town. On arrival he announced to the restaurateur that since he wished to entertain his friends in the lucky *Patron*'s establishment he should first inspect the kitchens. He then interviewed the owner to see if he was suitable to cater for such an august company and after tremendous ceremony we all enjoyed an excellent meal and left in high spirits, suspecting very much that Harry had not paid the bill...

The team had neither time to lick its wounds nor to rest upon its laurels. The Dutch GP at Zandvoort was being held the following weekend, so the ORO convoy set out direct from Monte Carlo with the three Austin Lodestar transporters accompanied by the Commer mobile workshop.

We spent a pleasant day checking-over the cars and then set off on the Tuesday for Zandvoort. I drove PB and Lorna, setting off after lunch, stopping at Macon overnight and the next

day lunching at Reims before a tedious run through Belgium, dinner at Antwerp and arrival in Zandvoort at midnight.

May 26, 1958 – Dutch Grand Prix, Zandvoort – 75 laps, 195.41 miles

The race was being run on Whit-Monday, first practice being held on the preceding Saturday. Behra and Schell drove their Monaco cars, and since both had survived Monaco intact ORO's intention had been to run a full three-car team in Holland, with Ron Flockhart present to race spare car '255'. However, RM appeared to have muddled the entries – the organizing KNAC officials explained none had been received, and it was only after some negotiation that even Behra and

1958 Dutch Grand Prix: BRM's best day yet in World Championship racing saw Harry Schell – here cornering his sleek new spaceframe-chassised/detachable-bodied '257' in the Hunzerug turn, behind the pits – finishing second ahead of team-mate Behra in '256'.

Behra was bitterly disappointed to have been out-performed and beaten by Harry Schell at Zandvoort and finished morose and silent. Here his '257' laps future BRM World Champion driver Graham Hill – experiencing an early F1 disappointment with his Team Lotus 1.9-litre Type 12...

1958 Dutch Grand Prix: "For us it was as if we'd actually won!" Harry Schell being greeted like a conquering hero as he brings his second-placed BRM back into the paddock, feted here by mechanics Dove, Newman (cap), Ayliff, Southcott (part-hidden), Salmon, Pat Carvath – whose sister Pam married Tony Rudd, Pat suffering in consequence as Tony attempted to prove that his brother-in-law would receive no special treatment – and Perkins amongst the photographers.

Schell were accepted – a most disgruntled Flockhart having to miss out yet again.

In first practice Moss demonstrated Vanwall's superiority, clocking 1:38.0 – 2 seconds inside Fangio's existing lap record (from 1955) with the Mercedes-Benz W196.

The BRMs again performed quite well, once fitted with replacement engines direct from Bourne. Behra slithered into the straw bales in the *Hunzerug* corner behind the pits – emerging without damage and grinning broadly – but as practice went on so he decided his engine was not performing as well as it should and his mood visibly changed, becoming quiet, dispirited, rather withdrawn. His main disappointment was that he could not keep pace with the Vanwalls along the main straight.

In fact the three works Vanwalls of Stuart Lewis-Evans, Stirling Moss and Tony Brooks proved to be in a class of their own – filling the front grid row in that order, with times of 1:37.1, 1:38.0 and 1:38.1 respectively. Behra was next up, fourth fastest overall in '256' with a 1:38.4. Jack Brabham flanked him in the works 2.2 Cooper, with Hawthorn's Ferrari sixth fastest on the inside of row three, flanked by Schell's 1:39.2 in '257'.

No fewer than 13 of the 17 starters had lapped inside the old lap record, and only 2.3 seconds covered the entire grid. Race day dawned bitterly cold and grey with torrential rain hosing the circuit clean. Fortunately the squalls blew away and the high wind dried the course, but the skies remained leaden and the wind cold. As engines ran up on the starting grid both BRMs puffed blue smoke, wafting into the pits upon the gale. BRM supporters held their breaths, were the Type 25s in trouble already?

They were soon to find out. When starter van Haaren dropped the flag the field bellowed away down into the braking area for the 180-degree *Tarzan* loop, where Schell immediately muscled his way into third place behind the Vanwalls of Moss and Lewis-Evans, followed by Brooks' Vanwall – with which he had touched wheels, fatally deranging the Acton car's rear end – and Behra, fifth.

Brooks made an early pit stop, Salvadori in the little Cooper displaced Behra, but while the two leading Vanwalls of Moss and Lewis-Evans were separated by 4 seconds, Schell kept pace, 4sec back in third. After 10 laps the Franco-American began forcing the pace, pressuring Lewis-Evans, and on lap 12 he took second place from him in the *Hunzerug*. Behra – dismayed to find his engine intermittently off-song, apparently with plug problems – had been passed by Hawthorn's Ferrari, but as the race pattern began to settle he fought back, took fifth place from the Italian car and tackled Salvadori for fourth.

After 20 laps Behra was mounting an attack upon Lewis-Evans for third. On lap 26, 13 seconds separated them, and while Moss and Schell were drawing away up front, Lewis-Evans was falling back, to allow Behra to close within 11 seconds until – on lap 46 – the Vanwall went out with a broken valve-spring.

At that point Moss led in the sole surviving Vanwall, 30 seconds ahead of Schell with Behra a distant but unchallenged third. Three British green cars 1-2-3 in a Continental *Grande Epreuve* – running reliably, running fast…

As the race had developed the ORO pit crew stood virtually agape at the astonishing sight of Moss' Vanwall purring its distinctively muted note, round and round, lap after lap, with the BRMs bellowing along apparently reliably in its wheel-tracks.

Schell, in fact, told journalists he had been worrying his way around, for '257' 's "oil pressure gauges were reading zero and 25psi instead of the usual 60", according to one report. Tony doubts this: There was only one pressure gauge – and Harry never looked at them anyway. He hoped the gauges were faulty – they were, although post-race the oil pressure was indeed found to be down – but their sombre message persuaded him not to press-on harder.

Hawthorn had been struggling all day with his unwieldy Ferrari Dino, battling vicious understeer round the swerving, undulating back stretch. Moss had lapped him – and indeed was threatening to do the same to Behra's BRM – but Schell was closing rapidly upon the red Ferrari – and in the pits the BRM boys relished the sight.

Gregor Grant:

> With six laps left…Schell caught Hawthorn, and went to pass him on the *Hoek van Tarzan*. He nearly lost his second place, for the B.R.M. shot onto the grass, and just missed going into the sand. A couple of laps later and Harry once again made to go through, and Mike waved him past at the hairpin. Moss could apparently have lapped Behra, but elected to stay…behind… Then it was over – complete and utter triumph for the green cars, with Moss scoring a magnificent victory, and the B.R.M.s silencing their critics by a really fine performance. Amidst scenes of wild enthusiasm, the Union Jack was run up on the finish line, and thousands of Dutchmen (and Dutch women) stood to attention to the strains of 'God Save the Queen'…

Heady stuff – but a genuine reflection of the way many British enthusiasts felt at the time…green cars ascendant was becoming an invigorating habit, and the new-spec BRMs finishing second and third against strong opposition in a full-length World Championship Grand Prix – the real thing – was a marvellous result.

Over in Sussex that afternoon at the Whit-Monday Goodwood meeting the race commentator announced that Stirling Moss had just won the Dutch GP for Vanwall. The crowd cheered and programmes fluttered. The commentator then broke the extraordinary news that BRMs had just finished second and third. There was a perceptible stunned silence…broken by an even louder and longer cheer.

At Zandvoort Schell eased himself stiffly from '257''s cockpit, beaming with delight as his team greeted him. But Behra drew to a halt grim-faced and sombre, despite his mechanics' delighted back-slapping. He seemed dismayed because he had been beaten by his team-mate, the same driver who in the Maserati works team the previous year had never been able to beat him. How could such a thing have happened in these green cars? Had Schell been given special attention, because he – unlike Behra – could speak good English? A nagging seed of suspicion had been sewn… The Frenchman had little to say about his car, which left Tony Rudd non-plussed since he had expected an enormous job list, yet none emerged. Both drivers reported some carburation trouble… associated with the new carburettor mounting, and Schell explained his oil pressure worries, but only the post-race strip-down back at Bourne would reveal the true lessons of this two-race trip…

MID-1958 – TROUBLE IN THE CAMP

Tested on the Folkingham dyno immediately after return from Zandvoort, Behra's race engine was found to deliver just 220bhp against the 254 with which it had been signed-off pre-race.

Tony Rudd's snag report covering the trip's two meetings at Monaco and Zandvoort ran to 30 items, the major of which were:

June 14, 1958 – Belgian Grand Prix practice, Spa-Francorchamps: The friendly relationship between BRM's two French-speaking drivers – Behra (left) and Harry Schell – deteriorated rapidly as this season progressed. Jean here has a dressing on his face, cut somehow during his high-speed spin at the Masta Kink, and the drivers are standing by his retrieved and essentially undamaged car, wondering what may have caused this demoralizingly high-speed incident…

All No. 4 timing gear bosses loose in the heads; both cars fluffing on right-hand corners, reduce carburettor angle…

– from 11 to 5° (the carburettors were inclined upwards at their outboard ends to maintain the part axis, this made them more prone to flood on right-hand bends):

> …all cars required rigid mirror mounts (like Behra's); bypassing of the main fuel filter had to be investigated (heavier spring required as per 'No. 7' car); better instruments, misfiring magnetos to be investigated; Weber-type throttle bell ends required; oil leaks from same places as last year, i.e. front of oil pump, 'O'-ring groove too deep rear of No. 5 main bearings – tacho drive sandwich and fuel pump mounting adaptor; propshaft UJ wear still bad; all engines leaked water from ends of Gaco cord in head joint; all header tank relief valves sticking due to electrolytic corrosion through dissimilar materials; radiator top connection very weak, 'No. 7' car's radiator split; double-diameter valve guides (*a la* V16) to be investigated to combat oily exhausts and possible breathing; electric starter shaft to be built-in to avoid damage to radiator and to facilitate pit adjustments; extra support under leading edge of bonnet, both cars had bonnets collapsed by spectators at Monaco; 'No. 7' car's gearbox mounting stiffness to be investigated; four half-shaft stars plucked; the gear drive clutch in engine '2582' cracked from all windows; cap half centre main bearing split in '2582'; old type inlet valve rotators were stuck and the valves were blowing in '2582'; a KLG280 plug was defective on '2584'; brake wear on Schell's left-front wheel double that of the right-front wheel at both Monaco and Zandvoort…

June 14, 1958 – Belgian Grand Prix practice: Dick Salmon and Pat Carvath prepare to push-start Schell's '257' on the downhill pit apron at Spa, Behra's '256' beyond, a characteristically pensive Tony Rudd between the cars. Note the latest nylon-carcass Dunlop R5 tyres – a great advance. Schell's battered white helmet bears BRM and USAC decals. An oddity of this Belgian race was the organizers' assigning of different numbers to the cars during practice to prevent pirate programmes being sold with the right numbers come raceday. Schell would race under number '10', Behra '8'. Number '14' on raceday would be Collins' Ferrari...

(denying Spear's attribution of this problem to the circuit at Monte Carlo).

Power loss over a full Grand Prix distance was clearly a problem with the new five-bearing P25 engines, and doubt was dawning over intrinsic power loss for which the mere change in fuel – from alcohol to AvGas – was not responsible. PB was desperately concerned, for the next race would be on the power circuit at Spa-Francorchamps, in Belgium. One of the old four-bearing engines was run on the dyno on AvGas, developing a happy and healthy 260bhp (!), so a current five-bearing unit was set up to burn alcohol and run in comparison, developing far inferior power than the '57 unit...

Clearly, either something was radically wrong with the new induction system or there was a major power loss somewhere... But again there was no time available to investigate further. High-speed tests were to be run on the long runway at RAF Cottesmore – between Stamford and Grantham – with Behra driving, but there were only 20 days between the Dutch and Belgian GPs, or 18 before practice would commence at Spa. BRM found itself – yet again – having to catch-up...

June 15, 1958 – Belgian Grand Prix, Spa-Francorchamps – 24 laps, 210.31 miles

Behra and Schell were to run their two regular 1958-spec cars, as at Monaco and Zandvoort, while the usual old '255' performed T-car duties. As at Zandvoort, the second '58-spec engine – '2584' – was fitted to Behra's car

But as PB and the team had feared, the Type 25s proved disappointingly slow in practice on this very fast course. Behra tried to compensate by driving desperately hard. Unfortunately, running the five-bearing engine flat-out for the long periods demanded at Spa raised the oil temperature to unprecedented heights, and on an early practice lap, after negotiating the high-speed right-hand curves at Burnenville and Malmedy, then hammering flat-out onto the long, slightly downhill back straight, hot oil was abruptly pumped out through the breather and over '256''s left-rear tyre.

Since Behra was by that time entering the legendary Masta kink – in the middle of that bullet-fast straight – '256' spun luridly through at least 720-degrees from around 160mph, gyrating wildly through the kink itself – miraculously slewing to rest amidst a billowing cloud of tyre smoke, without having touched anything hard...

Behra returned to the pits looking decidedly peaky, and it was noticed that his hand was trembling as he lit a soothing cigarette. Thereafter his times remained obstinately slow, thoroughly de-tuned by his experience.

The team spent an all-night session rearranging his car's oil system so that its oil tank breathed through the engine, in the belief – not quite correct as it turned out – that the oil breather system which worked on the '57 engines, cooled as they were by their alcohol fuel, was not going to work on the latest five-bearing units.

Peter Spear's report to Alfred Owen on what was to prove a disappointing race for BRM read, in part, as follows:

> During the three practices slight modifications were made to the car suspensions to suit the track, but the following points became apparent:
> 1. The 1st gear on the car was not quite the correct ratio.
> 2. The engines have insufficient power at higher revs. The real cause of this is not quite apparent.
>
> Schell started on the 3rd row of the grid and Behra on the 4th. Both our drivers were excellent in the start and Behra went round the pack, near the Pits, overtaking everyone and at the end of half a mile was in front of Moss who had been in the lead at the beginning. On the first long straight, however, he was overtaken by the Vanwalls, by two Coopers and a Lotus. This disheartened him and at the end of four laps he came into the Pits and refused to drive any more. He talked at first about oil pressure but this was satisfactory. His basic argument was that he is a first class driver and cannot afford to be in a race behind Coopers. As events turned out it was a pity he did not carry on as he would have probably finished third. However it means that the car is virtually untouched. Schell drove an excellent race, pressing on to the best of his ability all the time and finished 5th, gaining prize money of £70.

Both drivers were delighted with brakes and suspension. They reckoned that they gained 50 yards in braking. Even Schell could overtake Brooks on a corner but was almost immediately overtaken on the straight.

Behra had a nasty spin on the first day of practice which upset his confidence. He looked a very worried man as he went to the starting line…

…It is interesting to note that if there had been one more lap Harry Schell would have been first instead of fifth. Brooks' engine was failing and was incapable of another lap. Mike Hawthorn, who was second, blew up his engine on the last lap and coasted past the winning post in a wonderful display of smoke and sparks. Lewis-Evans, who was third, had broken the top wishbone at the rear end of his car, and Allison, who was fourth, had

a smashed exhaust. Schell was catching up on Allison rapidly towards the end of the race and would probably have caught him on another lap. On immediate post-race examination Schell's car, in spite of having done the equivalent of well over two races, including practices, was in very good condition…

PB felt badly enough about this disappointing performance to write to Owen, on June 19:

The Spa circuit is the fastest of all the Continental circuits in average, and this is actually the first time we have raced on a high-speed circuit with the present cars – and during practice and the race the following points came to light:

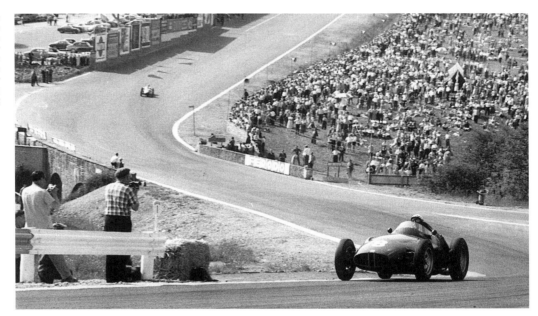

1958 Belgian Grand Prix: Behra, here loading-up '256' – with its fared-in carburettor trunk and internal intake – through the Raidillon bypass corner after Eau Rouge, was outraged to be passed on the straight by 2.2-litre Lotuses and Coopers and chose to retire rather than suffer further humiliation. This was hardly what any team would expect from an undeniably top-flight professional racing driver…

Harry Schell, in contrast, never lost his 'never-say-die' character despite declining capabilities (he was already 37 years old), and he soldiered-on in '257' to finish fifth and score World Championship points. Here throwing late-race shadows, he locks over for La Source hairpin ahead of Jo Bonnier – due to become Harry's team-mate before this season is out – in his ex-Fangio 'Lightweight' Maserati 250F, while eventual race winner Tony Brooks' Vanwall is poised to lap them both.

1) Road holding at speed was not good, there being a tendency for the cars to wander.

2) Serious engine breathing occurred on both the new cars in practice, and it was this that caused oil to be thrown on the rear offside tyre, and was responsible for Behra's skid.

3) Maximum speeds were very disappointing and our cars did not exceed the 160/165 mile per hour [sic], which was 10/15 miles per hour slower than the opposition.

During practice…it was found that rear axles were bottoming heavily on bump, so lifting the rear of the car off the road and displacing it relative to line of travel. As no practical means of increasing axle travel was available, a compromise was sought in using increased bump damping and making more use of the rubber bump stops, which are effectively a means of increasing spring rates at the end of the travel.

Finally the roadholding was said to be good by both drivers and our cars were able to outcorner and outbrake the opposition.

The oil breathing trouble was due to oil piling up at the rear of the oil tank on the long straights during acceleration, and being transferred into the engine via the breather pipe, which in turn was thrown out through the engine breather when the level rose sufficiently for the crank to dip.

A new breather system was fitted, which breathed the oil tank from both ends and omitted the return to the crank case…no trouble [thereafter].

Various reasons for possible lack of speed on the straights, leaving engine power aside, were investigated prior to the race, and variations of the air intake tried on Behra's car without improvement…"

PB announced that engine investigations were being pursued, "but time has been inadequate during the last three races to really explore the reasons". He maintained:

The only differences between the '57 and '58 type engines are:

1) 5 main bearings instead of 4 – the additional bearing costs approximately 3bhp

2) New carburettors with wider centres with a different type mounting.

3) A different type of exhaust system, which was developed as a result of winter test bed work.

4) Item 2 is suspected as carburettor flooding and severe emulsification of the fuel may be due to vibration.

During the race, Behra was so disgusted at being passed by the Cooper and the Lotus on the straight, that he felt it wasn't worth continuing to overdrive on the corners to keep his lap speeds up, and he eventually gave up. The car was mechanically sound…

He further reported that in post-race testing:

84. **Tony: This comment is rather cheeky since we had no idea whatsoever of the aerodynamic drag.**

Schell's engine was found to be down to 222hp, i.e. 50hp less than it should be…Assuming this power, and taking frontal area and drag figures[84] – this checks closely with the speed that was realised on the circuit, which exonerates air intakes and general car installation…the only defect…is a broken inlet valve spring on No. 4 cylinder…

Alfred Owen was simply shocked:

I cannot help feeling bitterly disappointed that we seem to go to race after race and always find some reason for not being successful. I was told that Behra was utterly disgusted at the maximum speed of his engine…and your letter confirms this. The failure of the cars at Spa was a bitter disappointment and the last thing in the world that I expected was to find the engines woolly!

Berthon explained:

My general policy on engine performance…has been the best possible range of useful torque at a small cost in maximum power. This…pays off handsomely on all average circuits…and all the Continental ones except Spa, Rheims [sic] and, to a lesser degree Monza.

Spa effectively caught us with our pants down, since the circuit has been considerably improved since the last Grand Prix was held there in 1956, with a big difference in lap times of nearly 10 miles per hour…

He argued that manipulating engine characteristics to suit such circuits was a "very elaborate problem", but "we will have a more suitable characteristic for Rheims; but we shall be lucky if we can alter it sufficiently in the time to secure any real advantage in maximum speed…".

He then observed, quite justifiably:

Behra should not have packed up on the eighth lap, as his car was mechanically perfect, and Spa is…hard indeed on engines and transmission. If in fact the race had been one lap longer, Jean could have been 1st and Harry Schell 2nd, as 2 Vanwalls and a Ferrari could not have run another lap, and when they came to take the sump off Allison's Lotus the centre main bearing and panel assembly dropped out on the floor (!)

This does not, of course, excuse our lack of performance; but I feel that a driver should not give up driving so early in a hard race of doubtful issue.

Owen vigorously scribbled *I agree* in the margin to this letter.

Veteran airflow expert Harry Weslake was then called in as consultant to investigate the five-bearing engines' mysterious power loss. He had extensive previous experience on Norton and Vanwall racing engines, "but has since rather fallen out with Vandervell" – Tony Vandervell, of course, not only heading Vandervell Products Ltd but also being on the board of Norton motorcycles. "Mr. Weslake said he would like to make an arrangement for a year, at an annual fee of £500, and charge for any actual work done on our cylinder heads, or in testing, at a bare labour charge, plus 175%, which is not more than 15/– per hour." PB recommended that this fee would be money well spent.

A number of cylinder heads were despatched to Weslake Research at Rye, where tests upon their airflow rig revealed considerable disparity between 'good' and 'bad' heads. One of the best-flowing heads was selected for improvement and it would be taken to Reims for Behra's use in the following French GP, time preventing a preparatory test-bed check.

Meanwhile, RM had been in touch with the *AC de Champagne* to arrange entries for their French GP on July 6. The Club was eager for BRM entries and offered outstanding start money as three cars were to be effectively French-driven, by Behra, Schell and guest driver Maurice Trintignant.

But at Bourne, ORO entered another of its periodic bouts of navel contemplation. Should BRM really make this trip – was the risk of running badly or unreliably too great to bear?

Would the time be better spent overcoming the engines' power loss to prepare for the British GP – to BRM, Rubery Owen and ORMA the year's most important event?

Tony: I had been put back in the tea pot at this time and was being kept out of the way as I was spreading rank heresy. Having found at Spa that the oil temperature went off the clock (135°C) and was still climbing despite our bigger oil cooler, I had measured the heat to oil in a five-bearing engine and had found it equal to some 20hp more than that of a four-bearing. I made the tactical mistake of telling PB and RM that my results were inaccurate and I had improvised some of the equipment in the brief time available. This had been turned into: "the whole winter development programme had been sloppy and rushed because I was obsessed with my new car design".

On July 1 Spear advised Owen:

> On balance I think we should go to Rheims [*sic*] for the following reasons:
> 1. Behra's engine will give 7% greater power than at Spa and Schell's engine 6%. I am not certain of... Trintignant's... It is hoped that a still more powerful

engine will be available nearer the end of the week, and this will be taken out by Peter Berthon, who is staying on at Folkingham for the next few days. It will then be fitted into Behra's car, all being well.
> 2. The gear ratios in the cars should be better than at Spa as there is not a slow corner on the Rheims circuit. Jean Behra is quite happy about this.
> 3. The team of mechanics that go out to Rheims could not help the engine situation if they stayed at Folkingham.
> 4. The Rheims race pays us more money than any other race of the year.
> 5. At the present time Harry Schell is fourth in the World Championship. If he gets a place at Rheims and the Vanwalls do not do too well, he could become third quite easily.
>
> On balance then, I think it would be better for the team to go to Rheims...

At Folkingham, the third of the 1958-spec, detachable-body spaceframe Type 25s – serial '258' – had just been completed. It would become not only the most successful individual car of the entire series, but it is today the only genuine survivor. It was fitted with a new-type oil cooler on the right side of the engine bay, in place of the previously standard heat-exchanger. Once again the team cars were race-prepared, and the ORO cavalcade set off for the Champagne country of northern France...

July 6, 1958 – *Grand Prix de l'ACF*, Reims-Gueux – 50 laps, 258 miles

The new car went finally to Harry Schell while Behra took over '257' which he had been eyeing with growing suspicion at Zandvoort and Spa when it apparently performed in Schell's

July 6, 1958 – Grand Prix de l'ACF, Reims-Gueux: Raymond 'Toto' Roche of the AC de Champagne prepares to start the race, Mike Hawthorn, head down, seeking a gear in his pole-position Ferrari Dino 246, Luigi Musso attentive and ready to go on the centre, Harry Schell just lowering his goggles in '258' on the outside of the rank. Beyond are Tony Brooks in the Vanwall and five-times World Champion Fangio about to start his farewell race in the Piccolo Maserati. Hawthorn will dominate and win, Schell will lead very briefly, but his BRM will fail him... Poor Musso will crash fatally.

1958 French Grand Prix: Jean Behra had an extremely difficult, controversial and contentious weekend in his home Grand Prix, demanding Schell's '257' for the race when it seemed faster to him than his own assigned '256'. This lovely study shows off the spaceframe Type 25 car's handsomely-balanced form at the Thillois corner. Note the massive oil cooler visible through those cut-outs – standard relief slots in the tail.

Harry Schell, leaving Thillois in '257', ended the Reims weekend incensed with Behra's prima donna behaviour and told Alfred Owen as much in the delightful letter reproduced here.

Maurice Trintignant accelerating the new '258' towards the timing line from Thillois; this dark lustrous green beauty has an internal carburettor air intake in place of the open-mouthed standard external scoop – producing the sleekest and most subtly beautiful Type 25 spec of all... Both the Behra and Trintignant original Type 25s arrived at Reims in this form, used by Behra at Spa. All three cars ran external intakes on raceday.

hands better than his own '256'. While '257' and '258' both had internal air intakes feeding their Weber carburettors, the 1958 prototype, '256', retained its external feed, drawing from the bonnet scoop. '258' was first entered for ORO's 'other Frenchman' – Maurice Trintignant. The three cars had downswept exhausts and repositioned and enlarged oil tanks with clever internal baffles.

Practice began in the cool of the Wednesday evening and, as Denis Jenkinson reported in *Motor Sport*:

> …Schell suddenly surprised everyone, not least himself, by putting in a lap at 2min 23.1sec, a new fastest time for the evening, and the only explanation B.R.M. could give was that they must have built a really good engine into that car…

On the Thursday evening Behra was running a works-entered sports Porsche RSK converted to centre-seat F2 form in practice for the supporting *Coupe de Vitesse*, clocking 2:37.4, handicapped by unsuitable gearing for acceleration away from the two slow corners while the enveloping-bodied car was fastest of all along the intervening straights. In the F1 session Hawthorn then stamped the Ferrari Dino 246's authority upon the scene, fastest in 2:21.7. Behra was unable to approach Schell's time in his BRM, while Trintignant ambled quietly round.

In the final sessions on Friday evening, Behra shattered his F2 rivals with a 2:24.0 lap in his re-geared Porsche while Trintignant suffered burns on the back of his neck when his Walker Cooper ignited. In the F1 session his BRM then died out on circuit, and Schell ferried the bandaged Mayor of Vergeze back to the pits. Behra remained slow and morose, disagreeably comparing his BRM's dismal performance with that of his pole-position F2 Porsche…

He now asserted his number one status, and since Schell's car – '257' – had seemed quicker on the straights Jean claimed it for the race. RM and PB initially backed Schell, then caved in to Behra's demands. Schell was outraged and the atmosphere within the team became appalling. Harry decided that as No. 2 he should have No. 3 driver Trintignant's car – the untried new '258' – while the placid and relaxed veteran said he was quite happy, confident the team would have built all the best parts into the No. 1's assigned car, so he was quite content to race Behra's discarded '256'!

On raceday, Hawthorn led throughout, while for three-quarter distance a great battle trailed him involving Vanwall, BRM and Maserati.

In his home event, Behra was at his best, duelling with Moss and Fangio and treating the crowd to a virtuoso display of real motor racing. He had run second just ahead of Moss before his car finally failed with engine trouble after completing 45 of the scheduled 50 laps. He was officially classified sixth, securing his first World Championship point for BRM. A gear in his engine's exhaust timing gear train had failed. The unit had been assembled with a 1957 head and '57-type gears to exploit better airflow and more power, although the crankcase was a '58-spec five-bearing unit. It had pulled 8,000rpm on the long straights and Behra expressed himself "very pleased with the performance…". He told RM and Spear he had now regained

his confidence and was looking forward to Silverstone; "Moss' Vanwall was faster on the straight but we were better on the corners and could brake 50 yards later…"

Schell had called at the pits after only five laps with an aluminium water pipe split. A temporary replacement was made and he limped around to complete the race. He stayed in the race because "…it was quite on the cards that Moss and Hawthorn could have blown up before the end of the race. The other two Vanwalls both failed, Tony Brooks' car before Trintignant's [BRM]. Both apparently had oil trouble. Moss came out of his car covered in oil below the waist and perspiration above…".

Trintignant's race ended after only 12 laps because "…the block securing the inlet valve camshaft was loose. The tab washers had sheared and the two steel bolts holding the end cap had broken. Eventually the camshaft broke and the engine just would not go…".

Harry Schell had arrived at Reims from Paris in a little four-wheeled Vespa minicar with his girlfriend Monique. After early morning practice he announced that it was his custom to go to the garage to check that his car was OK. This trip would be followed by a good lunch and bottle of Beaujolais. He would then retire with Monique to spend the afternoon in bed.

The first time Harry retired to rest he found his bedroom door locked from the outside and the room itself stripped absolutely bare. Carpets, bed, even the pictures from its walls had all been removed. This act was repeated with variations each day, the climax coming when he found his Vespa standing proudly in the middle of the room, several drivers – supervised by Fangio himself – having manhandled it up the stairs…

Harry then had the last laugh as he calmly found his keys, clambered into the little Vespa, started it up and drove it thump, bump, clump – back down the hotel stairway (Tony saw it being manhandled round the corner halfway down) and out through the foyer onto the street.

Despite such fun and games, the Franco-American was bitterly upset by Behra taking over his car after practice. Schell was lying fourth in the World Championship table at the time, and on the Monday after the race he one-finger typed the following intense letter to unburden himself to Alfred Owen.

He addressed it to "Mr Owen, Darlaston South Wal, England", which as Spear subsequently observed, meant "you must be well known to the Post office!"

Schell's one finger-typed English – exactly as follows – bristled with schoolboy dismay:

> Iam only sorry I din't win a race yet for you; it might be possible soion if luck comes on our side as the cars are getting very good; better every time.
>
> I hope thisletter will not ennoy you but I must let you know certain facts that might be the cause of our bad show in reims.
>
> As you know for the past three races Ihave allways been doing the best time in traing; due to better cars or better driving Ii don't know but the facts are there so at Reims the first day of training I made the best time fo the day on my own car 2.23 1/6 Behra 227. Ii tried Behra 's car and made 2.24 6/10 the next day I made an agreement with Mr Mays not to run my car as Ii was on

first line and like this we were savingthe car for the day of the race. On Friday the last day of training I did a few laps with my own car in 2.24 6/10 going very carefully; Behra was doing 2.27 2/10 with his own car and with the new engine which came at nite with Mr Berton XXXX I was asked by Mr Berha to try his own car I accepted this offer and put a time of 2.24 2/10 whih is three seconds dffaster than him. Mr Trintignant put a very good time of 223 6/10 which was the fourth time of the day; I still was on firts line and it was not necessary for me to do a better time Which Iwanted to do For my own satisfaction ; Iasked Mr Berthon the permission to run the car two laps which was refused by Mr Berton this was wise and we were saving the car for the race Iagree 100 % with Mr Berton.

Then five minutes before end of practice Mr Behra asked for my car; Mr Berthon ansered no so Mr Berha said in these conditions he was not started in the race and that he could not drive any more such a bad car anymore etc. etc.

The next day from IO am in the morning till 4 pm Mr Behra stayed at the garage tryingto persuade Mr Berton to give him my car by saying he wanted to cancel his contract and anyway he was not goingto start in the race at all.

I was then called in the garage by Mr Spear and Mr Berthon told me 'Harry . you must take another car as Berha refused to start in the race if he has not your car He has Threatened us to cancel his contract you understand the situation so Which car do you prefer of the remaining two cars '.

For the interest of the team Iaccepted this decision ; I Wanted to call you but Mr Spear told me Ionly couldget you at two in the XXX morning so I did not want to distub you.

Everybodyd was furious of theattitude taken by Mr Berha. I hope that all thefacts will be told to you exactly theway they happened Everybody has worked very hard to get the cars ready for This race. my c car was in perfect condition and prepared with care by the Mechanics,and at the last minute my car is taken away for no valuable reason; I am sure I could have won the race for you or at least be second anyway.

I want you for the future to let me know what is your decision about the choice of cars. I do not want to chose my car; I want to be given a car and keep this car for the training and for the r race; I never asked for any car from Mr Berton or Mr Mays and I allways did what Iwas told but I think for the intrest of the team thebest car goes to the faster driver; anyway for the future I hope things will be settle and that for the British Grand Prix We will see a BRM first.

I am very sorry to bother you with all these litle things but feel you should know about it…

Yours sincerely

[signed] Harry O'R Schell

P.S. Could you let me Know your decisions about this letter. I'll staying in Beaulieu s/Mer *Hotel Metropole* –

PB admitted to Owen:

Behra was disappointing in [the] result; but the initial efforts of Schell and the prolonged duel between Behra, Moss and Fangio created tremendous enthusiasm for the car and showed that our performance was up to the Vanwall on this the fastest in maximum speed of all road circuits…

Behra broke down plainly through over-revving. This I think he did, possibly justifiably, to confirm his view that the Schell practice car was faster…The Schell car failed primarily through a broken clutch and, secondly, through a broken water pipe. The water pipe would undoubtedly be due to extreme vibration set up through the broken clutch, which was fortunate, as had he continued the clutch would have disintegrated and caused him physical damage. The Trintignant car failed through a broken camshaft gear and camshaft, which was due to studs pulled out of the cylinder head holding the camshaft bearing adjacent to the timing gear (these studs have loosened before) and modifications are in hand…All three clutches were in varying states of collapse, which accents the fact that the present Lockheed clutch is entirely unsuitable for the job.

One engine had been rebuilt overnight for Reims and the second was brought out a day later – both with minor alterations as a result of Weslake's airflow testing.

After Reims all available cylinder heads were airflow-tested and Weslake brought them all up as close as possible to a common standard. PB pinpointed the differences between a 'good' and 'bad' head as follows:

a) Inlet port fettling was not being maintained to an accurate standard, and in some cases the bottom turn of the port had been spoilt by removing too much metal. Inlet port diameters tended to be over-large and too much metal generally was being removed.

b) Valve seat form and radius blending port to seat proper had not been properly finished after valve seats had been positioned by grinding, causing eddying at the seat.

c) In an attempt to promote longer valve seat life, seats had been left 'full' on new engines, which in effect brings the valves closer together and destroys the flow during the overlap period, and also the normal flow through the inlet port across the face of the exhaust valve.

Methods were investigated to replace metal in existing ports. Details and material for a low temperature soldering technique were speedily acquired by Peter Spear, but due to the shape of the port no satisfactory means was found to achieve this. Nevertheless, all heads were brought up to the best airflow standard possible…

Harry Weslake advised that filling should be improved by raising port velocity to a maximum compatible with no reduction in optimum airflow. Ports were then machined and sleeved to test varying diameters and blending shapes. All usable P25 heads would eventually be modified, "...to increase mid-range performance considerably, so that all current engines have outputs on the 4,000 to 6,000r.p.m. range comparable with the best 1957 alcohol engines".

Turbulence was also investigated:

> While mid-range...and maximum outputs [have been] increased to a consistent value of 250/260b.h.p. we have not managed to lift the B.M.E.P. figures above the original peak B.M.E.P. at 6,200 revs. crank – so that while considerably higher engine r.p.m. are available, the power tends to go down after 7,000r.p.m. crank. As the air flow figures are now considerably in excess of the Vanwall engine [so much for confidentiality, one presumes – DCN] it can only mean that the combustion characteristics at high r.p.m. are unsatisfactory, and we are not getting the full work back from the charge. This is borne out by the fact that current engines need more ignition advance than they should, which means that flame propagation and hence the pressure rise rate are too slow.

Weslake had warned that very high turbulence was necessary for efficient combustion on petrol at high rpm so efforts began to promote it. Weslake measured turbulence within the cylinder on a good head and found it already "of a high order due to the port angularity in two planes". The only avenue for improvement was to increase this angularity, so further sleeves were made and inserted in every head, providing optimum angularity in both planes plus maximum usable gas velocities. Back on the Folkingham dyno, mid-range torque was again improved and peak power spread over a wider rev band.

Piston shape was also examined, and the high-domed crowns used to ensure the highest usable compression ratio was suspected of damping incoming-charge turbulence upon compression. To minimize this damping effect meant lowering the dome. Naturally this reduced compression ratio – from around 10.9:1 to 9.9:1 but:

> Results showed that in spite of a lower compression a slight improvement in b.h.p. [was achieved] over the whole range on one engine tested. As this is the lowest compression consistent with obtaining the sort of power we want, it is not feasible to modify piston crown shapes further...

The final approach available was to introduce 'squish', by adopting a squish deck on top of the piston at right-angles to the valve cut-outs. High Duty Alloys modified the head pattern equipment to provide more meat in the cast blanks:

> ...so that the hemisphere can be counter-bored to permit a suitable 'squish'deck. At the same time the inlet port core is being altered to line up with the Weslake findings...It should be noted that, while the above modifications have improved 'bad' engines, additional turbulence is found to have no beneficial effect on 'good'

engines, which seems to indicate that previous 'good' engines have inherently higher turbulence than the present series engines. Weslake is at present investigating old cylinder heads to confirm whether this is so...

On August 21, 1958, PB concluded:

> Broadly speaking, all that can be done to improve existing engines has now been accomplished. Further improvements...can only come with modified heads and pistons to promote the 'squish' referred to above...

– however, he also admitted to the crucial factor which continued to separate BRM from Formula 1 victory during 1958:

> It is evident from differences in oil temperatures under road conditions that the frictional losses in the 1958 5-bearing engine are higher than those of the 4-bearing 1957 engine. This is straight test bed work, which is the first thing to be tackled at the end of the season...

Meanwhile, for the British Grand Prix at Silverstone, ORO was anxious to repeat its 1957 International Trophy success and to avoid any repetition of the disasters of '56. However, a rash decision had also been taken to return to Normandy the following day, for the Caen GP.

Grand Prix entries were made for Behra and Schell, with a third car for the bespectacled young Kansan Masten Gregory, who was regarded very much as the discovery of that season. He had impressed in *Centro-Sud*'s old Maserati 250F at the Silverstone May meeting and had been shining brightly in the Ecurie Ecosse Lister-Jaguar – but why Gregory and not Ron Flockhart?

The Scot had returned to the scene of his previous year's French GP capsize at Rouen-les-Essarts, and had again ended-up in hospital. He had been driving a John Coombs-entered Lotus 15 during practice for the *Coupe Delamare Deboutteville* meeting on June 7...

Peter Ashdown had spun his 1,100cc Lola in the slippery downhill swerves after the Rouen pits, his car overturned and his collar bone was broken. An ambulance drove to the scene on the narrow grass verge, but against circuit direction, Ashdown being loaded aboard accompanied by a friend, Arthur Cork. To their horror, the ambulance driver then headed uphill towards the pits, still on the verge but still against the direction of oncoming cars, and without any warning flag signals visible from the marshals ahead. Flockhart then arrived, drifting the Lotus 15 at very high speed, closely followed by George Burgraff's Porsche, which he had just overtaken. Confronted head-on by the ambulance – which he read as being on the road, not the verge – he lost control and broadsided clean into it, his wrecked car immediately catching fire. Ron probably owed his life to Arthur Cork, who leapt from the offending ambulance to pull him from the wreck and smother the flames on his burning overalls. Ron suffered concussion, several broken ribs, ligament damage which would take ages to heal, deep shock and some painful burns. He was to be sidelined for months... Hence the BRM vacancy prompting RM's invitation to Masten Gregory.

For Silverstone, the Type 25s' oil tanks were sited within the cockpit to the left of the seat, and the large oil coolers with their cool-air ducting were moved to the left of the engine behind the radiator.

July 18, 1958 – RAC British Grand Prix, Silverstone – 75 laps, 219.52 miles

BRM's hopes suffered an immediate blow in practice the preceding Thursday morning, even before the F1 sessions began. Masten Gregory was pressing hard for sports car pole position in the *Ecurie Ecosse* Lister-Jaguar when it embedded itself deep in the Beckett's bank – the American baling out the instant the car impacted, and being picked-up with broken ribs, a chipped shoulder blade and a cut scalp. He would not race a BRM until 1964...and then it would be an ex-works red-painted *Centro Sud* car.

Meanwhile, Behra returned to '257' and Schell '258' and in Friday practice Harry shone as at Reims – Denis Jenkinson observing how he "...recorded 1min 39.8sec with the B.R.M. using all the road and quite a lot of the grass, but having a real go nevertheless...".

This intense effort rewarded Schell and the team with second place on the starting grid, 0.4sec slower than Moss' Vanwall pole. Behra's best, in contrast, was only 1:41.4 – 2 seconds off Moss' pace and eighth fastest, on the inside of row three.

The GP began with Collins storming through from row two to lead for Ferrari, both he and Moss in second place opposite-locking their spectacular way around the aerodrome circuit in full-blooded power slides. Hawthorn was third in his Ferrari, pursued by Schell, well-placed in fourth. But as he scanned his gauges he noticed the BRM's water temperature was rising and the oil pressure sagging. He drifted back, behind Lewis-Evans' Vanwall, and the gauges stabilized, but meanwhile Behra had lost interest since his engine just wouldn't go!

He had never been in the hunt, and then he struck a hare galloping across the track. A few laps later, his BRM began to handle peculiarly, convincing the French driver that its suspension or chassis was somehow failing. After bringing it into the pits, he refused point blank to go out again, exclaiming: "There is no point – the car is outclassed." He was morose and miserable and not at all constructive, bothered more by the effect of another lack-lustre performance upon his public image...

Spear reported:

> It was not at all obvious that anything was wrong with the tyres as far as the pit examination was concerned and it was reasonable that the car was brought into the paddock [after which] one cannot put it back into the race. In any case he was complaining of his engine power. Undoubtedly his engine was low in power. This engine had been used in the car at practice on Thursday and was pulling reasonably well. There was some trouble with water flow, however, and it was necessary to send it back to Bourne to have the Wills ring replaced. This entails a fair amount of stripping of the engine, including

unscrewing the liners. It is quite obvious that in putting the engine back together there was insufficient time to re-bed in the valves. An attempt had been made to do this (by driving the car) on Saturday morning outside Brackley, but even then there was a fair amount of traffic on the road and there was insufficient time available to do the job properly. I am quite confident this is the reason why Behra had insufficient power and this has been confirmed to me from private sources...

Schell had slowed:

> ...because his thermometer showed the water to be overheating. This accounts for his losing several places after about 4 or 5 laps. He drove well and conscientiously to finish fifth. At one time he had a chance of finishing fourth but again he did not want to risk breaking his engine. It was better to finish fifth than to retire fourth... It was found that there was a considerable amount of oil at the back of the car and on the brakes. This was due to a poor pipe connection from the gearbox...there is a pipe around which goes a rubber hose, which is held in place by a clip. The metal tube was not far enough into the rubber pipe and had worked loose. This is bluntly bad fitting but, in the circumstances of the fantastic number of hours the mechanics have been working, is excusable as far as they are concerned and Harry Schell agreed this...

Immediately after the race the cars were returned to their Brackley garage where Schell's and the unused Gregory car were checked and gear ratios changed before being transported to Blackbushe Airport near Camberley on the Surrey/Hampshire border, from where a Bristol Freighter flew them to Deauville, meeting transport to carry them to Caen's *Le Prairie* circuit.

July 20, 1958 – Caen Grand Prix, *Le Prairie* – 86 laps, 188.11 miles

Behra was to drive '256' with '57-spec four-main-bearing engine and Schell '258' – the former seeming more ready to race before his home crowd than he had been at Silverstone, while in contrast Schell seemed dead on his feet, complaining he was tired out.

The organizers held a special Sunday morning practice session for British entries fresh from Silverstone, Stirling Moss promptly putting his Walker Cooper on pole position – fully 3 seconds faster than Behra's best. Schell qualified eighth amongst the F2 runners in the combined field.

The race began just before 4pm, Behra stealing an immediate lead from Moss with Schell hurtling through the pack into third place.

Passing the pits at the end of lap two, Keith Ballisat's F2 Cooper shed its right-front wheel, which struck and severely injured an unfortunate marshal before bouncing on into the BRM pit, bounding over the counter. It knocked off one of Mme

Behra's shoes, then hit the timing board, which whacked one of the mechanics on the head and virtually parted Tony Rudd's hair.

After four laps, Moss cut past Behra for the lead, only for the Frenchman to regain the place four laps later. He was repassed just as Schell headed for the pits. Moss then pulled away in an ever-growing lead from Behra until the second BRM's engine failed before half-distance. He was credited with fastest race lap at 1min 20.8sec.

The ORO team returned home, as Tony Rudd recalls, absolutely whacked physically, and very demoralized... Spear compiled a proxy report from Tony's information:

> Behra was driving a car with a 4-bearing engine and led for the first 4 laps. Moss was slipstreaming him and eventually he let Moss overtake him and slipstreamed him in turn. He retook the lead and was confident that he could have won the race if his car had held together [but] the timing gear failed...Harry Schell was not driving well because he was tired. I think this is reasonable; he normally has about 10 hours sleep and could only have had five at the most after an extremely fatiguing race at Silverstone. His car packed up after 16 laps. There was a little rear brake trouble in that taper wear was occurring slightly and the pads were rubbing... The serious thing was that the filter on the scavenge pump of the gearbox had collapsed and the gearbox was full of oil and overflowing. This meant that there was excessive churning of oil and he was losing power. It was wiser, in the circumstances, for him to retire...

Behra and Schell were at least on speaking terms again – not friendly but speaking, which was considered:

> ...a good sign since they have literally refused to even say 'good morning' to each other before. Also Behra gave £50 to be shared among the mechanics...to make it quite clear that although he had experienced trouble with his cars...he did not blame the mechanics in any way. This again is a good point...

– and one which Alfred Owen would have appreciated thoroughly.

However, concern was expressed at the French press' scathing comments on this poor BRM performance, expressing the view that Behra and Schell had been short-changed by the team since one car had come straight from Silverstone and the other was untried: "They felt that B.R.M. had not kept their commitments to the organisers of the car race meeting."

Back home Harry Weslake had made his recommendations to improve the engines by raising gas velocities with sleeves inserted into the cylinder-head ports. Tony: They made a small improvement, but not what we were really looking for. The worst engine was improved from around 225bhp to 235. Two weeks later BRM paid its first visit to the German GP at the formidable 14.2-mile Nurburgring, and I set off with a great boxful of assorted sleeves, but this as it transpired was not to be our problem...

August 3, 1958 – German Grand Prix, Nurburgring – 15 laps, 212.48 miles

The previous year – fresh from its maiden *Grande Epreuve* victory in the British GP at Aintree – the Vanwall team had made this journey for its own Nurburgring debut, and their cars had immediately been all at sea around the mountain circuit, woefully off the pace, unmanageable and uncompetitive.

ORO's men were quite aware of Vanwall's debacle, but it seems unclear whether RM or PB had ever thought about it. PB's mind was full of porting, sleeves and turbulence, that in the cylinder and also that from his development engineer who was vehemently arguing there was no such thing (!) and all the power loss was due to a major blunder in the design of the five-bearing crank, which he now said was costing over 30hp. However, Tony remembered. Mindful of Vanwall's problems the previous year, also Chapman-inspired, ORO had arrived armed with stiffer springs, dampers and a multiplicity of bump rubbers. All to no or little avail, the problem would prove to be the same as the Vanwall's – lack of wheel travel and lack of experience of the Nurburgring.

Denis Jenkinson wrote: "B.R.M...would have liked to have made some unofficial practice earlier but their drivers were not available, so they had to 'find out' just as Vanwalls had last year." When official practice began Jenks observed: "B.R.M. were in a sorry state, the cars being off the ground more than they were on it." Behra eventually crashed Schell's assigned car '258' through the hedge flanking the road near the *Karussel*. When the mechanics took one of the Lodestars round to retrieve it they drove straight by without noticing the car, for the hedgerow had sprung back upright after the car had ploughed through, and it was completely hidden from view.

Behra took over the spare '256' for final Saturday practice and he and Schell – in what had been Behra's intended '257' – ended up 8-9 on the inside of row three – Harry ahead with a best time of 9:39.6 against Hawthorn's Ferrari pole of 9:14.0, Behra on 9:46.8...

Peter Spear wrote the following detailed, and in parts haunting, report on this tragic race, which saw Peter Collins' fatal accident while challenging Tony Brooks' leading Vanwall in his Ferrari:

> In the first practice it was obvious that spring rates and damping were too low and they ran into vibration trouble. The gear ratios were satisfactory. Harry Schell was happy with his engine and his car. Behra tried all three cars; he was in Schell's car when it started to rain and, as you know, he came off the track, went through a hedge, jumped the ditch and the car was impaled on a stake forming part of the wire fence around a wood. The stake went through the undertray and a cross-member of the car rested on the top of it. I understand they had quite a time getting the car off and it was useless to try and put it back into race trim.
>
> The dampers were reset for the second practice and if anything it was reported the conditions were worse. The springs were jacked closer to try and improve matters. They gradually got practice times down from 9 minutes

August 1, 1958 – German Grand Prix practice, Nurburgring: Intra-team relations were further strained when Jean Behra bent Harry Schell's assigned new race car '258' in this Friday session, adding insult to injury by having punched his way through the roadside hedge which sprang back up to hide the bent car – actually impaled upon a stake – from the mechanics' view when they drove round to retrieve it. Here Pat Carvath has discovered the bent new BRM. Today it is the only surviving BRM-built Type 25...

50 seconds to 9 minutes 40 seconds.

Behra went out after the official practice at 7 o'clock in the evening with a revised suspension and said that if anything matters were worse. They worked all though Saturday night and the cars were tried again on Sunday morning when it was reported they were a little better. Both Schell and Behra's cars were given the same settings. At this stage Harry Schell felt that he could outbrake and out-accelerate Vanwalls but that he could not corner as well and was having more difficulty in driving due to suspension.

Race

It was a 4 3 4 grid start and Schell and Behra were in eighth and ninth positions, side by side on the third row. Harry Schell did a very good start, in close liaison with six mechanics who kept the marshals back to clear his pre-determined track. In fact it seems he jumped the start by an incredible amount, after which Moss led for half of the first lap and Harry Schell was in front of Brooks.

The race then settled down after a few laps with Moss in the lead followed 10 seconds later by Hawthorn and Collins who were racing together, changing positions, 10 seconds later was Brooks followed by Behra then Allison and Schell, who were fighting for position. Some considerable way behind followed a 'gaggle' of cars. We were then well placed.

In the fifth lap Moss blew up and Behra came in slowly five minutes after the main lot of drivers. He claimed that the car would not hold the road. They worked on the car for a quarter of an hour without success and Behra would not go on.

Harry Schell was lapping fairly consistently at about 9 minutes 35 seconds. Tony Brooks was leading at 9 minutes 20 seconds. In other words Schell was doing

quite reasonably. Then his times became 9.45 and 9.55. At about two-thirds of the race distance he came in claiming he had no brakes. On checking it was found that the left-hand front brake caliper was not operating properly. With the pedal full down there was an eighth to three-sixteenths inch gap between the disc and the pads. That is, it was fairly obvious that the automatic adjuster mechanism had failed and this was verified after the race. He was asked to go on driving and pumping the pedal but was not keen to go on because he would have been so far behind. He was behind Salvadori before he came in.

Shortly after this Collins crashed and Mike Hawthorn came round past the Pits driving on the inside of the road not attempting to race. His face was white as parchment. He stopped where Collins had crashed and got out and wanted to go in the helicopter with Collins but eventually went in the ambulance.

This left Tony Brooks in the lead. He was driving remarkably well and was outclassing the rest of the field.

Allison's radiator broke as his Lotus was bottoming at the front...This left Salvadori second but a lap (approximately 10 minutes) behind Tony Brooks. Thus if Behra had kept in the race and not refused to drive, he would have by then been second.

Schell would probably have been third or fourth if he had kept on going. Von Tripps [*sic*], who finished fourth, was without brakes for half the race.

Behra had engine [*sic* – 'car' in fact] '256', his old original, which he thought was the best. Harry Schell had '257' which is his old original, which he likes.

The needle fell off Harry Schell's thermometer but after the trouble in the last race, he knew enough to take no notice of it.

General

Behra won the Sports Car Race[85] and this pleased him. Harry Schell and Behra were talking together about technical matters but are still not friendly.

Harry Schell and Peter Collins came up together with their wives from Monte Carlo in a hired car. It was Harry Schell who took Louise [Collins] to hospital.

I understand that Behra has rather upset the mechanics because of his complaints about the car. I understand also that there was a long argument between Behra, Peter Berthon and Mays after the race but I know no details...

It was known that Nurburgring is very hard on suspension. My understanding was that we were going to take out a range of different dampers and springs but apparently an inadequate amount was taken. I cannot understand why but will try and find out..."

85. This was a 6-lap event for 1,300 and 1,600cc sports and GT cars – disputed overall between three works Borgward 1500RSs driven by Hans Herrmann, Jo Bonnier and Fritz Juttner, and two works Porsche RSKs of Behra and Edgar Barth. Behra started from pole, led throughout and set fastest lap at a record 9:48.9. At least he was happy when he *started* the Grand Prix.

'Jenks' provided a pearl of wisdom for BRM's number one in *Motor Sport*:

> Afterwards Behra ruefully regretted having given up due to temperament; had he kept going he would have been third for sure and possibly second. A race is never lost until the flag falls.

This Nurburgring failure prompted a gush of self-justification from RM:

> Schell informed us that the engine felt considerably more powerful than when he last drove it…However the power available was not able to be used at the Nurburgring…we made desperate efforts to alter shock absorbers, and although a slight improvement was made, the cars could not be driven to anything like their capacity.
>
> In the early stages of the race Behra and Schell settled down in 5th and 6th positions after a magnificent start by Schell, who held second place to Moss for the first seven or eight miles… Behra then settled down into 5th position, but shortly after that he came into the pits saying there was something wrong with the suspension. We had a hurried examination…but could find nothing wrong other than we knew about the suspension on this circuit… My own opinion is that Behra, in his present state of nervous irritability, coupled with the fact that the car was difficult to hold, preferred not to go on. This of course was most unfortunate because had the car continued at a similar speed or slightly slower than that at which Behra was driving, it could have finished second. Schell manfully carried on, but in the 8th lap he came into the pits with no front brakes…caused by a breakage in the adjusting mechanism…
>
> To emphasize my statement about the difficulties of a first appearance at the Nurburgring on any car, I must quote Vanwall last year, when they were just as bad, if not worse…

He cited the 1957 Vanwall on alcohol fuel, with 290bhp, with Moss driving, lapping at 9min 37sec; the 1958 Vanwall on AvGas with 30bhp less, but modified, and with Moss again driving, had just lapped in 9min 9sec. Behra and Schell's best were 9min 35sec.

Detailed examination of the Nurburgring cars back home at Folkingham, not unexpectedly in view of the amount of bottoming to which they had been subjected, revealed some minor frame cracks so they were stiffened up, notably in the front suspension cross bracing and the lower rear radius-arm anchorages, which projected on outriggers from the main frame.

A continuous procession of P25 cylinder heads was trailing to and fro between Weslake at Rye and Bourne when Harry Weslake suggested the cooling system should be investigated to explain why the engines lost power when thoroughly hot. This turned the spotlight on the fatal flaw of the screwed-in liner: it placed a great mass of uncooled metal around the upper circumference of the combustion chamber just where it was not wanted for optimum thermodynamic performance.

A colossal programme began to drill small holes around the thick band of metal where the cylinder liners screwed into the head, known as a poorly cooled area. Although the most visible sign of all this activity was increased water temperature, as more heat was being extracted from the engine, any power gain seemed doubtful, but all-round development pushed the best rebuilt engine up to 250bhp. Surely fortunes could now improve?

LATE 1958 – BRM MERELY THE BRIDESMAID

While Stirling Moss, Tony Brooks and Mike Hawthorn were all winning Grand Prix races, they were driving Vanwall, Ferrari – yes, and even *Cooper*! – cars, and instead of playing the starring part which Raymond Mays, and possibly the more realistic Peter Berthon too, had originally envisaged, BRM's was merely a supporting role. In fact, through the latter part of 1958 it was clear that BRM would not be that year's bride – indeed, the team' was struggling to qualify merely as a deserving bridesmaid…ready to catch the bouquet.

Two cars were prepared for the next Championship round to be run at Oporto in Portugal – chassis '256' fitted with engine '2582' being signed-off the Folkingham dyno on August 13 with 262bhp, for Behra, and '257' with engine '2584', giving 252bhp on August 12, for Schell. Brand-new engine '2586' "modified to latest technique" made the Portuguese trip as spare. Engine '2587' – the last complete unit of the 1958 programme – was due for build on August 31. Vaughan of AP Lockheed had fitted a completely overhauled brake system to Behra's '256'.

The cars were assembled with the intermediate cooling system tried at Reims, with suitably insulated oil tank beneath the exhaust manifold and a cylindrical oil cooler with horizontal air tubes running through it mounted on the right of the engine bay, beneath the Weber carburettors.

Meanwhile, car '258' was prepared and equipped with engine '2585', engine '2583' was earmarked for installation into Behra's car '256' ex-Oporto, ready for the Italian GP at Monza, while *The Vanguard* – old '255' – was prepared with four-bearing engine '2572' for despatch to Monza as team spare. The Oporto cars and equipment would be transported direct to Monza after the race, where they would meet the contingent travelling direct to Italy. Post-Portuguese GP strip-down, detailed examination, rebuild and race preparation of all cars would then be finalized at the Autodrome.

August 24, 1958 – Portuguese Grand Prix, Oporto – 50 laps, 230.14 miles

Six previous Portuguese GPs had been held since 1950, alternating between Lisbon's Monsanto Park and this public road course in the northern city of Oporto. Each one had catered for sports cars, but for 1958 the FIA accorded the event Formula 1 World Championship status. The Port-wine

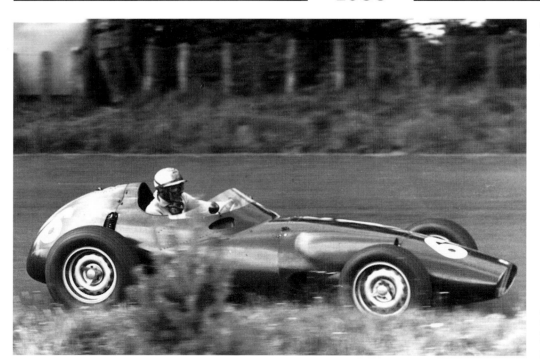

August 3, 1958 – German Grand Prix, Nurburgring: Harry Schell takes a tight line in '257' before brake trouble brought his retirement from this tragic race in which former BRM driver Peter Collins crashed in his Ferrari and lost his life.

August 24, 1958 – Portuguese Grand Prix, Oporto: Over the cobbles and tramlines Behra in '256' leads Brabham's 2.2 Cooper with Vanwall, Ferrari and Walker Cooper in pursuit beyond.

city's street circuit was one of the last of its heroic kind – its natural hazards including high kerbs, tramlines, trees, drain covers, power and telegraph poles, lamp-posts and even a section surfaced with cobblestones... It was fast, and long, and most demanding.

Drivers explored the course in hire cars from the moment they first arrived, practice beginning in hot weather on the Friday afternoon. Sports cars had lapped inside 3 minutes, and the F1 yardstick was established as Moss clocked 2:48, Hawthorn 2:49 and Harry Schell a rousing 2:46 for BRM. Cliff Allison broadsided his 'Vanwall'-shaped Lotus 16 on loose gravel in the *Avenida da Boavista* and the car's nose clipped a straw bale; the Lotus then spun and disintegrated against the kerbs and walls. The young Yorkshireman – who had attracted both RM's and Tony Rudd's attention as a potential BRM recruit – escaped unhurt, and 'Mimo' Dei of *Centro-Sud* would provide him with a Maserati 250F drive on race day.

Schell drove so hard that 'Jenks' described how he "...looked to be completely out of control", but late in the session Behra did a 2:36.17, FTD at that point, goading Moss into clocking 2:35.24.

On Saturday afternoon the final grid line-up was decided, with Moss' Vanwall on pole at 2:34.21, flanked by Hawthorn's Ferrari and Lewis-Evans' Vanwall, and with Behra behind him, fourth-fastest at 2:34.99. Schell started seventh on 2:37.05.[86]

Spear's eye-witness team report throws revealing light upon Formula 1 attitudes and practices of the period, telling the Boss:

86. Interestingly, while Behra's best practice time had been 2:34.99, his best race lap – fifth fastest overall – was completed in 2:33.52 (on lap 39), and Schell's grid time of 2:37.05 also improved to 2:34.48 (on lap 33)...

Doing [*sic*] practice, both Behra and Schell drove well, gradually increasing [also *sic*] their times. On the first day, Behra's best lap time was only just beaten by Moss, and Schell had about sixth best time. On the second day, the Vanwalls were practising with only enough fuel in the tanks to do three or four laps. As usual, we practised with the same amount of fuel in the tanks as might be expected half-way through the race. This is obviously the most sensible condition at which to practice. We finished up with Behra having fourth best time and Schell sixth [*sic* wrong – DCN] best time.

General

...The mechanics worked well and I am certain that Ayliffe, who is now in charge since Newman has left [following an almighty row with PB at Caen, over in Gordon's view the wasteful and inhuman treatment of the mechanics] is working very well, he has a sound idea of man-management and organises the men well into little units to do different jobs. He discussed various problems with me, and it is quite obvious that his ideas for the future are quite sound. I have told both Berthon and Rudd that I think he should be given a reasonably free hand to organise things as he thinks fit and have a good sense of responsibility. This they are doing. For example, we only have proper checklists for car preparation prior to races. He wants to institute check lists for the various jobs that are done on cars between races at Folkingham. This is a good idea. He wants new little gadgets of tools, trolleys, etc. All these are ideas which added together would make a much better working unit. He himself is quite happy with the work. From an appearance viewpoint, the cars were better prepared for this race than any other race I have seen.

For the first time I have been attending race meetings, every mechanic had a proper brasade. There seemed to be much less fluffing around, and R.M.'s absence was, as far as I can see, a benefit rather than a loss.

Race

As you know, we finished with Behra fourth and Schell sixth. In point of fact, Behra drove very much better than would appear from this result. He was baulked a little at the beginning but soon made his way to third place behind Hawthorn and Moss...At the end of seven laps Behra was thirty seconds behind Hawthorn and never really made this time up. Hawthorn came in for a pit stop halfway through the race and lost about forty seconds. This made Behra second but eventually Hawthorn caught him up. This was because a few laps from the end Behra's engine gave trouble and he lost about fifteen seconds in two laps. The position righted itself but by then he had been passed by Hawthorn and Lewis-Evans, who was lapped by Moss. Having lapped him, Moss then towed Lewis-Evans round the circuit, using the 'slip-streaming' technique. It was brilliantly done by both Moss and Lewis-Evans.

Schell was in the first three for the first two laps or so, but then trailed back a little. Nevertheless, he drove a very good hard race all the time, and was pressing on to the best of his ability.

...an hour before the race it was raining lightly. The circuit was wet, and with the combination of tarmac, cobblestones and tram lines, it was very dangerous in parts. We let Behra drive the Hillman car round the circuit three times with Schell, Berthon and I. Behra and Schell discussed each corner, how it should be taken and the tactics to use during the race relative to the conditions. Behra considered that it was likely that there would be an accident among the leaders. He therefore kept behind the leaders to be safe and to be able to take advantage of any accident that occurred. In fact the circuit dried as the race started. It was much faster than had appeared on our inspection. There was no accident to the leaders, and Behra never made up the early time lost. In addition, because it looked as though it was going to rain again, we used 280 plugs instead of 300 plugs. Towards the end of the race, one of these plugs, in Behra's engine, had the gas seal loosened, he was losing power from that cylinder, not burning all the fuel, and the carburettor was tending to flood. After two laps or so, carbon deposits or something made a temporary seal automatically and at the end of the race the engine was going better.

Certainly Behra tried harder than he has done in several races.

Both Behra and Schell were quite happy with the cars, were pleased with the power of the engine, road holding and the brakes. The brakes did wear during the race but no more than one would have wished them to.

After Race Examination

After the race it was found that Schell's engine was losing oil pressure and was down to about 35 lbs. per square inch. We believe that there was a little trouble with the big end bearing and this is being examined. On Behra's car, the rear cam bracket stud broke, but it was doubtful if it caused any trouble. There was also a slight crack in the steering box mounting bracket but again this was not serious.

Spear's account has some vital omissions. On the starting grid the race officials went round checking, by means of unfastening and refastening, that bonnets were secure. They made, as would be expected, a hash of this and several cars, Harry's included, had to come in to have them properly refastened, which cost him about 20 seconds.

Moss had won for Vanwall, but Hawthorn of Ferrari finished second and took a vital extra point by setting fastest race lap. At season's end that solitary point would prove decisive in making Hawthorn – rather than Fangio's natural heir, Moss – first British winner of the Drivers' World Championship.

From the drivers' comments it was clear that the rear dampers' performance had deteriorated as the race progressed. Tony, following the Nurburgring debacle, had found means of increasing rear wheel travel by 20 per cent. This meant that the dampers had to work that much harder. Colin Chapman had warned that, as he had made them the same length as the air struts which they replaced to simplify the conversion, they were on the limit for capacity, and should be watched. Increased wheel travel had pushed them over that limit. Tony and Willie Southcott, who flew back to England to prepare the Monza engine, took the dampers with them for investigation and possible modification. The Armstrong service representative, who was very much on the ball, had already telephoned his recommendations to the factory at York, and they were on

September 7, 1958 – Italian Grand Prix, Monza: Despite having gone to the start in an extremely agitated and distraught state after the loss of his beloved pet poodle, Jean Behra showed tremendous commitment and motivation for 28 laps and ran second in '256' before its clutch failed. Here he holds the position from Stuart Lewis-Evans' third-placed Vanwall entering the Curva Parabolica, the 180-degree turn leading back onto the pit straight.

the job immediately.

The ORO transporters, crewed by six mechanics, had meanwhile begun their planned drive eastward into Italy and to Monza to meet the two further cars plus two spare engines and extra mechanics travelling direct from Folkingham. The directors and drivers were to stay at the *Hotel Principe e Savoia*, the mechanics at the *Albergo Marchesi*, Villasanta.

Trintignant was unavailable to drive the intended third car entry – having accepted Rob Walker's offer of a Cooper instead – Jo Bonnier, the Swedish Maserati 250F privateer, being invited back to make his third BRM appearance. RM had approached Cliff Allison – Team Lotus' number one, and the slender 25-year-old Yorkshireman was keen, but nothing would come of the idea.

On the Tuesday following the Oporto race Peter Spear visited the convalescent Ron Flockhart in Edinburgh. After his Rouen sports car crash he had been discharged from hospital in France while still in great pain, and only when he returned home were quite severe back injuries properly diagnosed. He was taking action against the organizing *AC Normande,* whom he held responsible for his crash, but this would prove counter-productive as word went around Continental race organizers that the double Le Mans-winning driver was a contentious troublemaker…

After seeing Ron in Edinburgh, Spear reported he had enjoyed:

> …having tea with his father and step-mother. He is looking remarkably fit. He drove me around Edinburgh in his father's M.G. and his hands and feet were behaving perfectly…

A tentative date was made for him to test a BRM at Folkingham late the following month, with the possibility of an F1 comeback drive at Casablanca. The fear was that he would lack the stamina for a full-length Grand Prix…

In 'tween-race preparation at Monza, '256' 's brakes were found to have worn some 0.2-inch front and rear. Tony Rudd telephoned Fred Ellis of AP to assess the risks of attempting a second race "on the same linings" since the pads were half-worn. It was agreed to change the calipers, an overhauled spare set being mounted, and Behra was briefed and happy to bed them in gently during early practice. But the team expected their number one to be demoralized and not to try on this power circuit because of his engine's known clear deficit against the Vanwalls and the V6 Ferraris…

September 7, 1958 – Italian Grand Prix, Monza – 70 laps, 250.11 miles

Practice for the Italian classic was held on the Friday and Saturday afternoons. Behra was first away as the opening session began in hot sun, half an hour late, quickly getting his time down to 1 minute 46 seconds. New recruit Bonnier did some exploratory laps in his own Maserati 250F before taking out the spare lustrous green Type 25, while Masten Gregory was out in Temple Buell's new *Piccolo* Maserati in his first race since the Lister-Jaguar shunt at Silverstone's British GP meeting. Behra tried all three BRMs present as the session progressed, but could not approach some startling Vanwall laps clocked at around the 1:43 level.

Saturday afternoon then saw all four BRMs present in the pits, but try as they might neither Behra nor Schell could crack the 1:43 barrier, which had been penetrated by all three Vanwalls and all four Ferrari Dinos, Maranello spurred-on by the Moss-Hawthorn battle for the Championships. Moss finally took pole position for Vanwall at 1:40.5 while both Behra's and Schell's best was 1:43.2 each, making them eighth and ninth overall on row three of the grid, Bonnier right alongside on 1:44.7.

But BRM had a surprise in store for Vandervell's team, as RM told Owen:

In practice the cars ran well, and gave remarkably little trouble, and many improvements were made to the oil cooling, and it was most gratifying…on these fast courses, oil temperatures were reduced, and oil pressures increased. In the actual race Behra, who was in excellent form, was right up with the leaders from the very start, and he overtook all three Vanwalls, Brooks (the ultimate winner) first, then Lewis-Evans, and later on he overtook Moss right in front of the grandstands, and then they had a battle and overtook and re-overtook each other several times. Moss' Vanwall then retired with serious mechanical trouble, and Behra was then running about 10 seconds behind Hawthorn's Ferrari, which was in the lead. Behra then actually reduced the lead, and was about 5 seconds behind Hawthorn, and it was obvious that in a few laps Behra would overtake Hawthorn, and would lead the race. Then quite suddenly Behra comes into the pits with brake trouble…

The brakes were pumped up in the pits, and Behra went out again, and from quite a low position in the race worked his way through the field to fifth place again, and then he came in to the pits again through brake trouble. With this brake trouble he was having to use his gearbox to assist him in braking, and finally in addition to the brake trouble, on the inner front side wheel persisting [*sic*], clutch trouble, owing I imagine to having to use the gearbox and clutch for braking, developed.

The point is that both of the components in question are Automotive Products productions. Behra was driving well, he was delighted with the car, and from what I understand he thinks that the B.R.M. now is very near to being a real Grand Prix winner.

Schell had terribly bad luck. He made a good start, and at the end of the straight, approaching the fast curve, he was in third position, and as they rounded this curve Von Trips, the Number 2 Ferrari driver, rammed Schell, both cars seemed to lock together, and they somersaulted off the course. This was *in no way* Schell's fault, and it was an awful tragedy that one of the B.R.M.s was out though this unfortunate incident within a minute and a half of the start of the race. Schell's escape from serious injury was a miracle, and he speaks in the highest praise of the strength of the B.R.M., and of the special design of cross bracing above the cockpit, which he declares saved his life.

Bonnier ran well in practice and in the race, but very unfortunately the centre propeller shaft bearing gave trouble and heated up, and he was forced to retire.

Ray added:

If we run three cars at Casablanca I doubt if Flockhart, who has been absent so long, will be good enough to drive, and I personally should like to see Bonnier at the wheel. He is becoming really good, and after Monza I had a long talk with him, and his enthusiasm for the car was most gratifying. Bonnier stated to me that he considered that the B.R.M. now was the safest and best car that he has ever handled, and

extremely easy to drive…

Behra had in fact started this race distraught and distracted. His pet poodle – to which he was devoted – had been apparently stolen from his car. Unable to hunt for it he went to the grid deeply concerned, even more tense than usual. To the team's surprise he responded by "having a real go and fighting with the best of them amongst the leading bunch…".

After Harry Schell failed to complete the opening lap a runner had burst into the ORO pit to tell the crew that Schell's car had left the road entering "the first *Lesmo*", but the driver was OK. Tony: He appeared 15 minutes later with his overalls torn and the odd scratch and smear of blood, and informed us he had ridden up over the back of von Trips. Realizing he was in for a major crash he had grabbed the projecting ends of the cross-bracing tubes, and this prevented him being thrown out and saved him from serious injury. The car had ended up in a rose bush.

I found it very hard to credit there was a rose bush at *Lesmo*, and what we eventually found was in fact an enormous bramble bush with our car – badly battered – lying slap in the middle of it. Harry emerged with two broken ribs, very lucky to survive.

Tony had the post-race task of bearding AP about Behra's problems. He wrote to Fred Ellis:

When the car had covered about a third of the race and was holding a secure second place 7 seconds behind Hawthorn, who had to stop for tyres while we did not, Behra experienced a loss of brake efficiency, which a few laps later led to his coming into the pits, complaining that the pedal was going to the floor and he was unable to pump up the brakes. We checked that there was fluid in the system, all three calipers were operating and that there were no obvious leaks.

It was observed that there was rather more than usual clearance between the pads and the discs, so that the pedal was pressed violently to jump up the adjusting mechanism, which was successful in reducing the clearance and at the same time producing a normal solid pedal. The car was sent out again having dropped to sixth place, but soon climbing up to fifth place behind Tony Brooks in the Vanwall; but after 8 more laps was in again complaining of the same thing, together with slipping clutch. We jumped the adjusters up again, but could see nothing obviously wrong with the clutch other than a certain loss of free travel.

The car was sent out again to continue…but Behra was unable to use any power because if he did the clutch slipped; the car was therefore withdrawn.

After the race we changed the clutch and calipers and found a cracked plate in the clutch, but could see nothing wrong with the calipers. However, when attempting to bleed the system, with pedal removed and fully stroking the master cylinder, we found that we were unable to bleed the front system. The master cylinder assembly was changed and we then successfully bled the system.

I tried the car myself and found the brakes effective but was unable to pump up the pedal in the manner that Behra had described.

Upon the ORO convoy's return to Folkingham after this Oporto/Monza round trip, Tony's strip-down report found that 16 rockers had worn at Oporto during practice and the race, cured by oil feed holes and reduced oil temperature for Monza, where only three rockers wore unacceptably after 746 miles running compared with 16 worn over 622 miles in Portugal.

Behra's Oporto engine – '2582' – had broken both its inlet camshaft rear pedestal studs. No. 1 timing gear ball races were failing in his Monza engine, causing ±25 degrees timing variation. A KLG 280 spark plug body insulator had blown at Oporto and new gearbox '27/12' had seized 1st gear after one mile's running at Monza – the fourth such failure that season.

Considerable variation between gearboxes had been reported in lever movement necessary to make a gearchange. The drivers naturally preferred minimum movement, this variation leading to missed and slow changes.

Behra's Oporto gearbox showed heavy 3rd gear selector wear.

Schell's rear brake disc was badly cracked in Portugal, Behra's was crazed after Monza.

Eight hours work was wasted at Monza trying to fit a water rail to new engine '2586'. The rail had been tailored to '2583' which had water inlet centres 56-thou out of position, a hose-type rail eventually being required to compensate.

Car '258' had its prop-shaft centre bearing assembly come adrift during first practice at Monza – the bearing subsequently seized and overheated its rubber mounting within 17 race laps. This was the third time that the car had given such trouble. The corresponding bearing housing was also starting to move on Behra's '256' after 40 laps, the first time this one had given such trouble.

Schell's Oporto engine '2584' was found to have broken up badly from the pressure-plate windows, Behra's '2582' clutch at both Oporto and Monza broke up, "failure possibly accelerated by using engine as brake". Tony noted: "We always have clutch plate trouble at Monza (Brooks' 300-mile attempt 1956 – Flockhart/Bonnier 1957)".

BRM was still suffering chronic instrument problems – "two rev-counters U/S, seven thermometers and two oil pressure gauges had failed – Instrument panel on larger and better rubber mounting for these races."

There were the usual oil leaks from the fuel pump mounting, rev-counter drive, rear main bearing on engines '2582', '83 and '72; oil pump drive sleeve on '2572' and '2585', the last also leaking water from the head to block rear exhaust corner Gaco cord.

Radiators had leaked at both Oporto and Monza, from the centre of the header tank – "usual place". An additional oil cooler fitted for Monza reduced oil temperature 10°C, but the oil system then had 32 hose joints and each car so fitted blew off at least two scavenge hoses before the race, despite towing to start, warm oil, etc.

One inlet valve had a piece broken from its seat, one inlet valve spring broke after 80 miles, subsequent running producing another broken inlet valve seat.

There was much detail body trouble, loose rivets due to their not being deburred, cracks from sharp rough corners on side stressed holes. Tony recorded that Schell's bonnet had come adrift at Oporto – although as explained this was down to officialdom. The springs in the spring-loaded carburettor flow valves set down so that the spring housing operated the float after fuel level within the chamber had risen considerably. Weber supplied new 50gm spring valves for the race, which were better, but they too set down after 100 miles.

Car '256' 's rack mounting bracket had cracked at Oporto, was re-welded, but cracked again at Monza due to residual weld stress. This was the original 1958 spaceframe chassis whose cross-bracing tube had been welded in after the brackets, while subsequent frames had had the cross-tube welded in first, giving no trouble. Brackets were cut off chassis '256' and new ones were welded on to match the sister cars'.

Anti-roll bar brackets on '256' also broke up during practice, the welds were filed away to achieve clearance, while new box-section brackets were to be made.

Behra's Monza brake problem was due to failure of the front calipers to adjust for wear – and the team's inability to bleed air was eventually traced by them to a faulty front master cylinder. While no fault had been found by Lockheed's subsequent investigation, ORO's own search, perhaps triumphantly, located an incorrectly sited recuperator hole, missed by AP's engineers on their test rig.

It had conceivably cost BRM and Jean Behra a first *Grande Epreuve* victory at Monza… Tony: We prepared a special car for Jean to drive at Le Mans for a demonstration and attack on the lap record during a race weekend there. It had a four-bearing crank engine running on 17.5% nitro. The extra oil coolers and side fuel tanks were removed, it weighed 1,050lbs and had nearly 300bhp – but all to no avail as rain poured down the whole weekend.

Just one round of the 1958 World Championship remained to be run – the Moroccan GP at Casablanca. For the British motor racing fraternity it assumed crucial significance. The Drivers' World Championship could go only to one of two drivers, both English – Stirling Moss or Mike Hawthorn; the newly-instituted F1 Constructors' Cup would go to either Vanwall or Ferrari. BRM's bit-part role was being emphatically ground home – agonizingly so for its creators, RM, PB and Alfred Owen – but the Moroccan Club offered outstanding start money, so no fewer than four BRM entries were made, all for 1958-spec spaceframe cars, including the very latest chassis '259', brand-new for the recovered Ron Flockhart.

All four cars were equipped with huge spiral-tube oil coolers, known as 'boot scrapers', sited behind the radiators. Tony had at last got his message through concerning heat to oil and some of the '8' series engines had been rebuilt with four-bearing bottom ends, with enormous backlash in the timing gears. One of them went into Behra's car. There were also two additional 'eyebrow' air scoops formed into the top of the nose cowlings in anticipation of desert temperatures.

A C54 freighter 'plane was chartered from the French company TAI to fly BRM's entourage and equipment direct from Stansted to Casablanca. Representatives from the shippers visited Folkingham to explain how crucial it would be to load the cars forward to achieve a safe centre of gravity,

October 17, 1958 – Moroccan Grand Prix practice, Ain-Diab, Casablanca: Impressive BRM team line-up before the Atlantic coast course's pit row – Ron Flockhart and a drawn-looking Dick Salmon (left), Behra's '256' backed by Schell's '257', Bonnier's '258' and Flockhart's brand-new '259'... Vanwall beyond.

so an incredible new loading ramp was fabricated to place one car above another within the 'plane's fuselage. Their tyres were then wrapped in old inner tubes which were lubricated with soft soap so the cars could be slid sideways. Tony put the mechanics through dummy loading drill until they were expert at it, for TAI had warned the aircraft would not be available long on the ground at Stansted.

Tony: Imagine our dismay when the aircraft arrived and was nothing like the shape described to us. It was far more spacious and it proved quite easy to roll the cars in staggered, one alongside the other, and when we went through the motions of working out the C of G the pilot just ambled round to the nosewheel leg, eyed its extension compared with the main wheels, shrugged his shoulders, we all clambered aboard and after an enormously long run we were airborne and away to North Africa...

Extra hands were taken along from the engine and race shops, and some who had never been abroad before had to endure endless ribbing from the experienced travellers. Hired lorries were waiting for us in Casablanca. We still exercised our rule that the only person allowed to drive the cars other than the team drivers was me, so I had to warm them up before the race, and having to be push-started or towed in four cars drove me nearly mad. Another crisis arose when our Arab crew towing one of the cars hit a bridge, which swept the superstructure off the truck onto our car behind, doing considerable damage. Fortunately Dick Salmon, who was steering the car, escaped unhurt, but it caused a rare old row...

October 19, 1958 – Moroccan GP, Ain-Diab, Casablanca – 55 laps, 261.61 miles

The four BRMs were painted with alternative identification markings on their basic colour – a chequer-board nose band on '256' for Jean Behra, a plain white band on '257' for Schell,

and so on. Behra had won the inaugural non-Championship GP there the previous season and he was on top form as practice began on a sunny Friday cooled by a soothing breeze off the Atlantic. His best of 2:25.2 clipped 0.4sec off Fangio's 1957 record. Schell was fifth fastest with a 2:26.0. Ron Flockhart's new '259' developed brake troubles. On the Saturday the grid was decided with Hawthorn's Ferrari on pole for this crucial race, at 2:23.1, flanked by the Vanwalls of Moss and Lewis-Evans, with Behra fourth fastest on the inside of row two with 2:23.8. Jo Bonnier upon his return to the team qualified his car – '258' – eighth on the outside of row three with a 2:24.9 – with which the team was delighted – Schell was 10th on 2:26.4 and Flockhart 15th at 2:29.8.

All drivers were presented to the King of Morocco in a colourful ceremony before the start, portly 'Toto' Roche of Reims notoriety then giving one of his comic-cuts starts, dropping the flag without warning and running from the scene.

Phil Hill was first to react, leading for Ferrari from Moss, Hawthorn and Bonnier, fourth for BRM. While a battle for the lead would develop between Moss' Vanwall and the red Ferraris of Hawthorn and Phil Hill, Brooks moved forward to support his Vanwall team-mate while Bonnier kept his BRM in contention behind this group. At 20 laps the Swede lay fifth, Behra seventh and Schell ninth. Flockhart's engine abruptly shut down when a camshaft broke and on lap 26 Behra pulled into the pit, climbed from his car and walked away from it – and from BRM – in disgust. Unable to compete on a circuit he liked and on which he had won before, in front of a French-speaking crowd, his competitive urge had been overwhelmed by bitter frustration...

Brooks' Vanwall blew up, Gendebien spun his Ferrari and was rammed by Tom Bridger's F2 Cooper. Soon after Picard crashed his Cooper and was badly hurt.

While Moss led comfortably, Hawthorn merely had to finish second to clinch the World Championship and showed every sign of doing so in equal comfort. Bonnier's BRM was droning around fourth behind Moss, Phil Hill and Hawthorn.

1958 Moroccan Grand Prix: Opening lap with the midfield pack rushing up towards maximum speed out of Ain-Diab Corner after the pits – Ron Flockhart's '259' alongside Olivier Gendebien's Ferrari Dino, Masten Gregory's white-striped Temple Buell-entered Piccolo Maserati right behind.

On lap 41 the unfortunate Stuart Lewis-Evans suffered an engine failure in his Vanwall, locking its rear wheels. He crashed, the car's fuel tank burst and ignited and the popular – and extremely fast – Londoner sustained fatal burns.

Moss won the race to clinch the Formula 1 Constructors' Championship for Vanwall, Hawthorn was second to become the first Englishman ever to win the Drivers' World Championship – by one solitary point from a devastated Moss, regarded so much as the retired Juan Fangio's natural heir – Phil Hill was third for Ferrari, Bonnier fourth for BRM and Schell fifth, having unlapped himself from the winning Vanwall just before the finish. Harry Schell ended the season fourth-equal with Roy Salvadori of Cooper in the Drivers' table, both having accumulated 15 points to Hawthorn's winning 42. Behra ended up eighth-equal with Phil Hill and von Trips on nine points, Bonnier 14th with his three Casablanca points for BRM.

Tony: Jean came to say goodbye to the mechanics, and told me there was nothing personal in his having decided to join Ferrari. He believed I would build a Championship winner one day and said he hoped that he would be there to drive it... We attended a dinner party under the lighthouse that evening, where there was a very subdued Mike Hawthorn with 'Lofty' England – his former team manager at Jaguar and a great friend – obviously telling him of his decision to retire from racing. We all knew poor Lewis-Evans was in a bad way and the atmosphere was muted, strained and strange, in stark contrast with the fun and games the night before practice had begun when a party of us including Hawthorn had decided to go to a night club in the *Soukh* at which the key attraction was of course a belly-dancer.

A large tray was placed before us with a spirit lamp to keep our coffee warm and, as it was the custom, if you approved of the belly-dancer, to tuck a note or coin in what little clothing she wore, Hawthorn amused himself by heating coins on the spirit stove and slipping them into the dancer's pants, which did wonders for her tempo... Unfortunately she and the management both took a dim view and we were obliged to beat a rapid tactical retreat in the traditional British square, all back-to-back.

I had a sizeable hangover the morning after the race, but we had loaded the cars onto the aircraft and were poised to take off when I realized one of our party was missing. I was pretty furious and had just decided to leave him behind when a taxi delivered him to the tarmac – suffering from an even worse hangover than mine. Once airborne we then discovered the airline had provisioned the 'plane for a full complement of passengers, and when the crew told us that since our company had paid the bill we might as well take with us any wine left undrunk, one of our number loaded his case with it. Upon arrival at Stansted he was the unlucky person picked on by Customs to show what he had brought in. He of course said he had a camel saddle, but nothing else, and when they asked him to open his case they discovered it was packed with airline quarter bottles of wine, and he was obviously for it. Consequently, I unfortunately had to exercise our long-standing rule that anyone getting into trouble with HM Customs would be fired on the spot.

We finally arrived in Bourne very tired, still hungover, and both depressed and demoralized. BRM's first full season of World Championship Formula 1 racing was over. Their former driver Mike Hawthorn had become the first Englishman ever to win the Drivers' World Championship title – with Ferrari. Their former driver Stirling Moss had been runner-up – with Vanwall – and yet another of their former drivers, Tony Brooks, had finished third in the table – also with Vanwall.

To the mutual frustration of RM, PB and AGBO, former BRM backer Tony Vandervell's Vanwall team had clinched the inaugural Formula 1 Constructors' Championship, achieving in effect precisely what the rough-tongued tycoon had so loudly predicted he would do when he had stamped out of BRM's controlling Trust all those years before. And what did BRM have to show for its season?

BRM cars had made 29 starts in an unlucky 13 races, nine of them World Championship-qualifying rounds. They had yielded 19 retirements and 10 finishes – one second place, one third, three fourths, four fifths and a sixth. The team were placed fourth out of six in the final 1958-season Constructors' Championship table.

Such a record wasn't quite what Alfred Owen had had in mind... He now had to convince his employees at Bourne and Folkingham of the error of their ways.

ENTER GREGORY, MOSS, WALKER AND THE COOPER-BRM

By the end of 1958 – although Mike Hawthorn had become the first Englishman ever to win the Drivers' World Championship, and had announced his retirement soon after – it was Stirling Moss who was unchallengeably the world's finest racing driver.

His long-faithful friend and business manager was Ken Gregory, and during the winter of 1958–59 – while Alfred Owen was chewing over how at last to make BRM successful – Gregory and Moss were assessing possibilities for the coming season. Initially the situation had seemed settled. Stirling half-expected to drive again for Vanwall, but half-hearted noises emanated from Acton – just possibly Vandervell would not continue. In any case, just as he had won the year's Argentine GP in a Rob Walker-entered Cooper when Vanwall made no entries, alternatives had to be considered.

Tony Vandervell showed no sign of taking the rear-engined Coopers at all seriously – even less of building a smaller rear-engined car to combat them. Stirling knew just how quick they could be with Climax 2-litre and 2.2-litre engines, and now Leonard Lee of the Coventry company had authorized development of a full 2½-litre version for the coming year. These engines were to be supplied to Walker (for Moss), and to the works Cooper and Lotus teams. They could render the classical front-engined Grand Prix car entirely obsolescent – but in December 1958 such potential remained unproven.

Stirling recalled: "I had always been quite impressed by the four-cylinder BRM engine, it was light and practical – apart from those silly valves – and whenever it was on form it went like stink!"

He was attracted by the possibility of obtaining a P25 engine to power a Cooper chassis. Since the intended Argentine GP due early in 1959 had been cancelled, the new year's World Championship would not begin until Monaco in May. The BRM engine's power and torque in a Cooper frame could prove ideal for Monte Carlo's tight corners, swoops and climbs.

Rob Walker agreed to underwrite construction of such a car if BRM could be persuaded to loan an engine. Ken Gregory wrote to Alfred Owen, and a meeting was arranged between them by an enthusiastic Rivers Fletcher.

On December 17, they met in London where Owen was

chairing a Dr Barnardo's children's homes committee that day. He listened attentively to Gregory's ideas and said as they parted: "I will give you an answer in the next few days."

He drove his Bentley – hard as ever – back to the Midlands, cheered by the thought that here at last was an opportunity to see how a BRM engine could perform in the hands of a client team. The fact they would return to BRM the elusive services of Stirling Moss while also providing an insight into the option of rear-engined design was the sweetest cherry on the cake.

He consequently instructed Rivers to confirm acceptance, offering two Bourne-prepared engines, and on December 30, Ken wrote to Owen to thank him:

> ...firstly, for so kindly listening to my proposition... and, secondly, for your generosity in helping Stirling out at a time when help was badly needed.

He confirmed that:

> In return for the loan of two B.R.M. Formula 1 racing engines it was agreed that your unit should be fitted into a 1959 modified Formula 1 Cooper racing chassis by R.R.C. Walker of Pippbrook Garage, Dorking, Mr. Walker having already placed on order a five-speed gear box to his own design. The remainder of the car will consist of components of Cooper origin plus proprietary parts such as Girling disc brakes, suspension units, etc.
>
> The finished car will be called a Cooper-B.R.M. and will be driven exclusively by Stirling in the early events of 1959, a guarantee having been given to you that the combination of car and driver will be entered in the Grand Prix of America at Sebring on the 22nd of March (if held) – it was not – ...and the Grand Prix of Monaco on 10th of May. In the eventuality that the Grand Prix of America is cancelled or postponed I would suggest that the first race of the car should be at the Easter Meeting at Goodwood.
>
> Whilst the engines are on loan it was agreed that you should have full access to all data accruing from the installation of your unit in the Cooper chassis and, furthermore, that, as far as was practicable, the car should be used as a test bed for your engine research division.

After confirming his intention to issue press releases covering progress, to be agreed with Rivers Fletcher, Gregory undertook to keep Owen fully informed. Installation drawings had already been received from Peter Spear, and Ken's letter to Owen concluded with thanks:

> ...for your very great kindness and help on this matter and, furthermore, [I] sincerely hope that this association upon which we are all about to embark will be a happy, prosperous and successful one for all concerned...

In this, it would fail.

Its creators had high hopes of the car, especially for Monaco, where the big four's mid-range torque should have shone in such a compact and relatively lightweight car. Stirling's long-serving chief mechanic, Alf Francis, was to build the engine into a Cooper-based chassis with suitable adaptations as necessary to both power unit and frame. Finding a suitable gearbox to endure 2½-litre F1 engine torques was a problem. Cooper could not or would not supply their rival, BRM could offer nothing suitable, so Francis instead approached his old friend *Ing* Valerio Colotti, the former Maserati chassis and transmission specialist in Modena.

He had just set up his own *Studio Tecnica Mecanic* concern, from which he and Francis in partnership would develop Gear Speed Developments SpA to manufacture and market what would become the familiar series of Colotti rear-engined racing car transaxles. The prototype unit employed for Rob Walker's Cooper-BRM project would in fact found the new series.

Alf Francis converted a standard Cooper frame with help from Rob's other full-time mechanics, John Chisman and Mike Roach. The standard Cooper curved-tube engine bay structure was replaced by straight tubes, and all major tube junctions were boxed and gusseted. The driver position moved further forward as the BRM engine was longer than a Climax FPF.

Its standard magneto mounting, projecting forward at the front of the engine, had to be altered for this rear-engine installation, since the two mags would have cramped the driver's ears… They were resited and driven instead by internal-toothed rubber belts of the kind then familiar upon American dragsters but yet to gain widespread currency in Europe.

The car was completed with wider-than-standard front track, non-standard bodywork and Alf's distinctive brand of rear suspension with a single top radius rod each side, providing more than normally positive location for Cooper's transverse rear leafspring system.

In April the car was taken to Modena where its new Colotti Type 10 five-speed transaxle was fitted and Moss tested it at the famous *Aerautodromo*. It seemed promising, and was brought back to England in time for its debut in the Aintree '200' in which Stirling would be aiming at a fourth consecutive victory…

Unfortunately, when PB first saw it, he simply stood and studied it silently, then raised his eyebrows, turned, and walked away. It was, he would consider, "an appalling example of rank bad engineering – the design would barely do credit to a Shelsley special…". He was biased, of course, but in many ways he was right, and in the back of his mind he was beginning to suspect that perhaps this, after all, was the way to go – whatever Cooper could achieve in rear-engined racing car design, his boys at BRM could certainly do better.

CAT AMONG THE PIGEONS – A MATTER OF REGULATION

On October 28–29, 1958, a meeting of the International Sporting Committee – the CSI – of the *Federation Internationale de l'Automobile* – FIA – was held at the Royal Automobile Club's palatial headquarters in Pall Mall, London.

The year's World Championship and Formula 2 title awards were to be made there, but more importantly the CSI had been agonizing all season over the future of Formula 1 once contemporary regulations were due to expire at the end of 1960. Earl Howe and Dean Delamont of the RAC had organized this latest session to conclude the matter. While normally the CSI would merely recommend a course of action for formal ratification by the FIA itself, in this case the FIA had devolved complete executive power to its sporting commission.

The meeting was chaired by the CSI's French President, M. Augustine Perouse, and the countries represented, in addition to France and Great Britain, were Germany, Italy, the USA, Holland, Belgium and Monaco. The British delegation was led by Earl Howe, while absent – but presumably still voting – CSI members were the representatives of Switzerland, Mexico, Sweden and Portugal.

On October 28, the Committee first heard, for information, the views of three racing drivers – new World Champion Mike Hawthorn, Stirling Moss and Maurice Trintignant – and of two manufacturers – World Champion constructor Tony Vandervell and F2 Champion John Cooper. All were emphatically in favour of retaining the contemporary 2½-litre Formula, burning AvGas fuel. Italian manufacturer Enzo Ferrari did not attend, but sent an opinion in writing, reputedly favouring 3-litre cars designed specifically for the Indianapolis and Monza speedways and for such high-speed road courses as Reims and Spa, to attract American interest in European racing. He also suggested a secondary class for 2-litre cars with two-seater bodies….

Next day, the committee considered all views from various sources affecting Formula 1's future. In a first vote – to continue the existing 2½-litre Formula – only Great Britain, Italy and the USA were in favour. It was already apparent that the French and German representatives had come to London intent upon enforcing from 1961 a 1½-litre unsupercharged Formula.

The World Championship presentation ceremony was then held on the evening of Wednesday the 29th, an FIA cup and an RAC plaque going to Mike Hawthorn, the Constructors' Cup to Tony Vandervell and the F2 Cup to John Cooper.

Pat Gregory, RAC press officer, then rose to his feet and read the following statement announcing the majority decision of the CSI regarding Formula 1's future:

From the 1st January, 1961, Formula 1 will be for cars with a maximum cylinder capacity of 1,500cc unsupercharged and a minimum capacity of 1,300cc unsupercharged, running on commercial fuel.

A number of devices aimed at increasing safety and restricting the performance of the cars will also be compulsory. These are:

1. An anti-roll bar [*sic*, meaning 'roll-over bar'].
2. An automatic starter.
3. A double system of braking – one working on four wheels, and an emergency system working on at least the two front wheels.
4. No refuelling of lubricant [*sic* – meant 'refilling'] to be allowed during the race.
5. Safety type fuel tanks.
6. The drivers' cockpit to be open and all wheels exposed.
7. Cars to have a minimum weight including lubricant and coolant, but without fuel, of 500kgs – 1,102lbs or 9.83cwt, this weight not to be made up by ballast.

To cater for events with racing cars of greater performance a new Formula which, it is hoped, will strengthen co-operation between America and Europe, is to be considered in detail by a specialized Sub-Committee which has been set-up for this purpose. It will consist of delegates from Britain, Italy and U.S.A. For this Formula an engine capacity of three litres is contemplated.

Even before Gregory had completed this statement the room was in uproar – British interests, those with by far the greatest financial investment in 2½-litre F1, were furious.

Peter Garnier reported in *The Autocar*: "G.A.Vandervell, who has already suffered at the hands of the C.S.I. when they made a last-minute decision to change to hydro-carbon fuels at the beginning of this season, considers that this latest decision does not give sufficient consideration to the manufacturers' views... Raymond Mays...on behalf of B.R.M. says that it is the biggest blow ever dealt to Grand Prix racing. It eliminates ingenuity in chassis design, and would be prohibitively expensive if engines with a large number of small cylinders were built; this will be necessary to maintain the race speeds which the public expects to see... The method of voting on the C.S.I. should be changed, those nations with active Grand Prix cars, first-class drivers, and races, should have more power than those not similarly placed..."

David Brown of Aston Martin declared: "The whole question of our [impending] participation in Formula 1 racing now, and in the future, must come up for consideration...extraordinary [that] decisions of this kind can be reached in complete opposition to the views of the only countries interested in building racing cars". John Cooper made suitably unimpressed noises, but must have been thinking how handy the change could be since his cars had just dominated the 1½-litre F2 Championship, while Colin Chapman of Lotus echoed his seniors' disgust: "A minimum weight limit higher than the current weight attainable with 2½-litre engines is clearly a retrograde step because it rules out ingenuity in chassis design. A company like mine is forced to depend on a proprietary engine supplier who will certainly find it hard to compete in the horsepower race. The multi-cylinder engines which a 1½-litre Formula will demand has no commercial application and therefore nobody is likely to build one..."

The CSI's full statement concluded:

During its discussions, the Committee also reviewed other measures appertaining to the general safety of racing, and rules will be considered concerning inspection of tracks, improvements to signalling, selection of drivers, and protective clothing for drivers.

The Committee also, during its meeting, considered a breach of international regulations by the French driver

87. This storm burst over the unfortunate, just resigned BRM driver's head due to his appearance on October 12, 1958, in a 1,600cc Porsche RSK sports-racing car in the *Los Angeles Times* GP at Riverside, California. This was the first major postwar professional sports car race to be held in the US, but it was run with only a National licence, whereas Behra was a Group A graded driver, permitted by the CSI only to compete in International-status events. Hence the CSI's huffing and puffing in Pall Mall. Behra still emerged with a healthy profit, having drawn $2,000 start money plus $1,500 winnings for finishing fourth amongst Ferrari, D-Type Jaguar and Lister-Chevrolet opposition.

J. Behra who took part in a race in America without the necessary authority. It was decided to impose a fine of 100,000 Francs on Behra and to suspend his competition licence for six months should the offence be repeated. At the same time the race promoters were fined 1,000 dollars. [87]

The following drivers were listed as being able to compete outside their own country only in international events:

Hawthorn, Moss, Brooks, Brabham, Allison, Salvadori, Flockhart, G. Hill (Great Britain)
Behra and Trintignant (France)
P. Hill, Gregory, Shelby and Schell (U.S.A.)
Gendebien (Belgium)
Von Trips (Germany)
Fangio (Argentine)
Bonnier (Sweden)

On November 14, 1958, an ORO budget meeting was held at Bourne at which the proposed new 1961 Formula was discussed. Peter Berthon had digested the CSI's *diktat*, and on the 22nd compiled the following summary:

Due to the bad reception of the proposed 1½-litre Formula, it is not certain whether this or the proposed alternative 3-litre Inter-Continental Formula will be adopted.

In view of this doubtful position, I would not recommend any actual expenditure on either project at the moment other than Drawing Office investigation, preparing the way for both or either on the lines of the attached.

From the financial point of view, the 1½-litre formula is likely to prove the most costly in history, due to the type of engine required. The 3-litre formula, on the other hand, would be similar in cost to the present 2½-litre formula.

His attached report then reviewed available options for 1961–66 – as it was expected to be at that time, not 1961–65 as it turned out – and he opted for development of a 1½-litre unsupercharged update of...the BRM V16. He wrote:

The avenues left for continued development are: 1) Engine power; 2) Roadholding; 3) Transmission; 4) Brakes.

ENGINES

Engine power will be at a premium, as this will be the only fundamental difference between cars built to this Formula and that affects acceleration and maximum speed. The requirement then is for an engine to be of maximum output and of a design that has scope for development for a minimum of six years.

Minimum engine weight is of no importance, since chassis, transmission, etc., can be made lighter to suit the lower torques involved. The place to put the excess weight, to bring the total to the minimum requirement, is in the engine. This immediately calls for multi-cylinder engines; and as, broadly, the power from a given displacement varies almost directly to the maximum number of cylinders, the maximum number of cylinders consistent with keeping the overall car weight to the minimum requirement is essential, and generally development will follow the lines of current Italian motor-cycle engines that now use 8 cylinders for 500c.c.s. capacity.

We are fortunate in having the original 16-cylinder 1½-litre supercharged engine available and this in unsupercharged form, with altered cylinder heads to suit atmospheric intake conditions, simplified, generally, the supercharger and drive removed, adapted to take 4-cylinder ancillaries, water pumps, oil pumps, etc., which are already available, should prove the basis of an extremely reliable engine. This engine should be able to produce at the beginning of the new Formula, 250b.h.p. which is similar to that being used in the present 2½-litre class, with a possibility of development up to a maximum of 350b.h.p. as a peak.

This engine would be more costly initially to produce than the current 4-cylinder 2½-litre; but as it has been developed for 600b.h.p. should permit many races without dismantle and overhaul, i.e., without removal of engine from chassis.

PROCEDURE

The basis of the engine could be broadly kept as it is, using the same stroke/bore ratio, and new cylinder heads would be required as a result of air flow work by Weslake on a wooden model. At the moment drawings of a cylinder head arrangement are going ahead to determine optimum valve sizes, port shapes, etc., from which a wooden model would be sent to Weslake for flow tests. Weslake has already agreed the basis and this procedure.

It should be noted that any current 4-cylinder 1500c.c. engine will be quite useless for 1961, as the power potential of these engines is only about 160b.h.p. due to speed limitations.

CHASSIS, ROAD-HOLDING, SUSPENSION:

The best we know today is our 2½-litre car, which would obviously be the basis of a suitable layout after a further two years development has been carried out to improve road-holding, etc.

GEARBOX AND TRANSMISSION:

With a multi-cylinder engine, using very high R.P.M. it is probable that a 6-speed gearbox would be needed to keep the engine on its optimum torque range. This can be provided for in a light and simple manner by using a Schmidt arrangement (Cisitalia). The usual type of change would not be satisfactory with 6-speeds. Possibly an efficient hydraulic variable speed arrangement will be available in the future.

BRAKES:

These could follow the lines of normal development; but if a satisfactory hydraulic transmission is available within the period, this can also be used for braking.

Peter Berthon

He then added the following postscript:

ALTERNATIVE 3-LITRE INTER-CONTINENTAL FORMULA

The 1½-litre Formula decision has proved extremely unpopular with drivers, manufacturers of present Formula 1 cars, race promoters of the faster circuits, and the Americans. It has been hoped to get the Americans interested in Formula 1 road racing; but the proposed formula precludes this.

As it is finally in the hands of car manufacturers and race promoters to run races to suit racing drivers, circuits and their public, a very strong move is being made to support the proposed American and Italian proposal of 3-litres maximum capacity, with no other restrictions than the use of 100 Octane pump fuel. This was popular because the engine capacity is the same as the current sports car formula, and engines can be developed for both purposes.

The B.R.D.C. have shown their support to this formula by issuing the following statement:

The British Racing Drivers' Club, at a special committee meeting, unanimously agreed that the recent decision of the C.S.I. to limit Formula 1 to cars of less than 1,500c.c., and of not less than 500kg. in 1961 is a retrograde and short-sighted one, as it bears no relation to the wishes of the constructors, drivers, organisers, and the spectating public. It is resolved, therefore, that every support should be given to the R.A.C. in organising the proposed Inter-Continental (3-litre) Formula in the belief that races under this formula will not be confined to such circuits as Indianapolis.

Efforts should be initiated now to persuade B.R.M., Cooper, Ferrari, Lotus, Maserati, Vanwall and all other interested parties to support such a formula and, if agreement is reached, the nations likely to be of greatest importance in 1961 – that is, Britain, Italy and the U.S.A. – be convinced that they must announce now that their races in that year will be run for cars complying with the Inter-Continental Formula.

PB continued:

If this formula is accepted the range of development remains as it is with the present formula:

ENGINE

The requirement here is maximum power and minimum weight as with the present formula. Our current 2½-litre 4-cylinder engine could be increased to the capacity by adding approximately .5" to the stroke, with very little increase in weight. Current components generally would require little change. The engine would be much improved with the altered stroke-bore ratio and the increase would permit a better combustion chamber, due to the reduction in surface volume ratio. The present engine is the lightest 2½-litre yet constructed, and the increase to 3-litre would enhance this characteristic.

Similar remarks apply to chassis, brakes, etc., as with the 1½-litre formula, but with the exception of the gearbox, where 6 speeds would be necessary. Generally, the aim would be to reduce weight below present 2½-litre standard, which, with the increased engine size, would probably provide the maximum usable acceleration up to 150/60m.p.h. without recourse to a multi-cylinder engine.

'DOWN-UNDER' INTERLUDE – NEW ZEALAND, 1959

BRM's first race appearances of 1959 were made half a world away from home base – in New Zealand... This programme had been initiated when 'Buzz' Perkins of the New Zealand Grand Prix Association had first prompted ORO interest in a return down-under in September 1958.

Initially a BRM entry to be driven by Ron Flockhart was considered in the Australian race at Albert Park, Melbourne, on December 7, and RM's indefatigable secretary Miss Ingoldby provisionally booked space for a crated car and two mechanics on the *Stratheden* sailing from England on October 30 and arriving on December 1. PB wrote to Ron:

> The car will, of course, be ex-Casablanca and there is going to be little time after this event to prepare it with spare engine, gearbox etc., in time for crating and loading...

Works mechanic Roy Foreman had agreed – eagerly, one suspects – to make the long trip, accompanying former chief mechanic Gordon Newman, who was emigrating and was keen to operate for the team "on a one-way ticket...a lump sum payment for his services, plus living allowance..."

On October 13 the Australian race date was confirmed to RM as November 29, so plans were instantly rejigged – the car could not possibly arrive in time. It was decided instead to visit New Zealand only – where Rubery Owen owned an important subsidiary, Motor Specialties Ltd – starting with the well-regarded NZ GP outside Auckland on January 10.

'Buzz' Perkins had offered £1,500 start money for both the Melbourne and Auckland races, plus £500 for the Lady Wigram Trophy race at Christchurch, South Island, on January 24. Since there would not now be any Australian start money to share costs PB cabled Perkins' NZGP office at Ashington House, 75 Wakefield Street, Auckland:

> IMPOSSIBLE RUN 29 NOVEMBER MELBOURNE OWING SHIPPING DIFFICULTIES STOP AGREE RUN NEW ZEALAND EVENTS BUT COULD YOU AGREE INCREASE TO TWO THOUSAND FIVE HUNDRED FOR TWO OR THREE EVENTS STOP PLEASE CABLE REPLY – BERTHON – OWEN ORGANISATION.

Eventually the tour went ahead on this basis, but the often contentious Ron Flockhart picked another bone with the Bourne management before his departure. He had been paid a £500 retainer for the 1958 racing season, with the position to be reviewed in July when a further £500 payment would have been considered, dependent upon results.

In fact he had been injured in the June sports car meeting at Rouen, by which time BRM had run in six events but had only once provided him with a car. RM and PB suggested he should accept the £500 left in abeyance that season as a retainer for 1959. Ron felt that was unfair, and was further disgruntled since the New Zealand start money offered was well below that attracted by Ken Wharton with the V16 in '54,

meaning the forthcoming trip – for which Ron was paying his own way in return for start, prize and bonus money – might even show a loss. He instead requested £250 compensation "for lack of opportunity" through '58. RM found the diplomatic solution – since the NZ visit "...was undertaken solely from the point of view of Rubery Owen propaganda... Rubery Owen might be prepared to put up £250 for this journey". Ray felt Flockhart had a strong case and Alfred Owen ultimately agreed...

January 10, 1959 – New Zealand Grand Prix, Ardmore Aerodrome, Auckland – Two 15-lap, 30-mile Heats; Grand Prix 75 laps, 150 miles

Since these New Zealand races were being run to an effective *Formule Libre*, the Formula 1 AvGas aviation spirit restriction did not apply, and instead entries were permitted to burn old-style alcohol fuel, Flockhart's Type 25 '259' being jetted and tuned in consequence to burn specially supplied BP 'K' mix.

Ron was one of the first GP entries to practice at Ardmore early in the week preceding the race, lapping in 1:24.0, 85.7mph, according to his own timekeepers, but an independent watch made him even quicker, 1:23.1, 86.7mph, against Ross Jensen's official lap record of 1:26 in the ex-Moss Maserati 250F. Official practice began two days before the race, Moss getting down to 1:21.5 in the Walker Cooper, while Brabham in the works version and Flockhart matched each other on 1:23.7. Both BRM drivers Joakim Bonnier and Harry Schell were competing, in rival ex-works Maseratis 250Fs. Ron subsequently reported to Alfred Owen:

> ...as I had been careful to practise all the time with the fuel tanks fairly full I knew (my practice best lap) was no 'flash' time, but one which I could reasonably expect to hold during the race...

This Kiwi tour was being regarded very much as an important race-testing exercise and after practice at Ardmore it was noted that the base of '259''s oil cooler was found to be chafing on the radiator support bracket because the nose panelling fitted too tightly, forcing back the radiator and cooler as it went onto the car. However: "This was rectified by elongating the securing holes." The front roll bar bearing blocks were seizing on the bar, requiring .005-inch shims in the split block to provide adequate freedom. Initial tests on BP 'K' fuel saw the rear carburettor flooding, residue being found around the needle valve. Both carburettors were cleaned out and checked, rectifying the fault.

One front disc was fouling the shoulder of the caliper friction pad and backing piece. Grinding out both the pad material and backing piece helped, but left "excessive clearance between the pad and disc, resulting in too great travel". Consequently, the caliper was changed, the nicely bedded-in pads being re-used: "After this the brake performance was satisfactory."

Variations were found between wheels, one spare fouling

January 9, 1959 – New Zealand GP practice, Ardmore aerodrome: Ron Flockhart finds his way around the old Auckland area airfield circuit, driving '259', which still sports its extra hot-climate Moroccan cooling intakes atop the nose, and a prominent BP fuel company advertising decal upon its scuttle side. That bleacher would be packed come raceday…

the outside caliper, which had to be filed to clear. On another wheel the caliper securing bolts rubbed on rivet heads around the wheel rim. "Again filing gave the necessary clearance…"

No hand brake was fitted on the car, Flockhart commenting: "This did not cause any real inconvenience, but it is useful when starting up and on the grid."

Raceday dawned fine and overcast, humid with the threat of rain. As a vast, estimated 80,000, crowd packed around Ardmore's aerodrome circuit, races for motorcycles and saloon cars preceded two 30-mile qualifying heats for the Grand Prix.

The 2-litre Coopers of Brabham and McLaren finished 1-2 ahead of Bonnier's Maserati 250F in Heat One, Flockhart then lining up '259' for Heat Two alongside Moss' Cooper and the 250Fs of Ross Jensen and Carroll Shelby:

It was my intention to take the lead at the drop of the flag if at all possible, and force Moss to over-strain his car or engine in trying to pass me as I know he can never be content to stay in second place. This I managed without much difficulty and after a tussle he got by on lap 5…

passing in the course's Cloverleaf section.

They ran like this until the last lap when the Walker Cooper abruptly broke a half-shaft and Ron "…was not unduly surprised when, rather less than ¼ mile from the finish, I repassed Moss having kept him in sight some five seconds ahead of me during the 15 laps of the heat." He thus inherited victory, sharing fastest lap with Moss at 1:24.5.

We checked the car over between the heat and the final and found it to be in good order and I felt with any reasonable luck at all, I could at least expect a second place. However, due to circumstances completely out of my control, and which I understand will be the subject

of a letter to you by the Stewards of the Meeting, I found myself placed in a very difficult position indeed…

During the interval, Jack Brabham had sportingly loaned Moss a half-shaft even though the Walker driver would pose one of the greatest threats to the Australian in the Grand Prix itself. The Walker mechanics worked feverishly to fit it, their dark-blue Cooper being restarted barely in time to roll onto the back of the grid after the rest of the field had completed its warm-up lap.

Ron:

As my overall time as winner of my heat was better than Brabham…I was happy to find myself in pole position for the Final.

His lustrous green BRM was flanked by the Coopers of Brabham and McLaren and by Bonnier's Maserati, which refused to start, despite energetic pushing. From the back of the grid, Moss was gesticulating that the pushers around the car should keep out of his way. With 20 seconds to go the Swede's engine fired – to general relief. Mr Mathison, New Zealand Minister of Transport, raised the flag. Harry Schell – contemporarily renowned if uncrowned 'King of the Start Jumpers' – nosed forward from row two between Flockhart and Brabham, suddenly he had the clutch home and was accelerating furiously away with Bonnier in hot pursuit!

Nobody seemed sure whether Mathison had dropped the flag or not, the confused Ron Flockhart immediately stalled, while in contrast Moss joined the race from the grass verge, taking off like an artillery shell.

From the Scottish driver's rather prim viewpoint:

…due to certain drivers taking advantage of [Mr

Mathison's] lack of experience, the actual start was a very ragged affair altogether. Long before the flag dropped, cars were creeping forward all round me and in fact, an important official [Clerk of the Course] was knocked down as he was standing just beside my car. What with this and another car crowding through to avoid the accident, I could not move and went as far as allowing my engine to stop as it was quite an impossible situation altogether.

The officials in control did not see fit to declare a false start and I had to set off in pursuit of the fast disappearing field to the best of my ability…

As the tyre smoke cleared, his BRM and Gavin Quirk's elderly 250F both lay on the grid with dead engines, Ron restarting first. By the end of that opening lap Moss – from his back-row start, was in the lead! Flockhart lay 18th, passing six cars by the end of lap two. Ending lap seven his BRM lay sixth, then he displaced Shelby and Schell to run fourth. By lap 12 he was up into third place behind Brabham. He was clocked at 142mph along the straight, but the Coopers of Moss and Brabham hit 152 and 148mph respectively.

Ron:

Within 14 laps I had climbed back into fourth place and with another two or three laps had got into third place, still gaining on Jack Brabham in second, Moss being in the lead.

He was closing on Brabham under both braking and acceleration until lap 23, when he suddenly slowed, switched off and retired.

Officially, I have made out that in trying to retrieve the position, I over-strained the engine of the car, but in fact, the fracture of the main engine oil breather close to the engine crankcase, would have happened in any case in my opinion.

About the 23rd lap, oil was being blown back from the broken joint all over the car and particularly, over the rear tyres in such a way as I had no option but to retire much to my disappointment…

…as official representative of the Owen Racing Organisation here in New Zealand, I lodged a protest immediately after the race about the circumstances appertaining to the start of the race and had a hearing with the Stewards of the Meeting yesterday to state my case to register my disapproval. There was no question of any acrimony; they were most sympathetic and extremely apologetic for what had happened. I withdrew my protest on their assurance that they would write to you…I did not see the point of progressing further with this as I feel in the end, it would not do the name of the Organisation any good in the long run.

Car '259' was undamaged by any lack of lubrication but Roy Foreman and Gordon Newman were surprised to find a broken inlet valve spring on No. 1 cylinder:

Running mileage approximately 200 miles. Definitely no question of over-revving – maximum engine speed at any time was 8,200r.p.m. The restrictor was damaged. No spare included in the kit other than those on the spare engine. Foreman is certain that with careful dressing up, it is quite serviceable and will be refitted.

If I had continued, it is fairly certain that this would have caused a major breakdown of the engine before the end of the race (a total of 75 laps)…

The problem would be rectified with all speed "as we are due to leave for Christchurch on Friday…"

He enjoyed a dig at one former team-mate's Maserati 250F performance:

…The 'works' Temple Buell Equipe Maseratis driven by Schell and Shelby were completely outclassed to their undisguised disappointment and amazement…We have been paid the most sincere compliment by the Maserati team who are considering withdrawing from the next race [the Lady Wigram Trophy], if the B.R.M. is entered, as is our intention…

And so they did.

In pioneering style, 12,000 miles from home base, Ron Flockhart ended his despatch with the line:

Despite this setback, myself and the mechanics are in good spirits and I hope to have much better news for you…at Christchurch on the 24th…

In Wigram preparation, two of the three spare rear tyres were found to have pin-hole punctures, Dunlop (NZ) changing inner tubes while one tyre tread was found to be moulded "on a wobble" so it was rejected and returned to Erdington for examination.

At Ardmore, the engine had not exceeded 70°C, but oil pressure had fallen to 35–40psi after the breather had fractured around welds close to a flange. A new piece was made up utilizing the blanking flange from the spare engine. Oil tended to pile up in the gearbox when hot. Filters appeared to be clear, but were changed as a precaution. Useful power range had been up to 8,000rpm, no useful performance gain being apparent thereafter. Roadholding had been very good, but Ron "should like to have still a little more oversteer…". Tyre pressures of 33lbs front and 38lbs rear gave best performance. Spark plugs used were KLG 320s, Tony Rudd's recommended carburettor settings were found to be correct "and gave a very satisfactory performance", while "brake performance was satisfactory but no more than that."

January 24, 1959 – Lady Wigram Trophy, Christchurch, New Zealand – 71 laps, 150 miles

Out again in a fully fit '259', Flockhart tackled first practice on the South Island's major operational RNZAF base, the evening before the race. Peter Greenslade reported for *Autosport*:

Flockhart appeared to be on the limit of adhesion in the slightly off-cambered control tower bend, but was able to leaving his braking point for the chicane that closely follows it much later than anyone else...

The result was fastest time at 1:21.6, over 93mph.

Jack Brabham's Cooper was a second slower, followed by McLaren's, way behind on 1:25.3. Flockhart took pole on the left side of the grid, with Brabham, Bruce McLaren and Ross Jensen's Maserati arrayed to his right.

This time he made a perfect start, swooping across his neighbours' noses to take the wide line into the first left-hander. His standing lap was timed at 1:30.4, and he completed it with a 1.8sec advantage over Brabham. Once the leaders began to lap tail-enders, Brabham closed, passing Flockhart to take the lead after seven laps. Ron clung tight to the Cooper's tail, the pair of them pulling a second a lap away from McLaren, "...but they just did not seem to be racing".

Then, starting their 25th lap,

...right in front of the grandstand Flockhart took Brabham and raised a cloud of dust with the right-hand wheels as he went on to the grass to get by...Into the Hangar Bend, with bare daylight between them, Brabham held on to the B.R.M. like grim death...

and so it went on:

Time and time again they would take a slower car one on either side. The Wigram crowd had never seen anything like it before.

By half-distance, Brabham and Flockhart were miles in front of McLaren and on lap 39 the Cooper regained the lead, but there was absolutely nothing between the two cars...

Brabham was cutting surgically through back-markers until, on lap 47, out of the left-hander leading onto the pit straight:

Flockhart was wide out and there was not much room left. He put the right-hand wheels on the verge once more and went past Brabham. It looked exactly like a slow-motion film and again there was no daylight between them as they went into the Hangar Bend.

At 60 laps they were still wheel-to-wheel, and Brabham was realizing the BRM had the edge on outright speed and acceleration. Jack's pit hung out the 'Faster' signal and he clocked 1:22.6, 92.50mph, but on lap 69 Ron responded with 1:22.2. Brabham's crew waggled the *Faster* sign again, but as he went by he simply shook his head and waved his hand palm down. He was flat-out already and there was nothing more to give.

And so Flockhart was able to build a modest time cushion, eventually to win by 2.7 seconds from Brabham, with McLaren third, having been lapped twice by them both. It had taken a long time, but BRM was at last a winner in New Zealand...

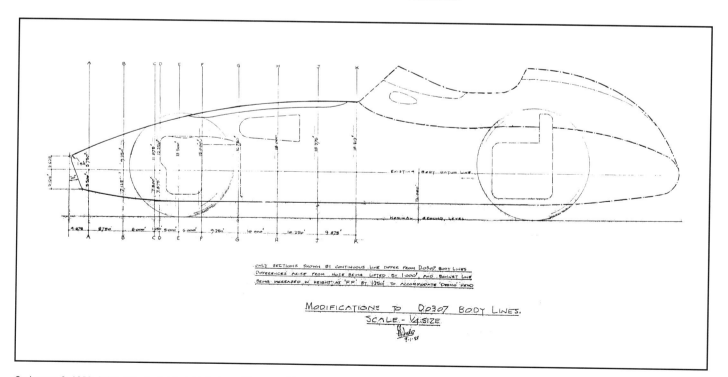

On January 8, 1959, Aubrey Woods sketched this body modification to lift the nose an inch and raise the bonnet at section F-F — just abaft the front suspension cut-out — by 1¼in to accommodate the 'desmo'-headed engine. But desmodromic valve gear showed no advantage. It would be the other end of cars '2510' and '2511' which changed shape, using taller headrests, smaller tails...

February 7, 1959 – Teretonga Trophy, Invercargill, New Zealand – Two 8-lap, 12-mile Heats; Trophy race – 40 laps, 60 miles; 'Flying Farewell' race – 8 laps, 12 miles

February 7, 1959 – Teretonga Trophy, Invercargill, New Zealand: Ron Flockhart completed his quite successful Kiwi tour here on the world's southernmost motor racing circuit, '259' by this time featuring a distinctive white noseband and screen-foot flash to make its dark green form a more eye-catching image in the mirrors of backmarker local drivers.

BRM's 1959 Tasman tour ended on the world's southernmost race circuit at Teretonga, near Invercargill, at the tip of New Zealand's South Island. The Southland Sports Car Club had attracted a record entry, and to cull the field two 12-mile qualifying heats were run on race morning, Flockhart lining up '259' on the front row for Heat Two, alongside McLaren, Tom Clark's ancient *Squalo* Ferrari and Sid Jensen's Cooper.

Bruce McLaren led away, he and Flockhart running 1-2 throughout the brief sprint, the BRM finishing second, fully 7.1 seconds adrift.

Grid positions for the feature race were decided by the fastest laps set in the two heats, Ron claiming pole on the left side of the front row, flanked by McLaren, Jack Brabham's Cooper and Ross Jensen's Maserati 250F. Flockhart fluffed his start – losing the advantage as the Coopers fled. He completed the lap fifth, behind Merv Neil's Cooper, but quickly moved into fourth, pressing Jensen's blue-and-yellow 'El Salvador' team Maserati. On lap five Ron took third place behind the Coopers of McLaren and Brabham.

Using all the BRM's available power, the Scot then reeled in Brabham and passed him right in front of the main grandstand on lap 12 to take second place. After 18 laps Flockhart had closed to within 3.8sec of McLaren, but Bruce promptly added an extra 3sec to the cushion in one lap and effectively Flockhart's challenge was over. The young Aucklander was dictating his own terms on this tight and abrasive course and there was nothing the BRM visitor could do about it. The chequered flag signalled Bruce McLaren's first International race win on his home soil.

Ron subsequently reported to Alfred Owen:

Teretonga is a short twisty circuit 1½ miles in length with a slow approach to the main straight, in length about 6 furlongs, and the surface is unusual, being a mixture of crushed and uncrushed river gravel dressing on tar which becomes very slippery and treacherous after a little racing. If the weather is hot the tar melts, and adds to the difficulties.

In practice we managed to return the fastest lap at 1 minute 9.3 seconds with McLaren at 1 minute 9.4 seconds and Brabham 1 minute 10 seconds, however it was discovered that the tread was shredding off the tyres in such a way as to make the car most unmanageable after a few laps. Fitting special D.3 [hard compound] covers on the rear cured the trouble as far as the rear was concerned but induced massive understeer on the worn fronts. Brabham was in similar streights [*sic*] to our-selves but McLaren apparently knew about Teretonga – hardly surprising, one suspects – and he had

on hand a set of covers nearly worn out on a smooth circuit which did not tear and gave him the correct handling characteristics. We arrived at a compromise by fitting a new set of unscrubbed covers on the front and reduced the understeer characteristics by increasing the front tyre pressure by a couple of pounds per sq. inch.

For some reason I could not engage first gear on the line and was forced to select 2nd gear before the flag fell and found myself in 5th position in the 1st lap. (Checking 1st gear appears to function quite normally.) After a few laps I got past Brabham into 2nd place (Race distance 40 laps, 60 miles) but as I gained on McLaren so the front tyres shredded and I had to content myself in that position until the end of the race. I would say that if a set of D.3 Covers had been available for the front wheels as well I reckon we could have gained 1st place. Otherwise the car behaved perfectly and we had no mechanical trouble of any sort. In fact I would say that the engine is running better now than it did when we first arrived out here in New Zealand and has covered some 550 racing miles… Water temperature was just over 70 degrees C. and oil pressure 55-60lbs Sq. In. The gearbox ratio of 23 driving 24 covered Ardmore and Wigram, 22 driving 25 was perfect for Teretonga giving only 2 gearshifts per lap – top to third and back again.

The day's race programme ended with a 'Flying Farewell' event for the eight fastest cars, which were lined-up on the grid behind a white Jaguar XK120 Roadster on which the starter perched precariously. The pack remained obediently in the pace car's wake round perhaps 90 per cent of a rolling lap, until Ross Jensen could contain himself no longer.

His Maserati promptly took off and burst past the hapless starter in his pace car, with Jack Brabham first to react, charging hard, right alongside. The whole pack then blasted by, the starter finally dropping his flag when the last runner was a clear 100 yards ahead of his Jaguar, hurtling across the startline.

This not-so-serious affair saw all eight cars covered by some three car lengths at the end of the lap, the ever-earnest Flockhart looking rather startled in fourth place. He eventually found a space wide enough to take third place behind the leader, Merv Neil, and Jack Brabham.

Out of the final turn of the eighth and final lap, Brabham dived for the inside of Neil's car, Flockhart for the outside, 'Black Jack' winning in a time of 9:55.1 while Flockhart, Neil and McLaren blurred across the timing line all second-equal on 9:56.6…

Ron reported generally on this New Zealand tour, as follows:

General Observations on the New Zealand trip

The car has proved to be fast, reliable and stable and has got that reputation generally with the sporting fraternity and motor racing public here in New Zealand. The spares apart from brake linings are intact, at no time were we faced with any great difficulty in getting the car ready for a race. Brakes are about the poorest part of the equipment, they always appear to need checking or some attention and never wear quite evenly. They are not as efficient as the Girling equipment fitted to the Cooper.

It has been my finding that no appreciable increase in performance is to be obtained by holding on to engine speeds of above 8,000–8,200r.p.m. either through the gears or in top.

There was no need at any time to alter the springs or dampers on any of the circuits and the good handling of the car was remarked upon on several occasions by knowledgeable observers not the least being Bertocchi of Maserati.

It was found that the colour of the car did not attract the attention of the drivers of cars in front, nor of flag marshals, and a white ring was painted round the nose and a white bar across the windscreen cowling, this helped considerably on overtaking slower cars on the tight circuits here.

…I would strongly recommend that for any future trip of this nature involving 1 car a simple two wheel trailer be constructed, this would act as a container of the car on the sea voyage and would greatly simplify transporting by road. This method was used during the stay in the South Island, a Land-Rover being hired as a tow car proved most successful. Car and spares must be shipped together as 'Special Storage' to obviate the inconvenience of waiting for unloading as part of the general cargo. The spares at Auckland were found separate at the very bottom of the hold in the *Rangitane*, no other overseas team was delayed as we were and all the other teams' cars were shipped uncrated without damage. One of our crates was stoved in but that fortunately without damage to the contents.

The mechanics Foreman and Newman have worked willingly and well, and have been popular with fellow competitors and organisers alike.

Taking everything into consideration, I would say without hesitation that the trip has been a success. Starts were made in five races including 2 heats resulting in:

Two – 1sts, Two – 2nds, Four times in pole position on the grid, and one lap record standing to our credit. The car was never in jeopardy (other than when the oil got on the rear tyres at Ardmore) and is in good condition and leaves the country with a greatly enhanced reputation.

Apart from the racing I have given 10 film shows and talks on Motor Racing and the Owen Organisation, and have been on radio broadcasts 5 times. The nett result can be summed up in the words of a prominent member of the motor trade at a recent function '£10,000 worth of newspaper advertising would not have done as much to bring the name of the Owen Organisation to the notice of the motor trade and public of New Zealand as this visit of the B.R.M. and team'.

BEGINNINGS OF BRM'S BEST-YET SEASON…

Meanwhile, back home, Bourne and Folkingham had been fully occupied with development of the Type 25s to the latest 1959 specification, with a return to four-main-bearing engines, Dunlop disc brake systems replacing AP/Lockheed, and what would prove to be the last pair of Type 25 cars – spaceframe chassis '2510' and '2511' – were completed at Folkingham. PB was not much in evidence, spending most of his time in Paris where he had an apartment, as the Talbot-Lago project had finally come together. The Bourne DO did some work on this, and in a desultory fashion investigated the new 1.5-litre Formula, due to take effect two years hence.

At Folkingham, much detail work was going on, refining the four-bearing engines with revised new '8' series heads. ORO had built its own version of Harry Weslake's airflow rig, minus the Rye gasometer, and had found that much smaller inlet valves gave more torque and power. A great deal of testing and car running was done by Tony to prove the new Dunlop brakes, which abandoned the ventilated rear disc. A NACA air intake duct similar to the Vanwall's was tried, but found to work too well for the carburettors, which it pressurized. The same problem did not afflict the Vanwall's injection system. Finally a much longer duct was found acceptable, adding some 4mph to the car's straight-line speed. A test session with Harry Schell at Silverstone confirmed that the winter's work had been effective, and the Folkingham team, blissfully unaware of contemporary rumblings with Cooper and BRP and of their expulsion from the airfield by the Air Ministry, looked forward to the new season with more confidence than usual.

On January 29, 1959, RM wrote to Owen, expressing his own reservations – and perhaps also his fears – regarding the arrangements made with Moss over the Walker Cooper-BRM project. He declared:

While I appreciate your thoughts behind the arrangements you have made on behalf of Moss, and have taken the decision, I naturally stand by it and fully support you in seeing this project through promptly and efficiently. Nevertheless, I think you would be the first to agree that I should state my views to you privately if I do not agree with the decision, and acquaint you with the likely repercussions. The decision seems to have been taken rather suddenly, and I think it would have been more in the spirit of the co-operation you so earnestly desire if I had had the opportunity of putting my views to you during the early stages of discussion.

The whole question of engine sales is constantly in my mind, and I agree the extreme importance of Bourne having a mission in life quite apart from motor racing, and this was the basic reason behind the Ford Conversion policy. As the 2½-litre engine now seems a reliable unit, it was agreed during your visit in September to try and promote sales with Lotus and Cooper, and a good deal of work was done in this connection. In fact both were interested and ready to purchase small quantities subject to definite service arrangements. This policy was disbanded during discussion when you visited Bourne in November on the grounds that the quantities were insufficient to be worthwhile.

In view of the change of Formula, the 2½-litre racing engine has virtually no future, and I feel I must make it clear to you that the arguments now being put to you of possible future sales are being used for purely selfish motives and without any practical foundation...

It is at the present extremely difficult to get precise information on any one subject, and a great deal of time is lost in reaching you through a third party [i.e. Peter Spear]. You must remember that the motor racing we are carrying out, and have worked very hard at to reach success, is your project, and your close direct authority and personal visits are absolutely essential to maintain the enthusiasm and morale that is so important, and is often a deciding factor in this type of project. An example of this is that *in spite of bad engineering* [my italics, DCN]...Vandervell got his success entirely through this.

If I could persuade you to come to Bourne at regular intervals, or that we could meet you at regular intervals, so that you know at first-hand what is going on and we know at first-hand what is in your mind, I am quite sure things would run more smoothly.

One can picture Alfred Owen smiling grimly as he read these words – perhaps his conscious effort to provoke some dynamism in RM and PB was beginning to pay off? He responded in part by talking further with Moss and Ken Gregory regarding the possibility of a still closer relationship. Stirling was interested in testing one of the works team's front-engined Type 25s in its latest 1959-spec form with the engine now returned to four-main-bearing configuration, with Dunlop brakes and perhaps also on 15-inch rather than 16-inch diameter Dunlop wheels and tyres...

Owen was still dealing with the Bourne executives through Peter Spear – keeping them at arm's length, playing them like fish on a line. In early March, following another meeting between Owen, himself, Moss and Gregory in London's *Mirabelle* restaurant, Spear briefed PB to arrange a suitable test session, for while it was Stirling's intention to give the new Walker Cooper-BRM its debut in the Aintree '200', he expressed an interest in driving a works BRM Type 25 at Silverstone in May – where it should be better suited to the faster circuit.

On March 11, Spear minuted to Owen:

> ...we would be far better to have this testing done after Goodwood. With the best will in the world there may be one or two minor bugs in the cars before Goodwood and I think it would be much better if Stirling tested them when they have been subjected to racing conditions.
>
> [Regarding] weight, I did not want to be specific in front of Stirling Moss and Ken Gregory. The dry weight of our car is just over 1,050lbs but this has now been increased a little. The Dunlop brakes put on about an extra 10lbs. If the 15" wheels are successful then we would save about 4lbs per corner.
>
> The 1959 engines should be just over 280 brake horsepower... The engine we have given to Moss is 240b.h.p. The weight of his car is going to be around 900lbs so that they are fairly evenly matched, if anything we would be better. Please do not be misled by the 240b.h.p. for Stirling Moss' engine. His torque/r.p.m. characteristic is very good indeed and his acceleration should be terrific. It is always the torque that matters...

On the 24th Spear reviewed BRM's car situation, gleaned from discussions with PB and Tony Rudd in Lincolnshire:

> For Goodwood we have two cars plus a training car. That is, Schell's '58 car made up to '59 standards plus the first of the '59 engines (No. 91), Bonnier's car, No. 10, which is brand-new with the second '59 engine (No. 92). Bonnier's car will probably be tried out on Wednesday at Goodwood or Folkingham. The spare car is No. 7, which is Behra's car[88] made to '59 standards with engine No. 84, which is the second Cooper-B.R.M. engine. The position on Friday was that we only had Dunlop disc brakes complete for two cars but the bits are following on.
>
> It is proposed to use these cars for Goodwood, Aintree and Silverstone. They will then be refurbished and again 2 plus 1 cars used at Monaco. These three cars will be No. 11 which is a new chassis, No. 6 which is an old chassis and No. 9 which is Flockhart's New Zealand car. After Monaco these cars will be refurbished for Zandvoort and the first batch from Goodwood will be ready for Spa and Rheims [sic], plus testing at Nurburgring. Broadly speaking the policy is to use 2 plus 1 cars wherever possible and to refurbish completely every second race with checking between individual races. This means that the mechanics do not have to travel so much and broadly there should be a more intelligent pattern on which to work...
>
> The following is the proposed policy:
> 1. With only one car available to offer Moss a drive at Silverstone, assuming he likes the car.
> 2. With two cars available to run, Schell at Aintree and

---

88. Spear is in error here – Behra's car, his favourite, was '256'. Car '257' was Harry Schell's.

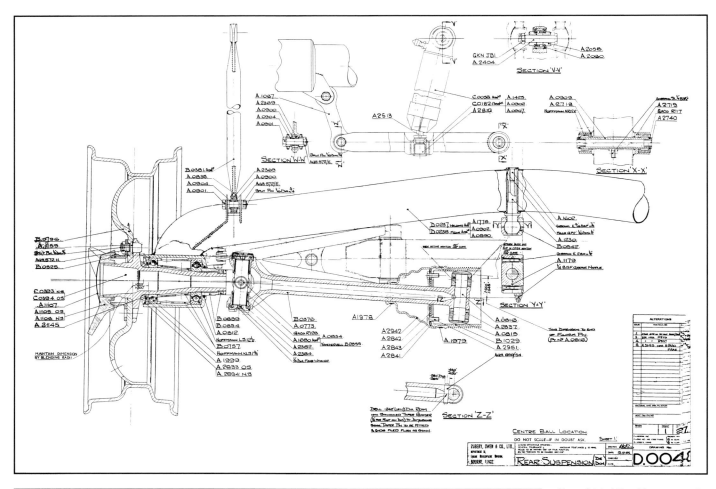

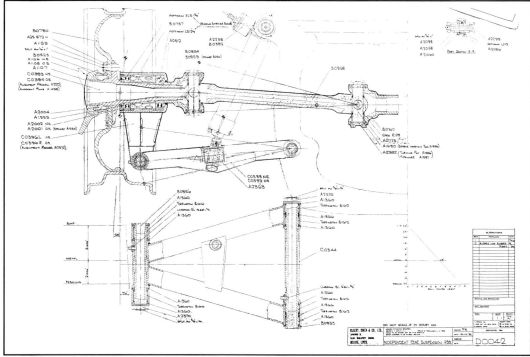

Above: Original Type 25 rear suspension layout, showing the de Dion tube with its centre locating ball to engage in the guide slot on the front of the P27 gearbox. Note fore-and-aft radius rod (top left) and the dreaded inboard 'pot joint' on the half-shaft — cause of so much tribulation.

Left: BRM's independent rear suspension system — depicted in this drawing of December 14, 1956 — was shelved, unsorted. The fixed-length half-shaft drives a stub-axle plunging within the hub carrier, located at its foot by a wide-based fabricated wishbone — three years ahead of Chapman's Lotus 18…

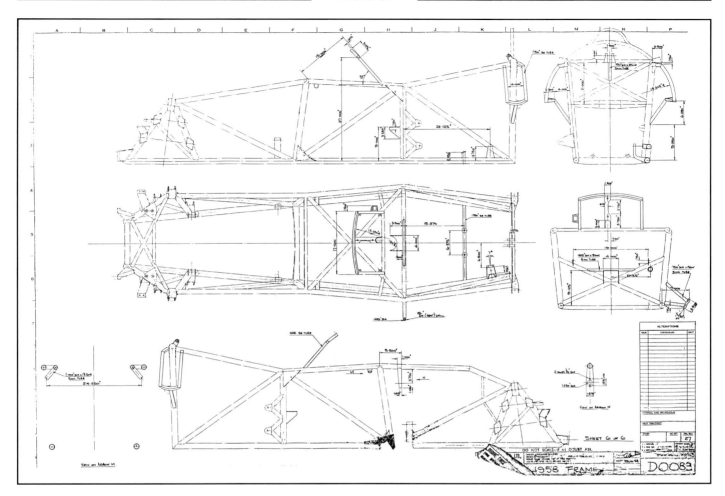

Above: Tony Rudd's original drawings for the 'Series 2' spaceframe, detachable-bodied Type 25s – chassis '256'–'2511' of 1958–59 – moulded away as mouse fodder at Folkingham, but the final frames were captured in the Bourne DO as in this surviving drawing, dated October 29, 1958.

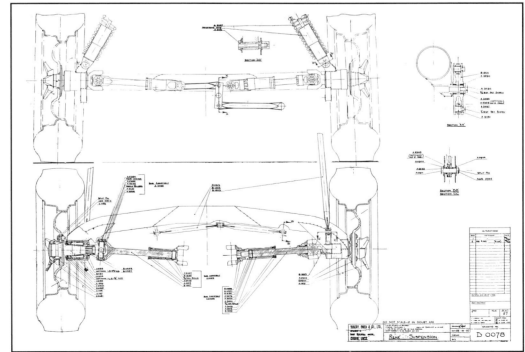

Right: Arguably the finest handling front-engined Formula I car of the 1950s – the 1958–59 series BRM Type 25s used this rear-end, the de Dion tube located laterally by Watt linkage, longitudinally by twin radius rods each side, and wheels driven by those exquisitely crafted low-friction ball-spline half-shafts – as drawn here, October 22, 1957.

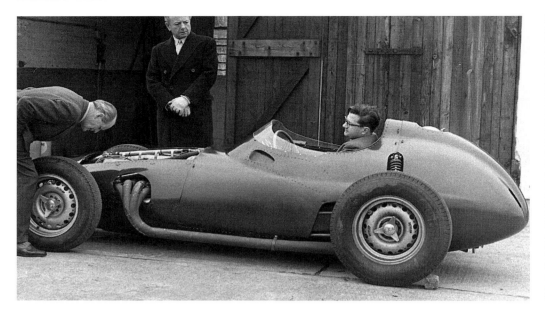

In the winter of 1958–59 BP despatched photographer John Ross to Folkingham to shoot BRM activities there. Here PB and RM examine one of the Type 25s – Tony Rudd aboard. These Type 25s were so painstakingly built to jig and drawing that – quite unlike the contemporary F1 Lotuses or Ferraris – they are exceedingly difficult to identify as individuals. We believe, however, that this is '258'. The detachable skin panels of these spaceframe Type 25s carried virtually no stress other than aerodynamic loads. The slightly spoon-shaped undertray was riveted to the bottom frame tubes and may have contributed to its stiffness, but was not so intended, diagonal bracing tubes performing that function. Governing principle was to provide a secure undertray as a firm base for the body proper, because its ultra-lightweight elektron panels were so floppy off the car they had to be stood on end to avoid damage. Below: RM, PB and emergent Type 25 outside the lock-up block in BRM's Folkingham compound where PB garaged his Raymond Mays-headed Zodiac. The poodle is recalled as having belonged to RM's garage manager, Henry Coy – Ray would often take him up to the aerodrome for a walk around.

Moss at Silverstone.

3. With three cars available, Bonnier and Schell at Aintree or Schell with Moss at Silverstone.

He admitted:

> …a lot of this depends on Moss' feelings on the car when he has tried it and your personal negotiations with him on starting money since I understood…that you would personally handle these negotiations.

March 30, 1959 – BARC Glover Trophy International '100', Goodwood – 42 laps, 100.8 miles

BRM's notional new number-one driver Harry Schell was provided with '257', and his new regular team-mate Jo Bonnier with '256' to face thin Goodwood opposition headed by Moss in Walker's latest Cooper equipped with one of the two prototype 2½-litre Coventry Climax FPF four-cylinder engines, the other powering Jack Brabham's bottle-green works Cooper.

As so often, F1 practice for the Easter Monday classic was run on a wet track. Schell was on top form and qualified his Type 25 on pole at 1:39.0 from Salvadori's Tommy Atkins-entered hybrid Cooper-Maserati, Brabham, and then Moss, whose car's steering had fallen apart in practice, sending him off into a fence – not only BRMs suffered silly failures…

Harry Schell took an immediate lead in the race, from Moss and Bonnier, until Brabham took third place from the Swede's BRM on lap three. Schell's car seemed faster than Moss' big-engined Cooper on the straights, but was visibly slower through the turns. On lap 10 Moss dived ahead entering St Mary's and began to pull away, and Brabham followed him through. Bonnier tried hard to close the gap on his team leader, but Moss was long gone – eventually completing the

42 laps some 15 seconds clear of Brabham, with a second between the works Cooper and each of the BRMs, which finished 3-4.

At the end of that season, Harry Schell would compile a summary of his last year's races for BRM, in his distinctively personal style. His entry for Goodwood read:

> Training: The car was going perfectly well 7,600RPM. Road Holding: perfect. Schell makes the fastest lap by 3 seconds faster than Moss and Brabham. RACE: Schell managed to stay in the lead for 15 laps but the car had no power 7,200RPM but was not staying on the road at all; understeering etc etc. Reasons for failure: The blame was put on DUNLOP who put on our two cars the special green spot tyres in the rear and not in the front. Why the BRM was not equipped with the same type of tyres all around? Who is to blame? Our own organisation? Mr Mays? Mr Berthon? Or Dunlop?…

In his parallel seasonal survey, Jo Bonnier contributed this entirely more polished and cheerful, if in comparison with

As previously arranged between Alfred Owen and Stirling Moss, the cars stayed at Chichester overnight and next morning returned to Goodwood, where Stirling tried them both. With the circuit dried by crisp spring sunshine, he clambered from one to the other, lapping ever faster as the day progressed. His best race lap in the new 2½-litre Walker Cooper had averaged at 94.12mph, but in the works BRM he was soon lapping faster, to mounting excitement from RM, PB and the mechanics. Then mechanic Arthur Hill held out the pit board showing the time '26-4' – with the magic '100' clipped above. Moss in the BRM Type 25 had just recorded the first-ever 100mph lap of Goodwood.

Next morning – April Fool's Day – in his office at 20 William IV Street, London WC2 – Stirling dictated the following for Alfred Owen. Just as PB and RM had discovered way back in the winter of 1951–52, followed by Maserati, Mercedes-Benz, Vanwall and the Walker team from 1954 to '58, when Moss drove anyone's car he simply bubbled with ideas and suggestions on how to improve it. He was extremely demanding, but his single-minded aim was to win:

> I was very pleased to be able to try the B.R.M. at Goodwood yesterday and felt that I should write to you with my findings.

Tuesday, March 31, 1959 – Goodwood testing, post-Easter Monday: The sensational session in which Stirling Moss tried both the Schell and Bonnier Type 25s – cars '256' and '257' – both retaining their International '100' race numbers from the previous day. 'Golden Boy' preferred the handling of this car – '257'…

Moss acknowledges the signal board brandished by 'Hill, A.' as he heads off towards Madgwick Corner through the spring mist in Bonnier's '256' – his previous timed lap has been clocked at 1:26.4, the first 100mph lap at Goodwood.

Schell's notes, perhaps chillingly Nordic view:

> Both racing cars as well as the practice car were very well prepared and we finished third and fourth. Personally I feel that I could possibly have won the race if Schell had been told – from the pits – to let me through.
>
> Schell had tried the cars at Silverstone earlier and broken the lap record several times, so after our good performance here the spirits were high, and we very much looked forward to the coming season…

Firstly, I thought the cars' roadholding were second to none, also the brakes. The first car I tested was Harry Schell's, which should have had 15h.p. more than Bonnier's car; however, this certainly was not the case when I began the tests; without wishing to malign Harry I think perhaps he stretched the elastic a bit far during the race. Anyway, I did the best time in Bonnier's machine, although I don't think the road holding was quite as good as the other car.

There are a few small modifications which I would suggest may be worthwhile:

1. A fitted fire-proof rubber tank.

2. I would like to see a slightly higher steering ratio with a steering wheel about ½ an inch smaller than at present fitted.

3. A gear box fitted with five speeds. I think this would be a great advantage at Spa and Reims.

4. Some form of catch on the gear change mechanism to help one change from 2nd to 3rd. At the moment it is rather easy to push the lever across the gate and go a little past the position for third gear and get between third and reverse.

5. For personal preference, I would like a seat made a bit narrower across the hips and a little wider across the shoulders to get support for the top of one's body.

6. I would like to try the car with a throttle linkage set up so that the throttle opens progressively.

7. There is a slight tendency for the car to understeer and one would therefore suggest putting slightly larger front tyres on. However, I feel that the 16 x 525 are already big enough and that the extra weight incurred by the use of 550s would be a disadvantage. I would like to try the car with 15 x 550 on the front and 15 x 700 on the back.

I would very much like to drive the car at Silverstone on May 2nd, if this would meet with your approval.

I would be very grateful if you would thank all those concerned for being so helpful in putting the car at my disposal.

Yours sincerely,

[signed] Stirling Moss

With the prospect of Moss – so carefully cultivated via the as-yet still unraced Cooper-BRM programme – almost back within the BRM camp, Owen enthused: "I note the modifications which you suggest should be made and I presume that Peter Berthon will be getting all these for your Car at Silverstone and engineering as much as it is possible to achieve before that date.

"We certainly look forward to your driving the Car that you name, i.e. the Chassis No. 7 fitted with the best engine and this again, no doubt, will be arranged..."

Moss had always cherished some superstitions – he believed his lucky number to be '7' and since '257' was the car he had preferred perhaps this was Kismet – fate smiling upon his chances. Entries would be arranged for Moss and Ron Flockhart to drive as BRM team-mates in the BRDC International Trophy at Silverstone, but first the works cars with regular drivers Schell and Bonnier were to face Moss in the debut of Rob Walker's new Cooper-BRM at Aintree...

April 18, 1959 – BARC Aintree '200', Liverpool – 67 laps, 201 miles

Jo Bonnier retained his Goodwood car, '256' while Schell appeared in the latest '2510', brand-new. Moss' rear-engined Cooper-BRM special, had engine '2584' installed.

While Masten Gregory qualified his works Cooper on pole at 1:59.6, Behra for Ferrari and Schell for BRM both clocked 2 minutes dead, and Bonnier took the inside of row two with 2:00.4 from Brabham, then Moss on 2:01.6.

It was BRM versus works Cooper on the opening lap as Gregory just held off Bonnier, then Moss, with Schell trying hard to pass him. On lap two Moss was second in the Cooper-BRM but Bonnier was missing...

After 10 laps, Gregory led Moss by 3 seconds, Schell being 9.8sec behind, third. On lap 19 Gregory retired with clutch failure, leaving Moss leading in the Cooper-BRM from Schell and Behra's Ferrari. Moss was able to pull away by a second a lap, Behra was right with Schell, and by lap 25 the Frenchman was second. Moss set a new lap record of 1:58.8, 90.91mph, but Schell's BRM clattered, coughed and died and he coasted to rest at Melling Crossing.

Meanwhile, Moss "...found it was all pretty hard work" in the Cooper-BRM, whose engine was running terribly hot and vibrating so violently that the frame vibrated in sympathy so that the entire dash-panel seemed a blur. But behind him a tab washer locating a nut on one of the brand-new five-speed Colotti transaxle's shafts had broken. This allowed the nut to unwind, enabling the shaft to slide axially until it simply pulled the gear wheels out of mesh. This happened just as Stirling was lapping a bunch of F2 cars – effectively in neutral he all but spun, but regained control, then hunted desperately for a gear. He found one, completed one more lap, then drew into the pits – and retired. "Colotti's sidekick Giorgio Neri – who had been a race mechanic at Maserati's when I was with them – was in our pit that day, and he was heartbroken. So was I."

Schell's view:

Aintree – Training: First line on the starting line the car was goingwell. Gear ratio wrong: second too low; third too hight [sic].

Race: nothing was done about the ratio for the day of the race.

After a few laps 15 Schell was second behind Moss on the Cooper BRM who was goin very well with Moss.

Schell broke a timing gear so did Bonnier I beleive.

Who is to blame for the timing gear?

Bonnier's view:

Schell and I talked about the organisation of the team, and we felt that we lacked a firm team-manager, as both Mr. Mays and Mr. Burthon [sic] told us what to do. At a brief meeting with...Mr. Spear, Mr. Mays, Mr. Burthon, Schell and myself, we were told that Mr. Mays was the manager and the one to tell us what to do. We both were rather uncertain, however, if this was to work out well. At the same time we were told that we were not going to Silverstone as Moss had expressed his wish to drive the BRM there. This was the morning of the race and neither Schell nor I felt too good about the whole thing.

During practice the cars went well except for my rear brake, which seemed to wear out extremely quickly. The Dunlop people thought the disc was sticking, but Mr.

April 18, 1959 – Aintree International '200': Moss in Rob Walker's Cooper-BRM 'special' leads the combined Formula 1 and 2 event at Liverpool upon the new car's debut before its prototype Colotti Type 10 transaxle failed. This basic Cooper frame carried its BRM engine in modified form to suit rear mounting, its requisite radiator – larger than a Climax engine's – demanding the nose blisters for clearance. That complex high-flung exhaust was necessary to provide adequately tuned-length pipes. Alf Francis' preferred single top radius rod location for the transverse-leafspring rear suspension was typical of the Walker cars – colours are Scots midnight-blue with Rob's distinctive brilliant-white noseband and number discs.

Burthon said there was nothing wrong, and gave me the rather strange explanation that I was accelerating and braking at the same time.

The race itself was a complete failure. My engine broke down on the second lap when I was just about to pass Gregory into first place, and Schell's car came to a halt a few laps later when running third. On both cars the timing gears had broken. I imagine the one to blame for that must be the manufacturer. I feel, however, that more tests on the bench could possibly have helped, and I was told the gears were of a new type.

In fact Bourne's Chief Inspector, A.C. Gordon, took the broken gears to Churchill Gear Machines Ltd, the suppliers, at Blaydon-on-Tyne, on Friday, May 1, brandishing the offending items before:

> Mr. Spraggon, who is I believe Foreman of Development at Churchills. He was disgusted with them and did find out the cause.
>
> It appears that the operator had somehow produced a bad step in the roots and decided to grind it out, and did not radius his wheel.
>
> Mr. Spraggon apologised to me for this and assured me it would not occur again as he himself had now taken over the job and would personally check each of our gears.
>
> Each gear, as it comes off the machine, is checked for concentricity round the pitch line of the teeth; it is then put on the 'Maag' tooth form checking machine. This machine produces a graph of the actual tooth form and is very accurate indeed…

PB had talked with Moss about the Cooper-BRM, whose performance – despite setting fastest race lap at Aintree – had deeply disappointed its creators. He then wrote frankly to Rob Walker that Moss:

> …seemed disappointed with the performance, and

what Alfred Moss had to say about the supply of rotten engines is nobody's business.

However, in spite of all the hard words, I am anxious that you make the car a success and we sort out as quickly as possible the temperature troubles, which in turn will cause the loss of power, coupled with an incorrect exhaust system and carburettor settings which show a 12b.h.p. drop on our test bed. This latter is probably due to an unsatisfactory air intake.

PB continued:

> Frankly…failure has been courted from the word Go, and it is not reasonable to expect satisfactory racing until at least the basic engineering has been established; and I would ask you to make a determined effort to get the fundamental installation correct, so that the engine can be given a chance to see what it can do.
>
> In spite of Ken Gregory's undertaking to our Chairman we have not had any precise information as to what has really happened; and as regards the clutch Shaft Support Bearing – while I appreciate Alf's remarks, I am not satisfied with what he says without sight of the drawings, as this manoeuvre, unless carefully carried out with a reasonable base between the bearings, will lead to certain clutch failure.
>
> When Alf came up here on the 23rd January, he was given the performance figures of the first engine on a typewritten sheet. I will send a further copy of this if it helps, but I am now quite convinced from what has been said that the engine is not giving the power in the car that it should. Unfortunately our detailed instructions regarding installation of the engine have been mainly ignored; but to help I would be prepared to take… responsibility for the oil and water systems if we could have the car here for a few days, to find out exactly what the flows and temperatures, etc., really are at the moment so that the root of the troubles can be eliminated.

You may remember that when you came back from Modena everybody was very thrilled with the performance, and for some odd reason this has now been replaced with disappointment and depression; and I feel strongly that it is up to us both to clear up the criticism and nonsense that will be spread about by this disappointment as speedily as possible.

One final point: We were asked singly and collectively by everybody connected with the project to supply two engines before Monte Carlo. I have been trying to contact someone in order to establish what was required for the second engine since early yesterday morning, and have been unable to get any satisfactory replies. It would seem from the fact that both the engine Carnets were left at Dorking that you are not using B.R.M. engines for Monte Carlo, and I think it only reasonable that somebody should have had the courtesy to save us a lot of work and time when we could ill spare it, in preparing the second engine. As I am without information we are taking the second engine to Monaco in our own transport in case you require it.

Meanwhile, Alf Francis was informed by the Walker mechanics that the spigot self-aligning bearing had broken up. I presume that the reason was not only one of the alignment, which I am sure was correct, but because in our input shaft – which is a very short one – we have reduction gears which cause a certain amount of vibration. Foreseeing this, I have already made provision to support the shaft for the self-aligning bearing and have made the necessary drawings to produce the input shafts supported on two ball bearings without any connection to the engine. Naturally, you have to understand that all these queries have to be solved with development, and it could hardly be expected that the car would go for the first time without any troubles.

Francis asked for a copy of the engine's power curve, while Rob Walker wrote to PB on April 30:

We have just tested the car at Goodwood, and I am afraid to say that I have to admit failure in every direction. The oil temperature and water temperature were very high again and the oil pressure went very low. The power didn't appear to be very great and we could not better the time of the old 2-litre Climax in the original chassis. So I am afraid to say I am very dejected about the whole affair, but perhaps we will manage to do something.

Typical Rob, he signed-off: "So sorry to write such a depressing letter…"

While the Cooper-BRM programme floundered, two works BRM Type 25s equipped with new-batch timing gears were to be driven by Moss and Flockhart at the May Silverstone meeting…

May 1, 1959 – BRDC International Trophy practice, Silverstone: 'Hill, A.' and colleagues push-start Moss in '2510' – the car he didn't want – under RM's gaze (right) as Stirling attacks pole positon upon his return to the BRM race team for the first time since his controversial disappointment at Dundrod in June 1952. At left is PB in conversation with Dick Jeffrey (upturned coat collar) of Dunlop.

Left: More disappointment – leading the race into lap 4, Moss' instincts warned him something was wrong as he came off the brakes and back on to the power at Woodcote Corner. Consequently he braked early into the next corner at Copse, and thanks his lucky stars he did; '2510''s brakes had failed. Here he deliberately spins the car, coming to rest unharmed – short of the bank – on the outside verge. This BRM preparation failure strengthened BRP's bid to prepare a Type 25 themselves for Moss.

May 2, 1959 – BRDC International Trophy, Silverstone – 50 laps, 146.35 miles

Moss immediately starred in early Thursday practice, lapping in 1:40.2, 105.16mph, just 0.2sec outside the course record, and a second faster than new team-mate Ron Flockhart. The BRMs were both faster than the works Ferraris and the Aston Martin DBR4s, and next day Moss broke the course record in both works Type 25s and preferred Flockhart's new '2510', clocking 1:39.2, 106.87mph – fully 1.4sec inside the lap record. In his own car he was then timed at 1:39.2 for pole position, Tony Brooks' Ferrari emerging second fastest on 40-dead, from Salvadori's new Aston Martin and Brabham's works Cooper, both on '40.4. Ron's best was a 1:41.2, on the inside of the second row.

But trouble was brewing…Ron had complained of a softening brake pedal, but Moss preferred the handling of that car, and the young Maestro told PB rather testily that he wanted to use it in the race. He was testy for good reason.

Ken Gregory: "When Stirling got to Silverstone, he found that chassis No. 7 had not been brought along…After practice, although he succeeded in making fastest time in both sessions, and unofficially broke the Silverstone lap record, Stirling decided that, although his engine was excellent, the chassis" – in fact Behra's old favourite '256' – "was not so good, and accordingly he asked BRM to put his engine into the chassis of the car to be driven by Ron Flockhart…" This was done, but of course it meant putting the engine from '2510' into Ron's car, which meant an all-nighter for everyone…

PB had in fact had chassis '256' and '2510' prepared for this event, under the pre-season plan to alternate race cars, thus extending preparation time between appearances. Moss' exercise of his choice of equipment had previously caused great friction within the Vanwall team, particularly on one occasion when he had demanded the engine from one team car and the gearbox from a second to be combined in the chassis of the third… But his purpose had always been simply to give his team the best chance of success, although he was now hot and steamy over what he saw as "another BRM double-cross…just like the time they swopped V16s on me at Dundrod". In fact this is almost grossly unfair, '257' – the car he had specified – was BRM No. 1 driver Schell's favourite. With the Monaco GP just one week after Silverstone, Moss' use of the car in the non-Championship race would have denied the regular driver his favourite car for a World Championship round. The fault lies almost certainly with RM or PB, who would not have explained as much to Moss.

On Saturday, the race was started by Juan Fangio, Brabham's rear-engined Cooper leading all the front-engined cars off the front row into Copse Corner, completing the lap with a narrow lead over Moss, the new Astons of Salvadori and Shelby, then Flockhart and Brooks. Stirling was already nosing left and right, feinting alongside the slithering Cooper, and on lap two he pushed '2510' into the lead. Next time round Brooks' Ferrari displaced Flockhart for fifth and completing lap four Moss came hurtling into the inviting,

open, curve before the pits at Woodcote Corner, his right foot hitting the brake pedal in his normal way.

But: "Something felt weird as I lifted off the brakes and went back onto the power. I could neither specify precisely what it was then, nor can I now, but I was sure something was far from right. Consequently, after accelerating along the short straight past the pits, I decided to brake about 100 yards early for Copse Corner. It was just as well I did, because the front brakes had failed completely…

"I was doing about 130mph, and had I braked at my normal point I would have been going even faster and would surely have rammed the bank very hard indeed. As it was I decided to spin it…coming to rest on the verge, about a yard short of the bank."

He would add, pointedly: "My doubts about BRM preparation had unfortunately been confirmed…"

He tramped back to the pits in considerable dudgeon and dismay, while Ron Flockhart raced on in Moss' originally assigned car '256' – in apparently perfect health. Stirling's insistence upon swapping cars had bitten him…

Jack Brabham was leading Salvadori's new six-cylinder Aston by over 3 seconds, with Brooks third, 5sec adrift, and Flockhart a further 2sec behind, fourth. The Ferrari then retired on lap 30, elevating Ron into third place, where he finished, 24.6sec behind Jack Brabham's winning works Cooper and 7sec behind Salvadori's new Aston Martin which – rubbing salt into the BRM wound – had also set fastest race lap, equalling the course record, at 1:40.0, 105.37mph. Having been beaten by the latest, enlarged, rear-engined Cooper-Climax was no disgrace, but giving best to former Trustee David Brown's brand-new similarly front-engined F1 car upon its public debut must have stung…

Alfred Owen was again dismayed. He felt a personal debt to Moss, having so painstakingly massaged him back into the fold, only for BRM's apparent disorganization and unreliability to shatter trust before it could grow.

Tony Rudd was charged with conducting a post-race investigation into '257's brake failure, and his report highlights not only his flair for such a task, but also the lengths to which ORO could go in identifying what had gone wrong *after* it had gone wrong. Tony attributed Moss' loss of brakes to:

1 …The bundy pipe joining the two cylinders of the offside front brake failed at the root of the flare fitted to the base of the outer cylinder.

2. Dunlop attribute this failure to the absence of an anti-vibration clip fitted to the lower rear corner of the inner cylinder.

3. The calipers were fitted with clips DAS.185/03 by Ayliffe, when drawn from the stores for all the cars. Fox fitted the caliper to the car, and Mr. G. Rowe, the Dunlop representative, shimmed the caliper to bring it into correct relationship with the disc.

4. Following your criticism of the fit of the clips on the pipe (29-4-59), I examined all the clips on each completed car, and as the rubber lining of the clip embraced more than 240° of circumference they were left in place.

5. Nos. 6, 7, 8 & 9 cars had clips in place on examination following this incident.

6. Several new calipers as received from Dunlop have been found where the union nut has been so severely overtightened that the end has belled out to such an extent that the nut could not be withdrawn from the threads, and the sealing face on the flare has been mutilated to the extent that the flash that runs down the tubing had been torn off and had scored a groove in the root of the flare, in the position where the failure occurred…this fault is much more common on offside than nearside, or rear calipers.

7) When the system on No. 10 car was bled, following replacement of the fractured pipe, a leak was found from the lower side of the outer cylinder, i.e. the position where the pipe fouled; the sealing face, examined in position, did not appear abnormal; the pipe was replaced and the nut re-tightened, without excessive force, and the leak apparently cured; but when the car was road tested fluid was noticed on the tyre; the pedal required pumping after three laps at Folkingham, and the joint found to be leaking again. A fresh caliper and pipe were fitted and the car tested satisfactorily.

8. On Friday evening, during an investigation of Ron Flockhart's complaint of loss of pedal on No. 10 car, following a pit stop during the second practice period, both master cylinders were changed by Mr. Rowe, after he had checked the entire system. The system was bled by Ayliffe, and after bleeding I noticed loss of pedal, due to leaks from the banjos on each master cylinder. The joint washers were checked, the faces on the cylinders for the washers refaced, and I personally shortened both banjo bolts by .050" as the threads were bottoming; after this the system held pressure with a solid pedal.

9. Vibration tests have been carried out with the Dawe-Goodman Oscillator unit on the offside system, with the brakes on and off, and with the pipe clipped and unclipped. The amplitudes, etc., were approximately the same whether the brakes were on or off.

With the pipe clipped, the maximum amplitude was .0008", vertically in the centre of the horizontal run of pipe at 40c.p.s. With the pipe unclipped the maximum amplitude was .0013" horizontal measured fore and aft in the corner of the pipe, about half-way from the two ends. This occurred at 28c.p.s. There were corresponding periods at times 2, times 4, etc., as would be expected, but much less amplitude – about 80% at times 2 and 40% at times 4.

A resonant period was found in the pedal between 33 and 40c.p.s. whether the brakes were on or not. This vibration must therefore be transmitted through the frame. The amplitudes were measured with the C.P. pick-up of the Standard Telephones C.R.O., which is rather difficult to calibrate for movements of less than .001" – but as the settings of the instrument were not changed, the amplitudes are absolutely comparative, although the values may not be affected.

10. The material used for these brake pipes was identified as 'Bundy' by the copper film inside the tube, and the same visible inside and outside the tube.

11. The cars have been sent to Monaco with DAS.185/04

clips over a Hellerman sleeve on the pipe, which completely grips the pipe and cannot cause distortion of the pipe.

> 5th May, 1959   A.C.Rudd

Tony: I was very upset over this incident, as I felt it could have so easily been avoided. Dunlop later reported that they had found a damage mark on the failed pipe and suggested to me that it might have occurred during the engine changes. As usual so many people were conducting witch hunts and fabricating alibis that the root cause of the problem became obscured.

If Stirling had either been given the car he asked for or told he could not have it and why, there would have been no overnight double engine change, and he would have had a car which did not fail its brake pipe, and we and Dunlop would have had the opportunity to inspect the brakes thoroughly without getting caught up in the engine change. I personally thought '257', which had been crashed several times, was a bit of an old dog compared with the newer and tauter '2510' and '2511'. I noticed when the BRP deal was finally done that '2510' was the car chosen…

I thought when the season began we had a good chance. The car was competitive, in the right hands. It was well sorted and instead of panic last-minute modifications to fix problems, we could go to the startline with well-prepared cars, and at least pick up points with Harry and Jo. But it was not to be, Alfred Owen felt it was time his cars started winning and he thought he could see how to do just that.

He had been building up the Organisation and at the same time pressuring us to develop engines and cars. He could never see why we didn't run an engine at full power and maximum rpm for a full race duration – then two hours. He would never accept Peter Berthon's explanation that a racing engine only spent a few seconds at maximum power and rpm as it is accelerated up and down through the gears, and this became a bone of contention, and his Darlaston engineers were always asking me to explain why it could not really be done.

As his frustration grew – so that of his brother Ernest grew even more rapidly, and to a greater degree because Ernest had long since lost what little interest he had ever really had in BRM.

I think in common with many in the Rubery Owen Organisation he resented the fact that the Chairman seemed simply to be throwing money down the drain by keeping faith with the Racers. He accepted the fact that some good might come out of it one day, but he watched us carefully to ensure it was all kept within limits – which unfortunately, it was not.

Perhaps we didn't appreciate the full extent of Alfred Owen's frustration until after the Silverstone brake failure on Moss' car, when the storm really burst around our heads.

All Stirling's doubts about the quality of BRM's preparation seemed to have been confirmed, but so had his faith in the car itself as a very fine proposition, while it lasted. Alfred Moss and Ken Gregory were running their own private F2 team under the British Racing Partnership title – BRP – using fuel-injected Borgward-engined Coopers prepared under the direction of Chief Mechanic Tony Robinson. They appreciated better than most that to finish first, one must first finish, and therefore gave high priority to painstaking race preparation. They now proposed to take two cars and engines and prepare them away from Bourne for Moss to drive one when available, and they implied they could do it far better than we could.

This was taken by the BRM mechanics and all our rank and file as a complete slur upon their abilities – implying that BRP could provide better race preparation than we could. I doubt if this was intended, but this was certainly the way it was interpreted. BRP had painted a picture to Alfred Owen of employing a far more methodical method of setting-up the car and of sorting out its problems away from the works team pressures of continuing experimentation and development. They predicted that by this means they would be in a better position to finish races than we were, and with Moss in the cockpit they'd obviously stand a better chance of winning.

Alfred Owen – almost in desperation, one suspects – was attracted by the idea. Ken Gregory felt "that BRM [were] always endeavouring to do more than they can efficiently accomplish; they will not let the design rest and concentrate upon making it completely race-worthy, but seem rather to mix development and racing at the same time… If development must continue during the Grand Prix season, then the activities should be entirely separated; design and development on one side, and the racing programme on the other…".

This had been, almost word for word, the ethic preached over so many years by Peter Spear and Cliff Mander amongst many other high-ranking Rubery Owen engineers who had become involved with BRM activities.

PB, backed by RM, had always vigorously resisted such pressure to slow development, to freeze design and to race only a proven specification. Alfred Owen had always hitherto been persuaded of their view. Motor racing had always seemed some special kind of engineering, an arcane science that ordinary engineers such as his could never grasp. But now this other set of Racers from BRP were telling him a different story – the kind his Darlaston engineers had long advised. Owen told RM and PB he was thinking of acceding to BRP's proposal…

Tony: Great friction was thus being generated at all levels, and meanwhile Mr Owen's sister, Jean, and her husband, Louis Stanley, had become closely interested in the team's activities – and the motor racing scene in general. We believed they were curious to see what had been happening to a significant proportion of the Group's profits.

I believe it was initially at Alfred Owen's request that they came to Bourne and Folkingham to have a close look at what was happening, and at the Chairman's request they were shown everything and we answered all their questions. But to our intense relief they perhaps saw more of the BRM camp's viewpoint than they did BRP's, and would come down very heavily on our side.

We were due to set off for the Monaco GP just 24 hours after the Silverstone fiasco, which certainly had some bearing on the car allocations, so right in the middle of this hotbed of intrigue, off we went to Monte Carlo, and promptly gave ammunition to the BRP faction as we sustained a Great Brake Disaster…

May 10, 1959 – Monaco Grand Prix, Monte Carlo – 100 laps, 195.41 miles

BRM arrived in the Principality with four cars, three to be raced by Schell ('257' – the car Stirling had wanted at Silverstone), Bonnier ('256') and Flockhart ('259'), the fourth ('2510' ex-Moss at Silverstone) as team spare. All were identical apart from modified rear radius rods on one chassis. Walker Racing fielded three cars, 1958 and '59-spec Coopers – both fitted with the latest 2½-litre Climax FPF engines – plus the hybrid – and already unloved – Cooper-BRM special which had, of course, been specifically conceived with Monaco in mind.

May 10, 1959 – Monaco Grand Prix, Monte Carlo: Harry Schell boots '257' out of the Station Hairpin, chased by Tony Brooks' Ferrari Dino 246 in its latest Fantuzzi-bodied 1959 form – here modified with abbreviated 'Monaco nose', a measure BRM would not adopt until 1962, considering it unnecessary in their compact and by this time extremely nimble Type 25s. But Harry has already dented '257's nose against Bruce McLaren's Cooper at the chicane and after running third he will bend his car terminally against the bales.

During first practice on a dull and cloudy Thursday afternoon, Moss preferred Walker's Cooper-Climax to the Cooper-BRM, while Schell was the first to return a reasonable time, of 1:47, in his works BRM, but Moss then began motoring seriously in the midnight-blue Cooper-Climax, and Schell could not match him. Behra was very fast in the latest Ferrari and the session ran out with the Ferraris of Behra and Brooks accompanying Moss at the top of the list.

Full Ferrari and BRM teams – including their spare cars – and Walker's Cooper-BRM all ran on the Friday afternoon. But Moss found the still-vibrating Cooper-BRM soon in gear selection difficulties, its temperatures were as feverish as ever and it was set aside – forever…

Schell, Bonnier and Flockhart were circulating reliably in the works Type 25s, without threatening top times, and they remained some 3 seconds off the pace on the third practice day, Saturday. Having set a furious pace in the Walker Cooper, Moss consented to take out the spare works BRM '2510' for 10 rapid laps, but was only fractionally quicker than the team drivers. Denis Jenkinson observed: "To go from rear-engined Cooper to the front-engined B.R.M. and expect to do equal times on such an exacting circuit as Monte Carlo was asking too much, even for Moss…"

'The Boy' emerged on pole with his Walker Cooper at 1:39.6, from Behra's Ferrari and Jack Brabham's works Cooper, while Bonnier's was the fastest BRM, on the centre of row three at 1:42.3, and Schell and Flockhart formed row four, on 1:43.0 and 1:43.1 respectively.

Under a blazing sun, Behra led from the start with Moss and Brabham close behind. Bonnier led a midfield group of eight, including Schell and, bringing up the tail, Flockhart. Harry bounced his BRM off McLaren's works Cooper at the chicane, without apparent damage. Tony Brooks' ugly Monaco-nosed Ferrari was sandwiched between the BRMs of Bonnier and Schell "and was obviously being held up". On lap 11 he finally found a way past the Swede and quickly rushed away from the Bourne cars. By 20 laps, Schell was ahead of Bonnier and trying hard to close the gap on Brooks for fifth.

Behra lost the lead when his Ferrari's engine expired, and Moss moved ahead with Brabham pacing along several lengths behind, while Schell, having worn down Brooks, had taken fourth place. Bonnier was in trouble, later telling journalists that the rear of his BRM had begun bouncing around as the dampers had failed. Flockhart ran third-last ahead of only the delayed Trintignant and McLaren.

At 40 laps, Moss led Brabham, with Schell third and Bonnier drifting back through the field, eventually calling at the pits on lap 45, doing one more lap, then retiring due to ailments variously reportedly as 'ineffective brakes', 'an oil pipe adrift' and 'mechanical damage'. Tony: Jo came in and said he had lost rear brakes and was trying to keep going but he had spun and damaged the car. We could not see anything obvious so he said he would keep going, but gave up after one more lap.

Barely had the BRM pit realized the first of their cars was missing than Schell failed to reappear; he had slithered head-on into the straw bales in the Casino Square. He manhandled his car out, headed it down the slope towards Mirabeau and roll-started its stalled engine, but its nose was battered, both

oil and water radiators were split, and he too retired.

At half-distance, 50 laps, only eight cars – half the field – had survived. On lap 55 Flockhart came rushing into the Gasworks Hairpin with brakes locked, tyres streaming smoke, using all the available roadway to get round as Trintignant slipped by on the inside, together with Moss, the leader, both lapping the BRM. Ten laps later Ron spun entering the Casino Square. He stalled his engine and, unable to restart without assistance, had to abandon on the spot.

Moss seemed set for certain victory until his Walker Cooper's Colotti transaxle failed, Brabham inheriting the lead in the works Cooper to score his first *Grande Epreuve* victory, and the first for the Cooper Car Company's works team.

Harry Schell subsequently reported:

> Monte Carlo – Training: Schell broke a timing gear on his own car.
> Bonnier: Brakes failure.
> RACE: Schell went off the road on an oil spot when in Third position on the 65th lap; it was entirely my fault.
> BONNIER: Brakes failure.
> FLOCKHART: Off the road because of brakes failure.
> After the race we checked my car and found out that the brakes were worn out and I could'nt [sic] have done another five laps.
> Who is to blame for the brakes failure of the Three cars?

Bonnier's view:

> After Silverstone where Moss had a very close escape after a brakepipe had broken, the enthusiasm among us drivers was not too great. Some people told me I must be crazy to drive a BRM at Monte Carlo and others just laughed, which neither cheered me up much.
> During practice I was accused, not directly, but through Schell, which is typical, of not putting my heart into the driving. It might and might not have been true, but anyway I went faster than both Schell and Flockhart and equalled Moss' time in the practice BRM, so I did not really understand what they expected from me. What hardly made me happier is that one of the radius arms broke on my car after only a few laps of practice, which I think was caused by faulty mounting.
> The race itself was a new failure, and personally I had a close escape when a flexible oil pipe came loose. Flockhart too was near disaster when he spun into the bales after a brake failure. The athmosphere [sic] was very tense when we met after the race. Nobody seemed to want to take the responsibility for the continuing brake trouble. Mr. Burthon [sic; Jo never came to grips with PB's surname] …blamed Dunlop and Dunlop told me it was not their fault. I have a very strong feeling that Dunlop was not the one to blame.

The rear brakes had simply eaten their pads, which lent ammunition to the pro-BRP faction who pointed out that they would of course have carefully measured pad wear during practice and would never have been caught out in such a manner. They were the professionals – all good politics…

Tony: After every practice the Dunlop brake specialists, who had been running disc brakes nearly as long as we had, and in much longer races, came to our garage and with us measured and logged the pad wear. From this we both predicted that we would finish with about one third of the rear pad thickness remaining. What we did not appreciate was that the brakes did not get up to full working and wearing temperature in 10 or 12-lap practice runs, neither did we appreciate that as the pads got thinner with wear they wore faster. The first tenth of an inch of pad lasted more miles than the third tenth. However, it was a case that the dog had a very bad name, and despite the skill and experience of PB and RM, was now up against really master politicians…

The Cooper-BRM never again ran in Formula 1 after being discarded by Moss during Monaco practice. The chassis was eventually sold to wheeler-dealer Cliff Davis for his client, the lanky Count Steven Ouvaroff, and subsequently went to South Africa. On May 22, following his return from the minor race at Pau, Rob Walker wrote to Alfred Owen about their hybrid project:

> I must firstly thank you most sincerely for your great kindness in letting us have the B.R.M. Engine, and for all the enormous co-operation that we had.
>
> I very much regret that we did not make a success of it, but the fault has been entirely due to ourselves and I have made every effort to make this known to the press and everybody else.
>
> I feel that it was a project that might have worked first time if we were lucky and everything went well, but unfortunately as you know we met certain snags and I feel they would take time to overcome. I don't think that any of these would be particularly difficult, but unfortunately we have not got the time to spend and I, myself, feel that the biggest snag of all is the rather large amount of vibration from the Engine, and I think this might cause things to go wrong in many unexpected places and one would never be quite certain what might fail next…this question of vibration is the most outstanding reason why I would rather not accept your very kind offer to continue this project, but I do hope you will not feel that I have been ungrateful in any way…

He went on:

> I do very much regret articles that have been written in both the daily newspapers and the motoring press, but as far as I am concerned I have never expressed any feelings that we were either displeased with the Engine or with the treatment we were receiving… *Autocar* has this week come out with some story about us not getting the latest and most powerful Engine. I cannot imagine where this came from or who made it up. Whether Stirling has been saying anything different I would not know, but whatever he does say I'm afraid I have no control over…!

Owen had already told Peter Spear he was keen to persuade

Walker to sell ORO the chassis "…for us to experiment with it as I feel it has potentialities for certain courses". Very quickly PB persuaded the Chairman that whatever Cooper could do in rear-engined chassis design, BRM at Bourne could do better, and from this beginning emerged Bourne's Project 48 – their own rear-engined 2½-litre Formula 1 car…

Meantime, in the interval between Monaco and the forthcoming Dutch GP at Zandvoort, high-powered negotiations had continued between Alfred Owen and BRP, to the intense disgust of Folkingham and Bourne. Tony: As part of Dunlop's investigation into the brake failures, a day's testing was organized at Zandvoort, the circuit for the next race and fairly convenient for Bourne. Dunlop arranged for Stirling to drive, on the grounds that he was the fastest driver in the business, therefore he could put the most load onto the brakes. To defray their costs, tests of new tyres, intended for the Dutch GP, were to be run coincidentally. Apart from the fact that Dunlop would not consider my ventilated disc, which would have reduced the temperatures, and thus the rate of wear, substantially, I agreed with the whole plan.

We ran for a whole day, covering well over race distance with no trouble of any sort, and producing very good times. All the mechanics' blood was up and we went to the race there more determined to finish and to do well than for donkey's years.

His own blood was up after a gearbox seizure while testing the spare car. This had sent him spinning backwards off the Folkingham circuit through a pile of steel scaffolding stacked by Air Ministry contractors who had moved onto the site in order to restore it to operational status as a Thor nuclear missile site. After more than a decade at Folkingham Aerodrome, BRM had been given notice to quit.

Tony: Since so much pressure seemed to be building up against us I think BRM at that point was more united as an organization than it had ever been. Everybody was on the same side – itself a rare state of affairs – and the incentive to excel was tremendous!

May 31, 1959 – Dutch Grand Prix, Zandvoort – 75 laps, 195.41 miles

During the team's private pre-race testing at the Dutch seaside circuit the week before the race, Moss had covered 105 laps at very high speed. The car seemed admirably suited to the course and Moss had unofficially improved the lap record. During race week, Walker Racing then ran Moss in their Cooper-Climax, and he was soon lapping almost – but not quite – as quickly as he had in the BRM.

Official practice began at 4.30 Friday afternoon, and although spare cars were available to both teams the organizers refused to accept any more than two entries each from both BRM and Cooper – the KNAC was not a wealthy club, and there was simply no more start money available. In any case, they felt there were enough green cars in the field, and so instead they accepted Dutchman Carel Godin de Beaufort's sports Porsche, triggering a terrific row – which the Club would win.

Moss then began driving the Walker Cooper incredibly

May 30, 1959 – The ORO garage, Zandvoort, pre-race Dutch Grand Prix preparation: Spaceframe 1959-spec Type 25 unveiled – that structurally infelicitous kinked top-right chassis longeron over the engine bay was demanded by practicality, to clear the Weber carburettor bell-mouths; note suspension pick-up and body mount bracketry as welded-on by 'Flash Alf' Martin, high-mounted steering rack, coolant swirl-pot and de-aerator with those distinctively BRM wafer-thin, flat, finger-gripped filler caps, riveted-on undertray and engine bay bulkhead, cockpit flank fuel tank just visible…Rear welded fuel tank skewered upon its bolt-together support frame, minimalist instrument panel, detail of co-axial coil-spring/damper suspension and sculptured rear brake caliper with 'bird's beak' cooling duct around the opposite side of that ventilated rear disc.

quickly, "…going at such a speed round the back swerves", 'Jenks' reported in *Motor Sport*, "…that it was beginning to look dangerous, even for Moss…but he had to keep an eye on the B.R.M. team as Bonnier was driving incredibly smoothly and quickly at the same time; Schell was working hard, but not getting anywhere near his team-mate". Moss finished the session with a best of 1:36.8, Bonnier a 1:37.6.

During Saturday practice most teams became concerned about tyre wear on the abrasive circuit, and several practised tyre-changing pit stops. BRM, using the regulation two mechanics and hide hammers to avoid damaging their aluminium wheel nuts, managed changes in under 30 seconds, predicting that on race day using copper hammers they could do it in 20 seconds. For the other teams with bolt-on wheels a tyre stop would have spelled disaster, including the Coopers. However, with their recent testing behind them BRM knew that it was unlikely that they would need to change. Possibly Stirling could read his BRM test experience across to a Cooper for wear, but if he could, he was not talking either.

After that pre-race test experience, the BRM Type 25s were

May 31, 1959 – Dutch Grand Prix, Zandvoort: Jo Bonnier made a superb start in '258' and here leads the field out of the first 180-degree turn at Tarzan, back behind the paddock and pits. Masten Gregory (Cooper) leads the pursuit from Ferrari, Schell's '259', Lotus and the rest…

being run on 15-inch rear wheels with 7.00-section tyres in place of their usual 16-inch size, which partly explains the tyre wear, but handling was improved on the smaller wheels – saving about 0.2sec per lap.

In the Walker Cooper, Moss whittled his times down to 1:36.2, Ferrari, Cooper and Lotus chased him, and then – as 'Jenks' reported:

"Bonnier went out with the B.R.M. and did 1min. 36.0sec dead…Before practice finished for lunch, Schell went out to try and get near Bonnier's time, but the best he could do was 1min 37.3sec."

In the final two-hour session that afternoon, Moss and the BRM team rested upon their laurels, while Brabham finally matched the Swede's time, but BRM was to start from pole position, Schell sixth fastest on the inside of row three.

Race day was dry and sunny, the Type 25s retaining 15-inch wheels. Tony – whose responsibility it was – knew there was little risk of requiring a tyre stop.

Bonnier immediately led through the first corner at *Tarzan*, but Masten Gregory's works Cooper cut ahead through the swerves behind the pits. Gregory and Bonnier drew out the length of the main straight from Brabham, while behind him seven cars were battling frantically over fourth position, including Schell, who was successively elbowed down a place each lap by Behra, Graham Hill and Moss, who had made a poor start.

On lap 12 Bonnier denied Gregory his line into the left-handed *Hunzerug* behind the pits, and accelerated away in the lead. Gregory's Cooper gearbox was jumping out of engagement.

On lap 15 Brabham took second place from his team-mate, and at 20 laps Bonnier held a 3sec lead over Brabham, Gregory was third, the length of the straight behind, and Behra's Ferrari fourth, blocking and baulking an enraged Moss through the swerving back stretch, then storming away from the Cooper along the straight. Stirling eventually passed the Frenchman on the outside at *Tarzan* on lap 24 and then tore into the leaders' third-of-a-lap advantage, proving how badly the Ferrari had delayed him.

1959 Dutch Grand Prix: Bonnier locking '258' over into the Hunzerug corner as the crouching Jack Brabham rushes ever closer in his Monaco GP-winning works Cooper-Climax.

the circuit, Jo was driving superbly, utterly impassive, but Moss was gaining all the time. So much depended upon the outcome I found the excitement almost unbearable..."

On lap 49 Moss out-braked Brabham's works Cooper into *Tarzan* and set about catching Bonnier for the lead. The dour Swede was driving with his typical smoothness, bearded face set, impassive. Moss closed, Brabham dropped back with his gearbox jumping out of second gear. As Bonnier began his 60th lap Moss was right on the BRM's tail. They were rushing up upon Behra to lap his Ferrari, and as the cars came together Moss took advantage of Bonnier being momentarily blocked, and cut by.

It seemed then to be all over – Moss must surely win, Bonnier and BRM second. Moss drew away, while Bonnier settled back to finish reliably, matching Schell's performance the previous year.

The Walker Cooper led the race ending lap 60, lap 61, and

Right: Lap 30 – Bernard Cahier captured this evocative shot as 'JoBo' flicks on opposite lock to correct an incipient tail-slide, clipping the inside verge at the Hunzerug, 'Black Jack's oversteering Cooper having just passed the BRM temporarily to take the lead. Note the Type 25's 1959-spec tail slots, and its single rear disc brake on the gearbox tail protruding into the airstream down below.

Brabham was inching closer to the leading BRM. By lap 30 he was on Bonnier's tail and he took the lead in a late-braking duel at the end of the straight. But Bonnier responded in kind, and out-braked the Australian into the *Hunzerug* four laps later to regain the lead.

During this duel, Moss gained on both of them. Gregory was falling back in fourth place, Behra was tiring, fifth, and Schell set to pass him, doing so on lap 37, only to abandon his car with the gearbox seized in second gear after 46 laps, when lying fifth behind Gregory. Harry disconsolately clambered out to watch his nominal 'number two' team-mate racing on, and on...

Moss had caught Brabham on the previous lap and was trying to find a way by, then Bonnier was shown a tyre-warning pit signal, but as oil and rubber had coated the circuit the wear rate had stabilized, his car felt good and he was happy.

Raymond Mays "...found it impossible to remain in the pits. I walked about watching the race from different points on

lap 62. But towards the end of lap 63 it was the green BRM's nose which appeared in the lead at the start of the main straight. Moss' Colotti gearbox had failed again...

'Jenks':

> Bonnier was now securely in first place and the B.R.M. pits hardly dare breathe as the car continued to reel off the laps, for already Schell had gone out with a seized gearbox, but the Swedish driver was more alive to the situation than anyone, and driving with perfect restraint and almost loving care for the car he completed the 75 laps amidst enormous enthusiasm, for if ever a team were due for a major victory, the B.R.M. team were. As Bonnier stopped after his lap of honour the B.R.M. sounded as healthy as ever and it had run a perfect race, driven by a new Grand Prix winner who had handled the car and all the situations that arose with remarkable coolness...

1959 Dutch Grand Prix: Four laps to go, 2.3sec lead over Brabham, Pat Carvath signals Bonnier as BRM's maiden Grande Epreuve victory draws agonizingly near. Tony offers a reassuring thumbs-up, Schell is behind him on the pit apron, Phil Ayliff tense to the right, Vic Barlow of Dunlop (jacket and tie) far right...

Victory: The historic moment as J.H. van Haaren of the organizing KNAC club drops the chequered flag, Jo Bonnier punches his gloved hand skyward in triumph – and '258' (still in superb order) secures BRM's first-ever World Championship Grand Prix victory.

Savouring the moment. Below left: A cheerful and philosophical Jack Brabham congratulating the coolly exultant Jo Bonnier. Below: Tony Rudd and Bonnier as the Anthems are played – right and proper British phlegm in triumph, no vulgar champagne showering pre-'67 when ex-BRM driver Dan Gurney and A.J.Foyt first drenched the photographers so uncouthly at Le Mans...

Jo had finished 14.2 seconds ahead of Brabham at a speed of 93.46mph.

RM: "After 10 years of effort and failure, and of narrow defeats, we had won our first World Championship event...He had never been out of first or second place and never made a mistake.

"My first reaction was to burst into tears of joy. This victory meant so much, all the world to Peter Berthon and me. Our mechanics danced a jig about us...Tavoni of Ferrari's, John Cooper, Colin Chapman and others...came up to say how thrilled they were, and we knew they meant it...We celebrated

that night in the *Bouwes Hotel*...at a party given by the Stanleys. Jean Behra came to join us after the dinner, and added his congratulations. The mechanics celebrated with us and with the dawn were seen being driven back to their hotel sitting on the roof of a lorry..."

Tony: For all of us at that time this was the best day of our racing lives. And amidst all the celebrations Jean Behra shyly came up to add his congratulations and he told me rather wistfully how he'd always felt sure our car would win a Grand Prix one day and how disappointed he was that he hadn't been driving it.

He was driving for Ferrari that season and was very unhappy there, not really fitting in at all with the way they went about things. He shook me warmly by the hand and told me to buy the mechanics a drink on him and when he let go and walked away I realized there was still something in my hand and I found he'd given us about £100 in Dutch *Guilders* – which was a lot of money in those days – and the mechanics certainly had a rare old celebration.

Meanwhile, 'Jenks' had ended his *Motor Sport* report with this pointed postscript:

> Shortly before the race the B.R.M. team were given a 'vote of no confidence' by Mr. A.G. Owen when he handed over two cars to the Alfred Moss/Ken Gregory team known as the British Racing Partnership, having been convinced that they would do better than the Bourne people. After the Dutch G.P. one could not help feeling that Bourne had 'cocked a snoot' at all concerned…

Bonnier's personal round-up of the season subsequently added startling perspective to both BRM's and his own maiden victory in this World Championship-qualifying Grand Prix race. He would explain to Owen:

> After Monte Carlo I went down to Sicily to drive the Targa Florio for Porsche. I spent twelve days there before the race in order to learn the course and prepare myself. I led the race overall and put up the fastest lap and, in spite of that we had to retire only a few miles from the finish. I feel that I had driven my best race ever. I tell you this, not in order to brag, but to give you the background to what happened at Zandvoort a week later.
>
> When I arrived at Zandvoort before practice I met Mr. Denis Druitt, who told me about the BRM BRP arrangement. Personally I did not mind this, and I very well understood your feelings, but I felt that the BRM camp would be in uproar.
>
> The same night I dined with Mr. Burthon and Schell, and we were both frankly told that we were no good, and that we did not know anything about driving, and that the BRM failure was entirely our fault. I did not say anything at the moment, as I only felt sorry for him, as I think he is a good designer. I still think, however, it was a little bit much in view of my performance a week earlier in the Targa Florio.
>
> Anyway, I was second fastest the first day of practice and put up f.t.d. the next day. The cars were absolutely perfect and it was a real pleasure to drive them. After we had won the race I felt very happy and in my childishness I thought this was the turning point. Unfortunately it proved to be entirely the other way round.
>
> There is no doubt that our success was due to the pressure that had been put on the team. The BRM:s wanted to show you and the BRP:s that they could do well, at the same time as they were scared of completely loosing [sic, and so very *Swedish*] your faith.
>
> For a long time I had asked them to enter only two cars in the races and bring a training car, which would give them more time for preparation. This proved to be right and with five long weeks to go, I was very hopeful for the G.P. of France.

Schell's view, meanwhile, was expressed like this:

> Zandvoort – Bonnier's car was going very well and the training Schell's car was bad on road holding because it was his own car which was damaged at Monte Carlo.
>
> RACE: Bonnier was in the lead and was going very well till Moss start catching up Two to Three seconds a lap and broke down. Schell's car broke down on the 50th lap when in Third position. – minor exaggeration here, he was really running fifth, having completed only 46 laps.
>
> REASONS: GEARBOX SEIZED
>
> Who is to blame for this failure of the gear box?
>
> When the car went back to BOURNE we found out that one of the mechanic connected the oil pipies [sic] the wrong way into the gear box.
>
> This victory din't [sic] prove anything as the average of the winning B.R.M. was slower than BERHA [sic] and SCHELL last year.

Bonnier certainly had a point when he described how the team had been energized by the BRP deal. Spear to Owen, June 3, 1958:

> At Zandvoort the mechanics and Tony Rudd expressed to me their very great fears over the B.R.P. venture. They had to put up with a great deal of leg-pulling from other equipes. I have a strong suspicion that the project was not put over to them very well by R.M. last week. The basic argument used to them was that Stirling Moss and his associates were not satisfied with the preparation of cars and that that was the only point worrying them. I explained to the Head Mechanic, Ayliffe and Rudd that this was not so and that there were a large number of factors involved.
>
> I have explained as much as was appropriate of your feelings and pointed out that as yet no details have been finalised, although a general agreement on principles had been reached…

Spear was nettled to hear that Rivers Fletcher had approached the mechanics the night before the race "firstly to ask them generally what they felt about things and secondly, to see who would like to go and work for Alfred Moss. This caused quite an upset…". Spear felt that Rivers, having merely made the introductions between BRP and BRM, should then have stepped out of the picture.

That same day, Alfred Owen received the following from 'Pa' Moss, a diplomatic masterpiece which at a stroke cut the ground from beneath the feet of RM and PB's major objections to their Chairman's proposed deal with BRP, while being couched in sufficiently equivocal terms to present a most generous recognition of Bourne's newfound *Grande Epreuve*-winning stature.

'Pa' Moss wished first to:

...congratulate all concerned on the victory of the works B.R.M. at Zandvoort, a victory which must, to some degree, represent the fulfilment of many of your hopes over the past years.

I feel that in view of the negotiations which took place between us prior to Zandvoort and in view of this success it maybe necessary for us to review the arrangements which we have made...I feel it would be most unwise to jeopardise the chances of B.R.M. from a works point of view, at a time when the incentive for victory is probably higher than ever before. I have discussed this matter with Stirling at some length and he feels that, if the British Racing Partnership were to be handed over two cars and a spare engine plus mechanics and a transporter from Bourne, this would seriously weaken the team's chances and may split the available resources of Bourne to such a degree that neither Bourne nor ourselves would be sufficiently equipped to achieve victory.

On the other hand, if the British Racing Partnership were purely to retain the present car [chassis No. 10] – selected, Tony felt, on merit as a new car – "and to prepare and enter the car independent of Bourne without any further call upon their services other than in the preparation of its engine, and possibly its gearbox, I feel this would have no harmful effect upon Bourne or its chances, and would, in fact, continue to provide a competitive incentive for the future.

We are of the opinion that we are able to employ sufficient direct labour of a suitable nature to assist (our chief mechanic) Mr. Robinson in the preparation of a single car, the main difference of this revised suggestion is that if Stirling chooses to drive a B.R.M. he would now be free to choose either a B.R.M. prepared by Bourne or the car prepared by ourselves, whereas if the British Racing Partnership have two cars plus a spare engine this would not be possible.

Finally, there is no doubt in my mind that this situation would be welcome at Bourne in promoting the friendly spirit of competition, which I think is desirable for the continued success of B.R.M. this year, which is the common objective of us all...

Although Ken Gregory recalls how the elder Moss was always...a very clipped and to-the-point character who normally said exactly what he thought and seldom wrote letters to anyone, never mind anything so long and eloquent, I suspect this one was a joint BRP and Stirling effort, which Alfred simply signed!

Irrespective, BRP's eloquence worked just fine.

In mid-June they met at Rubery Owen's London office, Kent House, and the arrangement outlined above was confirmed. Owen wrote to 'Pa' Moss on June 17:

I want to express my appreciation of your proposals which will not jeopardise Bourne one iota in their preparation of the Cars. My one great hope is that we shall persuade Stirling to drive the B.R.M. both now and in the future. May I, at the same time, express

ZANDVOORT – THE INSIDE STORY

Rivers Fletcher's report of BRM's victory in the 1959 Dutch GP in *ORMA Bulletin No. 33* enthused:

The cars were racing against the cream of drivers and machines... Jo Bonnier's pole position thoroughly shocked the opposition. Nearly all the Grand Prix 'circus' seemed to be forecasting a B.R.M. win. The B.R.M. cars were put away early after practice with just nothing to do to them... altogether there was an air of confidence about the whole equipe...Bonnier's victory was immensely popular... The mechanics were absolutely jubilant and it was a pleasure to see that when Tony Rudd lifted the bonnet of the winning car the engine was as immaculately clean as when it had started the race...

This telling final comment was absolutely true, and is confirmed by ORO's own strip-down report on what went on inside the cars that day... This historic document read as follows:

GRAND PRIX OF HOLLAND – ZANDVOORT
31st May, 1959

J. BONNIER'S CAR, RACE No. 7:

Total mileage including practice – 294.

Post Race Check – 3 galls. remaining in rear tank; 2 in side tanks; oil consumption 6 pints. No water lost; no engine external oil leaks whatever; slight oil leak from gearbox selector shaft. Tyre wear – L.H. front 60% tread worn; R.H. front 25% tread worn; L.H. rear 75% tread worn; R.H. rear 50%. No oil in cockpit; rev. counter tell-tale at 7,900r.p.m.; oil pressure 80; water temperature 70, 75°. Driver complained of vibration in steering wheel. Heavy sand deposits in air intakes.

ROAD TEST:

Pulled 7,800r.p.m. in top at Folkingham; performance slightly better than when car was tested prior to departure. Some vibration felt in pedals 5,000 to 4,000r.p.m. decelerating, due to wear in front propshaft universal joint; no vibration at all at full throttle above 5,000r.p.m. but some vibration felt in steering wheel around 7,000r.p.m. part throttle, due to front and rear

every hope that the friendliest of spirits will exist between Bourne and B.R.P.

He added:

I am sure you will understand when I say I wish I had more time to give to racing venture [*sic*] but with all my business responsibilities and my determination to keep my finger on the pulse together with Local Authority work I am prevented from giving as much time as I would like. Nevertheless, I am behind it all and keen to keep in close touch whenever I can.

carburettor butterflies not being in alignment – due to heavy wear of front carburettor operating rod ball ends, probably due to ingress of sand. Brakes good; road holding, etc., all normal. Clutch very rough in operation, particularly at low r.p.m. Reverse stop spring very weak.

BRAKE WEAR:

All discs in good condition, only lightly scored; fit for further use.

Total including practice and race:

Front L.H.S. outer .060"   Inner .050" tapered
       R.H.S. inner .065" tapered Outer .065" tapered

Rear Front .120"
     Rear .125"

GEARBOX to Bourne for Strip – Superficial check indicates box in very good condition.

Engine to Shop for Strip – Clutch Plate teeth – teeth on drum and output shaft, particularly latter, very badly worn. Clutch spider cracked across withdrawal shaft bosses. Pistons scored on sides – no signs of valves touching – heavier carbon deposits than usual. Most rings feathered, B.1196 inlet valves all guttered, rotators free – 1958 timing gears in good condition. Bearings very slightly scored – can be replaced.

Some minor body cracks, lower edge of cockpit section – one crack under nose, but body in generally better condition than usual.

Propshaft universal end floats, front .012" x .006" with .022" T.I.R. run out (inc. end float) .012" end float bearings spread .010". Rear .006" x .006" run out .012" (in end floats).

Centre bearing alignment changes .005" with full rear and empty side tanks to full side empty rear. Changes .002" with full to empty rear tank with empty sides.

Inner L.H. track rod ball badly scored and picked up.

4th June, 1959

And Schell's sister car:

POST ZANDVOORT, 1959

H. SCHELL'S CAR, No. 6:
202 miles, including practice.
    Post Race Check – 10 to 11 galls. remaining in rear tank; oil consumption 7 pints; no water lost. Slight engine oil leak from rear main bearing; moderate oil leak from gearbox selector shaft. Rev. counter tell-tale at 8,200. Seized in first gear. Carburettor lower side panel adrift, section pulled out, complete with rear Djus [*sic* – means Dzus fastener] …spring broken on front lower djus, tufts of grass and earth embedded around bracket, etc., around front carburettor side, indicating panel had been damaged by running over grass, etc. (Note: After race several large clods of turf noticed on the road between Scheiolak corner [*sic*, actually *Schievlak*] and the woods – said to have been dislodged by Brooks early in the race.)
    Driver reported unusual noises on L.H. curves – thought transmission was in trouble. Slight traces of oil from rear engine breather.

BRAKE WEAR:

All discs in good condition, only lightly scored and fit for further use.

Front L.H.S. Outer .040" tapered Inner .040"
       R.H.S. Inner .040" tapered Outer .030"
Rear: Front .070"
      Rear .050"

GEARBOX – sent to Bourne for investigation. Usual quantity of oil drained from Box; internal condition indicates general oil shortage – oil pump in working order.
ENGINE – to Shop for Strip. Preliminary examination shows engine in very good condition, particularly latest type pistons and B.1555 inlet valves – no tipping or other usual seat faults, rotators free. Clutch stalk quill broken. Sintering breaking upon centre plate; drum teeth badly worn. Clutch spider cracked across withdrawal race bosses. Top compression ring broken in two pieces, No. 3 piston; no serious damage to pistons.
    Heavy oil leak from N.S. old type rack end fitting.

Propshaft within running limits, i.e., .006".

Steering box mounting cracked R.H.S.

4th June, 1959

Car '2510' had been handed over to BRP and delivered to their London workshops in Lots Road, Chelsea, as Ken Gregory would recall: "I was considerably stirred when the BRM lorry arrived at Chelsea, and the car was wheeled in…Hardly twelve months earlier Alfred Moss and I had begun our partnership with one Formula 2 Cooper, and now here we were preparing a full-blown Formula 1 car, for Stirling to drive…*the* test for all our ideals of ultra-careful preparation and good workmanship."

The car "was stripped to the bare chassis and completely rebuilt. Everything possible was renewed, and all components carefully checked for faults. The rather grim dark green paintwork was removed, and the car repainted in the BRP colours of pale green, with white wheels…".

It was also during June that PB met Alfred Owen and ran his suggestions for building a prototype rear-engined BRM past him. In mid-month, as he recalls, Tony was detailed to commence design and construction: I think it was felt at this time that I was having rather too much to say for myself, and getting too big for my boots. Certainly I was convinced that I was a suspension design genius, but the result of all this was that they did not involve me in design at all, but merely set me to organize the team which built the car.

Of course, our newfound unity in face of the BRP threat had certainly been a major factor in winning at Zandvoort, and it definitely changed the course of BRM history – or perhaps *prevented* it being changed too radically. But immediately after the win we all relaxed. Now we were off to Reims for the French GP, to run three works cars against Moss in BRP's. With the Zandvoort win we had clearly found the magic so we would now continue to win automatically.

And, of course, it didn't work like that.

July 5, 1959 – *Grand Prix de l'ACF*, Reims-Gueux – 50 laps, 258 miles

The BRP team's '2510' emerged repainted and with its gateless gearchange modified to Moss' preference, with a reverse lock-out catch. Its engine was fresh from Bourne, cared for by a works mechanic seconded to BRP. The Chelsea team also fielded two Cooper-Borgwards for the supporting Formula 2 race, while ORO's works team comprised two race cars and a spare, the brand-new '2511' just completed. Although the third car had been intended only as a T-car, and completed over 50 practice laps, it was then fitted with a fresh engine and run in what would prove to be an immensely gruelling Grand Prix race.

Practice began at Reims-Gueux at 4pm on the Wednesday, the conditions being warm and dry, with a breeze blowing down the long hill towards Thillois Hairpin – ideal for fast times. Schell was out early on – not in the BRM but in his own brand-new F2 Cooper-Climax. At 6pm the F1 session commenced, the immediate target being Hawthorn's existing lap record of 2:24.9.

Schell went out first in the BRM, and promptly clocked 2:24.3, then followed up with a 2:23.5 – a startling improvement in performance, but still outside Hawthorn's '21.7 1958 pole time. Moss clocked '23.3 during his first run in the pale-green BRP-BRM, then unofficially broke the record

at 2:22.4, but Tony Brooks put the BRM performances in stark perspective, and lent weight to Ferrari's claims of over 290bhp, with 2:19.7, followed by a '19.6, then '19.4. "…which made Moss and his B.R.M. look as sick as its colour" as one report put it.

Moss had his tailored seat removed from the pale-green '2510' and fitted instead into the works spare car, practising in it so extensively that PB was forced to approach Ken Gregory and 'Pa' Moss to ask: "Please could we have our car back before your man wears it out…?"

Trying really hard in '2510' Moss then managed 2:20.5, followed by a '19.9. Meanwhile, Bonnier and Schell were both lapping in 2:21s.

The following day's two-hour F1 session ran again from 6 to 8pm, BRP not running '2510' as Moss considered "it reached its limit yesterday". Bourne's three Type 25s were all out, with Flockhart running the spare '2511' which the organizers had now accepted for the race, so in final Friday practice a fresh engine was fitted and Flockhart's times counted.

Moss waited until the track was clear and the evening had cooled, and he lapped on both 15in and 16in wheels, intentionally overshooting the Thillois Hairpin, going around the island at the road junction there to make a virtual drag start out of the return road to run a few extra rpm across the timing line to start his next flying lap. He found as much as

July 5, 1959 – Grand Prix de l'ACF, Reims-Gueux: Ron Flockhart was a last-minute extra entry in ORO's 'spare car', the latest '2511' with its 'small tail' tucked-under body, which style it shared with '2510', the BRP car of Moss. Ron would finish sixth.

Screaming into the braking area for the Muizon corner out on the back stretch of the circuit, in roasting heat, Phil Hill's Fantuzzi-bodied Ferrari Dino 246 leads Moss' BRP-entered pale-green '2510'.

an extra 300rpm that way, but the rest of the course was slower than in previous sessions, and he could not improve on '20-dead.

Brooks' 2:19.4 retained pole for Ferrari, with Brabham's Cooper and Phil Hill's sister Ferrari completing the front row, Moss being fourth fastest on row two, while Bonnier's '258' was sixth with 2:20.6 on the inside of row three, Schell's '259' ninth on '21.5 and Flockhart's '2511' 13th on row five with a '23.4.

Following his torrid Reims weekend for BRM the previous year, Jean Behra – driving for Ferrari this time – had again demanded a junior team-mate's car after setting slow times. He had taken over Gendebien's, was in a highly agitated state and the race would end for him in professional disaster as he felled team manager Tavoni with a punch, which got him fired by Ferrari.

Tony: At Reims we failed to appreciate that our car's strong point was its exceptional roadholding and brakes, but it had neither tremendous power nor a very good shape aerodynamically, despite its being such a handsome car. Its frontal area was large, it generated high lift and high drag, and although we had as much horsepower as the previous season's Vanwall, that car had a better shape and had always left us trailing along the straights. In corners we were nearly as good and under brakes probably better – when they worked. After the elation of Zandvoort, Reims was about to destroy our complacency, and Bonnier of course became very confused by this whole business – particularly since he had qualified on pole in Holland; from celebrated new ace to also-ran in just two weeks…

The Champagne circuit was bathed in broiling sunshine on race day, the thermometer hovering around the 100°F mark, the track surface reaching 130°. Before the race somebody remarked: "*I* wouldn't like to be a racing driver today" – to which someone else responded: "I wouldn't like to be a racing *tyre* today!" Both had a point…

As 'Toto' Roche flagged the race away in his usual comic-cuts style, Brooks shot into the lead he would hold throughout, and Behra was left on the grid with his Ferrari's engine stalled. Moss' pale green BRM was running in Brooks' slipstream, and Schell and Bonnier passed the pits 6-7. In midfield, Flockhart was involved in a gaggle of cars disputing ninth place. Masten Gregory's works Cooper was fast enough on the long straights to tow past Moss, and on the next lap both Trintignant's and Brabham's Coopers went by. "The speed of the Climax-engined Coopers was surprising everyone, especially B.R.M. and Ferrari drivers…"

After five laps Brooks led three Coopers, Moss and Phil Hill's sister Ferrari. After a gap Bonnier and Schell slammed by in close company.

Moss lowered the lap record to 2:23.6, while several drivers stopped for attention to damage – both vehicular and personal – caused by flying granite chips. Then Bonnier went missing and was seen to have stopped at Thillois. Despite the roasting heat he began to push his car the undulating mile to the pits.

Moss was running fourth, behind Brooks, Trintignant's Walker Cooper and Brabham's works car. Phil Hill began to press the BRP-BRM and Behra had ripped through the field to occupy sixth place; Schell was ninth and Flockhart 11th. On lap 12 Schell slithered off into a roadside field, losing over

a lap in regaining the circuit. Then Phil Hill displaced Moss – who was troubled by an inoperative clutch.

On lap 20 Trintignant spun and stalled on melted tar at Thillois. Ambient temperature even in the shaded pits was 100°F, in the open it was hovering around 110! Starting lap 24 Behra passed Moss and Phil Hill for third place, but ending lap 25 he tried to take second place from Brabham under braking into Thillois, overshot and slithered around the grass triangle, dropping to fourth. Only eight cars remained on the leader's lap, the last being Flockhart's BRM. On lap 29 Behra's Ferrari V6 engine faltered badly, Moss inheriting fourth place, while Behra struggled on to complete the three more laps necessary to qualify as a finisher.

Flockhart suddenly recoiled in his cockpit as a flying stone shattered the left lens of his goggles, a sliver of glass penetrating his eyeball. He clawed the goggles from his face and pressed on, only to be struck and cut by another stone.

With 14 of the 50 laps remaining, Moss made his move, closing on the near-exhausted Phil Hill and Brabham ahead of him. Phil was driving in a daze, broadsiding away from the two tight corners, his judgment of braking distances completely shot. On lap 38 Moss passed Brabham for third place, the Australian offering no resistance, then on lap 40 Stirling set a new lap record at 2:22.8 – 209.207km/h – and attacked Hill's second place, but at the end of lap 43 – no Moss…

He had spun on melted tar at Thillois, and with the BRM's clutch inoperative was unable to prevent its engine stalling. He tried hard to restart the car, building up impetus before scrambling into the high-cowled cockpit and crunching-in second gear. He tried repeatedly, tried until exhausted, but it was quite impossible to restart unaided and he finally collapsed on the trackside verge, where journalist friends and photographers revived him with showers of mineral water.

Knowing it would cause disqualification, he eventually had the car push-started by the marshals, and simply drove the basically still-healthy '2510' back to the pits to retire.

The *Motor Sport* report read:

> The scene at the pits when the race was over was indescribable, with prostrate drivers everywhere, many of them cut and bleeding from flying stones and lumps of molten tar; some lucky enough to be able to relax, others having to recover sufficient energy to start in the F2 race which was due to follow…!

Moss ran the equipe Walker Cooper-Borgward in that event, and won it…

Bonnier's view:

> In spite of Schell's and my wishes, three cars were entered for the French G.P.
>
> As expected our cars were slower than the others but they ran very well otherwise, so we hoped to be somewhere in the money. It did not turn out this way, however, as a very high temperature caused the water to overheat. Due to a sudden increase in water temperature, I took the escape road and stalled the engine. After pushing the car almost a mile the mechanics found out that they could not do anything to get the car restarted.

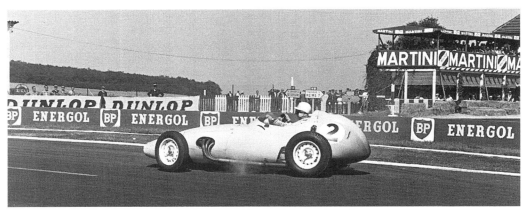

1959 Grand Prix de l'ACF: Moss' clutchless '2510' completes the half-spin under braking on melting tar at Thillois, which cost the British star a fine chance of a high-scoring finish in the BRP BRM – but Tony Brooks proved quite uncatchable that day in the works Ferrari V6.

Stirling clambered out and pushed '2510' back into the slip road to face it in the right direction for an attempted unassisted restart.

Except the tendency the BRM has to loose [sic] power in hot weather, I felt that my failure to finish was mainly my own fault.

Schell, who finished seventh, 3 laps behind the winner, reported:

Reims – First day of training the car was going rather well, best time at training.
Second day the car was going slower.
Race: the car was going nicely except very slow compare to the Ferrarris [sic].

He really put his back into getting the car rolling, then attempted to jump back in, snatch a gear and bump-start it. But in such heat, on sticky tar – its bubbles cracking and popping beneath his feet – and with the Type 25's cockpit enclosure he stood no chance…

Exhaustion won, even the super-fit Moss collapsing beaten on the infield verge. Dousing with bottled mineral water revived him and he accepted an assisted push-start, which disqualified him, to bring '2510' back to the paddock…

Fuel troubles when coming out of fast right hand curves.

Schell went off the road when a stone hit his eyes and lost a lot of time.

BRM finished 6th seventh and eight after Moss spun. No power in the Engine WHY?

Peter Spear's report observed:

A lot happened at this race, but I think it can be summarised broadly as follows:

1. The B.R.P./B.R.M. relationships were very good indeed. On one occasion their Head Mechanic tried to get a bit of extra work done, but it was more a matter of enthusiasm than awkwardness.

2. We got 6th, 7th and 8th places officially and the defeat was an honourable one. Moss would have been second but freely admits he made a mistake and had to take the escape road.

3. Bonnier's engine failed, we believe, due to Wills ring failure. [A ring had failed but as a result of overheating, due to loss of coolant from a cracked aluminium side water pipe.] He pushed the car a mile under terrible heat conditions. It was over 100°F in the shade of the Pits.

4. Both Ron and Harry Schell smashed two pairs of goggles during the race with flying stones. Everyone had trouble with granite chips on a badly-made part of the circuit. Trintignant has three cuts on his forehead, Behra one, and plenty of other people were damaged. Both Harry and Ron cut their left eyeballs. Ron had a piece of glass literally in his eyeball for a considerable portion of the race, otherwise he would have been at least fifth if not fourth, because even with blurred vision he drove quite reasonably. Schell lost 500secs. with a spin and a penalisation for assistance in starting. He was told to keep running because of the possibility of other cars failing.

5. Both Ron and Stirling had a linkage failure on the clutch pedal and both drove most of the race not using the clutch, which both are used to doing and are not perturbed about.

Spear's next point perhaps raised a brief smile on the Chairman's face, regarding Mrs Berthon:

6. Lorna came on the Saturday but, to be fair, was not much of a nuisance…

Moss again elected to drive '2510' in preference to the Walker Cooper for the British GP at Aintree, but the race would provide further disappointment, as ORMA were told: "…all the engines were a little down on power. After Reims all the engines were stripped and quite a lot of damage had been caused inside, particularly to valves and valve seats, owing to the enormous number of little bits of stone etc. that had gone through the engines at Reims. There was not time between Reims and Aintree to make good all this damage and to reseat engines…". Cooper-Climax did not share this problem.

July 18, 1959 – RAC British Grand Prix, Aintree – 75 laps, 225 miles

Moss in the pale green BRM set fastest time in first Thursday practice at 2:08.4, while Schell ('257'), Bonnier ('258') and Flockhart ('259') ran the works Type 25s. Jack Brabham took pole position for Cooper at 1:58.0, flanked by Roy Salvadori's Aston Martin DBR4 on the same time and Schell on the outside of the front row with a '59.2. Moss was seventh fastest in the centre of row three with a '59.6, Bonnier 10th on two minutes dead and Flockhart 11th, 0.2sec slower.

Brabham made the best race start to lead from Schell and Bonnier, with Moss initially sixth. By 10 laps Moss was through into second place, pursuing Brabham's Cooper, with Schell third and Bonnier locked in combat with the Coopers of McLaren and Gregory.

On lap 17 the Cooper's lead was 17sec from the pale-green BRM, but Moss was speeding up as his car's fuel load diminished and the tyres wore down. Schell was battling for third place with Trintignant and as they slowed each other up so McLaren was catching them in his works Cooper.

Moss set a new lap record of 1:58.6 on lap 24, whittling 2sec off Brabham's lead. McLaren was up into third ahead of Trintignant and Schell. Moss then lowered his lap time to 1:58.0, but Brabham was able to maintain a 14-16sec lead. By lap 35 he was matching Moss' times, while Bonnier had not featured until – ending lap 37 – his BRM stammered onto idle as its throttle linkage parted and he coasted into retirement.

Moss closed to within 12 seconds of Brabham, "but it was taking all his skill to reduce this distance by a few tenths of seconds, and he had the B.R.M. in some pretty wild-looking full-lock slides…".

McLaren was firmly third, ahead of Schell. As Moss – who had started on part-worn tyres to obtain maximum grip – completed his 50th lap the gap was down to 10sec, but he then shot into the BRP pit and had his car's left-rear wheel changed, rejoining after a 31sec stop. Dunlop had estimated the tyres would survive race distance, but had not allowed for Moss improving upon his fastest practice time by 2sec. The BRM was now 51sec behind Brabham, whose Cooper was not wearing its tyres at the same rate, despite the Australian's luridly tail-wagging cornering style.

In the ORO pit Tony Rudd and his men were making disparaging comments on the time it took BRP to change Moss' wheel. Confident they could have done it quicker, and with Schell lonely and unchallenged in fourth place, they decided to make their point. Tony gave Schell the 'IN' signal and as the puzzled driver came flurrying angrily into the pit to ask what the Hell was going on the mechanics flung a jack beneath the car and began pounding away at the hub-nut. Harry objected, bawling it was unnecessary, the tyres were fine. He put his hand out on the tyre and received a sharp rap from the wheel-hammer for his pains. The fresh wheel was hammered home, '259' thumped back down off the jack and Harry – still mystified – tore back into the race. Stop time 18secs, position retained; a small but savoured victory for ORO that day…

At 54 laps Brabham still led Moss by 50 seconds, McLaren

July 18, 1959 – British Grand Prix, Aintree: Moss power-sliding the BRP-prepared and entered car '2510' in vain pursuit of Jack Brabham's fleeing rear-engined Cooper-Climax. Note the revised – and complete – BRM badge on the pale-green car's nose, complete with Rubery Owen & Co's eagle emblem – a Roc. The wheels were white. Above: Harry Schell in his favourite '257' at Aintree, wondering where his rivals have got to. He was furious to be called in for an unnecessary wheel change – but BRM pride was riding on it…

Imperturbable, unfathomable – the patrician Swede Jo Bonnier retired his Zandvoort-winning '258' at Aintree with throttle linkage adrift, after running third.

was a distant third, Schell an even more distant fourth. Flockhart should have been eighth, but he had spun out in the country at Village Corner, dropped the car into a shallow ditch and stalled. His cockpit was coated in oil, the pressure gauge having blown, spreading lubricant over the foot pedals.

On lap 59 Moss clocked 1:57.8, a new record, the gap to the leading Cooper was down to 46 seconds and he continued to close at 2sec per lap. With bolt-on wheels there was no question of Cooper being able to make a competitive in-race tyre change, but Brabham had the situation under perfect control. On lap 65 Schell was called in to have the left-rear tyre changed. With nine laps to go the Brabham-Moss gap was down to 32 seconds, but Stirling felt his engine hesitate twice and, recognizing fuel starvation, he rushed unexpectedly into the BRP pit for extra fuel. Five gallons were thrown into the tail tank, the car was pushed off, but did not fire immediately as Moss had left the fuel tap switched to side tanks. McLaren was closing fast in third place, the tap was flicked to tail tank and the P25 engine fired as the Cooper fled by into second place behind its team leader.

By this time Brabham had lapped Schell, so these two were the only others on the leader's lap. Moss was quickly up onto

McLaren's tail, he passed on the next lap, but could not get away from the young New Zealander. On lap 71 Bruce drew alongside the BRM passing the pits. Next time round they were barely a foot apart, and as they accelerated towards the finish line on the final lap photographers were blocking the roadway there leaving only space for one car, and Stirling aimed straight at their legs on the right of the road, forcing them to jump back, actually making space for Bruce to attempt a pass on the left. Jack Brabham won, while the BRP-BRM and number two Cooper blurred across the line as one – 0.2sec being the official margin between Moss' second place and Bruce's third. Schell was fourth, one lap behind.

Moss and McLaren shared fastest race lap – on lap 75 – at 1:57.0, 92.31mph.

Next day at Chelsea, BRP's mechanics carefully drained the remaining fuel from '2510', 10 gallons 2 pints of it. Since five gallons had been added in that precautionary stop there would still have been over five gallons remaining had Stirling maintained his pursuit of Brabham's leading Cooper. He could, perhaps, have caught and passed it. So why had his engine starved?

Practice had indicated the Type 25s' fuel consumption as

being 8.9 miles per gallon, so the corresponding amount, plus a 5-gallon margin for warming-up and errors, had been loaded pre-race. Stirling had found that he preferred the car's handling with a larger load in the much lower midship tanks, and less in the high tail tank into which they vented. To top-up the three tanks, one in the tail and one each side of the cockpit, fuel filled through the higher-floored tail tank from which it drained down into the side cells. Once they were full, the tail tank itself would begin to fill. A three-position fuel cock on the floor between the driver's legs permitted him to select from which tank the engine would draw.

Moss had been instructed to run on '2510''s side tanks until Tony Robinson signalled him to switch to the tail tank, which should then have sustained the car to the finish. But when he switched to the tail tank, some fuel had surged through the air-bleed pipes into the side tanks. The engine had misfired and faltered, Stirling had tried switching back onto the side tanks which should have been empty, and it picked-up again – thoroughly confusing him. Hence his precautionary stop.

RM: "Before the race BRP had checked with us about the fuel load. They put in the same quantity as us, but whereas we always filled the back tank and put the balance in the side tanks, Stirling preferred his car with the back tank about three-quarters full, and some of this fuel had surged through to the side tanks…"

Bonnier's view of this British GP was remarkably balanced:

> In the beginning of the season it was clearly said that there were three races where we absolutely had to do well – Zandvoort, Aintree and Portugal.
>
> It had started well at Zandvoort and in view of our experience from the Aintree 200, we were optimistic about our chances in the British G.P.
>
> In spite of some very inaccurate time keepers, practice went fairly well. We seemed, however, to be down on power since the April meeting, a tendency that had been increasing from race to race.
>
> The race went fairly well with Moss finishing second and Schell fourth. My own car, however, was in pretty bad shape. After I had been running third for some time in the beginning of the race, my rear brake started locking up and I had to slow down which lost me two places. It was later found out that the disc itself was moving. I do not know whose fault it could have been, but I imagine with a more thorough preparation it could not have happened. As it turned out it did not matter as when half the race was run, my throttle pedal broke, which I imagine was just bad luck.

Schell's view was impressively factual and concise:

> Aintree – British GP
> Training: "3 BRM"
> Schell in first row
> Bonnier in second
> Moss in third
> The car was going rather well the day of the race except for fuel troubles for Schell: coming out of the

right hand corners.
> Moss finished second
> Schell fourth
> Bonnier broke down.

Immediately after Aintree, PB, Jo Bonnier and Vic Barlow of Dunlop flew out to Berlin, where a small ORO crew awaited them with '2511' and a stack of alternative Dunlop racing tyres. The German GP was about to be held on the city's daunting AVUS speedway. Barlow was gravely concerned about the effects of high speeds and high G-loadings upon his tyres generated around the AVUS banking. Bonnier had considerable racing experience there and since the pre-Dutch GP Zandvoort test had proved so fruitful ORO was again adopting the right approach to modern GP racing.

To reach Berlin by road required use of the corridor *autobahn* through East Germany and it was quite a dramatic – but trouble-free – experience for the BRM boys as they drove the Lodestar through Communist territory via the Cold War frontier checks.

These tests were successful, and resulted in Dunlop producing a special batch of tyres modified with specially thin treads to restrict temperature build-up. The Grand Prix was in any case to be run in two Heats with an eye upon tyre distress, and two suitably-adapted Type 25s – '258' and '259' – were flown-out in an Eagle C54 freighter to join '2511' (earmarked as spare) for race weekend, the team being better-prepared than any other for AVUS' challenge.

August 2, 1959 – German Grand Prix, AVUS, Berlin – Two 30-lap Heats, 309.46 miles

Financial and political manoeuvrings within the German clubs had led to the traditional Nurburgring being abandoned as the home of the German GP, and this race being run instead at AVUS. The track comprised two legs of prototype *autobahn*, linked at the North Turn by a vast wide-radius brick-built banking, and at the South Turn by a flat, ungraded loop. The organizing AvD foresaw average lap speeds of around 150mph and over-rode the standing regulations for FIA World Championship races by arranging their event into two one-hour Heats, the overall result being decided by the addition of drivers' results from each, only finishers in the first Heat being allowed to start the second. Race regulations specifically forbade any attempt at streamlining the wheels, so the entire entry arrived in effective 'Nurburgring' form, apart from further-stiffened suspensions, high axle ratios and engines tuned for peak-revolution, flat-out speed.

Only Schell and Bonnier were to drive the works cars, while BRP's '2510' reappeared, but Moss had elected to drive the Walker Cooper instead, 'Pa' Moss and Ken Gregory doing a deal with the organizers to run Hans Herrmann in his home GP.

Formula 1 cars had last competed at AVUS in 1954, so the old record of 2:13.4 was lowered with ease during practice. The works Ferraris dominated the entire meeting, challenged only by the Coopers, while BRM and Lotus were both

July 31, 1959: Loading the BRMs onto the Eagle Airways C54 freight 'plane for the flight to Berlin's Tempelhof Airport, ready for the only postwar German Grand Prix ever to be run on the appallingly unsuitable autobahn 'speedway' of AVUS. Bonnier's '258' on the forklift, Willie standing by, 'Sheriff' seems concerned facing camera.

Below: Chained-down to hard points in the Douglas transport's cabin floor, the T-car is '257', race number '9' Bonnier's '258'...

overwhelmed on maximum speed.

During Saturday lunchtime's one-hour F1 session Moss clocked 2:6.8 in the blue Cooper, second fastest to Brooks' Ferrari Friday pole time of 2:5.9, while Dan Gurney's Ferrari and Brabham's works Cooper completed the front row. Both Bonnier and Schell set identical times of 2:10.3 – the Swede lining up seventh on the outside of row two, Schell on the inside of row three.

A 25-lap 1,500cc sports car race was run that grey and dank afternoon, in drizzle, and during it Jean Behra's private Porsche RSK duelled with the works cars driven by Jo Bonnier and 'Taffy' von Trips.

Tony: At AVUS, before Behra had gone out to practice in his Porsche I had quite a talk with him. He said he had heard that we were building a rear-engined car and he hoped very much indeed that he'd be invited back into the team to drive it in 1960. I think that had we had him, it would certainly have helped...

On the second lap of that sports car race, Fritz von d'Orey spun his Porsche coming off the North Turn banking, and pirouetted helplessly into the concrete wall fronting the grandstands, without hurting himself.

On the following lap, Godin de Beaufort lost his sister Porsche in the middle of the steep brick-paved banking, spun up to the top...and disappeared clean over the lip. To general astonishment the giant Dutchman reappeared unabashed at the paddock entrance, with the front of his car smashed in, having careered down the reverse side of the banking into the *Fahrerlager*, and then, having picked his way out between the parked transporters and F1 cars, he rejoined the race – the organizers spending two laps recovering from their amazement before black-flagging him.

Meanwhile, Jean Behra had been slipstreaming the two

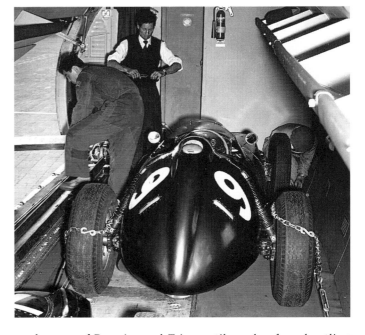

works cars of Bonnier and Trips until, on lap four, hurtling onto the slick banking, his RSK's rear tyres lost adhesion and the blue car spun tail-first up to the top of the banking, but in this case it smashed into a concrete block house upon the lip with thunderous impact. The unfortunate French ex-BRM driver was hurled from the cockpit high into the air, and died instantly as he struck, and snapped, a towering flag pole standing on the lip.

Bonnier and von Trips in their works RSKs then simply completed the distance, swapping places between themselves and treading gently round the fatal banking, Jo finally backing off to allow the German a home win. Behra's death threw the entire meeting into deep gloom.

The organizers subsequently decreed that should it rain during the Grand Prix a yellow light would be shown at the entry to the banking. If the light was on it was forbidden to run above the median white line, and overtaking within the banking area would also be forbidden.

The weekend was becoming a nightmare. RM: "Everyone connected with the team had to have a red cord around the wrist, sealed with a lead seal embossed with the crest of the AvD. We were told that as we had flown out, and consequently had no transport vehicles, we could drive the cars to and from the course. At first the police objected…this contravened the traffic laws. Then they relented, and escorted us to and from practice, until another team outpaced their police escort, who promptly withdrew the privilege, insisting on cars being towed or carried in lorries…"

The Formula 1 cars had to be removed speedily after practice to make way for the sports cars arriving for the next session, authority insisting they use a spectator overflow exit, but forgetting that they opened onto a flight of steps. The Berlin police chief had also stipulated a limit of only three pit passes per car – including one for the driver – while the pits were separated from the paddock by almost a mile, with myriad pass checks in between.

Above all, the pits themselves were in depressingly filthy condition…literally 'the pits'.

On race day RM and PB took up station there, while Tony Rudd marshalled his service crew at the paddock: "Louis and Mrs Stanley particularly wished to see the start", RM would later recall "…but they became very involved in an argument with a high-up Berlin police authority. Finally Louis Stanley completely out-Prussianed the jackbooted police and arrived at the track in good order…". Tony: During practice the star for me had been Rob Walker, who spoke very sharply in military German to the very senior Berlin police officer who had been causing so much trouble. It had an amazing effect. The man flushed and snapped to attention and clicked his heels. Apparently, Rob had ordered him to "Stand up *straight* when you're talking to *me*!" And, do you know, he did…

In Heat One Moss' Colotti transmission failed on only the second lap to ruin his return from BRM to the Walker Cooper while Brooks' Ferrari proved utterly dominant, pursued by the works Coopers of Gregory and Brabham. On lap three the fearless Masten Gregory took the lead, his Cooper drifting visibly all the long way round the North Wall. Meanwhile, Bonnier fell away from the leaders – his BRM simply outclassed, but also in trouble with (of all things) a wearing throttle linkage.

Brooks and Gurney in Ferraris and Gregory's bold Cooper took turns at leading while Schell had caught Bonnier in a bunch of cars disputing fifth place.

Flat-out on the straight after 24 laps, Gregory's tremendous challenge ended as a Climax big-end bolt broke and literally sawed his engine in two. The three Ferraris of Brooks, Gurney and Phil Hill emerged unchallenged – wailing round 1-2-3, while McLaren tucked his Cooper into their slipstream when the group he was duelling with – including Bonnier and Schell – was lapped. Bruce finished fourth, Schell fifth by 0.3sec from Trintignant's Walker Cooper, and Bonnier seventh, 2.9sec further back. Hans Herrmann, meanwhile, had driven a quiet race in the BRP-BRM, finishing eighth, 14 seconds behind Bonnier.

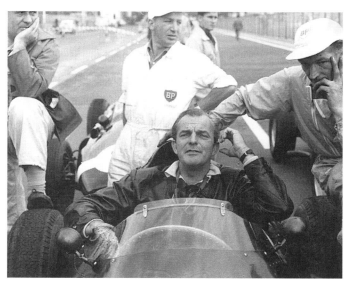

August 2, 1959, German Grand Prix, AVUS: Harry Schell waiting for the start in '259' – as opposed to his regular car '257' – the small Perspex lip added to the top of his windscreen having been applied to minimize buffeting around his head on this tremendously high-speed course.

Since Moss had elected to return to Rob Walker's rear-engined Cooper-Climax here at AVUS, BRP accepted attractive start money for Stirling's former Mercedes-Benz teammate Hans Herrmann to drive '2510' instead. Here he has the pale-green car hunched down hard against its bump stops on the fearsome brick-surfaced banking of AVUS' infamous North Wall – on which Jean Behra had just lost his life…

1959 German Grand Prix. Above left: Bernard Cahier's camera captures all three BRMs together on the North Wall banking, Schell's '259' leading Trintignant's Walker Cooper, McLaren's works car, Jo Bonnier's '258' and Hans Herrmann's '2510' hurtling as near flat-out as the drivers dared between the bowl's safety lines. Behra's crashing Porsche on the Saturday had hurled its driver against a flagpole similar to that in the foreground. Top: Herrmann's crash which destroyed '2510' at the South Curve – the BRM somersaulting after bursting through straw bales directing traffic off the autobahn stretch into this Sudkehre loop. Herrmann has already been thrown out as '2510' pinwheels to rest on its tail, its front end destroyed, radiator and oil cooler flailing skyward, left-rear wheel rim and tyre airborne. Herrmann scrambles to his feet, miraculously little harmed – shaken marshals running to his aid as the steam-shrouded wreck of '2510' has come to rest. Left: The shredded straw bale barrier which had launched '2510' in the background, Herrmann skidding to a halt on his heels and backside, watching '2510' as it bounces into history. The Sudkehre corner loops left to right across the foreground, then away again parallel to the outward leg visible here.

The starting grid for Heat Two comprised only nine cars, arranged in their finishing order from Heat One. During the half-hour interval between the heats, Bonnier's troublesome throttle linkage was part-replaced, while Harry Schell – terribly distressed by Behra's violent death the previous day – reported that his clutch had frozen. There was nothing the crew could do to free it as the plates had broken up and jammed, but Harry was determined to finish.

Judging the start carefully, the mechanics wheeled back his BRM, and with around 15 seconds to go before the flag was likely to fall they began a charge to push-start the car. Its engine fired and Harry drove up to the back of the grid. Just as he reached its back row, the flag fell so he had an immediate 50mph on all his rivals and led them all down towards the South Turn before Bruce McLaren, the Ferraris and the rest hurtled by!

Brooks took the lead on lap two, but Bonnier split the Ferraris before dropping to sixth, then McLaren's Cooper broke its drop-gears. The Ferraris circulated in imperious formation, while Bonnier disputed fourth place with Trintignant, half a minute behind, and by this time Schell's clutch was slipping furiously.

On lap seven, Herrmann came hurtling into the South Turn flat-out in BRP's '2510' to find only its rear brakes were working. Travelling at least 40mph too fast to take the turn, he had a choice between a row of straw bales closing off the *autobahn* straight ahead, or a low concrete wall. He chose to burst through the straw into the escape road, but upon impact the bales rolled-up beneath the pale-green BRM, it reared up over them high into the air and began rolling, bouncing and somersaulting – tossing out its driver and happily missing him as it pounded itself into a steaming, smoking shower of scrap.

The only remaining interest in the race, save for Ferrari, lay in the duel for fourth place between Bonnier and Trintignant, but this was resolved on lap 21 when the throttle linkage on one of Bonnier's Weber carburettors came adrift and he limped into the pits with only one carburettor operative.

Spear's technical report later confessed that, despite the team's thoughtful preparation:

> Our cars are just not powerful enough to meet with the opposition, but both Schell and Bonnier and for that matter Herrmann drove well in the circumstance. Our engines are still a little down in power. Relative to the design of engine there does not seem to me to be a fundamental technical reason for this. The prime cause is the speed of the racing season and the lack of time to build engines accurately and to really sort them out individually on dynamometer test.
>
> The circuit is very punishing on cars as it gives rise to a fair amount of vibration and we suffered various cracks in the body and chassis.
>
> In the first heat of the race Bonnier's engine was a little off tune towards the end as a ball-joint on the front linkage of the carburettor end was wearing badly and the hole had elongated. This was repaired during the half hour between heats. Schell at the end of the first heat complained of loss of clutch. During the second heat Bonnier had to come into the Pits as a replacement

unit in the front linkage had come undone and the nut had fallen off. This was repaired on the spot and the car then behaved quite well. Schell's clutch got worse and worse and he was doing lap times at 2 mins 45secs which was about 30secs slower than the slowest Ferrari towards the end of the race when the tempo was dying down. In the end he stopped just before the finishing line and pushed his car over to finish an official seventh.

Because Lockheed had not supplied new components as requested, Schell's clutch had old slotted type plates and these broke up through the slots during the race. The Lockheed spares position is now ridiculous and there are still no signs of when the new clutch will be available.

The B.R.P. car went quite well and Herrmann's failure was due to loss of brakes on the front. He was just approaching the very slow hairpin off the *autobahn* and realising he had insufficient brakes, steered back on to the *autobahn* and tried to take the straw bales head on. This he did but the car somersaulted in a spectacular fashion and is in effect a complete write-off. Herrmann was not seriously injured but was very, very lucky.

Our own examination of the car at Bourne shows the pipe broken under the clip used on the front caliper. This is the clip which was not fitted on the Stirling Moss car at Silverstone. We suspect that the clip was too tight so that the pipe was restrained completely rather than being resiliently mounted.

After the race the B.R.P. personnel were, as far as I can make out, very awkward about arrangements for the removal of the broken vehicle and did not try to use their initiative. With the exception of the mechanics the whole party left two hours after the race finished to get back to England for a Formula II race on the Monday…

Tony: I went to see the wreckage of the BRP car, having been told it was a front brake failure. The car was badly damaged, bits strewn everywhere, although most of it had been collected up by the marshals. I did not find any evidence of a pipe or other failure, other than from the crash.

I could not stay long as I had to get back to the garage to sort out the trip home. Apparently BRP had taken the line: "It's your car, you get it back", and on that basis had decided to terminate the whole arrangement. It had come out in the Eagle C54 with us, so I arranged for Arthur Hill and his transporter crew, who had brought '2511' out for the tests, to collect '2510' and bring it back, while '2511' came back in the C54 with us. I never saw the wreckage back in England, neither did anyone involve me in the post mortem and rows, as I was then working 18 hours a day on the new rear-engined prototype.

I was not very sociable during this period. '2511' had bottomed badly during the tests at AVUS and if I had known, we could have modified the other cars before leaving Bourne and taken a kit along for '2511'. I had also been closer to Jean Behra than most of the team. The build of the new rear-engined car was intensely frustrating; apart from the usual crop of DO errors, it appeared to me that all we had learned had been deliberately thrown away as being of no value, and how Spear and I were kept apart I have no idea, except that I would have probably tried to blame him for some of the chaos, as the build programme had been properly planned, as he had rightly been preaching.

The surviving BRMs had been loaded onto the chartered Eagle Airlines freighter at Tempelhof Airport and flown home. RM: "Everyone was glad to leave Berlin, vowing never again to race at AVUS".

Ken Gregory: "That was an awful weekend, a meaningless race on a stupid circuit. What I remember most is a trip we made through Checkpoint Charlie and down *Unter den Linden* in the Eastern zone where we noticed that only the facades of the buildings along each side had been spruced up, while the actual structure behind was virtually derelict, cracked and crumbling. It was a chilling insight into what the Communist *bloc* was all about.

"In fact when we got back to Chelsea without the BRM someone asked one of our mechanics what had happened to it, and he said that when Hans Herrmann had gone straight on through the straw bales and the car took off, it had rolled so far it ended up in the Russian Zone and they wouldn't give it back…"

Poor Jean Behra was taken home. A memorial service for him was held in Paris on the following Wednesday, and he was buried in Nice on the Friday. Amongst the wreaths were those from his old friends at BRM…the team he had wished to rejoin.

Bonnier's view of this tragic German GP meeting was expressed as follows:

> Long before going to Germany we knew that we would not be able to challenge the much faster Ferraris at AVUS. We did not know about the Coopers, but we felt that even they would be quicker than the BRM.
>
> However, this time we did not leave anything unchecked before the race, as we went there a week early in order to get the suspension right. This we did, and during the race the BRM proved to be the best car on the banking, though, as we had thought, it was not fast enough on the straights.
>
> Schell broke his clutch and I was very lucky to finish fifth after all the works Coopers had broken down. Herrmann's crash in the BRP BRM after a brake pipe had broken did not make us much more confident in the car, and this, in combination with Behra's tragic accident, left a very dull impression of the whole race.

Schell's analysis was the most crisp and distinctive yet:

> AVUS – Nothing to say except the car was so terribly SLOW.

A post-race analysis written by PB for Owen on August 10 then offered more detail and twisted the knife which he had long been sharpening for BRP:

> The German Grand Prix at AVUS proved to be the unfortunate event of the season, while the tragic death of Jean Behra and numerous other accidents filled everybody with despondency. The circuit was a speed track and quite unsuitable for modern road racing cars, and the race generally was a technique of making

the cars stand up to the appalling condition of the antiquated banking at the expense of road holding on the straights and south curve. Fortunately our tests with Dunlop the week before the race enabled us to make provision for the banking and our cars together with the British Racing Partnership car, were specially modified before despatch.

Our cars proved to have the stamina to stand up to 300 miles of full throttle and severe banking conditions, but the cars were not fast enough to compete with the Ferraris, who had about 10 miles an hour in hand on the straights over all comers. The clutch on Schell's car proved the only unreliable feature, and this was due to the use of old type slotted drive plates, which broke up through the bottom of the slots. In spite of promises they let us down on delivery of replacements of the current type plate and proper spares were not available until after the cars had left for AVUS.

Herrmann's accident was due to a cracked brake pipe, which caused loss of fluid to the front brake system, and finally complete loss of front brakes. The brakes are only used once a lap for the south curve, which is a tight corner approached at maximum speed without any escape road [on] either section of the course. Due to lack of braking Herrmann felt he had more chance by going into the straw bales rather than heading for a concrete wall which nearly surrounds this particular corner. The chassis is a total write-off, and very few chassis components can be salvaged. The engine has a broken sump, rocker box covers and mounting feet; but with replacements this unit can be salvaged, together with the gearbox, which has broken mounting feet and other superficial damage.

An unpleasant situation developed between our team and B.R.P. concerning the salvaging of Herrmann's crash [car]. In spite of the fact that they had hired and had available a large lorry from Borgward, and had a breakdown lorry available with lifting tackle at the crash, they insisted that they could not manage it and it was up to us to collect. I had arranged that our one transporter when allowed to go to the pit, would remove our personnel-equipment and get our cars back to our garage, and after the transporter was unloaded two of our mechanics would go to the accident and load it into our transporter with the help of their three mechanics. After considerable delay, due to bad race organisation, this eventually happened; but in the meantime Robinson remonstrated to Alfred Moss who came to me with the attitude that as it was Alfred Owen's car, we had better worry about it and not keep his mechanics hanging about. Both he and Ken Gregory left for England immediately and the crash [car] was brought back to England in our transporter. However, since AVUS, Stirling Moss has confirmed to me personally that he will drive Rob Walker's new Cooper, both at Lisbon and at Monza; and in view of this, I have taken no steps to replace the B.R.P. car.

As if this had not been sufficient aggravation for one

PETER BERTHON ON THE 1959 GRAND PRIX SCENE

On August 12, 1959, PB wrote the following observations and analysis of the contemporary Formula 1 scene for Alfred Owen. It makes interesting background reading when considering the happenings of that season:

I have been giving a good deal of thought to our racing activities, as the last three events clearly show the pattern for the immediate future.

While our cars show a better reliability factor than those of the opposition, we have now lost the edge on performance. Both Coopers and Ferraris have about 240b.h.p. or 35b.h.p. less than our minimum acceptance bases; but the torque and the torque range is very similar to our engine and, in consequence, they will have the same acceleration as our car, possibly slightly better under certain conditions due to their lower weight. In maximum speed they have the advantage of the smaller car presenting a lower frontal area by nearly 2 square feet.

The Ferraris, with their 6-cylinder engines, have similar torque with a higher speed range, which with the gearing that can be employed gives them a rear wheel torque of approximately 15% higher than ours. They are heavier than we are; but this is offset by the lower gearing – the acceleration is fairly similar but they have the advantage over both the Cooper and ourselves in maximum speed by about 12 miles an hour.

The second point is that the standard of driving in our team is lower than that of the Ferrari and Cooper teams. Bonnier, due to Zandvoort, has moved up into category I, so that he is actually the senior driver of our team (Schell still being in category II). He is driving well and is keen and intense, and I am certain with more experience he will make an excellent No. 1. While Schell is a good team driver, he is not a race winner, and at his age will not improve and must then in the course of time be replaced as No. 2 driver. Flockhart is a category III driver and, with due respect to him, will not make a higher grade, as he is unlikely to improve at his age. I know that you are anxious we try young drivers. There are young drivers coming up, and I feel we should be frank, and generous, with Flockhart, and appoint a younger man in his place as quickly as possible, so that we have more driver scope for next year.

Our technical progress, which is related directly to the finance available, has been at the lowest ebb ever during the past two years. In attempting to meet the budget figure our labour, and particularly drawing office, has been cut to the lowest possible level; and beyond routine modifications and general steady improvement of the breed, the new work that has been done and is in progress covers the 5-speed gearbox, a new 1½-litre engine, and the rear engine car.

In view of the limited facilities, the policy has been to concentrate on the requirements of the new formula rather than continue the development of the present engine. The 4-cylinder engine has had its day in racing, irrespective of size, and although the present engine could be improved for next year, any real increase would have to come through a new multi-cylinder design. Nevertheless, the new rear engine car should considerably improve both maximum speed and acceleration with the present engine. We anticipate reduction of approximately 3 square feet and a weight saving of approximately 1cwt. The rear suspension is independent, a new departure, and has to be as it is not practicable to cross the engine with a de Dion tube. However, on paper the stability characteristics of this new suspension are rather better than those of the present car. This rear engine project is a direct step towards a new formula car…

Upon the top of this letter's first page, Alfred Owen wrote four drivers' names in his characteristically florid scrawl. They were Gurney…Graham Hill…Innes Ireland…Bruce McLaren…

weekend, PB further reported that:

Ron Flockhart came out to Berlin with the team and arrived in a very belligerent state. When I explained that in spite of three days arguing on my part, the Race Organisers refused to accept his entry, which they have a right to do without giving any reason, and they had already written to the R.A.C. to this effect, this calmed him to some extent, but he took the whole thing in very bad part. I am afraid he has been black-marked by the F.I.A. as a result of the claims he made against the Race Organisers after his last incident at Rouen, although, of course, they do not say this officially…

In this interesting document, PB further explained that after the loss of BRP's chassis '2510', the team's car position was as follows:

We now have four current cars, No. 6 car, Jean Behra's 1958 machine has been dismantled, and the components are built into the first rear-engine car, which is due to run at Monza. Three cars are entered at Lisbon, and we are only taking three, in view of the distance and expense of the journey. If any incident arises, our fourth car will have to be picked up as replacement to act as an available car for Monza, in case the rear engine machine is not in a raceworthy state…

Matters came to a head with BRP after this Berlin disaster. PB wrote to Ken Gregory complaining about BRP's invoices to BRM:

…up to and including the British Grand Prix…we are not entirely in agreement with some of the charges you have made…

Berthon complained to Owen:

While their charges are outrageous and not compatible with the arrangement you made with them, the matter goes somewhat deeper. At Rheims [sic], for instance, they ran two cars in the Formula II race, an important event, driven by Bueb and Bristow,

August 22, 1959 – Portuguese Grand Prix practice, Monsanto Park, Lisbon: Jo Bonnier's assigned race car '258' after the Swede's practice indiscretion, which dented its tail against the straw bales and bounced Jo down this embankment. He was then given '259' for the race, allegedly without being warned it had suffered a similar practice excursion... Ron Flockhart raced '258' suitably beaten out – the car looking immaculate here in the brilliant late afternoon sun, and set to finish.

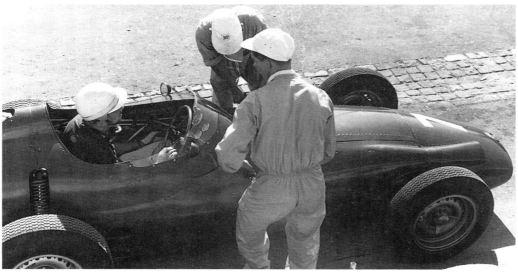

Left: A thoroughly disgusted 'JoBo' at the pits with his race car '259' tended by Pat Carvath (far side) and Jimmy Collins. This shot demonstrates shape and detail of the long 1959-spec Type 25 carburettor air intake, dash panel layout and tail and cockpit cowl fixtures and fittings.

using time-keepers and mechanics to be paid for by O.R.O.

During the Saturday preparation, prior to the race, I spent considerable time in their garage while our mechanics were carrying out the routine engine checks on their car, and only one mechanic during this period was working on the B.R.M.

While I fully agree the terms of the arrangement you made with them, I feel that every effort should be made to reduce their charges to proper proportions as, in any case, these costs will drive our expenditure further over Budget limits, in which I have a personal responsibility.

I feel that [at] any meeting to be held somebody should have the responsibility of settling a final figure with B.R.P. as otherwise no agreement would be reached, and Alfred Moss will revert to you personally to agree a compromise figure.

At over 30 years' range Ken Gregory could only recall that RM and PB had always resented his team's arrangement with Alfred Owen for the ill-fated Type 25, and they would always do their best to paint BRP black in Owen's eyes: "The business at AVUS about our chaps refusing to retrieve the wreck while Alfred and I simply rushed back to England is utter Berthon balls. Our post-race movements were governed by the charter flight we were all booked onto, we had no choice. As for time-keepers and mechanics to be paid for by ORO at Reims, our timekeeper and lap-scorer were Cyril Audrey of RAC fame and his wife Doreen, and they went around with us unpaid, while we paid for our mechanics.

"As for *our* charges being outrageous, I think the boot was on the other foot! At Reims, we always stayed at an economical little place called the *Hotel Crystal*, while Mays and Berthon lorded it at the five-star *Lion d'Or* on the Owen Organisation's expense account...and the same kind of thing was true everywhere else we raced.

"I don't recall any bad blood between BRP and BRM, our mechanics always got on very well with their's and Alfred Moss and I had a particularly warm relationship with Alfred Owen. I certainly recall Raymond Mays as being tremendously charming, a great personality, but I would admit we always had reservations about Berthon. He was always conjuring up exercises in self-justification..."

August 23, 1959 – Portuguese Grand Prix, Monsanto Park, Lisbon – 62 laps, 206.56 miles

ORO sent almost a skeleton crew to Lisbon's combined parkland and *autostrada* course as the rear-engined prototype P48 car was taking shape in the threatened race 'shop at Folkingham with its target two weeks hence – the Italian GP at Monza. As in 1958, BRM's Portuguese GP contingent were to drive direct to Monza immediately after the race.

The Lisbon cars were '257' for Schell, '258' for Bonnier and '259' for Flockhart. Bonnier was on fine form, lapping in 2:10.8 in early practice. On the Saturday evening he then clocked 2:7.86 in the "notably steady looking" BRM, while in contrast "Schell was obviously trying as hard as he could, but only just got below 2:10, and Flockhart was driving well and almost keeping up with his team-mate." Schell had a narrow escape when local driver Mario Cabral spun his Cooper-Maserati in the BRM's path.

Both Moss and Brabham were using new Mark II high-compression-headed Climax FPF engines – as at AVUS – yielding an extra 12-15bhp, Moss of course using the five-speed Colotti gearbox against Brabham's four-speed Citroen-ERSA.

The four fastest practice times were set by Cooper-Climax cars, driven by Moss, Brabham, Gregory and Trintignant – Bonnier's BRM then being the fastest front-engined runner, 4.03sec slower than Moss' Cooper pole time…

'The Rear-Engined Revolution' was beginning to bite with a vengeance.

Just as practice ended, Carroll Shelby crashed his Aston Martin into the straw bales on the *Estrada dos Parcos* and Bonnier spun his BRM, nudged some bales, and came to rest down a slope, only bales jammed beneath its front suspension saving the car from diving into a field. For the race next morning, Bonnier took over Flockhart's '259', and the Scot drove Bonnier's '258'. Within this change a demon lay hidden for the Swede.

1959 Portuguese Grand Prix: Harry Schell in '257' has just lapped local driver Mario Araujo Cabral's Scuderia Centro-Sud Cooper. The Portuguese is watching anxiously for Schell's pursuers to follow him through – as well he might, having just cut across second placeman Jack Brabham to send him crashing head-on into a roadside power pylon.

After retiring his mysteriously stricken Type 25 with fuel feed problems, Jo Bonnier and journalist Bernard Cahier – who took this photograph – set up a refreshment depot on the inside of the hairpin, Jo emptying bottles of mineral water into his crash hat and showering needy drivers at this slowest part of the circuit – Masten Gregory receiving the full service here in his works Cooper-Climax. He will finish second behind Moss.

At the start his engine faltered and he was engulfed by the accelerating pack, Brooks having to brake hard to prevent his Ferrari ramming the BRM's tail. Jo trailed away dead last, while Schell ran a lonely seventh as the race settled down with Coopers 1-2-3-4 and already drawing away. Graham Hill spun his Lotus 16 in the cutting, mounted the roadside bank, then careered back across the road, to be rammed squarely upon its right-rear wheel by Phil Hill's Ferrari.

As the stricken cars cannoned apart, Flockhart's BRM arrived upon the scene streaming rubber smoke from all four tyres, but shooting gratefully through the widening gap, unscathed.

Meanwhile, Bonnier was limping round at the back of the field, his engine misfiring and stammering, and on lap nine he stopped at the pits, subsequently tried one more lap but then had the engine die completely. He coasted to rest at the hairpin, from where he watched the rest of the race. With photo-journalist Bernard Cahier he collected bottles of fruit juice and water, overheated drivers stopping or slowing long enough to grab a drink or to be doused with cold water slung from Bonnier's crash helmet! Gregory was his first customer, followed by Moss. Bonnier was amusing himself, while harbouring immense resentment towards his team…

BRM's interest in the rest of the race was limited. Schell's brakes became inconsistent, Flockhart pressing him ever harder before taking seventh place on lap 16, going well in spite of a tightening gearchange. The two BRMs were quickly lapped by Moss.

Flockhart was screaming around stuck in third gear for long periods, making a precautionary stop on lap 36 to add fuel, which elevated Schell to sixth. McLaren's retirement then elevated both BRMs one more place. Moss ran out the winner of his first *Grande Epreuve* that season in such an overwhelming manner that he had lapped every other surviving runner. Schell finished fifth, and Flockhart seventh.

Bonnier was justifiably enraged by what he saw as the shambles within the BRM team surrounding this event, and he pulled no punches when in October he wrote his season's summary for Alfred Owen:

> In this race everything went wrong starting with the cars arriving a day late. The mechanics were exhausted by the quick and long trip. I do not understand why the cars were not sent a day or two earlier.
>
> The first day of practice went fairly well and we were among the fastest. Nobody went very fast except those who had been there before. The course reminds very much of Zandvoort, so we were optimistic about our chanses [sic].
>
> During the second day of practice we started getting fuel trouble with the engine cutting off in the corners. It got gradually worse till when I was going back to the pits, the engine stopped between shifting from second to third gear, which caused me to spin and end up in the bales slightly bending the front. It all happened on a short straight and practice was over, so I did not think it could have been my fault. However, I know that behind my back I was blamed for the spin.
>
> All this caused the poor mechanics a lot of extra work. Through a lack of parts (which surprised me) the car

could not be repaired properly, so it was mutually decided that I should drive Flockhart's car and he take the crippled one. I felt sorry about this, which I also told him but there was no other solution.

> The day before the race came, and I was going to drive a car I had never tried before, but Mr. Burthon assured me it was in a very good shape.
>
> Fifty yards from the starting line my engine stopped. I went downhill slowly and shifted over to main tank. The engine started again and I went a few laps with the engine stopping and starting all the time until it stopped entirely. The reason for this I still do not know, but there must have been a stoppage in the fuel system.
>
> This all was very fortunate, however, because *after* the race, when the car came back to the garage, they found that the rear of the chassis was considerably bent and one of the arms locating the de Dion-tube broken. I was simply told that Flockhart had been off the road during practice and that they had not had time to check the car. After they had changed a bent wheel they obviously thought everything was allright [sic].
>
> Naturally I was quite upset about it and I think it was allmost [sic] criminal to put a car on the grid in that shape. If the engine had not stopped, I would almost certainly have gone off the road.
>
> If only two cars had been entered and a training car brought, the whole trouble could have been avoided.

Schell's brief view:

> Lisbon – Race: Right hand brakes locking all the time; impossible to use the brakes. [The brakes were completely changed a few hours before the race. Why?]
> FLOCKHART: fuel starvation.
> Bonnier broke down

The Lisbon cars were transported direct to Monza where the team was reunited with the contingent travelling out direct from Folkingham – with the brand-new experimental rear-engined prototype – new chassis '481'.

September 13, 1959 – Italian Grand Prix, Monza – 72 laps, 257.26 miles

BRM's prototype rear-engined car became the sensation of Monza practice, but only the three Type 25s would be starting the race. Schell's '257' was easily fastest for the team while Bonnier spent much of his time driving the new car. On the Saturday afternoon '481' lapped the *Autodromo* in 1:44, but the afternoon dragged by until the sun began to lower in the western sky and the air began to cool.

Moss then went out and qualified his Walker Cooper on pole at 1:39.7, from Brooks' Ferrari on 1:39.8 and Brabham's Cooper with a '40.2. Schell's 1:41.6 was only seventh fastest, on the centre of row two, while Bonnier's best Type 25 time – in his regular '258' – was 1:43.1, 11th fastest on the inside of row five, and Flockhart's '2511' a poor 15th on the outside of row six with 1:43.6.

Brooks' Ferrari failed at the start and the Grand Prix developed into a straight battle between the torquey rear-engined Coopers of Moss and Brabham and the works Ferraris of Phil Hill and Dan Gurney. Schell was involved in a second group running wheel-to-wheel with the Ferraris of Gendebien and Cliff Allison and Innes Ireland's Lotus 16, while Bonnier was embroiled with McLaren and Salvadori, just behind.

Bonnier displaced Schell, but later in the long race Gendebien managed to fight his way back past the two BRMs, Schell and Bonnier finishing 7-8, twice lapped, not only by the victorious Moss, but also by Phil Hill, Brabham and Gurney who finished 2-3-4. Flockhart, 13th, was five times lapped…

Bonnier's view was typically, and justifiably, uncompromising:

> The Italian G.P. was to be our worst race during this season. We spent the whole week before the race trying the cars and they got gradually worse. The Ferraris and the Coopers were considerably much faster than the BRM on the straights and in the corners all our engines were cutting out so badly that it was difficult to keep the car on the road.
>
> The night before the race the engine was changed in my car, but this one proved to be even worse.
>
> Our cars finished 7th, 8th and 13th which I think is absolutely disgraceful. It would definitely have been much better if we had not finished at all. I was very upset after the race, and I might have been a little too frank about my opinions about the car, which I later told them I was sorry for, but I think I was right.

One can sympathize entirely with the earnest Swede's attitude, and there is little doubting the comments which followed, while he was also obviously making a strong pitch to protect his own employment in the coming season… He wrote:

> There was, however, one thing during all these sad things, that made me very optimistic about the future of the BRM – the rear engined car. After only a few laps in it I was down to times not far from the previous lap record, a very good performance for a new car. There are, of course, quite a few things to do to it, but I definitely think it will have a great future.

Harry Schell's jaundiced view:

> MONZA – Training: the car was going very well but slow.
>
> Second row at the start.
>
> RACE. The car was going very well for two laps then start missing RPM; fuel troubles coming out of right hand corners same thing on Bonnier Car.
>
> Schell's car was going much better toward the end. Why?

And here at the end of the season – in fact at the end of his lengthy BRM career, Harry Schell wrote his epitaph for the team:

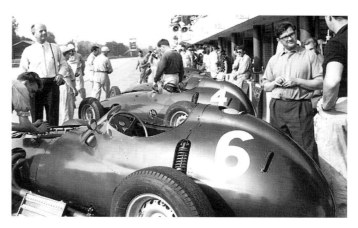

September 12, 1959 – Italian Grand Prix practice, Monza: RM – in shirtsleeve order – surveys this impressive BRM team line-up before what proved to be one of ORO's most disappointing outings of the year. Bonnier's '258' – race number '6' – is backed by Flockhart's new '2511' ('4') with its late-style tucked-down 'small tail', Schell's '257' beyond. Tony Rudd with Bonnier at right, Flockhart (dark shirt) pensive beyond his car.

CONCLUSION

> I believe the cars are well prepared by the Mechanics.
> The engines are giving a reasonable amount of Horse power; but I am sure we are losing this amount of Horse power after the two days of training. We always [sic] started in training with about 265 H.P.; we do good times the first day and then we loose [sic] power gradually every day; I am positive that we never started in a race with more than 260 H.P. which means that during the race we have around 250H.P. and probably maximun [sic] 240 by the end of the race.
>
> The proof of it: The BRM are allways in FIRST, second or Third row maximun at training and during races we allways laying around the seventh of eight [sic] place.
>
> It is possible too that the engines are giving a reasonable of HORSE power on the test bench and we are losing [sic] power when the engine is placed in the chassis by friction etc. etc.
>
> As far as I am concerned the other failures we had at every race: Brakes failure, fuel starvation is due to bad management.

He completed these reports with the following commentary upon the new rear-engined car…whose successors' story is to be told in our companion volume. It stands in stark contrast with Jo Bonnier's opinion expressed above.

NEW CAR

> After many test at Monza the car was much slower than the old one, no power whatsoever; WHY?
>
> I believe we loose the power by friction.
>
> Technically on paper this car should be unbeatable according to the ratio weight and power 450 kilogrammes and 275 H.P.
>
> It should be the fastest car there is; on the contrary it is the slowest
>
> WHY?

The road holding is good up to a limit then the car goes suddenly from the back, then you loose her immediately; I believe there is too much weight on the tail of the car. The back is too good on the road compare to the front which is too light.

The chassis twist during fast curves and we broke for this reason four or five time the fuel tanks.

In two words I believe there is a lot of work to do before we can get this car right.

I believe the COOPER-BRM was a much better reesult for the first time on the road; if you remember that Stirling Moss was leading the 200 miles of Aintree with a car badly prepared in a hurry with a very bad engine of last year which had maximum 245 horse power.

Bonnier made his own, eminently reasonable, pitch to Alfred Owen in the covering letter with his summary report:

I am very serious about motorracing, and I have a great wish to do well. I believe in you, your desire to find success and in your cars. Therefore it is very discouraging to see good intention and good money be wasted on a bad organisation.

I have nothing personal against Mr. Mays, on the contrary I like him very much, and I think he is a charming person. Perhaps, however, he is a little too nice, and I think you need somebody younger and firmer to lead your racing-team.

I am sure, however, it would do the team spirit a lot of good, if Mr. Mays could be found a position in the team where he could stay as an inspiring symbol of the creation of the BRM.

Mr. Burthon too is a nice man and above all I think he is a brilliant designer. This year, hwoever, his duties have ben too many and in fact he has been our team-manager.

My opinion is that he should stay at the factory to be able to do continual research work and let Mr. Rudd put the cars on the grid with an efficient man to keep the team under control.

Yours faithfully,

[signed] Joakim Bonnier

This clear-sighted, penetratingly brief, note crystallized within Owen's mind much of the frustration accumulated over many years. He would still sustain what he still regarded as a personal commitment to Raymond Mays and Peter Berthon, but 'JoBo''s missive written in Stockholm that October day was perhaps the beginning of the end for their executive regime which had endured so long...

After Monza, the 1959 World Championship titles were to be decided by the United States Grand Prix, to take place at Hendrick Field, Sebring, Florida on December 12. But that would be a long and costly trip. With no hope of winning either the Drivers' or Formula 1 Constructors' Championships, BRM made no entries...

One race remained in ORO's 1959 season – at Snetterton during the *Autosport* Three Hours meeting in October. Two cars were entered for Ron Flockhart – in his BRM swansong –

and Maserati 250F privateer Bruce Halford – making what would prove to be a one-off appearance for the team.

October 10, 1959 – Silver City Trophy, Snetterton – 25 laps, 67.75 miles

Before Formula 1 practice began at the Norfolk aerodrome circuit, the lap record there stood to Brian Naylor's JBW-Maserati – effectively a private owner's special – at 98.99mph. As practice began for the Silver City Trophy, Graham Hill of Team Lotus became the first driver to lap Snetterton at over 'The Ton', and by the end of that session six men had broken that magic barrier – 1min 37sec. Ron Flockhart qualified '2511' on pole at 1:34.8 from Roy Salvadori's Tommy Atkins-entered Cooper-Maserati on 1:35 and Hill on 1:35.2. Bruce Halford was making his mark with Peter Spear – but not apparently with the Bourne management – with 1:36.4, 0.2sec faster than Innes Ireland's Lotus 16. The only decent prize money was for the first 100mph lap in the race. It was clear from practice that this would be the leader on the first lap. And so it was...

The two BRMs ran 1-2 first time round, from Hill, Jack Brabham in a 2.2-litre Cooper and Ireland. Flockhart averaged over 100mph on his first flying lap in '2511', and Hill and Brabham – cornering at angles approaching 30 degrees in his small-engined Cooper – had found their way around Halford's '259'. The F1 cars were exceeding 160mph along the Norwich Straight, and Graham Hill was pressing Flockhart hard.

Graham had suffered an appallingly unreliable first two Formula 1 seasons with Team Lotus. Most recently at Monza he had found his Lotus 16's steering left loosely clamped as he was pushed back onto the grid and on only the second lap of the race the car's quill-shaft connecting clutch to gearbox had snapped in two. Now at Snetterton, with RM's blandishments ringing in his ears, he was giving Colin Chapman's team what he viewed as one last chance.

Flockhart's sixth lap was a record 1:33.6, 103.85mph, yet on lap seven Hill found a way by and already the tail-enders were being lapped. Flockhart fought back, regaining the lead on lap nine. But Hill was out, his always fragile Lotus having again broken its quill-shaft. Graham recalled: "At last I seemed to be in a Formula 1 race with a chance to win. But the quill-shaft broke...Well, that for me was the end – I had just about had enough. I had endured so many failures and so much disappointment and I didn't see any end to it. In two whole seasons of Grand Prix racing, I had finished once and scored just two World Championship points and I didn't want to face another season of constant failures..."

Flockhart emerged in a secure lead from Brabham's hybrid Cooper, with Halford comfortably third. Flockhart lapped fourth place man David Piper's private Lotus 16 and ran out as winner for BRM at an average speed of 101.71mph – faster than the preceding lap record, 11sec ahead of Brabham, with Bruce Halford third and troubled by unpredictable braking.

Thereafter, ORO concentrated entirely upon 1960, and all Folkingham's and Bourne's energies were thrown into the rear-engined Project 48 programme to be described in our companion volume.

Active planning was proceeding at Bourne and Darlaston to fix the driver team for 1960. RM: "Peter and I decided that in addition to new cars we needed a team of young drivers. We signed two new ones: first Graham Hill, whom I had met in 1956 with his wife, through the widow of Mackay Fraser, when they brought her to Bourne to see me and my mother. Graham then was little known. The next thing I knew he was driving for Lotus and I considered he was going to be a very good driver. The second driver to be signed was Dan Gurney from California. At Zandvoort Jean Behra had told us about this new young Ferrari pilot who was to be his co-driver in the forthcoming sports car races. Dan's drive in Portugal impressed Peter Berthon and me, and we hoped for great things from him…"

Of course, securing these new drivers, and shedding the old, was neither a simple nor painless exercise.

Peter Spear had compiled his own analysis of driver possibilities for Alfred Owen, who had arranged to meet Jack Brabham, whom Spear properly considered "an excellent driver for us next year as No. 1", but Jack of course would clinch that season's World Championship – in BRM's absence – in the US GP at Sebring and would then remain with Cooper, to defend his title successfully through 1960.

Spear's assessment of the alternatives was typically emphatic:

1) Stirling Moss…the greatest of them all. If we could get him to drive for us then I would have him every time, but not on a grasshopper principle as 1959. One cannot plan and work properly on that basis.
2) Jo Bonnier…has already shown that he can win a Grand Prix race. He is capable of winning further races. I do not think he will ever be a team leader. He is far too selfish and thinks far too little about the mechanics, and everybody else concerned…To my mind he is not a very good test driver. His comments always appear to be biased by whatever other people have said. In simple terms, things are never 10/15% wrong: they are either reasonable, or hopeless.
3) Harry Schell…I do not think Schell will ever improve now. He is too old. He has certainly not proved himself to be a good No. 1. This year, in my opinion, he has never tried to lead Bonnier. There has always been some kind of rivalry between them. Furthermore he does not have the 'tiger' instinct and is perfectly happy if Harry Schell can be in the first six and never disappointed that he isn't in the first three…
4) Graham Hill. Subject to test I would say he is one of the best potential British drivers for us and, of course, reasonably anxious to come in.
5) Bruce Halford. This man impressed me enormously at Snetterton and may well be worth a further trial. He is 28, has quite a lot of experience and so far has acted very intelligently.
6) Ron Flockhart – He will never be a world beater in Grand Prix racing though, considering the cars he has had, he has driven fairly well this year. He drove very well at Snetterton but would not have beaten Brabham or Moss etc. in proper Formula I cars. As you will have seen…he has apparently done very well indeed at

Goodwood on car testing but he must bear in mind there that he has been testing out special tyres. Flockhart is about the best test driver we have had on the car next to, say, Behra. Before we lose Flockhart I think we should make quite sure we have a proper team.
7) Gurney – He is a remarkably promising American driver who has already been approached by Mays. He is only 24, I understand, and is potentially very good. On the other hand he is quite a tall man and may not be suitable for the newer cars for '60, 61 and 62 where undoubtedly the premium will be on the small man.
8) McKee. The Norwich driver mentioned by Mays… I know nothing about this driver.[89]
9) Tony Brooks – I very much doubt if Tony Brooks would drive for B.R.M. If he does carry on in Grand Prix racing I think he will stay with Ferrari…"

Only four days after the Snetterton race, Tony ran a test session at Goodwood in which not only Graham Hill, but also young Mike McKee, had his first, exploratory drive for BRM. Tony reported, with typical care:

GOODWOOD TESTS – 14TH OCTOBER, 1959

The object of these tests were threefold – to evaluate new drivers, test new rubber compound tyres, and obtain temperature data for the winter development programme.

Two cars were used, Nos. 259 and 2511; both cars have previously competed at Snetterton, where they had each covered over 170 miles. Car No. 2511 was fitted with fuel, temperature and pressure gauges, oil tank temperature gauge, temperature gauges across the oil cooler and gearbox, together with a gearbox pressure gauge.

Car No. 259 was fitted with a fuel pressure and oil tank temperature gauge. Tyre pressures were 34 front and 35 rear throughout, 15" wheels.

Climatic conditions – barometer 29.90ins; air temp. varied from 17° to 19°C; wind S.E., 8m.p.h.

CAR 2511: Driver R. Flockhart; 5 laps on tyres used at Snetterton to prove car, and warm up.
1) *Car 2511* – Driver R. Flockhart, 10 laps on standard 1959 tyres as used throughout the year; best lap 1-28-3 – car tends to oversteer, brakes not as good as at Snetterton. Pulling 7,500, 7,600r.p.m. on straight (152m.p.h. compared with 150, during tests with Stirling Moss). Engine etc., very good.
2) *Car 2511* – Driver R. Flockhart, 10 laps on special lightweight low resilience compound tyres – best 1:25.8. Handling very good; driver feels what he believes to be de Dion tramp during hard acceleration in second from Lavant; car on throttle earlier with these tyres; wear on outer rear 2.2mm. per 10 laps.
3) *Car 2511* – Driver R. Flockhart, 10 laps on special lightweights, low resilience compound with additives to increase wear [*sic*, presumably meant 'to improve wear'].

89. Mike McKee, son of a leading Norwich surgeon and a promising sports and later Formula Junior and Lotus Elite driver, whose career would be cut short by a serious, but survived, accident.

Best 1:26.0 – handling may not be quite so good – does not give same feeling of security. Engine pulling 7,600 on straight. Wear 1.4mm.

4) *Car No. 2511* – Driver R. Flockhart. 10 laps on light-weights from test 2; best 1:26.0. handling not quite so good – conscious of rapid tyre wear, pattern nearly disappeared.

5) *Car No. 2511* – Driver R. Flockhart. 10 laps on standard 1959 tyres; best 1:28.6. car oversteers, handling poor.

6) *Car No. 2511* – Driver R. Flockhart. 10 laps on lightweights hard wearing compound; best 1:25.1. handling very good. Wear for 20 laps 3.0mm.

Car 2511 – Driver Graham Hill. 10 laps between tests 3 and 4 on standard tyres; best 1:28.4.

Car No. 2511 – Driver Graham Hill, 7 laps on tyres from test 6; best 1:27.6.r.p.m. only 7,200 on straight and misfiring – found that distributor covers on experimental Lucas outer magneto had rotated due to vibration wear of locating groove – magneto unserviceable.

Car 259 – Driver Graham Hill, on tyres used at Snetterton; 6 laps; best 1.30.7 – bedding brakes.

Car 259 – Driver Graham Hill on same tyres, 11 laps – best 1:27.4 – feels big heavy car after Lotus – tail seems to hang out a long way on corners.

Car 259 – Driver Graham Hill on Snetterton tyres from 2511 – 16 laps, best 1:26.8. maximum r.p.m. 7,200 – oil tank temperature 110°C; gearbox outlet temp. 85°C.

Car 259 – Driver M. McKee on standard tyres – 18 laps, best 1:30.8, limited to 7,000r.p.m.

Car 259 – Driver M. McKee, same tyres, 14 laps. rev. limit raised to 8,000; driver told to change at 7,500. best 1:29.3, only getting 7,100 on straight.

Car 259 – Driver M. McKee, same tyres, 13 laps. Best 1:31.5; engine not pulling 7,000 in top, centre mag. found to be U/S. Standard type of mag.

23rd November, 1959   *A.C.Rudd*

The day this report was typed, a second series of Goodwood tests was conducted to compare the front and rear-engined cars, and as it happened to obtain the impressions of none other than Jack Brabham – the works Cooper number-one – of BRM's new rear-engined contender, as Cooper were also present that day. RM asked Jack to try the new prototype. He reported: "It understeers like hell, but they all do at first!" Type 25 chassis '2511' – as used in the first series Goodwood tests – provided a baseline reference, and in this volume I record only its performances in detail:

Climatic conditions, bar: 29.60, air temp. 14°C. to 16°C. Wind S.W. slight.

Car No. 2511 – Ron Flockhart, with normal tyres on 15" wheels at 34, 35p.s.i. to establish comparative times. 6 laps, best 1:27.2; driver commented slight oversteer conditions comparable with first series of tests on these tyres.

Ron then took out the P48 prototype and spun off between St Mary's and Lavant! The car was recovered, Jack Brabham

ran it for seven laps and while its suspension was being readjusted he tried the Type 25…

Car No. 2511 – Jack Brabham, 8 laps, best (last) 1:28.1. Car seemed big and clumsy. Best to avoid driving it as it confused his impressions of rear engined car…

Perhaps a telling epitaph for the dying dinosaur? It was not run again that day…

While Ron Flockhart and 'Black Jack' were sawing their way around the Sussex circuit, in his office at Darlaston, Peter Spear wrote formally to Joe Wright, Managing Director of Dunlop, about problems with the company's disc brakes, which had persisted even into the Snetterton finale race:

> …we have run into certain difficulties this year, particularly on what appears to be inspection of components…we have run into one or two odd mysterious troubles on caliper cylinders and the question of failures of flares on brake pipes has never been solved satisfactorily…when we have passed over various failed specimens for Laboratory report, I have never yet seen a copy of any…report nor officially have I ever had any information as to the cause of failure…

He forwarded a front caliper bridge pipe from the rear-engined prototype car, used at Monza:

> The caliper was new out of stores…it was found there was a crack behind the flare…exactly the same trouble which Moss had at Silverstone this year…exactly the same trouble as on the sample pipes handed over to your people some months ago for Laboratory report… If the crack had not been quite so bad and if the weeping had not been observed, this failure could have led to complete destruction of a car.
>
> …On Bruce Halford's car at Snetterton, during the race, he complained of a grabbing front right-hand caliper. On the face of it, since I do not know the cause, this seems a little 'naughty' at the end of the season.
>
> …We might as well face facts now before the 1960 season. On balance [your equipment] has been vastly superior to that supplied by any other company with whom I have been associated on the B.R.M… As far as I am concerned I want to see Dunlop brakes on the car in 1960 subject to your agreement.
>
> At the same time I do not think we should blind ourselves to the fact that there have been one or two troubles of a relatively routine nature, which I am quite sure can be sorted out but which could be the 'nail' which loses the 'Kingdom'…

In mid-November PB was summoned to a meeting with Alfred Owen at the Junior Carlton Club in London. On November 17 Owen confirmed the gist of the meeting to him at Bourne:

> This is to confirm…I want all the cars altered and turned over to rear engined by the end of January which

would give us the month of February free to do any testing that might be necessary at Folkingham and the cars should be ready for track testing from the 1st March onwards. I want to have your assurance that all this work could be accomplished by the personnel at Bourne. If not, then the work should be sub-contracted to one or other firms in the Group to enable the cars to be all renovated by the 31st January without fail.

I hope that you will get everybody working to this end at Bourne so that, as I have said earlier, everyone of our cars for next season's racing will be rear engined.

You told me you thought the challenge was achievable with Bourne personnel but I would like your assurance in writing to this effect…

On November 23 PB responded as follows:

In the broad picture I gave you when we met at the Carlton Club, I told you of the intention to convert all cars to the new rear-engined version and bring up the total strength to six by the beginning of the season. Requirements to do this are already laid down and the work is in hand; but for the time being I have kept one front-engined car (No. 2511) intact, which is being held at the ready for testing as required, since this is really the yardstick by which we can assess any real improvement with the rear-engined car on any given circuit.

A second front engined chassis [this would have been '258' since Alfred Owen had given the strictest instructions literally to everyone that as the Zandvoort winner it was to be preserved in running order, as nearly as possible in its Dutch GP trim – DCN] has been completely overhauled and is being held intact, less engine, just in case there is any requirement to race a car during the winter. (Argentine, January 31st, now looks fairly certain and their delegates are coming to discuss possible entries on the 25th.)

Of the remaining three car sets – one constitutes the prototype rear engine car, and the other two are now being converted – the first production chassis being just complete. This will leave two cars to be converted and one to build (replacement of the B.R.P. car).

The first part of this programme will be accomplished by the 1st March and will give three units for testing and preliminary English races.

The remaining three units will be completed by mid-May and will incorporate any modifications found necessary as a result of early spring testing…

PB bemoaned the Air Ministry's continuing determination to evict ORO from their Folkingham site "…which unless faced up to at once may prove a disruptive factor to the above programme…".

Despite a rather plaintive letter from Team Lotus manager Stan Chapman, Colin's father, to Alfred Owen claiming that Graham Hill was under contract to them for 1960 "just in case you should be thinking of making an approach to this driver", RM had done the deal. Graham: "I told Colin I had been approached by BRM and that I wanted to leave; and I told him why…"

On the evening of November 22, PB confirmed to Owen that Dan Gurney had also agreed to join BRM, for a three-year period, covering the seasons 1960–62. Next day PB wrote:

He had already been offered £5,000 for next year by Aston Martin, made up of £2,500 contract fee, and a further £2,500 guaranteed through Shell. Bryan Turle says this is not true and Aston Martin would pay the additional £2,500; but this arrangement was used to keep the actual contract fee in line with their other drivers (Salvadori, etc). He turned down the Aston Martin offer because he did not think their car good enough.

As an American, living in California with a wife and two children, his cost of living compared with ours is considerably higher and he is faced with expensive flights to and from during the year to see his family. With this consideration and the Aston Martin offer, it was not possible to secure him on a lower basis, but he has agreed this figure at your discretion on results over a period of three years. The contract he has signed is worded so that the sum of £3,000 is the basic contract figure, and an additional £2,000 is a consideration for tying himself to the use of fuels, oils, accessories, etc., we specify.

I have done this to keep the contract figures the same as the other drivers; and as he is not driving sports cars, etc., he will have no other direct remuneration from the Oil Companies, so that his overall remuneration is on broadly similar lines to Hill and Bonnier.

I think we are very fortunate to have signed him as he is the only young driver with the long-term potential of a Stirling Moss, and is a simple straightforward young man whom I know you will like.

I sincerely hope you understand my feelings on the subject of Bonnier; and while he has yet got it in him to be a real asset to the team, he does not yet appreciate that a contract is a two-sided arrangement. He is difficult to deal with and I was a little afraid that he would seek your agreement on being made No. 1 driver, at a number 1 fee. This year Bonnier was paid £3,000 contract fee, plus a further £750 bonus as a result of Zandvoort. I would suggest he be put on the same footing as Graham Hill at a contract fee of £3,000 with no variations. As he will be driving for Porsche with Graham Hill in their sports car team, he will get a further £1,500 paid through Shell, as is the case with Hill. This gives him £4,500 total contract fees, plus 50% of all starting money and prize money, which permits him on a reasonable season to gross towards £10,000.

His efforts last year were unfortunately more directed to showing us that he was worth more to us than Schell than producing the best possible results for the team; and having thought about the matter a great deal on the basis of making the drivers work for us as a team, I would make the following points for your consideration: 1) No driver be nominated as No. 1 – the three are of equal potential race winning value to us, with Gurney ahead on brilliance but down on experience.

2) Irrespective of the Frankfurt category – decided at a previous CSI conference there – of drivers, the three drivers be placed on an equal footing, and the starting money for three-car entries be paid to them on an equal basis of one-sixth each, of total Starting Money.

3) There be no preference in cars. 2 cars can be allocated to each driver for the season, each pair being arranged to suit their own individual peculiarities. The same mechanics of the racing team be allocated to the drivers, so whichever of their two cars be in use they have the same mechanics. This ensures competition within the team and between the mechanics, and enables drivers and mechanics to have mutual confidence.

4) You consider putting up a bonus or special purse to the driver who comes out highest in the markings for the Championship table. This to encourage friendly competition between drivers during the season, and to stop the consistent bleat you get from drivers for more money as soon as they make any form of success. The Championship marking is acceptable and well understood by all as a fair basis.

On November 24, RM conveyed his thoughts to Owen concerning drivers for the coming season, heading his letter "STRICTLY CONFIDENTIAL". It read as follows, revealing Ray's own by that time increasingly antiquated values, and perhaps demonstrating some of his own misgivings, and fears:

Dear Alfred,

I was extremely pleased that you were able to see Dan Gurney last Sunday, and I appreciated your coming to Tamworth to meet us. From our experience of Gurney during the few days he was in Bourne, and from what other people say, he is a very nice young man, with a very high moral character, and I am delighted that you agreed to the terms which enabled him to join us. I am convinced he will be 100% loyal in every way.

…as regards the driver position: I have discussed this with Peter many times just recently, and I have thought a great deal about this myself. Obviously driving standard is of paramount importance, but loyalty and team spirit also must play a very prominent part in the success of the team as a whole.

I have been trying to weigh up…who would be the best third member of the team now that we have two young and promising people in Gurney and Graham Hill, and I think this matter wants most careful consideration. In my opinion, the three people to consider are Bonnier, Phil Hill and Maurice Trintignant, and it is very important that we weigh up the true merits of these three people from every point of view…

1. Bonnier.
a) Until we gave Bonnier a drive in a good car at Casablanca in 1958, where he finished third, he was never considered in any way near top flight. In this race he drove well, and it was chiefly for this reason, and the fact that he is so comparatively young, that we decided we would try to obtain his services.

b) On thinking very carefully concerning every individual race this year, other than Zandvoort, Bonnier has never shown any real brilliance, nor has he been…100% loyal. At Zandvoort…it was really only when Brabham lost a gear…that Bonnier showed his superiority, in other words it was the reliability of the B.R.M. that helped Bonnier to take first place.

c) On reviewing all the other races this year there has been remarkably little difference in the lap practice times and race times of Schell and Bonnier, and only on the Lisbon circuit did Bonnier show any superiority over Schell. Here you will remember that right at the end of the last day's practice some peculiar incident happened, when he crashed his car, and no trace could ever be found to blame the car.

d) Bonnier has proved himself to be of a rather cold and unfriendly nature, not very popular with those who work with him or for him.

e) All at Bourne have always done their very best for Bonnier, and he has had full co-operation and every consideration, but both he and Schell have not been what I call really loyal to the team, which is so necessary to success.

f) If it is thought that Bonnier is the best man to complete the team we would still give him every co-operation and help, which I can assure you has been done in the past, but equally if we can find another driver whom we consider could be at least as good as Bonnier, I think a complete team change would be advisable.

2. Phil Hill.
This driver has apparently fallen out with Ferrari. Phil Hill is a good all-round driver, particularly good on the fast circuits, and although he has not shown brilliance at Silverstone and Lisbon, I think this is…due to his lack of knowledge of the circuits…he always seems to drive hard, and this was confirmed by Dan Gurney, when we were discussing Hill. I think he would make a good member of the team…would work well with the other two drivers, and furthermore the inclusion of a second American in the team, not being able to find a British driver at the moment, would probably do no other than good.

3. Maurice Trintignant.
Trintignant's Manager…Bernard Cahier…has written saying that Maurice would very much like to join the B.R.M. team, because he has high hopes of the car, and was always happy when with us. Trintignant is one of the nicest and best-behaved (in every way) drivers of today; he has always been an extremely good and reliable driver, and easy to work with. My one fear about Trintignant is the fact that he must now be around forty…

I think we want to get away from this Number 1, 2 and 3 idea. Ferrari, although giving a certain seniority as regards publicity in programme order, do not ever state their Number 1 Driver. In other words, they try to create friendly rivalry, which I think is an excellent thing to have in the team…

The services of Graham Hill, Dan Gurney and old hand Jo Bonnier – for all his perceived faults – were ultimately secured for the new season, and production of the new P48 rear-engined cars charged ahead. The stock of obsolescent Type 25s, in all but two cases, were in the throes of being torn down, cannibalized and scrapped, and so the Owen Racing Organisation entered the busiest closed-season of its entire history.

Tony: It had become characteristic for BRM to go into virtual hibernation each winter, then to approach the start of each new season in a frantic last-few-weeks burst of feverish activity. The winter of 1959–60 was different – it was feverish throughout, and the entire matter was complicated by the fact that the Air Ministry really was evicting us from the Folkingham site, and to take its place we had to build a brand-new race 'shop beside the Old Maltings behind Eastgate House at Bourne – and that building would become our home for the rest of my time with BRM.

We spent the winter getting to know our new drivers, while they acclimatized themselves first to us, then to the existing front-engined cars and finally to the prototype rear-engined car, while all the time Stan Hope's fabrication team and the panel bashers all together at Folkingham were working flat-out to complete the first production P48s – and the programme was inevitably sliding further and further behind schedule.

END OF AN ERA – FRONT-ENGINED SWANSONG, 1960

Having taken to heart Jo Bonnier's comments regarding the need for an adequate Team Manager to run ORO 'in the field' in succession to Peter Berthon, Alfred Owen had briefed Peter Spear to sound out opinion at Bourne in a visit there on November 25, 1959.

Spear reported:

> I had another session on the question of Team Manager. Berthon tells me privately that R.M. is resigned to the fact that he will take less executive action…Although I have a lot of misgivings, on balance, provided he is well tied down, there is a lot to be said for Flockhart in some kind of Assistant Team Manager capacity. If he was responsible for testing of the cars before they went out, for discussing technical matters with drivers and so on, it might be a useful thing. If there was an argument we would at least have a man who could get into a given car and take it round. His technical knowledge is good relative to the other drivers and he does give intelligent observations on car performance. If he accepts retirement from active racing except in an emergency and, as I said before, is well tied down, there could be possibilities. There are very few real team managers available. The strength of Mercedes in the past was that their Chief Engineer, Ullenhart [sic, actually 'Uhlenhaut'] was also a very competent fast driver.

But when approached with such a proposition Ron Flockhart preferred to continue racing as a driver, and he would appear occasionally in the new year for Team Lotus before retiring, expanding his flying interests and ultimately losing his life early in 1962 when the P51 Mustang he had prepared for a second attack upon the London-to-Sydney solo record crashed into hills in Australia.

Eventually, and quite startlingly, Alfred Owen appointed neighbouring Walsall enthusiast and (comparatively minor) industrialist Bertie Bradnack – owner of Walsall Pressings – to the position. The ebullient, burly Bradnack had considerable experience in racing, having driven in sprints and hill-climbs from prewar with a twin-supercharged Frazer Nash, and subsequently – despite his generous girth – in Cooper 500s.

Raymond Mays was formally confirmed as Racing Director of BRM, but Bradnack was to accompany the small team which PB would be leading out to Argentina for the opening round of the new year's World Championship, taking cars '2511' and '258' to run in two events for drivers Joakim Bonnier, Graham Hill and Dan Gurney – Graham being due to return home after the first race to continue P48 testing, while Gurney would take his place for the second engagement.

Before being despatched, the Type 25 cars in this, their final form, were weighed back-to-back against the replacement rear-engined P48 car, '481'.

As shipped to Argentina, on 15-inch wheels with D9 Dunlop Racing tyres and assuming a standard driver weight of 180lbs, the Type 25s were weighed with oil, water and 15 gallons of fuel on board, 3 gallons in each side tank, 12 in the rear, revealing a front weight of 680lbs, rear 801lbs, totalling 1,481lbs.

Dry, less driver, but with brake fluid, front weight was 549lbs, rear 571lbs, totalling 1,120lbs.

In contrast, the rear-engined prototype P48 with 10 gallons of fuel aboard (72lbs) weighed front 570lbs, rear 790lbs – total 1,360lbs, 121lbs less than the front-engined Type 25.

Dry, less driver, but with brake fluid, P48 front weight was only 338lbs, rear 690lbs – total 1,028lbs, or 92lbs less than the front-engined Type 25.[90]

Tony Rudd was left in charge of the rear-engined car build and development programme, amidst the move from Folkingham to Bourne, while RM recalled ORO's second South American foray like this: "Peter Berthon and a few mechanics – all that could be spared from the rear-engined car build programme – and Bradnack flew out to Buenos Aires. As usual, even this was fraught, there was an airline strike and they had to fly via Germany. When they finally arrived, Buenos Aires was in a state of political ferment, with bombs going off all over the city…"

February 7, 1960 – Argentine Grand Prix, Buenos Aires Autodrome – 80 laps, 194.4 miles

The *Parque Almirante Brown* course was opened for practice on Wednesday, February 3, local star Froilan Gonzalez – that old friend of BRM – being credited with fastest time that day, 1:41, while Graham Hill – making his BRM debut – set second fastest time for the day at 1:41.8 in '2511'.

90. **Tony: These weights for the front-engined car are about right, but I suspect the rear-engined figures are early estimates and not actual. At this time I was in extremely hot water for having told Spear that '481' was in fact *heavier* than the front-engined cars, which I swear it was, by about 20lbs…**

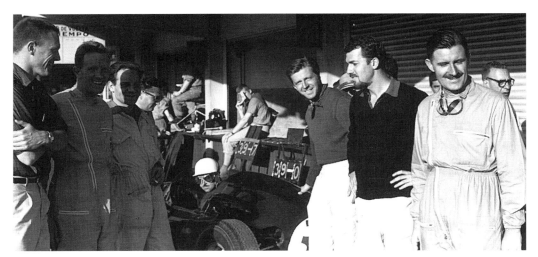

February 6, 1960 – Argentine Grand Prix practice, Buenos Aires Autodrome, Parque Almirante Brown: Under the at this time futuristic permanent pit block's broad canopy, BRM newboy Dan Gurney with his replacement at Ferrari, Cliff Allison, new Lotus number-one Innes Ireland, Walker oldboy Maurice Trintignant seated in the Walker Cooper, 'Taffy' von Trips of Ferrari, Bonnier of BRM and Bourne's second newboy Graham Hill – fresh ex-Lotus – on the right.

Below: February 7, 1960 – Argentine Grand Prix: Rear-engined sensation – Innes' hastily-assembled new prototype Lotus-Climax 18 led as the race began from the BRMs of Bonnier – '258' – and Graham Hill – '2511' – in close contention, Phil Hill's Ferrari 256 fourth.

In second day's practice Bonnier's faithful '258' bettered Gonzalez' time with a 1:39.8. Qualifying was organized on the Saturday, February 6, Moss taking pole at 1:36.9, from Ireland's new rear-engined Lotus 18 on 1:38.5, while the BRM Type 25s of Graham Hill and Joakim Bonnier – in their farewell World Championship Grand Prix – tied for third fastest time on 1:38.9 each, Hill well satisfied, one would suspect, while the Swede would have been eyeing this newcomer with suspicion...

For the first time, an international Argentine GP would start without a Ferrari on the front row of the grid...

But practice at the BA Autodrome had been dominated by the astonishing speed of Innes Ireland's brand-new rear-engined F1 Lotus-Climax 18, shipped there in kit form and assembled in the paddock garages. Graham Hill: "When I decided to leave Lotus, in an effort to persuade me not to go Colin showed me all the designs for his new Formula 1 car, which was the first rear-engined Lotus. But I had had just about enough...I thought a clean break was necessary.

"The new Lotus was down at Buenos Aires, entered for its first Grand Prix. It showed terrific form and you can well imagine my feelings at the time. I had jumped out of one team to join another and now I was finding myself being left behind by my ex-No. 2 driver – it was a pretty galling experience."

Ireland actually led the Argentine race from the fall of the flag, trailed by Bonnier's Type 25 and Moss, biding his time in the Walker Cooper. The hastily-assembled new Lotus eventually began to fall apart and after 40 laps Bonnier still led

1960 Argentine Grand Prix: Jo Bonnier held a seven-second lead in the Buenos Aires Championship-opening race before breaking a valve spring in '2511' – here showing off the extra cooling holes cut into its windscreen coaming base as a touch of opposite-lock controls a tail slide on the sun-soaked circuit's super-heated, treacly tarmac.

Right: Not bad company – Graham Hill acquitted himself very well in his BRM debut, holding second place behind his number-one, the Type 25 by this time acknowledged to be one of the best handling cars in Formula 1. Graham looks smooth and unhurried compared to the crouching World Champion Jack Brabham, skating his works Cooper round in the background, with Moss' Walker Cooper following through.

February 14, 1960 – Buenos Aires City GP, Cordoba, Argentina: The Formule Libre race field sets off on the Cordoba boulevard circuit – Bonnier's '2511' snatching an initial advantage from Jack Brabham's works Cooper-Climax (left), Trintignant's ultimately victorious Walker Racing entry (38) and Dan Gurney (far right) in '258'. Ireland's Lotus 18 is race number '20'; behind is Menditeguy's Cooper ('6') with Bruce McLaren just between the two BRMs.

Left: Cordoba, 1960 – Dan Gurney also put in a praiseworthy BRM debut, finishing second behind Trintignant's Cooper in '258', despite muscling the car's gearchange to destruction. "You can't afford to Gran'ma a shift…" Dan would recall…

Moss, but then Stirling made his attack, he displaced the BRM and pulled away at the rate of a second a lap until a wishbone broke, putting him out.

Bonnier inherited a comfortable lead, just as at Zandvoort nine months previously. He eased off, but his engine abruptly stuttered, popped and banged and he was forced to peel off into the pits – a valve spring had broken, and with it had gone BRM's chance of a second Grande Epreuve victory.

Bruce McLaren inherited the lead in his second-string works Cooper. Trintignant was third behind Cliff Allison's Ferrari in the second Walker car, but when he was unable to respond to 'Faster' signals brandished by Alf Francis he was

Cordoba, 1960: Ultimate winner Maurice Trintignant in his Walker Cooper holds off Jo Bonnier's '2511' in 100-degree heat as they dispute third place early in the 75-lap Argentine Libre race. Cooper's rear-engined revolution had rendered front-engined F1 car design – amongst which BRM's Type 25 was one of the very best – obsolescent.

called in, Moss took over and finally finished third overall, 15 seconds behind Allison.

Bonnier was placed seventh, while Graham Hill ran fourth before pulling in with a split water hose, which had sent the temperature off the clock, and another case of broken valve-springs, retiring after 38 laps.

February 14, 1960 – Buenos Aires City *Formule Libre* Grand Prix, Cordoba – 75 laps, 142.5 miles

This traditional international *Formule Libre* race had normally been run at the BA Autodrome as part of the Argentine GP/BA 1,000Kms sports car classic tour, but in 1960 it was instead organized up-country to run on a 1.9-mile circuit laid out around the city of Cordoba's municipal park, some 450 miles from the capital whose name it carried.

Moss had declared he would not enter, not wishing to run again amongst local *Libre* specials since one had rammed him at high speed during the last previous International City GP at the BA Autodrome in 1958. Ferrari also opted out, and the only sign of *Formule Libre* as the meeting began was the sweet and heady smell of alcohol fuel while Gonzalez's Ferrari-Chevrolet V8 provided the only 'big-bore' opposition to the 2½-litre F1 cars, and would retire early in any case.

Practice began on Friday, February 12, but two truck loads of competing cars had been delayed on the long haul from Buenos Aires, including both BRMs, and they missed qualification scheduled for Saturday afternoon.

RM: "Peter had returned to England, as did Graham Hill, to get on with testing the rear-engined cars, whilst Bradnack and the mechanics flew to Cordoba. Bradnack was much troubled by the intense heat, as were most people…" When the cars failed to arrive on their vast locally hired transporters: "The race organisers raised a real hue and cry and police all over

Argentina were alerted. There was still no trace of the vehicles, which seemed to have disappeared into the blue. Finally, and terribly late…the vehicles arrived. The drivers of the lorries had encountered some senoritas and had digressed to a fiesta! Our mechanics were furious, but said afterwards that as each truck driver weighed about 15 stone they decided to contain their anger…"

The race organizers gave a special dispensation for drivers Dan Gurney and Jo Bonnier to qualify for the race in one car, there being no time to get both BRMs running.

Jack Brabham emerged as fastest qualifier with a lap in 1:27.9, Trintignant close behind, then Bonnier's 1:28.2, which was 0.4sec faster than Gurney's best upon his BRM debut.

Raceday temperatures hovered around 100deg F as the cars lined up for the start with the Coopers of Brabham and Trintignant and the two BRMs forming the front row. Bruce McLaren shot through from row two to latch onto his number one's tail at flagfall, the two works Coopers leading Trintignant's Walker entry and the BRMs, though Gurney – driving Bonnier's usual '258' – rapidly established himself in front of Trintignant.

Bonnier – having opted to drive '2511' instead of his regular car – lay fourth on Gurney's tail, Brabham was forced out by fuel-feed problems, enabling Gurney to take the lead, 15 seconds ahead of Trintignant, while Bonnier pulled in on lap 45 with his car's rear brake cooked in the roasting conditions.

At 50 laps Dan still led comfortably but, soon after, his muscular driving style first bent, and then broke, the car's gearchange. On lap 60 Trintignant went by. He pulled out 5 seconds, then as the Cooper's clutch began to slip dropped back into Gurney's grasp. Local former Maserati works driver Carlos Menditeguy closed rapidly in his Cooper-Maserati until his gearbox broke on lap 63. Despite Gurney's car being stuck in top gear he still managed to retake Trintignant for the lead, but held it for just one lap before the Walker Cooper forged back in front and then held its advantage to the finish. As only four cars were still running near the end, Bonnier, having

1960: THE CHIEF MECHANIC'S VIEW OF ARGENTINA

Even by ORO standards, the Argentine tour of 1960 became an epic. Jackie Greene – son of the late Eric Forrest Greene who had played such a prominent role in securing Fangio's services for the team in 1952 – handled negotiations with the Argentine Club.

Phil Ayliff, Chief Mechanic at the time, recalls: "PB and RM discovered we could save a bond with the Argentine Customs if the cars went in as 'accompanied baggage' and I was volunteered to accompany them.

"Space was booked on a ship sailing from London to Buenos Aires via Lisbon, where I was to join it after helping with the rear-engined car build then pressing ahead at Folkingham…"

Phil's diary entry for Saturday, January 2, 1960, records Type 25 chassis '2511' and '258' completing preparation that day – fitted respectively with engines '2595' and '2596', with '2594' as spare. At 09.00 on Monday, January 4, he then handed them over to the shippers at London's Albert Dock, and returned to London on Friday the 8th to collect his visa from the Argentine Embassy. On Friday the 15th he left home in Bourne at 17.00, caught the train to London and spent the night in the *Cumberland Hotel* before flying next day from London Heathrow to Lisbon via Schiphol (Amsterdam) and Rome…

But he found himself cooling his heels in Lisbon – with no ship arriving. "I telephoned PB and he told me it was going direct, and I should come home, so I flew back via Lisbon, Rome, Schiphol and Heathrow only to be told there I should report direct to the *Aerolineas Argentinas* desk – I was going straight to Buenos Aires. Only in those days you didn't fly direct – the Argentine Comet 4 flew back to Schipol, Rome, Madrid, then Dakar, Recife (Brazil) and then down to BA.

"When I got there and was met by Jack Greene I'd spent about four days airborne… And then we discovered the ship had been delayed by a strike in England, and while I'd been waiting for it in Lisbon it had been sent to Liverpool – and was still there! Jack Greene was going on holiday in Mar del Plata and invited me to join his family on their boat. Very nice it was, too…

"When we returned to Buenos Aires I found PB had been trying desperately to contact me and couldn't find me anywhere, so he'd sent Arthur Hill down to help. By this time all the BA dockers were on strike, and through Jack Greene we enlisted Fangio's help to get the ship into port and the cars unloaded. To qualify our cars as accompanied baggage I then went out to the ship in the pilot cutter and sailed into port as a passenger…

"Hilly, Jack and I then brought all the cars – the Coopers and Lotuses, too – from the docks to the *Autodrome*, ready for the main Grand Prix circus to arrive…

"By that time PB had arrived and was in charge, but Bertie Bradnack had been sent out by Alfred Owen as Team Manager. Nice enough bloke, but he didn't seem to have a clue about what was involved. He was a great big feller and couldn't stand the heat. At one point he and PB went off and found us some sandwiches from a place which we decided would do nicely again next day. PB asked Bradnack to get them, but after a while he returned empty-handed and owned-up that he couldn't find the place, could Berthon help? So they went off together in their hire car, PB went in to get the order and when he came back Bradnack had dozed off in the heat. So PB just left him there and he played no further part that day. I'm afraid we didn't miss him…

"Then PB was offered tremendous start money for Cordoba, but he was needed back in England, so he asked if I'd take the cars up there.

"It was a free-Formula race, which meant we could run nitro fuel instead of AvGas, so we spent two or three days at the *Autodrome* getting one engine running on fresh valve springs and re-tuning it for about 2½ per cent nitro. I test-drove it at the *Autodrome* and after a few laps PB flagged me in and said: 'Either DRIVE IT or get out!' so off I went for some fast laps and frightened myself silly…

"We were still awaiting fresh valve springs for the second car when PB left for England, then the trucks arrived for Cordoba, but the only two spaces left on them were on the top deck where some cross-pieces would be directly beneath the engines. I was frightened our cars would bounce over the rough roads and might damage their sumps so I insisted on having another truck.

"The rest of the lads flew up to Cordoba on February 11 while I hung around waiting for the new valve springs. I finally collected them at the airport at 2.30 on the Friday and caught a Dakota to Cordoba. By coincidence Fangio was on the same flight. He invited me to sit with him, and when we walked off the 'plane at Cordoba with me clutching my parcel of valve springs it was like the Beatles arriving at New York – the reception they gave 'us' was tremendous – I felt ten feet tall!

"But the cars hadn't arrived. Fangio got the Club revved up, the police were called and they sent out a helicopter to search for the truck. It finally turned up at 3.30 on Saturday with only a couple of hours' practice left. The driver had picked up a bird just outside Buenos Aires and had had a tiring journey… Bits had been pilfered from one of the cars, which had to be replaced before we could run it, and he was still in jail when we left.

"Jo and Dan qualified in the same car – we swopped the numbers. Gonzalez saw what we were doing, but didn't let on, and when one car lost oil in the race and he saw me carefully ladling oil into its tank out of a 5-gallon drum he just barged me out the way, hefted the entire drum into the air as if it was a featherweight and gushed in a load, I banged the cap shut and sent Dan away – we had no idea how much had gone in but it certainly saved some time…

"Then I stayed behind with Arthur Hill to attend the prizegiving and collect our start money – and we won an enormous cup for the best-prepared cars. That was a good end to an epic trip. On the way home on the Comet 4 we slept…"

The Argentine tour was a long, hot, rugged torture for both men and cars – here in the BA Autodrome garage are Willie Southcott, Graham Hill, the comprehensively sun-tanned Phil Ayliff – fresh from his 'holiday' with Jack Forrest Greene – and Arthur Hill. The car is Graham's '258' with driver cooling mods apparent.

watched this race of the walking wounded for several laps, clambered back into his BRM and while Dan finished second in this promising debut against second-string opposition, Bonnier was placed fifth, having completed only 53 of the full 75-lap distance.

Back home from the Argentine *Temporada*, on April 2, in the Jakobs Kyrka, Stallmastaregarden, Stockholm, Jo Bonnier married Marianne Ankarouna.

At Bourne work progressed feverishly to complete two rear-engined 'production' P48s in time for the opening race of the new season, at Easter Monday Goodwood. Further test series were conducted, concentrated entirely upon the P48 without a Type 25 front-engined comparator while the only two assembled front-engined machines were completing the Argentine trip.

A final pre-Goodwood test was then conducted at Snetterton on Wednesday, April 13 – a bitterly cold day, with sharp westerly winds gusting up to 50mph at nearby Lakenheath Air Base. Sand was blowing across the hairpin, and there were large puddles on the track. Air temperature was only 8deg C, and the barometer hovered at 29.88. Dan Gurney had a bitter introduction to English test conditions…

Cars '482' and '258' – the Dutch GP-winning chassis – were present, Dan initially running 10 laps in the Type 25 to learn the circuit and re-acquaint himself with the car, bed-in the brakes, etc. He reported:

> 'Car very good indeed, brakes coming up, windscreen not high enough', extension fitted to screen, car checked over.

After six laps in '482' he returned to '258' for eight laps, best 1:35.0, reporting:

> …car loosening up, and handling exceptional [*sic*] well. Engine has more power than Cordoba…brakes very good… Exhaust sounded clear, pick up and part throttle carburation very good, no complaints apart from windscreen being too low.

April 18, 1960 – International '100', Easter Monday Goodwood: Drifting into history – swansong of the BRM Type 25s as works entries came here under the Sussex sun, Jo Bonnier preferring '258' – still sporting its Argentine ventilation holes – to the alternative new rear-engined BRM P48s, which made their debut in this same race, driven by Hill and Gurney.

After four laps in '482' had returned a best time of 1:37.0, Dan did six more in '258,' getting down to a '33.7, then another seven laps in '482,' returning 1:35.0.

On Friday, the 15th, a colder but less windy day, with merely damp patches on the track, Dan tried '483', but it proved troublesome and was very slow.

And so to Easter Monday Goodwood, with Jo Bonnier insisting on racing one of the obsolescent front-engined Type 25s in what would be its final works team appearance. He had completed as many test miles as any in the rear-engined P48s, and was confident that at least he stood some chance in the Type 25, against no chance in the latest design…

April 18, 1960 – Glover Trophy, Goodwood – 42 laps, 100.8 miles

RM's report upon this race would admit:

> The performance of the B.M. cars was disappointing. Two of the new rear engine cars and one front engine car were entered to be driven by Graham Hill, Gurney and Bonnier respectively…

While the story of the rear-engined cars will appear in our companion volume, Bonnier's experiences in the Type 25 concern us here.

RM reported:

> The front engine car was in the same condition in which it ran successfully in the Argentine, and although Bonnier lapped in just over 1 minute 26 seconds in practice he was not able to repeat this figure in the race, and for the majority of the race was lapping between 2 and 4 seconds slower than this time. On the completion of the race Bonnier complained that on occasions he had to pump the brake pedal, and immediately we knew this the Dunlop brake experts were contacted, and an on the spot investigation made. Dunlop could find nothing wrong with the system, and when this car was returned to Bourne, a further examination was made, and subsequently the car [was] tested again at Snetterton with Gurney and Hill driving, and no brake trouble occurred. Bonnier [had] finally finished the race in sixth place…
>
> The times during practice and the race were disappointing, because during previous test at Goodwood the old front engine car had lapped in 1 minute 25.2 seconds, and had done many, many continuous laps at 1 minute 26 seconds.

Immediately after Goodwood, the disgruntled Bertie Bradnack issued the following statement to the press:

> After special practice early on Easter Monday morning I considered the matter very carefully and decided to resign my position as B.R.M. racing manager, as the whole outfit had completely changed from when I had sole control in the Argentine.

Since then there has been complete lack of co-operation by the organization at Bourne, and although I made countless enquiries regarding tests of the 1960 rear-engined B.R.M. the first time I saw the cars was Saturday morning at Goodwood Circuit.

I felt that my appointment by Mr. A.G.B.Owen was deeply resented by the organization at Bourne and consequently the team spirit which is so essential in an enterprise of this kind was completely absent.

It was, of course, with deep regret that I had to make this decision prior to the Formula 1 event on Easter Monday afternoon.

The test session which RM mentioned was organized at Snetterton on April 22 in an attempt "to confirm the theory that the poor performance of the cars at Goodwood had been due to a loss of cornering power, as a result of camber change with roll".

Bonnier's Goodwood Type 25 – chassis '258' – was driven by Dan Gurney for six laps, under instruction to follow Graham Hill in '482' to observe the rear-engined car's cornering behaviour. Tony's test notes on Gurney's car reported: "Best 1:36.3..." – against Hill's best of '36.5 in the P48 – "...Brakes very good, better than on his car at Goodwood. Engine seems to be rough and down on power and rear road-holding not quite as good as pre-race tests."

When Graham then drove '258' untimed – he completed five laps – he reported: "Brakes very good, pedal may be a trifle spongey." Later in the day '258' was fitted with "pre-Goodwood race rear tyres, with D9 code number included in tyre serial number, 5 laps, best 1:34.8. Driver convinced that these tyres give better handling characteristics than the ones used for the Goodwood race – the difference being between half and one sec per lap."

BRM's long-faithful 2½-litre front-engined Grand Prix cars were not run again by ORO on serious test nor ever again in anger. And in parallel with their passing as significant contenders, another era in BRM history also reached its end, as RM's monthly Bourne Report for April 1960, related:

The new Bourne shop is now in working order, but there have been unavoidable delays through the removal from Folkingham, but everything possible is being done to make up time. The engine test house at Folkingham was kept going to the last possible moment, and then this building was dismantled with a view to being rebuilt in another position at Folkingham, outside the security area. This work is proceeding with all possible speed, but the delay through not being able to test any engines is serious. Engines are now built and waiting for test and all endeavours are being made for the test house to be working before the end of this week...

The passing of the front-engined era, and the introduction of the new generation of rear-engined cars, had coincided with closure and demolition of the ex-aerodrome control tower, complete with the flat that had been PB's, all the converted wartime Maycrete buildings and the Salopian race 'shop which had for so long formed the BRM Folkingham compound.

The long-used if ever crumbling runway and perimeter track test circuit was also now denied to the team, and as an Air Ministry sub-contractor's bulldozer crashed and splintered its way through the building in which the original V16-cylinder BRM had been unveiled to the press that long-gone December day in 1949, the first long volume of British Racing Motors' history could be closed.

There would be more, much more, to follow...

Tailpiece: Debut of the rear-engined Project 48 design had come in practice and testing here at Monza, around the 1960 Italian Grand Prix. Maurice Dove, Dick Salmon and Tony Rudd (hidden) wheel the team's makeshift prototype '481' back into line with its variably successful front-engined predecessors. Here is a whole new story waiting to be written...

TELEGRAMS: "RUBEROWEN, DARLASTON".
TELEPHONE: No 130 DARLASTON.
(P.B.EX)

DARLASTON,

Our ref: Chairman's Office.   SOUTH STAFFS.
O.R.J.

6th May, 1955.

Raymond Mays,Esq.,
Eastgate House,
Bourne,
Lincs.

Dear Ray.,

        I have received a letter from a Mr. E. J.
Lawrence, Mec/(E). P/K 931492, 14 Mess, H.M.S. Vigo
c/o F.M.O. Portsmouth, Hants, and am quoting this below.

        "I am writing to you hoping that you need
a driver for your B.R.M.   I have been driving since I
was 12 years old and although I do not hold a current
annual licence, it would not be any trouble to pass a
test.   I haven't a clue as to the qualifications of a
Formula "1" racing driver, as I know there must be some
I would be able to pass any of these tests.   If I can
be of any help to you please use me to your advantage.
On the 5th May I am proceeding on 14 days leave, therefore if you would like to interview me I will be only
too pleased to travel up to your Works.   The address
at which I can be reached whilst on leave is "The Crown
Hotel", Soham. Ely, Cambs.

        "I made the firm decision to break into
racing so therefore if you cannot use me, could you
recommend somebody who might be interested in a "Green"
driver so to speak, You might consider this letter a
liberty as I understand there must be plenty of experienced drivers who can and will drive your cars, but as
you must agree everyone has to start somewhere and sometime as I am only 20 years old it is best to start young".

        "Trusting you can help me".

        Will you please write to this young man and
let him know what the exact position is.

        Yours sincerely,

        A.G.B. Owen

The BRM project, Raymond Mays' brainchild – Alfred Owen's article of faith – made the British public more motor racing minded than ever before; establishing a stage upon which others might star, but BRM would eventually triumph…

No letter to him, no matter how naive its content, ever passed unanswered… A most unusual captain of industry, Alfred Owen always had time for the interested, for the enthusiastic, above all for the young. Because he cared…

May 13, 1950 – 'Royal Silverstone': Photographer Guy Griffiths had loaded a rare roll of colour film for this British Grand Prix meeting, aiming mainly at the works Alfettas. Guy recalled: "I believe the programme was slipping a little, everyone was terribly tense with the King and Queen present... In a great rush the BRM people suddenly wheeled out Ray for his demonstration laps and I just had the chance for one shot..." This is it. Movement, drama, the urgency of the great occasion as the BRM V16 runs in public for the first time.

September 27, 1952 – Goodwood Trophy: Rich, low, autumn sunshine made this a day on which the slow-speed colour film of the period could be used successfully for action – Guy Griffiths capturing Ken Wharton's V16 'No 2' heading towards third place in support of his team-mates, Gonzalez (first in 'No 3') and Parnell, second in 'No 1'.

February 7, 1954 – Lady Wigram Trophy, Christchurch, New Zealand: Private enthusiast – and later Alfa Romeo Monoposto owner – Bill Clark captured Ken Wharton's V16 'No 2' here. Willie Southcott and Gordon Newman cared for the car with keen local help. Typical Willie, he caused consternation during one pit stop after clouting the hub nut with a copper hammer, carefully checking the nut for damage before clouting it again... Note the disc brakes, splash guards and outboard sweep of the exhausts to project hot gases wide of the rear tyres.

1954 Lady Wigram Trophy, Christchurch, New Zealand: Willie Southcott and Gordon Newman refasten the bonnet on V16 'No 2' before sending Ken Wharton back into the fray, blue smoke spluttering from its exhausts, the tread centre section on that right-rear tyre already worn bald. This was, of course, the BRM which – next time out – would achieve the rare distinction of winning a motor race as a write-off...

THE BRM V16 MARK I

Tony Matthews' wonderful cutaway artistry at its finest in this detailed depiction of the sole surviving contemporary BRM P15, or V16 Mark I chassis 'No 1'. The author was part responsible for this car's acquisition – with assistance from the National Heritage Memorial Trust Fund and The Science Museum – for preservation within the National Motor Museum at Beaulieu as an indispensable item of British automotive history. His only regret is that the car had been restored by BRM at Bourne with stub exhausts and has retained them since, although no Mark I ever ran such a system in anger, outswept long side-pipes being the rule – stubs were purely a later Mark II 'sprint car' preserve.

April 7, 1958 – Glover Trophy, Easter Monday Goodwood: Colour photographs of Jean Behra driving a BRM are extremely rare. Here Edward Eves recorded the French star lining up his ill-fated interim Type 25, chassis '253', on the Sussex grid flanked by Moss' Walker Cooper on pole – which is refusing to restart – with Hawthorn's Ferrari V6 and Jack Brabham's Cooper-Climax completing the rank.

May 18, 1958 – Monaco Grand Prix, Monte Carlo: Jean Behra in '256' beside the deep-blue harbour on the Cote d'Azur course, driving his heart out as he always would before what was effectively his home crowd. This car was the first of BRM's new design of spaceframe-chassised/detachable-bodied Type 25s, fresh for the 1958 season.

May 2, 1959 – BRDC International Trophy, Silverstone: Stirling Moss' BRM comeback attracted enormous interest here at the beginning of the new season. Tom March caught Phil Ayliff (left) and Jimmy Collins (cap) with Moss on the startline in '2510'. Rivers Fletcher (extreme right) had worked assiduously behind the scenes to massage Moss back into a BRM drive…

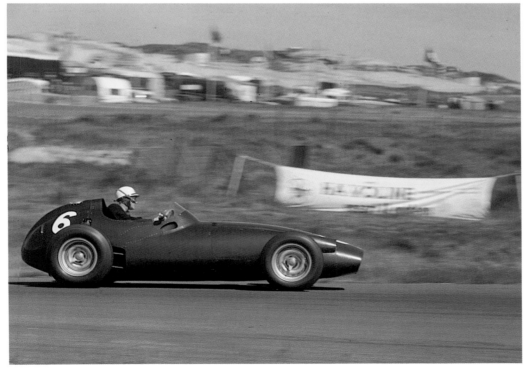

May 31, 1959 – Dutch Grand Prix, Zandvoort: On the great day when Jo Bonnier scored BRM's first-ever victory in a World Championship-qualifying Grand Prix, Harry Schell demonstrates the lovely lines of the spaceframe-chassised '259' while briefly holding fourth place. From the driver's seat the Type 25 seems remarkably short-nosed, he has a commanding view of the front wheels, the car feels taut, but everything vibrates with that lusty engine. The day will be spoiled for 'Arree' by gearbox failure.

May 31, 1959 – Dutch Grand Prix, Zandvoort: Jo Bonnier's winning '258' is the only contemporary Type 25 to have survived, owned in 1994 by the Hon. Amschel Rothschild. Team mechanic Pat Carvath recalled its debut had been scheduled for the 1958 German GP. However, after '253' – aka '27/3' – had been written-off at Goodwood, '258's debut was brought forward to the French GP. Jim Sandercombe, who organized Customs carnets, was not told '258' was going abroad until too late, so the new chassis was stamped '27/3' to use the write off's redundant carnet. This is why this unique historic BRM Type 25's frame is stamped '27/3', not '258'.

July 18, 1959 – British Grand Prix, Aintree: Stirling Moss, in BRP's '2510'. This car and '2511' both featured simplified frames and 'small tank/high headrest' tails. Some parts later provided the basis of the most faithful of three Type 25 replicas built in the early 1970s for Tom Wheatcroft's Donington Collection. Enthusiast Mike Stowe had already commissioned Stan Hope and Allan Ellison to build him a more accurate reconstruction around original parts – later completed by new owner Robs Lamplough, who added a further sister replica.

Bourne, October 1981: The sole surviving contemporary V16 BRM Mark I – chassis 'No 1' – ready-prepared for the BRM Collection auction sale at the London Motorfair in which it passed from Rubery Owen into private hands, and eventually for posterity on to the National Motor Museum. Here with their handiwork are, left to right, Dick Salmon, 1970s F1 team mechanic Gerry van der Weyden, Cyril Atkins, Aubrey Woods and the late Stan Hope.

Donington Park, September 1985: 1961 World Champion Driver – and subsequent Scuderia Centro-Sud BRM pilot – Phil Hill, track testing Tom Wheatcroft's V16 Mark II for the American magazine Road & Track. Tom acquired this car at the 1981 Motorfair auction and it subsequently accumulated an enormous mileage while removing the earwax from numerous drivers, including the author. And it was essentially trouble-free – prepared and maintained mainly by Hall and Fowler...of Folkingham aerodrome.

Surviving V16 Mark I 'No 1' stripped for preparation to full running order in Tony Merrick's workshop at Waltham St Lawrence, Nick Mason's Mark II 'No 5' alongside – the Rubery Owen four-longeron, all-welded chassis, Porsche-type trailing arm front suspension, Girling disc brakes, offset driveline and the Mercedes-Benz inspired transaxle assembly were all quite beautifully made.

The rear end of 'No 1', with its de Dion axle tube located laterally by the guide channel cast into the rear of the transaxle casing, and longitudinally by twin-tube radius arms each side. The Lockheed air-strut spring/dampers are absent. It was the final-drive output shafts deep within those pot-joint housings which sheared at Silverstone in 1950 – Sommer left waggling that right-hand gearchange in vain.

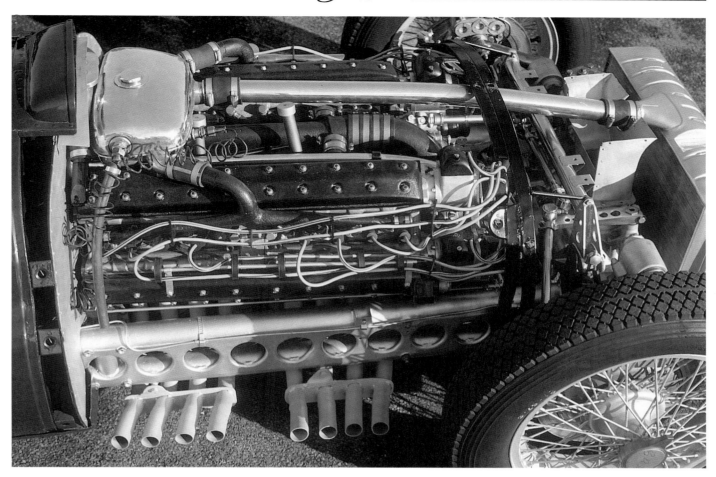

"That bewildering box of tricks" – V16 engine 'No 20/1' installed in car 'No 1' – photographed at Bourne in 1981... As previously mentioned, the stub exhausts are out of place on a Mark 1, but in demonstration an adoring and deafened public have approved...

Stripped bare – the 135-degree wide-angle V16-cylinder BRM engine looks almost reminiscent of a 1970s Ferrari flat-12 in this form – yet to be united with its lower crankcase half and output mechanism, ignition magnetos incomplete on the camshaft noses, Rolls-Royce supercharger yet to be added.

High angle on V16 'No 1' at the end of its long life at Bourne, showing its engine offset across the chassis, giant radiator and the mechanism's general resemblance to an aero engine installation. For an entire generation of race-goers the V16 BRM had become an enduring legend…

PART FIVE

Appendices

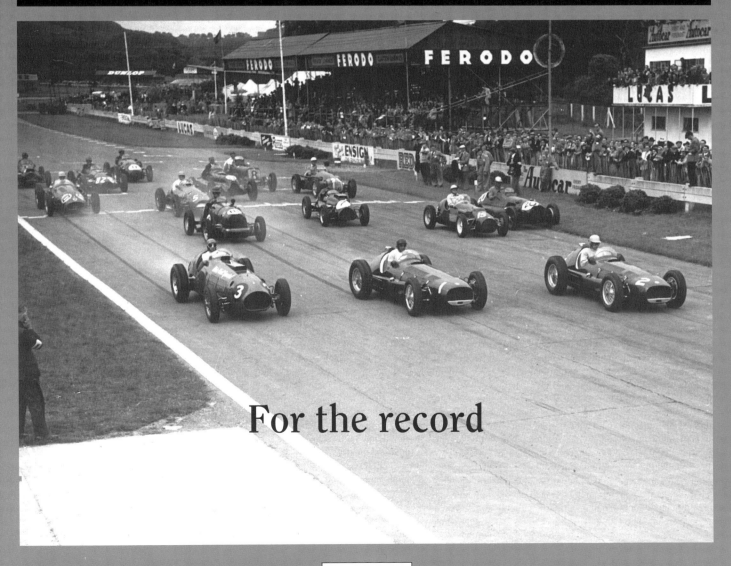

For the record

APPENDIX A:
FRONT-ENGINED BRMs – THE RACE RECORD

Date	Event & Venue	No	Car	Engine	Driver(s)	Grid	Result	Notes
1949								
29-11-49	Folkingham Aerodrome	None	Prototype	10/1	Ken **Richardson**	–	–	*Unlouvred body – pale green – first run*
15-12-49	Folkingham Aerodrome	None	Prototype	10/1	Raymond **Mays**	–	–	*Unlouvred body – pale green – press launch*
1950								
13-5-50	**British GP meeting demonstration run, Silverstone**	None	Prototype	10/1	Raymond **Mays**	–	–	*Public debut, two small scuttle scoops – pale green*
26-8-50	**International Trophy, Silverstone**	'8'	V16 Mk I No 1	10/1	Raymond **Sommer**	Back row No time	Rtd –	*0 laps – sheared both inboard UJs at start, louvred bonnet & side panels, large under-nose intake*
30-9-50	**Woodcote Cup, Goodwood**	'1'	V16 Mk I No 1	10/2	Reg **Parnell**	2nd (Row 1)	**1st**	*5-lap race – beat Maserati 4CLTs of 'Bira' and de Graffenried*
30-9-50	**Goodwood Trophy, Goodwood**	'1'	V16 Mk I No 1	10/2	Reg **Parnell**	7th (Row 2)	**1st**	*12-lap race – beat 'Bira' and Gerard's ERA – both races on flooded track*
29-10-50	**Pena Rhin GP, Pedralbes, Barcelona, Spain**	'8'	V16 Mk I No 1	10/1	Reg **Parnell**	4th (R1)	Rtd	*2 laps – sheared supercharger drive – ran 4th, pale green with red nose-band & tail-tip*
		'10'	V16 Mk I No 2	10/2	Peter **Walker**	5th (R1)	Rtd	*33 laps – gearbox seizing after oil loss – ran 4th, three pit stops – blue nose-band & tail tip.* LAST RACE IN PLAIN PALE GREEN.
1951								
14-7-51	**BRITISH GP, Silverstone**	'6'	V16 Mk I No 1	10/1	Reg **Parnell**	Back row No time	5th	*5 laps behind Gonzalez's winning Ferrari – opened-up nose cowl*
		'7'	V16 Mk I No 2	10/2	Peter **Walker**	Back row No time	7th	*7 laps behind Gonzalez's winning Ferrari – opened-up nose cowl.* FIRST RACE IN METALLIC PALE GREEN.
16-9-51	**ITALIAN GP, Monza**	'30'	V16 Mk I No 1	10/1	Reg **Parnell**	8th (R2)	DNS	*Open nose – did not start – see text*
		'32'	V16 Mk I No 2	10/4	Ken **Richardson** Hans **Stuck**	10th (R3)	DNS	*Slatted grille in nose – did not start – see text*
1952								
1-6-52	**Albi GP, Les Planques, France**	'2'	V16 Mk I No 1	20/1	Juan **Fangio**	**1st**	Rtd	*Disc brakes – led 15 laps until boiled, pits, 1 final lap – snapped head studs*
		'4'	V16 Mk I No 2	20/3	Froilan **Gonzalez** (R1)		Rtd/FL	*Disc brakes – ran 2nd before engine failure after 5 laps – both cars raced with extra-large nose top and scuttle intakes, louvred side panels, slatted grilles*
7-6-52	**Ulster Trophy, Dundrod, N. Ireland**	'7'	V16 Mk I No 1	20/4	Juan **Fangio**	12th (R5)	Rtd	*25 laps of 34 – fuel contamination – 2nd by lap 4 stoneguards added since Albi*
		'8'	V16 Mk I No 2	20/2	Stirling **Moss**	13th (R5)	Rtd	*3 laps – stalled at start, pit stop after 2 laps, terminal overheating*
17-7-52	*Formule Libre* **Trophy, Silverstone**	'7'	V16 Mk I No 1	20/4	Froilan **Gonzalez**	1st	Rtd	*Spun when 2nd, damaged radiator/steering – took over Wharton's car*
		'8'	V16 Mk I No 2	20/2	Ken **Wharton**	3rd (R1)	Rtd/FL	*Ran 3rd – Gonzalez took over – gearbox failure – both cars colour-coded nose-top intake extension, slatted grille, extensive louvring.*
2-8-52	**International Trophy, Boreham**	'25'	V16 Mk I No 1	20/4	Froilan **Gonzalez**	2nd (R1)	Rtd	*Crashed when 2nd, in rain, at Hangar Bend entering lap 3*
		'26'	V16 Mk I No 2	20/2	Ken **Wharton**	4th (R1)	Rtd	*Gearbox trouble at 61 laps after being lapped by Formula 2 runners.* FIRST RACE IN DARK METALLIC LUSTROUS GREEN, COLOUR-CODED NOSE-TOP BLISTERS.
23-8-52	**National Trophy, Turnberry, Scotland**	'53'	V16 Mk I No 3	–	Reg **Parnell**	2nd (R1)	**1st**	*DRUM BRAKES – OLD-STYLE GEARBOX – 20-laps, beat prewar cars*
		'52'	V16 Mk I No 2	–	Ken **Wharton**	3rd (R1)	Rtd	*7 laps – steering failure while leading.* DARK LUSTROUS GREEN OVERALL.

Date	Event & Venue	No	Car	Engine	Driver(s)	Grid	Result	Notes
27-9-52	Woodcote Cup, Goodwood	'5'	*V16 Mk I* No 3	–	Froilan **Gonzalez**	1st	1st/FL	*5-lap race – Farina 2nd in 'Thin Wall Special' Ferrari*
		'6'	*V16 Mk I* No 1	–	Reg **Parnell**	3rd (R1)	3rd	
		'7'	*V16 Mk I* No 2	–	Ken **Wharton**	4th (R1)	DNS	*Car failed to restart on grid – see text*
27-9-52	Goodwood Trophy, Goodwood	'5'	*V16 Mk I* No 3	–	Froilan **Gonzalez**	1st	1st	*15 laps – led BRMs home ahead of unsupercharged Formula 2 cars*
		'6'	*V16 Mk I* No 1	–	Reg **Parnell**	3rd (R1)	2nd/FL	*All three cars in similar trim with definitive top-blistered, large radiator nose, louvred bonnets and side panels, all on disc brakes*
		'7'	*V16 Mk I* No 2	–	Ken **Wharton**	2nd (R1)	3rd	
11-10-52	International Trophy, Charterhall, Scotland	'1'	*V16 Mk I* No 2	–	Reg **Parnell**	3rd (R1)	Rtd	*6 laps of 40-lap race – transmission problem*
		'2'	*V16 Mk I* No 1	–	Ken **Wharton**	2nd (R1)	2nd/FL	*Spun while leading – Gerard's pre-war ERA won*

1953

Date	Event & Venue	No	Car	Engine	Driver(s)	Grid	Result	Notes
6-4-53	Chichester Cup, Goodwood	'1'	*V16 Mk I* No 1	–	Reg **Parnell**		4th	*5-lap race won by de Graffenreid's Plate-Maserati*
		'2'	*V16 Mk I* No 2	–	Ken **Wharton**		2nd/FL	*Ron Flockhart's ERA finished 3rd*
6-4-53	Glover Trophy, Goodwood	'1'	*V16 Mk I* No 1	–	Reg **Parnell**	4th (R1)	Rtd	*After 4 laps – supercharger quill-shaft sheared*
		'2'	*V16 Mk I* No 2	–	Ken **Wharton**	1st	1st/FL	*15-lap race – new lap record – beat Taruffi in 'ThinWall'*
23-5-53	*Formule Libre,* Charterhall, Scotland	'2'	*V16 Mk I* No 2	20/1	Ken **Wharton**	1st	3rd/FL	*20-lap race – led, spun, broke lap record in pursuit of Flockhart & Gerard ERAs*
31-5-53	Albi GP, Les Planques, France – F1 Heat	'7'	*V16 Mk I* No 1		Juan **Fangio**	1st	1st/FL	*10-lap race – Fangio set new lap record*
		'9'	*V16 Mk I* No 3	–	Ken **Wharton**	4th (R2)	2nd	
		'11'	*V16 Mk I* No 2	20/2	Froilan **Gonzalez**	3rd (R1)	5th	*Delayed by pit stop on lap 4 to replace stripped tyre*
	Albi GP – Final	'7'	*V16 Mk I* No 1	–	Juan **Fangio**	1st	Rtd	*15-lap race – Fangio led until tyre failed, brake and hub damage*
		'9'	*V16 Mk I* No 3	–	Ken **Wharton**	2nd (R1)	Crash	*Over-ambition on outward leg of course – CAR DESTROYED, WRECK SCRAPPED – Salvage into V16 Mark II*
		'11'	*V16 Mk I* No 2	20/2	Froilan **Gonzalez**	9th (R4)	2nd	*15 laps – beaten by Rosier's Ferrari 375 after tyre change*
18-6-53	Douglas demonstration, Isle of Man	None	*V16 Mk I* No 2	20/2	Reg **Parnell**	–	–	*British Empire Trophy sports car race meeting – 6 practice laps, 4 in earnest*
18-7-53	*Formule Libre* Trophy, Silverstone	'2'	*V16 Mk I* No 2	20/1	Ken **Wharton**	3rd (R1)	3rd	*16 laps – beaten by Farina's 'ThinWall' and Fangio*
		'3'	*V16 Mk I* No 1	–	Juan **Fangio**	1st	2nd	*Engine compromised by race-eve preparation muddle – see text*
25-7-53	USAF Trophy *F. Libre,* Snetterton	'1'	*V16 Mk I* No 1	–	Ken **Wharton**	1st	1st/FL	*15-lap F1 race – beat Flockhart's ERA – set first 90mph Snetterton lap*
		'1'	*V16 Mk I* No 1	–	Ken **Wharton**	1st	1st/=FL	*10-lap Libre race – beat Marr's Connaught, shared FL with Flockhart*
15-8-53	*Formule Libre* Trophy, Charterhall, Scotland	'35'	*V16 Mk I* No 1	–	Ken **Wharton**	2nd (R1)	1st/FL	*50-lap race – took lead when Farina's 'ThinWall' failed*
		'34'	*V16 Mk I* No 2	20/1	Reg **Parnell**	T-Crash	DNS	*Car damaged beyond immediate repair on-site in practice 'off'*
29-8-53	Shelsley Walsh hill-climb demonstration	None	*V16 Mk I* No 1	–	Ken **Wharton**	–	–	*At RAC British Hillclimb Championship-round meeting*
26-9-53	Woodcote Cup, Goodwood	'1'	*V16 Mk I* No 1	–	Juan **Fangio**	1st	2nd	*5-lap race – won by Hawthorn in 'ThinWall'*
		'2'	*V16 Mk I* No 2	20/1	Ken **Wharton**	3rd (R1)	3rd	*Ran 2nd before spin at chicane*
26-9-53	Goodwood Trophy, Goodwood	'1'	*V16 Mk I* No 1	–	Juan **Fangio**	1st	Rtd	*12 laps of 15-lap race – gearbox*
		'2'	*V16 Mk I* No 2	20/1	Ken **Wharton**	4th (R1)	2nd	*15 laps – beaten by Hawthorn's 'ThinWall'*
3-10-53	Hastings Trophy, Castle Combe	'62'	*V16 Mk I* No 2	20/1	Ken **Wharton**	1st	1st/FL	*15 laps – beat Gerard's ERA & Gould's Cooper-Bristol*

1954

Date	Event & Venue	No	Car	Engine	Driver(s)	Grid	Result	Notes
9-1-54	New Zealand GP, Ardmore, N. Island	'1'	*V16 Mk I* No 2	20/2	Ken **Wharton**	1st	3rd	*100 laps – led until partial brake failure*
7-2-54	Lady Wigram Trophy, Christchurch, NZ S. Island	'3'	*V16 Mk I* No 2	20/3	Ken **Wharton**	1st	3rd	*Led 42 laps of 48-lap race until engine seized – pushed across line*

Date	Event & Venue	No	Car	Engine	Driver(s)	Grid	Result	Notes
19-4-54	Chichester Cup, Goodwood	'4'	*V16 Mk II No 4*	20/2	Ken **Wharton**	1st	1st/=FL	*DEBUT OF MARK II 'SPRINT CAR' – 5 laps – beat Salvadori & Parnell in Maserati 250F & Ferrari 625*
		'5'	*V16 Mk I No 2*	20/5	Ron **Flockhart**	2nd (R1)	4th/=FL	*Spun in first corner on BRM debut, lost 25secs – first four shared FL*
19-4-54	Glover Trophy, Goodwood	'4'	*V16 Mk II No 4*	20/2	Ron **Flockhart**	1st	4th	*Led first lap, but magneto trouble told…*
		'5'	*V16 Mk I No 2*	20/5	Ken **Wharton**	2nd (R1)	1st/=FL	*21 laps – won after duel & collision with Salvadori's Maserati 250F – CAR DAMAGED BEYOND ECONOMIC REPAIR, STRIPPED & SCRAPPED – LAST RACE APPEARANCE OF WORKS-ENTERED V16 BRM MARK I.*
24-4-54	*Formule Libre, Snetterton*	'1'	*V16 Mk II No 4*	20/2	Ron **Flockhart**	1st	1st/FL	*10 laps – beat Gould and Marr, Cooper-Bristol & Connaught – new record lap*
8-5-54	*Formule Libre, Ibsley*	'102'	*V16 Mk II No 4*	–	Ron **Flockhart**	1st	1st/FL	*15 laps – beat two C-Type Jaguars & Whitehead's ERA*
20-5-54	Aintree circuit opening ceremony	None	*V16 Mk II No 4*	–	Ken **Wharton**/ Ron **Flockhart**	–	–	*Wharton ran 5 laps, Flockhart 2 in company with Parnell's Ferrari 625*
31-5-54	Aintree '200' F. Libre Heat One	'9'	*V16 Mk II No 5*	–	Ken **Wharton**	6th (R2)	4th	*DEBUT OF SECOND MARK II 'SPRINT CAR' – 17-lap Heat – behind Parnell, Collins & Moss (Ferrari 625, 'ThinWall' & Maserati 250F) – in rain did not risk car*
	Heat Two	'10'	*V16 Mk II No 4*	–	Ron **Flockhart**	4th (R1)	1st	*Second 17-lap Heat – beat Salvadori's Maserati 250F – in rain*
	Final	'10'	*V16 Mk II No 4*	–	Ron **Flockhart**	3rd (R1)	3rd	*17 laps – behind Moss & Parnell after Collins retired – spin cost one lap*
		'9'	*V16 Mk II No 5*	–	Ken **Wharton**	6th (R2)	Rtd	*16 laps – Front brakes locked-on – ran 3rd*
7-6-54	Whitsun Trophy, Goodwood	'1'	*V16 Mk II No 5*	–	Ken **Wharton**	2nd (R1)	4th	*15 laps – race won by Collins' 'ThinWall', Salvadori's 250F 2nd*
		'2'	*V16 Mk II No 4*	–	Ron **Flockhart**	3rd (R2)	2nd	*15 laps – beaten by Collins – led first 3 laps*
17-6-54	Shelsley Walsh hill-climb practice	None	*V16 Mk II No 5*	–	Ken **Wharton**	–	–	*Three climbs, second fastest at 37.8secs – brakes locked*
4-7-54	FRENCH GP, Reims-Gueux	'42'	*Maserati 250F '2509'(1)*	'2509'	Ken **Wharton**	16th (R7)	Rtd	*After 19 laps – damaging propshaft vibration – ran 10th – DEBUT OF 'OWEN MASERATI'*
17-7-54	BRITISH GP, Silverstone	'8'	*Maserati 250F '2509'(1)*	'2509'	Ken **Wharton**	9th (R3)	8th	*86 laps of 90-lap race – ran 7th – oiled plugs, driver trouble…LAST RACE OF ORIGINAL '2509' AS ORO ENTRY – car swopped with 'Bira's crashed 250F in compensation for Flockhart driver error…see text.*
14-8-54	*Formule Libre, Snetterton*	'21'	*V16 Mk II No 4*	–	Ron **Flockhart**	2nd (R1)	3rd	*36 laps of 40-lap race – three spins, lost 128secs in pit stops, car battered!*
22-8-54	SWISS GP, Bremgarten, Berne	18'	*Maserati 250F '2509'*	'2509'	Ken **Wharton**	8th (R3)	6th	*64 laps of 66 – hit Mantovani's 250F lap 4, lost 31secs, 6th to 11th – DEBUT OF REBUILT Ex-'BIRA' 'OWEN MASERATI'…*
28-8-54	Hastings Trophy, Castle Combe	'54'	*V16 Mk II No 5*	–	Ron **Flockhart**	2nd (R1)	2nd	*15 laps – Gerard's Cooper won by 0.4sec – led, brakes poor, magneto fault*
4-9-54	*Formule Libre, Charterhall, Scotland*	'?'	*V16 Mk II No 4*	–	Ron **Flockhart**	1st	Rtd	*0 laps – carburettor piston jammed by stone – Gerard's Cooper-Bristol won*
13-9-54	Folkingham test	None	*V16 Mk II No 4*	–	Juan **Fangio**	–	–	*Drove on visit – 10 laps – best 1:39.0 – averaged 100mph over last 7*
25-9-54	Woodcote Cup, Goodwood	'3'	*V16 Mk II No 4*	–	Ken **Wharton**	2nd (R1)	2nd	*10 laps – misfiring – beaten by Collins' 'ThinWall'*
		'4'	*V16 Mk II No 5*	–	Ron **Flockhart**	Back row	Rtd	*No time – 0-laps – deranged suspension after lap 1 driver error at Woodcote*
2-10-54	*Formule Libre, Aintree*	'3'	*V16 Mk II No 5*	–	Ron **Flockhart**	4th (R1)	3rd	*17 laps – beaten by Moss & Mantovani Maserati 250Fs – No 3 plug cracked.*
		'4'	*V16 Mk II No 4*	–	Ken **Wharton**	2nd (R1)	Rtd/=FL	*4 laps – spun and rammed by Schell's Maserati 250F*
2-10-54	SPANISH GP, Pedralbes, Barcelona	'28'	*Maserati 250F '2509'*	'2509'	Ken **Wharton**	14th (R4)	8th	*74 laps of 80-lap race – ran distant 6th*

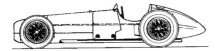

Folkingham launch car, 1949

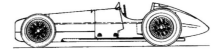

Mays, British GP demonstration, 1950

Sommer, 'Daily Express' Silverstone, 1950

Parnell, Goodwood, 1950

Parnell, Pena Rhin GP, 1950

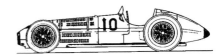

Walker, Pena Rhin GP, 1950

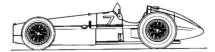

Walker, British GP, 1951

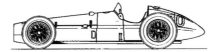

Parnell, Italian GP, 1951

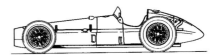

Richardson/Stuck, Italian GP, 1951

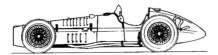

Fangio, Albi GP, 1952

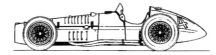

Gonzalez, Albi GP, 1952

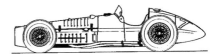

Fangio, Dundrod, 1952

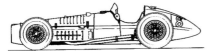

Moss, Dundrod, 1952

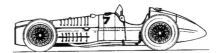

Gonzalez, Silverstone, 1952

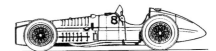

Wharton/Gonzalez, Silverstone, 1952

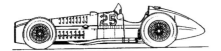

Gonzalez, Boreham, 1952

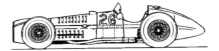

Wharton, Boreham, 1952

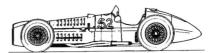

Wharton, Turnberry, 1952

Parnell, Turnberry, 1952

Gonzalez, Goodwood, 1952

Parnell, Goodwood, 1952

Wharton, Goodwood, 1952

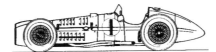

Parnell, Easter Goodwood, 1953

Wharton, Easter Goodwood, 1953

Wharton, May Charterhall, 1953

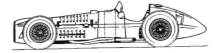

Fangio, Albi GP, 1953

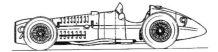

Wharton, Albi GP, 1953

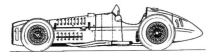

Gonzalez, Albi GP, 1953

Wharton, Silverstone, 1953

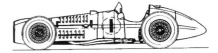

Wharton, Snetterton, 1953

Date	Event & Venue	No	Car	Engine	Driver(s)	Grid	Result	Notes
1955								
11-4-55	Chichester Cup F. Libre, Goodwood	'25'	V16 Mk II **No 5**	–	Peter **Collins**	1st	1st/FL	7 laps – beat Salvadori & Moss 250Fs
11-4-55	Easter Handicap, Goodwood	'25'	V16 Mk II **No 5**	–	Peter **Collins**	Scratch	5th/FL	5 laps – behind Gerard, Salvadori & Connaughts of Young & Beauman
7-5-55	International Trophy, Silverstone	'3'	Maserati 250F '2509'	'2509'	Peter **Collins**	5th (R2)	1st/=FL	60 LAPS – ORO'S FIRST F1 WIN SINCE ALBI HEAT, 1953 – NEVER LOWER THAN 2ND IN DICE WITH SALVADORI'S SISTER 250F
28-5-55	Formule Libre, Snetterton	'97' '96'	V16 Mk II **No 5** V16 Mk II **No 4**	– –	Peter **Collins** Ron **Flockhart**	1st 5th (R2)	Rtd/FL 2nd	7 laps – collided with Cunningham-Reid's Lister-Bristol 10-laps – beaten by Salvadori's 250F – grid positions by ballot
30-5-55	London Trophy F. Libre Crystal Palace Heat One	'8'	Maserati 250F '2509'	'2509'	Peter **Collins**	1st	1st/FL	12 laps – again beat Salvadori
	Heat Two	'8'	Maserati 250F '2509'	'2509'	Peter **Collins**	1st	1st/FL	12 laps – beat Gerard's Cooper-Bristol after Salvadori's 250F failed
	Aggregate		Maserati 250F '2509'	'2509'	Peter **Collins**	–	1st	From Gerard – Owen Maserati ran without tail cowl.
16-7-55	BRITISH GP, Aintree	'42'	Maserati 250F '2509'	'2509'	Peter **Collins**	23rd (R10)	Rtd	30 laps – 'clutch failure' – con-rod, engine almost in two – ran 7th
13-8-55	Formule Libre, Snetterton	'146'	V16 Mk II **No 5**	–	Peter **Collins**	–	Rtd	After only 1 of 25-laps – broken l/h driveshaft UJ
2-9-55	Daily Telegraph Trophy, Aintree (practice)	'9'	Type 25 '252'	'252'	Peter **Collins**	–	DNS	TYPE 25 PUBLIC DEBUT – Oil on rear tyres, minor crash at Melling New car '252' – 2-piece propshaft, air-strut suepension, Dunlop servo-assisted disc brakes
3-9-55	Aintree F. Libre	'22'	V16 Mk II **No 5**	–	Peter **Collins**	2nd (R1)	1st	17 laps – beat Salvadori's 250F & Brooks' Connaught
24-9-55	International Gold Cup, Oulton Park	'10'	Type 25 '252'	'252'	Peter **Collins**	13th (R4)	Rtd	10 laps – ran 3rd – false reading from faulty oil pressure gauge
1-10-55	Avon Trophy, Formula 1, Castle Combe	'14'	Maserati 250F '2509'	'2509'	Peter **Collins**	Back row (DNP)	Rtd	13 laps of 55 – de Dion tube broke when 2nd
1-10-55	Empire News Trophy, Formule Libre, Castle Combe	'48'	V16 Mk II **No 5**	–	Ron **Flockhart**	2nd (R1)	2nd	20 laps – split Schell's winning Vanwall & Gerard's Cooper-Bristol FINAL RACE APPEARANCE OF WORKS-ENTERED BRM V16
1956								
22-1-56	ARGENTINE GP, Buenos Aires Autodrome	'14'	Maserati 250F '2509'	'2509'	Mike **Hawthorn**	8th (R3)	3rd	96 of 98 laps – behind Fangio/Musso's Lancia-Ferrari & Behra's 250F
5-2-56	Buenos Aires City Libre GP, Mendoza, Argentina	'14'	Maserati 250F '2509'	'2509'	Mike **Hawthorn**	–	9th	54 of 60 laps – delayed by steering problems
2-4-56	Richmond Trophy, Goodwood	'4'	Type 25 '253'	–	Mike **Hawthorn**	3rd (R1)	Rtd	23 of 32 laps – led, then crashed when half-shaft pot-joint seized, rolled in at Fordwater. DEBUT RACE OF NEW CAR '253' – Lockheed disc brakes – damage repairable
		'5'	Type 25 '252'	–	Tony **Brooks**	No time	Rtd	9 laps – ran 5th, oil pressure – '252' rebuilt in winter – Connaught-link de Dion location, negative camber de Dion tube, lever-type air-strut front suspension, air short ram intake
21-4-56	Aintree '200'	'1'	Type 25 '253'	–	Mike **Hawthorn**	2nd (R1)	Rtd	4-laps only – brake pedal pivot pin dropped out – negligent fitting '253' repaired since Goodwood inversion.
		'2'	Type 25 '252'	–	Tony **Brooks**	6th (R3)	2nd/FL	67-laps – led, beaten by Moss's 250F after stop in search of effective brakes FIRST RACE FINISH BY BRM TYPE 25
5-5-56	International Trophy, Silverstone	'9'	Type 25 '252'	–	Mike **Hawthorn**	4th (R1)	Rtd/=FL	14-laps of 60 – timing gears – led, shared FL with Moss's winning Vanwall

Wharton, August Charterhall, 1953

Wharton, New Zealand GP, 1954

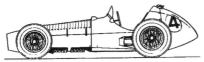

Wharton/Flockhart, Easter Goodwood, 1954

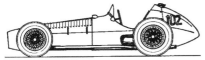

Flockhart, Ibsley, 1954

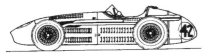

Wharton, French GP, 1954

Wharton, Swiss GP, 1954

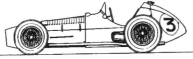

Flockhart, October Aintree, 1954

Collins, May Silverstone, 1955

Collins, British GP, 1955

Collins, Type 25, Aintree, 1955

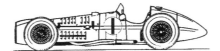

Fangio, September Goodwood, 1953

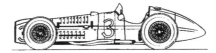

Wharton, Christchurch, NZ, 1954

Flockhart/Wharton, Easter Goodwood, 1954

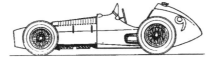

Wharton, Aintree '200', 1954

Wharton, British GP, 1954

Flockhart, Castle Combe, 1954

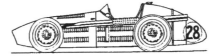

Wharton, Spanish GP, 1954

Flockhart, May Snetterton, 1955

Collins, August Snetterton, 1955

Collins, September Aintree, 1955

Wharton, Castle Combe, 1953

V16 Mark II prototype, 1954

Flockhart, April Snetterton, 1954

Wharton, Whit-Monday Goodwood, 1954

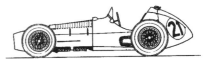

Flockhart, August Snetterton, 1954

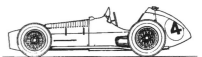

Flockhart, September Goodwood, 1954

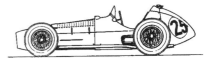

Collins, Easter Goodwood, 1955

Collins, Crystal Palace, 1955

Type 25 first prototype, 1955

Collins, Oulton Park, 1955

Date	Event & Venue	No	Car	Engine	Driver(s)	Grid	Result	Notes
13-5-56	MONACO GP, Monte Carlo	'10'	Type 25 '253'	–	Mike **Hawthorn**	10th (R4)	DNS	*Both cars withdrawn after practice valve failures – see text*
		'12'	Type 25 '252'	2561	Tony **Brooks**	12th (R5)	DNS	
24-6-56	Aintree '100'	'1'	Type 25 '252'	–	Tony **Brooks**	–	DNS	*'Valves' after brief practice appearance – 2:04.8 lap good enough for pole position*
14-7-56	BRITISH GP, Silverstone	'23'	Type 25 '251'	–	Mike **Hawthorn**	3rd (R1)	Rtd	*24-laps of 101 – pot-joint seal failure after leading DEBUT RACE OF FIRST PROTOTYPE '251' – previously used only in testing, rebuilt to rocking-lever front suspension, Connaught-link de Dion location, long-wheelbase to accomodate Hawthorn – first short ram air intake*
		'24'	Type 25 '252'	–	Tony **Brooks**	9th (R3)	Rtd	*41-laps – crashed, overturned & burned-out at Abbey Curve, sticking throttle – CAR '252' DESTROYED – WRECKAGE STRIPPED AND SCRAPPED*
		'25'	Type 25 '253'	–	Ron **Flockhart**	17th (R5)	Rtd	*3-laps only – timing gear failure*

1957

Date	Event & Venue	No	Car	Engine	Driver(s)	Grid	Result	Notes
22-4-57	Glover Trophy, Goodwood	'1'	Type 25 '253'	–	Roy **Salvadori**	6th (R2)	Rtd	*0 laps – brakes jammed on, spun at Woodcote – '253' rebuilt with high cockpit sides, centre-pivot transverse leaf springs and anti-roll bars f&r (no roll stiffness), piston-type dampers, in Issigonis-Moulton experimentation*
		'2'	Type 25 '251'	–	Ron **Flockhart**	4th (R2)	3rd	*32 laps – beaten by Connaughts of Lewis-Evans & Fairman – '251' rebuilt over winter with centre-pivot transverse leaf springs – still low cockpit*
19-5-57	MONACO GP, Monte Carlo	'6'	Type 25 '254'	–	Ron **Flockhart**	11th (R5)	Rtd	*60 of 105 laps – ran 5th – DEBUT RACE OF NEW CAR '254' with fixed high-sided cockpit surround, centre-pivot rear leaf-spring, anti-roll bars f&r*
		'8'	Type 25 '253'	–	Roy **Salvadori**	DNQ	–	*Driver demoralization largely due to unpredictability of brakes*
7-7-57	FRENCH GP, Rouen-les-Essarts	'26'	Type 25 '254'	–	Ron **Flockhart**	11th (R5)	Rtd	*3-laps of 77 – crashed and rolled car on spilled oil when 11th – '254' just rebuilt with coil-spring/tele-damper suspension, Watt-link de Dion location WRITTEN OFF, STRIPPED & SCRAPPED – salvaged parts went into new '255'*
		'28'	Type 25 '253'	–	Herbert **Mackay Fraser**	12th (R5)	Rtd	*25-laps – rear pot-joint near seizure – ran 6th – '253' rebuilt with coil-spring/tele-damper suspension, Watt link de Dion location – roller-pot half-shaft joints*
20-7-57	BRITISH GP, Aintree	'24'	Type 25 '253'	–	Jack **Fairman**	15th (R5)	Rtd	*48 of 90 laps – ran 11th – '253' fitted with roller-pot half-shaft joints*
		'26'	Type 25 '251'	–	Les **Leston**	12th (R7)	Rtd	*45 laps – ran 9th – '251' rebuilt with elektron body, high cockpit sides, coil-spring/tele-damper suspension with Watt link de Dion location*
27-7-57	Caen GP, Le Prairie, France	'2'	Type 25 '253'	–	Jean **Behra**	1st	1st/FL	*86 laps – beat Salvadori's 1.96 Cooper & four private 250Fs BRM's FIRST SIGNIFICANT FORMULA 1 RACE WIN. '253' fitted with first ball-slider half-shaft joints, plain-bearing universals*
		'4'	Type 25 '251'	2574	Harry **Schell**	5th (R2)	Rtd	*59 laps – engine failure after swopping lead with Behra*
14-9-57	International Trophy, Silverstone, **Heat One**	'6'	Type 25 '251'	2574	Jean **Behra**	2nd (R1)	1st/FL	*15 laps – led throughout, broke lap record – '251' running ball-slider half-shafts with needle-roller UJs*
		'8'	Type 25 '255'	254	Ron **Flockhart**	3rd (R1)	2nd	*15 laps – 2nd throughout behind Behra – beat three private 250Fs – DEBUT RACE OF '255' – LAST STRESSED-SKIN TYPE 25 – cannibalized salvage from '254' (written-off at Rouen) – ball-spline half-shafts from new*
	Heat Two	'7'	Type 25 '253'	2573	Harry **Schell**	1st	1st	*15 laps – beat Brabham's 1.96 Cooper, two private 250Fs*
	Final	'6'	Type 25 '251'	2574	Jean **Behra**	1st	1st/FL	*35 laps – led throughout*
		'7'	Type 25 '253'	2573	Harry **Schell**	2nd (R1)	2nd	*35 laps – in absence of works Vanwall, Ferrari, Maserati after Italian GP*
		'8'	Type 25 '255'	254	Ron **Flockhart**	4th (R1)	3rd	*35 laps – ahead of four private 250Fs – Bonnier, Gregory, Gould & Halford*
21-9-57	Modena GP, Modena *Aerautodromo*, Italy, **Heat One**	'10'	Type 25 '255'	2574	Ron **Flockhart**	5th (R2)	7th	*38 of 40 laps – lost time in spin & stop to investigate low oil pressure*
		'12'	Type 25 '251'	–	Jo **Bonnier**	7th (R3)	6th	*39 laps – behind works & private 250Fs & hybrid Ferrari Dino V6s*

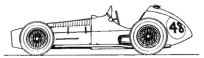

Flockhart, Castle Combe, 1955

Collins, Castle Combe, 1955

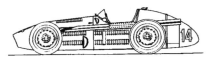

Hawthorn, Argentine GP, 1956

Hawthorn, Easter Goodwood, 1956

Brooks, Easter Goodwood, 1956

Hawthorn, Aintree '200', 1956

Hawthorn, May Silverstone, 1956

Hawthorn, Monaco GP, 1956

Hawthorn, British GP, 1956

Brooks, British GP, 1956

Flockhart, British GP, 1956

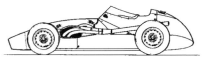

1956 Monza tests 'Howdah'

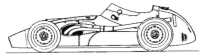

Salvadori, Easter Goodwood, 1957

Flockhart, Easter Goodwood, 1957

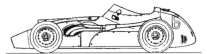

Flockhart, Monaco GP, 1957

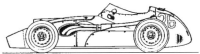

Flockhart, French GP, 1957

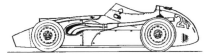

Fairman, British GP, 1957

Behra, Caen GP, 1957

Behra, International Trophy, 1957

Flockhart, Modena GP, 1957

Trintignant, Moroccan GP, 1957

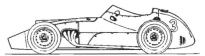

Behra, Easter Goodwood, 1958

Schell, Easter Goodwood, 1958

Behra, Aintree '200', 1958

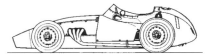

Behra, May Silverstone, 1958

Flockhart, May Silverstone, 1958

Behra, Monaco GP, 1958

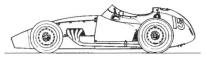

Schell, Dutch GP, 1958

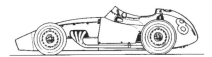

Behra, Belgian GP, 1958

Schell, French GP, 1958

Date	Event & Venue	No	Car	Engine	Driver(s)	Grid	Result	Notes
	Heat Two	'10'	Type 25 '255'	–	Ron **Flockhart**	7th (R2)	Rtd	23 laps – fuel pump drive – ran 6th
		'12'	Type 25 '251'	–	Jo **Bonnier**	6th (R3)	Rtd	27 laps – broken universal joint – ran 5th
27-10-57	Moroccan GP, Ain-Diab, Casablanca	'26'	Type 25 '251'	–	Maurice **Trintignant**	8th (R3)	3rd	55 laps – beaten by Behra's works 250F & Lewis-Evans' Vanwall
		'28'	Type 25 '255'	2572	Ron **Flockhart**	10th (R4)	Rtd	27 laps – jamming throttles, intake bird-strike – ran 6th – 253' also present as team T-car

1958

Date	Event & Venue	No	Car	Engine	Driver(s)	Grid	Result	Notes
7-4-58	Glover Trophy, Goodwood	'3'	Type 25 '253'	–	Jean **Behra**	2nd (R1)	**1st**	Crashed on 4th lap of 42 – brakes jammed off, rammed chicane while leading – '253' rebuilt over winter with long-wishbone front suspension on new forward frame. CAR WRITTEN-OFF, STRIPPED, SCRAPPED
		'4'	Type 25 '251'	–	Harry **Schell**	5th (R2)	Rtd	7 laps - brakes seized on! - '251' suspension modified – softer a/r bar, etc
19-4-58	Aintree '200'	'1'	Type 25 '251'	–	Jean **Behra**	**1st**	Rtd	27 of 67 laps – further brake problems
3-5-58	International Trophy, Silverstone	'1'	Type 25 '256'	–	Jean **Behra**	5th (R2)	4th/=FL	50 laps – led until stone injured eye – shared FL with Collins' Lancia-Ferrari – DEBUT OF DETACHABLE BODY SPACEFRAME CAR '256' – long-wishbone front suspension, short ram intake
		'2'	Type 25 '251'	–	Ron **Flockhart**	6th (R2)	Crash	19 laps – crashed avoiding Halford's 250F being pushed by marshals – '251' DAMAGED BEYOND ECONOMIC REPAIR – STRIPPED, SCRAPPED
18-5-58	MONACO GP, Monte Carlo	'6'	Type 25 '256'	2584	Jean **Behra**	2nd (R1)	Rtd	30 of 100 laps – led early stages, brake and driver self-image problems
		'8'	Type 25 '257'	2582	Harry **Schell**	11th (R5)	5th	91-laps – walking wounded, behind Trintignant Cooper, Moss Vanwall Collins Ferrari & Brabham 2.2 Cooper DEBUT OF NEW DETACHABLE BODY SPACEFRAME CAR '257' – non-servo brakes, short ram air intake
26-5-58	DUTCH GP, Zandvoort	'14'	Type 25 '256'	2584	Jean **Behra**	4th (R2)	3rd	BRM's BEST GRANDE EPREUVE TO DATE – 75 laps – beaten only by Moss's Vanwall
		'15'	Type 25 '257'	2582	Harry **Schell**	7th (R3)	2nd	
15-6-58	BELGIAN GP, Spa-Francorchamps	'8'	Type 25 '256'	2584	Jean **Behra**	10th (R4)	Rtd	5 of 24 laps – driver morale – 'oil pressure'
		'10'	Type 25 '257'	–	Harry **Schell**	7th (R3)	5th	23 laps – behind Brooks, Hawthorn, Lewis-Evans and Allison 2.2 Lotus 12
6-7-58	FRENCH GP, Reims-Gueux	'14'	Type 25 '257'	–	Jean **Behra**	9th (R4)	Rtd	41 laps of 50 – fuel pump failure after leading
		'16'	Type 25 '258'	–	Harry **Schell**	3rd (R1)	Rtd	41 laps – water rail , led briefly – DEBUT OF NEW DETACHABLE BODY SPACEFRAME CAR '258', upswept tail
		'18'	Type 25 '256'	–	Maurice **Trintignant**	7th (R3)	Rtd	24 laps – oil pipe breakage after running 7th
19-7-58	BRITISH GP, Silverstone	'19'	Type 25 '257'	2584	Jean **Behra**	2nd (R1)	Rtd	20 of 75 laps – tyre punctured, driver deflated – ran 10th
		'20'	Type 25 '258'	–	Harry **Schell**	8th (R3)	5th	75 laps
20-7-58	Caen GP, Le Prairie, France	'2'	Type 25 '256'	2572	Jean **Behra**	2nd (R1)	Rtd/FL	Engine failure after leading
		'6'	Type 25 '258'	–	Harry **Schell**	8th (R4)	Rtd	Engine failure after not even looking like leading
3-8-58	GERMAN GP, Nurburgring	'5'	Type 25 '256'	2584	Jean **Behra**	9th (R3)	Rtd	4 of 15 laps – 'suspension', driver shaken – ran 5th
		'6'	Type 25 '257'	–	Harry **Schell**	8th (R3)	Rtd	9 laps – brake failure
24-8-58	PORTUGUESE GP, Oporto	'8'	Type 25 '256'	2582	Jean **Behra**	4th (R2)	4th	49 of 50 laps – behind Moss, Hawthorn, Lewis-Evans
		'10'	Type 25 '257'	2584	Harry **Schell**	7th (R3)	6th	49 laps – ran 3rd
7-9-58	ITALIAN GP, Monza	'8'	Type 25 '256'	2586	Jean **Behra**	8th (R3)	Rtd	43 of 70 laps – clutch failure after Behra "had a real go" – ran 2nd
		'10'	Type 25 '257'	2582	Harry **Schell**	9th (R3)	Crash	0 laps – collision with von Trips' Ferrari in the Curva Grande
		'12'	Type 25 '258'	–	Jo **Bonnier**	10th (R3)	Rtd	15 laps – transmission failure
19-10-58	MOROCCAN GP, Ain-Diab, Casablanca	'14'	Type 25 '256'	–	Jean **Behra**	4th (R2)	Rtd	27 of 53 laps – ran 6th
		'16'	Type 25 '257'	2585	Harry **Schell**	10th (R4)	5th	53 laps – repanelled with upswept-tail body since Monza
		'18'	Type 25 '258'	2584	Jo **Bonnier**	8th (R3)	4th	53 laps – behind Moss, Hawthorn & Phil Hill – ran 3rd
		'20'	Type 25 '259'	–	Ron **Flockhart**	15th (R6)	Rtd	16 laps – engine – ran 11th – DEBUT OF NEW DETACHABLE BODY SPACEFRAME CAR '259' – upswept tail, first to have shunt water system.

Date	Event & Venue	No	Car	Engine	Driver(s)	Grid	Result	Notes
1959								
10-1-59	New Zealand GP Heat Two, Ardmore, N. Island	'12'	Type 25 '259'	2586	Ron **Flockhart**	2 (R1)	1st/=FL	15 laps – won after Moss' 2.2 Cooper retired
10-1-59	New Zealand GP, Ardmore, N. Island	'12'	Type 25 '259'	2586	Ron **Flockhart**	1st	Rtd	23 of 75 laps – oil system failure after delayed at start – ran 3rd
24-1-59	Lady Wigram Trophy, Christchurch, NZ S. Island	'1'	Type 25 '259'	2586	Ron **Flockhart**	1st	1st/FL	71 laps – beat Brabham's 2.2, McLaren's 1.96 Coopers
7-2-59	Teretonga Trophy Invercargill, NZ S. Island Heat One	'1'	Type 25 '259'	2586	Ron **Flockhart**	1st	2nd/FL	8 laps – beaten by McLaren's 1.96 Cooper
7-2-59	Teretonga Trophy Final, Invercargill, NZ S. Island	'1'	Type 25 '259'	2586	Ron **Flockhart**	1st	2nd	40 laps – beaten again by McLaren's better-suited Cooper
7-2-59	'Flying Farewell', Teretonga, Invercargill, NZ S. Island	'1'	Type 25 '259'	2586	Ron **Flockhart**	2nd	2nd	8 laps – beaten by Brabham, virtual dead-heat with Neil & McLaren Coopers – rolling start
30-3-59	International '100', Goodwood	'1'	Type 25 '257'	2591	Harry **Schell**	1st	3rd	42 laps – beaten by new 2 ½-litre Coopers of Moss & Brabham after leading – '257' rebuilt over winter with Dunlop disc brakes, shunt water system etc, long ram air intake, modified cockpit enclosure
		'2'	Type 25 '256'	2592	Jo **Bonnier**	4th (R1)	4th	42 laps – less than 1sec behind Schell – '256' converted during winter to Dunlop brakes, long ram air intake T-car NEW DETACHABLE BODY SPACEFRAME CAR '2510' built new with long air intake, small tail, extra-large head faring, simplified frame
18-4-59	Aintree '200'	'14'	Type 25 '2510'	2593	Harry **Schell**	3rd (R1)	Rtd	28 of 67 laps – major engine breakage (timing gears) – ran 2nd
		'15'	Type 25 '256'	2592	Jo **Bonnier**	4th (R2)	Rtd	1 lap – engine failure – timing gears – led very briefly
		'7'	Cooper-BRM	2584	Stirling **Moss**	6th (R3)	Rtd/FL	30 laps – Colotti transmission failure – led, new lap record
2-5-59	International Trophy, Silverstone	'4'	Type 25 '256'	2585	Ron **Flockhart**	5th (R2)	3rd	50 laps – beaten by Brabham's Cooper & Salvadori's new Aston Martin
		'7'	Type 25 '2510'	2586	Stirling **Moss**	1st	Rtd	4 of 50 laps – brake failure, spun entering Copse Corner while leading
10-5-59	MONACO GP, Monte Carlo	'16'	Type 25 '257'	2594	Harry **Schell**	9th (R4)	Rtd	49 of 100 laps – damage after spin into straw bales – ran 3rd
		'18'	Type 25 '256'	2586	Jo **Bonnier**	7th (R3)	Rtd	46 laps – brakes – ran 5th – '258' rebuilt over winter with Dunlop disc brakes, shunt water system, modified cockpit, long ram air intake
		'20'	Type 25 '259'	2592	Ron **Flockhart**	10th (R4)	Rtd	65 laps – spun & stalled – briefly ran 5th – '259' rebuilt over winter like '258'
31-5-59	DUTCH GP, Zandvoort	'7'	Type 25 '258'	2594	Jo **Bonnier**	1st	1st	BRM'S FIRST GRANDE EPREUVE VICTORY – 75 laps, beat Brabham & Gregory Coopers after Moss' had retired while leading
		'6'	Type 25 '259'	2586	Harry **Schell**	6th (R3)	Rtd	47 laps – gearbox – briefly ran 4th – 15in instead of 16in wheels
5-7-59	FRENCH GP, Reims-Gueux	'6'	Type 25 '257'	2586	Harry **Schell**	9th (R4)	7th	47 of 50 laps – spun early on, rejoined and simply persevered
		'4'	Type 25 '258'	2594	Jo **Bonnier**	6th (R3)	Rtd	7 laps – head seal failure due to water loss from broken top pipe – ran 6th
		'44'	Type 25 '2511'	2595	Ron **Flockhart**	13th (R5)	6th	50 laps – behind Brooks, Phil Hill, Brabham, Gendebien, McLaren – NEW DETACHABLE BODY SPACEFRAME CAR '2511' – similar to '2510'
		'2'	Type 25 '2510'	2585	Stirling **Moss**	4th (R2)	8th/FL	43 laps – spun when 3rd, clutch had failed, legal restart impossible – ran 2nd
18-7-59	BRITISH GP, Silverstone	'8'	Type 25 '257'	2586	Harry **Schell**	3rd (R1)	4th	74 of 75 laps – ran 2nd
		'10'	Type 25 '258'	2595	Jo **Bonnier**	10th (R4)	Rtd	38 laps – throttle linkage – ran 3rd
		'42'	Type 25 '259'	2594	Ron **Flockhart**	11th (R5)	Rtd	54 laps – spun & stalled – ran 8th
		'6'	Type 25 '2510'	2585	Stirling **Moss**	7th (R3)	2nd/=FL	75 laps – beaten by Brabham – virtual dead heat with McLaren, shared FL

Date	Event & Venue	No	Car	Engine	Driver(s)	Grid	Result	Notes
2-8-59	GERMAN GP, AVUS, Berlin, Heat One	'9'	Type 25 '258'	2594	Jo **Bonnier**	7th (R2)	7th	*29 of 30 laps – ran 6th*
		'10'	Type 25 '259'	2595	Harry **Schell**	8th (R3)	5th	*29 laps – behind three Ferraris & McLaren's Cooper*
		'11'	Type 25 '2510'	2585	Hans **Herrmann**	11th (R3)	8th	*29 laps – the ill-fated BRP entry*
	Heat Two	'9'	Type 25 '258'	2594	Jo **Bonnier**	7th (R1)	5th	*29 laps – ran 4th behind Ferraris – passed by Trintignant's Cooper*
		'10'	Type 25 '259'	2595	Harry **Schell**	5th (R2)	7th	*20 of 30 laps – briefly ran 2nd – pit stop with carburettor linkage adrift – clutch failure – pushed across finish line*
		'11'	Type 25 '2510'	2585	Hans **Herrmann**	8th (R3)	Rtd	*7 laps – crashed in South Curve after brake failure – CAR DESTROYED, STRIPPED, WRECKAGE SCRAPPED*
	Aggregate	'9'	Type 25 '258'	2594	Jo **Bonnier**	–	5th	*Behind works Ferraris of Brooks, Gurney, Hill & Trintignant's Cooper*
		'10'	Type 25 '259'	2595	Harry **Schell**	–	7th	*And last – 12 laps behind Brooks' winning Ferrari*
23-8-59	PORTUGUESE GP, Monsanto Park, Lisbon	'6'	Type 25 '257'	2595	Harry **Schell**	9th (R4)	5th	*59 of 62 laps – behind Moss, Gregory, Gurney, Trintignant*
		'7'	Type 25 '259'	–	Jo **Bonnier**	5th (R2)	Rtd	*11 laps – fuel feed – ran 13th – see text re car-change controversy*
		'8'	Type 25 '258'	2594	Ron **Flockhart**	11th (R5)	7th	*59 laps – behind Salvadori's Aston Martin – ran 6th*
13-9-59	ITALIAN GP, Monza	'2'	Type 25 '257'	2595	Harry **Schell**	7th (R3)	7th	*70 of 72 laps – ran 5th – CAR'S LAST RACE, THEN BROKEN-UP*
		'6'	Type 25 '258'	2594	Jo **Bonnier**	5th (R2)	8th	*70 laps – ran 6th*
		'4'	Type 25 '2511'	2593	Ron **Flockhart**	15th (R6)	13th	*67 laps – ran 11th*
		T-car	P48 '481'	2586	–	–	–	*DEBUT OF REAR-ENGINED EXPERIMENTAL PROTOTYPE*
10-10-59	Silver City Trophy, Snetterton	'2'	Type 25 '2511'	–	Ron **Flockhart**	1st	1st/FL	*25 laps – beat Brabham's 2.2 Cooper, set Snetterton's first 100mph lap*
		'3'	Type 25 '259'	–	Bruce **Halford**	4th (R2)	3rd	*25 laps – beat Piper's 2.0 Lotus – CAR'S LAST RACE, THEN BROKEN-UP*

1960

Date	Event & Venue	No	Car	Engine	Driver(s)	Grid	Result	Notes
7-2-60	ARGENTINE GP, Buenos Aires Autodrome	'40'	Type 25 '258'	2596	Jo **Bonnier**	4th (R1)	7th	*79 laps – led until valve-spring trouble, limped round until engine failed*
		'42'	Type 25 '2511'	2595	Graham **Hill**	3rd (R1)	Rtd	*38 laps – valve-gear failure – holed rocker cover, lost oil and pressure – ran 2nd*
14-2-60	'Buenos Aires City' *Libre* GP, Cordoba, Argentina	'40'	Type 25 '2511'	2595	Jo **Bonnier**	3rd (R1)	5th	*53 of 75 laps – rear brakes jammed on, exhaust system broke up – ran 3rd*
		'42'	Type 25 '258'	2594	Dan **Gurney**	4th (R1)	2nd	*75 laps – beaten by Trintignant's Cooper – limped round with gearbox failing*
18-4-60	International '100', Goodwood	'3'	Type 25 '258'	2597	Jo **Bonnier**	10th (R3)	6th	*41 of 42 laps – LAST WORKS ENTRY OF BRM TYPE 25*
		'4'	P48 '483'	2591	Dan **Gurney**	7th (R2)	Rtd	*2 laps – RACE DEBUT OF REAR-ENGINED BRM P48 – collision with Salvadori's Cooper while disputing 3rd place*
		'5'	P48 '482'	2586	Graham **Hill**	9th (R3)	5th	*41 laps – behind Ireland's Lotus 18, & Moss, Bristow & McLaren Coopers*

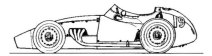

Behra, British GP, 1958

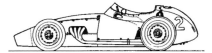

Behra, Caen GP, 1958

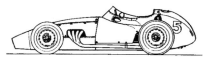

Behra, German GP, 1958

Behra, Portuguese GP, 1958

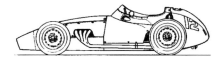

Bonnier, Italian GP, 1958

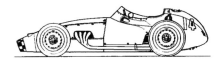

Behra, Moroccan GP, 1958

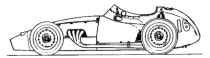

Schell, Moroccan GP, 1958

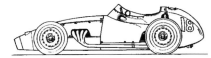

Bonnier, Moroccan GP, 1958

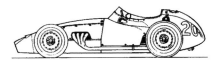

Flockhart, Moroccan GP, 1958

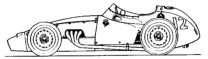

Flockhart, New Zealand GP, 1959

Flockhart, Christchurch, NZ, 1959

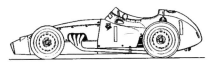

Flockhart, Teretonga, NZ, 1959

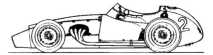

Bonnier, Easter Goodwood, 1959

Schell, Aintree '200', 1959

Moss, May Silverstone, 1959

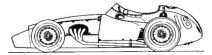

Schell, Monaco GP, 1959

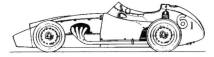

Schell, Dutch GP, 1959

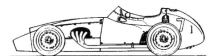

Bonnier, Dutch GP, 1959

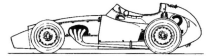

Moss, French GP, 1959

Flockhart, French GP, 1959

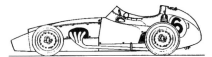

Moss, British GP, 1959

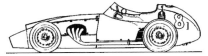

Schell, British GP, 1959

Bonnier, German GP, 1959

Herrmann, German GP, 1959

Schell, Portuguese GP, 1959

Bonnier, Italian GP, 1959

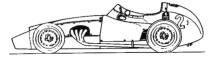

Flockhart, Snetterton, 1959

Bonnier, Argentine GP, 1960

Graham Hill, Argentine GP, 1960

Bonnier, Easter Goodwood, 1960

APPENDIX B:
TYPE 25 BRMs, 1955–59

Tony Rudd compiled the following summary of the individual Type 25 car histories early in 1960, at the end of a winter through which the surviving cars had been – with one exception – dismantled and scrapped or cannibalized in favour of the P48 rear-engined car programme. Tony's report read as follows:

No. 251: Prototype, first ran 25th June 1955; 7'3" wheelbase, 4'0" track, engine 251 with S.U. fuel Injection. 4 separate butterflies at outer ends of ram pipes. Dunlop disc brakes with servo pump driven from centre of rear disc, air struts all round, direct acting on front wishbones, operating rear through small wishbones and links, slide-located de Dion. Stressed-skin aluminium body with tail fin and high cockpit sides and wrap-round screen, steel side fuel tanks contributing to frame stiffness. Water-cooled heat exchanger in oil tank; one-piece propshaft. Converted to 52mm Weber carburettors and two-piece propshaft, July 1955 – track increased to 4'2". Air bottles fitted to air struts.

1st Rebuild: October-November 1955; new body with cutaway cockpit sides – no fin, small screen, aluminium side fuel tanks threaded onto frame tubes; Lockheed disc brakes, servo pump driven from inlet camshaft, and larger radiator. Driven during tests at Silverstone and Folkingham by Mike Hawthorn.

2nd Rebuild: January 1956, converted to independent rear suspension for experimental purposes, using half-shafts as a locating member.

3rd Rebuild: March to June 1956, converted to rocking-lever air-strut front suspension. Connaught link location to de Dion, additional side tails, wheelbase increased to 7'6" especially for J.M. Hawthorn; driven by him in the British Grand Prix, Silverstone, July 1956, with first short ram air intake.

4th Rebuild: August 1956, with transverse leaf-spring in rollers, Connaught link location, and Armstrong piston-type rear dampers, used for Monza tests.

5th Rebuild: December 1956, with centre-pivot leaf-springs front and rear (no roll stiffness). Driven R. Flockhart, Easter Goodwood, 1957, (3rd).

6th Rebuild: May to June 1957. Elektron body, high cockpit sides, wrap-round screen, coil-spring and telescopic damper suspension, Watts link de Dion location. Driven by Les Leston, British Grand Prix 1957, with roller pot joints. Driven by H. Schell, Caen 1957.

Converted to ball-slider half-shafts with needle-roller universals, August 1957. Driven by J. Behra, *Daily Express* Trophy, Silverstone, September 1957, (1st – new lap record). Driven by J. Bonnier, Modena, September 1957, and Maurice Trintignant, Casablanca, October 1957, (3rd).

Used for R.5 tyre tests by H. Schell and J. Behra. Detail modifications made to suspension in winter, track 4'3" front 4'2" rear, softer roll bar, increased castor, etc. Driven by H. Schell, Goodwood, Easter 1958. Converted to non-servo braking system, April 1958. Driven by J. Behra Aintree '200' – driven by R. Flockhart *Daily Express* Trophy, May 1958, and crashed avoiding another car – front suspension damaged beyond economic repair – *Car written-off.*

No. 252
1st series version. 7'3" wheelbase; air-strut suspension, Weber carburettors; low cockpit sides, aero screen, aluminium side fuel tanks, threaded on frame tubes. Dunlop disc brakes, engine-driven servo pump. Two-piece propshaft. Shown to press, Bourne, August 23rd 1955, first ran August 30th 1955. Driven by Peter Collins Oulton Park Gold Cup, September 1955. Driven by Stirling Moss Oulton and Silverstone test October 1955.

1st rebuild December 1955, converted to Connaught link de Dion location, negative camber de Dion, lever-type air strut front suspension, short ram air intake; driven by Tony Brooks Goodwood Easter, converted to revised oil pump system April 1956. Driven by Tony Brooks Aintree '200' (2nd). Driven by J.M. Hawthorn *Daily Express* Trophy May (new lap record). Driver Tony Brooks Monaco and British G.P. Silverstone, where it crashed and was completely burnt out.

No. 253
2nd series version, completed Easter 1956, Lockheed brakes, and carburettor air feed from centre of radiator intake, otherwise identical specification to '252'. Crashed by J.M. Hawthorn Goodwood Easter Monday.

Repaired – driven by J.M. Hawthorn, Aintree '200' and Monaco; Ron Flockhart British G.P. Silverstone.

1st rebuild, with high cockpit sides, centre pivot transverse leaf spring at rear, co-axial Armstrong piston-type dampers, front and rear roll bars (Issigonis suspension). Driven R. Salvadori Easter Goodwood and Monaco.

2nd rebuild – converted to coil-springs and telescopic dampers with Watts link de Dion location, May 1957. Driven Mackay Frazer, French G.P., Rouen 1957; Jack Fairman British G.P. Aintree – with roller pot joints. Converted to ball slider half-shafts with plain bearing universals night before race, at Caen, July 1957, driven by J. Behra (1st and new lap record). Driven H. Schell, Silverstone 1957 (2nd). 'T' car Casablanca, October 1957.

3rd rebuild – converted to new-type long wishbone front suspension with new-type frame forward of bulkhead, retaining old oil system. Used for R.5 tyre tests Behra and Schell; driven by J. Behra Goodwood Easter 1958, *crashed and written-off.*

No. 254
Completed September 1956, 7'6" wheelbase with transverse rear leaf spring, coaxial Armstrong piston-type damper, lever-type air-strut front suspension, normal cut-away cockpit body, all other details as '252' and '253'. Detachable high-sided cockpit enclosure, provided with wrap-round screen; car never ran without this in place; duplicated rear brake cooling ducts. Used for majority of Monza tests.

Rear suspension modified to provide adjustable spring and roll ratio for tests Silverstone, January 1957.
1st rebuild: February-April 1957; given permanent high-sided cockpit with wrap-round screen, centre-pivot rear leaf spring, front and rear roll bars (Issigonis suspension). Driven by R. Flockhart, Monaco, May 1957.
2nd rebuild: June 1957. Converted to coil-spring suspension, with telescopic dampers and Watts link de Dion location. Crashed and written-off French G.P. Driven by Ron Flockhart.

No. 255
Last stressed-skin chassis, completed September 1957, using parts salvaged from '254'. Built with coil-spring suspension, etc., complete. Similar specification to '253' and '254'. Started life with ball-spline half-shafts. Driver R.Flockhart, Silverstone *Daily Express* Trophy, September 1957, (3rd); and Modena, September 1957; and Casablanca, October 1957.

Modified to same standard as '251', January 1958; track 4'3" front, 4'2" rear; softer roll bar, increased castor, etc. Converted to non-servo brakes April 1958. Never raced 1958, but used as 'T' car Goodwood, Easter, Aintree '200', Monaco, Zandvoort, Spa, Monza – known to drivers as the 'Vanguard'.

No. 256
First 1958 true space frame car – completed May 1958. Normally driven by J. Behra. Incorporated long wishbone front suspension as used on '253', side tanks threaded on detachable frame tubes, carb. air intake feeding from centre of radiator duct; all body panels detachable except undertray. Heat exchanger for oil cooling in water pipe from radiator to pump. Many detail modifications to improve reliability and road-holding. Built with servo brakes but converted to non-servo before it ran. Converted to short ram air intake during practice for Silverstone *Daily Express* Trophy, 1958. Driver Jean Behra (4th). New lap record (still stands) jointly with Peter Collins.

Driven by J. Behra, Monaco and Zandvoort (3rd). Spa (crashed in practice). Driven M. Trintignant French G.P. Reims.

Oil heat exchanger removed, and honeycomb oil cooler fitted under carburettors. J. Behra Nurburgring. Caen (new lap record – still stands). Oporto (4th). Fitted series oil cooler Monza and Casablanca.

Overhauled winter 1958 and converted to Dunlop brakes, shunt water system, and long ram air intake, with detail modifications to improve reliability and road-holding. Driven J. Bonnier, Goodwood Easter 1959, Stirling Moss in subsequent tests – first Goodwood 100 m.p.h. lap. Ron Flockhart *Daily Express* Trophy 1959 (3rd). 'T' car Zandvoort 1959.

Car not used again and has now been rebuilt with unserviceable pieces as an exhibition car. Serviceable parts have gone into rear-engined prototype.

No. 257
Completed May 1957 and normally driven by H. Schell. Built with non-servo brakes and short ram air intake, otherwise identical with '256'. Driven by H. Schell Monaco (5th), Zandvoort (2nd); Spa (5th). Oil heat exchanger removed and replaced by honeycomb oil cooler located under carburettors. Driven French G.P. Reims and British G.P. Silverstone by J. Behra. Driven Nurburgring, Oporto (6th) by H. Schell. Fitted with series oil cooler in addition to honeycomb cooler for Monza; driven by H. Schell; crashed on first lap after collision with Von Trips Ferrari.

Repaired, given upswept tail; fitted with 'footscraper' series oil cooler only. Driven Casablanca, October 1958, by H. Schell (5th).

Rebuilt winter 1958–59 with Dunlop disc brakes and shunt water system, and used for development work on them at Folkingham and Silverstone (driven by H. Schell); fitted with long ram air intake and modified cockpit enclosure.

Driven by H. Schell, Goodwood Easter 1959 (3rd) and S. Moss on subsequent tests. Driven H. Schell Monaco (crashed), French G.P. Reims (7th), British G.P. Aintree (4th), Lisbon (5th), Monza (7th).

Car now broken up and serviceable pieces used to build 2nd rear-engined car.

No. 258
3rd full space frame car, completed June 1958, built to same standard as '257' except for upswept tail. Driven by H. Schell, French G.P. Reims, July 1958; and British G.P. Silverstone July '58, (5th), and Caen July 1958. 'T' car Nurburgring – crashed by J. Behra. Modified to include series oil cooler for Monza, September 1958; driven by J. Bonnier, who subsequently always drove this car, with one exception. Honeycomb oil cooler removed and series 'footscraper' cooler fitted for Casablanca 1958 (4th).

Converted to Dunlop disc brakes, shunt water system, modified cockpit and long ram air intake winter 1958/59. Zandvoort, June 1959, Avus August 1959, Lisbon August 1959, driven by R. Flockhart after a crash in practice (5th), Monza (8th).

Has since been overhauled and sent to Argentina.

No. 259
4th space frame car, completed October 1958. Usually driven by R. Flockhart. Similar to other cars with upswept tail and series 'footscraper' oil cooler. First car to have shunt water system. Driven by R. Flockhart Casablanca October '58. Overhauled and sent to New Zealand in 1958 trim. Driven R. Flockhart, Ardmore, Wigram Trophy (1st). Terr Tonga [*sic*!] Park (2nd).

Overhauled and converted to Dunlop disc brakes and long ram air intake, and modified cockpit, April 1959. Driven R. Flockhart Monte Carlo. Driven H. Schell Zandvoort, June 1959. R. Flockhart British G.P. Aintree. H. Schell German G.P., Avus (6th). J. Bonnier Lisbon. B. Halford Snetterton (3rd). Car now reduced to spares.

No. 2510
5th space frame car, built to 1959 standard with 'footscraper' oil cooler, long air intake, small tail with extra large head fairing, and simplified frame. Completed March 1959. 'T' car Goodwood Easter Monday.

Driven H. Schell Aintree '200'; S. Moss *Daily Express* Silverstone, 'T' car Monaco. Delivered to British Racing Partnership June 1959, and driven by Stirling Moss under their colours; French G.P. Reims, (fastest lap and new lap record). Driven by H. Herrmann at German G.P. Avus, crashed and completely destroyed.

No. 2511
6th space frame car, to 1959 standard, identical to '2510'. Completed June 1959. Driven R. Flockhart French G.P. Reims (6th), 'T' car Avus. Driven R. Flockhart Monza (13th), Snetterton (1st and new lap record). Subsequently used for Goodwood tests where it has lapped at 1–25.1. Driven by R. Flockhart.

Since been overhauled and sent to Argentina. The only car that all team drivers agree to be a good one, i.e., Bonnier says '258' is the best but would have '2511' if '258' wasn't available. Schell said if he could not have '257' would like '2511'; Flockhart thinks '2511' is as good as '259'.

9th February 1960   *A.C.Rudd*

[A full chassis register of all BRMs built will be found in Volume 2.]

─────────────────────

APPENDIX C:

TECHNICAL SPECIFICATIONS, FRONT-ENGINED BRMs

1.5-litre BRM Type 15

Engine:

Bore & stroke:	49.53mm × 47.8mm – 1.95in × 1.9in
Displacement:	1,496cc
Compression ratio:	c.7.5:1
Supercharger:	Rolls-Royce two-stage centrifugal
Max. boost:	5.7 ata
Carburettors:	Twin horizontal 3in choke SUs
Fuel:	Petrol/alcohol mix
Consumption:	c.3mpg
Max. fuel load:	75 gallons
Ignition:	Lucas coil/distributors; Quadruple Lucas magnetos
Firing order:	1-10-6-13-2-16-5-11-8-15-3-12-7-9-4-14
Plugs:	16 Lodge 14mm 320/340
Piston area:	47.8sq in
Piston speed:	3,800ft/min @ 12,000rpm
Valves:	Two per cylinder at 80deg included angle; two overhead camshafts per cylinder; finger followers, hairpin springs; camshafts driven by spur gear train from crankshaft centre
Valve head dia:	Inlet 1.25in; exhaust 1.0937in
Valve timing:	Inlet: Opens 55deg BTDC, closes 70deg ABDC
	Exhaust: Opens 70deg BBDC, closes 46deg ATDC
Cylinders:	Disposed at included angle of 135deg: Cast-iron wet liners inserted in alloy block at base, spigoted into alloy head
Connecting rods:	Nickel-chrome steel forgings, 4.125in between centres, Vandervell ThinWall big-end/phosphor-bronze little-end bearings
Crankshaft:	Two-piece counterbalanced, running in eight Vandervell ThinWall and two roller main bearings, later in 10 Vandervell bearings.
Lubrication:	Dry-sump; two pinion pumps feeding 20galls/min each at 50/70psi
Power output:	c.100bhp – 105lb.ft torque @ 5,000rpm
	c.175bhp – 153lb.ft @ 6,000rpm
	c.250bhp – 187lb.ft @ 7,000rpm
	c.335bhp – 220lb.ft @ 8,000rpm
	c.412bhp – 241lb.ft @ 9,000rpm
	c.525bhp – 262lb.ft @ 10,000rpm

Max bmep:
c.585bhp – 278lb.ft @ 11,000rpm
c.600bhp – 262lb.ft @ 12,000rpm
c.462psi

Driveline:

Clutch:
7½in three-plate driven by engine output shaft taking power from crankshaft centre

Transmission:
By jointed prop-shaft, through right-angle drive to all-indirect transverse-shaft five-speed gearbox, final-drive spur gears, ZF differential, universally-jointed half-shafts

Chassis:

Frame:
Side members built up from parallel tubes and sideplates forming box section; four crossmembers

Front suspension:
Porsche-type trailing arms and Lockheed air struts

Rear suspension:
de Dion rear axle with rotating tube located laterally by sliding block in diff housing; longitudinally by torque arms; springing and damping by Lockheed air struts

Steering:
By jointed column above engine to worm-and-nut steering box on left side of centre cross-rod, two half track rods, 2½ turns lock-to-lock

Brakes:
Girling hydraulic servo-operated three-shoe Girling 14in drums; later Girling discs, front 13½in diameter, rear 13in diameter

Wheels & tyres:
Dunlop wire-spoked; front 5.25 × 18 Dunlop; rear 7.00 × 17 Dunlop

Wheelbase:
8ft 2in (V16 Mark II P30 – 7ft 7in)

Front track:
4ft 4in

Rear track:
4ft 3in

Unladen weight:
1,624lb (V16 Mark II P30 – 7ft 7in)

Startline weight:
2,128lb (V16 Mark II P30 – 1,904lb)

Frontal area:
9.5sq ft

Hp per sq ft:
c.55.2

Hp per ton unladen:
c.546

Hp per ton startline:
c.525

2.5-litre BRM Type 25

Engine:

Bore & stroke:
102.87mm × 74.93mm – 4.05in × 2.95in

Displacement:
2,497cc

Compression ratio:
c.10.25:1

Carburettors:
Two twin-choke Weber 58DCOEs

Fuel:
1955–1957 50% alcohol mix; from 1958 AvGas

Consumption:
c.7mpg on alcohol/c.10mpg on Avgas

Max fuel load:
38 gallons

Ignition:
Two Lucas magnetos

Firing order:
1-3-4-2

Plugs:
Four Lodge, 10mm 280/300

Piston area:
51sq in

Piston speed:
4,425ft/min @ 9,000rpm

Valves:
Two per cylinder at 79deg included angle; two overhead camshafts with finger followers, hairpin springs, spur camshaft drive at rear of unit

Valve head dia:
Inlet 2.4in; exhaust 2.0in

Valve timing:
Inlet: Opens 55deg BTDC, closes 72deg ATDC
Exhaust: Opens 75deg BBDC, closes 46deg ATDC

Cylinders:
Four in line spigoted into alloy block, 0.4–0.5% carbon steel tube

Connecting rods:
Nickel-chrome EN 25V forgings, 4.825in between centres, four-bolt big-end cap, Vandervell lead-indium shell bearings

Crankshaft:
Forged Nitralloy, four main bearings with centre

balance, counterweighted; 1958 five main bearings – Vandervell lead-indium shell bearings

Lubrication:
Dry-sump; one pinion pump feeding 18 galls/min at 80psi

Power output:
1955 Max c.248bhp @ 9,000rpm
1956 Max c.270bhp @ 7,500rpm
1957 Max c.288bhp @ 8,250rpm
1959–60 Max c.270bhp @ 8,000rpm
Max torque c. 1,981lb.ft @ 7,000rpm

Max bmep:
210psi

Driveline:

Clutch:
7¼in two-plate driven from crankshaft tail

Transmission:
By open-jointed prop-shaft to crownwheel and pinion, output through overhung four-speed indirect gearbox

Chassis:

Frame:
Combination welded tube baseframe/stressed-skin semi-monocque fuselage (1955–57); welded multi-tubular spaceframe, detachable magnesium-alloy skin panels (1958–60)

Front suspension:
Double wishbones with inclined Lockheed air struts – later co-axial coil-spring/damper unit

Rear suspension:
Single-piece de Dion rear axle located laterally by sliding block in diff housing, later Connaught link, later Watt linkage, twin radius arms; early Lockheed air struts replaced by transverse leafsprings, later telescopic damper struts with co-axial coil-springs

Steering:
BRM rack-and-pinion with short track rods

Brakes:
Lockheed or Dunlop hydraulic discs – initially servo-operated – front discs 10½in diameter, rear single disc on gearbox output shaft, 10¼in diameter

Wheels & tyres:
Dunlop dural forged wheels; front 5.25 × 16 Dunlop; rear 7.00 × 16 Dunlop – 1959 move to 15in diameters

Wheelbase:
7ft 3in (later 7ft 6in)

Front track:
4ft 4in

Rear track:
4ft 2in

Unladen weight:
c.1,520lb

Startline weight:
c.1,900lb

Frontal area:
9.5sq ft

Hp per sq ft:
c.28.8

Hp per ton unladen:
c.400

Hp per ton startline:
c.320